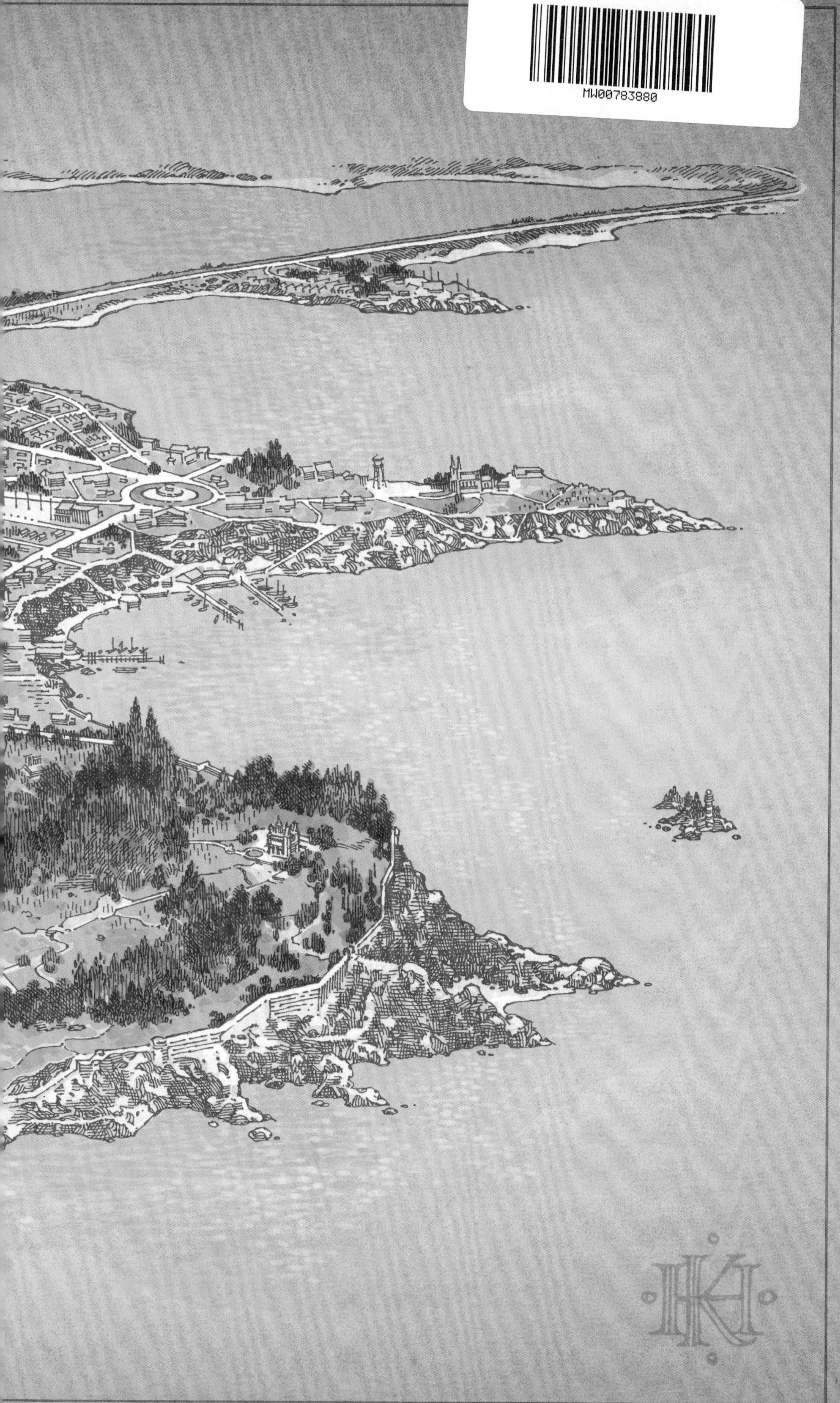

LOCKE & KEY

- VOLUME ONE -

MASTER EDITION

IDW

IDW ®

@IDWpublishing
IDWpublishing.com

ISBN: 978-1-63140-224-1   26 25 24 23   10 11 12 13
For international rights, contact licensing@idwpublishing.com.
Ted Adams and Robbie Robbins, IDW Founders

Nachie Marsham, Publisher
Blake Kobashigawa, SVP Sales, Marketing & Strategy
Mark Doyle, VP Editorial & Creative Strategy
Tara McCrillis, VP Publishing Operations
Anna Morrow, VP Marketing & Publicity
Alex Hargett, VP Sales
Jamie S. Rich, Executive Editorial Director
Scott Dunbier, Director, Special Projects
Greg Gustin, Sr. Director, Content Strategy
Kevin Schwoer, Sr. Director of Talent Relations

Lauren LePera, Sr. Managing Editor
Keith Davidsen, Director, Marketing & PR
Topher Alford, Sr. Digital Marketing Manager
Patrick O'Connell, Sr. Manager, Direct Market Sales
Shauna Monteforte, Sr. Director of Manufacturing Operations
Greg Foreman, Director DTC Sales & Operations
Nathan Widick, Director of Design
Neil Uyetake, Sr. Art Director, Design & Production
Shawn Lee, Art Director, Design & Production
Jack Rivera, Art Director, Marketing

JOE HILL
&
GABRIEL RODRÍGUEZ
Storytellers

JAY FOTOS
Colors

ROBBIE ROBBINS
Lettering

CHRIS RYALL   JUSTIN EISINGER
Series Editor   Collection Editor

TED ADAMS
Publisher

Locke & Key created by
Joe Hill & Gabriel Rodríguez

Master Edition designed by Gabriel Rodríguez

LOCKE & KEY
- Book One -

WELCOME TO LOVECRAFT

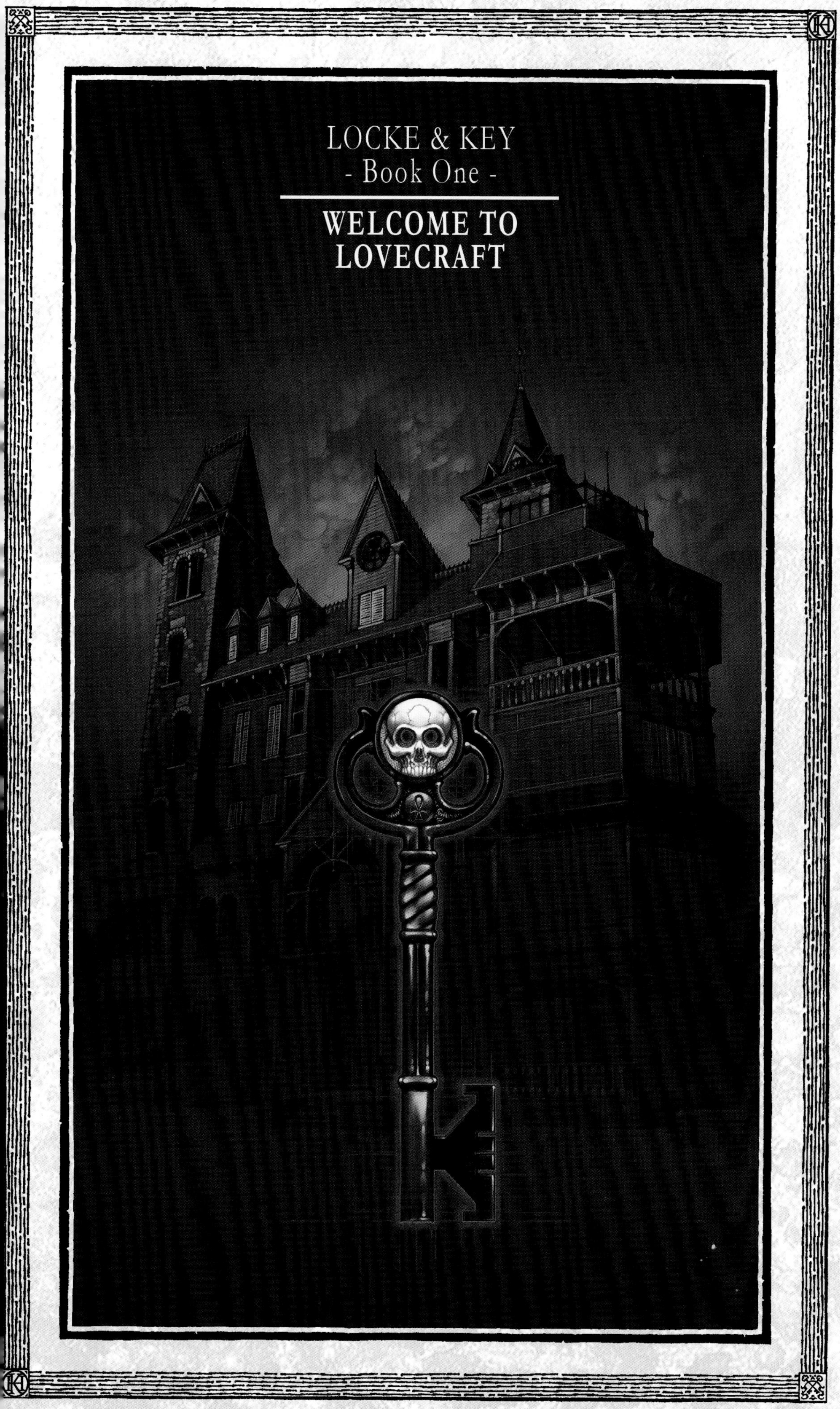

For Tabitha Jane King:
Literary locksmith, mother, friend. Love you.
- Joe

————————————————

To Catalina:
You unlocked my dreams.
- Gabriel

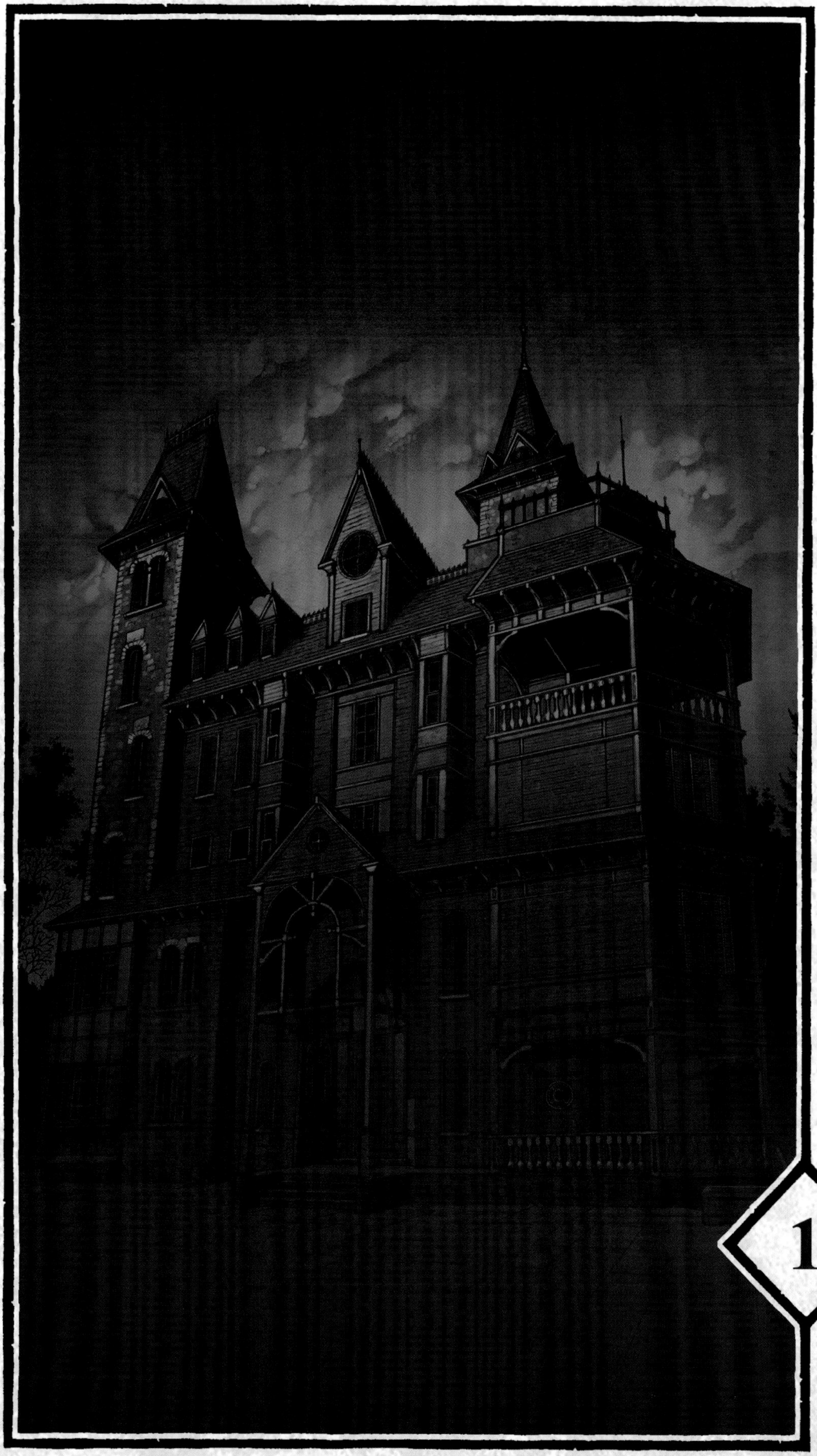

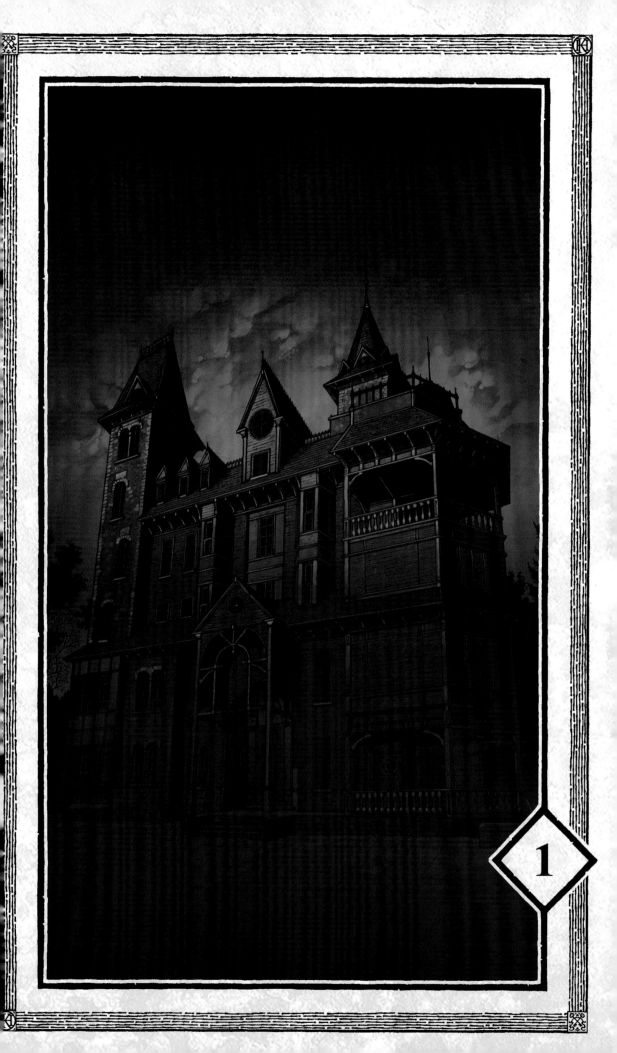

1

WELCOME TO LOVECRAFT
- ONE -

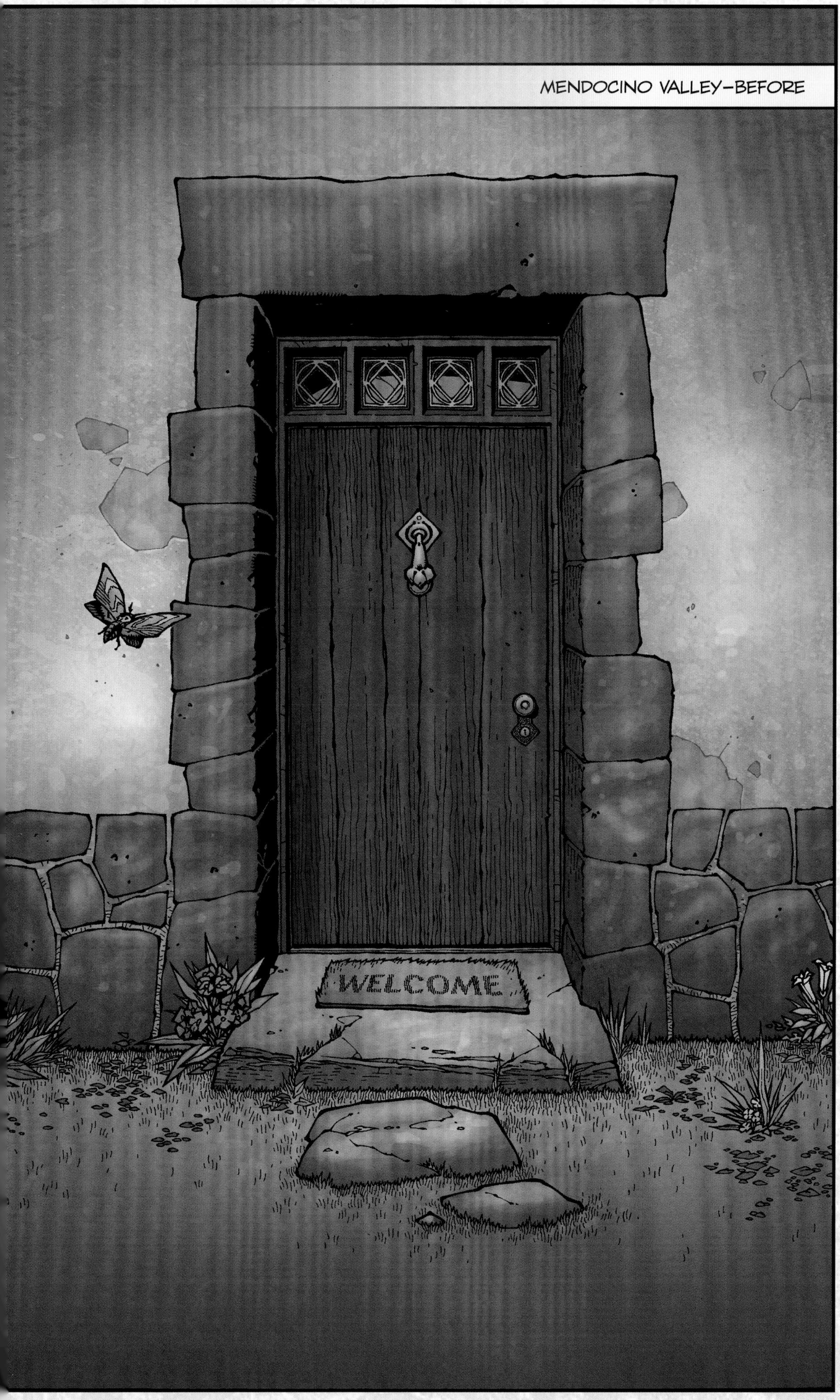
MENDOCINO VALLEY–BEFORE
WELCOME

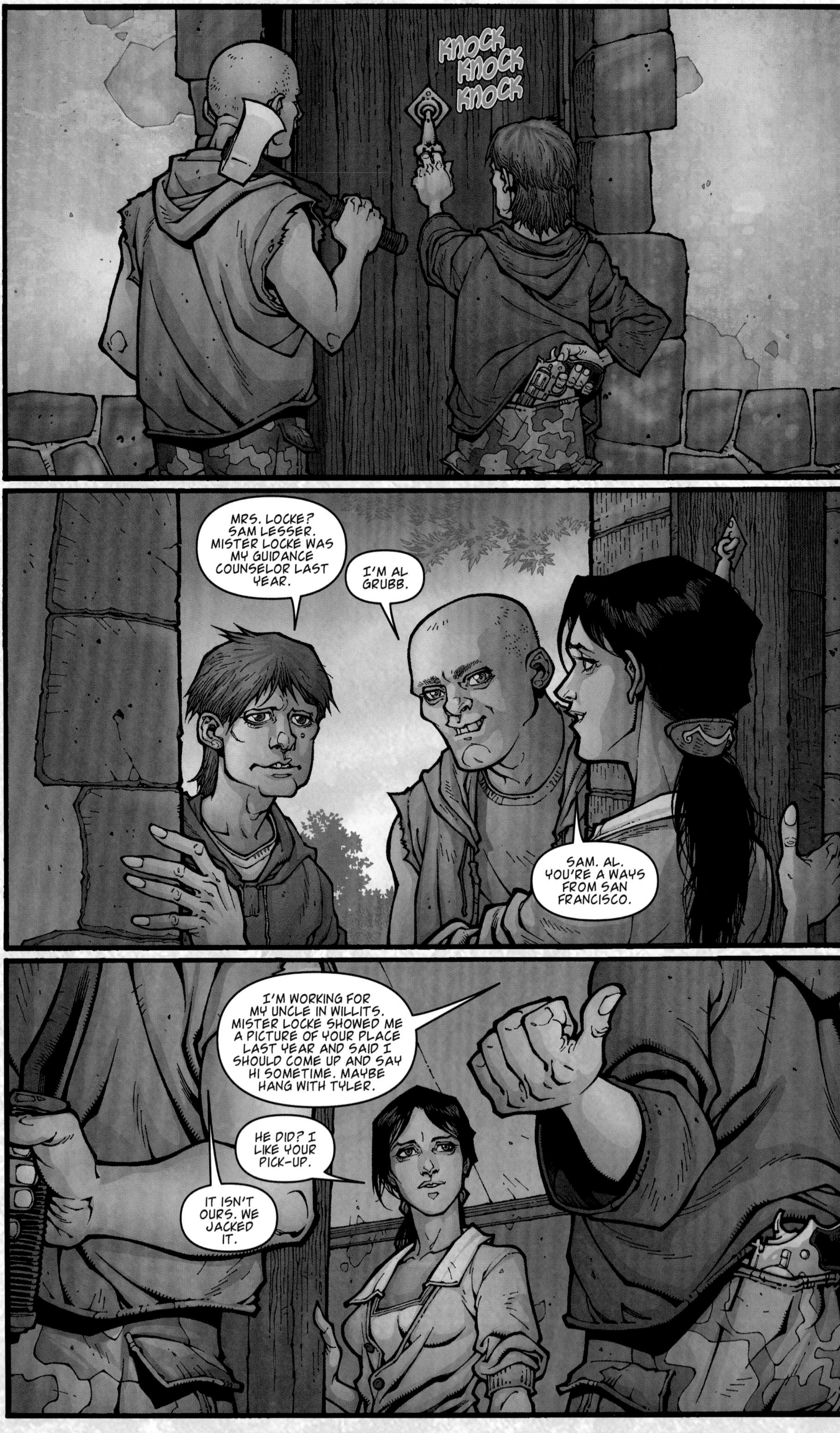
KNOCK KNOCK KNOCK
MRS. LOCKE? SAM LESSER. MISTER LOCKE WAS MY GUIDANCE COUNSELOR LAST YEAR.
I'M AL GRUBB.
SAM. AL. YOU'RE A WAYS FROM SAN FRANCISCO.
I'M WORKING FOR MY UNCLE IN WILLITS. MISTER LOCKE SHOWED ME A PICTURE OF YOUR PLACE LAST YEAR AND SAID I SHOULD COME UP AND SAY HI SOMETIME. MAYBE HANG WITH TYLER.
HE DID? I LIKE YOUR PICK-UP.
IT ISN'T OURS. WE JACKED IT.

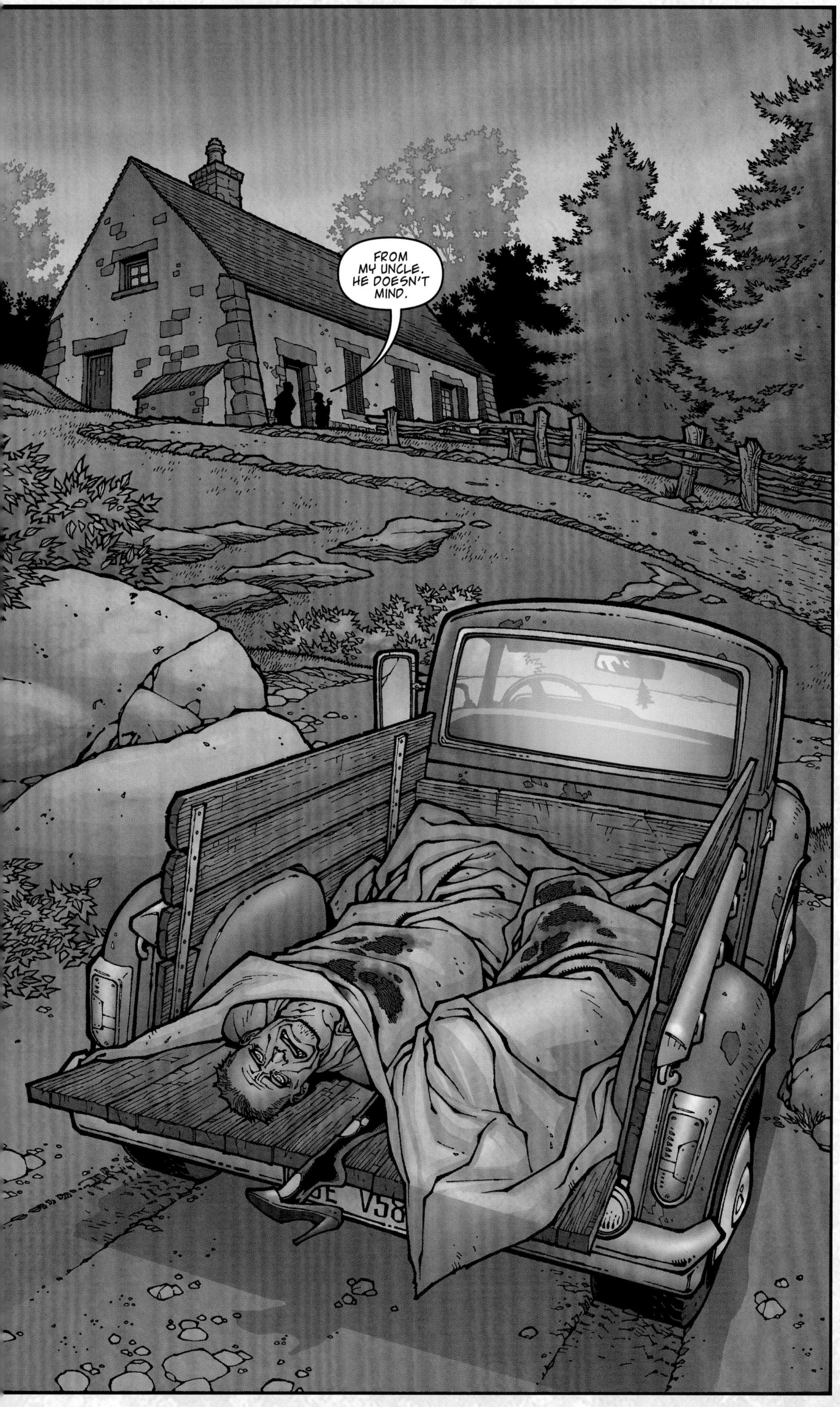
FROM MY UNCLE. HE DOESN'T MIND.

PLEASE, GOD, ALL I WANT IS AN EARTHQUAKE.

JUST ONE LITTLE QUAKE THAT MAKES THE ROOF FALL IN ON MY BEDROOM, SO I CAN'T STAY HERE ANYMORE AND MY PARENTS HAVE TO SEND ME TO BAJA TO LIVE WITH ROD FESS AND THEN I CAN LEARN TO SURF.

MORE LIKE THEY'D SEND ME TO STAY WITH MY COUSIN ORIN WHO WALLPAPERS HIS ROOM WITH THE OBITUARIES OF FAMOUS PEOPLE, BECAUSE HE SAYS THE ONLY THING COOLER THAN BEING A CELEBRITY IS BEING A DEAD CELEBRITY.

ALTHOUGH... AT LEAST ORIN HAS A PS3.

I FOUND A LITTLE TURTLE BUT IT WENT CRAP IN MY HAND AND GOT AWAY. LOOKAT.

WHAT ARE YOU TWO DOING?

A TURTLE SHIT IN BODE'S HAND AND HE WANTS TO KEEP IT AS A SOUVENIR OF OUR UNFORGETTABLE SUMMER HERE.

SO HE'S EXPERIENCING NATURE. WHAT ARE *YOU* DOING?

EXPERIENCING BOREDOM AND EXISTENTIAL ANGST.

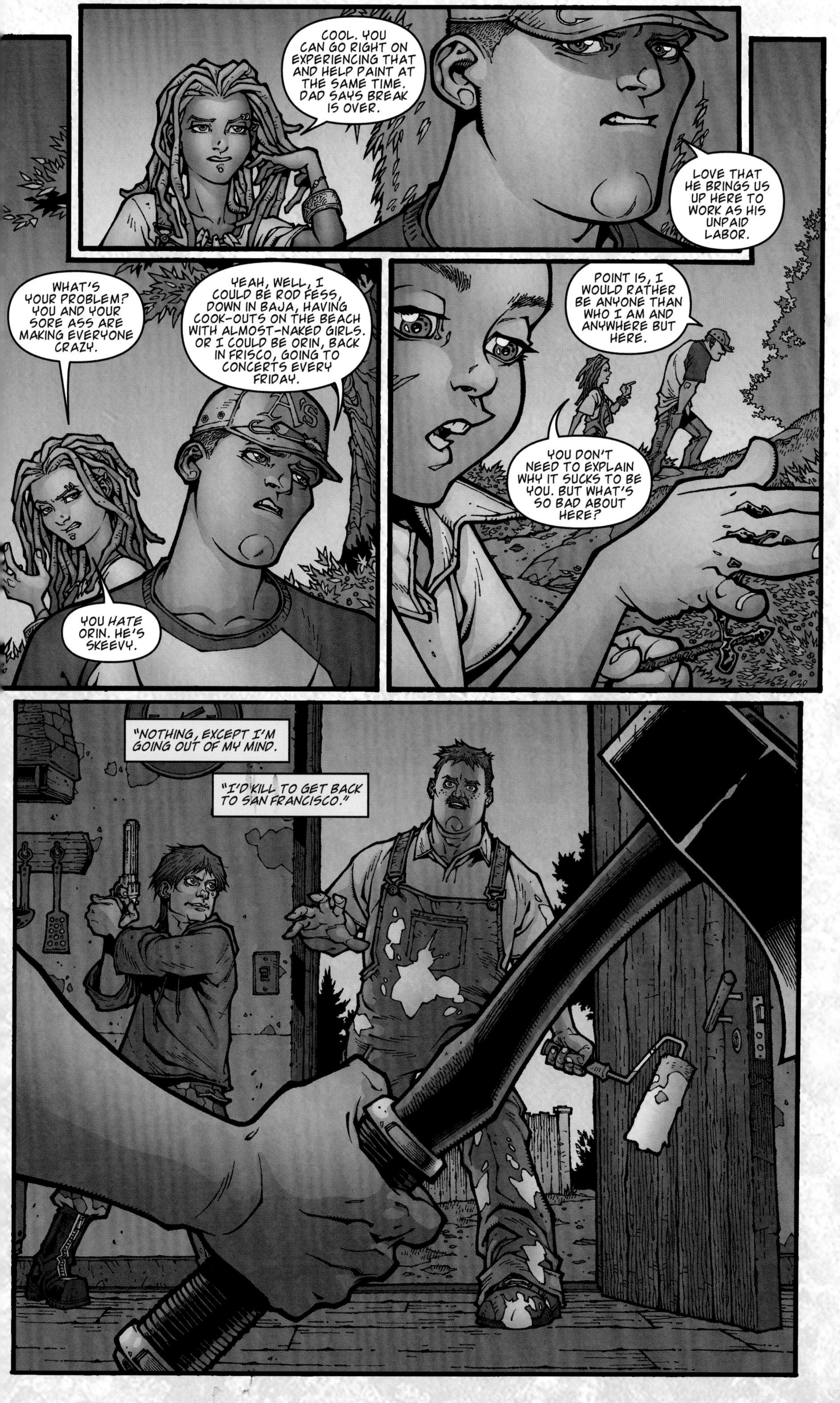

COOL. YOU CAN GO RIGHT ON EXPERIENCING THAT AND HELP PAINT AT THE SAME TIME. DAD SAYS BREAK IS OVER.
LOVE THAT HE BRINGS US UP HERE TO WORK AS HIS UNPAID LABOR.
WHAT'S YOUR PROBLEM? YOU AND YOUR SORE ASS ARE MAKING EVERYONE CRAZY.
YEAH, WELL, I COULD BE ROD FESS, DOWN IN BAJA, HAVING COOK-OUTS ON THE BEACH WITH ALMOST-NAKED GIRLS. OR I COULD BE ORIN, BACK IN FRISCO, GOING TO CONCERTS EVERY FRIDAY.
YOU HATE ORIN. HE'S SKEEVY.
POINT IS, I WOULD RATHER BE ANYONE THAN WHO I AM AND ANYWHERE BUT HERE.
YOU DON'T NEED TO EXPLAIN WHY IT SUCKS TO BE YOU. BUT WHAT'S SO BAD ABOUT HERE?
"NOTHING, EXCEPT I'M GOING OUT OF MY MIND.
"I'D KILL TO GET BACK TO SAN FRANCISCO."

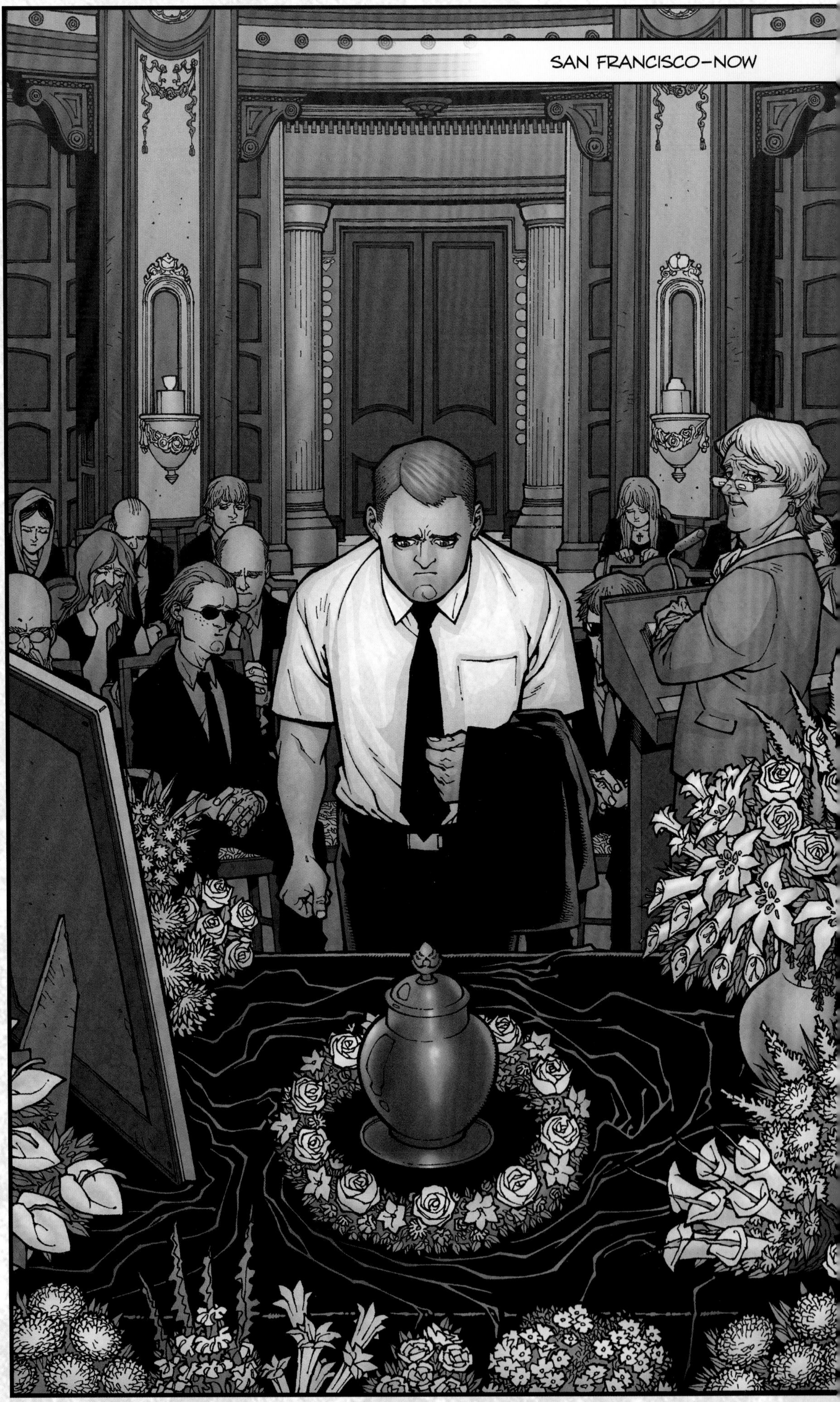
SAN FRANCISCO–NOW

HEY, DUDE. HOW YOU DOING?

I MEAN... SORRY. WHAT A STUPID-ASS QUESTION.

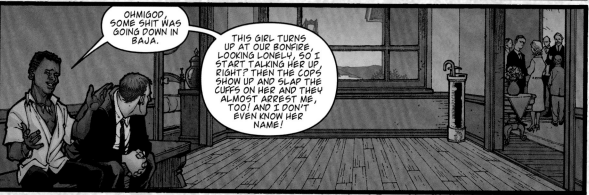

OHMIGOD, SOME SHIT WAS GOING DOWN IN BAJA.

THIS GIRL TURNS UP AT OUR BONFIRE, LOOKING LONELY, SO I START TALKING HER UP, RIGHT? THEN THE COPS SHOW UP AND SLAP THE CUFFS ON HER AND THEY ALMOST ARREST ME, TOO! AND I DON'T EVEN KNOW HER NAME!

TELL YOU ABOUT IT SOMETIME IF YOU WANT. IT WAS CRAZY.

I'M HERE FOR YOU, MAN. DON'T TRY AND GO THROUGH THIS ALONE.

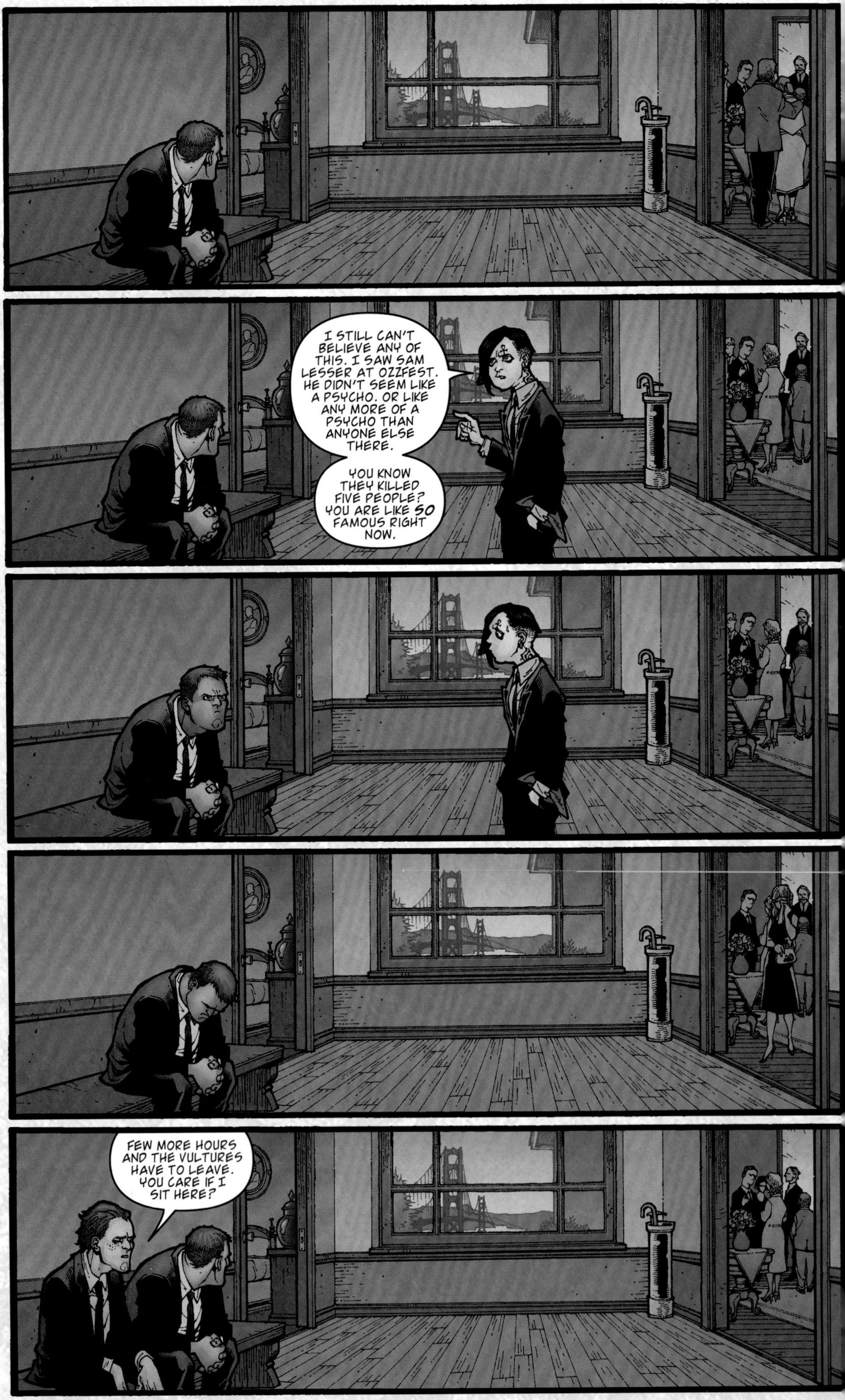
I STILL CAN'T BELIEVE ANY OF THIS. I SAW SAM LESSER AT OZZFEST. HE DIDN'T SEEM LIKE A PSYCHO. OR LIKE ANY MORE OF A PSYCHO THAN ANYONE ELSE THERE.
YOU KNOW THEY KILLED FIVE PEOPLE? YOU ARE LIKE SO FAMOUS RIGHT NOW.
FEW MORE HOURS AND THE VULTURES HAVE TO LEAVE. YOU CARE IF I SIT HERE?

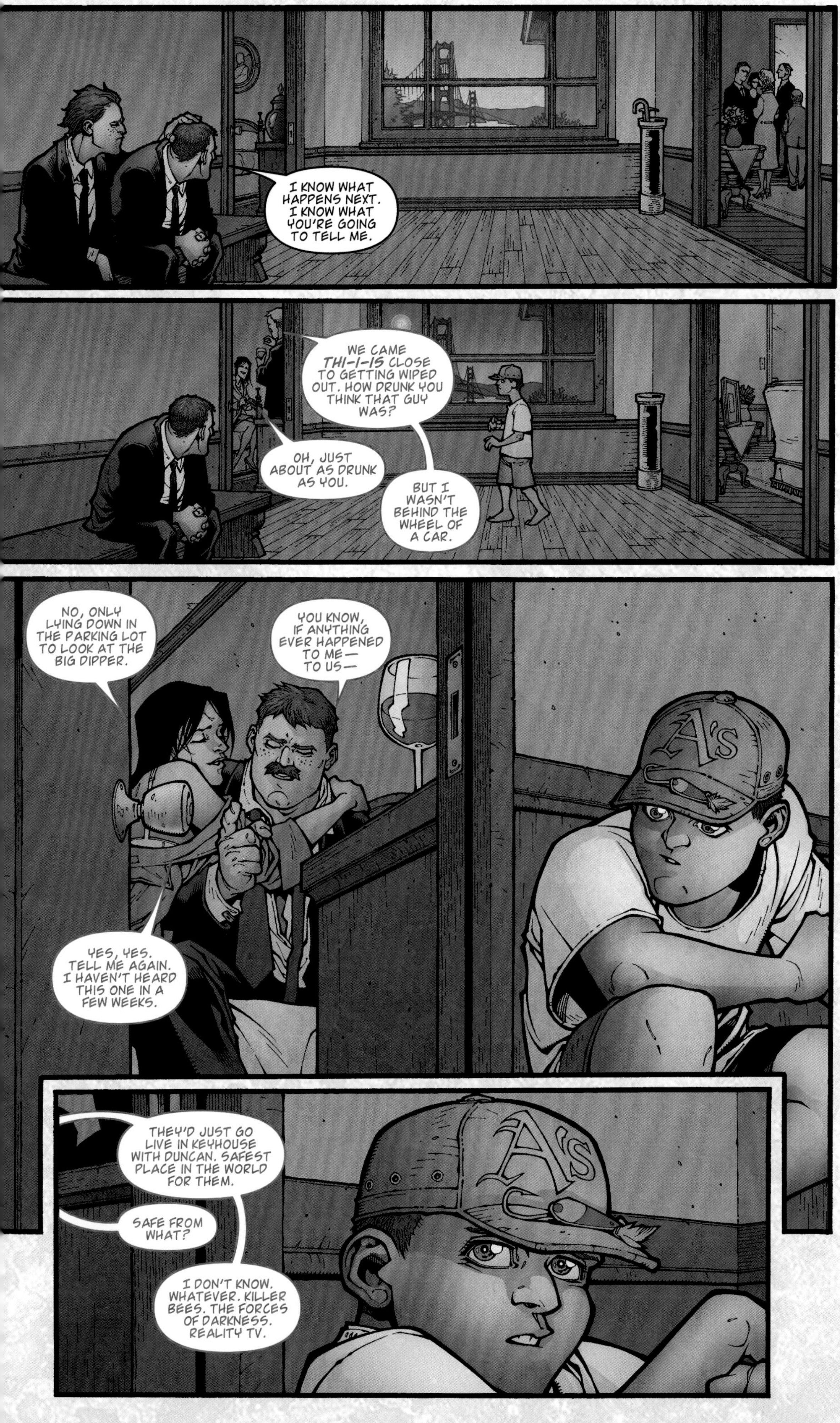
I KNOW WHAT HAPPENS NEXT. I KNOW WHAT YOU'RE GOING TO TELL ME.
WE CAME *THI-I-IS* CLOSE TO GETTING WIPED OUT. HOW DRUNK YOU THINK THAT GUY WAS?
OH, JUST ABOUT AS DRUNK AS YOU.
BUT I WASN'T BEHIND THE WHEEL OF A CAR.
NO, ONLY LYING DOWN IN THE PARKING LOT TO LOOK AT THE BIG DIPPER.
YOU KNOW, IF ANYTHING EVER HAPPENED TO ME— TO US—
YES, YES. TELL ME AGAIN. I HAVEN'T HEARD THIS ONE IN A FEW WEEKS.
A'S
THEY'D JUST GO LIVE IN KEYHOUSE WITH DUNCAN. SAFEST PLACE IN THE WORLD FOR THEM.
SAFE FROM WHAT?
I DON'T KNOW. WHATEVER. KILLER BEES. THE FORCES OF DARKNESS. REALITY TV.
A'S

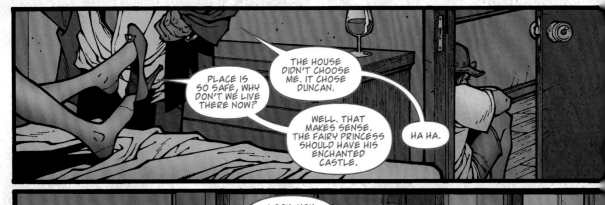

PLACE IS SO SAFE, WHY DON'T WE LIVE THERE NOW?

THE HOUSE DIDN'T CHOOSE ME. IT CHOSE DUNCAN.

WELL. THAT MAKES SENSE. THE FAIRY PRINCESS SHOULD HAVE HIS ENCHANTED CASTLE.

HA HA.

LOOK, YOU DON'T HAVE TO BELIEVE ME. HELL, WHEN I'M SOBER *I* DON'T BELIEVE— YOU THINK I SOUND CRAZY?

YES. LUCKY FOR YOU, PSYCHOSIS TURNS ME ON. AND TO THINK THEY LET YOU WORK WITH CHILDREN.

MY DAD KNEW. SOMEHOW HE KNEW SOMETHING LIKE THIS WOULD HAPPEN. HOW COULD HE KNOW THAT?

AW, KID. YOUR POP WAS THE ORIGINAL BOY SCOUT. ALWAYS BE PREPARED. THAT'S ALL.

WE'RE GOING WITH YOU. TO MASSACHUSETTS. TO KEYHOUSE.

YEAH. THAT'S THE PLAN. IS THAT ALL RIGHT, TYLER?

CHRIST, YES. PLEASE LET'S JUST GET THE HELL OUT OF THIS PLACE.

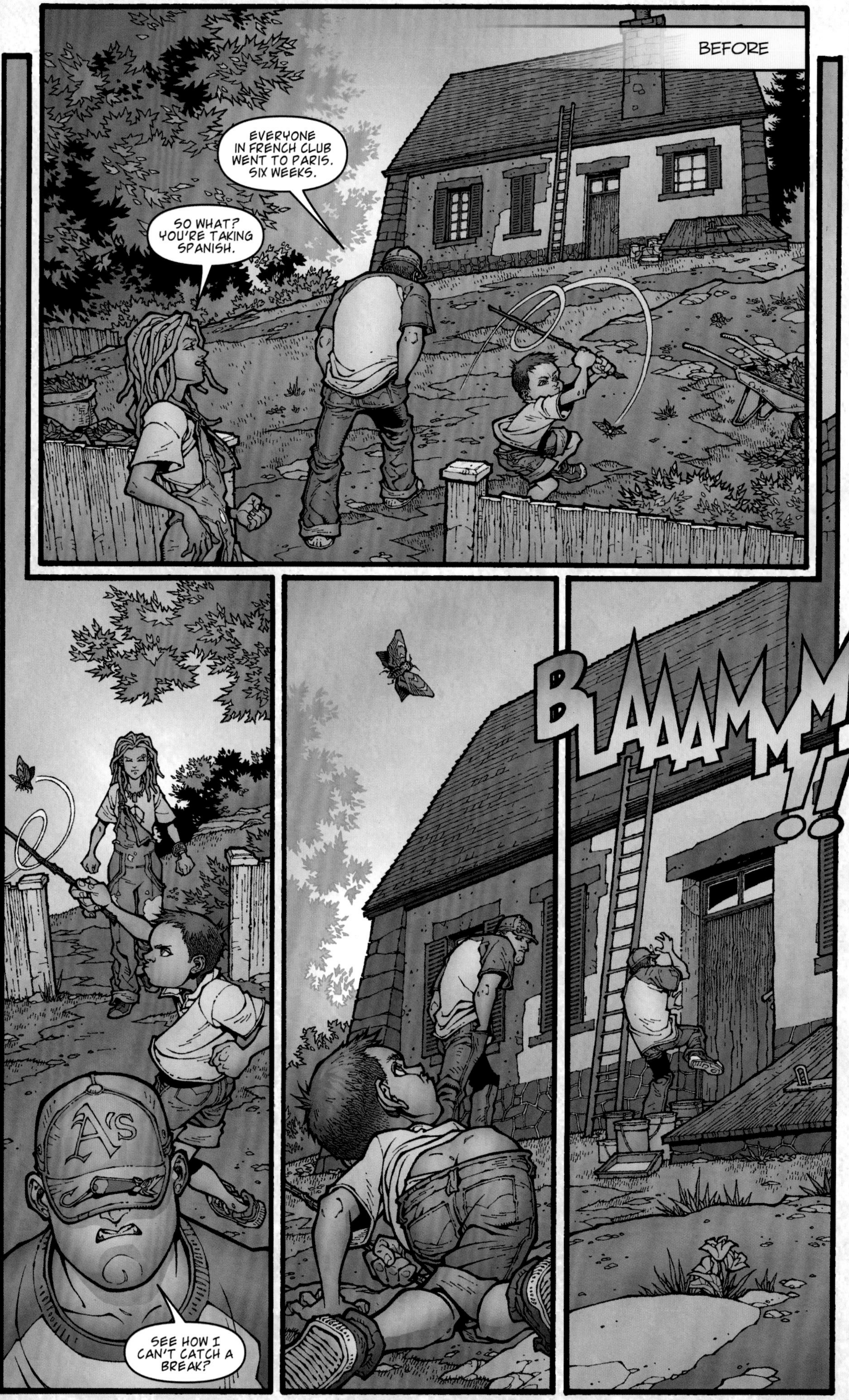
BEFORE
EVERYONE IN FRENCH CLUB WENT TO PARIS. SIX WEEKS.
SO WHAT? YOU'RE TAKING SPANISH.
A'S
SEE HOW I CAN'T CATCH A BREAK?
BLAAAMM!!

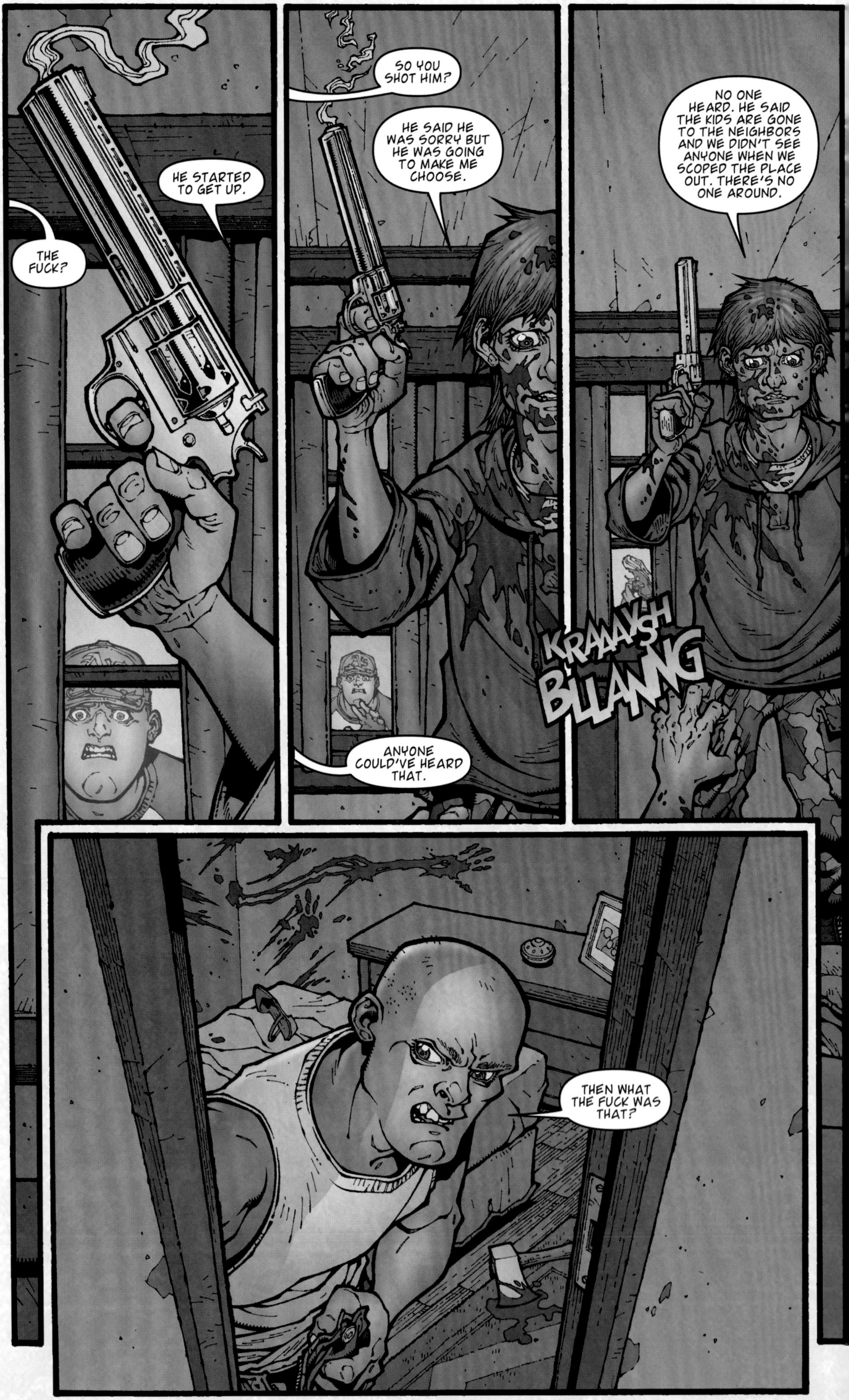
HE STARTED TO GET UP.
THE FUCK?
SO YOU SHOT HIM?
HE SAID HE WAS SORRY BUT HE WAS GOING TO MAKE ME CHOOSE.
ANYONE COULD'VE HEARD THAT.
NO ONE HEARD. HE SAID THE KIDS ARE GONE TO THE NEIGHBORS AND WE DIDN'T SEE ANYONE WHEN WE SCOPED THE PLACE OUT. THERE'S NO ONE AROUND.
KRAAAYSH
BLLANNG
THEN WHAT THE FUCK WAS THAT?

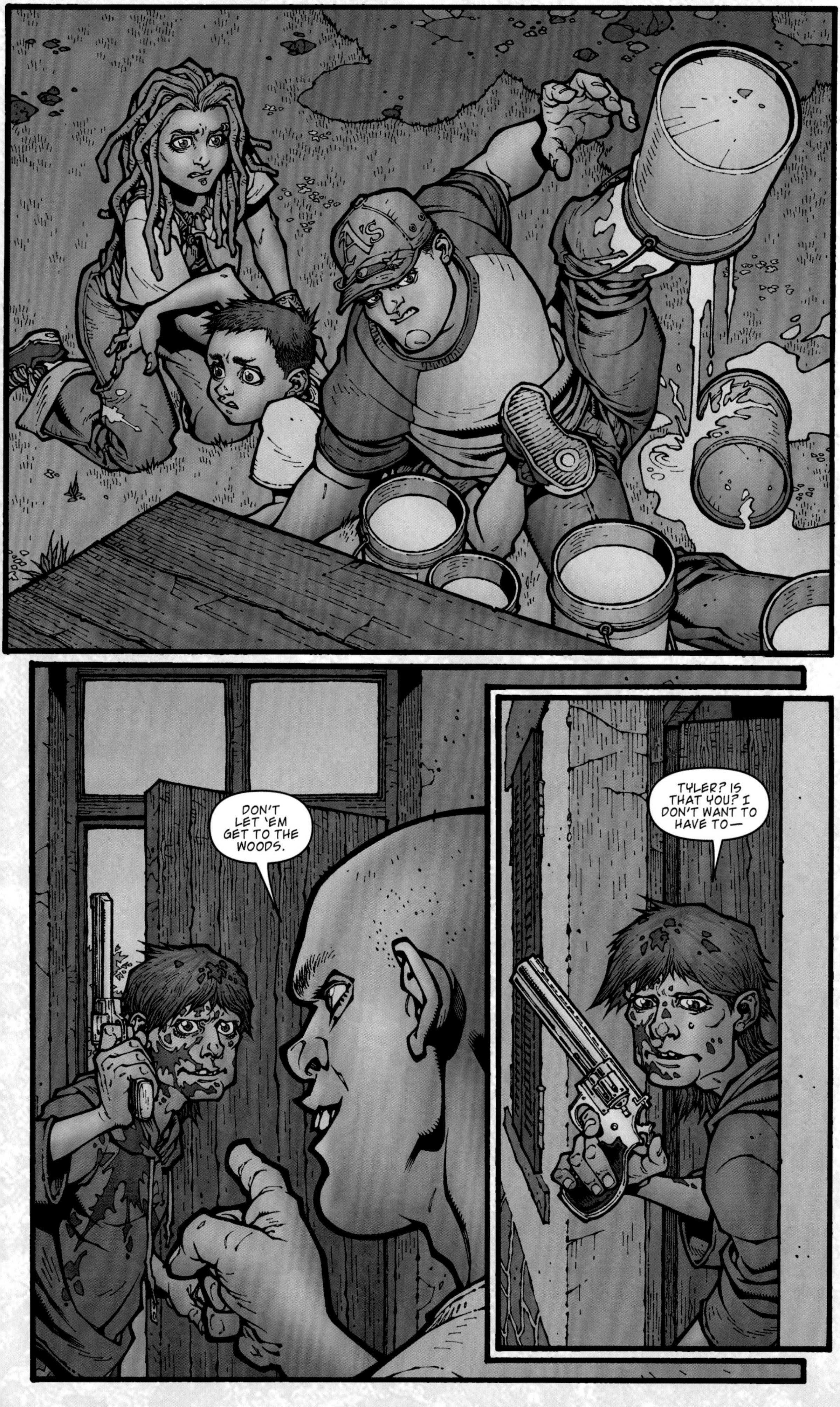
DON'T LET 'EM GET TO THE WOODS.
TYLER? IS THAT YOU? I DON'T WANT TO HAVE TO—

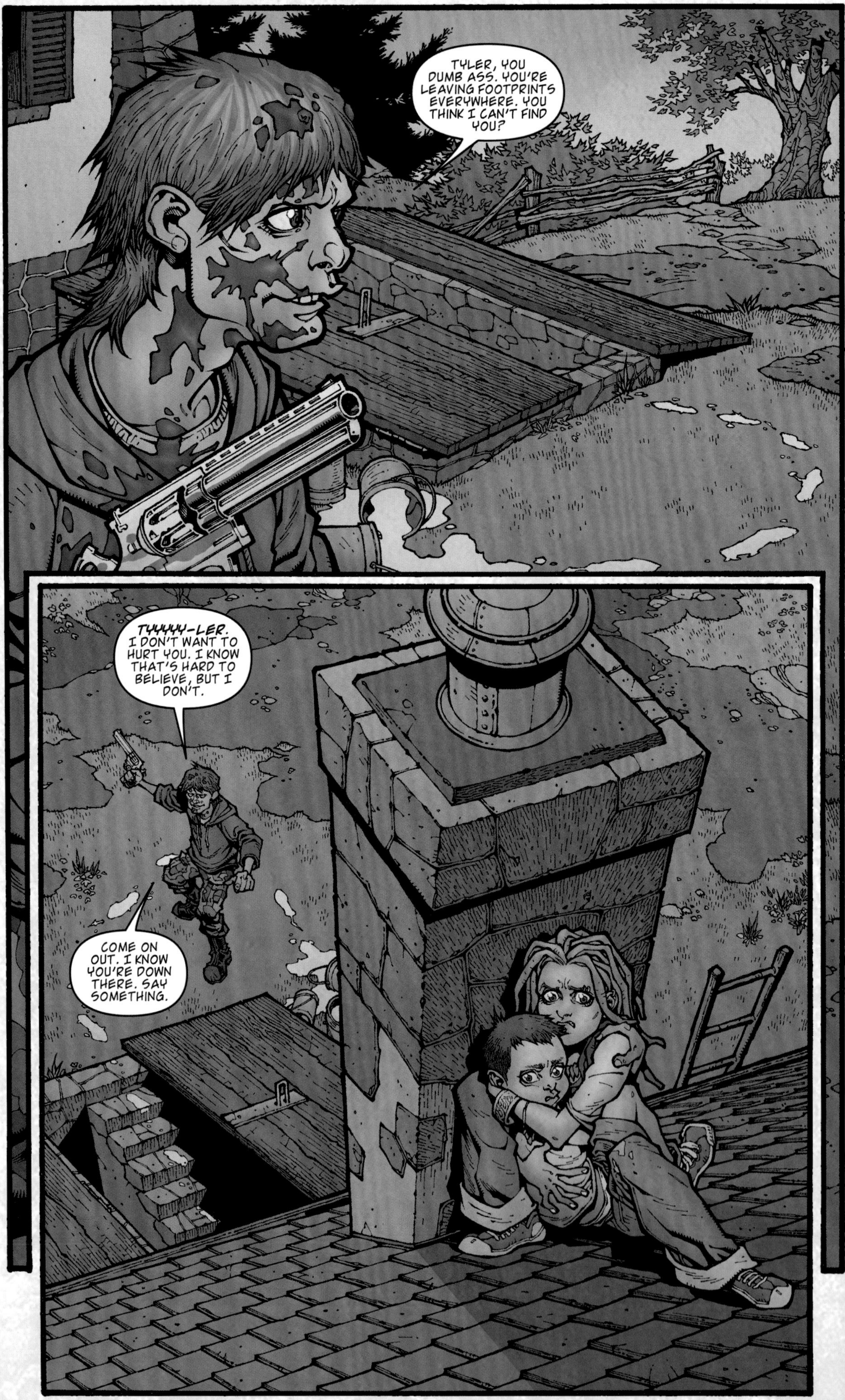
TYLER, YOU DUMB ASS. YOU'RE LEAVING FOOTPRINTS EVERYWHERE. YOU THINK I CAN'T FIND YOU?
TYYYYY-LER. I DON'T WANT TO HURT YOU. I KNOW THAT'S HARD TO BELIEVE, BUT I DON'T.
COME ON OUT. I KNOW YOU'RE DOWN THERE. SAY SOMETHING.

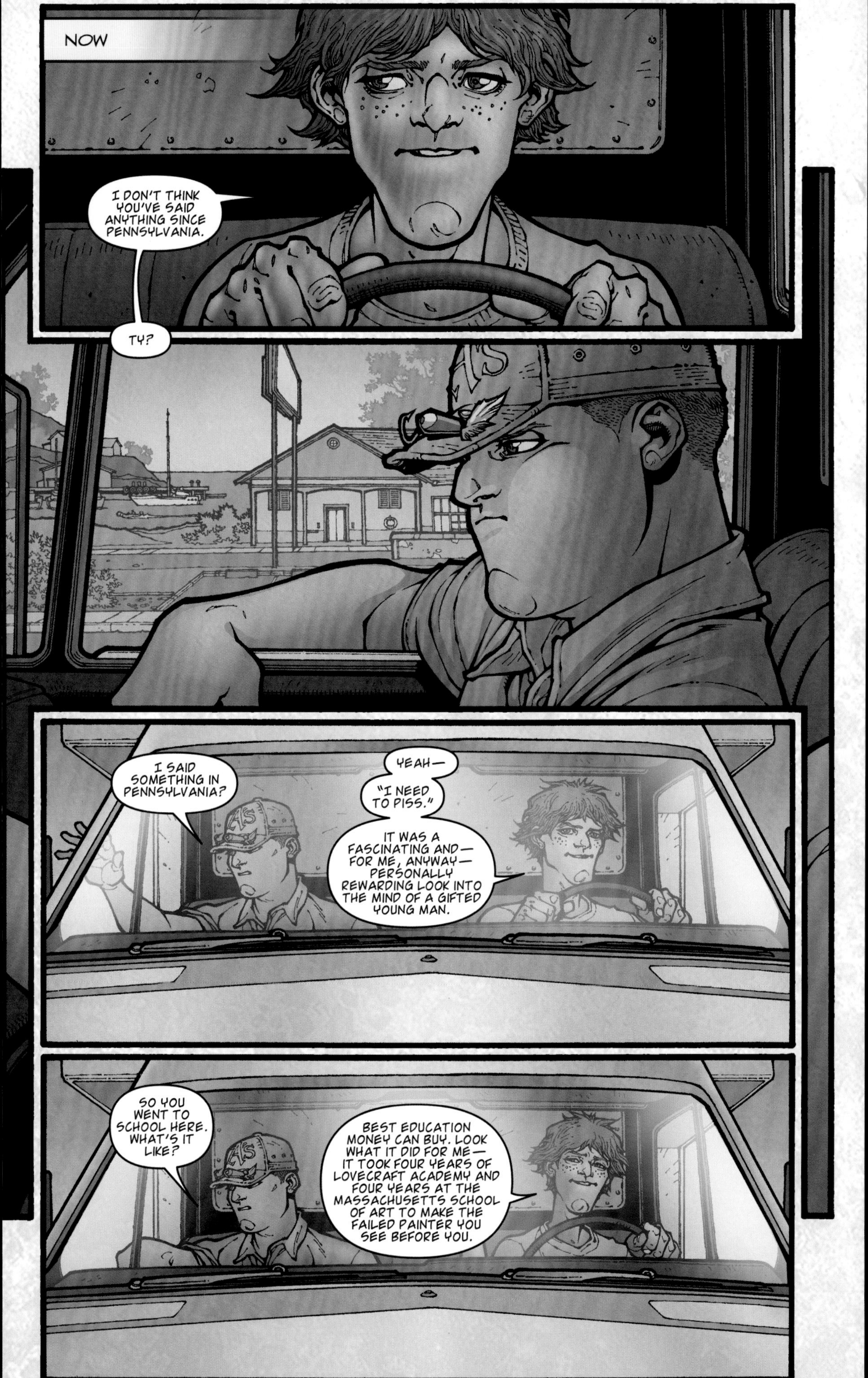
NOW
I DON'T THINK YOU'VE SAID ANYTHING SINCE PENNSYLVANIA.
TY?
I SAID SOMETHING IN PENNSYLVANIA?
YEAH—
"I NEED TO PISS."
IT WAS A FASCINATING AND— FOR ME, ANYWAY— PERSONALLY REWARDING LOOK INTO THE MIND OF A GIFTED YOUNG MAN.
SO YOU WENT TO SCHOOL HERE. WHAT'S IT LIKE?
BEST EDUCATION MONEY CAN BUY. LOOK WHAT IT DID FOR ME— IT TOOK FOUR YEARS OF LOVECRAFT ACADEMY AND FOUR YEARS AT THE MASSACHUSETTS SCHOOL OF ART TO MAKE THE FAILED PAINTER YOU SEE BEFORE YOU.

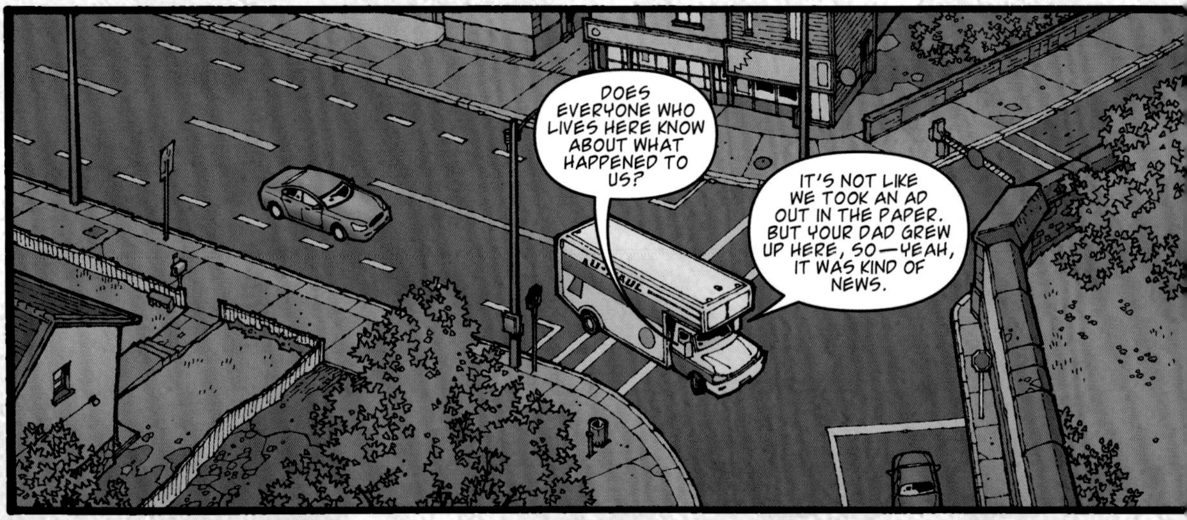
DOES EVERYONE WHO LIVES HERE KNOW ABOUT WHAT HAPPENED TO US?
IT'S NOT LIKE WE TOOK AN AD OUT IN THE PAPER. BUT YOUR DAD GREW UP HERE, SO—YEAH, IT WAS KIND OF NEWS.

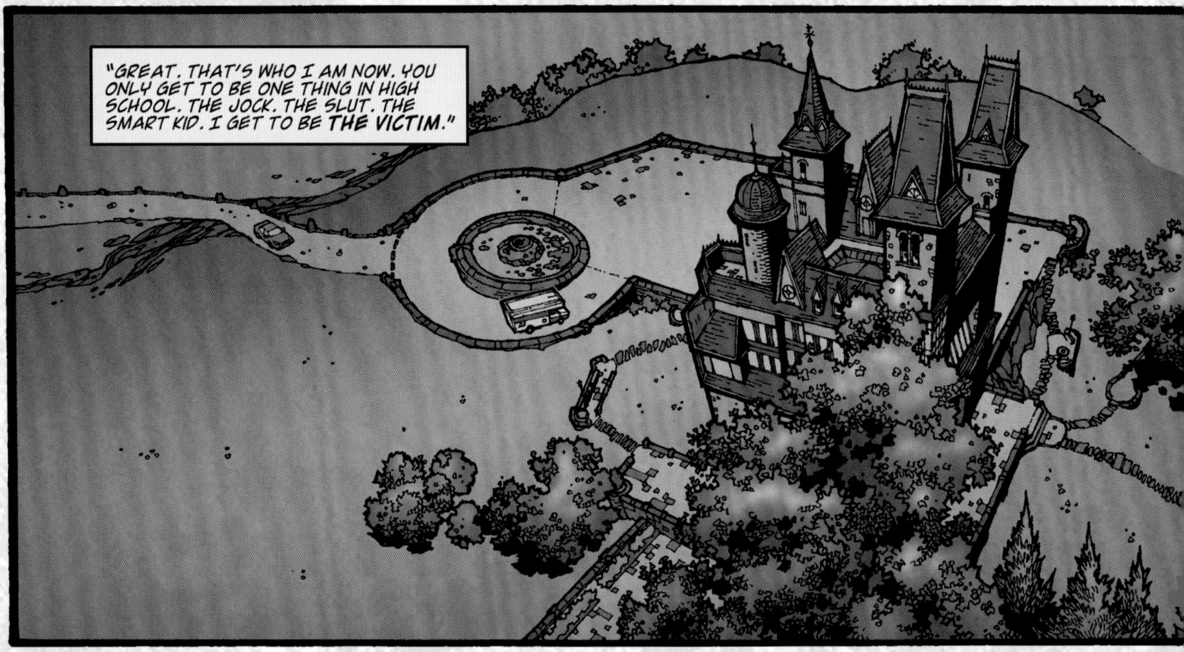
"GREAT. THAT'S WHO I AM NOW. YOU ONLY GET TO BE ONE THING IN HIGH SCHOOL. THE JOCK. THE SLUT. THE SMART KID. I GET TO BE THE VICTIM."

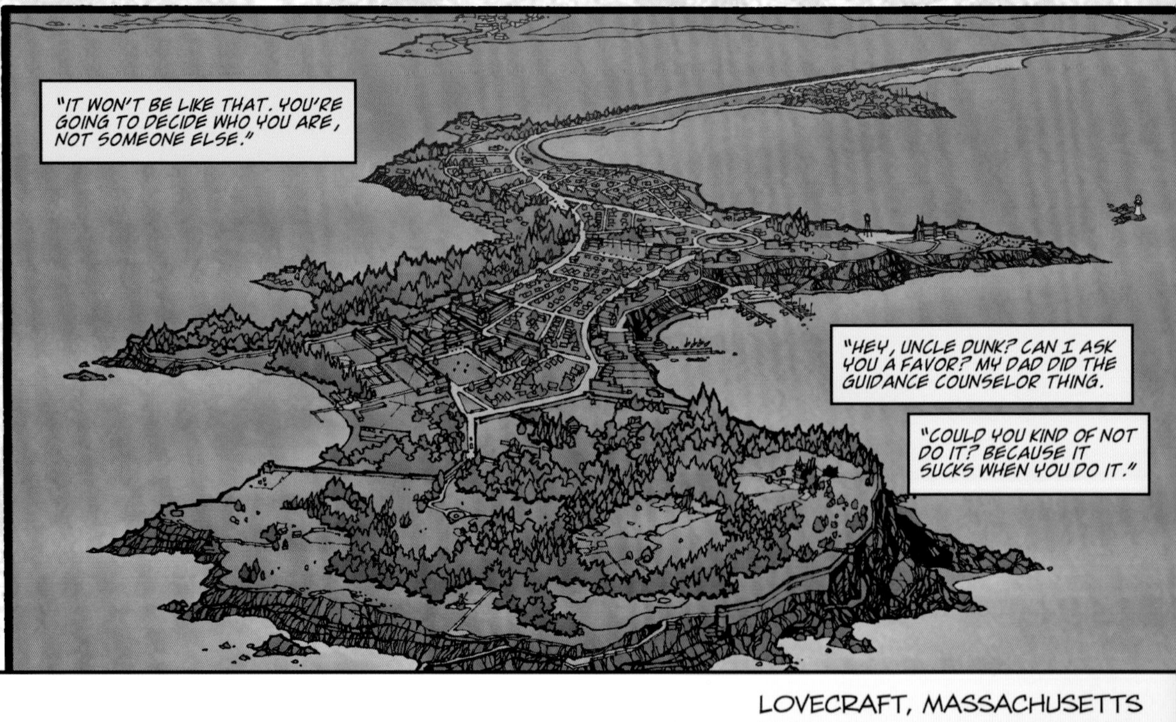
"IT WON'T BE LIKE THAT. YOU'RE GOING TO DECIDE WHO YOU ARE, NOT SOMEONE ELSE."
"HEY, UNCLE DUNK? CAN I ASK YOU A FAVOR? MY DAD DID THE GUIDANCE COUNSELOR THING.
"COULD YOU KIND OF NOT DO IT? BECAUSE IT SUCKS WHEN YOU DO IT."
LOVECRAFT, MASSACHUSETTS

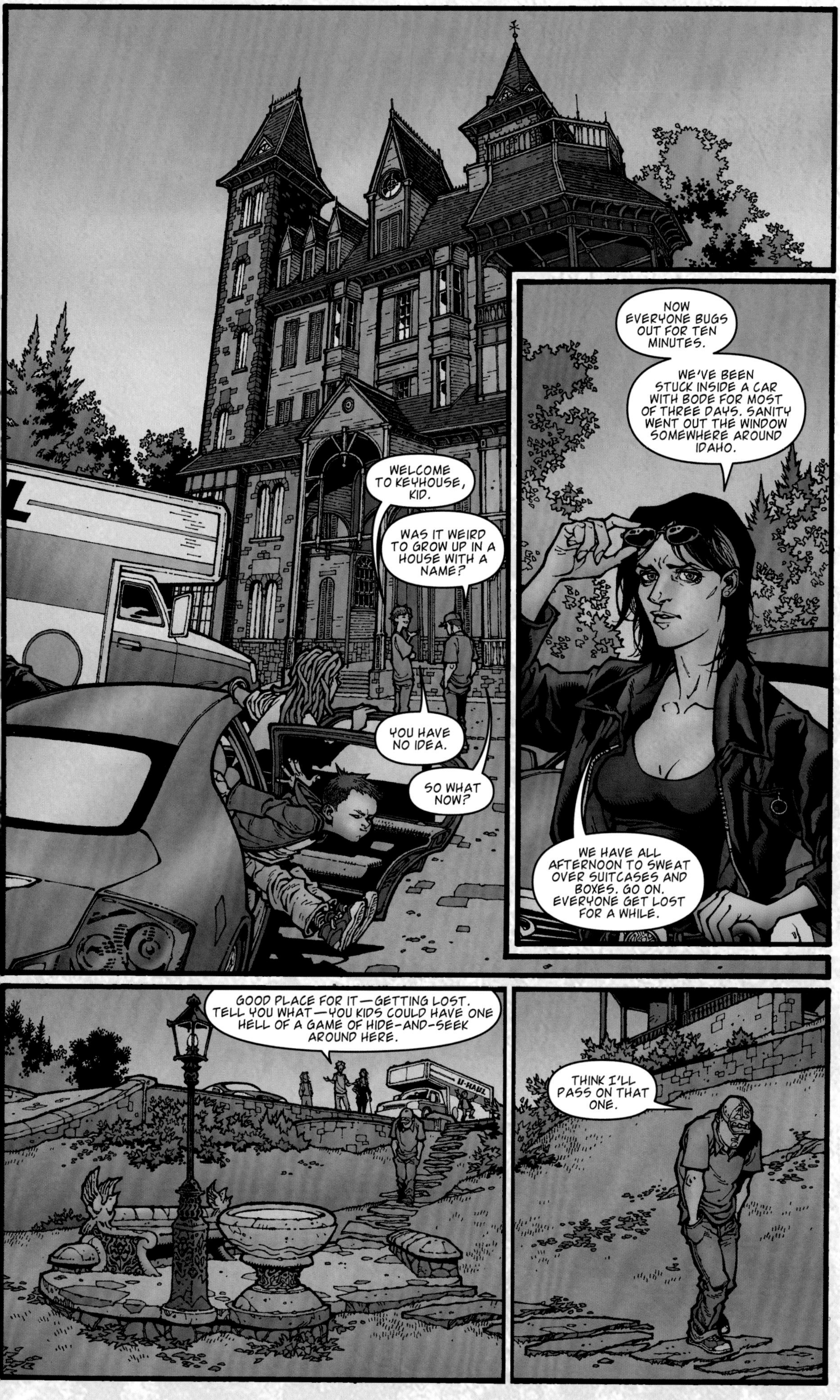
WELCOME TO KEYHOUSE, KID.
WAS IT WEIRD TO GROW UP IN A HOUSE WITH A NAME?
YOU HAVE NO IDEA.
SO WHAT NOW?
NOW EVERYONE BUGS OUT FOR TEN MINUTES.
WE'VE BEEN STUCK INSIDE A CAR WITH BODE FOR MOST OF THREE DAYS. SANITY WENT OUT THE WINDOW SOMEWHERE AROUND IDAHO.
WE HAVE ALL AFTERNOON TO SWEAT OVER SUITCASES AND BOXES. GO ON. EVERYONE GET LOST FOR A WHILE.
GOOD PLACE FOR IT—GETTING LOST. TELL YOU WHAT—YOU KIDS COULD HAVE ONE HELL OF A GAME OF HIDE-AND-SEEK AROUND HERE.
U-HAUL
THINK I'LL PASS ON THAT ONE.

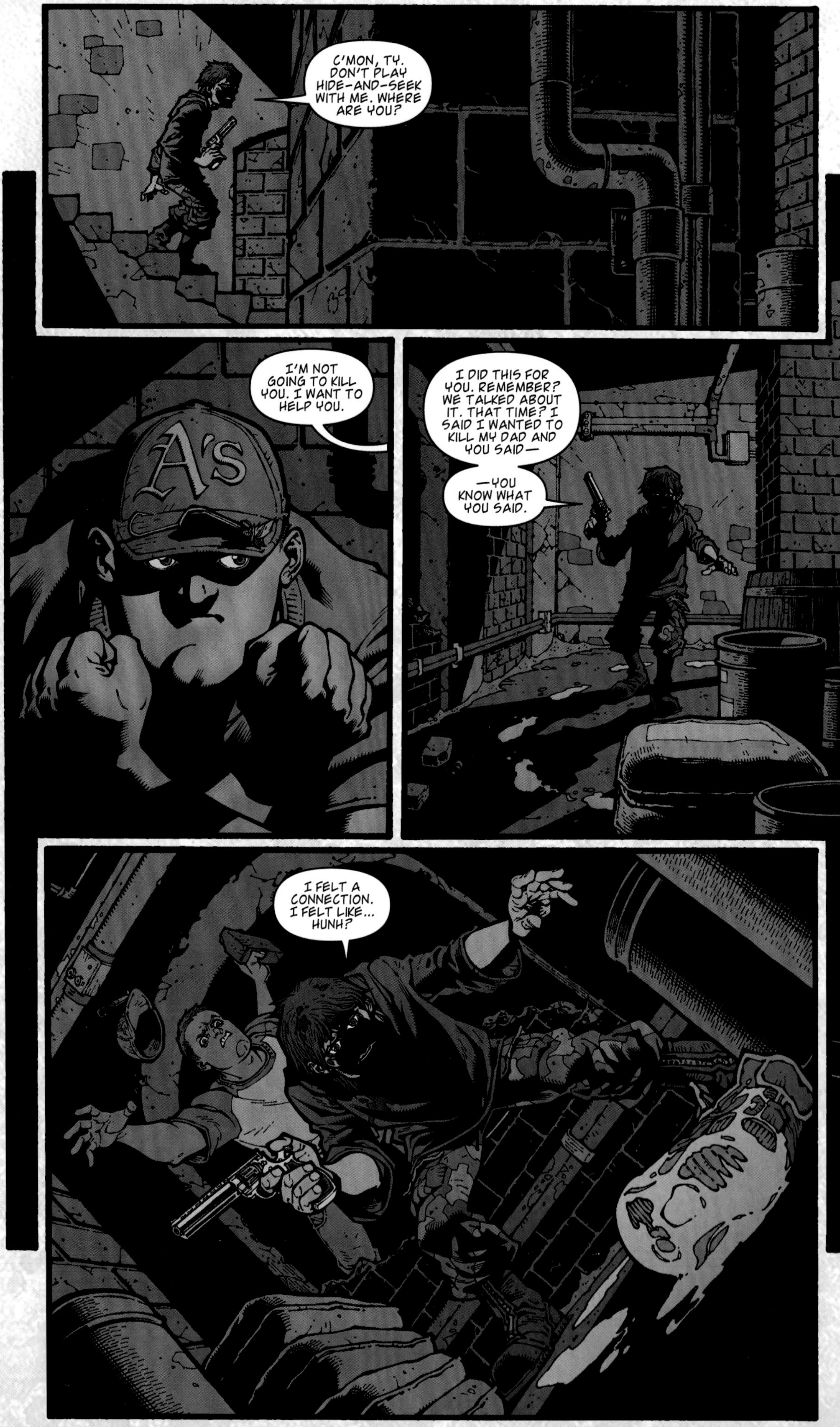
C'MON, TY. DON'T PLAY HIDE-AND-SEEK WITH ME. WHERE ARE YOU?
I'M NOT GOING TO KILL YOU. I WANT TO HELP YOU.
I DID THIS FOR YOU. REMEMBER? WE TALKED ABOUT IT. THAT TIME? I SAID I WANTED TO KILL MY DAD AND YOU SAID—
—YOU KNOW WHAT YOU SAID.
I FELT A CONNECTION. I FELT LIKE... HUNH?

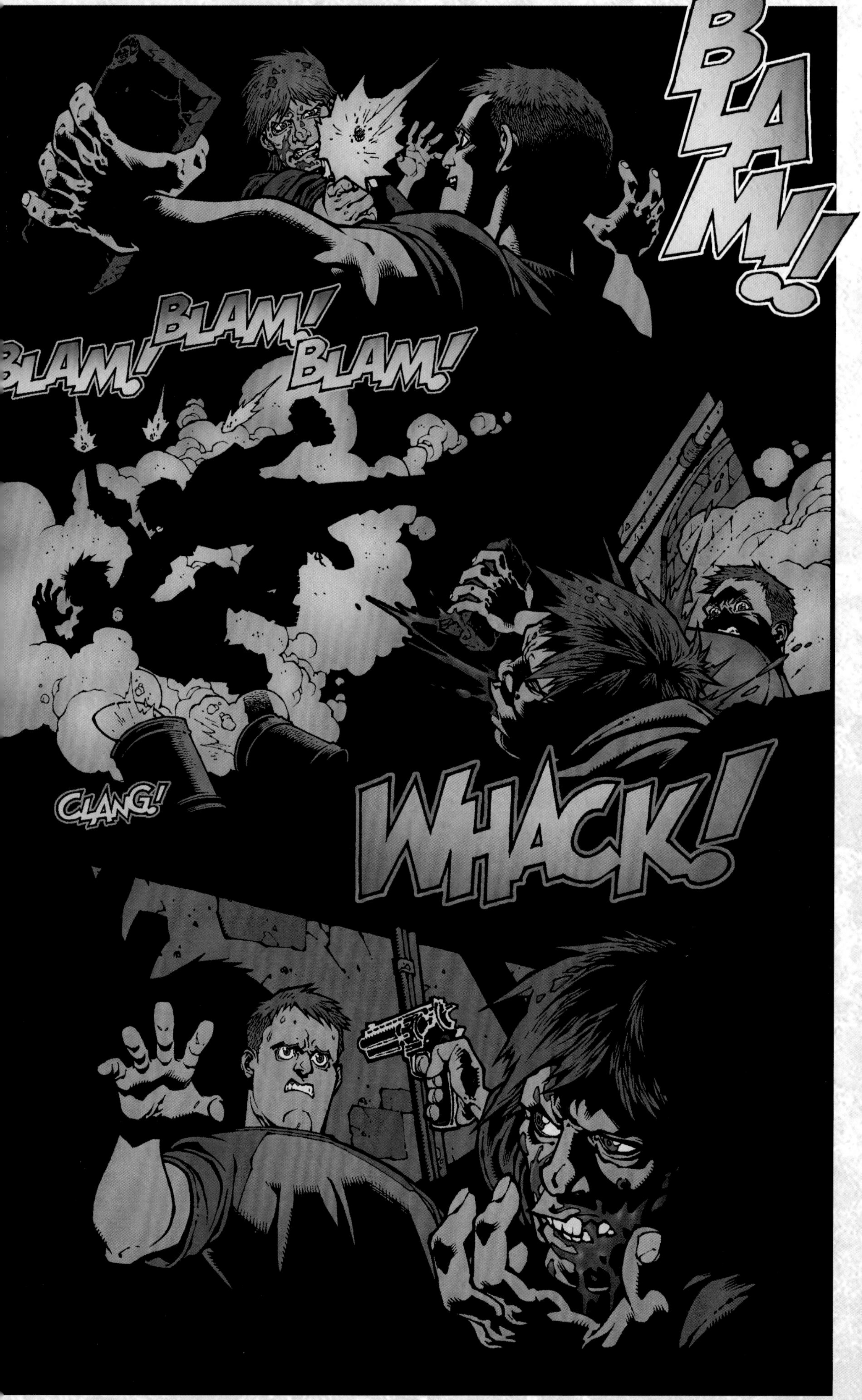
BLAM!
BLAM! BLAM! BLAM!
CLANG!
WHACK!

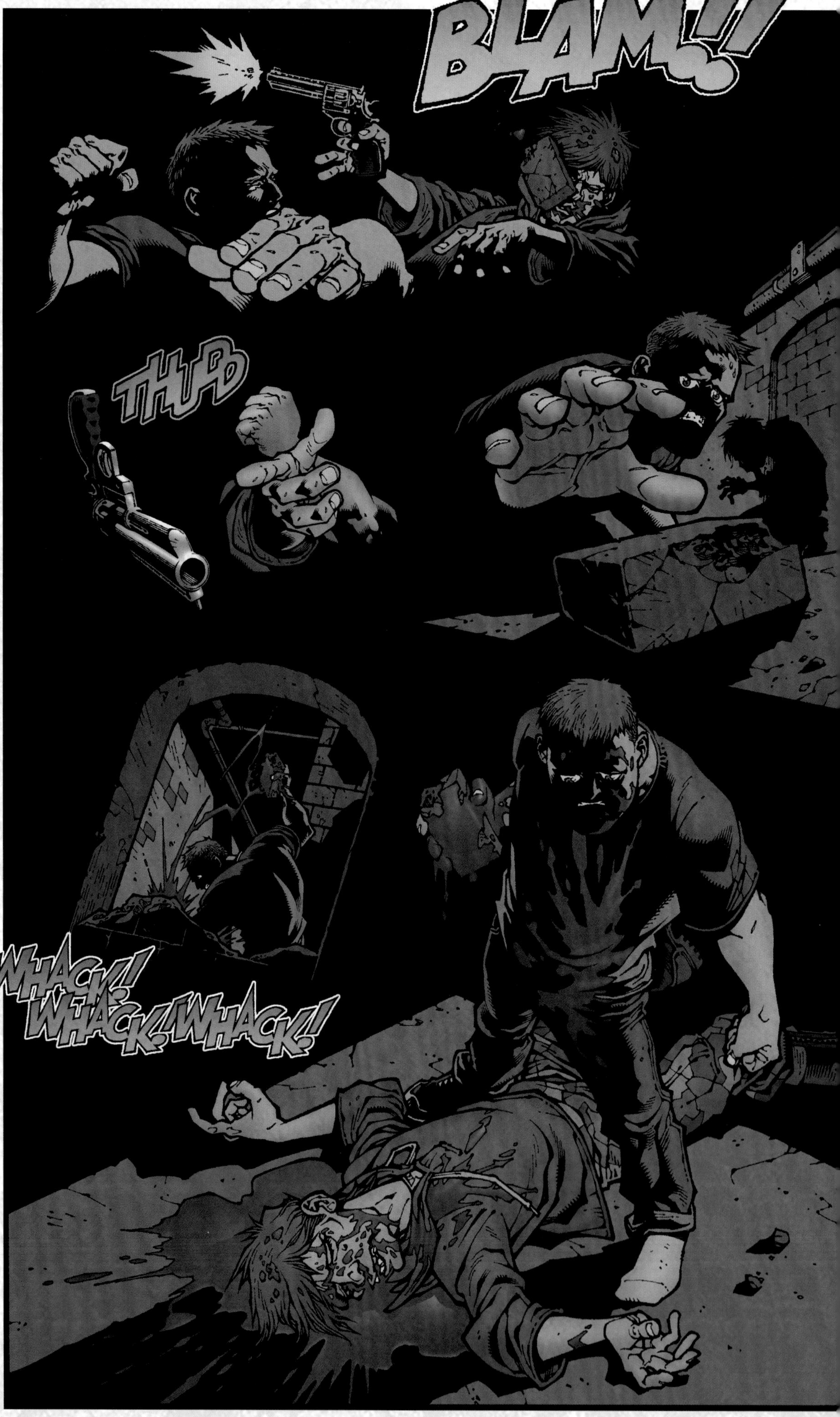
BLAM!!
THUD
WHACK! WHACK! WHACK!

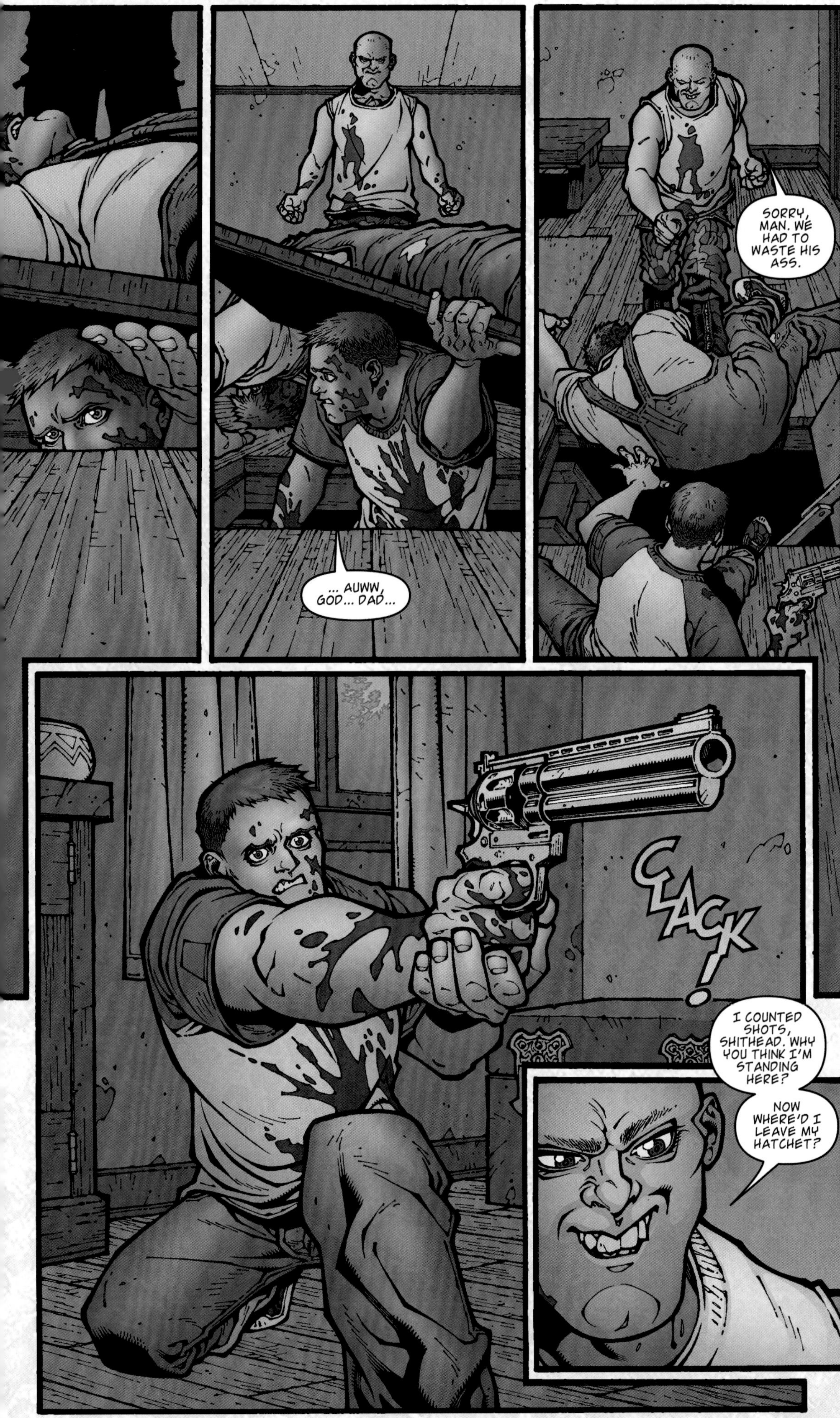
... AUWW, GOD... DAD...
SORRY, MAN. WE HAD TO WASTE HIS ASS.
CLACK!
I COUNTED SHOTS, SHITHEAD. WHY YOU THINK I'M STANDING HERE?
NOW WHERE'D I LEAVE MY HATCHET?

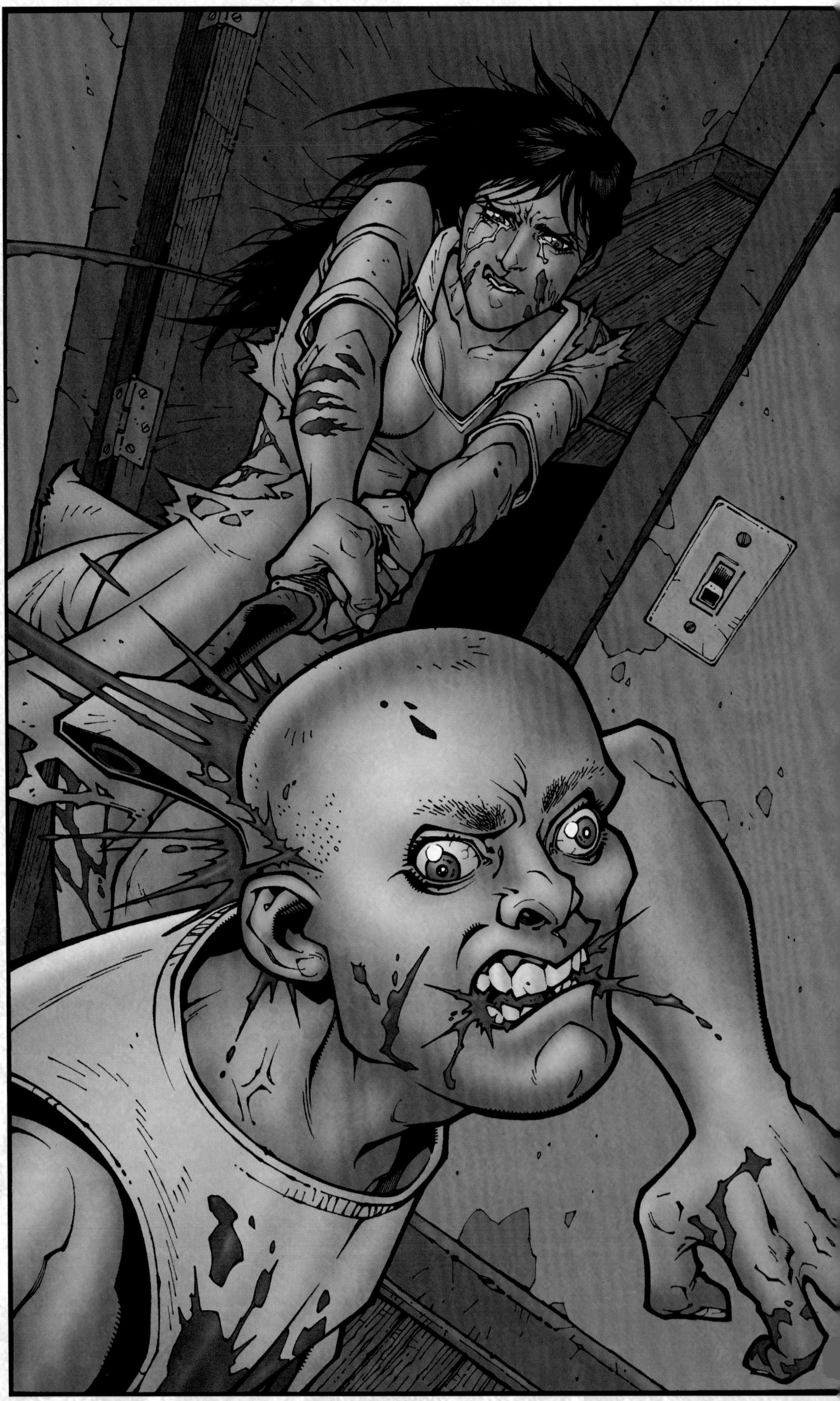

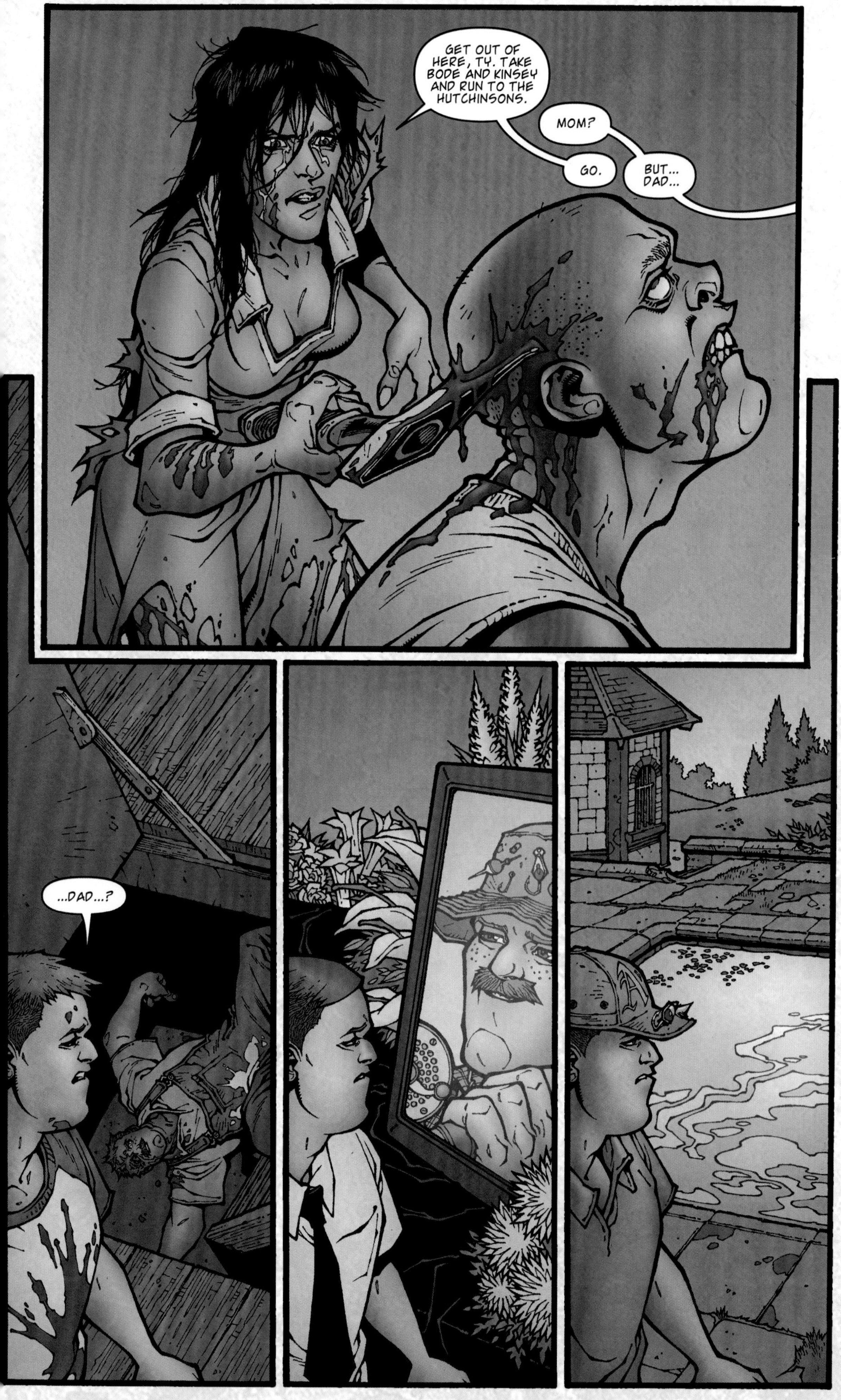
GET OUT OF HERE, TY. TAKE BODE AND KINSEY AND RUN TO THE HUTCHINSONS.
MOM?
GO.
BUT... DAD...
...DAD...?

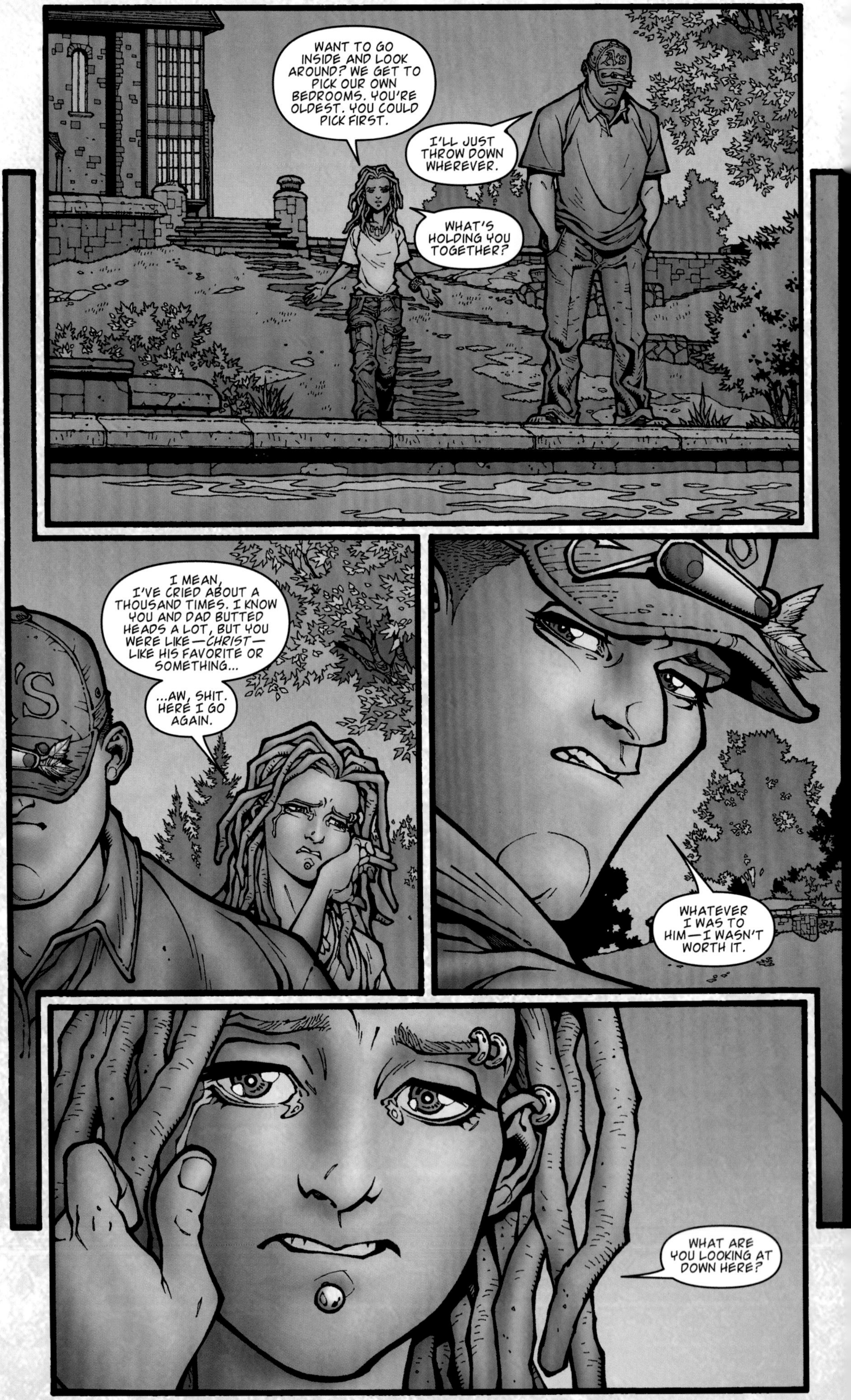
WANT TO GO INSIDE AND LOOK AROUND? WE GET TO PICK OUR OWN BEDROOMS. YOU'RE OLDEST. YOU COULD PICK FIRST.
I'LL JUST THROW DOWN WHEREVER.
WHAT'S HOLDING YOU TOGETHER?
I MEAN, I'VE CRIED ABOUT A THOUSAND TIMES. I KNOW YOU AND DAD BUTTED HEADS A LOT, BUT YOU WERE LIKE—*CHRIST*—LIKE HIS FAVORITE OR SOMETHING...
...AW, SHIT. HERE I GO AGAIN.
WHATEVER I WAS TO HIM—I WASN'T WORTH IT.
WHAT ARE YOU LOOKING AT DOWN HERE?

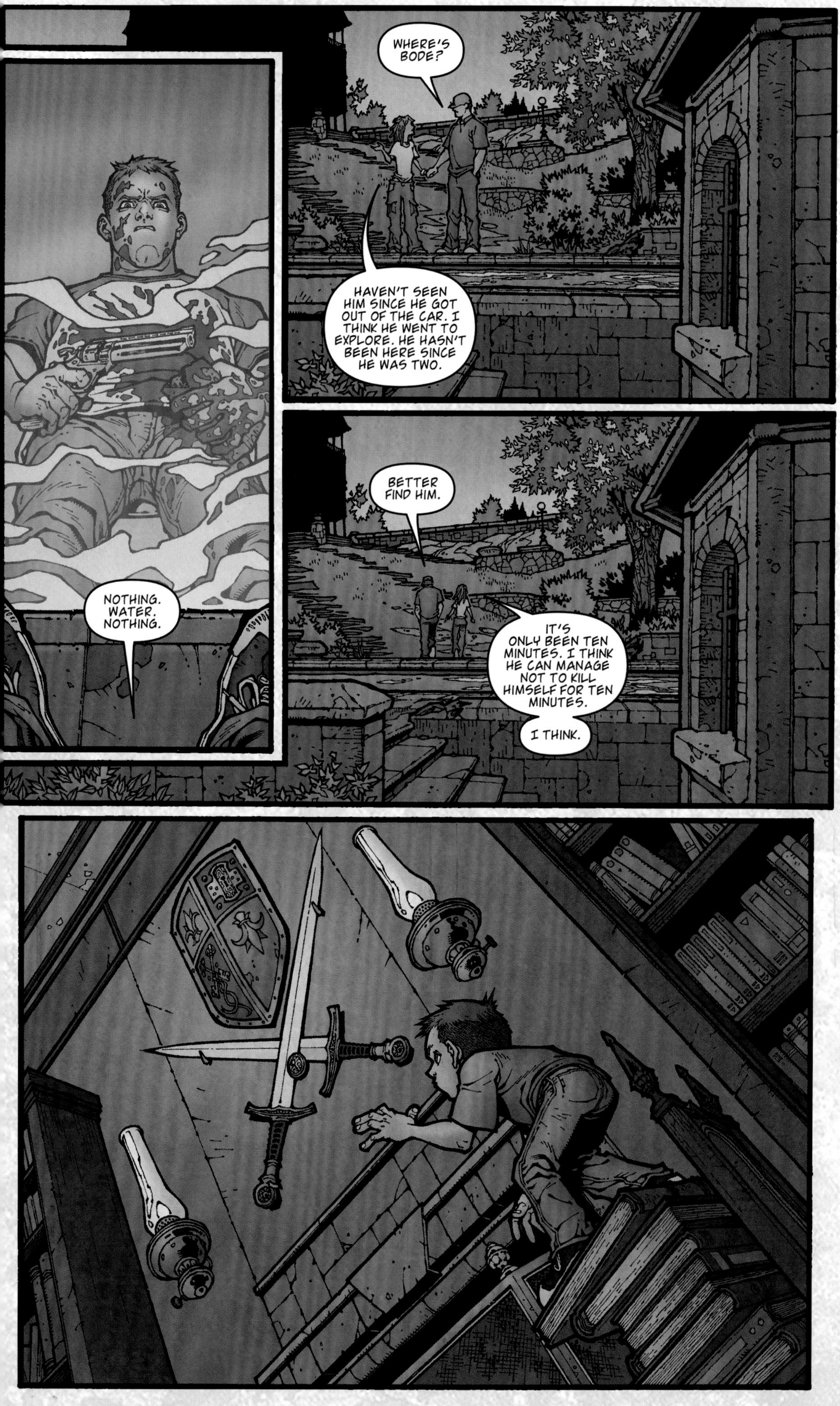
WHERE'S BODE?
HAVEN'T SEEN HIM SINCE HE GOT OUT OF THE CAR. I THINK HE WENT TO EXPLORE. HE HASN'T BEEN HERE SINCE HE WAS TWO.
NOTHING. WATER. NOTHING.
BETTER FIND HIM.
IT'S ONLY BEEN TEN MINUTES. I THINK HE CAN MANAGE NOT TO KILL HIMSELF FOR TEN MINUTES.
I THINK.

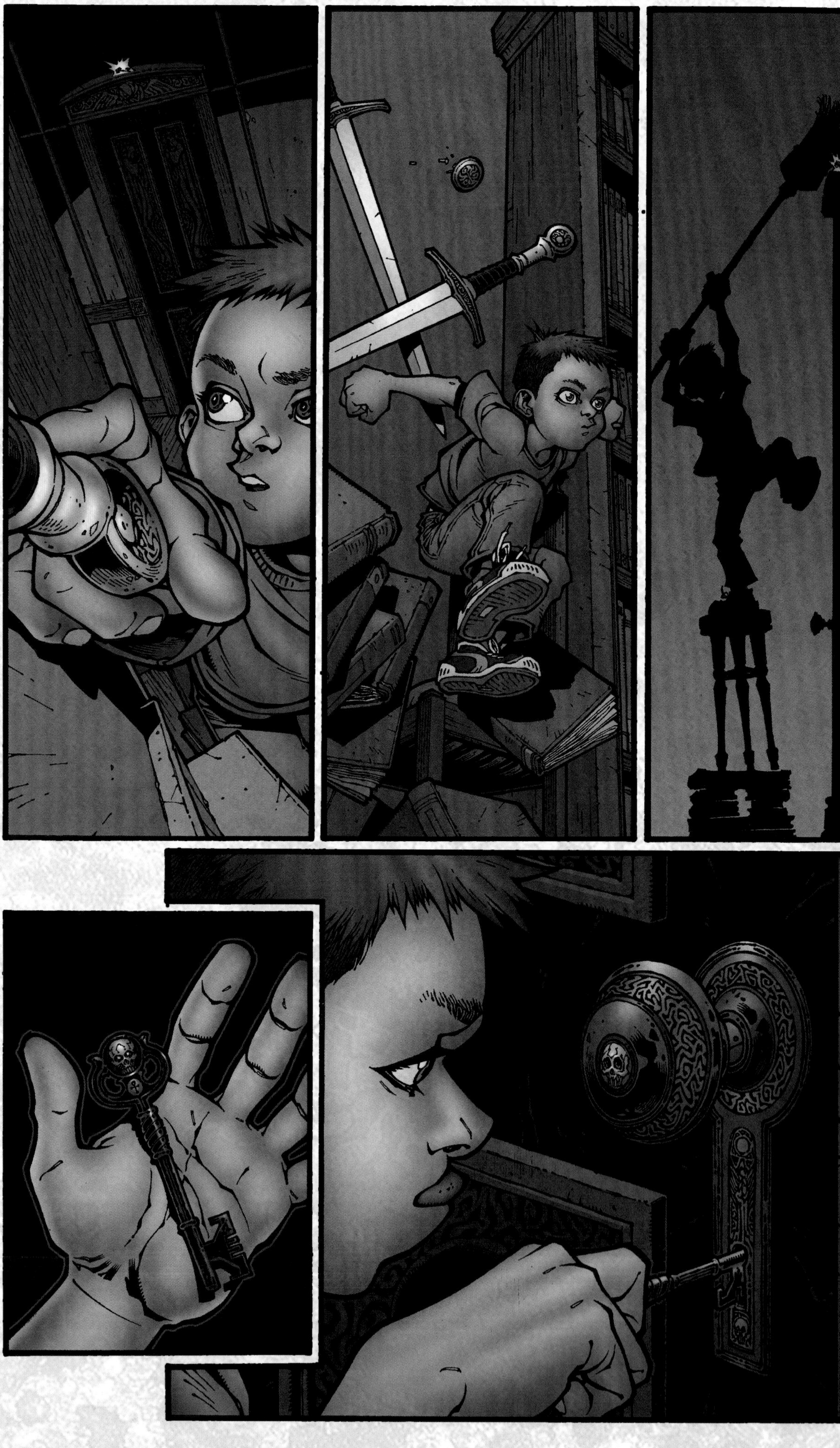

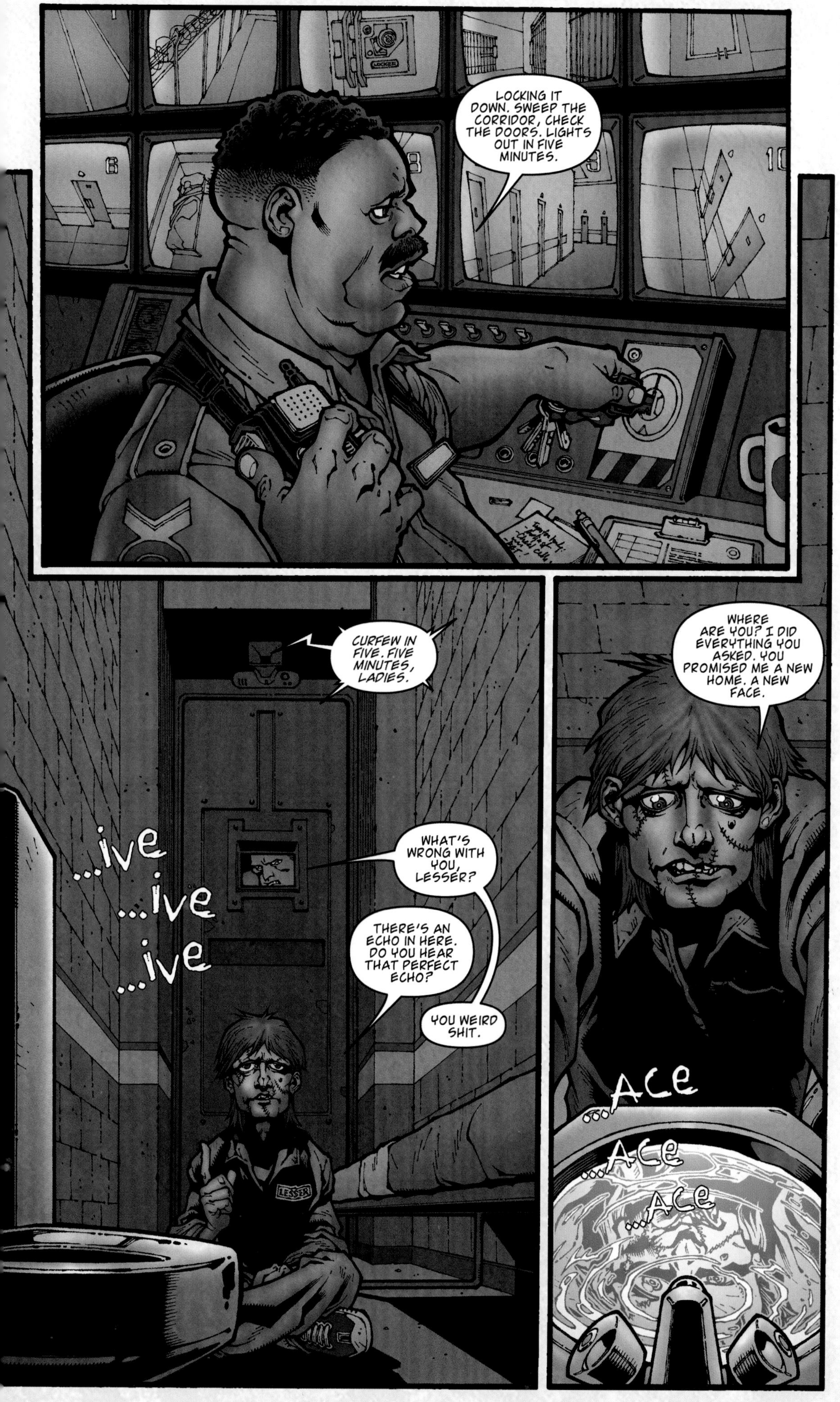
LOCKING IT DOWN. SWEEP THE CORRIDOR, CHECK THE DOORS. LIGHTS OUT IN FIVE MINUTES.
CURFEW IN FIVE. FIVE MINUTES, LADIES.
...ive
...ive
...ive
WHAT'S WRONG WITH YOU, LESSER?
THERE'S AN ECHO IN HERE. DO YOU HEAR THAT PERFECT ECHO?
YOU WEIRD SHIT.
WHERE ARE YOU? I DID EVERYTHING YOU ASKED. YOU PROMISED ME A NEW HOME. A NEW FACE.
...ACE
...ACE
...ACE

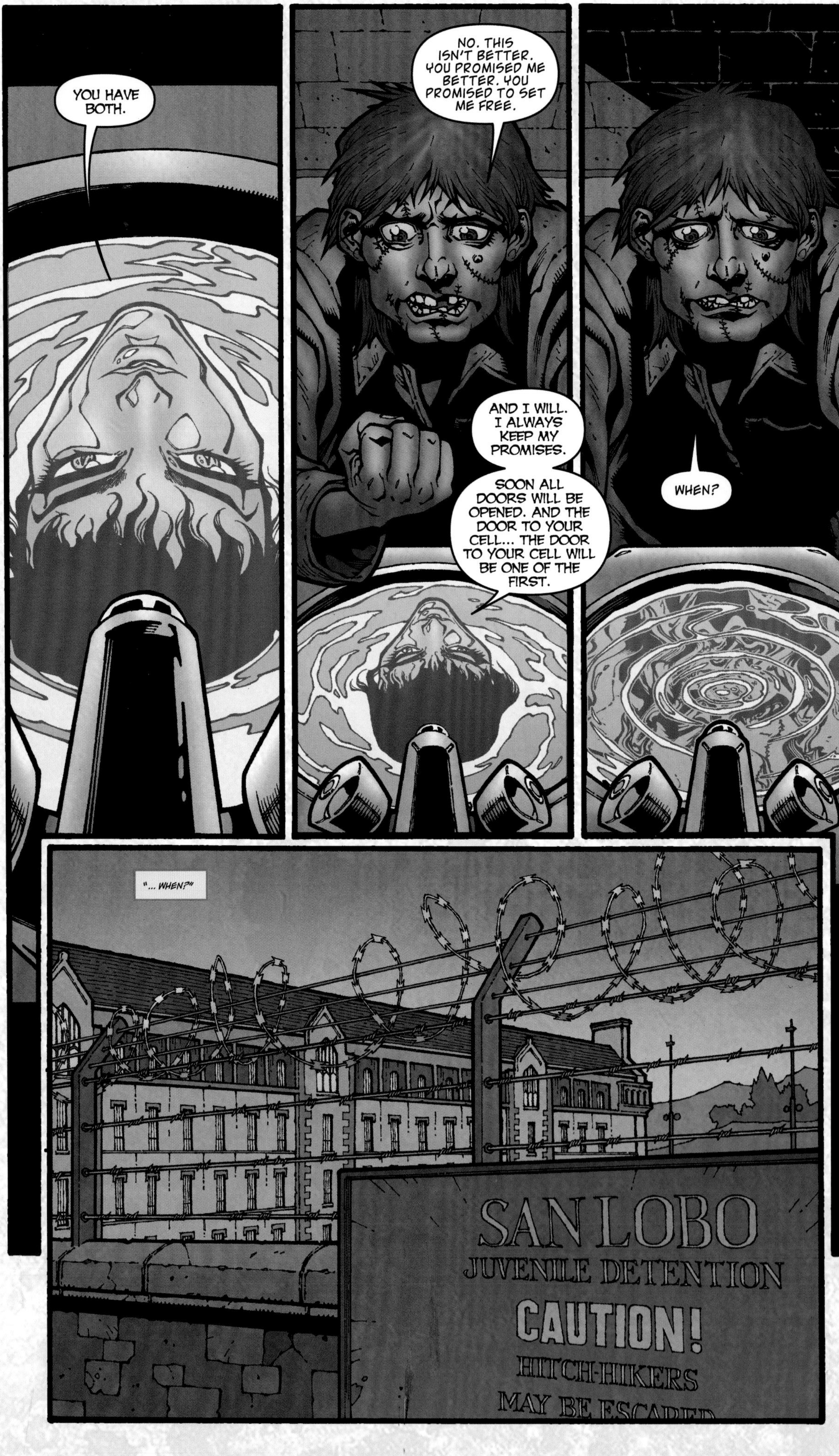
YOU HAVE BOTH.
NO. THIS ISN'T BETTER. YOU PROMISED ME BETTER. YOU PROMISED TO SET ME FREE.
AND I WILL. I ALWAYS KEEP MY PROMISES.
SOON ALL DOORS WILL BE OPENED. AND THE DOOR TO YOUR CELL... THE DOOR TO YOUR CELL WILL BE ONE OF THE FIRST.
WHEN?
"... WHEN?"
SAN LOBO
JUVENILE DETENTION
CAUTION!
HITCH-HIKERS

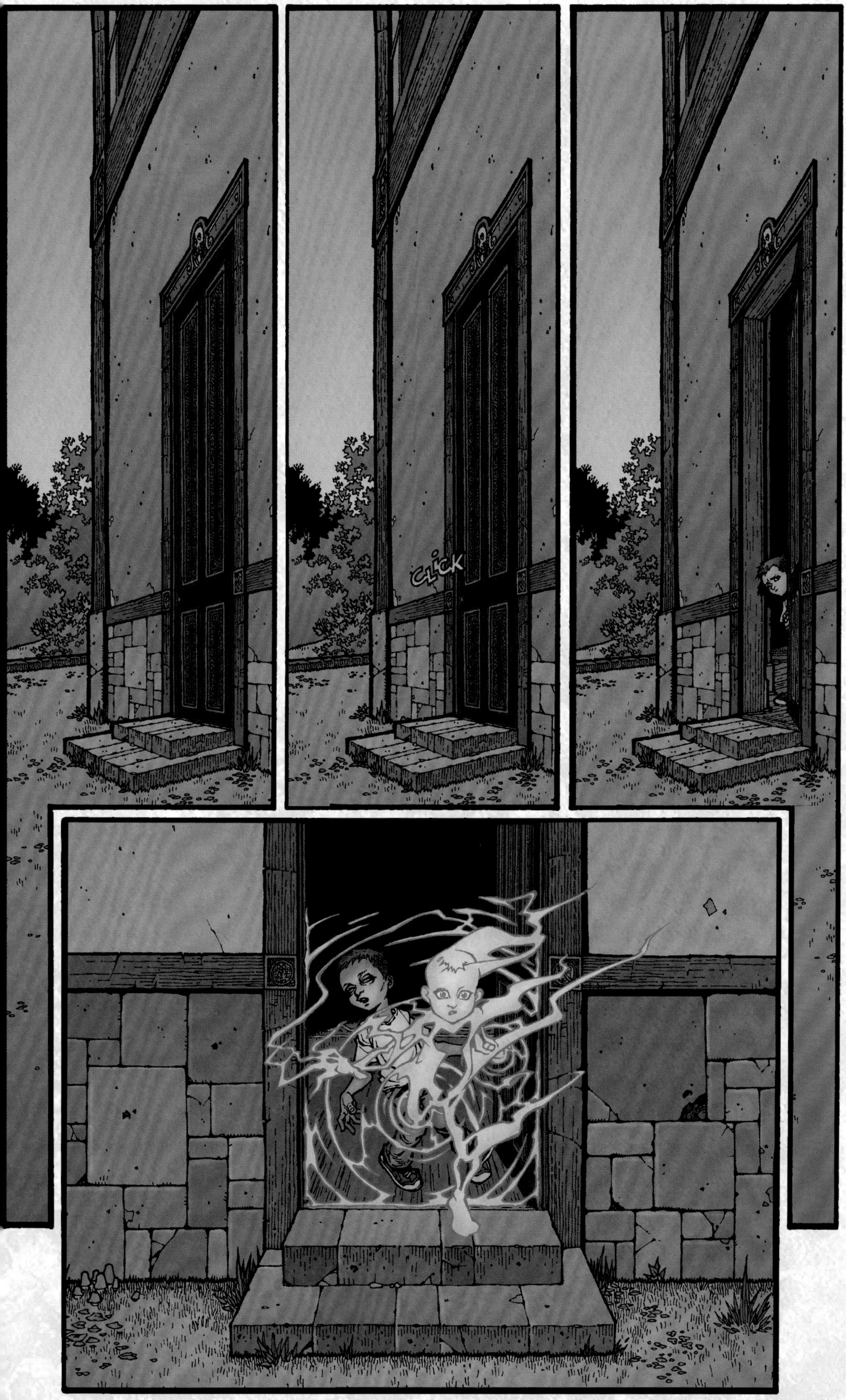
CLICK

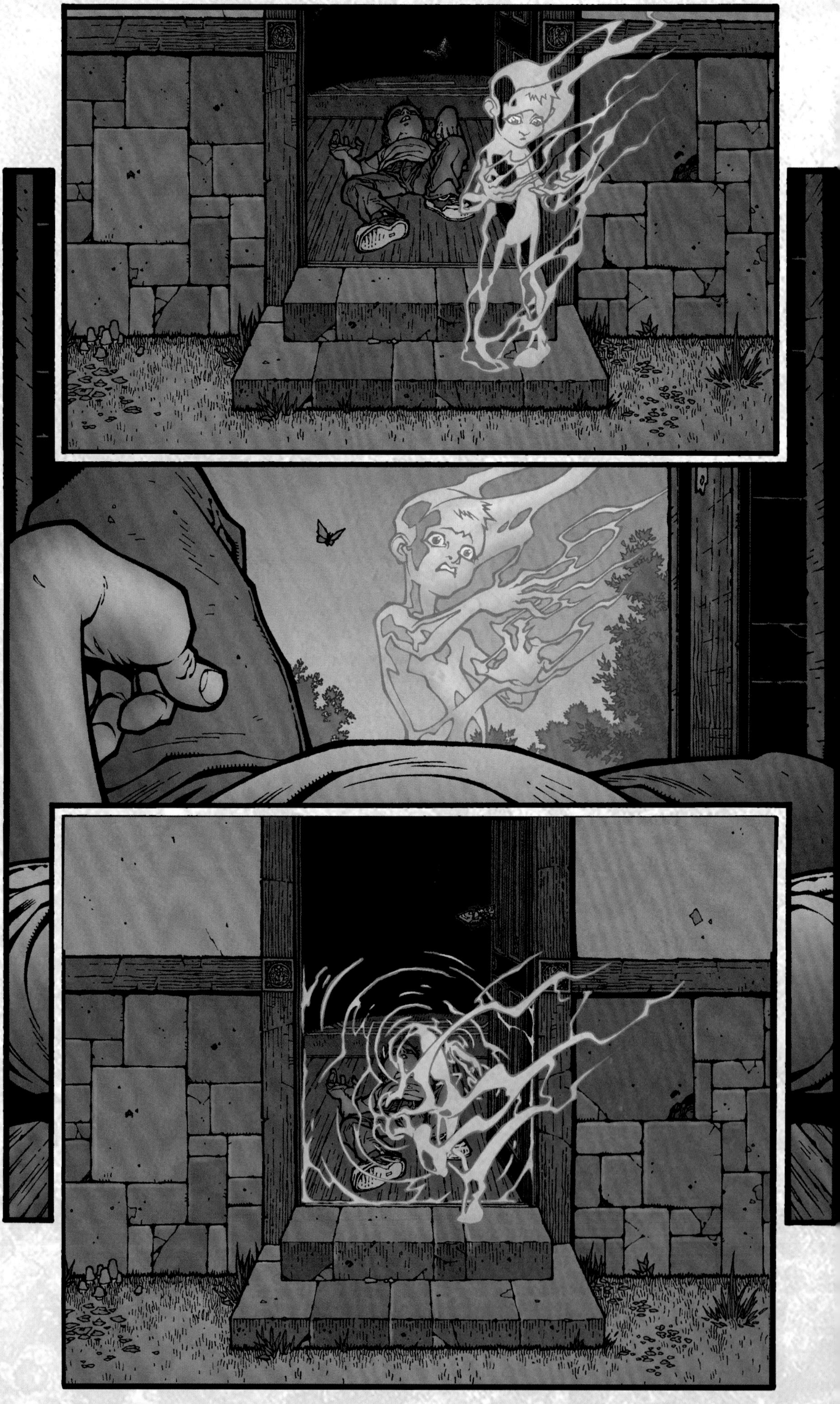

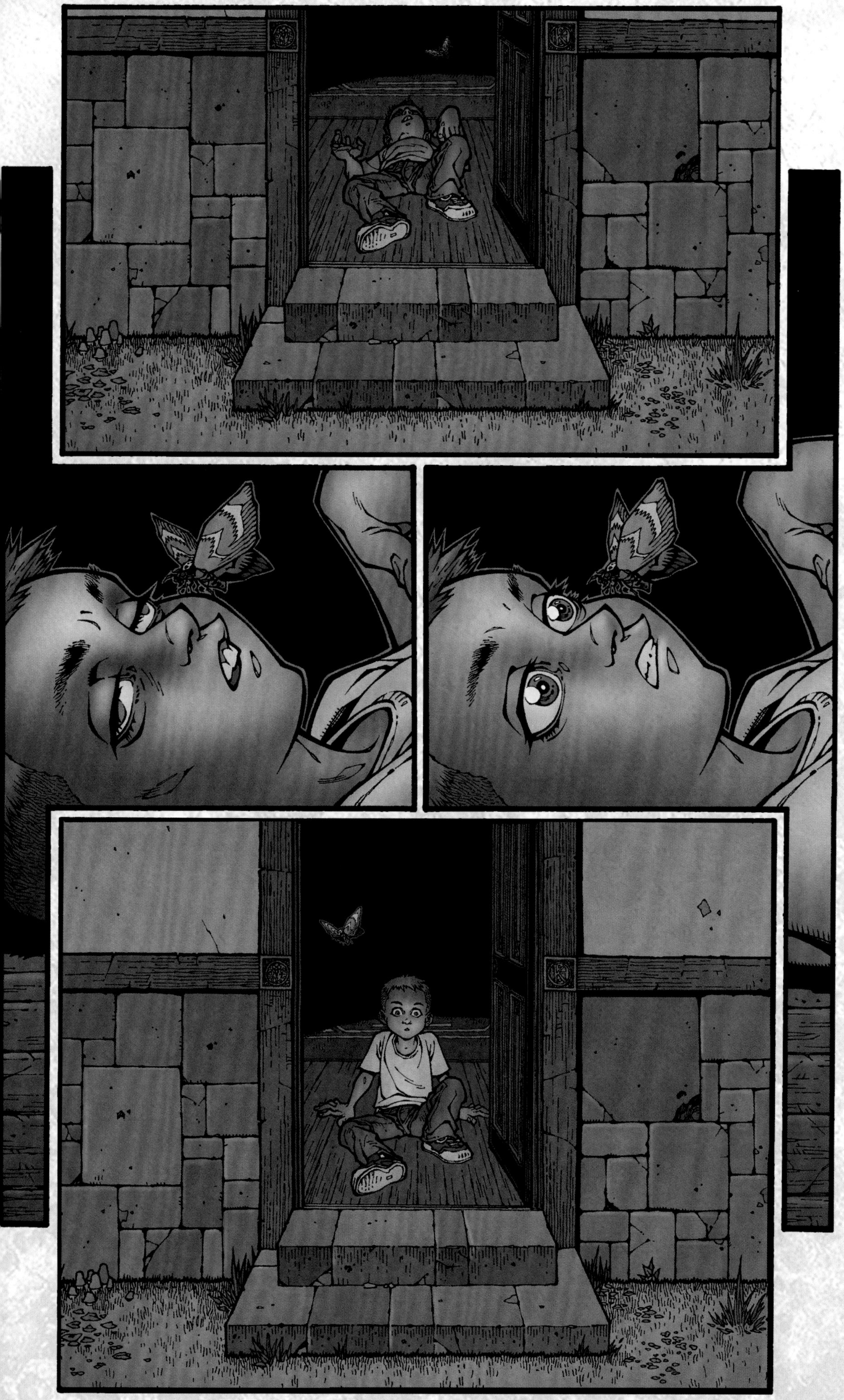

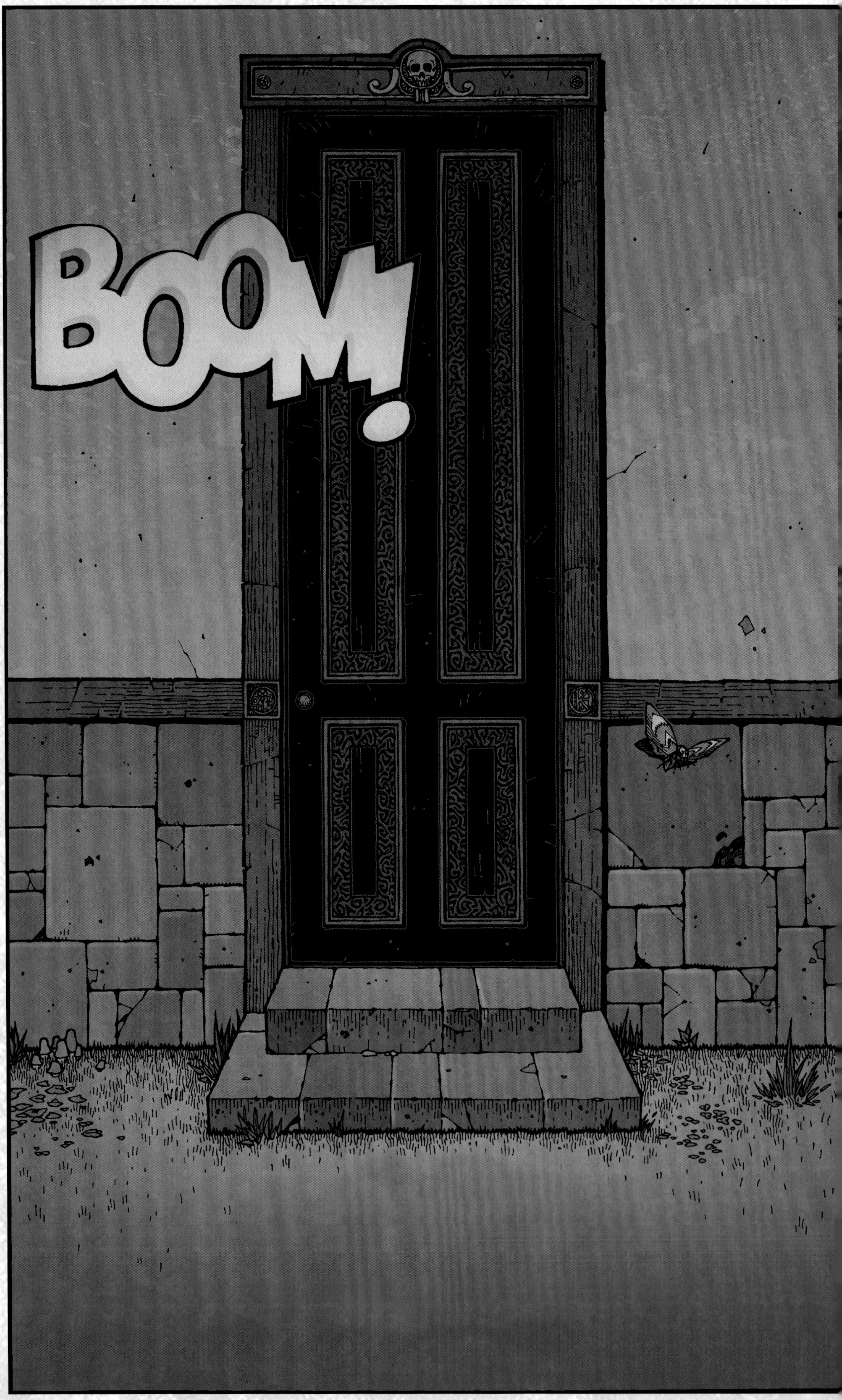
BOOM!

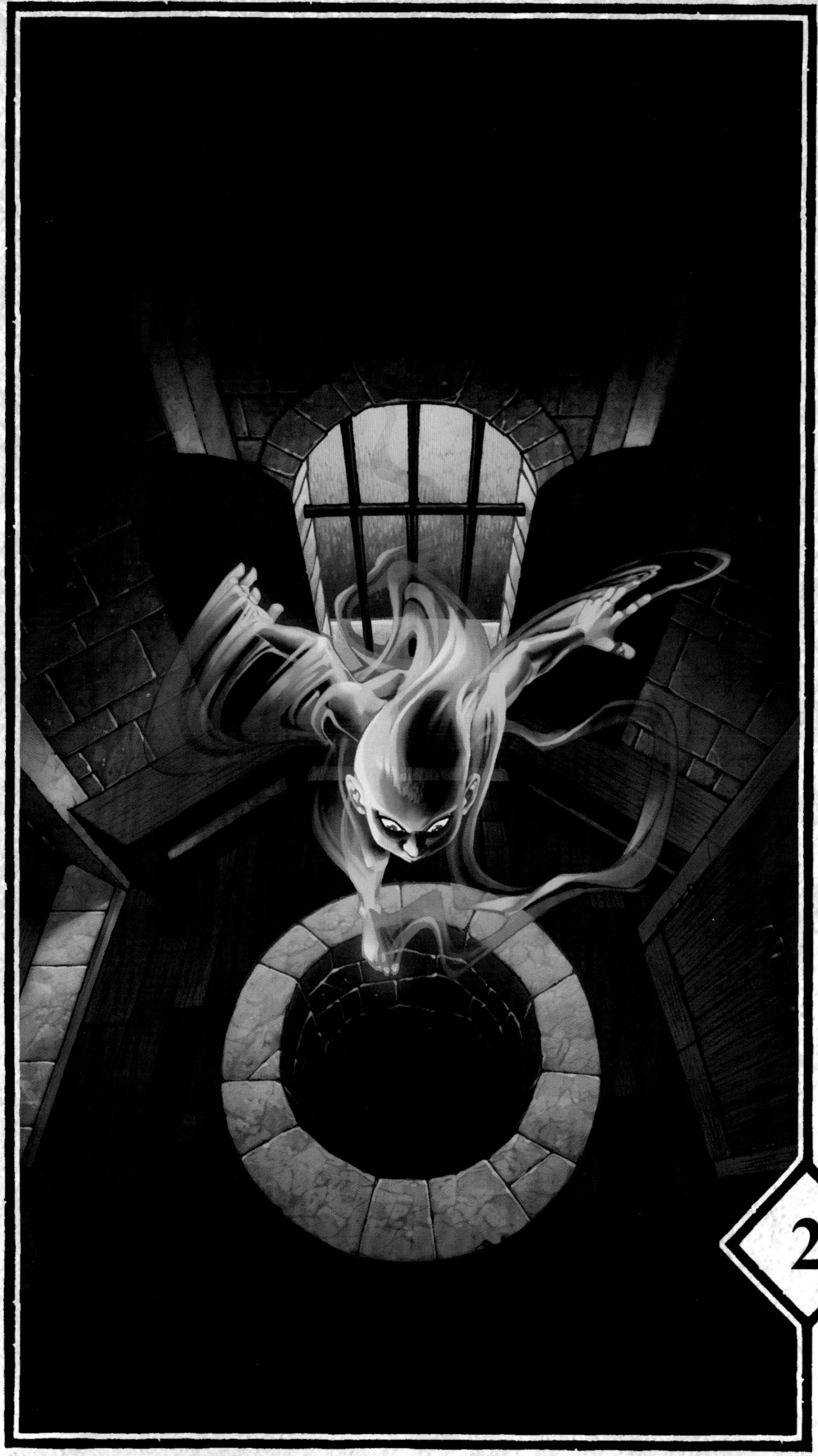

2

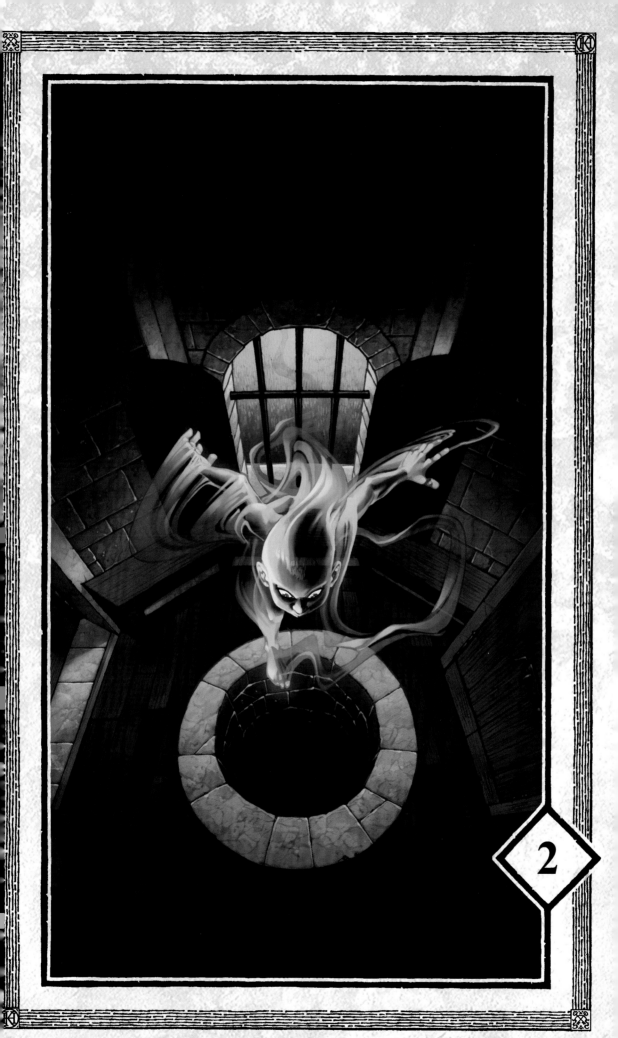

WELCOME TO LOVECRAFT
- TWO -

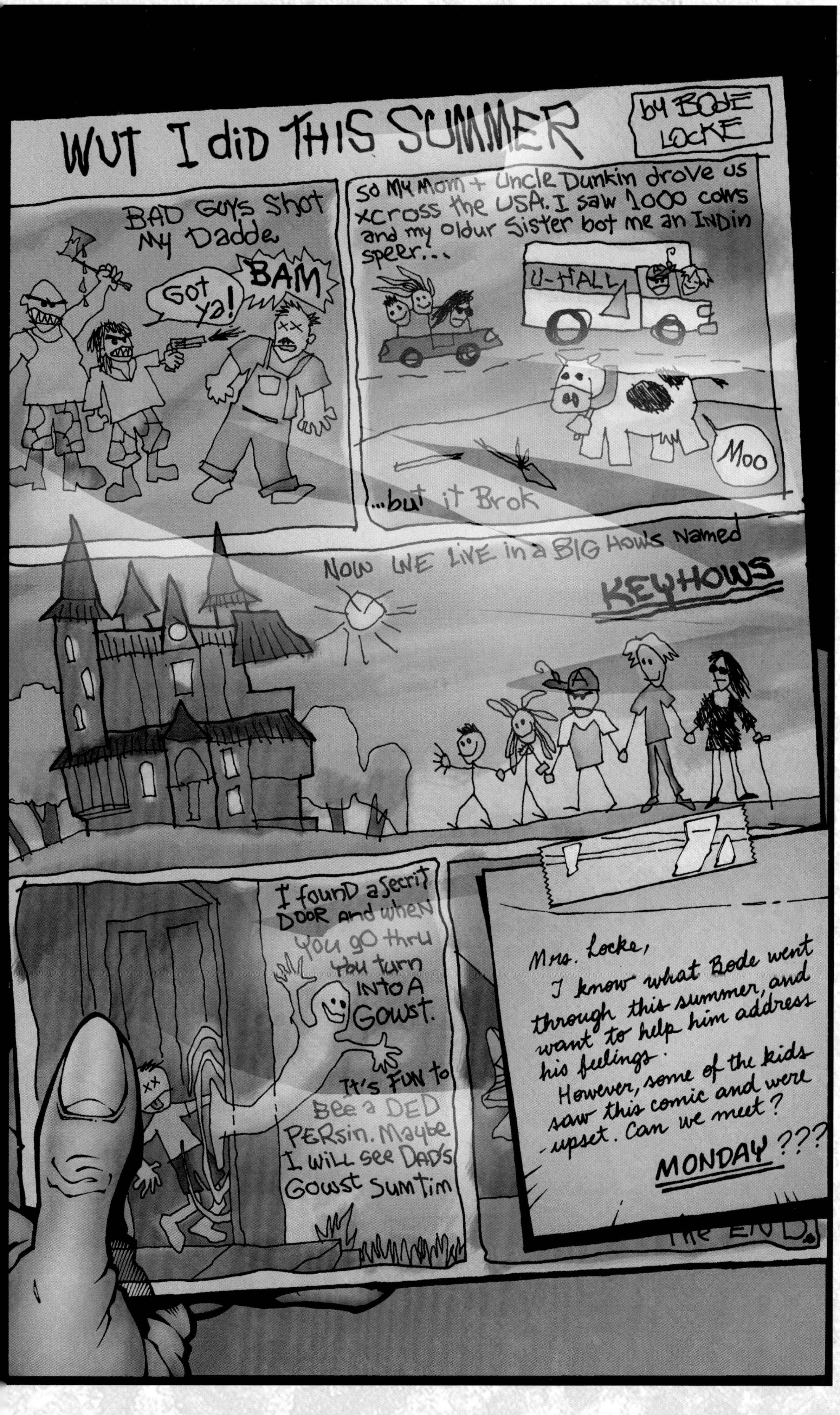
WUT I diD THIS SUMMER
by BODE LOCKE
BAD GUYS Shot My Dadde
Got ya!
BAM
So My Mom + Uncle Dunkin drove us xcross the USA. I saw 1000 cows and my oldur Sister bot me an INDin speer...
U-HALL
Moo
...but it Brok
NOW WE LIVE in a BIG HOWS Named
KEYHOWS
I founD a Secrit DOOR and when You gO thru You turn INTO A GOWST.
It's FUN to Bee a DED PERsin. Maybe I WILL see DAD'S Gowst SumTim
The END
Mrs. Locke,
I know what Bode went through this summer, and want to help him address his feelings.
However, some of the kids saw this comic and were upset. Can we meet?
MONDAY???

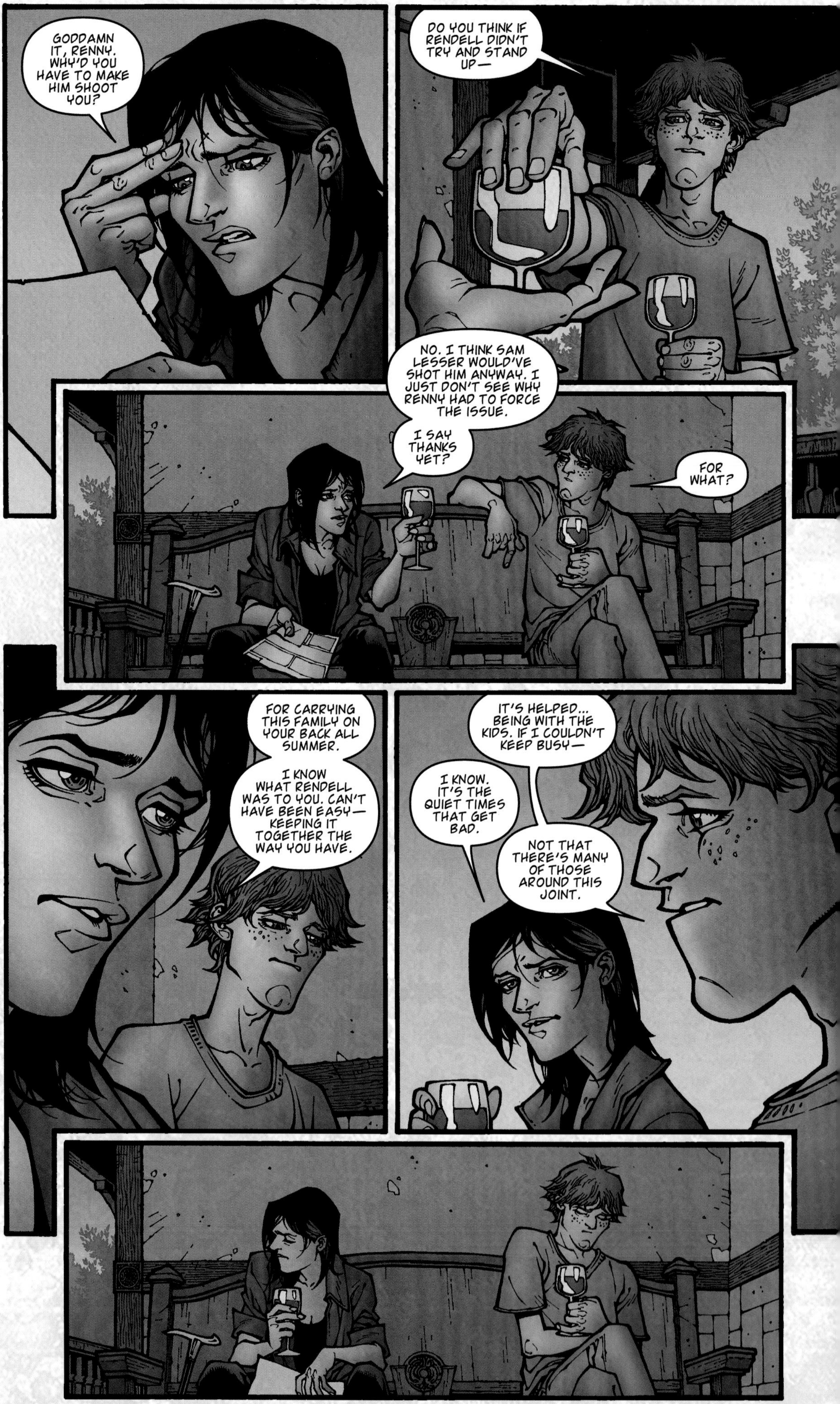
GODDAMN IT, RENNY. WHY'D YOU HAVE TO MAKE HIM SHOOT YOU?
DO YOU THINK IF RENDELL DIDN'T TRY AND STAND UP—
NO. I THINK SAM LESSER WOULD'VE SHOT HIM ANYWAY. I JUST DON'T SEE WHY RENNY HAD TO FORCE THE ISSUE.
I SAY THANKS YET?
FOR WHAT?
FOR CARRYING THIS FAMILY ON YOUR BACK ALL SUMMER.
I KNOW WHAT RENDELL WAS TO YOU. CAN'T HAVE BEEN EASY— KEEPING IT TOGETHER THE WAY YOU HAVE.
IT'S HELPED... BEING WITH THE KIDS. IF I COULDN'T KEEP BUSY—
I KNOW. IT'S THE QUIET TIMES THAT GET BAD.
NOT THAT THERE'S MANY OF THOSE AROUND THIS JOINT.

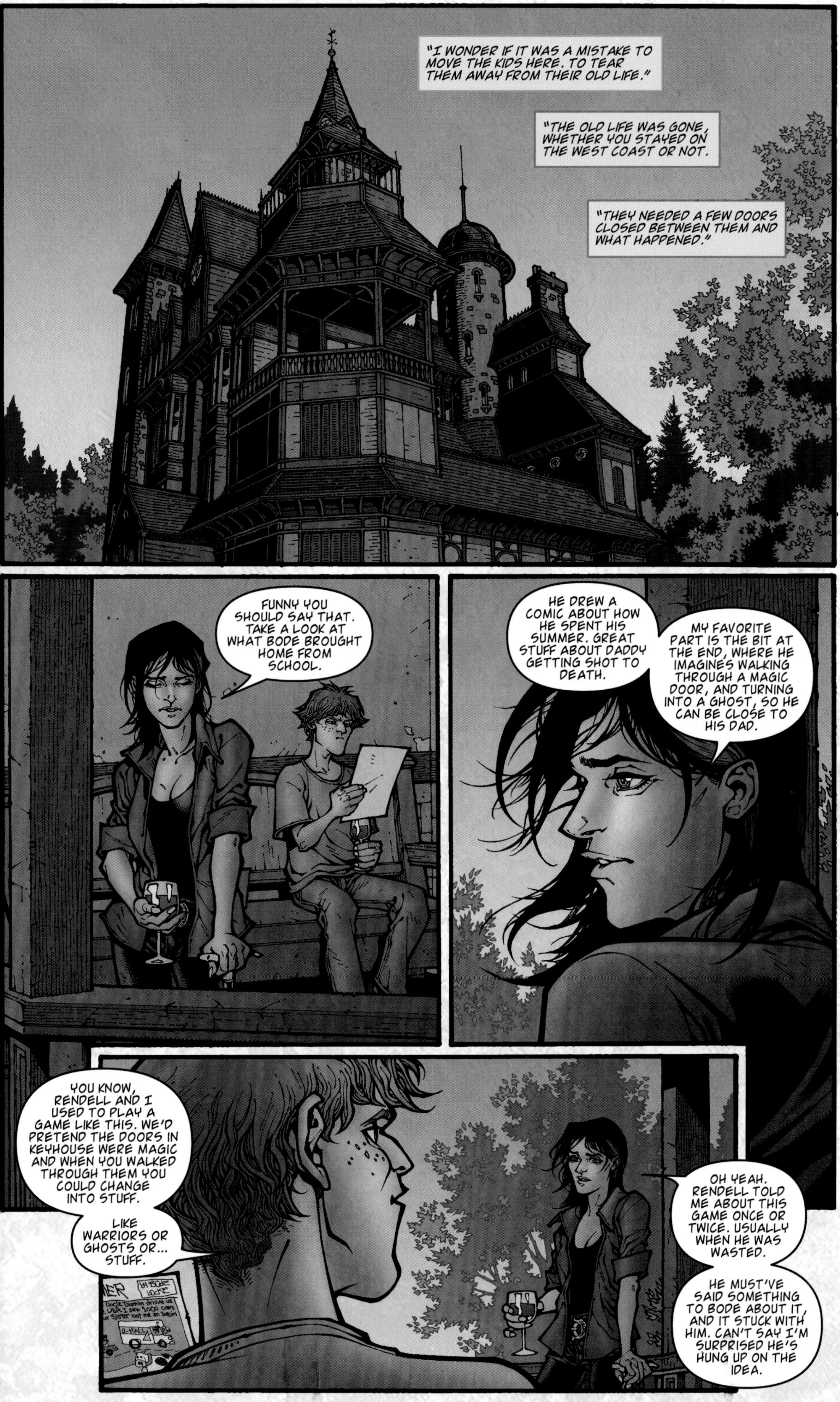
"I WONDER IF IT WAS A MISTAKE TO MOVE THE KIDS HERE. TO TEAR THEM AWAY FROM THEIR OLD LIFE."
"THE OLD LIFE WAS GONE, WHETHER YOU STAYED ON THE WEST COAST OR NOT.
"THEY NEEDED A FEW DOORS CLOSED BETWEEN THEM AND WHAT HAPPENED."
FUNNY YOU SHOULD SAY THAT. TAKE A LOOK AT WHAT BODE BROUGHT HOME FROM SCHOOL.
HE DREW A COMIC ABOUT HOW HE SPENT HIS SUMMER. GREAT STUFF ABOUT DADDY GETTING SHOT TO DEATH.
MY FAVORITE PART IS THE BIT AT THE END, WHERE HE IMAGINES WALKING THROUGH A MAGIC DOOR, AND TURNING INTO A GHOST, SO HE CAN BE CLOSE TO HIS DAD.
YOU KNOW, RENDELL AND I USED TO PLAY A GAME LIKE THIS. WE'D PRETEND THE DOORS IN KEYHOUSE WERE MAGIC AND WHEN YOU WALKED THROUGH THEM YOU COULD CHANGE INTO STUFF.
LIKE WARRIORS OR GHOSTS OR... STUFF.
OH YEAH. RENDELL TOLD ME ABOUT THIS GAME ONCE OR TWICE. USUALLY WHEN HE WAS WASTED.
HE MUST'VE SAID SOMETHING TO BODE ABOUT IT, AND IT STUCK WITH HIM. CAN'T SAY I'M SURPRISED HE'S HUNG UP ON THE IDEA.

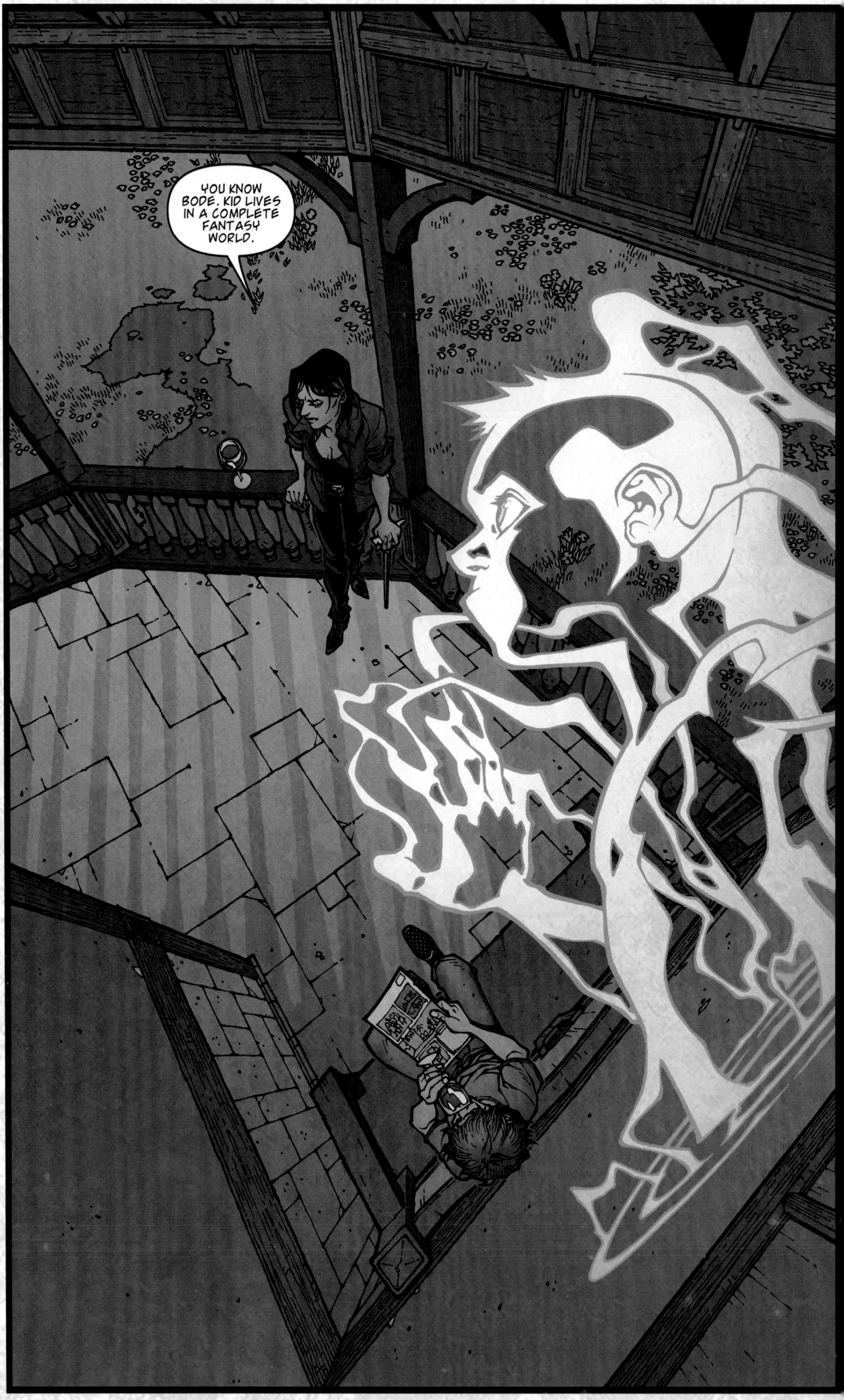
YOU KNOW BODE. KID LIVES IN A COMPLETE FANTASY WORLD.

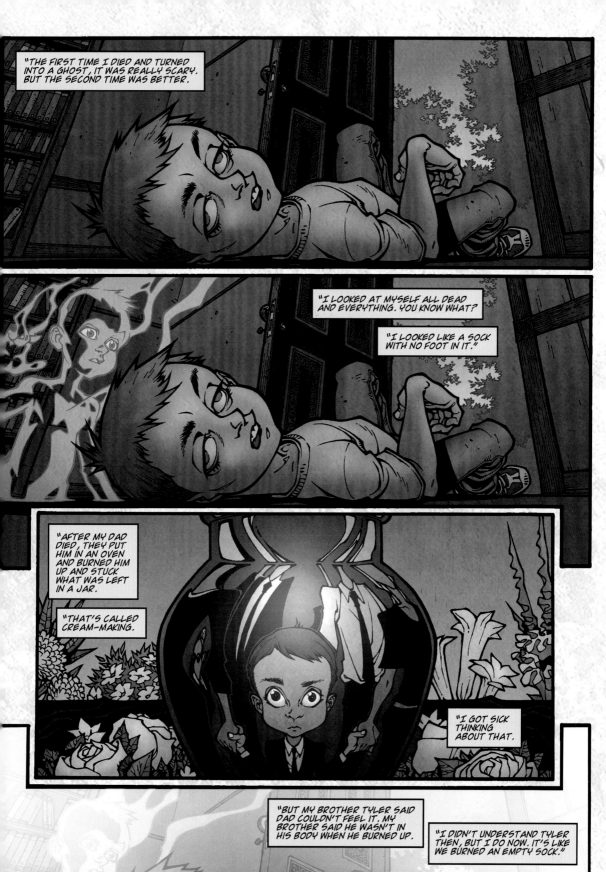

"THE FIRST TIME I DIED AND TURNED INTO A GHOST, IT WAS REALLY SCARY. BUT THE SECOND TIME WAS BETTER.

"I LOOKED AT MYSELF ALL DEAD AND EVERYTHING. YOU KNOW WHAT?

"I LOOKED LIKE A SOCK WITH NO FOOT IN IT."

"AFTER MY DAD DIED, THEY PUT HIM IN AN OVEN AND BURNED HIM UP AND STUCK WHAT WAS LEFT IN A JAR.

"THAT'S CALLED CREAM-MAKING.

"I GOT SICK THINKING ABOUT THAT.

"BUT MY BROTHER TYLER SAID DAD COULDN'T FEEL IT. MY BROTHER SAID HE WASN'T IN HIS BODY WHEN HE BURNED UP.

"I DIDN'T UNDERSTAND TYLER THEN, BUT I DO NOW. IT'S LIKE WE BURNED AN EMPTY SOCK."

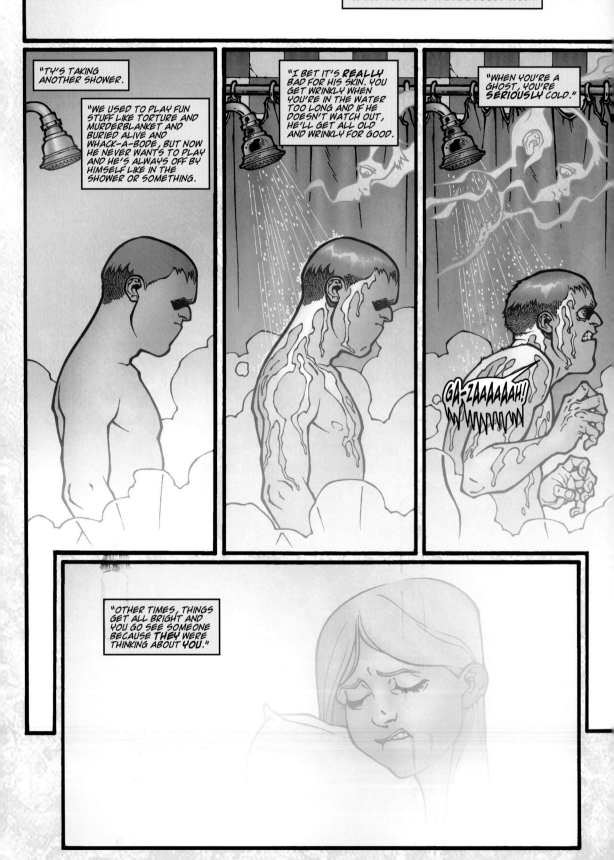

"TYLER.

"WHEN YOU'RE DEAD, YOU GO PLACES IN BRIGHT FLASHES.

"SOMETIMES YOU GO TO SOMEONE JUST 'CAUSE YOU WERE THINKING ABOUT THEM.

"TY'S TAKING ANOTHER SHOWER.

"WE USED TO PLAY FUN STUFF LIKE TORTURE AND MURDERBLANKET AND BURIED ALIVE AND WHACK-A-BODE, BUT NOW HE NEVER WANTS TO PLAY AND HE'S ALWAYS OFF BY HIMSELF LIKE IN THE SHOWER OR SOMETHING.

"I BET IT'S REALLY BAD FOR HIS SKIN. YOU GET WRINKLY WHEN YOU'RE IN THE WATER TOO LONG AND IF HE DOESN'T WATCH OUT, HE'LL GET ALL OLD AND WRINKLY FOR GOOD.

"WHEN YOU'RE A GHOST, YOU'RE SERIOUSLY COLD."

GA-ZAAAAAAH!

"OTHER TIMES, THINGS GET ALL BRIGHT AND YOU GO SEE SOMEONE BECAUSE THEY WERE THINKING ABOUT YOU."

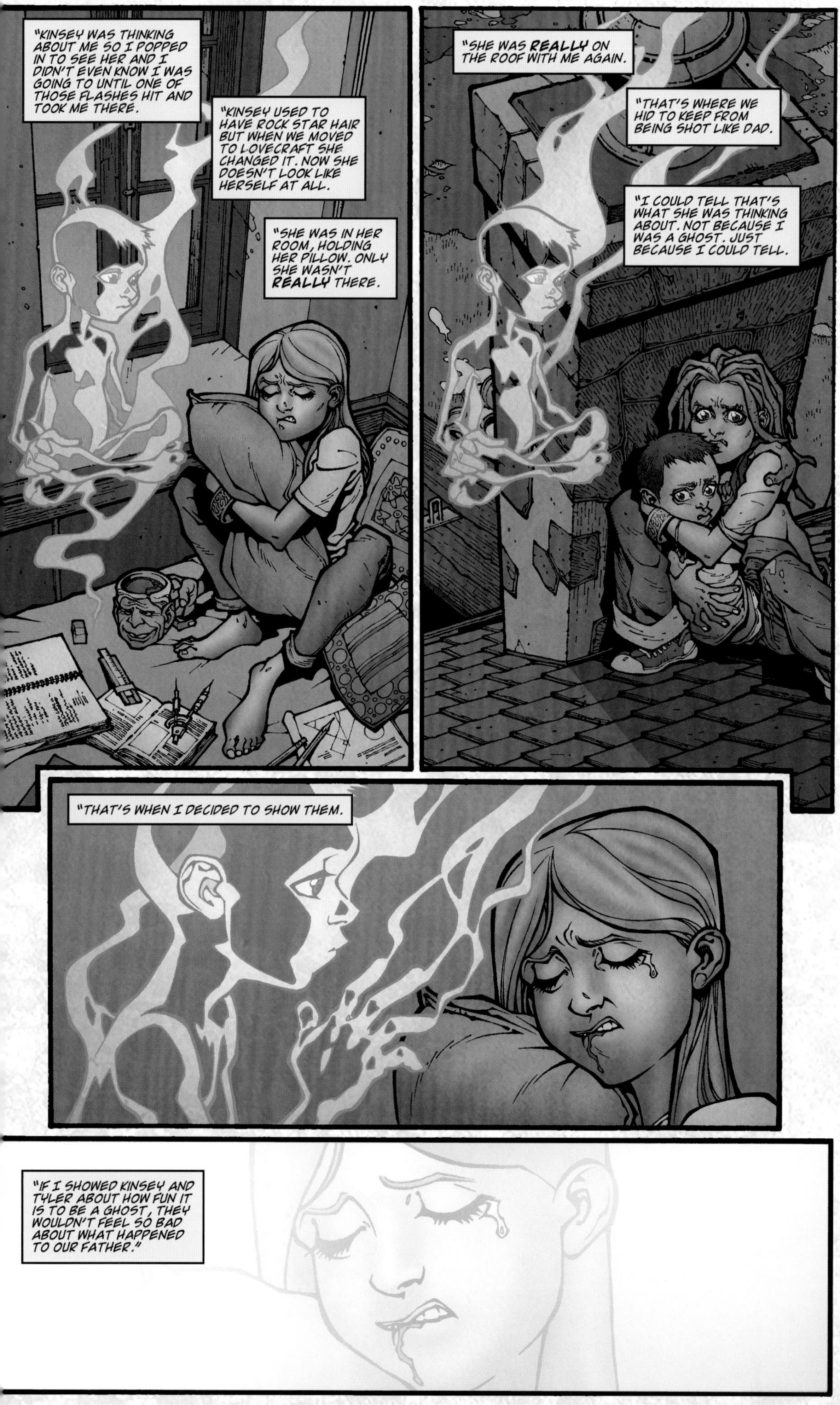
"KINSEY WAS THINKING ABOUT ME SO I POPPED IN TO SEE HER AND I DIDN'T EVEN KNOW I WAS GOING TO UNTIL ONE OF THOSE FLASHES HIT AND TOOK ME THERE.
"KINSEY USED TO HAVE ROCK STAR HAIR BUT WHEN WE MOVED TO LOVECRAFT SHE CHANGED IT. NOW SHE DOESN'T LOOK LIKE HERSELF AT ALL.
"SHE WAS IN HER ROOM, HOLDING HER PILLOW. ONLY SHE WASN'T REALLY THERE.
"SHE WAS REALLY ON THE ROOF WITH ME AGAIN.
"THAT'S WHERE WE HID TO KEEP FROM BEING SHOT LIKE DAD.
"I COULD TELL THAT'S WHAT SHE WAS THINKING ABOUT. NOT BECAUSE I WAS A GHOST. JUST BECAUSE I COULD TELL.
"THAT'S WHEN I DECIDED TO SHOW THEM.
"IF I SHOWED KINSEY AND TYLER ABOUT HOW FUN IT IS TO BE A GHOST, THEY WOULDN'T FEEL SO BAD ABOUT WHAT HAPPENED TO OUR FATHER."

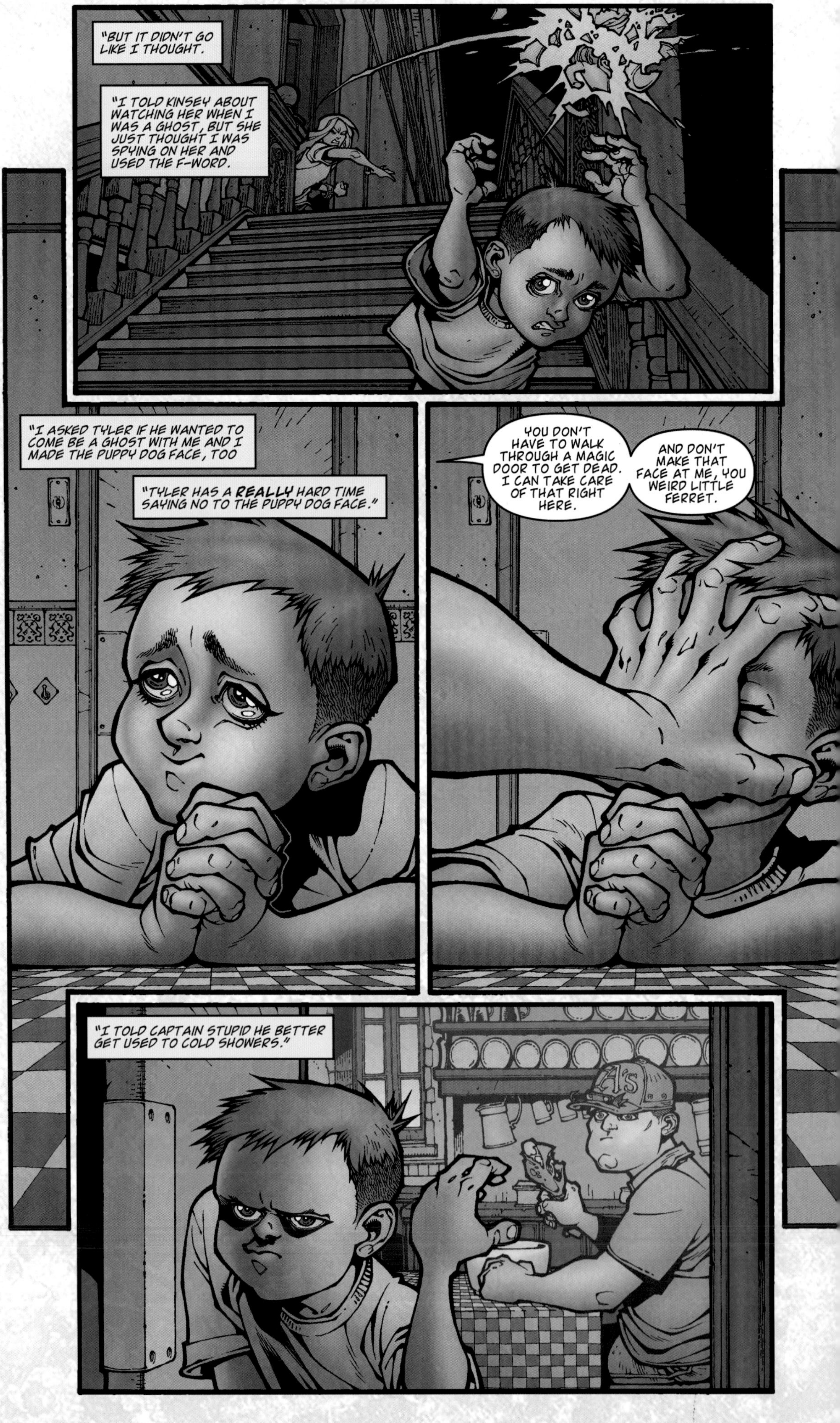
"BUT IT DIDN'T GO LIKE I THOUGHT.
"I TOLD KINSEY ABOUT WATCHING HER WHEN I WAS A GHOST, BUT SHE JUST THOUGHT I WAS SPYING ON HER AND USED THE F-WORD.
"I ASKED TYLER IF HE WANTED TO COME BE A GHOST WITH ME AND I MADE THE PUPPY DOG FACE, TOO
"TYLER HAS A **REALLY** HARD TIME SAYING NO TO THE PUPPY DOG FACE."
YOU DON'T HAVE TO WALK THROUGH A MAGIC DOOR TO GET DEAD. I CAN TAKE CARE OF THAT RIGHT HERE.
AND DON'T MAKE THAT FACE AT ME, YOU WEIRD LITTLE FERRET.
"I TOLD CAPTAIN STUPID HE BETTER GET USED TO COLD SHOWERS."
A'S

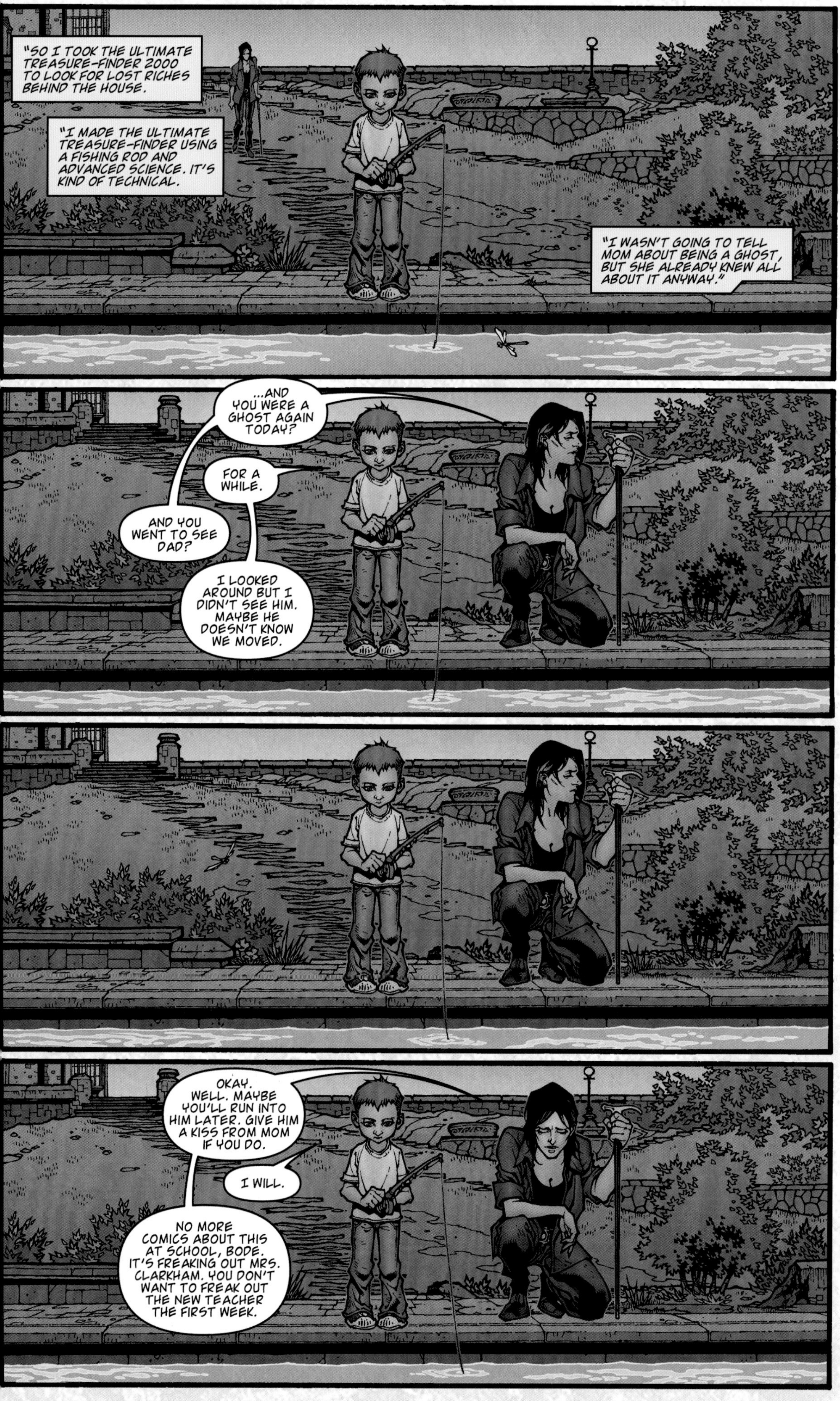
"SO I TOOK THE ULTIMATE TREASURE-FINDER 2000 TO LOOK FOR LOST RICHES BEHIND THE HOUSE.
"I MADE THE ULTIMATE TREASURE-FINDER USING A FISHING ROD AND ADVANCED SCIENCE. IT'S KIND OF TECHNICAL.
"I WASN'T GOING TO TELL MOM ABOUT BEING A GHOST, BUT SHE ALREADY KNEW ALL ABOUT IT ANYWAY."
...AND YOU WERE A GHOST AGAIN TODAY?
FOR A WHILE.
AND YOU WENT TO SEE DAD?
I LOOKED AROUND BUT I DIDN'T SEE HIM. MAYBE HE DOESN'T KNOW WE MOVED.
OKAY. WELL. MAYBE YOU'LL RUN INTO HIM LATER. GIVE HIM A KISS FROM MOM IF YOU DO.
I WILL.
NO MORE COMICS ABOUT THIS AT SCHOOL, BODE. IT'S FREAKING OUT MRS. CLARKHAM. YOU DON'T WANT TO FREAK OUT THE NEW TEACHER THE FIRST WEEK.

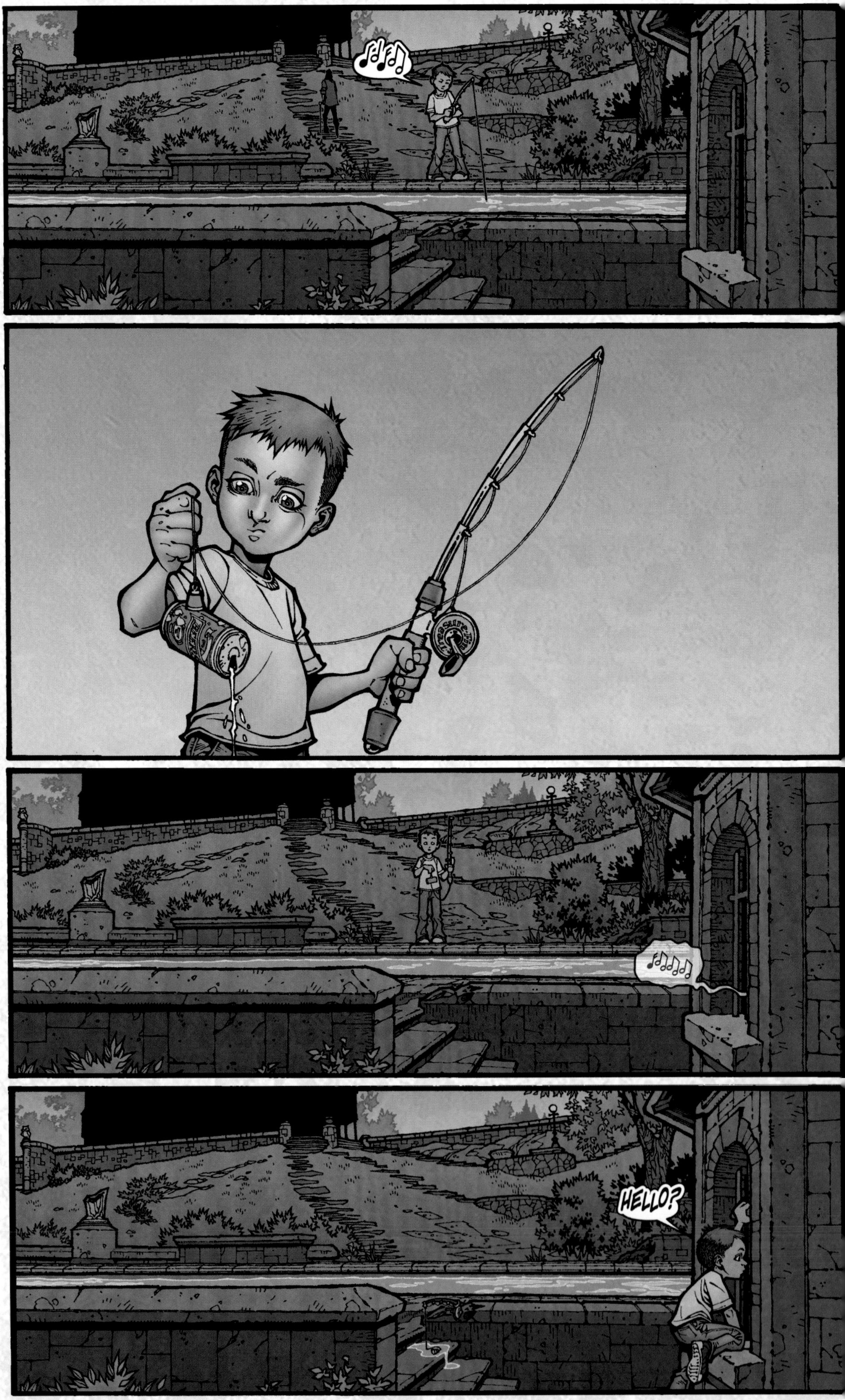
HELLO?

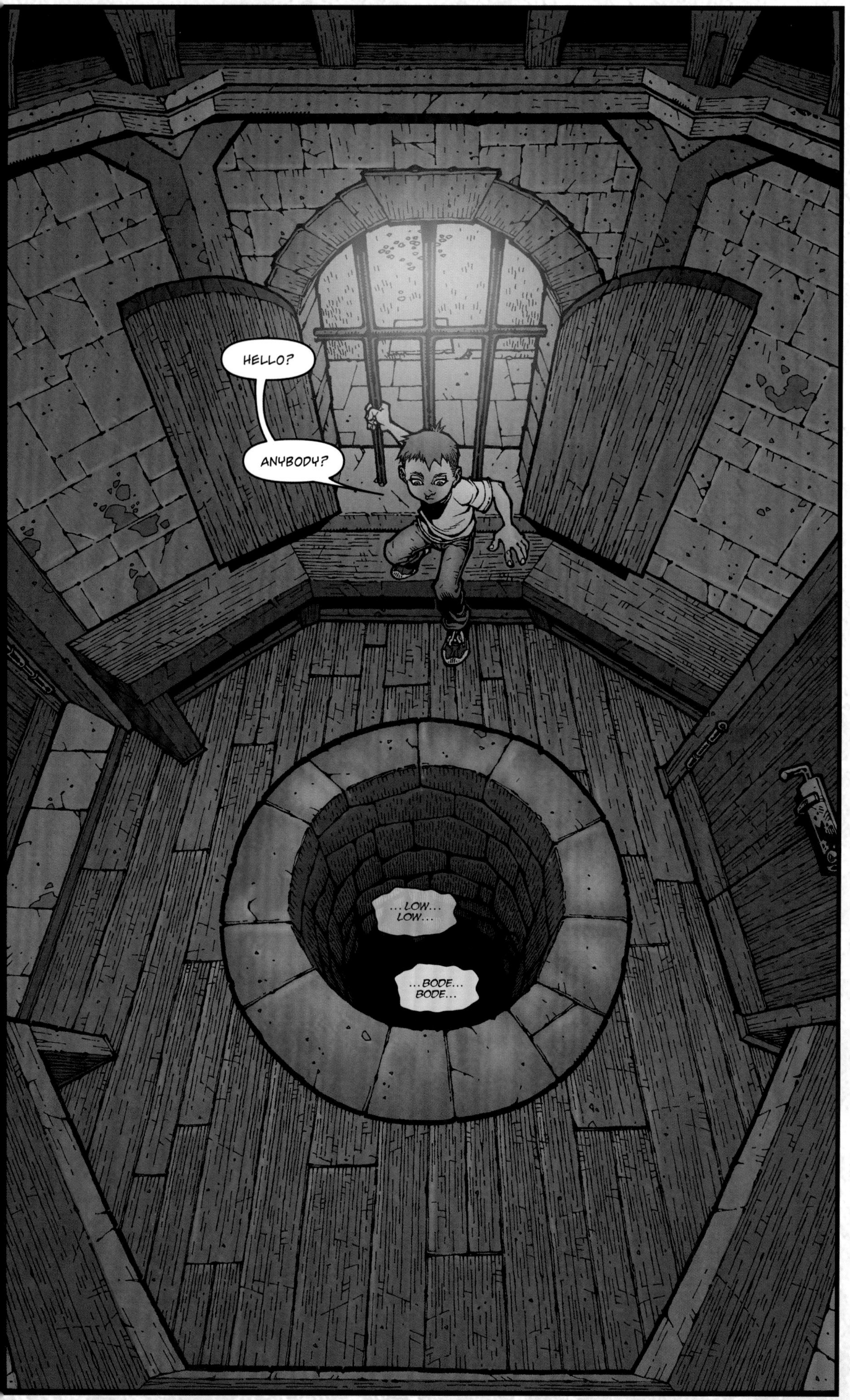
HELLO?
ANYBODY?
...LOW... LOW...
...BODE... BODE...

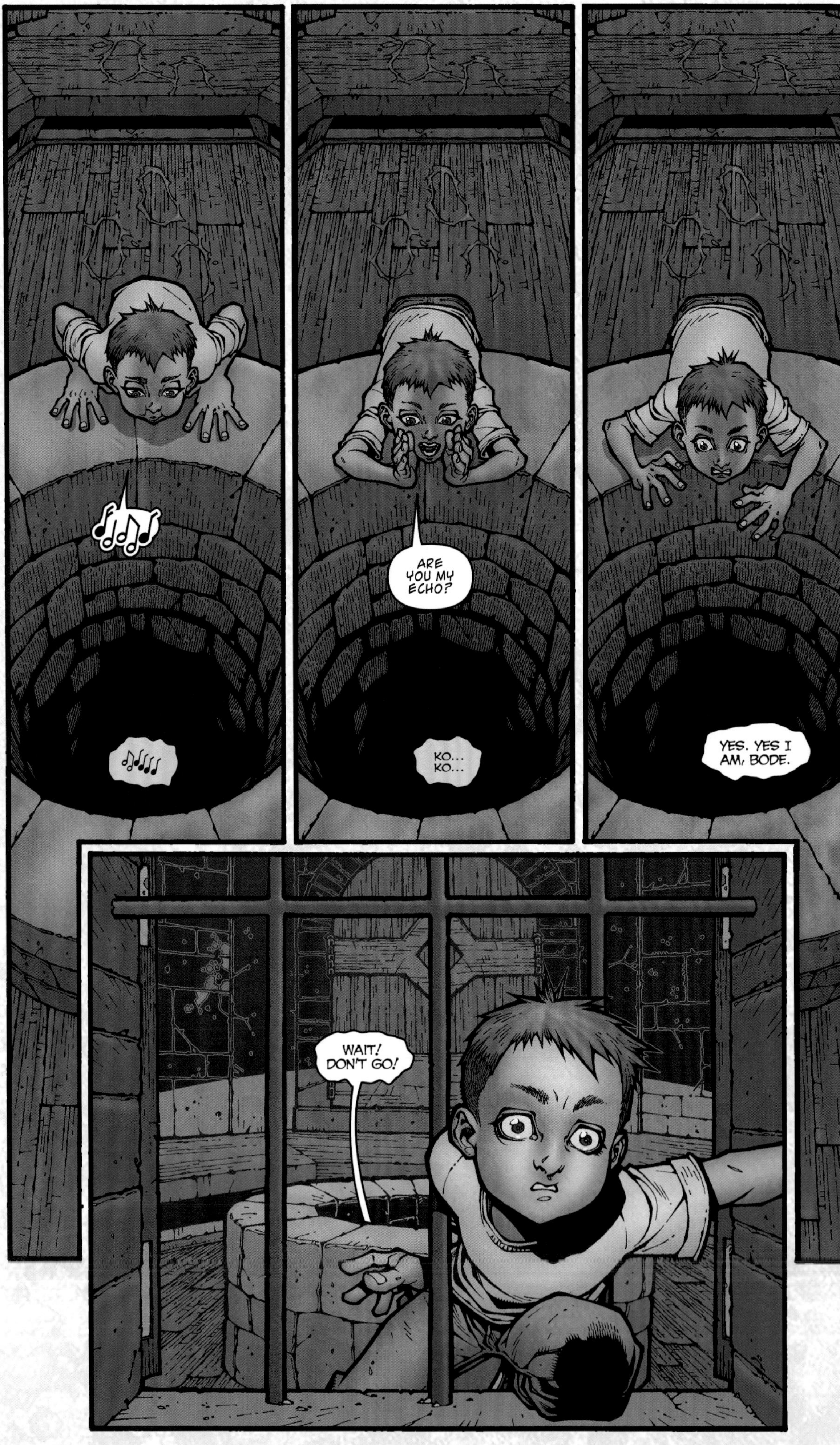
ARE YOU MY ECHO?
KO... KO...
YES. YES I AM, BODE.
WAIT! DON'T GO!

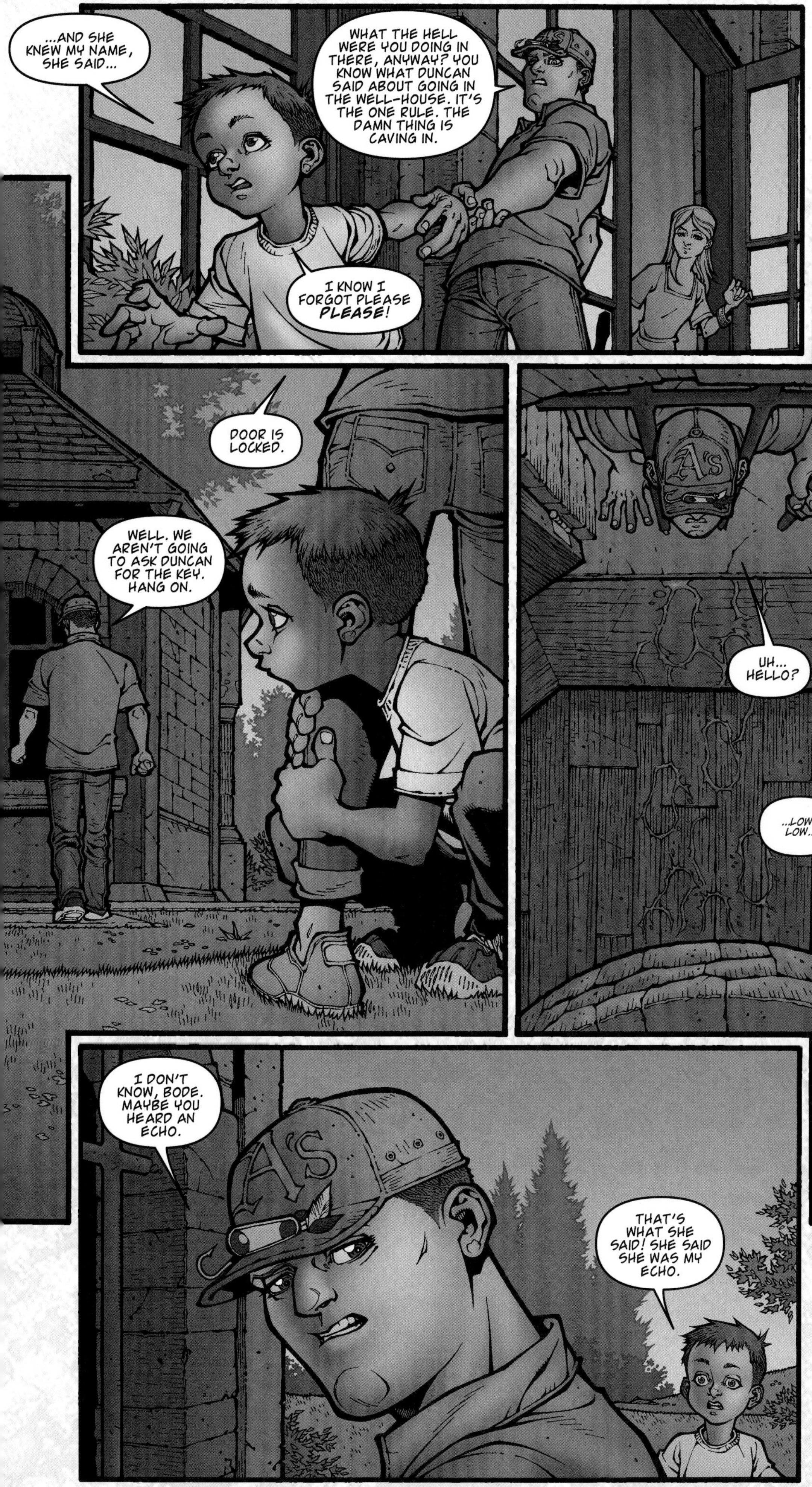
...AND SHE KNEW MY NAME, SHE SAID...
WHAT THE HELL WERE YOU DOING IN THERE, ANYWAY? YOU KNOW WHAT DUNCAN SAID ABOUT GOING IN THE WELL-HOUSE. IT'S THE ONE RULE. THE DAMN THING IS CAVING IN.
I KNOW I FORGOT PLEASE *PLEASE*!
DOOR IS LOCKED.
WELL. WE AREN'T GOING TO ASK DUNCAN FOR THE KEY. HANG ON.
UH... HELLO?
...LOW... LOW...
I DON'T KNOW, BODE. MAYBE YOU HEARD AN ECHO.
THAT'S WHAT SHE SAID! SHE SAID SHE WAS MY ECHO.

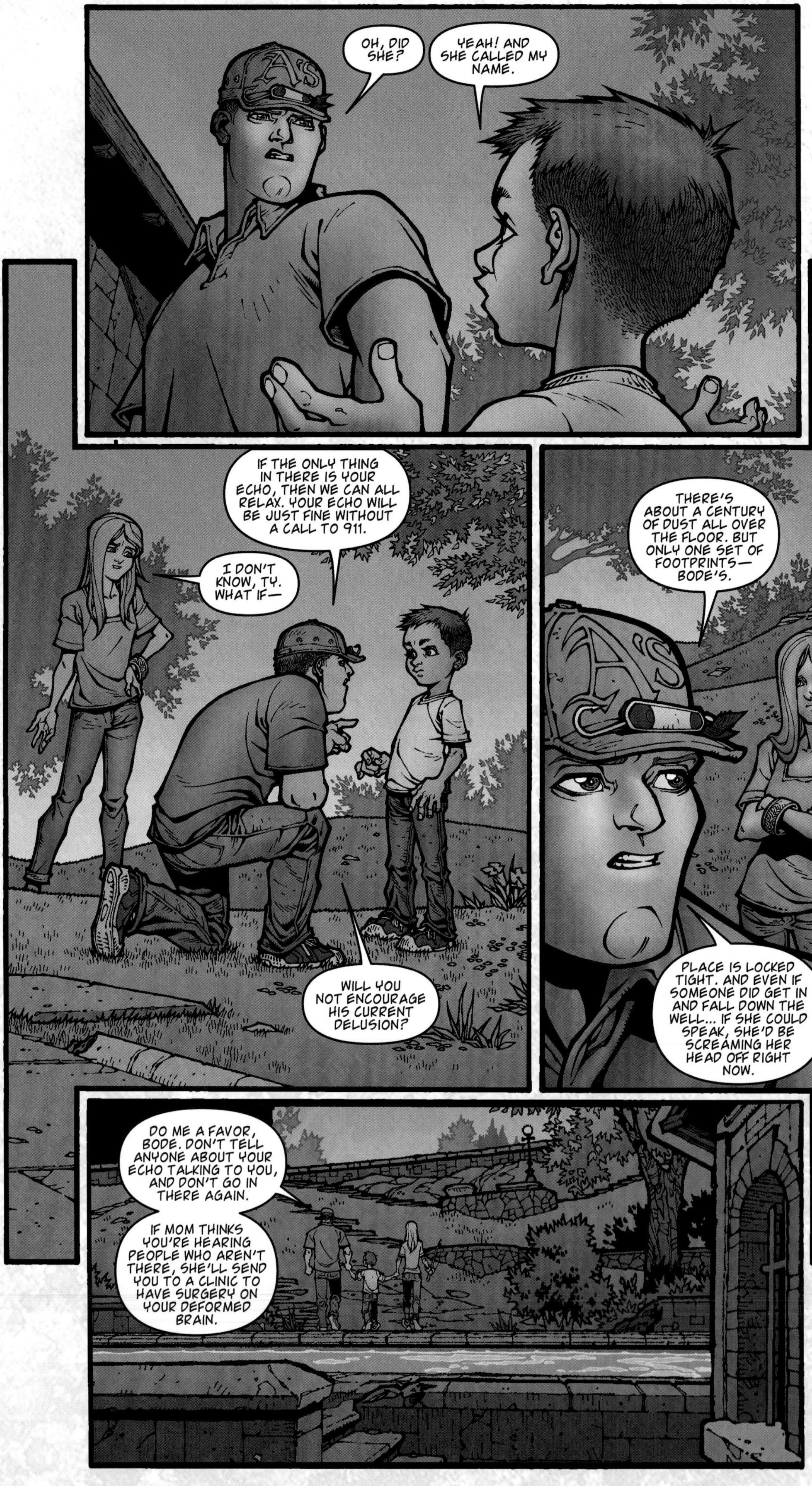
OH, DID SHE?
YEAH! AND SHE CALLED MY NAME.
IF THE ONLY THING IN THERE IS YOUR ECHO, THEN WE CAN ALL RELAX. YOUR ECHO WILL BE JUST FINE WITHOUT A CALL TO 911.
I DON'T KNOW, TY. WHAT IF—
WILL YOU NOT ENCOURAGE HIS CURRENT DELUSION?
THERE'S ABOUT A CENTURY OF DUST ALL OVER THE FLOOR. BUT ONLY ONE SET OF FOOTPRINTS—BODE'S.
PLACE IS LOCKED TIGHT. AND EVEN IF SOMEONE DID GET IN AND FALL DOWN THE WELL... IF SHE COULD SPEAK, SHE'D BE SCREAMING HER HEAD OFF RIGHT NOW.
DO ME A FAVOR, BODE. DON'T TELL ANYONE ABOUT YOUR ECHO TALKING TO YOU, AND DON'T GO IN THERE AGAIN.
IF MOM THINKS YOU'RE HEARING PEOPLE WHO AREN'T THERE, SHE'LL SEND YOU TO A CLINIC TO HAVE SURGERY ON YOUR DEFORMED BRAIN.

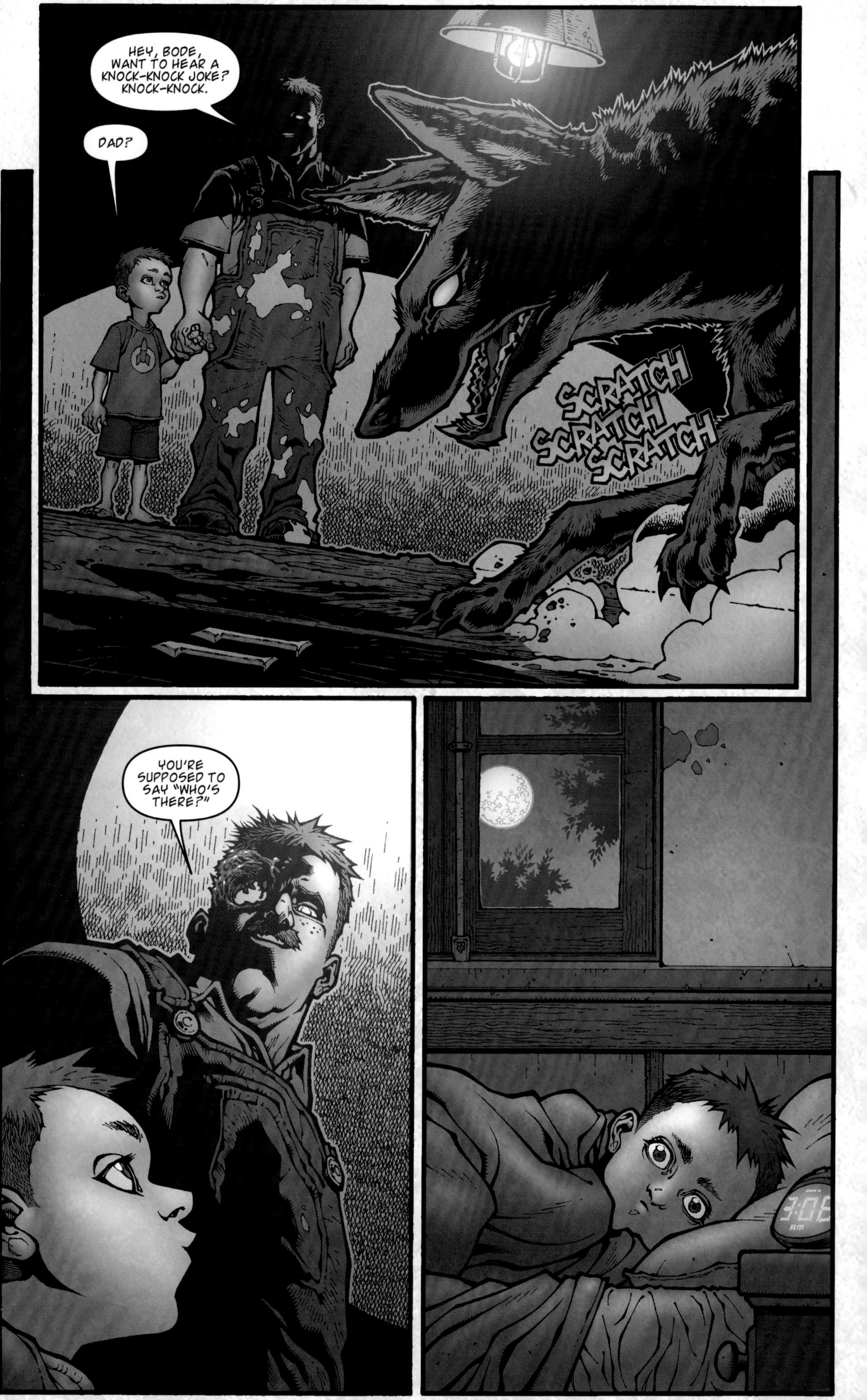
HEY, BODE, WANT TO HEAR A KNOCK-KNOCK JOKE? KNOCK-KNOCK.
DAD?
SCRATCH SCRATCH SCRATCH
YOU'RE SUPPOSED TO SAY "WHO'S THERE?"

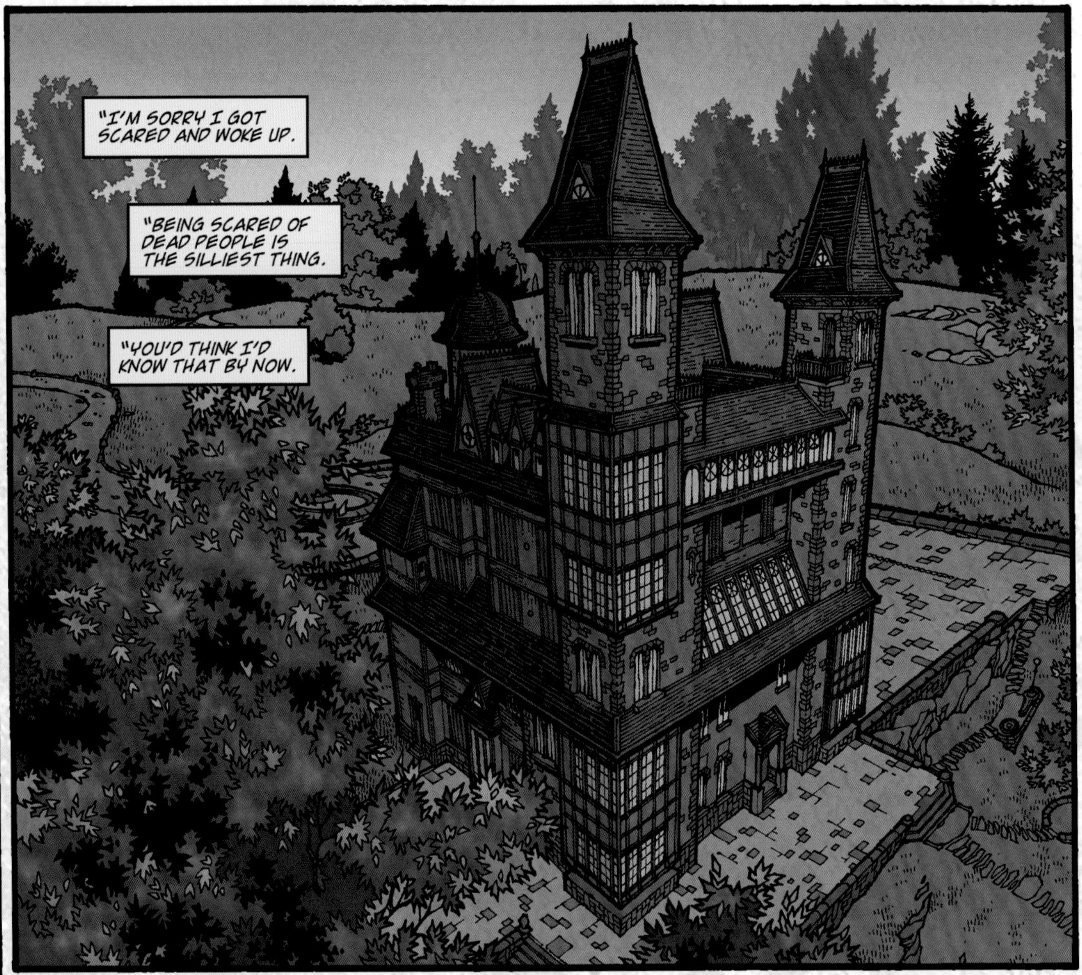
"I'M SORRY I GOT SCARED AND WOKE UP.
"BEING SCARED OF DEAD PEOPLE IS THE SILLIEST THING.
"YOU'D THINK I'D KNOW THAT BY NOW.

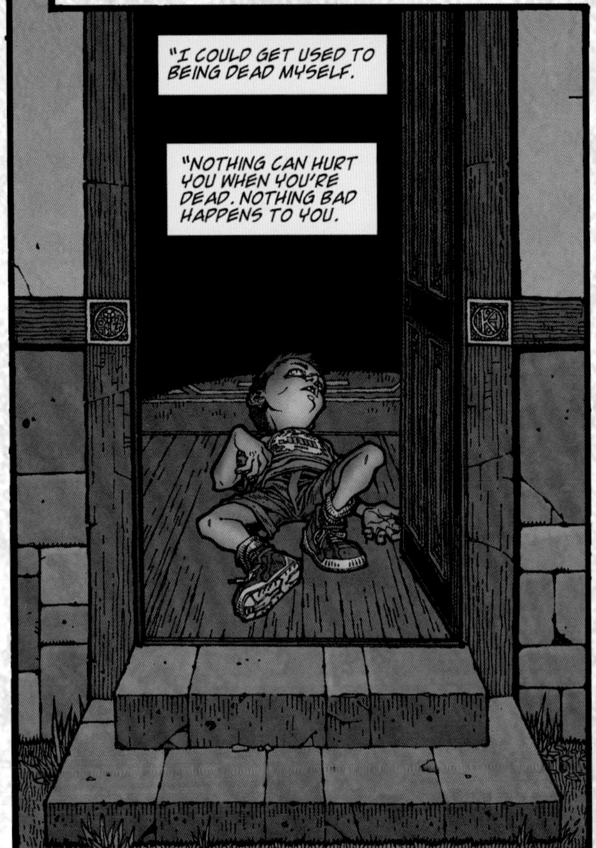
"I COULD GET USED TO BEING DEAD MYSELF.
"NOTHING CAN HURT YOU WHEN YOU'RE DEAD. NOTHING BAD HAPPENS TO YOU.

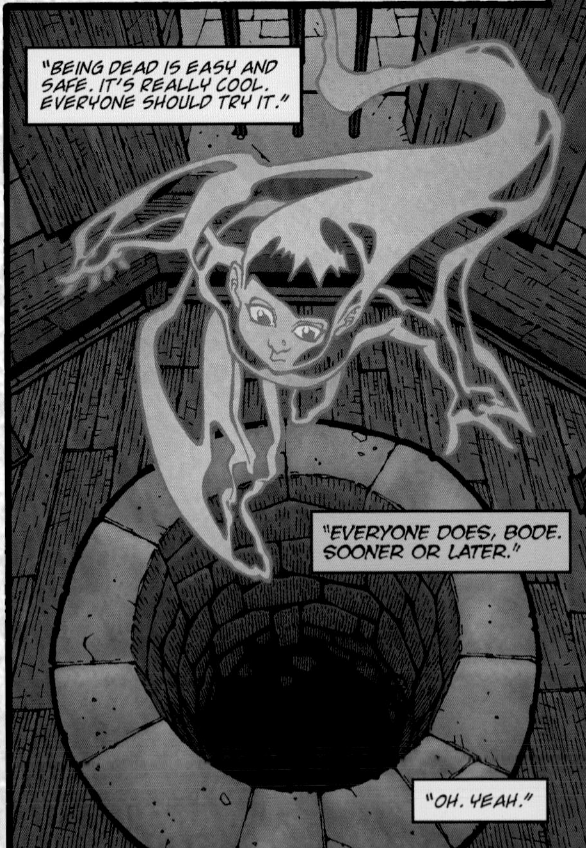
"BEING DEAD IS EASY AND SAFE. IT'S REALLY COOL. EVERYONE SHOULD TRY IT."
"EVERYONE DOES, BODE. SOONER OR LATER."
"OH. YEAH."

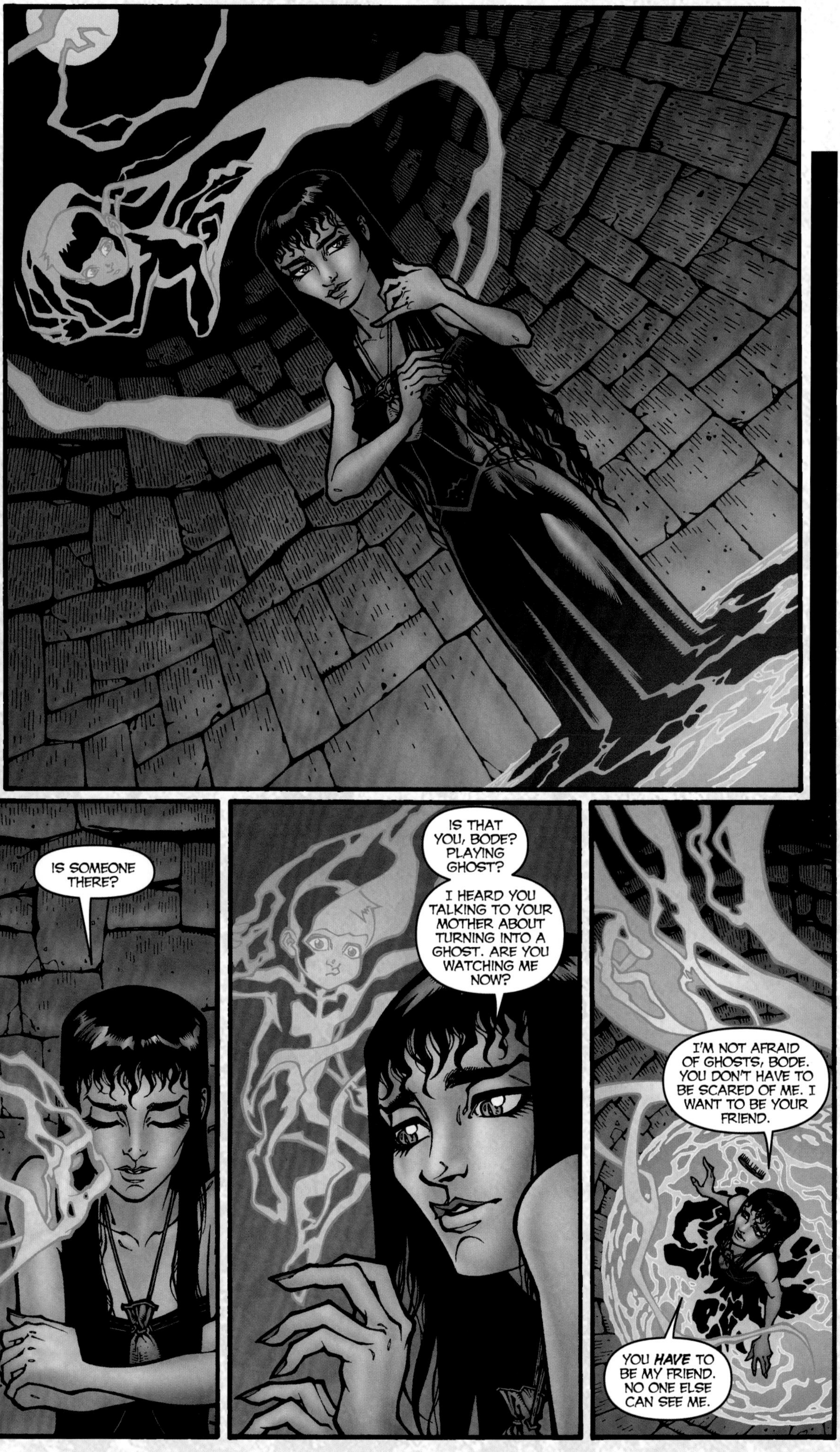
IS SOMEONE THERE?
IS THAT YOU, BODE? PLAYING GHOST?
I HEARD YOU TALKING TO YOUR MOTHER ABOUT TURNING INTO A GHOST. ARE YOU WATCHING ME NOW?
I'M NOT AFRAID OF GHOSTS, BODE. YOU DON'T HAVE TO BE SCARED OF ME. I WANT TO BE YOUR FRIEND.
YOU *HAVE* TO BE MY FRIEND. NO ONE ELSE CAN SEE ME.

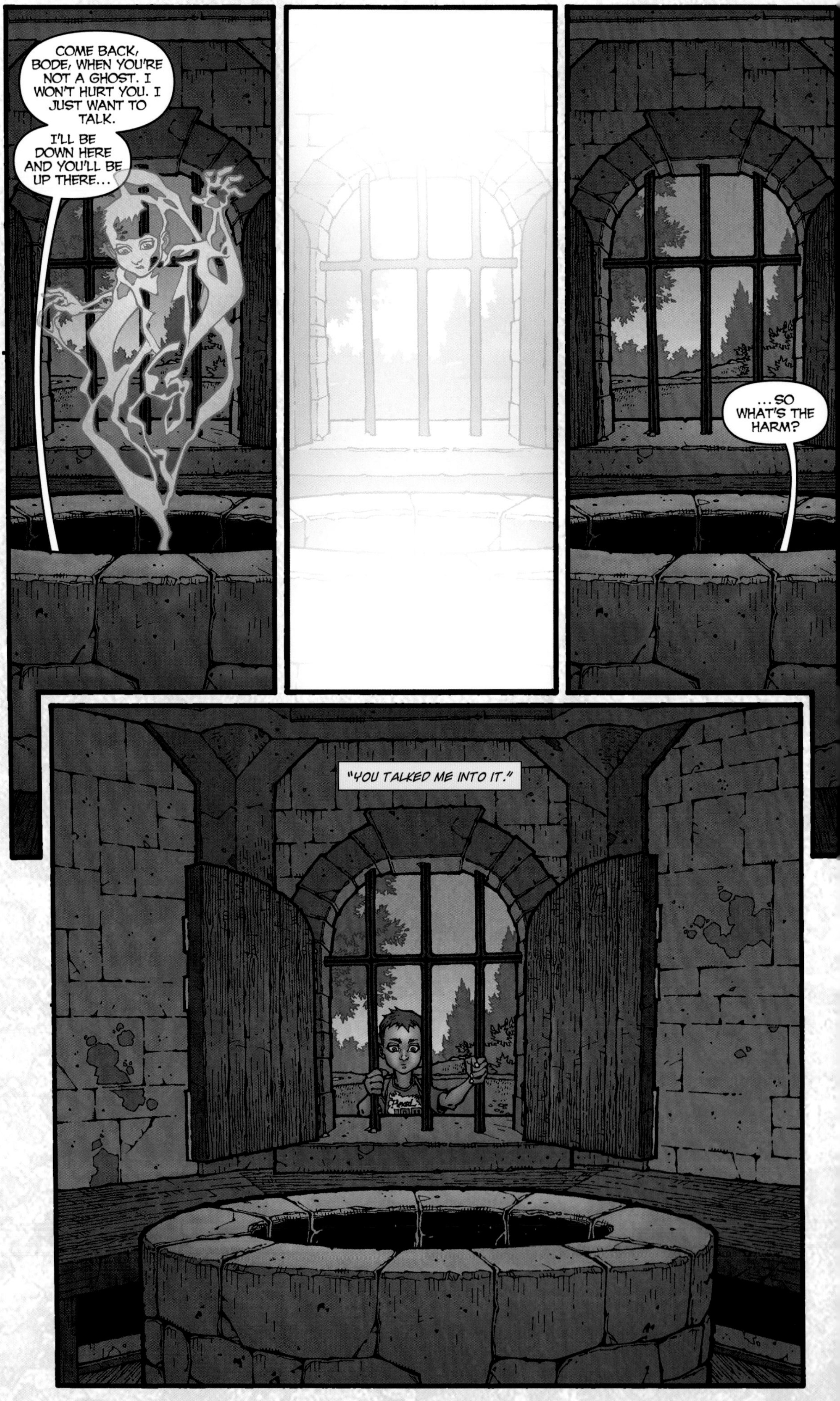
COME BACK, BODE, WHEN YOU'RE NOT A GHOST. I WON'T HURT YOU. I JUST WANT TO TALK.
I'LL BE DOWN HERE AND YOU'LL BE UP THERE...
...SO WHAT'S THE HARM?
"YOU TALKED ME INTO IT."

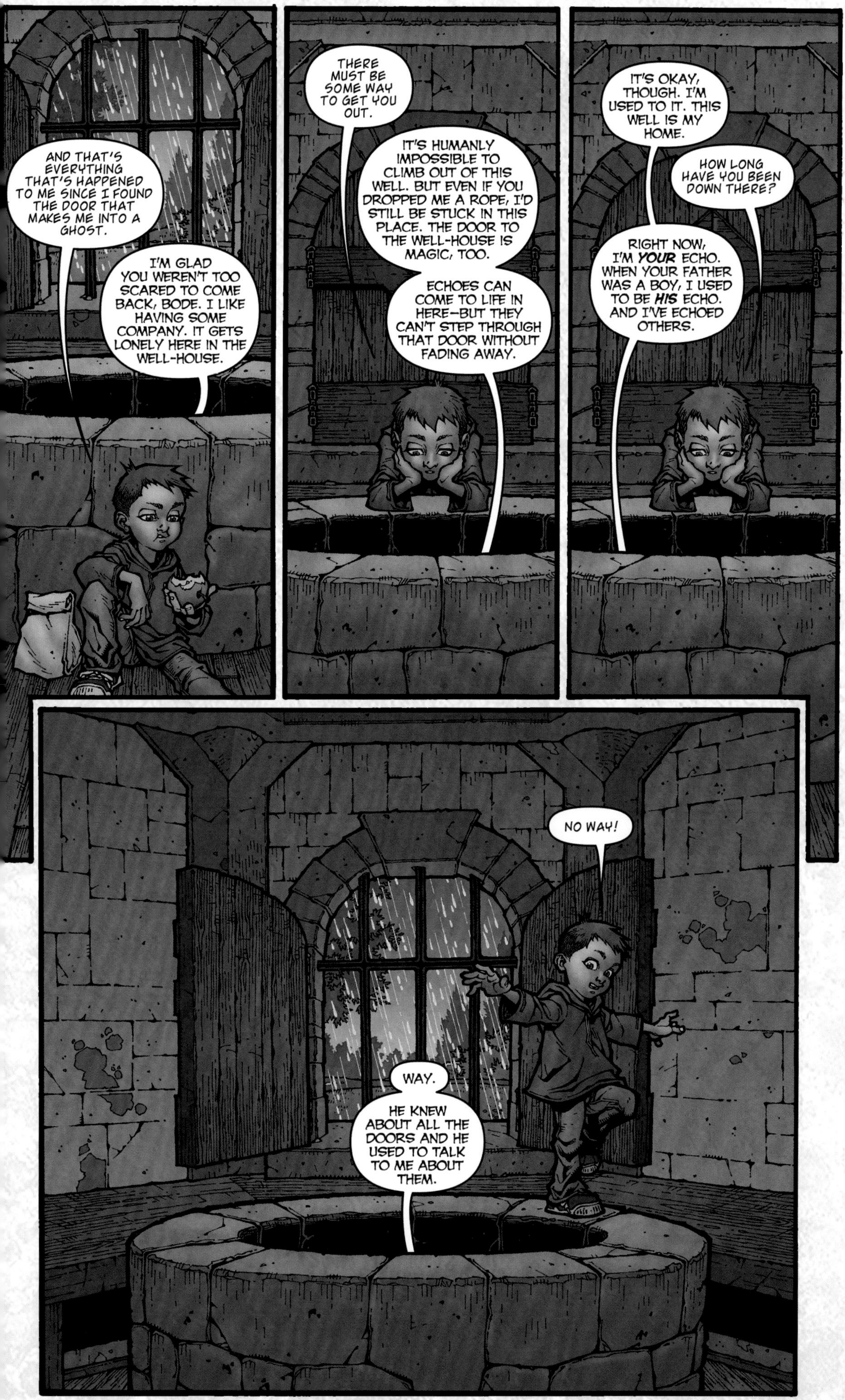
AND THAT'S EVERYTHING THAT'S HAPPENED TO ME SINCE I FOUND THE DOOR THAT MAKES ME INTO A GHOST.
I'M GLAD YOU WEREN'T TOO SCARED TO COME BACK, BODE. I LIKE HAVING SOME COMPANY. IT GETS LONELY HERE IN THE WELL-HOUSE.
THERE MUST BE SOME WAY TO GET YOU OUT.
IT'S HUMANLY IMPOSSIBLE TO CLIMB OUT OF THIS WELL. BUT EVEN IF YOU DROPPED ME A ROPE, I'D STILL BE STUCK IN THIS PLACE. THE DOOR TO THE WELL-HOUSE IS MAGIC, TOO.
ECHOES CAN COME TO LIFE IN HERE--BUT THEY CAN'T STEP THROUGH THAT DOOR WITHOUT FADING AWAY.
IT'S OKAY, THOUGH. I'M USED TO IT. THIS WELL IS MY HOME.
HOW LONG HAVE YOU BEEN DOWN THERE?
RIGHT NOW, I'M YOUR ECHO. WHEN YOUR FATHER WAS A BOY, I USED TO BE HIS ECHO. AND I'VE ECHOED OTHERS.
NO WAY!
WAY.
HE KNEW ABOUT ALL THE DOORS AND HE USED TO TALK TO ME ABOUT THEM.

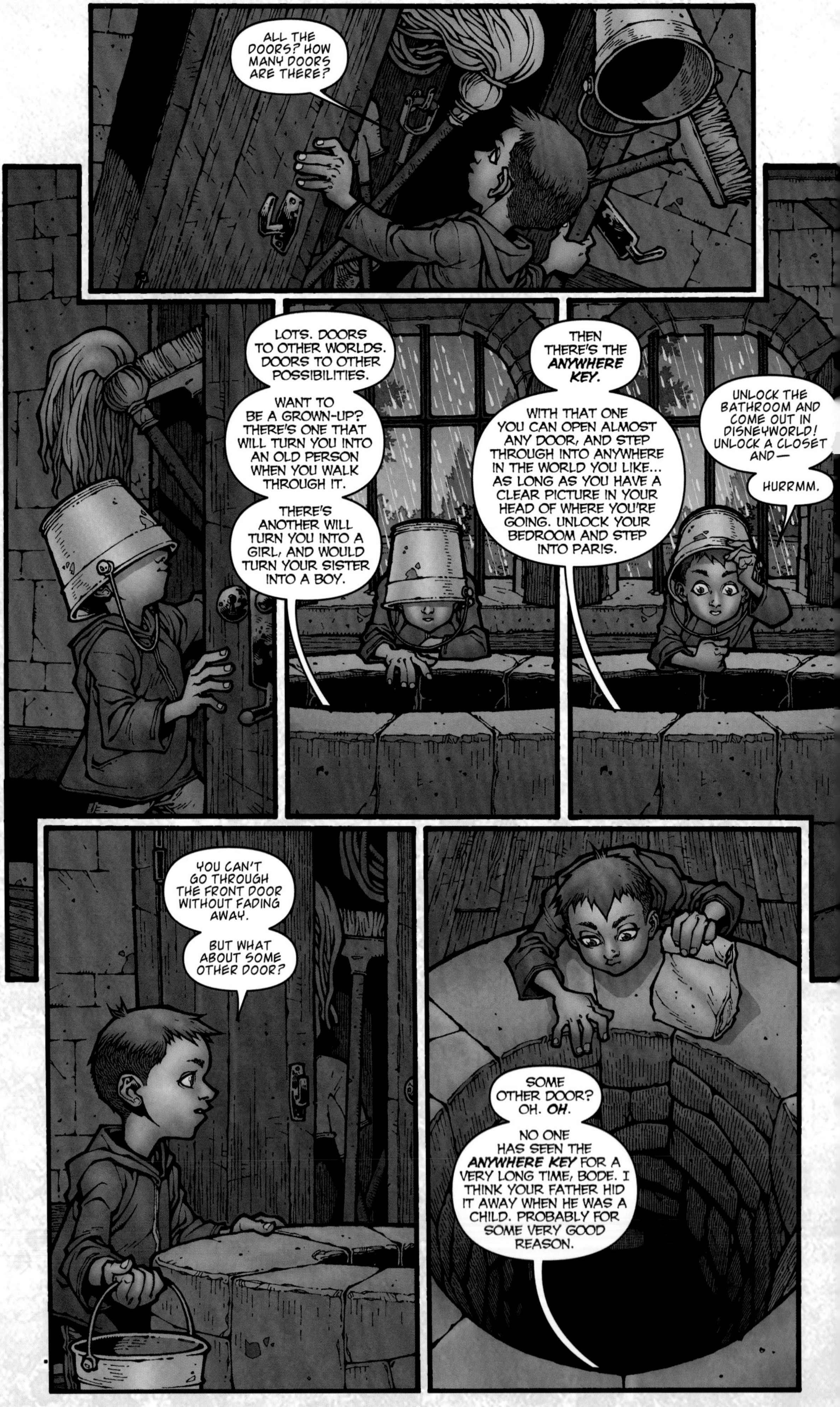
ALL THE DOORS? HOW MANY DOORS ARE THERE?
LOTS. DOORS TO OTHER WORLDS. DOORS TO OTHER POSSIBILITIES.
WANT TO BE A GROWN-UP? THERE'S ONE THAT WILL TURN YOU INTO AN OLD PERSON WHEN YOU WALK THROUGH IT.
THERE'S ANOTHER WILL TURN YOU INTO A GIRL, AND WOULD TURN YOUR SISTER INTO A BOY.
THEN THERE'S THE ANYWHERE KEY.
WITH THAT ONE YOU CAN OPEN ALMOST ANY DOOR, AND STEP THROUGH INTO ANYWHERE IN THE WORLD YOU LIKE... AS LONG AS YOU HAVE A CLEAR PICTURE IN YOUR HEAD OF WHERE YOU'RE GOING. UNLOCK YOUR BEDROOM AND STEP INTO PARIS.
UNLOCK THE BATHROOM AND COME OUT IN DISNEYWORLD! UNLOCK A CLOSET AND—
HURRMM.
YOU CAN'T GO THROUGH THE FRONT DOOR WITHOUT FADING AWAY.
BUT WHAT ABOUT SOME OTHER DOOR?
SOME OTHER DOOR? OH. OH.
NO ONE HAS SEEN THE ANYWHERE KEY FOR A VERY LONG TIME, BODE. I THINK YOUR FATHER HID IT AWAY WHEN HE WAS A CHILD. PROBABLY FOR SOME VERY GOOD REASON.

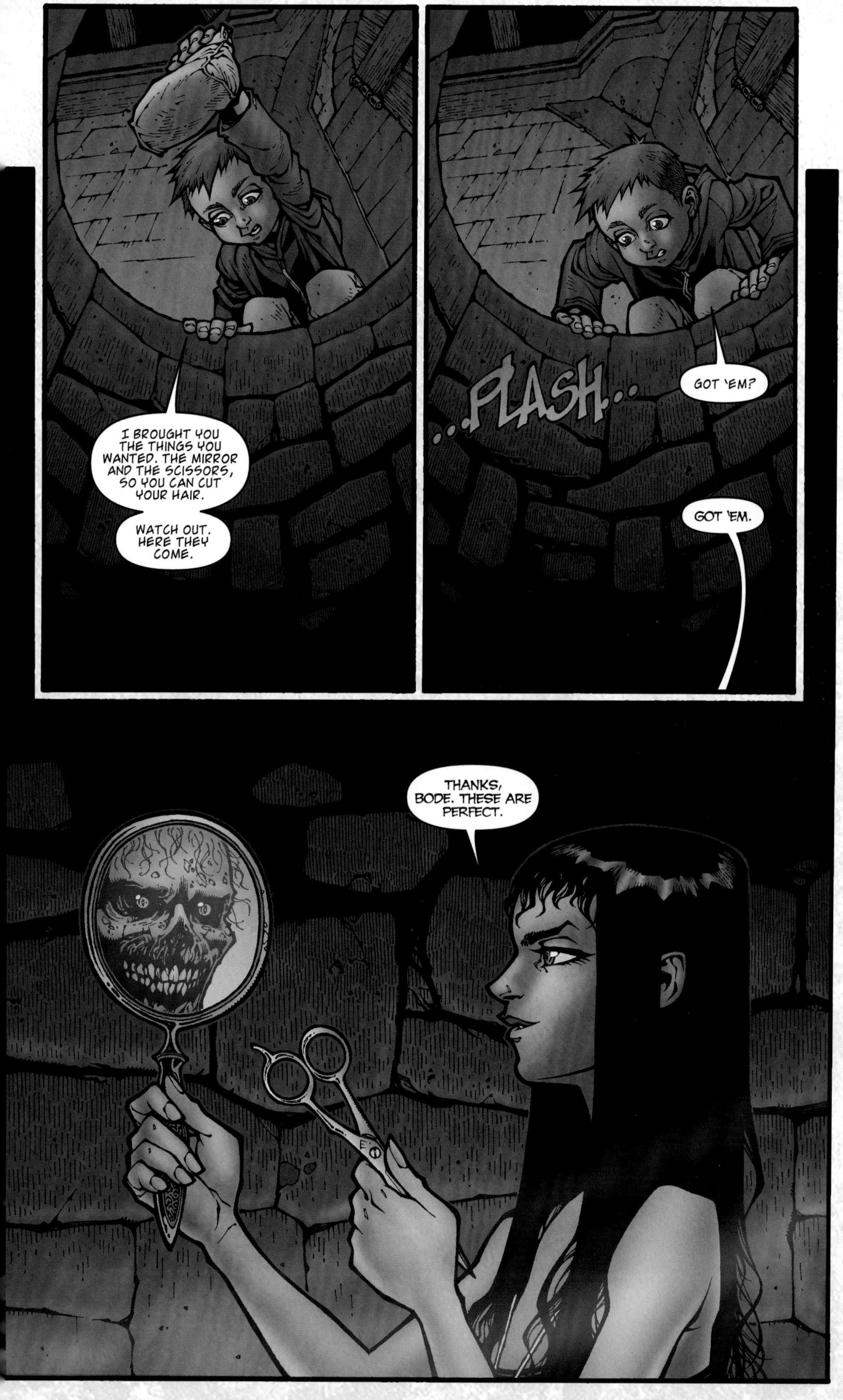

I BROUGHT YOU THE THINGS YOU WANTED. THE MIRROR AND THE SCISSORS, SO YOU CAN CUT YOUR HAIR.
WATCH OUT. HERE THEY COME.
...FLASH...
GOT 'EM?
GOT 'EM.
THANKS, BODE. THESE ARE PERFECT.

SAN LOBO
JUVENILE DETENTION
CAUTION!

SAM. I'VE GOT SOMETHING FOR YOU, SOMETHING I PROMISED.

WHAT ARE YOU TALKING ABOUT? I DIDN'T ASK FOR THIS.

YES, YOU DID, SAM. YES, YOU DID.

IT'S THE KEY TO YOUR CELL.

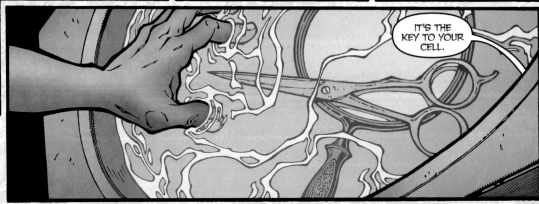

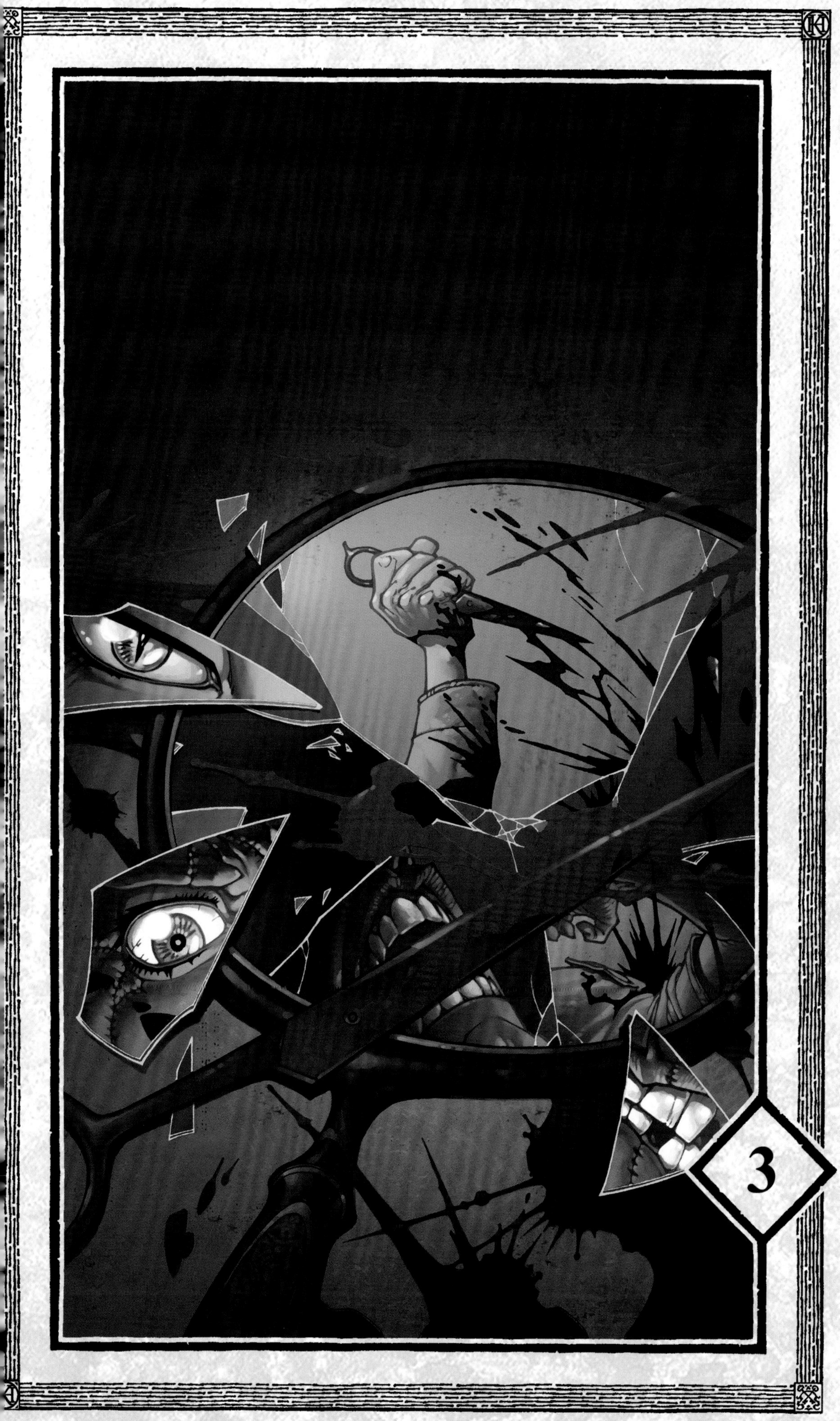
3

WELCOME TO LOVECRAFT
- THREE -

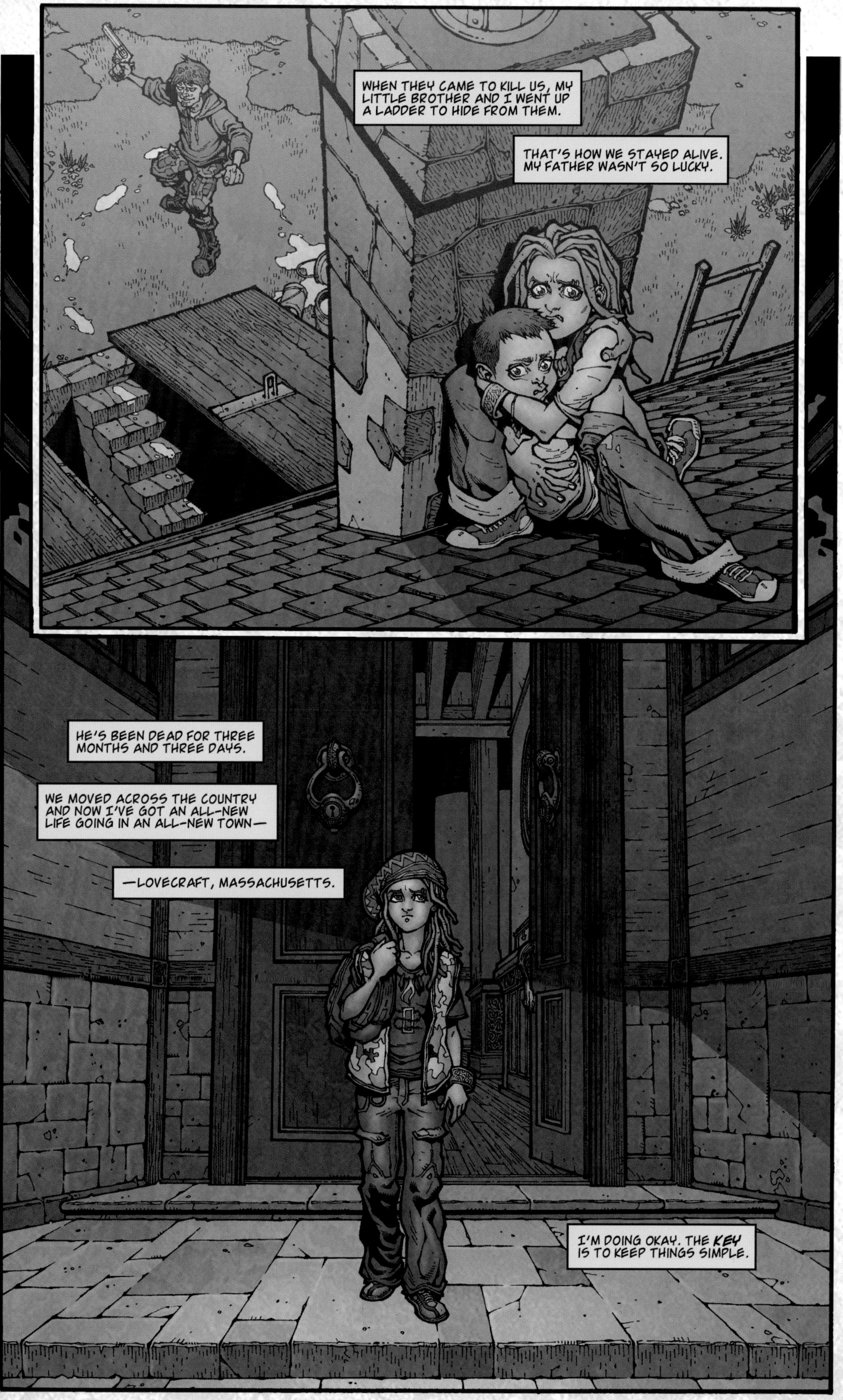
WHEN THEY CAME TO KILL US, MY LITTLE BROTHER AND I WENT UP A LADDER TO HIDE FROM THEM.
THAT'S HOW WE STAYED ALIVE. MY FATHER WASN'T SO LUCKY.
HE'S BEEN DEAD FOR THREE MONTHS AND THREE DAYS.
WE MOVED ACROSS THE COUNTRY AND NOW I'VE GOT AN ALL-NEW LIFE GOING IN AN ALL-NEW TOWN—
—LOVECRAFT, MASSACHUSETTS.
I'M DOING OKAY. THE KEY IS TO KEEP THINGS SIMPLE.

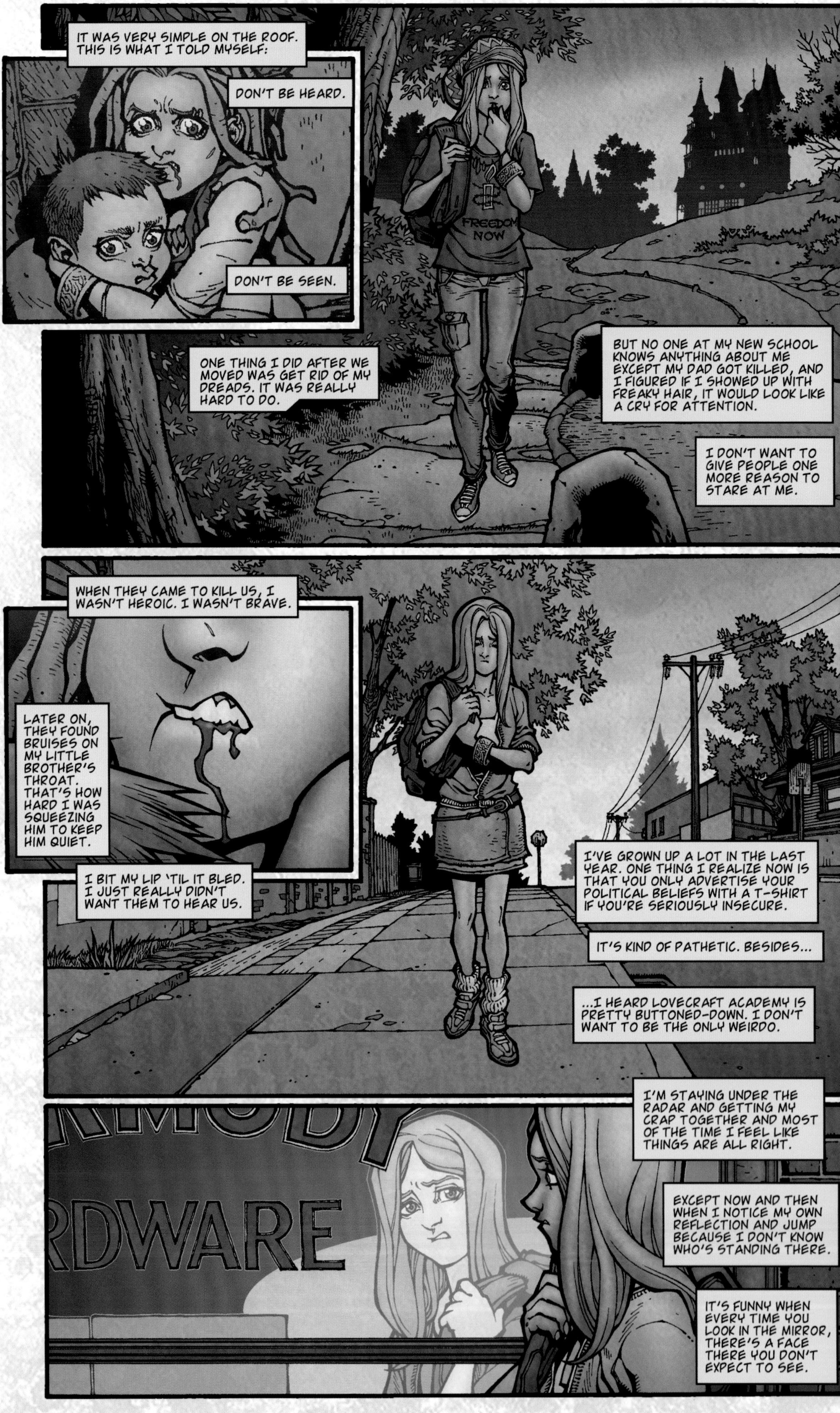
IT WAS VERY SIMPLE ON THE ROOF. THIS IS WHAT I TOLD MYSELF:
DON'T BE HEARD.
DON'T BE SEEN.
FREEDOM NOW
ONE THING I DID AFTER WE MOVED WAS GET RID OF MY DREADS. IT WAS REALLY HARD TO DO.
BUT NO ONE AT MY NEW SCHOOL KNOWS ANYTHING ABOUT ME EXCEPT MY DAD GOT KILLED, AND I FIGURED IF I SHOWED UP WITH FREAKY HAIR, IT WOULD LOOK LIKE A CRY FOR ATTENTION.
I DON'T WANT TO GIVE PEOPLE ONE MORE REASON TO STARE AT ME.
WHEN THEY CAME TO KILL US, I WASN'T HEROIC. I WASN'T BRAVE.
LATER ON, THEY FOUND BRUISES ON MY LITTLE BROTHER'S THROAT. THAT'S HOW HARD I WAS SQUEEZING HIM TO KEEP HIM QUIET.
I BIT MY LIP 'TIL IT BLED. I JUST REALLY DIDN'T WANT THEM TO HEAR US.
I'VE GROWN UP A LOT IN THE LAST YEAR. ONE THING I REALIZE NOW IS THAT YOU ONLY ADVERTISE YOUR POLITICAL BELIEFS WITH A T-SHIRT IF YOU'RE SERIOUSLY INSECURE.
IT'S KIND OF PATHETIC. BESIDES...
...I HEARD LOVECRAFT ACADEMY IS PRETTY BUTTONED-DOWN. I DON'T WANT TO BE THE ONLY WEIRDO.
I'M STAYING UNDER THE RADAR AND GETTING MY CRAP TOGETHER AND MOST OF THE TIME I FEEL LIKE THINGS ARE ALL RIGHT.
RDWARE
EXCEPT NOW AND THEN WHEN I NOTICE MY OWN REFLECTION AND JUMP BECAUSE I DON'T KNOW WHO'S STANDING THERE.
IT'S FUNNY WHEN EVERY TIME YOU LOOK IN THE MIRROR, THERE'S A FACE THERE YOU DON'T EXPECT TO SEE.

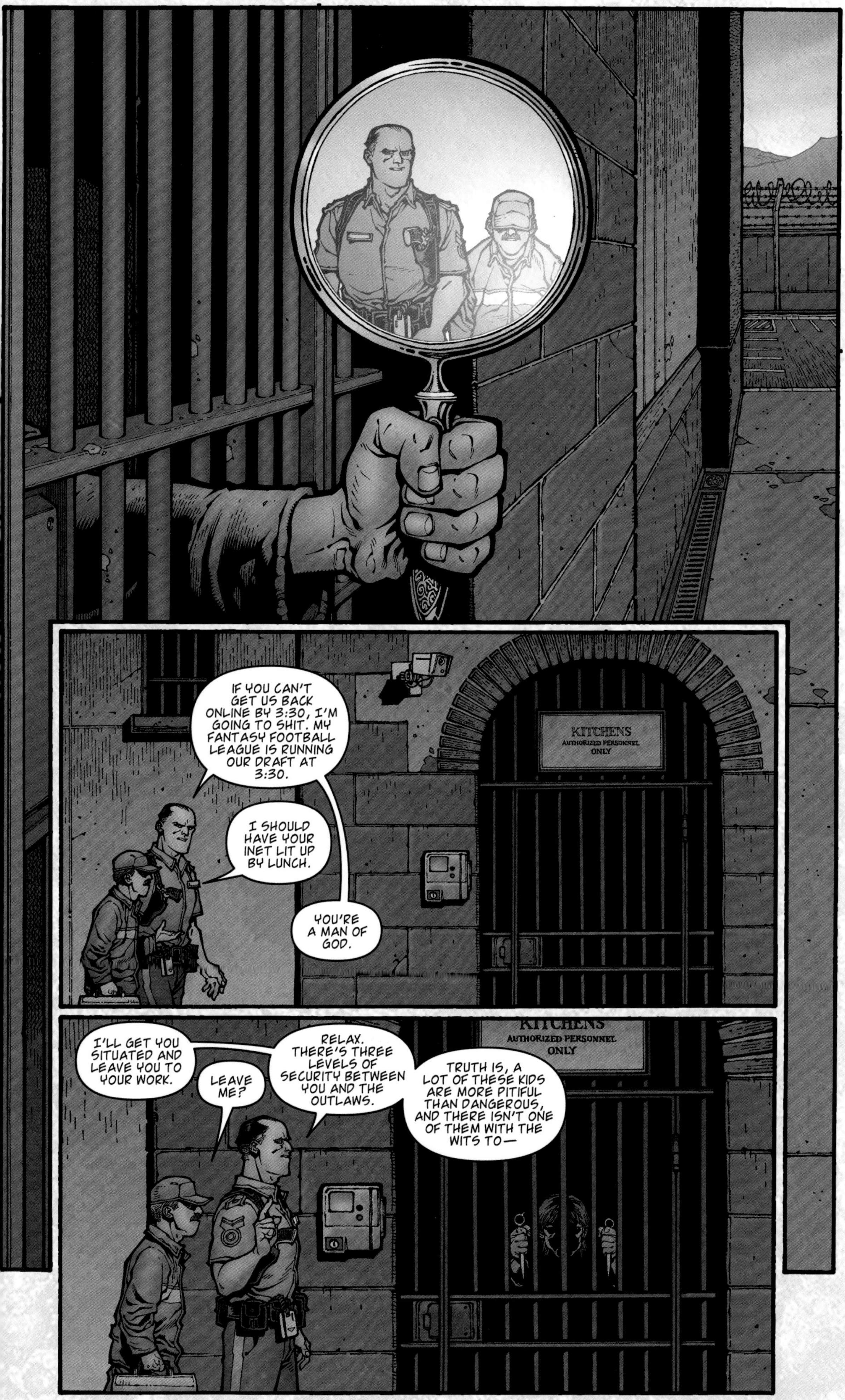
IF YOU CAN'T GET US BACK ONLINE BY 3:30, I'M GOING TO SHIT. MY FANTASY FOOTBALL LEAGUE IS RUNNING OUR DRAFT AT 3:30.
KITCHENS AUTHORIZED PERSONNEL ONLY
I SHOULD HAVE YOUR INET LIT UP BY LUNCH.
YOU'RE A MAN OF GOD.
KITCHENS AUTHORIZED PERSONNEL ONLY
I'LL GET YOU SITUATED AND LEAVE YOU TO YOUR WORK.
LEAVE ME?
RELAX. THERE'S THREE LEVELS OF SECURITY BETWEEN YOU AND THE OUTLAWS.
TRUTH IS, A LOT OF THESE KIDS ARE MORE PITIFUL THAN DANGEROUS, AND THERE ISN'T ONE OF THEM WITH THE WITS TO—

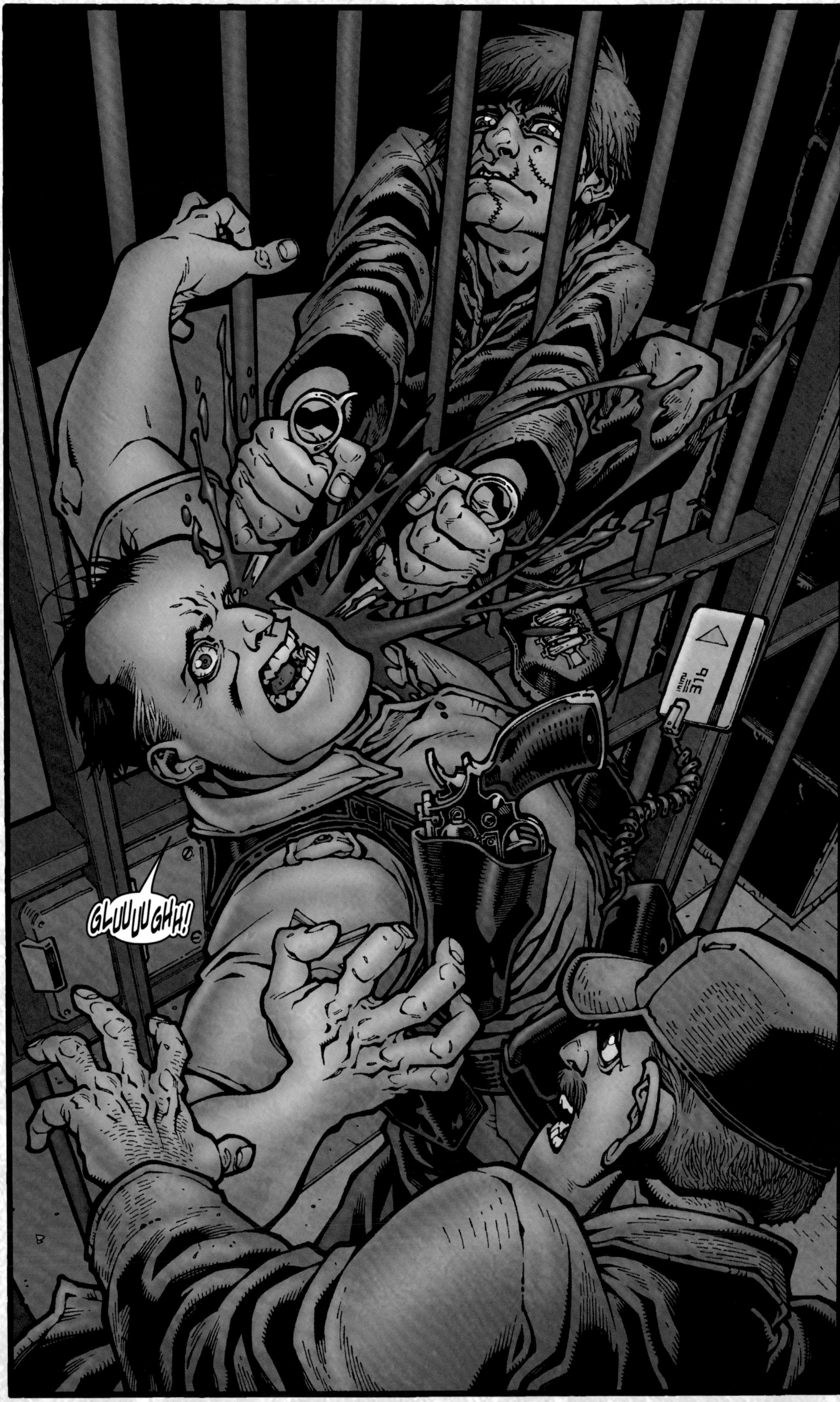
GLUUUUGHH!

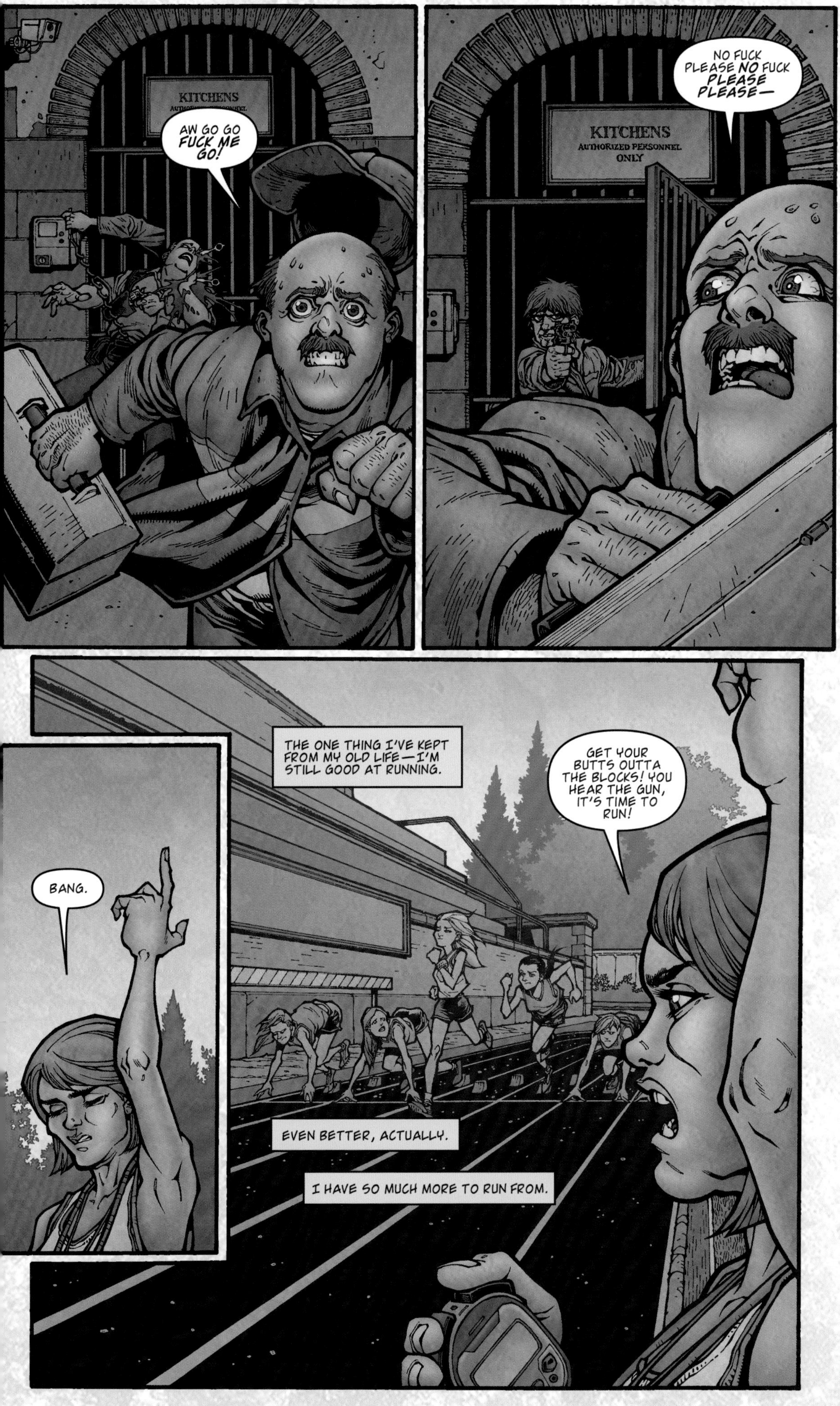
KITCHENS
AW GO GO FUCK ME GO!
NO FUCK PLEASE NO FUCK PLEASE PLEASE—
KITCHENS AUTHORIZED PERSONNEL ONLY
THE ONE THING I'VE KEPT FROM MY OLD LIFE—I'M STILL GOOD AT RUNNING.
GET YOUR BUTTS OUTTA THE BLOCKS! YOU HEAR THE GUN, IT'S TIME TO RUN!
BANG.
EVEN BETTER, ACTUALLY.
I HAVE SO MUCH MORE TO RUN FROM.

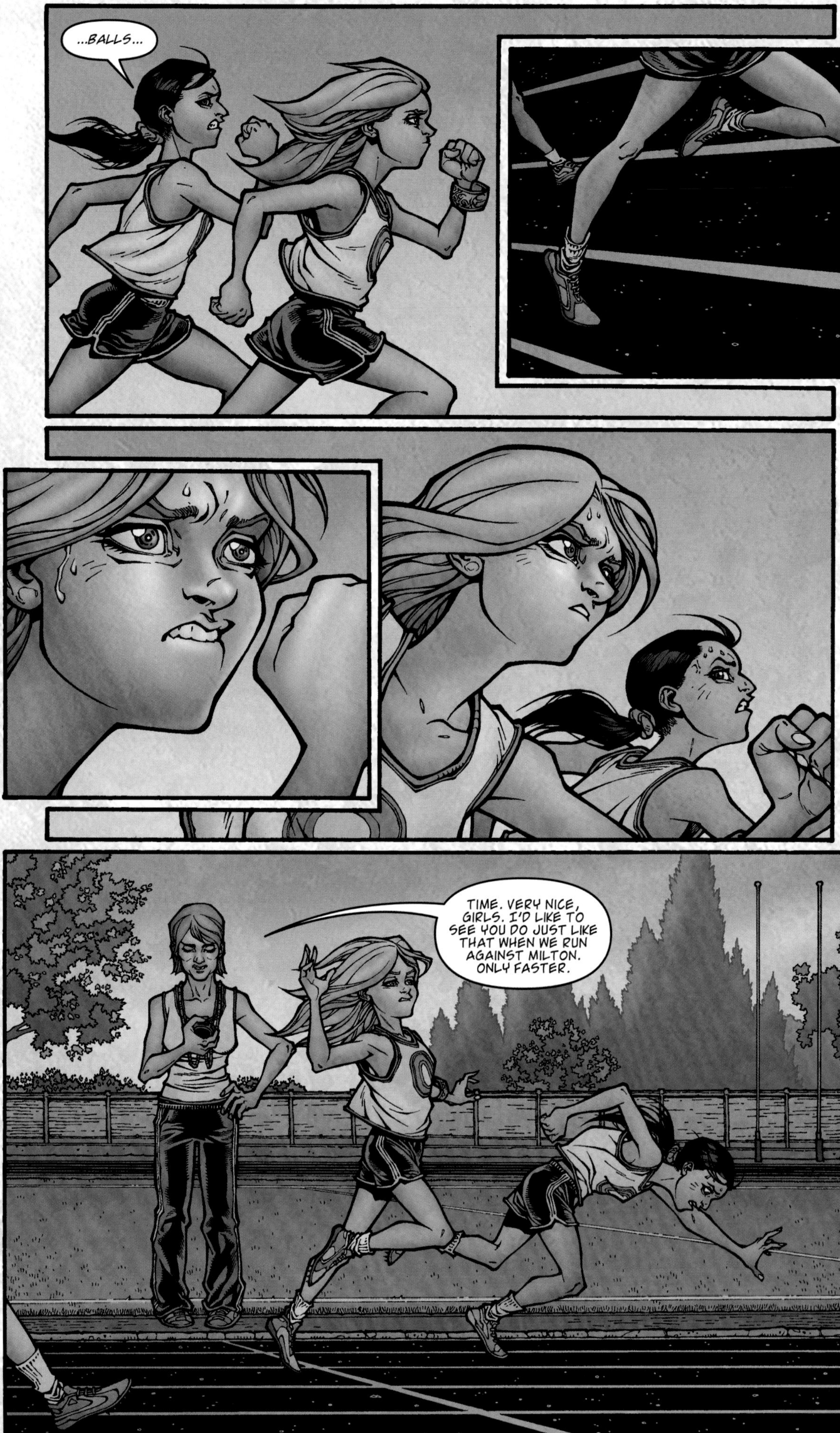
...BALLS...
TIME. VERY NICE, GIRLS. I'D LIKE TO SEE YOU DO JUST LIKE THAT WHEN WE RUN AGAINST MILTON. ONLY FASTER.

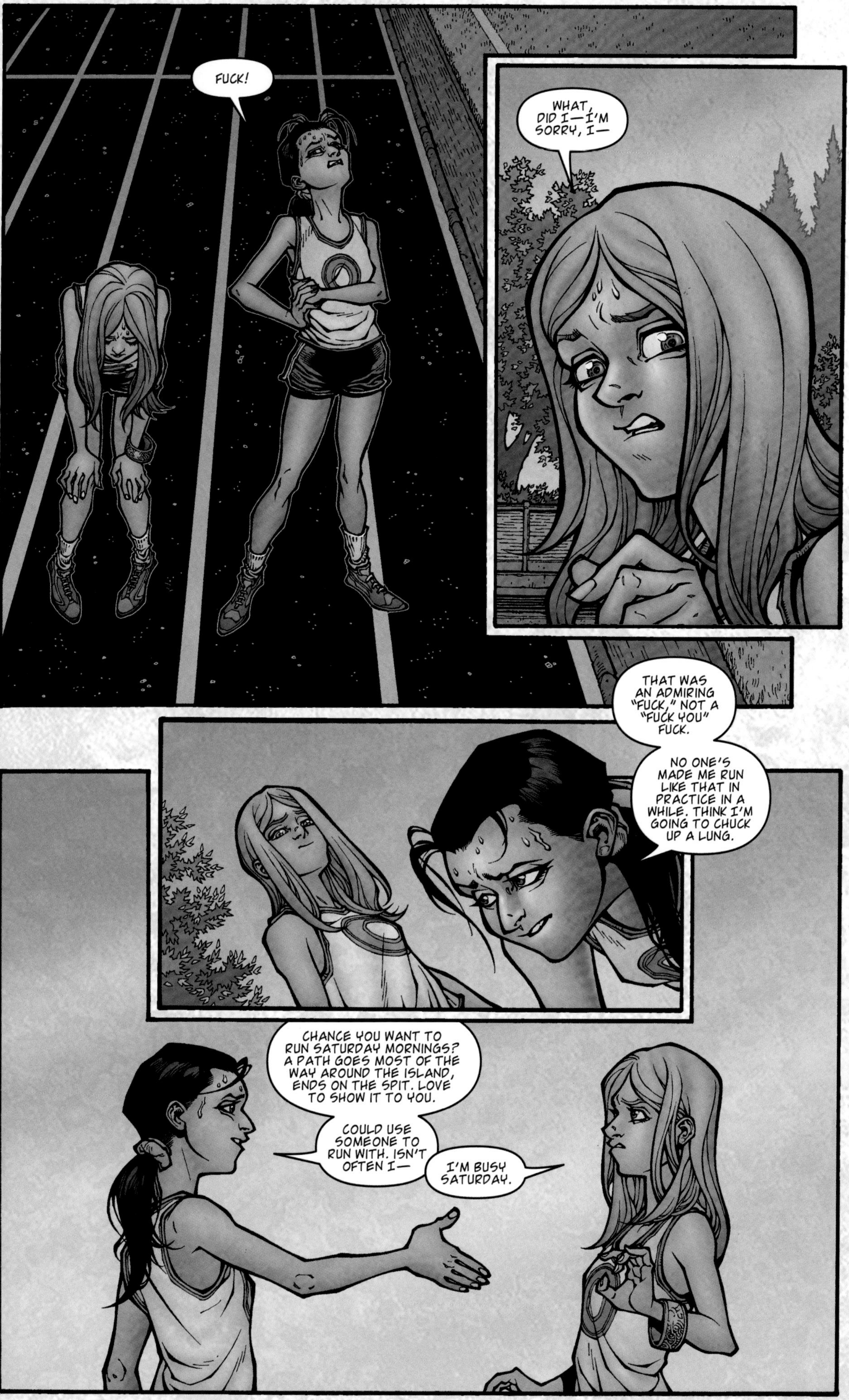
FUCK!
WHAT, DID I—I'M SORRY, I—
THAT WAS AN ADMIRING "FUCK," NOT A "FUCK YOU" FUCK.
NO ONE'S MADE ME RUN LIKE THAT IN PRACTICE IN A WHILE. THINK I'M GOING TO CHUCK UP A LUNG.
CHANCE YOU WANT TO RUN SATURDAY MORNINGS? A PATH GOES MOST OF THE WAY AROUND THE ISLAND, ENDS ON THE SPIT. LOVE TO SHOW IT TO YOU.
COULD USE SOMEONE TO RUN WITH. ISN'T OFTEN I—
I'M BUSY SATURDAY.

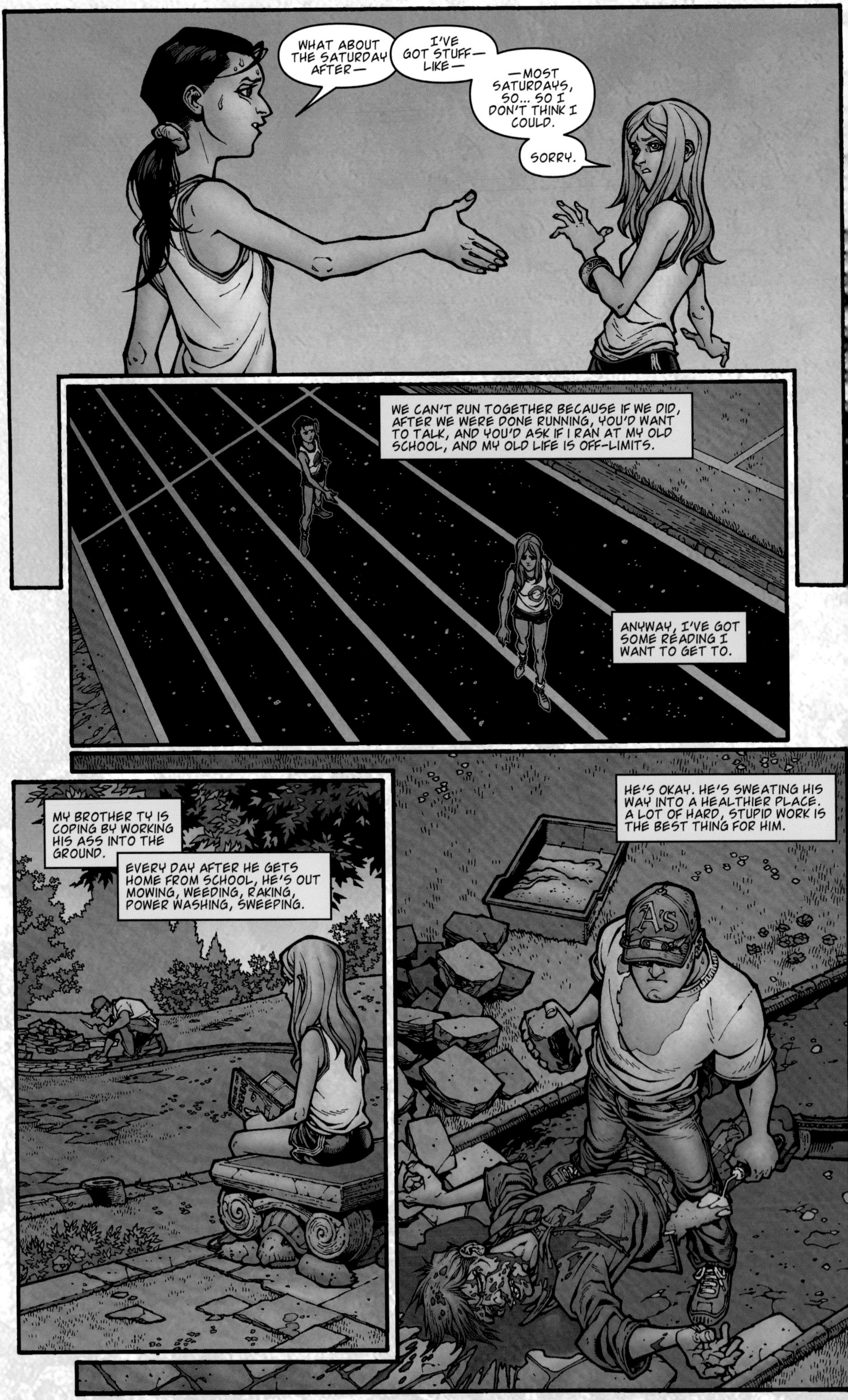

WHAT ABOUT THE SATURDAY AFTER—
I'VE GOT STUFF— LIKE—
—MOST SATURDAYS, SO... SO I DON'T THINK I COULD.
SORRY.
WE CAN'T RUN TOGETHER BECAUSE IF WE DID, AFTER WE WERE DONE RUNNING, YOU'D WANT TO TALK, AND YOU'D ASK IF I RAN AT MY OLD SCHOOL, AND MY OLD LIFE IS OFF-LIMITS.
ANYWAY, I'VE GOT SOME READING I WANT TO GET TO.
MY BROTHER TY IS COPING BY WORKING HIS ASS INTO THE GROUND.
EVERY DAY AFTER HE GETS HOME FROM SCHOOL, HE'S OUT MOWING, WEEDING, RAKING, POWER WASHING, SWEEPING.
HE'S OKAY. HE'S SWEATING HIS WAY INTO A HEALTHIER PLACE. A LOT OF HARD, STUPID WORK IS THE BEST THING FOR HIM.

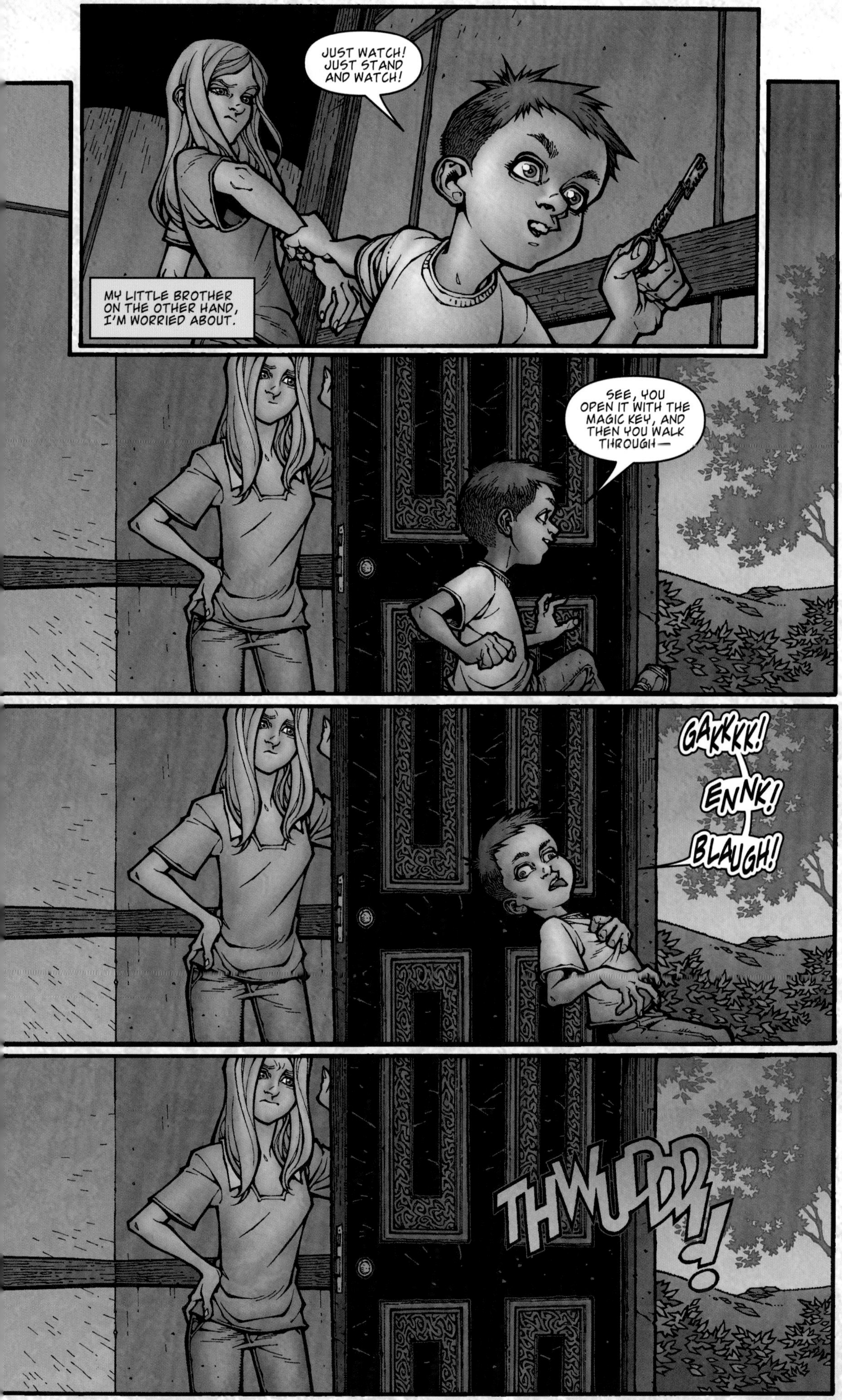
JUST WATCH! JUST STAND AND WATCH!
MY LITTLE BROTHER ON THE OTHER HAND, I'M WORRIED ABOUT.
SEE, YOU OPEN IT WITH THE MAGIC KEY, AND THEN YOU WALK THROUGH—
GAKKKK!
ENNK!
BLAUGH!
THWUDD!

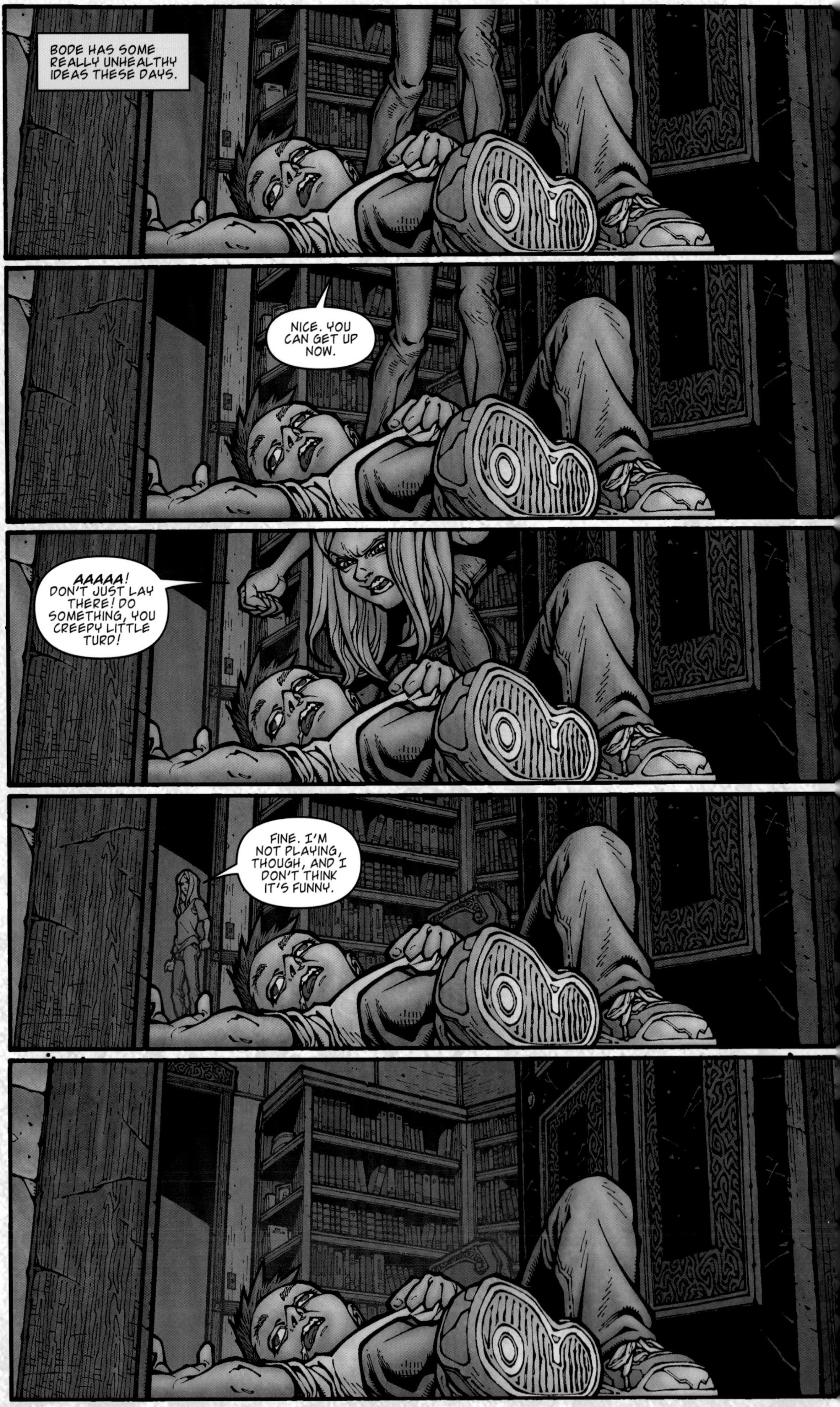

BODE HAS SOME REALLY UNHEALTHY IDEAS THESE DAYS.
NICE. YOU CAN GET UP NOW.
AAAAA! DON'T JUST LAY THERE! DO SOMETHING, YOU CREEPY LITTLE TURD!
FINE. I'M NOT PLAYING, THOUGH, AND I DON'T THINK IT'S FUNNY.

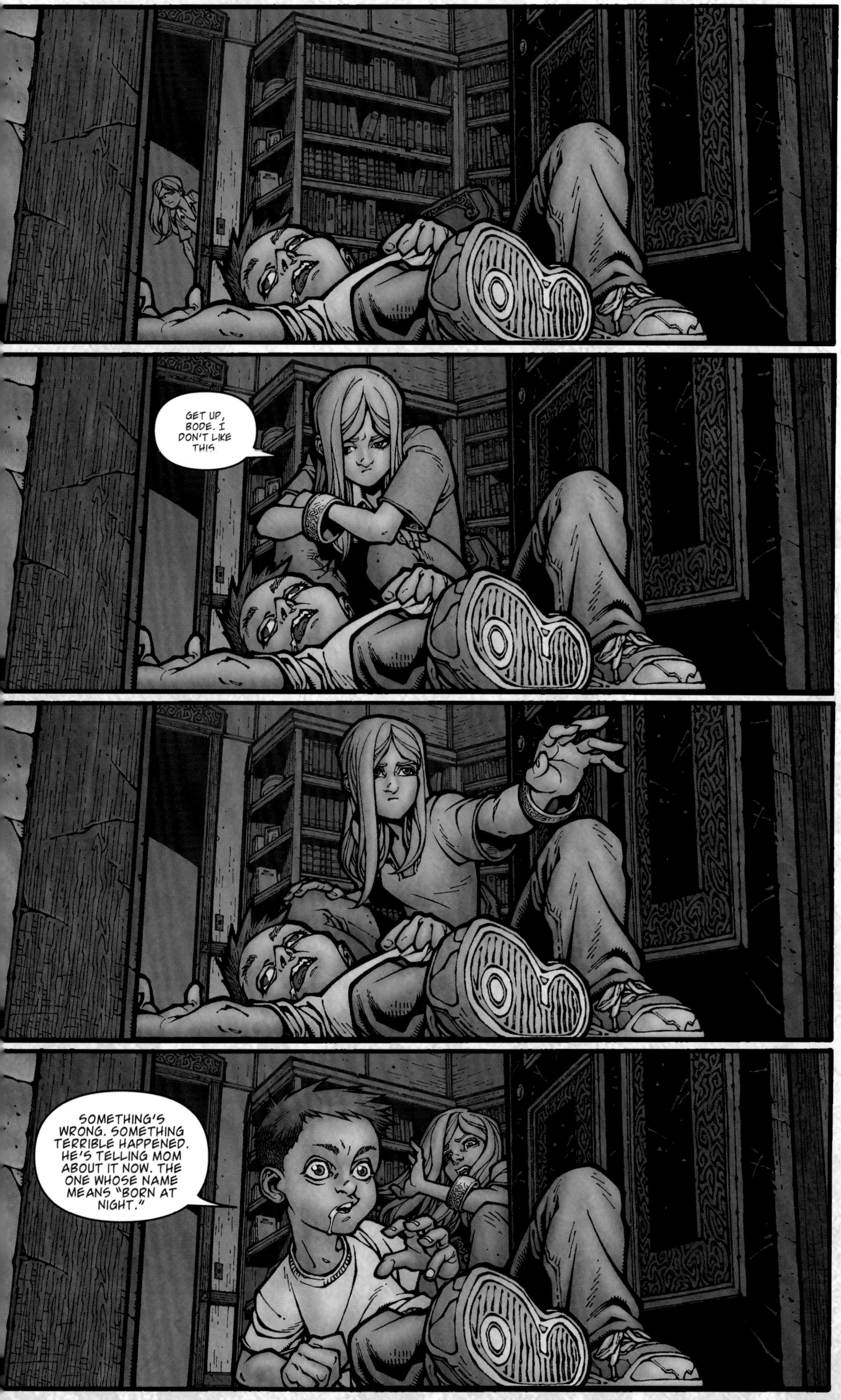
GET UP, BODE. I DON'T LIKE THIS.
SOMETHING'S WRONG. SOMETHING TERRIBLE HAPPENED. HE'S TELLING MOM ABOUT IT NOW. THE ONE WHOSE NAME MEANS "BORN AT NIGHT."

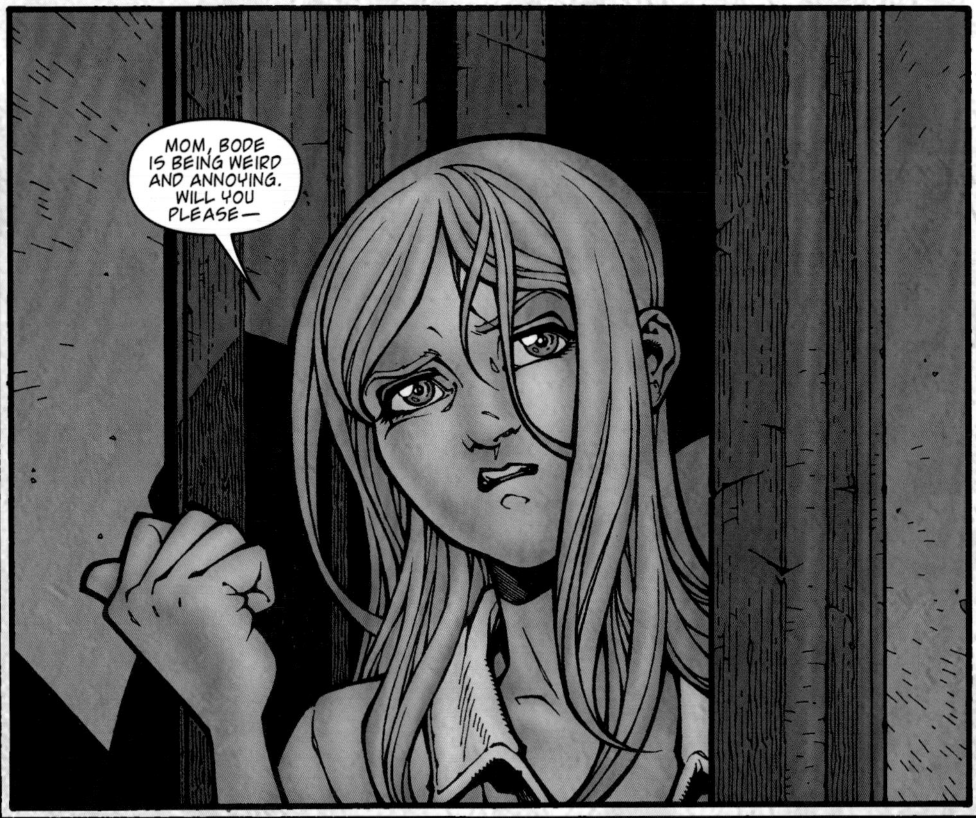
MOM, BODE IS BEING WEIRD AND ANNOYING. WILL YOU PLEASE—

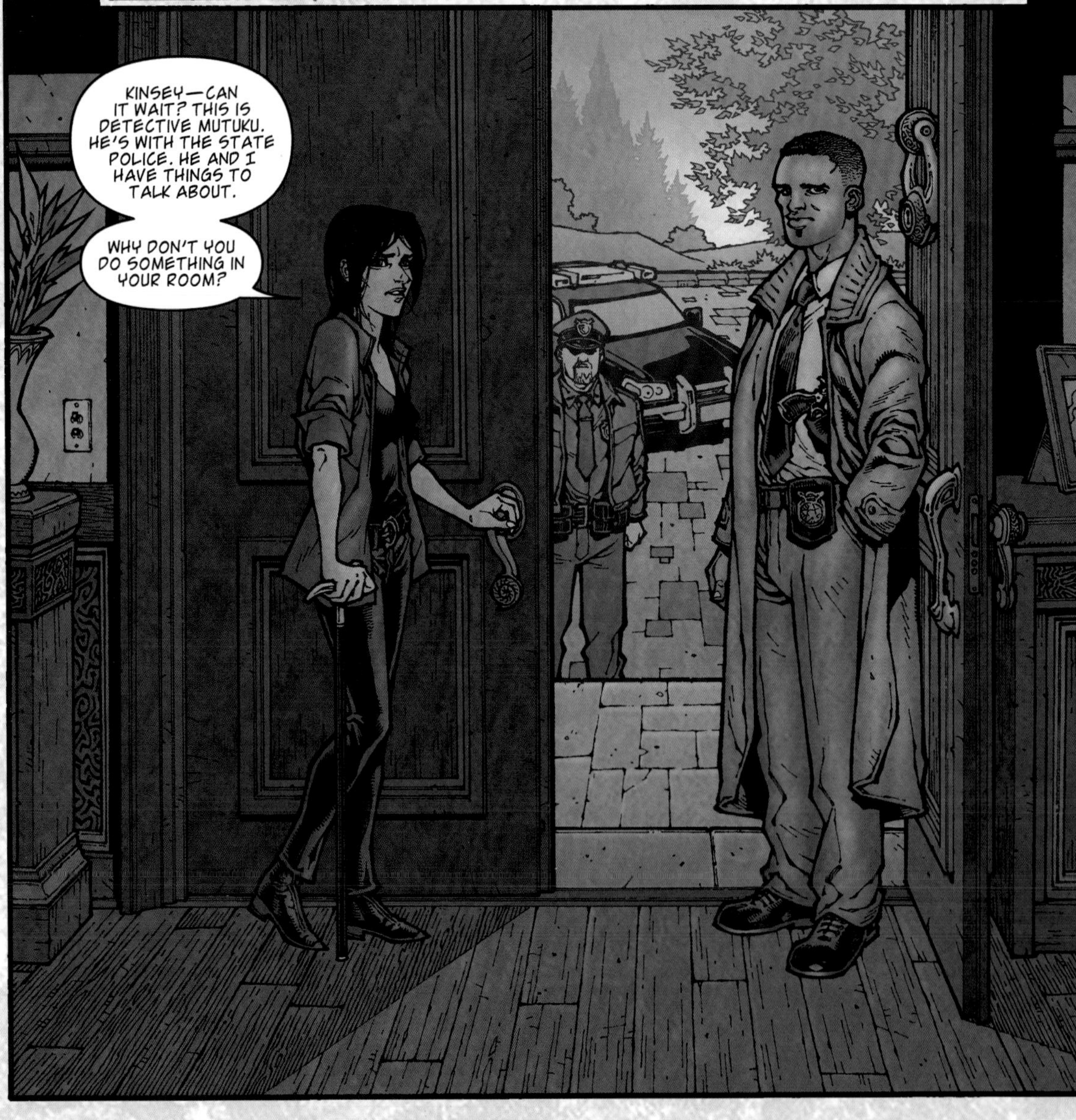
KINSEY—CAN IT WAIT? THIS IS DETECTIVE MUTUKU. HE'S WITH THE STATE POLICE. HE AND I HAVE THINGS TO TALK ABOUT.
WHY DON'T YOU DO SOMETHING IN YOUR ROOM?

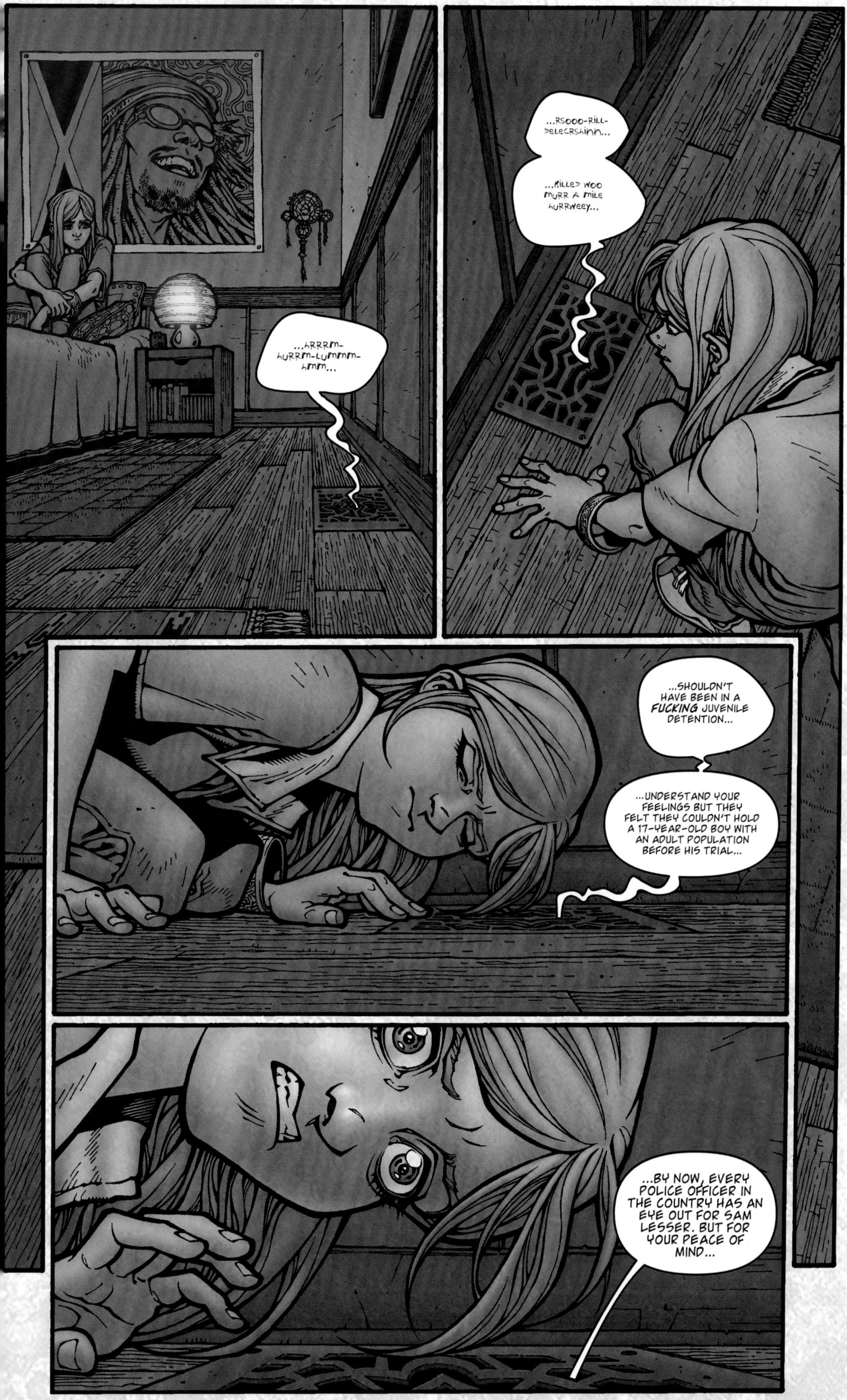

...ARRRM-HURRM-LUMMM-HMM...
...RSOOO-RILL-DELECRSHINN...
...KILLED WOO MURR A MILE HURRWEEY...
...SHOULDN'T HAVE BEEN IN A FUCKING JUVENILE DETENTION...
...UNDERSTAND YOUR FEELINGS BUT THEY FELT THEY COULDN'T HOLD A 17-YEAR-OLD BOY WITH AN ADULT POPULATION BEFORE HIS TRIAL...
...BY NOW, EVERY POLICE OFFICER IN THE COUNTRY HAS AN EYE OUT FOR SAM LESSER. BUT FOR YOUR PEACE OF MIND...

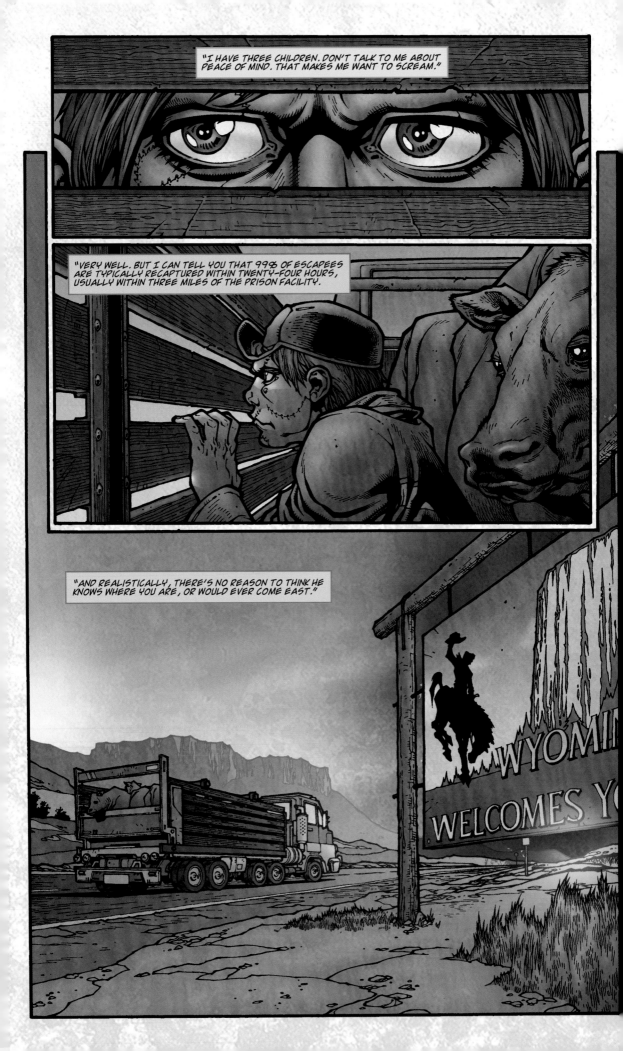

"I HAVE THREE CHILDREN. DON'T TALK TO ME ABOUT PEACE OF MIND. THAT MAKES ME WANT TO SCREAM."

"VERY WELL. BUT I CAN TELL YOU THAT 99% OF ESCAPEES ARE TYPICALLY RECAPTURED WITHIN TWENTY-FOUR HOURS, USUALLY WITHIN THREE MILES OF THE PRISON FACILITY."

"AND REALISTICALLY, THERE'S NO REASON TO THINK HE KNOWS WHERE YOU ARE, OR WOULD EVER COME EAST."

WYOMI...
WELCOMES YO...

MOM?

YOU GET MOST OF THAT?

A BUNCH.

COME HERE.

"HOW LONG ARE THERE GOING TO BE COPS PARKED IN FRONT OF OUR HOUSE?"

"I DON'T KNOW. FOR NOW."

"SO THEY THINK—"

"NO."

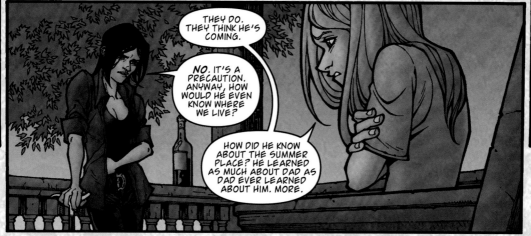

THEY DO. THEY THINK HE'S COMING.

NO. IT'S A PRECAUTION. ANYWAY, HOW WOULD HE EVEN KNOW WHERE WE LIVE?

HOW DID HE KNOW ABOUT THE SUMMER PLACE? HE LEARNED AS MUCH ABOUT DAD AS DAD EVER LEARNED ABOUT HIM. MORE.

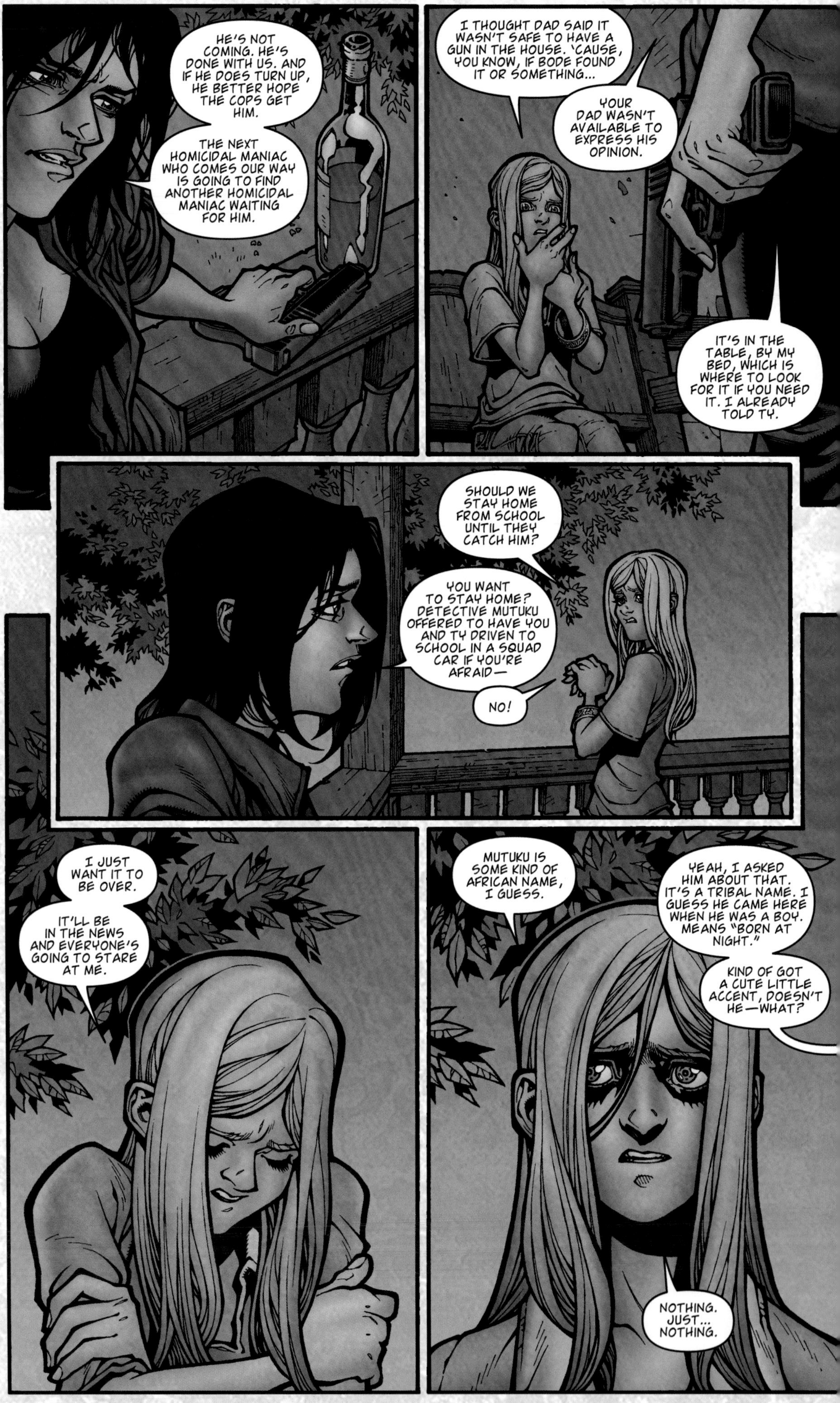
HE'S NOT COMING. HE'S DONE WITH US. AND IF HE DOES TURN UP, HE BETTER HOPE THE COPS GET HIM.
THE NEXT HOMICIDAL MANIAC WHO COMES OUR WAY IS GOING TO FIND ANOTHER HOMICIDAL MANIAC WAITING FOR HIM.
I THOUGHT DAD SAID IT WASN'T SAFE TO HAVE A GUN IN THE HOUSE. 'CAUSE, YOU KNOW, IF BODE FOUND IT OR SOMETHING...
YOUR DAD WASN'T AVAILABLE TO EXPRESS HIS OPINION.
IT'S IN THE TABLE, BY MY BED, WHICH IS WHERE TO LOOK FOR IT IF YOU NEED IT. I ALREADY TOLD TY.
SHOULD WE STAY HOME FROM SCHOOL UNTIL THEY CATCH HIM?
YOU WANT TO STAY HOME? DETECTIVE MUTUKU OFFERED TO HAVE YOU AND TY DRIVEN TO SCHOOL IN A SQUAD CAR IF YOU'RE AFRAID—
NO!
I JUST WANT IT TO BE OVER.
IT'LL BE IN THE NEWS AND EVERYONE'S GOING TO STARE AT ME.
MUTUKU IS SOME KIND OF AFRICAN NAME, I GUESS.
YEAH, I ASKED HIM ABOUT THAT. IT'S A TRIBAL NAME. I GUESS HE CAME HERE WHEN HE WAS A BOY. MEANS "BORN AT NIGHT."
KIND OF GOT A CUTE LITTLE ACCENT, DOESN'T HE—WHAT?
NOTHING. JUST... NOTHING.

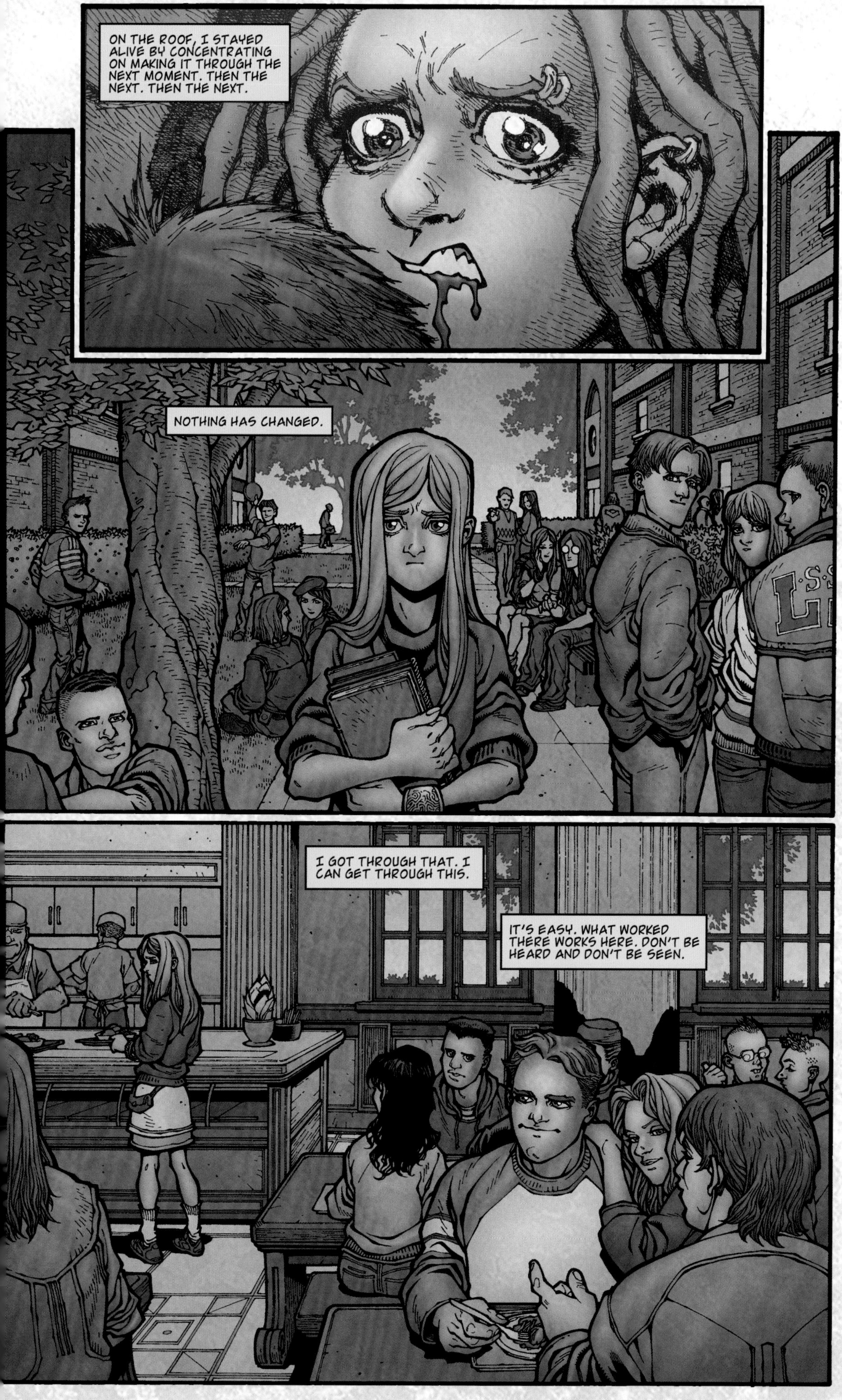
ON THE ROOF, I STAYED ALIVE BY CONCENTRATING ON MAKING IT THROUGH THE NEXT MOMENT. THEN THE NEXT. THEN THE NEXT.
NOTHING HAS CHANGED.
I GOT THROUGH THAT. I CAN GET THROUGH THIS.
IT'S EASY. WHAT WORKED THERE WORKS HERE. DON'T BE HEARD AND DON'T BE SEEN.

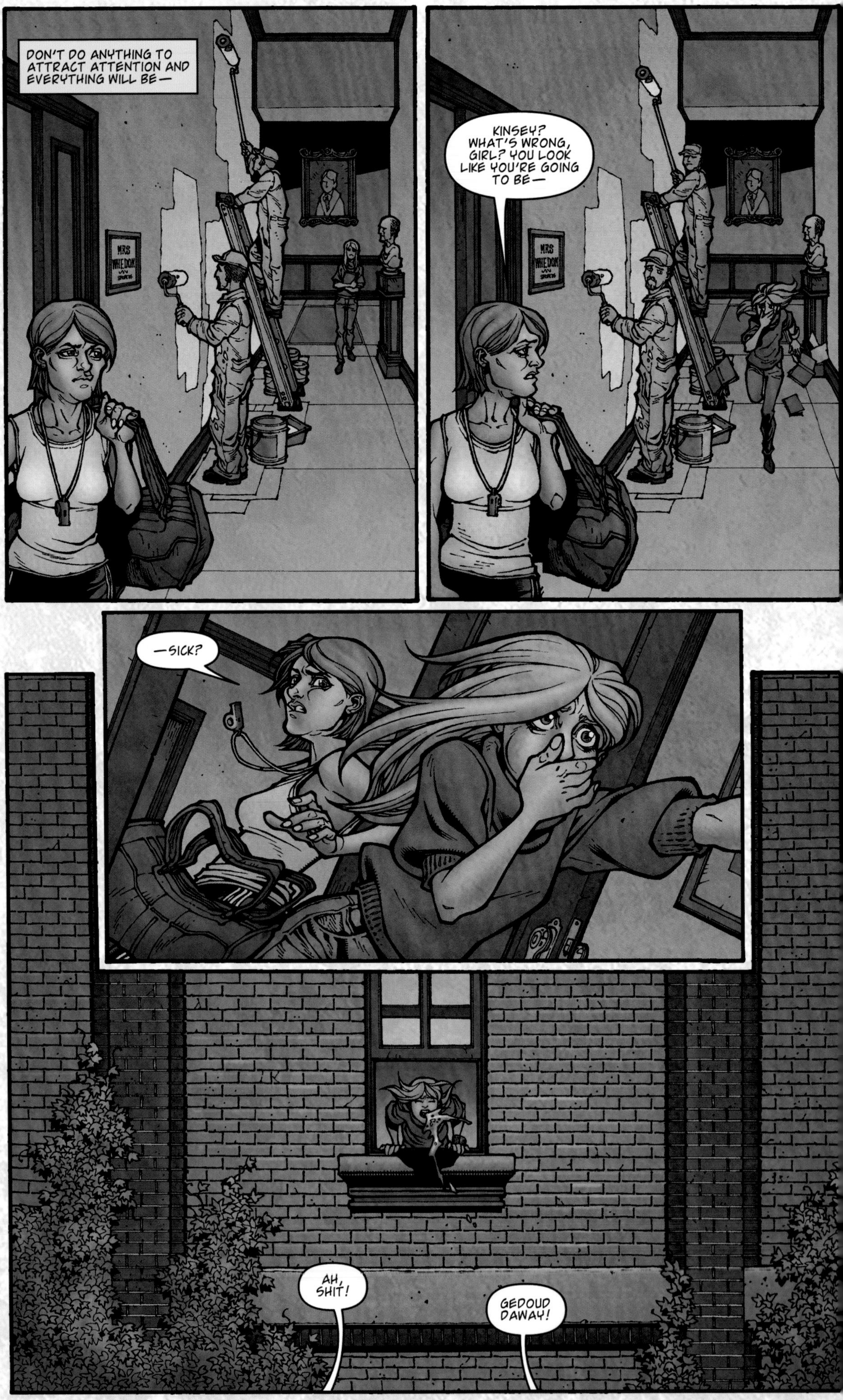
DON'T DO ANYTHING TO ATTRACT ATTENTION AND EVERYTHING WILL BE—
MRS WHEDON
KINSEY? WHAT'S WRONG, GIRL? YOU LOOK LIKE YOU'RE GOING TO BE—
—SICK?
AH, SHIT!
GEDOUD DAWAY!

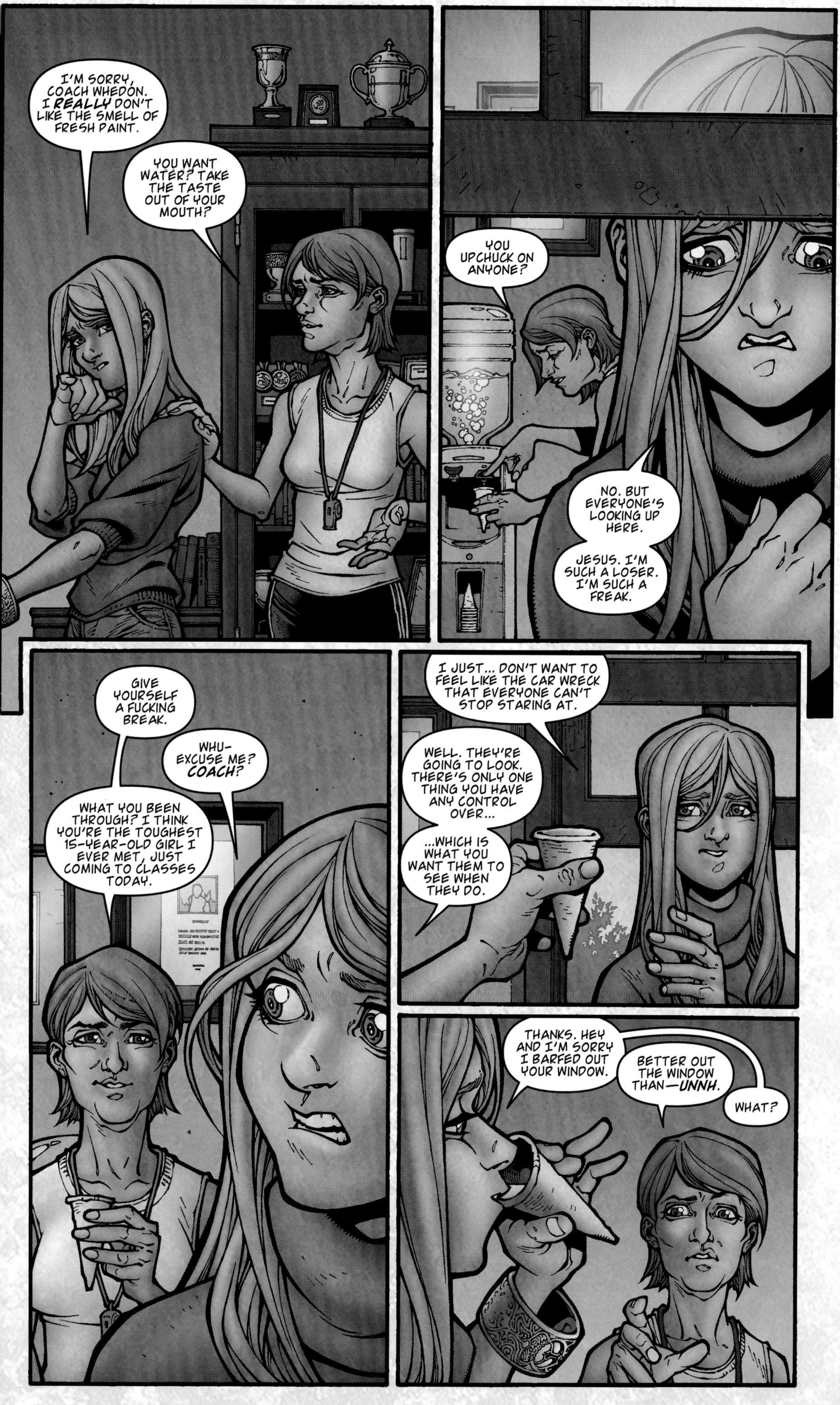
I'M SORRY, COACH WHEDON. I REALLY DON'T LIKE THE SMELL OF FRESH PAINT.
YOU WANT WATER? TAKE THE TASTE OUT OF YOUR MOUTH?
YOU UPCHUCK ON ANYONE?
NO. BUT EVERYONE'S LOOKING UP HERE.
JESUS. I'M SUCH A LOSER. I'M SUCH A FREAK.
GIVE YOURSELF A FUCKING BREAK.
WHU- EXCUSE ME? COACH?
WHAT YOU BEEN THROUGH? I THINK YOU'RE THE TOUGHEST 15-YEAR-OLD GIRL I EVER MET, JUST COMING TO CLASSES TODAY.
I JUST... DON'T WANT TO FEEL LIKE THE CAR WRECK THAT EVERYONE CAN'T STOP STARING AT.
WELL. THEY'RE GOING TO LOOK. THERE'S ONLY ONE THING YOU HAVE ANY CONTROL OVER...
...WHICH IS WHAT YOU WANT THEM TO SEE WHEN THEY DO.
THANKS. HEY AND I'M SORRY I BARFED OUT YOUR WINDOW.
BETTER OUT THE WINDOW THAN—UNNH.
WHAT?

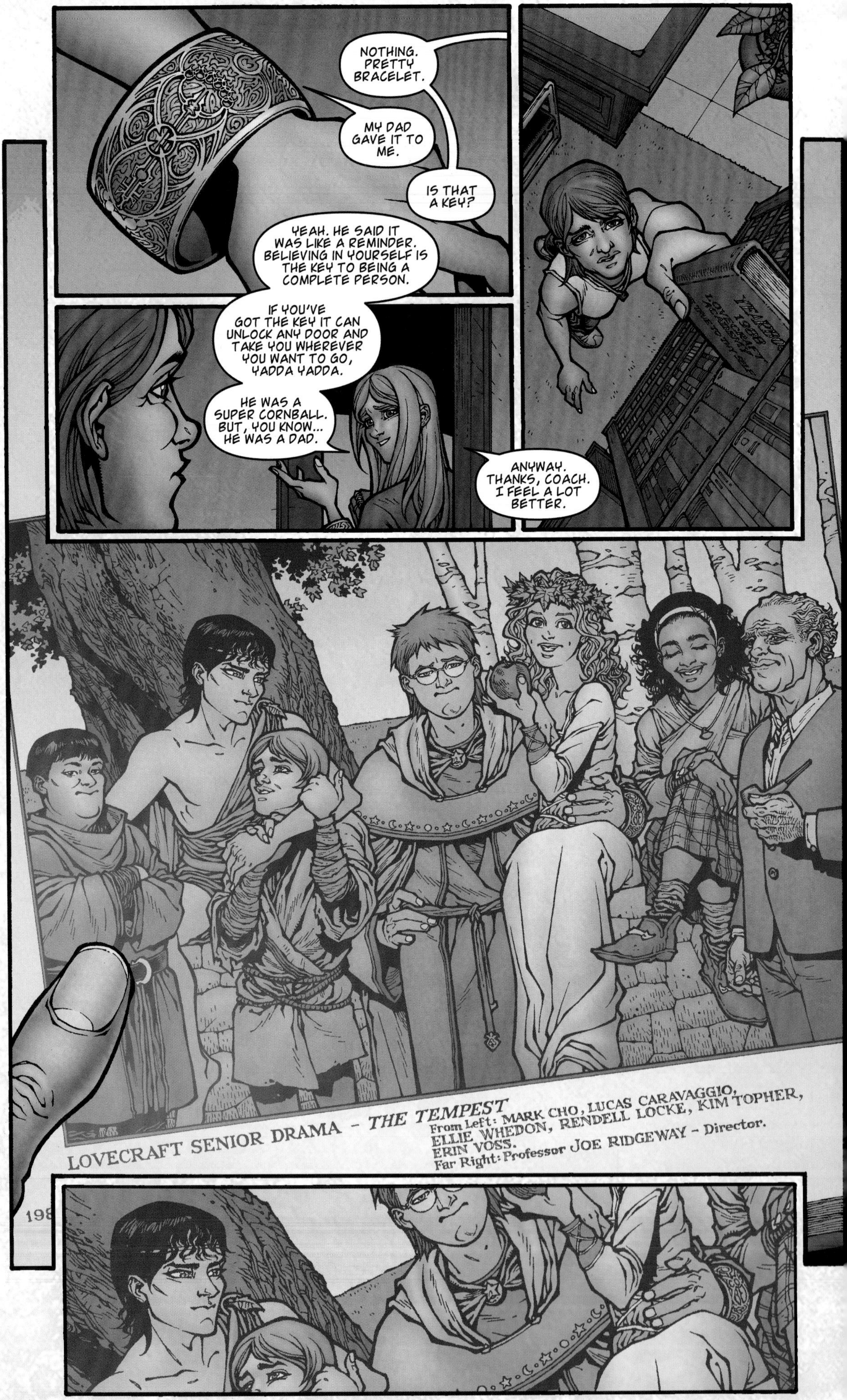
NOTHING. PRETTY BRACELET.
MY DAD GAVE IT TO ME.
IS THAT A KEY?
YEAH. HE SAID IT WAS LIKE A REMINDER. BELIEVING IN YOURSELF IS THE KEY TO BEING A COMPLETE PERSON.
IF YOU'VE GOT THE KEY IT CAN UNLOCK ANY DOOR AND TAKE YOU WHEREVER YOU WANT TO GO, YADDA YADDA.
HE WAS A SUPER CORNBALL. BUT, YOU KNOW... HE WAS A DAD.
ANYWAY. THANKS, COACH. I FEEL A LOT BETTER.
LOVECRAFT SENIOR DRAMA - *THE TEMPEST*
From Left: MARK CHO, LUCAS CARAVAGGIO, ELLIE WHEDON, RENDELL LOCKE, KIM TOPHER, ERIN VOSS.
Far Right: Professor JOE RIDGEWAY - Director.
198

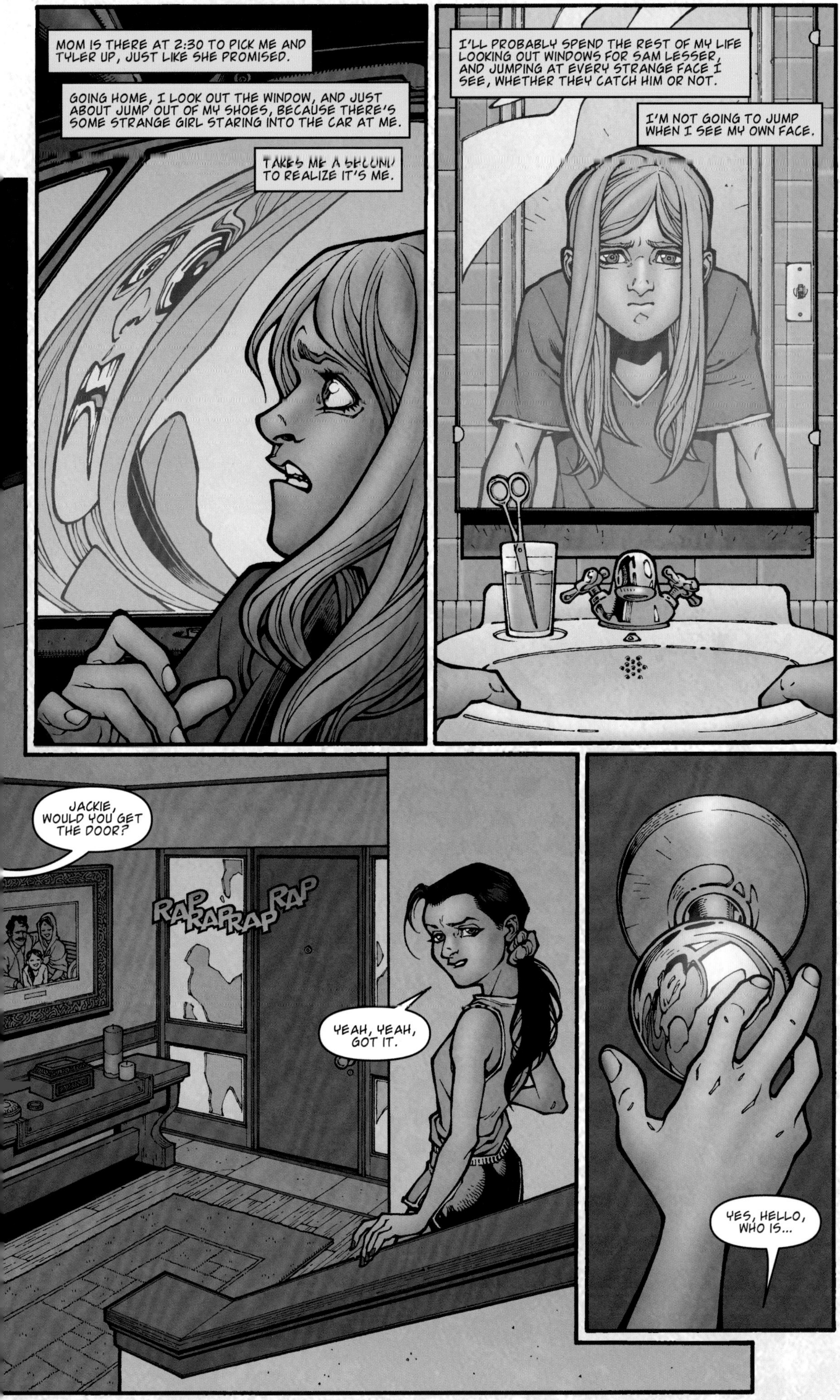
MOM IS THERE AT 2:30 TO PICK ME AND TYLER UP, JUST LIKE SHE PROMISED.
GOING HOME, I LOOK OUT THE WINDOW, AND JUST ABOUT JUMP OUT OF MY SHOES, BECAUSE THERE'S SOME STRANGE GIRL STARING INTO THE CAR AT ME.
TAKES ME A SECOND TO REALIZE IT'S ME.
I'LL PROBABLY SPEND THE REST OF MY LIFE LOOKING OUT WINDOWS FOR SAM LESSER, AND JUMPING AT EVERY STRANGE FACE I SEE, WHETHER THEY CATCH HIM OR NOT.
I'M NOT GOING TO JUMP WHEN I SEE MY OWN FACE.
JACKIE, WOULD YOU GET THE DOOR?
RAP RAP RAP RAP
YEAH, YEAH, GOT IT.
YES, HELLO, WHO IS...

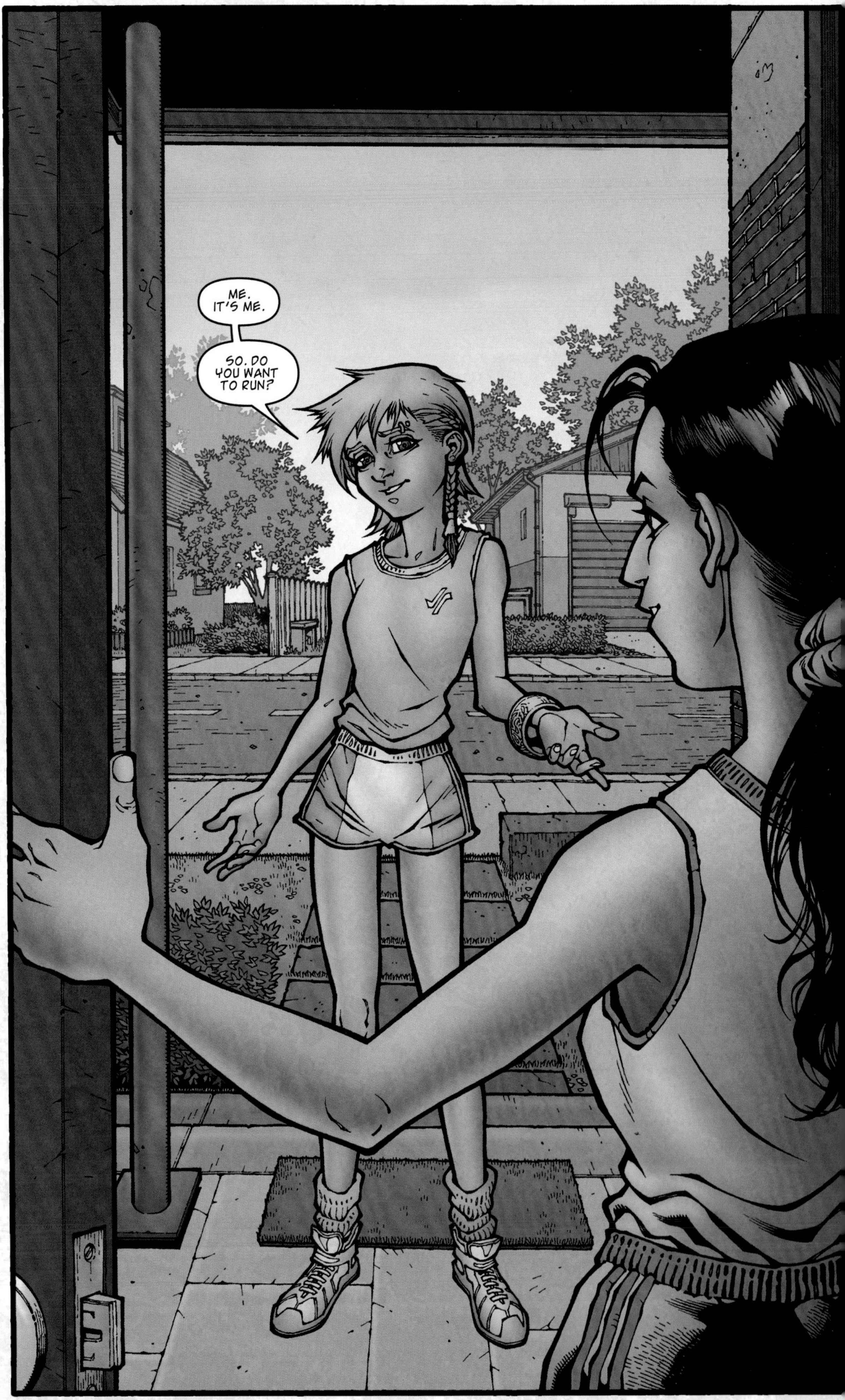
ME. IT'S ME.
SO. DO YOU WANT TO RUN?

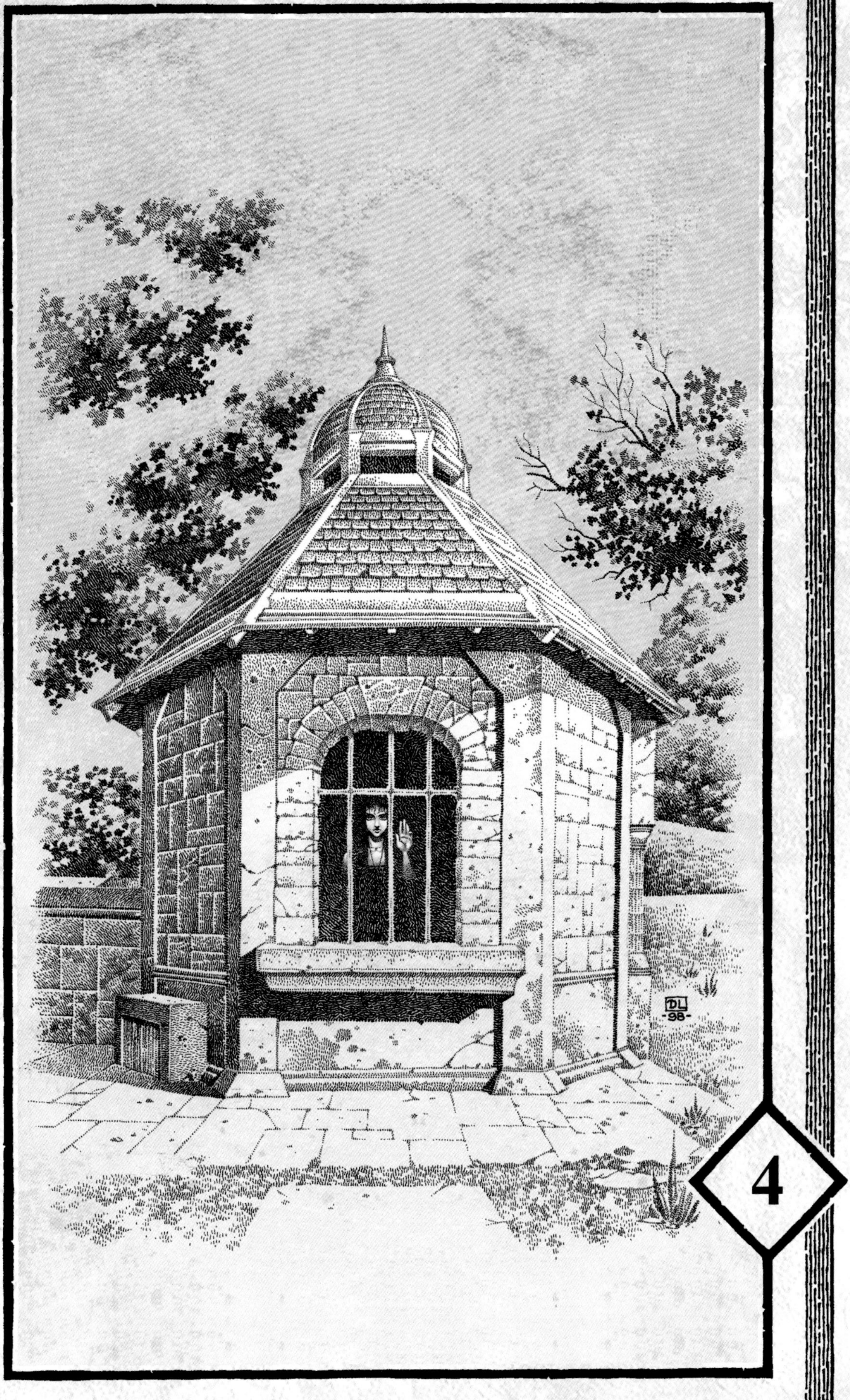
4

WELCOME TO LOVECRAFT
- FOUR -

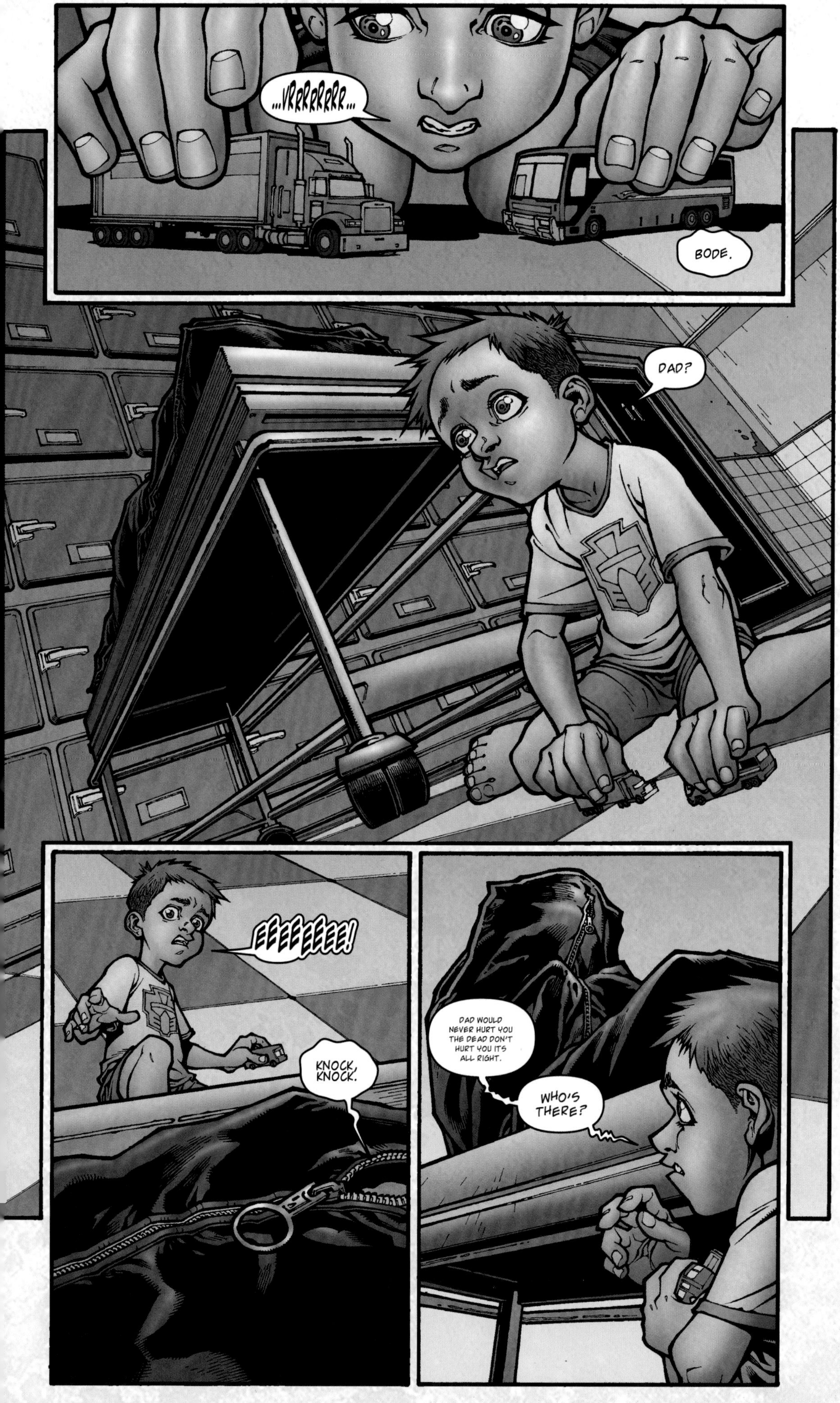
...VRRRRRRRR...
BODE.
DAD?
EEEEEEEE!
KNOCK, KNOCK.
DAD WOULD NEVER HURT YOU THE DEAD DON'T HURT YOU ITS ALL RIGHT.
WHO'S THERE?

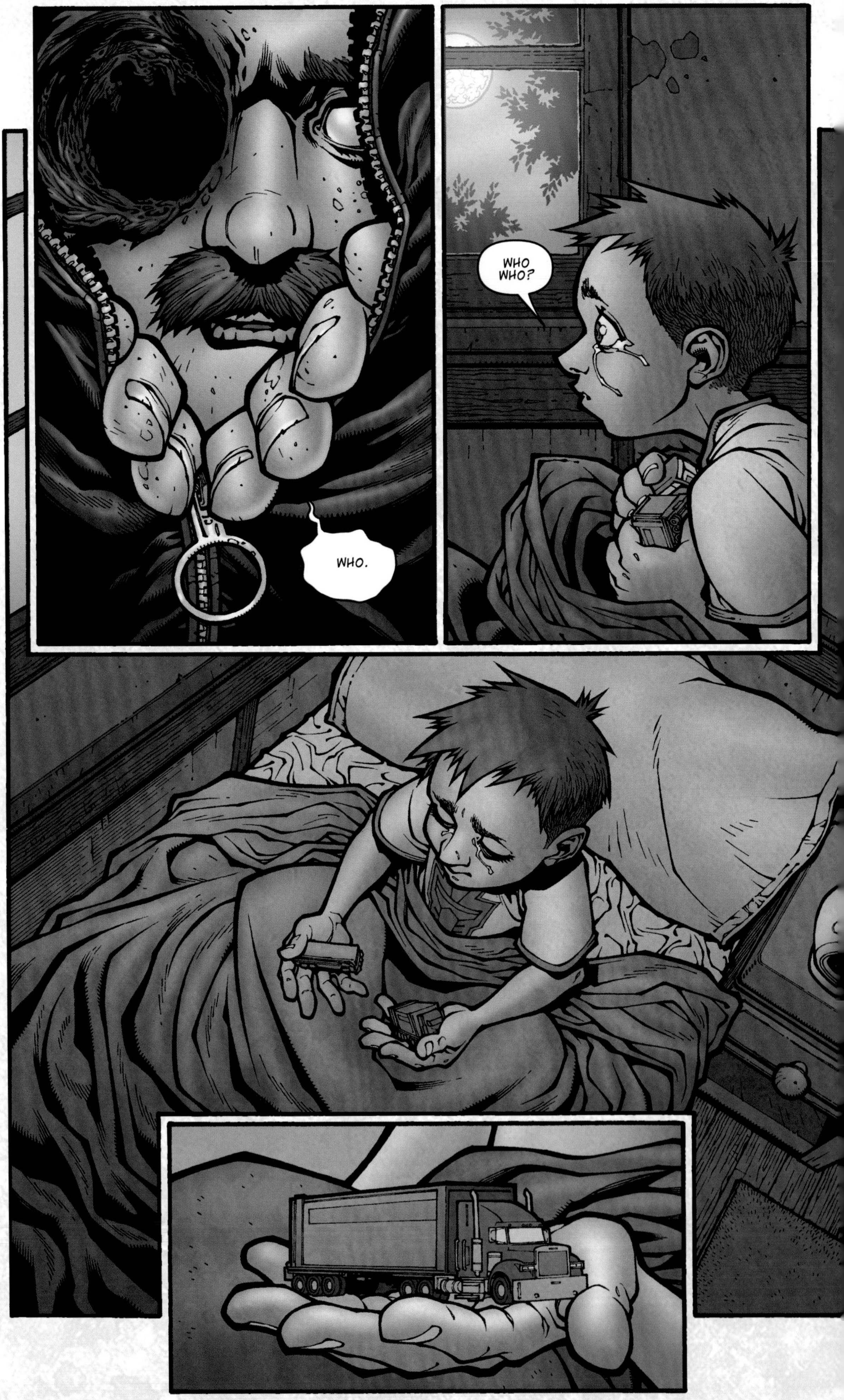
WHO.
WHO WHO?

NNNNNNURRRA

...AAAAAAAHHH YEAH!

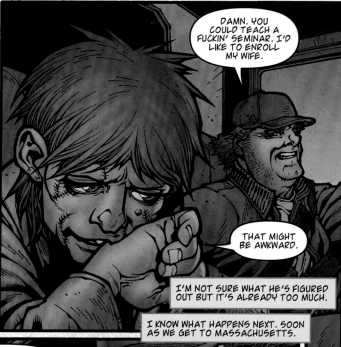

DAMN, YOU COULD TEACH A FUCKIN' SEMINAR. I'D LIKE TO ENROLL MY WIFE.

THAT MIGHT BE AWKWARD.

I'M NOT SURE WHAT HE'S FIGURED OUT BUT IT'S ALREADY TOO MUCH.

I KNOW WHAT HAPPENS NEXT. SOON AS WE GET TO MASSACHUSETTS.

YOU REALLY SHOULDN'T BE STOWING AWAY IN TRUCKS. YOU COULD EASY BE TALKING TO COPS RIGHT NOW. NOT EVERYONE'S AS UNDERSTANDING AS ME.

YOU'RE A LITTLE YOUNG FOR LIVING ON THE ROAD. MUST BE SOMEONE WORRYING ABOUT YOU SOMEWHERE. YOUR MOM... YOUR DAD... FOLKS AT SCHOOL...

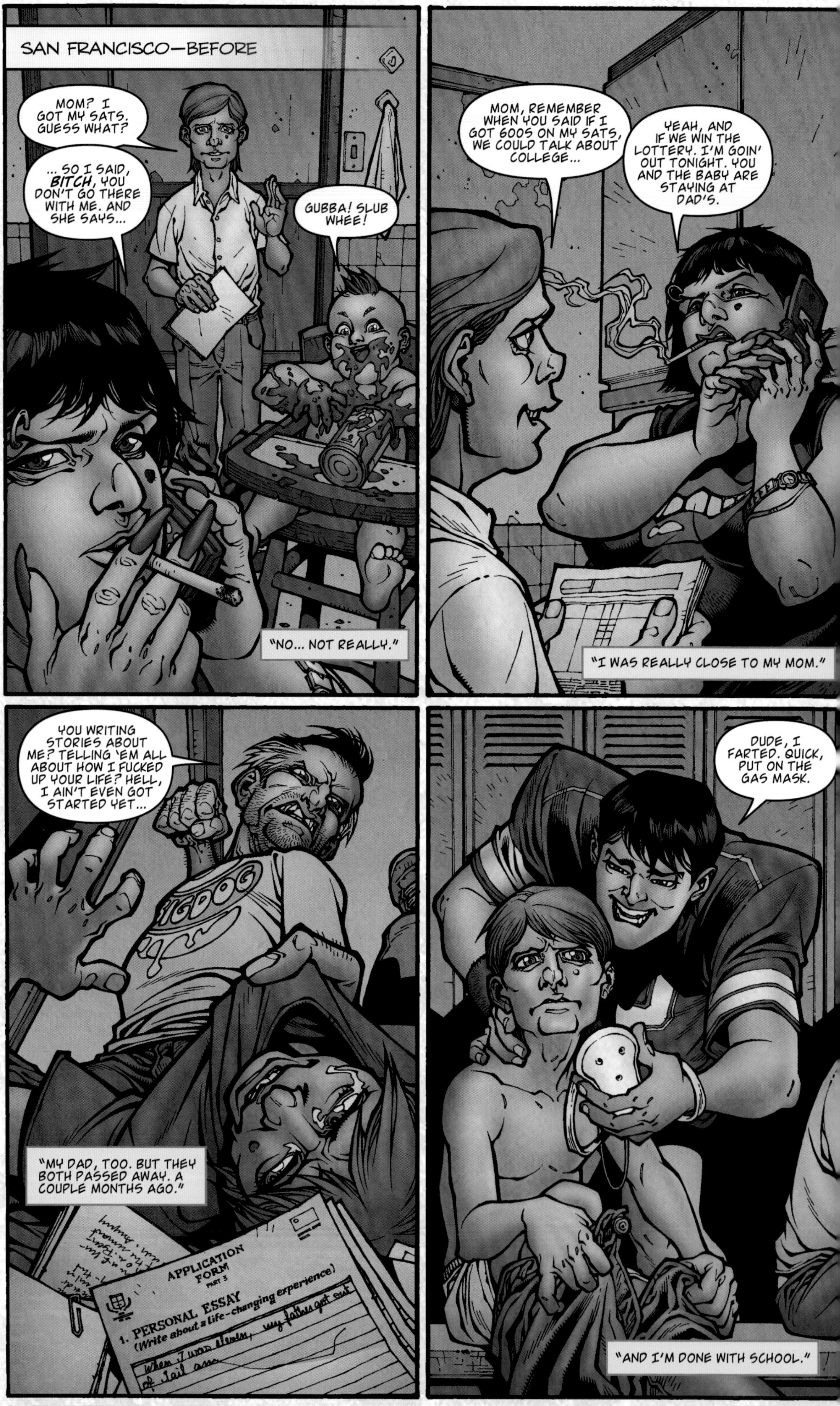
SAN FRANCISCO—BEFORE
MOM? I GOT MY SATS. GUESS WHAT?
... SO I SAID, BITCH, YOU DON'T GO THERE WITH ME. AND SHE SAYS...
GUBBA! SLUB WHEE!
"NO... NOT REALLY."
MOM, REMEMBER WHEN YOU SAID IF I GOT 600S ON MY SATS, WE COULD TALK ABOUT COLLEGE...
YEAH, AND IF WE WIN THE LOTTERY. I'M GOIN' OUT TONIGHT. YOU AND THE BABY ARE STAYING AT DAD'S.
"I WAS REALLY CLOSE TO MY MOM."
YOU WRITING STORIES ABOUT ME? TELLING 'EM ALL ABOUT HOW I FUCKED UP YOUR LIFE? HELL, I AIN'T EVEN GOT STARTED YET...
"MY DAD, TOO. BUT THEY BOTH PASSED AWAY. A COUPLE MONTHS AGO."
APPLICATION FORM
PART 3
1. PERSONAL ESSAY
(Write about a life-changing experience)
DUDE, I FARTED. QUICK, PUT ON THE GAS MASK.
"AND I'M DONE WITH SCHOOL."

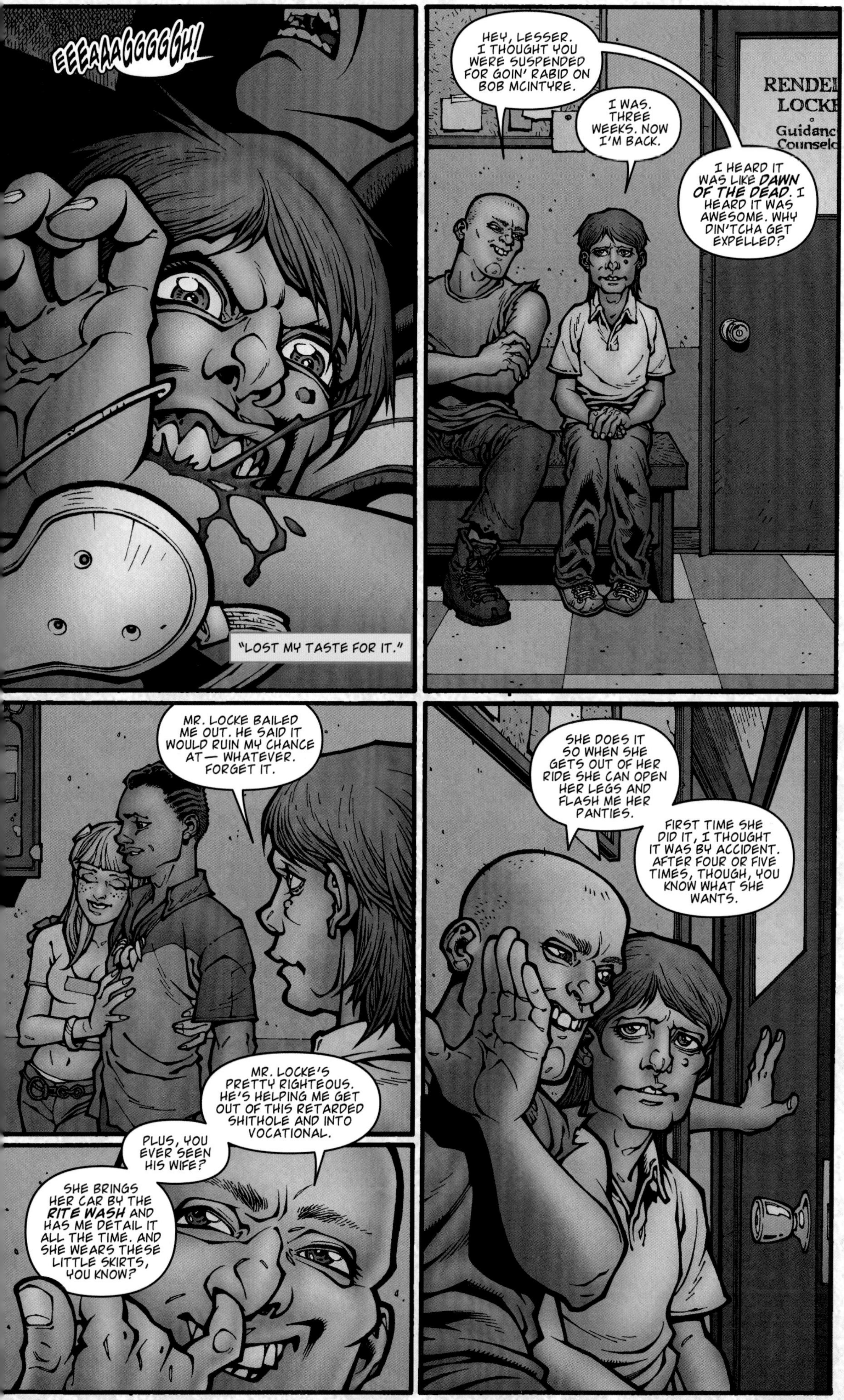
EEEAAAGGGGGH!
"LOST MY TASTE FOR IT."
HEY, LESSER. I THOUGHT YOU WERE SUSPENDED FOR GOIN' RABID ON BOB MCINTYRE.
I WAS. THREE WEEKS. NOW I'M BACK.
RENDEL LOCKE Guidanc Counselo
I HEARD IT WAS LIKE DAWN OF THE DEAD. I HEARD IT WAS AWESOME. WHY DIN'TCHA GET EXPELLED?
MR. LOCKE BAILED ME OUT. HE SAID IT WOULD RUIN MY CHANCE AT— WHATEVER. FORGET IT.
MR. LOCKE'S PRETTY RIGHTEOUS. HE'S HELPING ME GET OUT OF THIS RETARDED SHITHOLE AND INTO VOCATIONAL.
PLUS, YOU EVER SEEN HIS WIFE?
SHE BRINGS HER CAR BY THE RITE WASH AND HAS ME DETAIL IT ALL THE TIME. AND SHE WEARS THESE LITTLE SKIRTS, YOU KNOW?
SHE DOES IT SO WHEN SHE GETS OUT OF HER RIDE SHE CAN OPEN HER LEGS AND FLASH ME HER PANTIES.
FIRST TIME SHE DID IT, I THOUGHT IT WAS BY ACCIDENT. AFTER FOUR OR FIVE TIMES, THOUGH, YOU KNOW WHAT SHE WANTS.

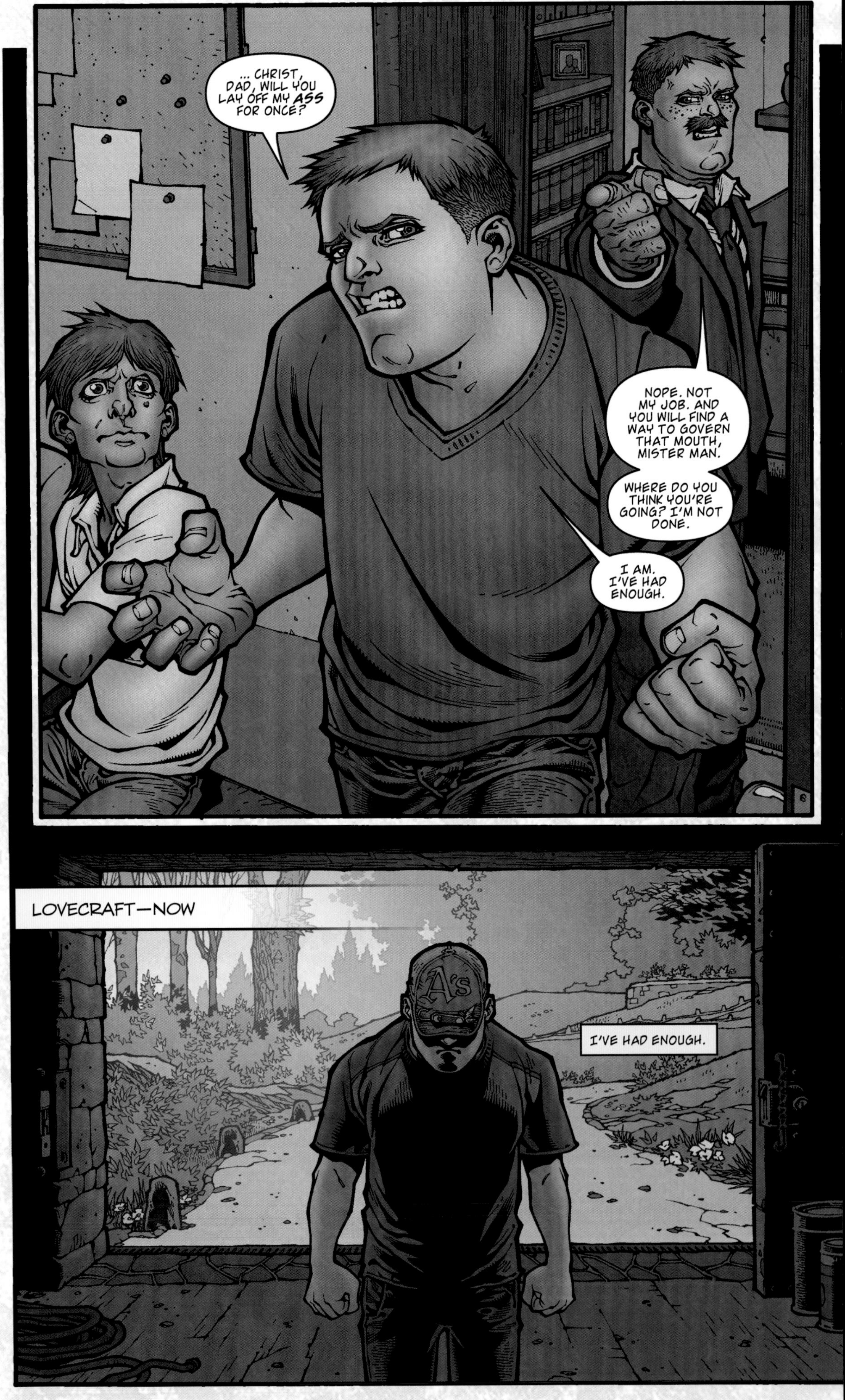
... CHRIST, DAD, WILL YOU LAY OFF MY ASS FOR ONCE?
NOPE. NOT MY JOB. AND YOU WILL FIND A WAY TO GOVERN THAT MOUTH, MISTER MAN.
WHERE DO YOU THINK YOU'RE GOING? I'M NOT DONE.
I AM. I'VE HAD ENOUGH.
LOVECRAFT—NOW
I'VE HAD ENOUGH.

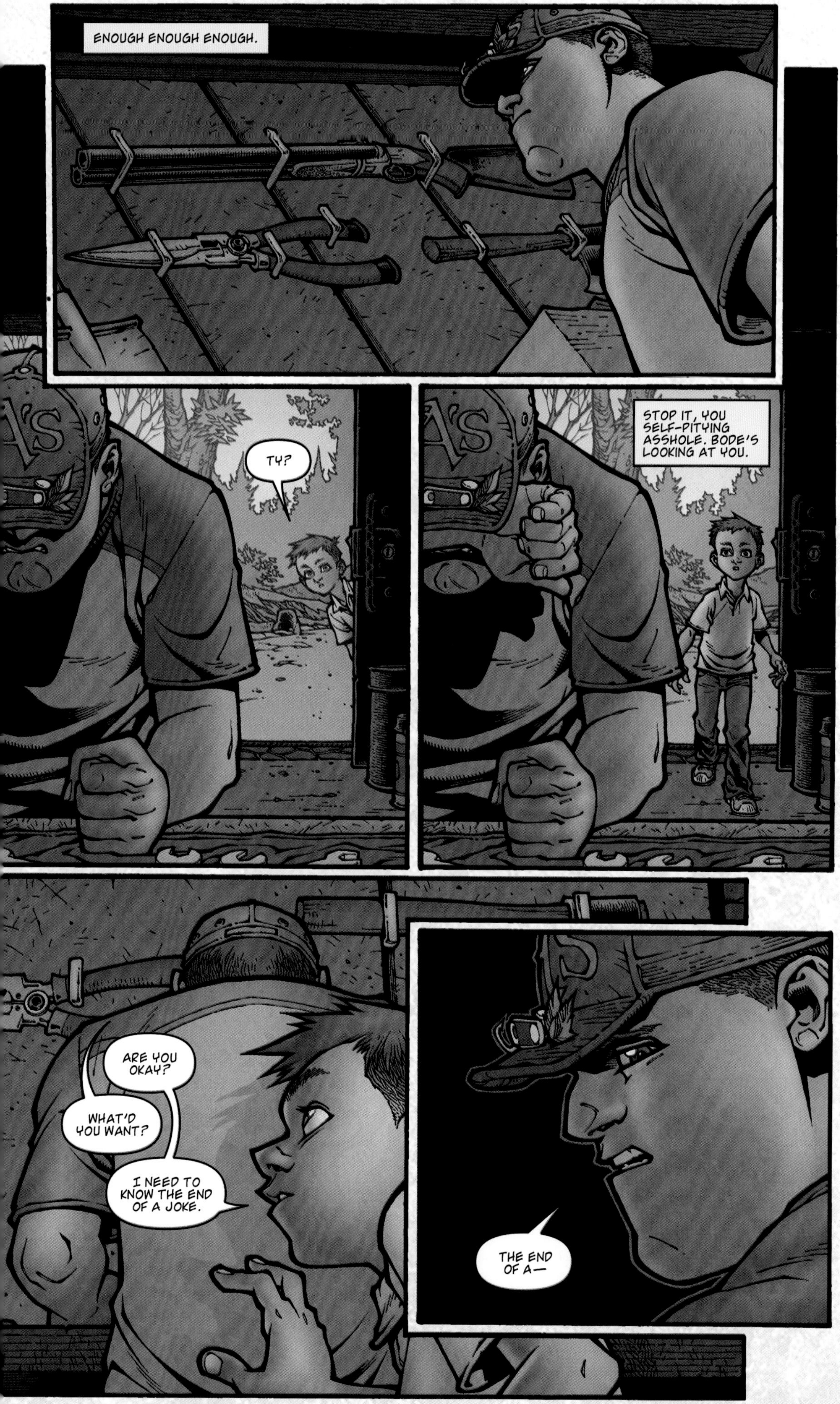
ENOUGH ENOUGH ENOUGH.
TY?
STOP IT, YOU SELF-PITYING ASSHOLE. BODE'S LOOKING AT YOU.
ARE YOU OKAY?
WHAT'D YOU WANT?
I NEED TO KNOW THE END OF A JOKE.
THE END OF A—

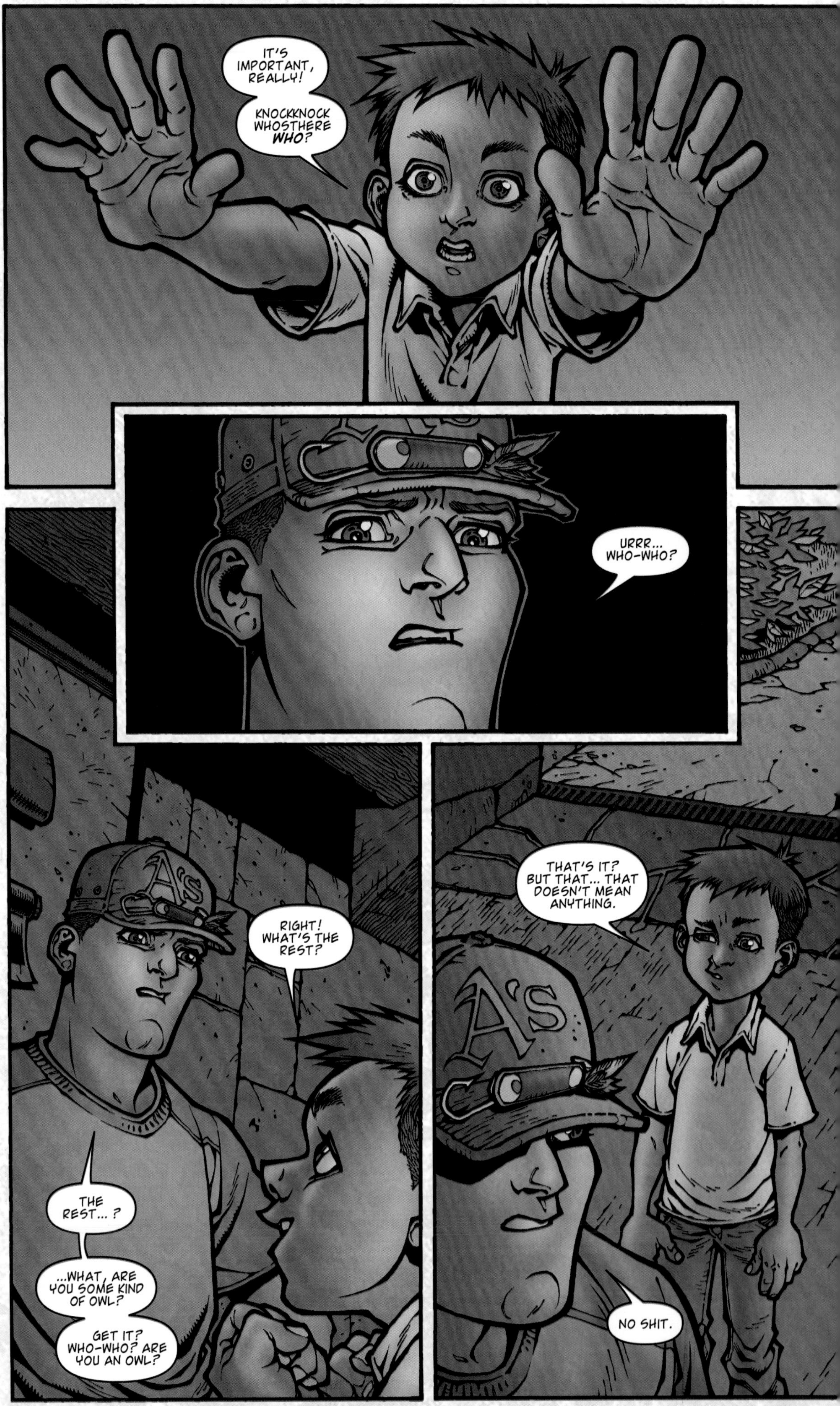
IT'S IMPORTANT, REALLY!
KNOCKKNOCK WHOSTHERE WHO?
URRR... WHO-WHO?
RIGHT! WHAT'S THE REST?
THE REST... ?
...WHAT, ARE YOU SOME KIND OF OWL?
GET IT? WHO-WHO? ARE YOU AN OWL?
THAT'S IT? BUT THAT... THAT DOESN'T MEAN ANYTHING.
NO SHIT.

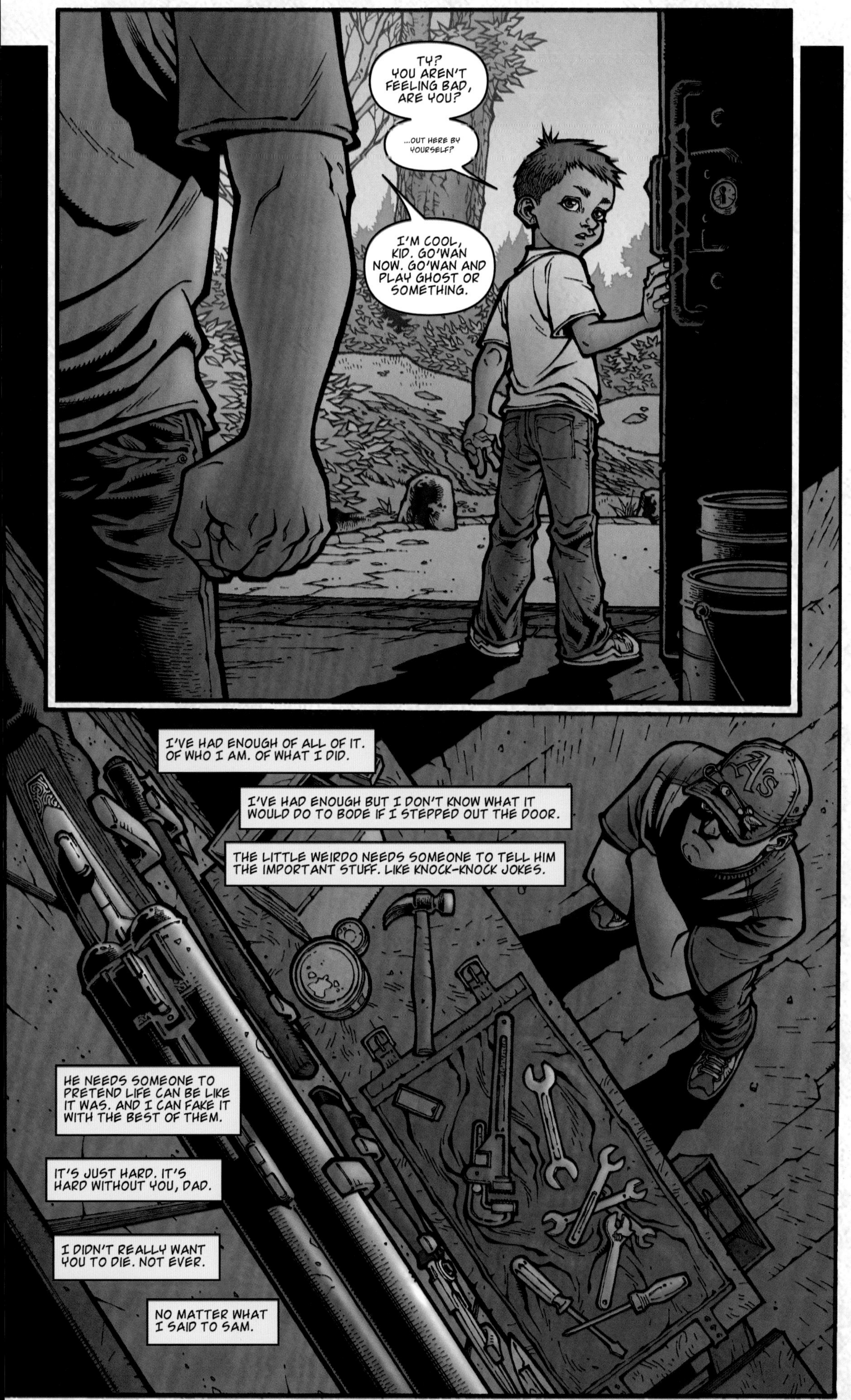
TY? YOU AREN'T FEELING BAD, ARE YOU?
...OUT HERE BY YOURSELF?
I'M COOL, KID. GO'WAN NOW. GO'WAN AND PLAY GHOST OR SOMETHING.
I'VE HAD ENOUGH OF ALL OF IT. OF WHO I AM. OF WHAT I DID.
I'VE HAD ENOUGH BUT I DON'T KNOW WHAT IT WOULD DO TO BODE IF I STEPPED OUT THE DOOR.
THE LITTLE WEIRDO NEEDS SOMEONE TO TELL HIM THE IMPORTANT STUFF. LIKE KNOCK-KNOCK JOKES.
HE NEEDS SOMEONE TO PRETEND LIFE CAN BE LIKE IT WAS. AND I CAN FAKE IT WITH THE BEST OF THEM.
IT'S JUST HARD. IT'S HARD WITHOUT YOU, DAD.
I DIDN'T REALLY WANT YOU TO DIE. NOT EVER.
NO MATTER WHAT I SAID TO SAM.

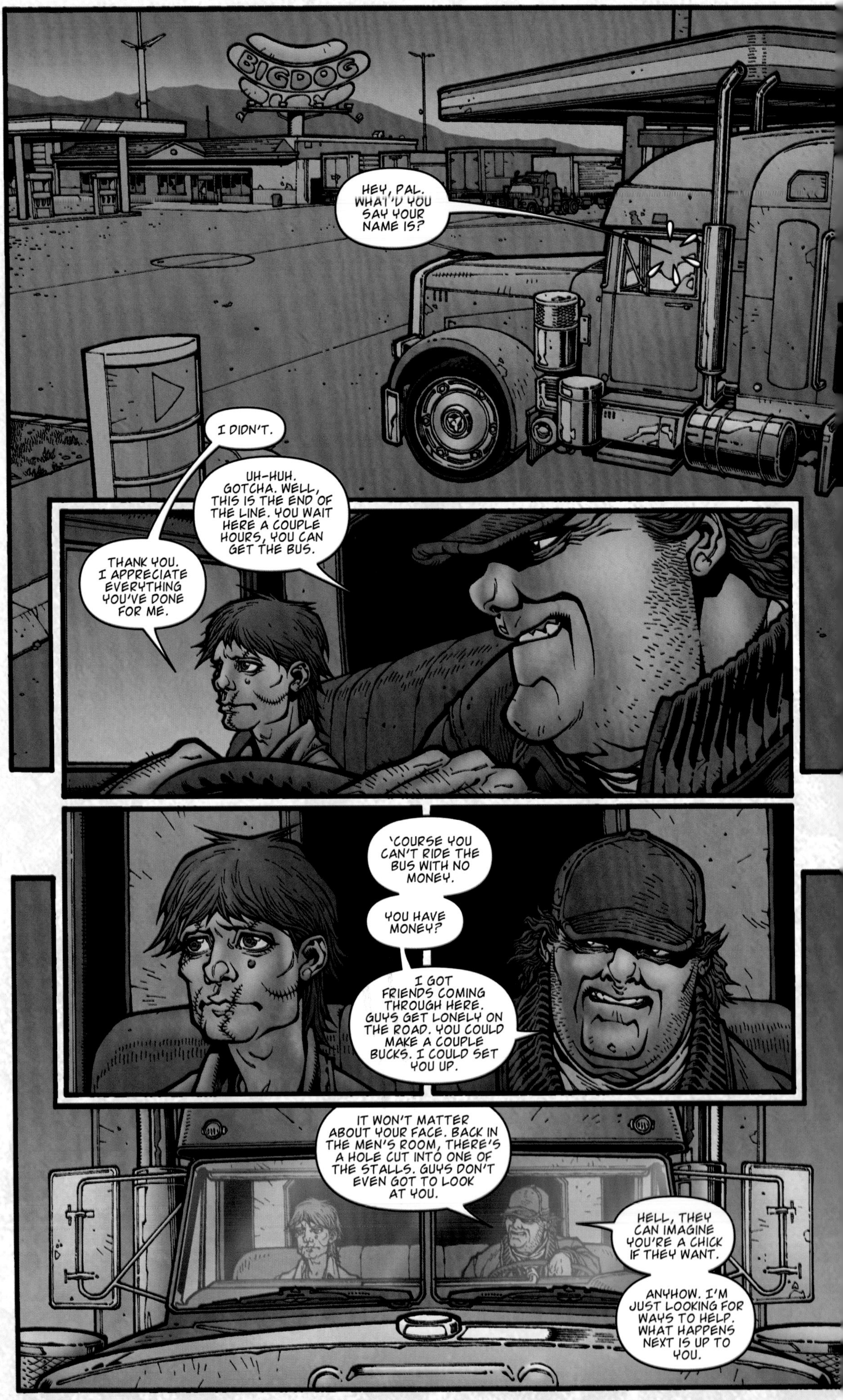
BIG DOG
HEY, PAL. WHAT'D YOU SAY YOUR NAME IS?
I DIDN'T.
UH-HUH. GOTCHA. WELL, THIS IS THE END OF THE LINE. YOU WAIT HERE A COUPLE HOURS, YOU CAN GET THE BUS.
THANK YOU. I APPRECIATE EVERYTHING YOU'VE DONE FOR ME.
'COURSE YOU CAN'T RIDE THE BUS WITH NO MONEY.
YOU HAVE MONEY?
I GOT FRIENDS COMING THROUGH HERE. GUYS GET LONELY ON THE ROAD. YOU COULD MAKE A COUPLE BUCKS. I COULD SET YOU UP.
IT WON'T MATTER ABOUT YOUR FACE. BACK IN THE MEN'S ROOM, THERE'S A HOLE CUT INTO ONE OF THE STALLS. GUYS DON'T EVEN GOT TO LOOK AT YOU.
HELL, THEY CAN IMAGINE YOU'RE A CHICK IF THEY WANT.
ANYHOW. I'M JUST LOOKING FOR WAYS TO HELP. WHAT HAPPENS NEXT IS UP TO YOU.

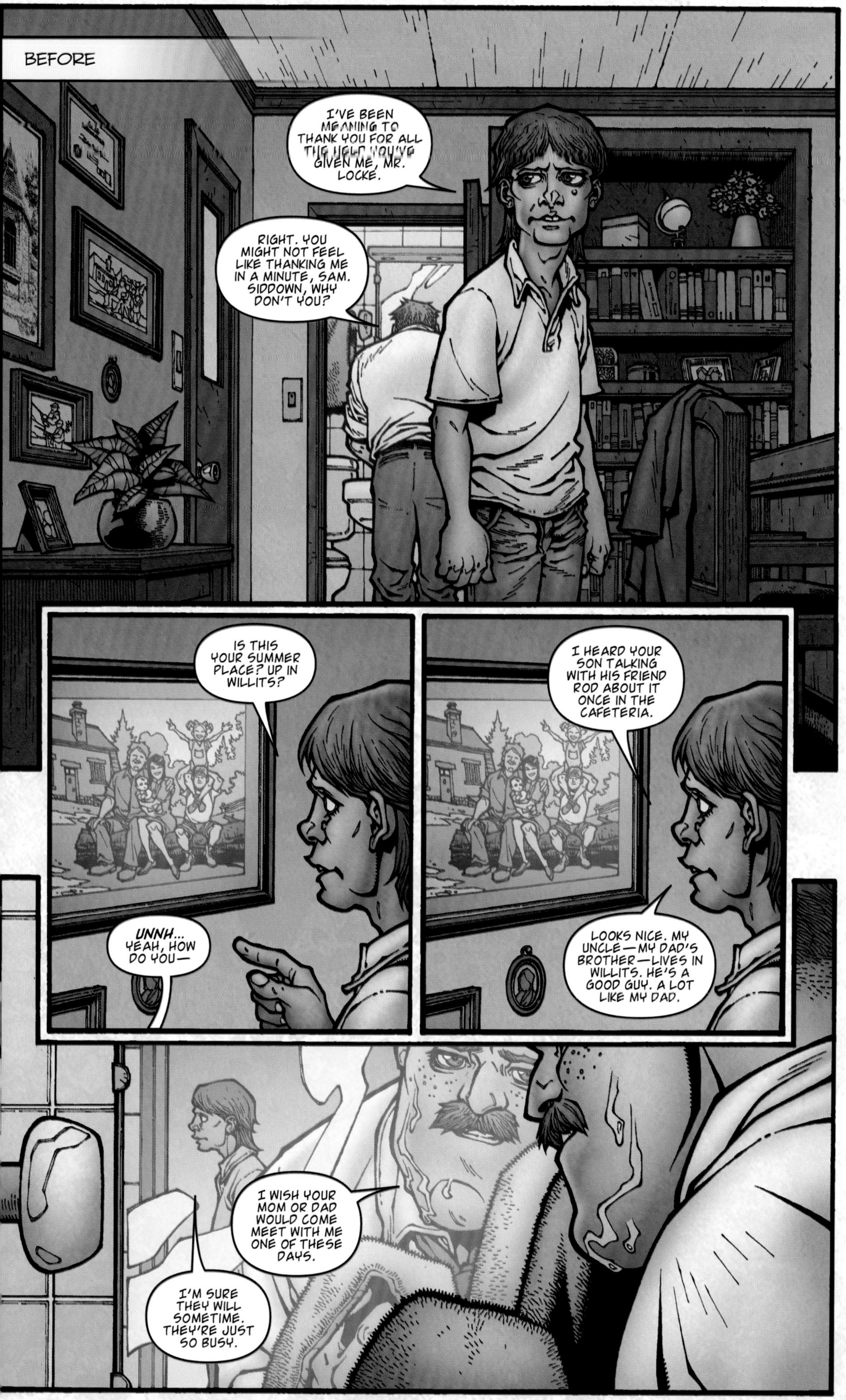
BEFORE
I'VE BEEN MEANING TO THANK YOU FOR ALL THE HELP YOU'VE GIVEN ME, MR. LOCKE.
RIGHT. YOU MIGHT NOT FEEL LIKE THANKING ME IN A MINUTE, SAM. SIDDOWN, WHY DON'T YOU?
IS THIS YOUR SUMMER PLACE? UP IN WILLITS?
UNNH... YEAH, HOW DO YOU—
I HEARD YOUR SON TALKING WITH HIS FRIEND ROD ABOUT IT ONCE IN THE CAFETERIA.
LOOKS NICE. MY UNCLE—MY DAD'S BROTHER—LIVES IN WILLITS. HE'S A GOOD GUY. A LOT LIKE MY DAD.
I WISH YOUR MOM OR DAD WOULD COME MEET WITH ME ONE OF THESE DAYS.
I'M SURE THEY WILL SOMETIME. THEY'RE JUST SO BUSY.

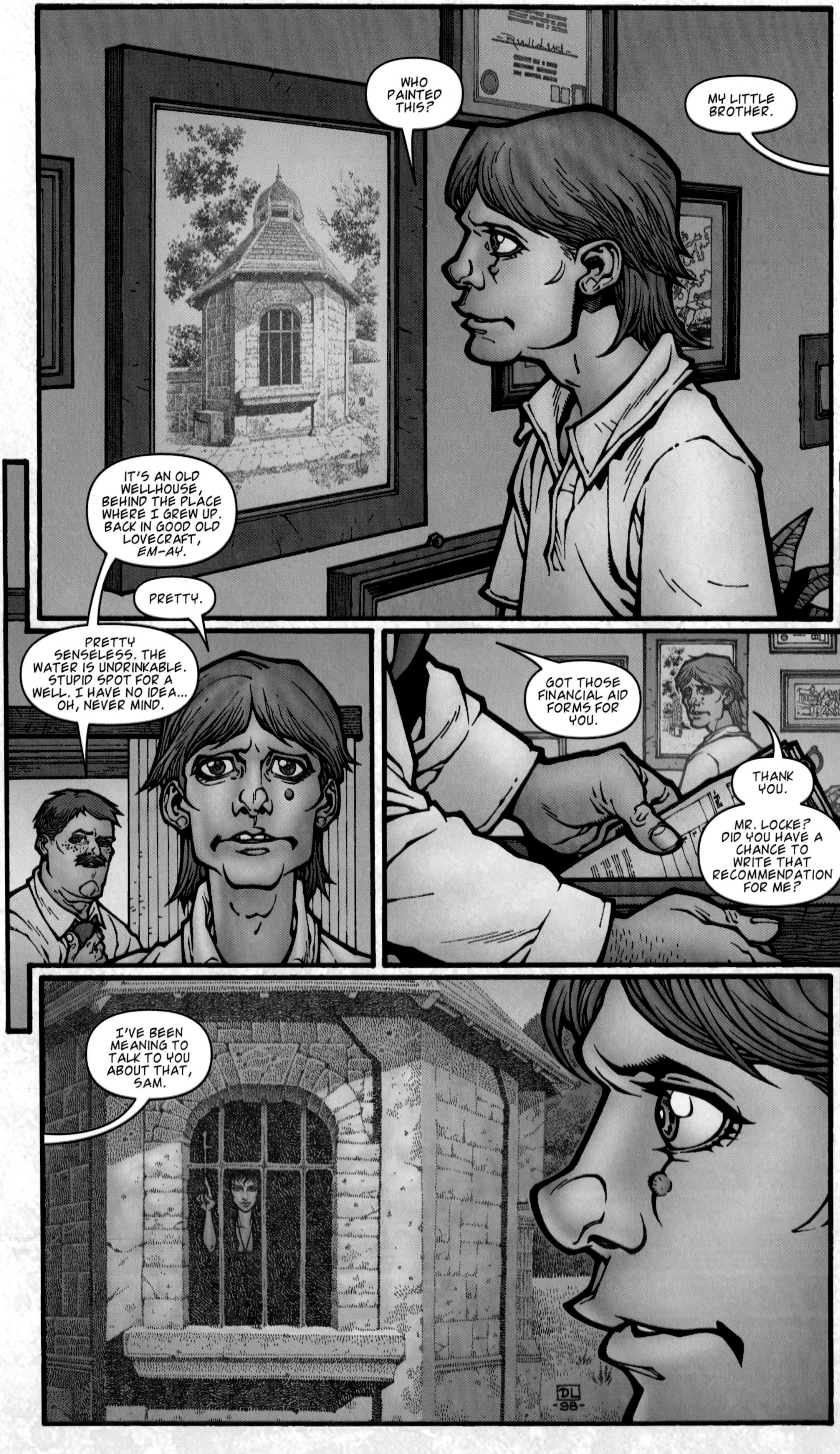

WHO PAINTED THIS?
MY LITTLE BROTHER.
IT'S AN OLD WELLHOUSE, BEHIND THE PLACE WHERE I GREW UP. BACK IN GOOD OLD LOVECRAFT, EM-AY.
PRETTY.
PRETTY SENSELESS. THE WATER IS UNDRINKABLE. STUPID SPOT FOR A WELL. I HAVE NO IDEA... OH, NEVER MIND.
GOT THOSE FINANCIAL AID FORMS FOR YOU.
THANK YOU.
MR. LOCKE? DID YOU HAVE A CHANCE TO WRITE THAT RECOMMENDATION FOR ME?
I'VE BEEN MEANING TO TALK TO YOU ABOUT THAT, SAM.

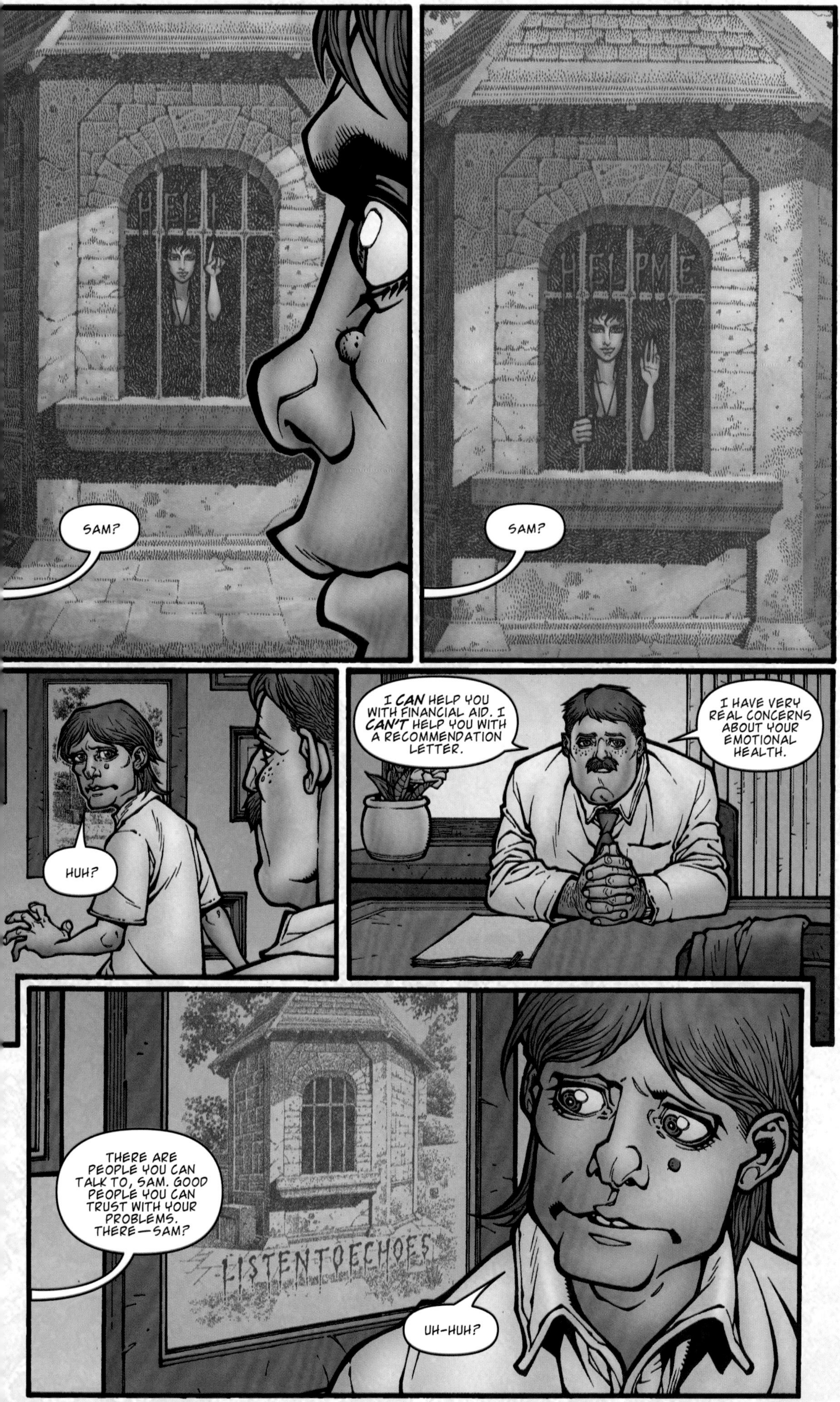
HELP
SAM?
HELPME
SAM?
HUH?
I CAN HELP YOU WITH FINANCIAL AID. I CAN'T HELP YOU WITH A RECOMMENDATION LETTER.
I HAVE VERY REAL CONCERNS ABOUT YOUR EMOTIONAL HEALTH.
THERE ARE PEOPLE YOU CAN TALK TO, SAM. GOOD PEOPLE YOU CAN TRUST WITH YOUR PROBLEMS. THERE—SAM?
LISTENTOECHOES
UH-HUH?

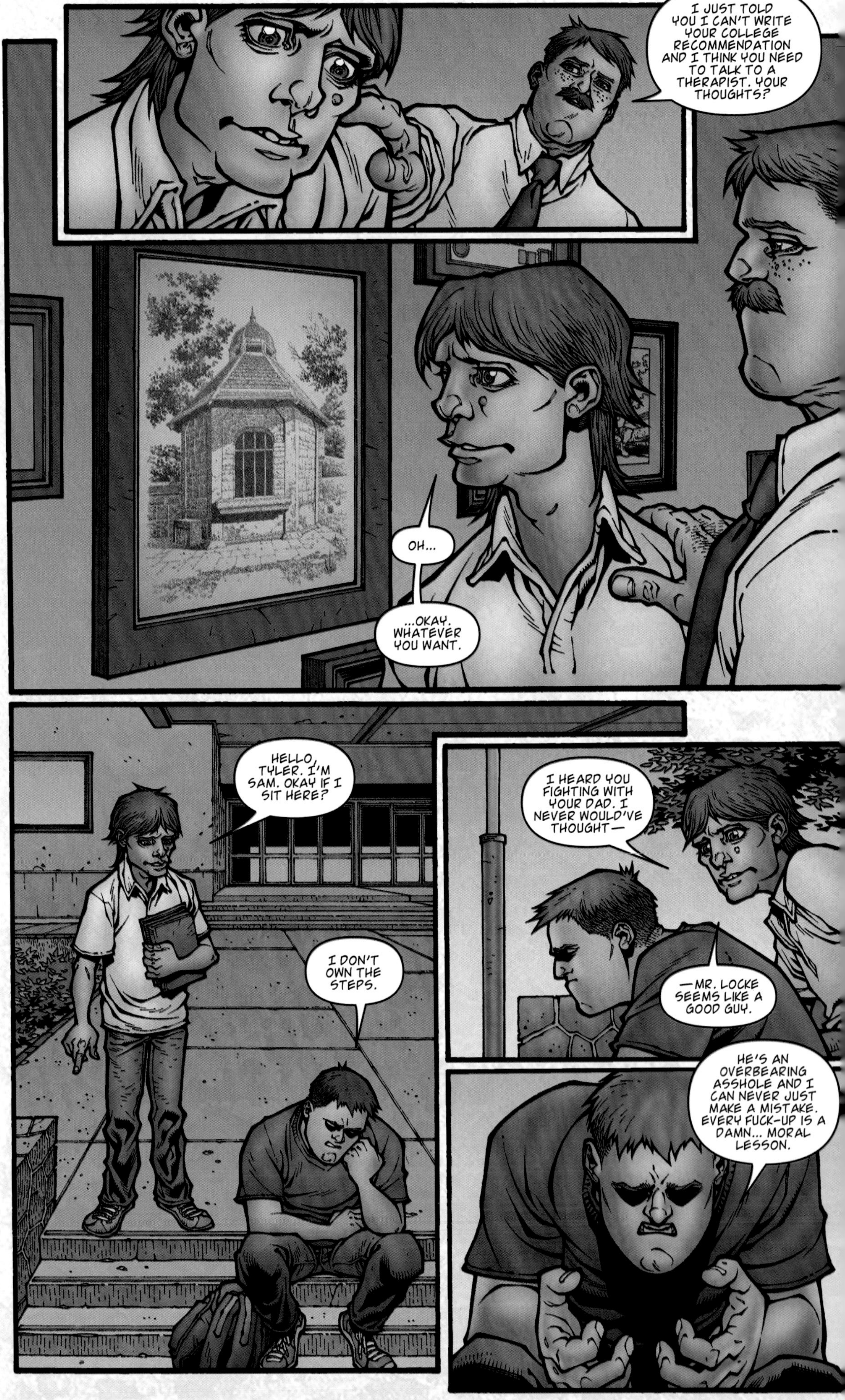
I JUST TOLD YOU I CAN'T WRITE YOUR COLLEGE RECOMMENDATION AND I THINK YOU NEED TO TALK TO A THERAPIST. YOUR THOUGHTS?
OH...
...OKAY. WHATEVER YOU WANT.
HELLO, TYLER. I'M SAM. OKAY IF I SIT HERE?
I DON'T OWN THE STEPS.
I HEARD YOU FIGHTING WITH YOUR DAD. I NEVER WOULD'VE THOUGHT—
—MR. LOCKE SEEMS LIKE A GOOD GUY.
HE'S AN OVERBEARING ASSHOLE AND I CAN NEVER JUST MAKE A MISTAKE. EVERY FUCK-UP IS A DAMN... MORAL LESSON.

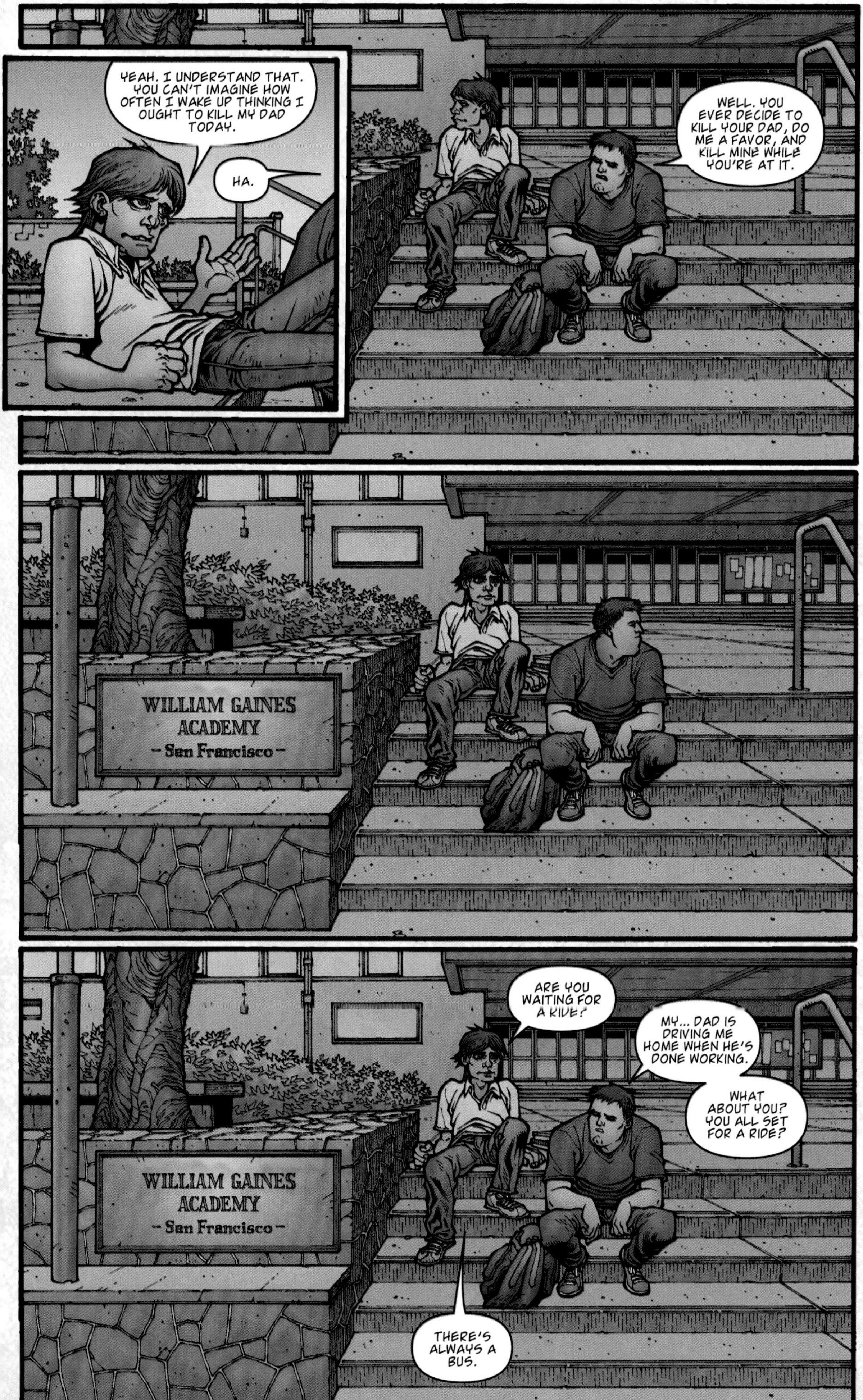
YEAH. I UNDERSTAND THAT. YOU CAN'T IMAGINE HOW OFTEN I WAKE UP THINKING I OUGHT TO KILL MY DAD TODAY.
HA.
WELL. YOU EVER DECIDE TO KILL YOUR DAD, DO ME A FAVOR, AND KILL MINE WHILE YOU'RE AT IT.
WILLIAM GAINES ACADEMY
~ San Francisco ~
ARE YOU WAITING FOR A RIDE?
MY... DAD IS DRIVING ME HOME WHEN HE'S DONE WORKING.
WHAT ABOUT YOU? YOU ALL SET FOR A RIDE?
THERE'S ALWAYS A BUS.
WILLIAM GAINES ACADEMY
~ San Francisco ~

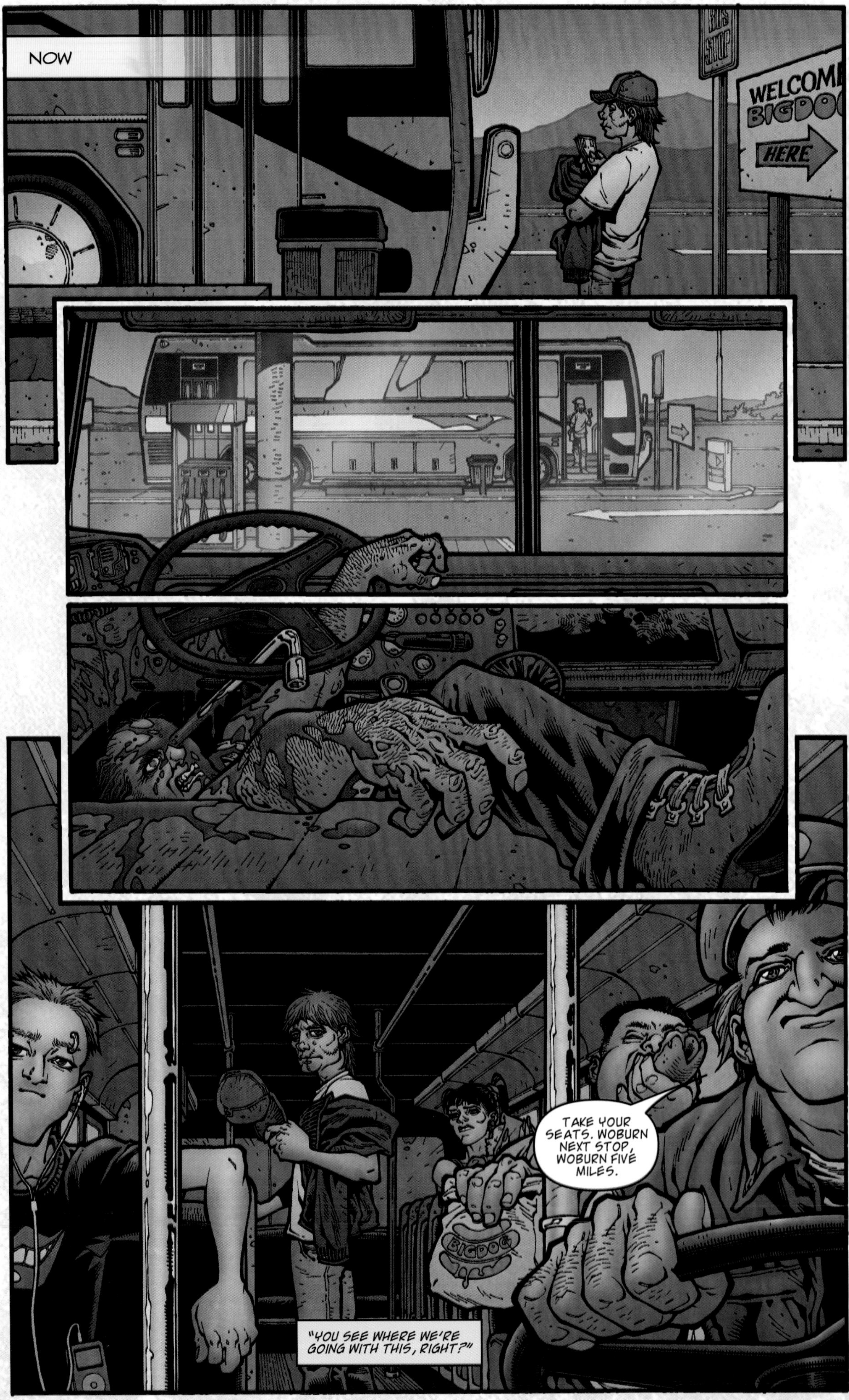
NOW
BUS STOP
WELCOME BIGDOG
HERE
TAKE YOUR SEATS. WOBURN NEXT STOP, WOBURN FIVE MILES.
BIGDOG
"YOU SEE WHERE WE'RE GOING WITH THIS, RIGHT?"

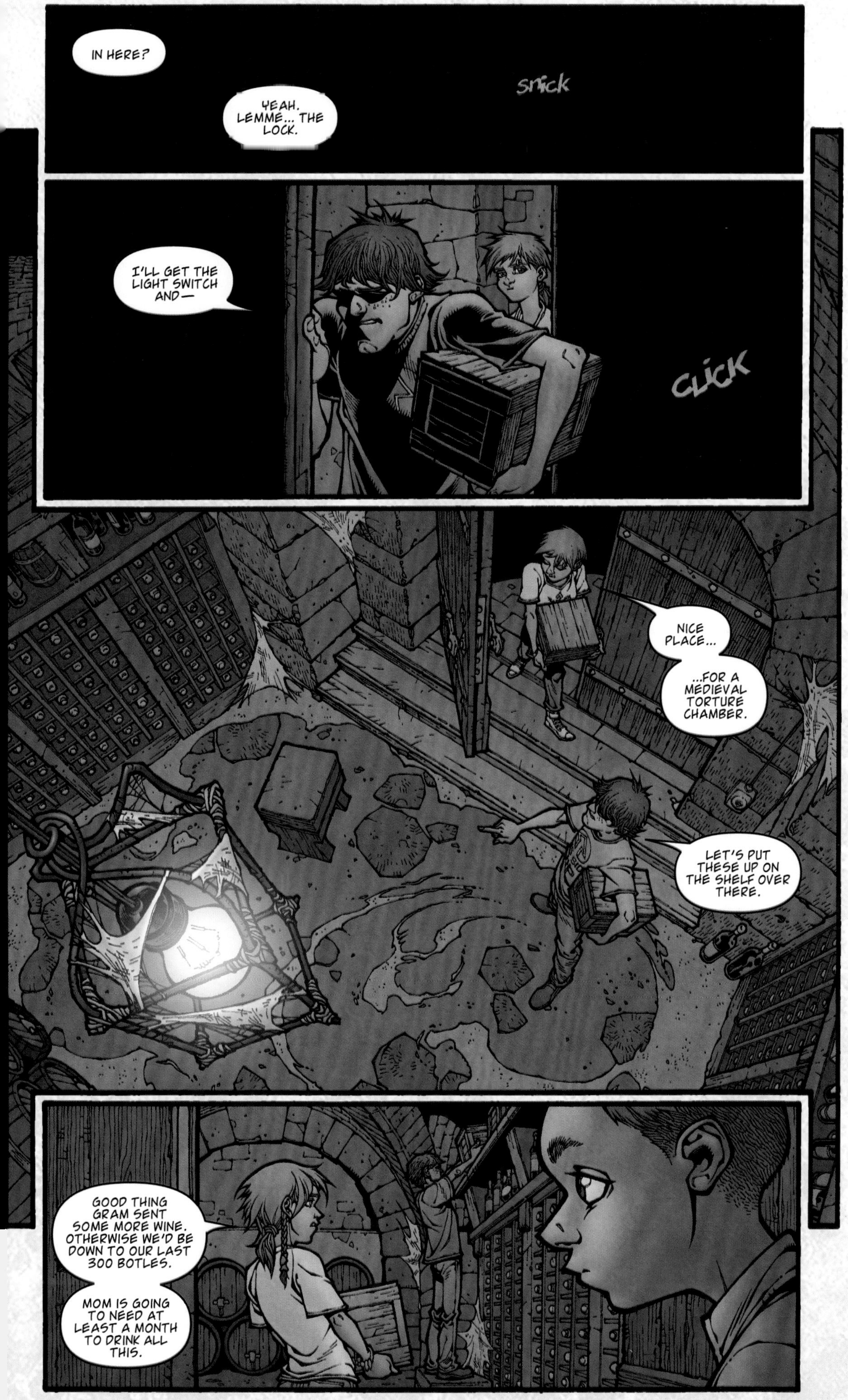
IN HERE?
YEAH. LEMME... THE LOCK.
snick
I'LL GET THE LIGHT SWITCH AND—
CLICK
NICE PLACE...
...FOR A MEDIEVAL TORTURE CHAMBER.
LET'S PUT THESE UP ON THE SHELF OVER THERE.
GOOD THING GRAM SENT SOME MORE WINE. OTHERWISE WE'D BE DOWN TO OUR LAST 300 BOTLES.
MOM IS GOING TO NEED AT LEAST A MONTH TO DRINK ALL THIS.

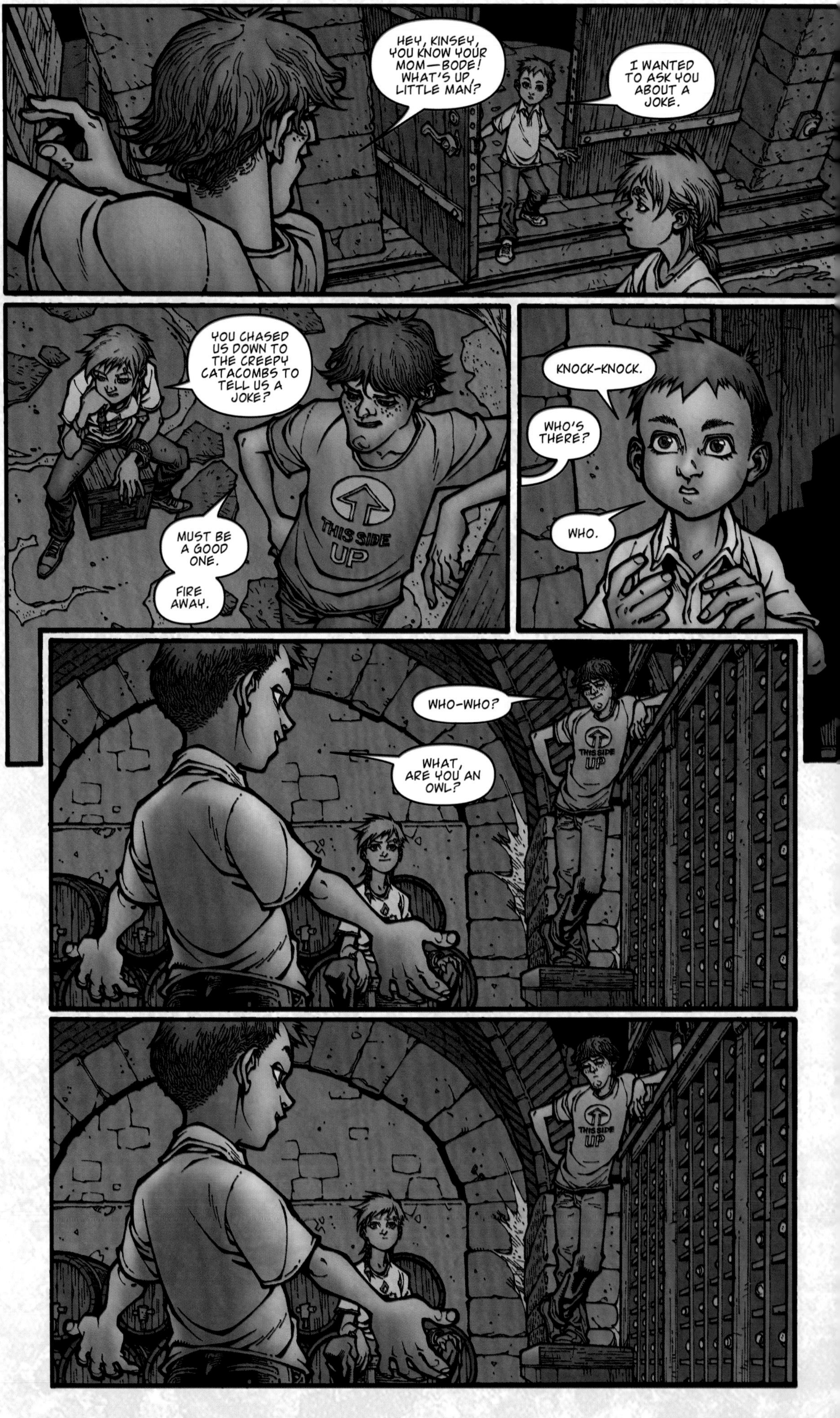
HEY, KINSEY, YOU KNOW YOUR MOM—BODE! WHAT'S UP, LITTLE MAN?
I WANTED TO ASK YOU ABOUT A JOKE.
YOU CHASED US DOWN TO THE CREEPY CATACOMBS TO TELL US A JOKE?
MUST BE A GOOD ONE.
FIRE AWAY.
THIS SIDE UP
KNOCK-KNOCK.
WHO'S THERE?
WHO.
WHO-WHO?
WHAT, ARE YOU AN OWL?
THIS SIDE UP
THIS SIDE UP

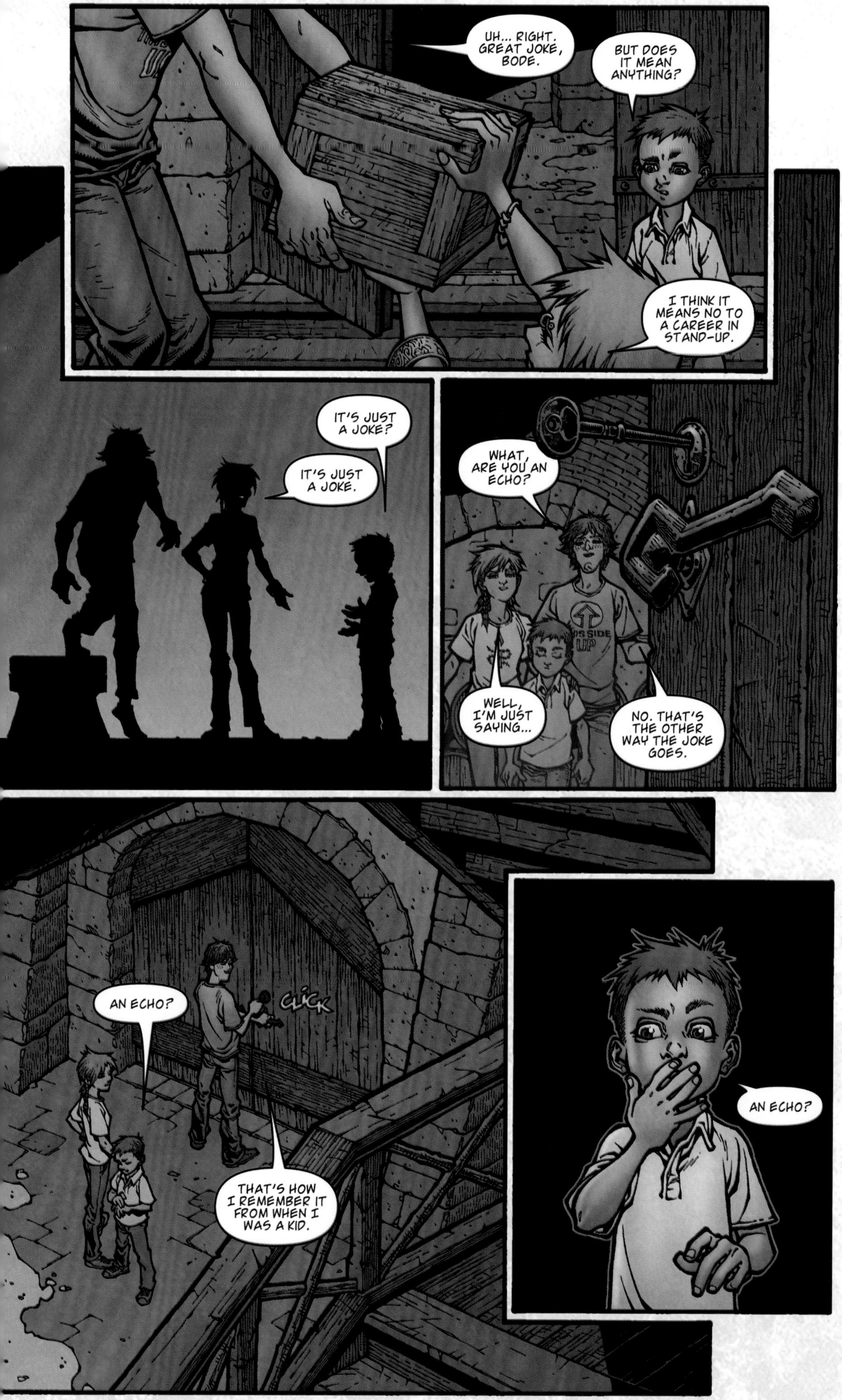

UH... RIGHT. GREAT JOKE, BODE.
BUT DOES IT MEAN ANYTHING?
I THINK IT MEANS NO TO A CAREER IN STAND-UP.
IT'S JUST A JOKE?
IT'S JUST A JOKE.
WHAT, ARE YOU AN ECHO?
WELL, I'M JUST SAYING...
NO. THAT'S THE OTHER WAY THE JOKE GOES.
AN ECHO?
CLICK
THAT'S HOW I REMEMBER IT FROM WHEN I WAS A KID.
AN ECHO?

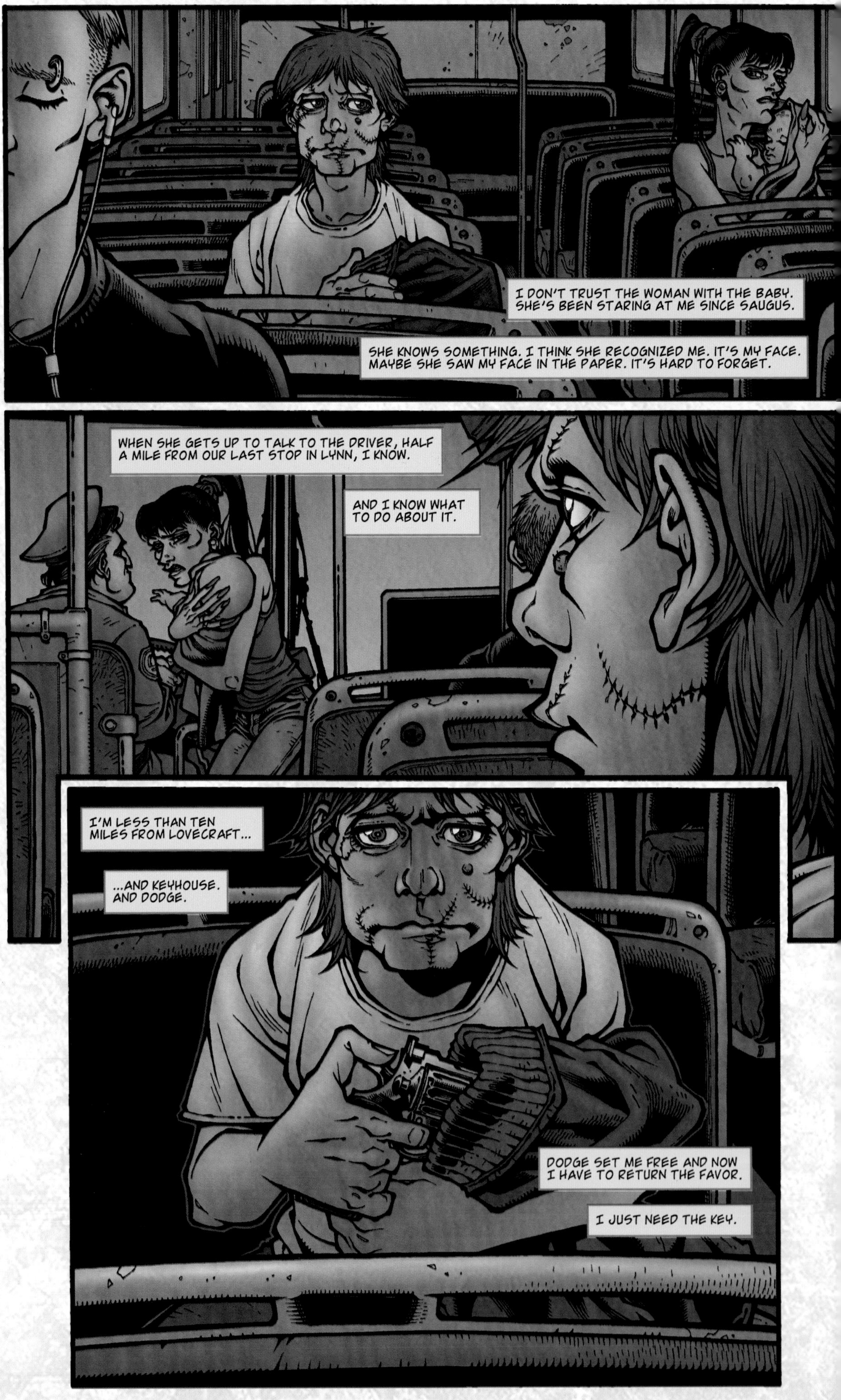
I DON'T TRUST THE WOMAN WITH THE BABY. SHE'S BEEN STARING AT ME SINCE SAUGUS.
SHE KNOWS SOMETHING. I THINK SHE RECOGNIZED ME. IT'S MY FACE. MAYBE SHE SAW MY FACE IN THE PAPER. IT'S HARD TO FORGET.
WHEN SHE GETS UP TO TALK TO THE DRIVER, HALF A MILE FROM OUR LAST STOP IN LYNN, I KNOW.
AND I KNOW WHAT TO DO ABOUT IT.
I'M LESS THAN TEN MILES FROM LOVECRAFT...
...AND KEYHOUSE. AND DODGE.
DODGE SET ME FREE AND NOW I HAVE TO RETURN THE FAVOR.
I JUST NEED THE KEY.

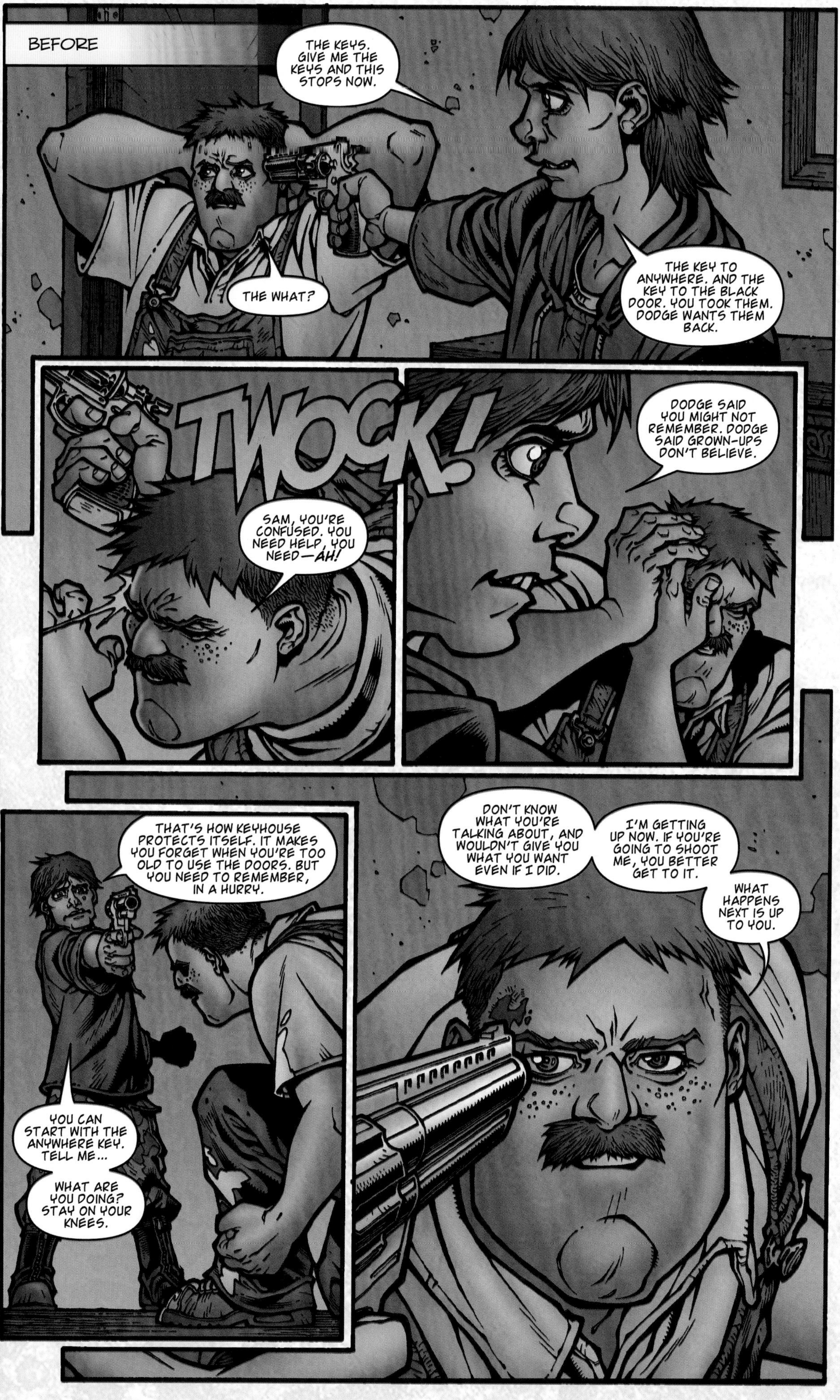
BEFORE
THE KEYS. GIVE ME THE KEYS AND THIS STOPS NOW.
THE WHAT?
THE KEY TO ANYWHERE. AND THE KEY TO THE BLACK DOOR. YOU TOOK THEM. DODGE WANTS THEM BACK.
TWOCK!
SAM, YOU'RE CONFUSED. YOU NEED HELP, YOU NEED—AH!
DODGE SAID YOU MIGHT NOT REMEMBER. DODGE SAID GROWN-UPS DON'T BELIEVE.
THAT'S HOW KEYHOUSE PROTECTS ITSELF. IT MAKES YOU FORGET WHEN YOU'RE TOO OLD TO USE THE DOORS. BUT YOU NEED TO REMEMBER, IN A HURRY.
YOU CAN START WITH THE ANYWHERE KEY. TELL ME...
WHAT ARE YOU DOING? STAY ON YOUR KNEES.
DON'T KNOW WHAT YOU'RE TALKING ABOUT, AND WOULDN'T GIVE YOU WHAT YOU WANT EVEN IF I DID.
I'M GETTING UP NOW. IF YOU'RE GOING TO SHOOT ME, YOU BETTER GET TO IT.
WHAT HAPPENS NEXT IS UP TO YOU.

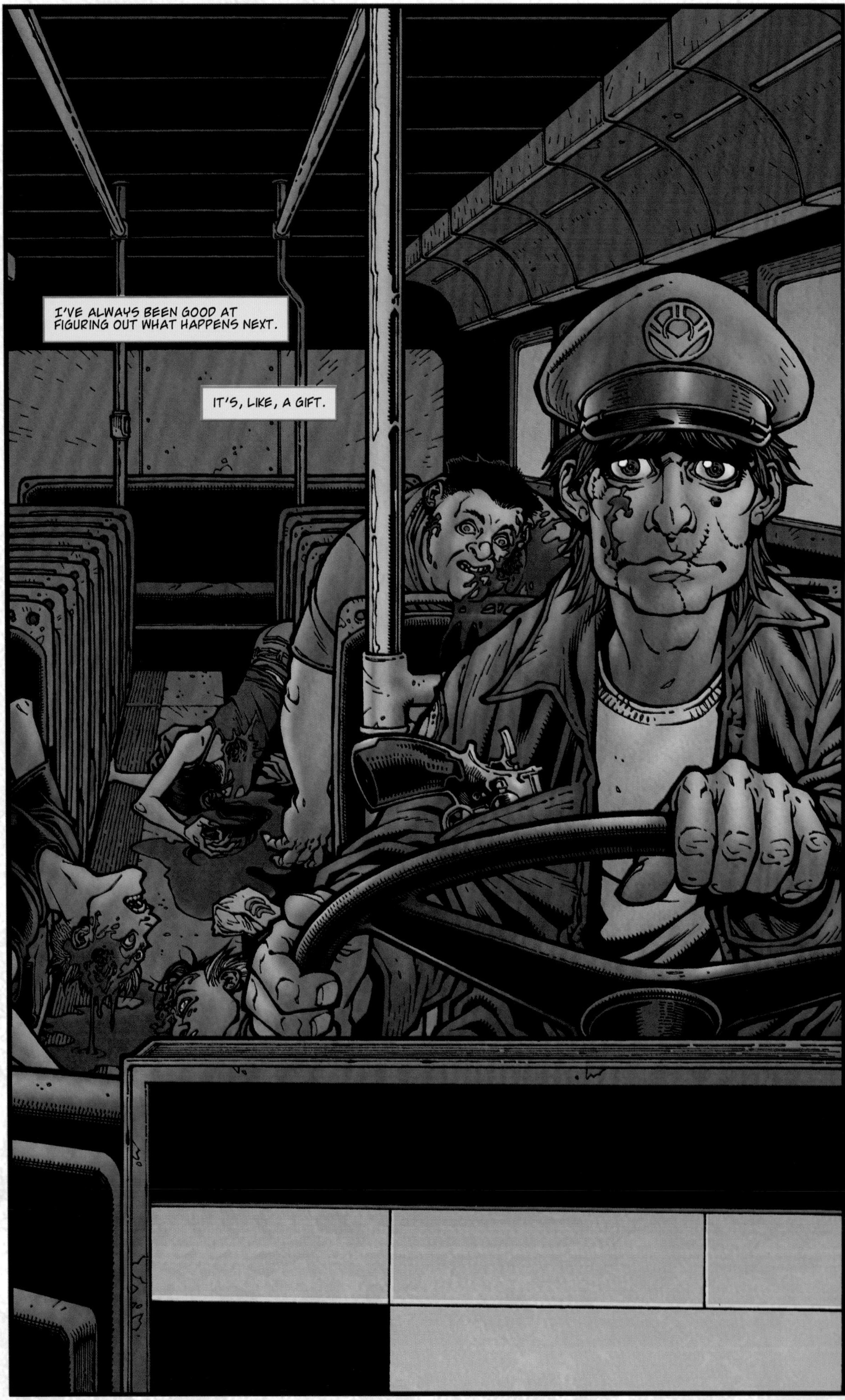
I'VE ALWAYS BEEN GOOD AT FIGURING OUT WHAT HAPPENS NEXT.
IT'S, LIKE, A GIFT.

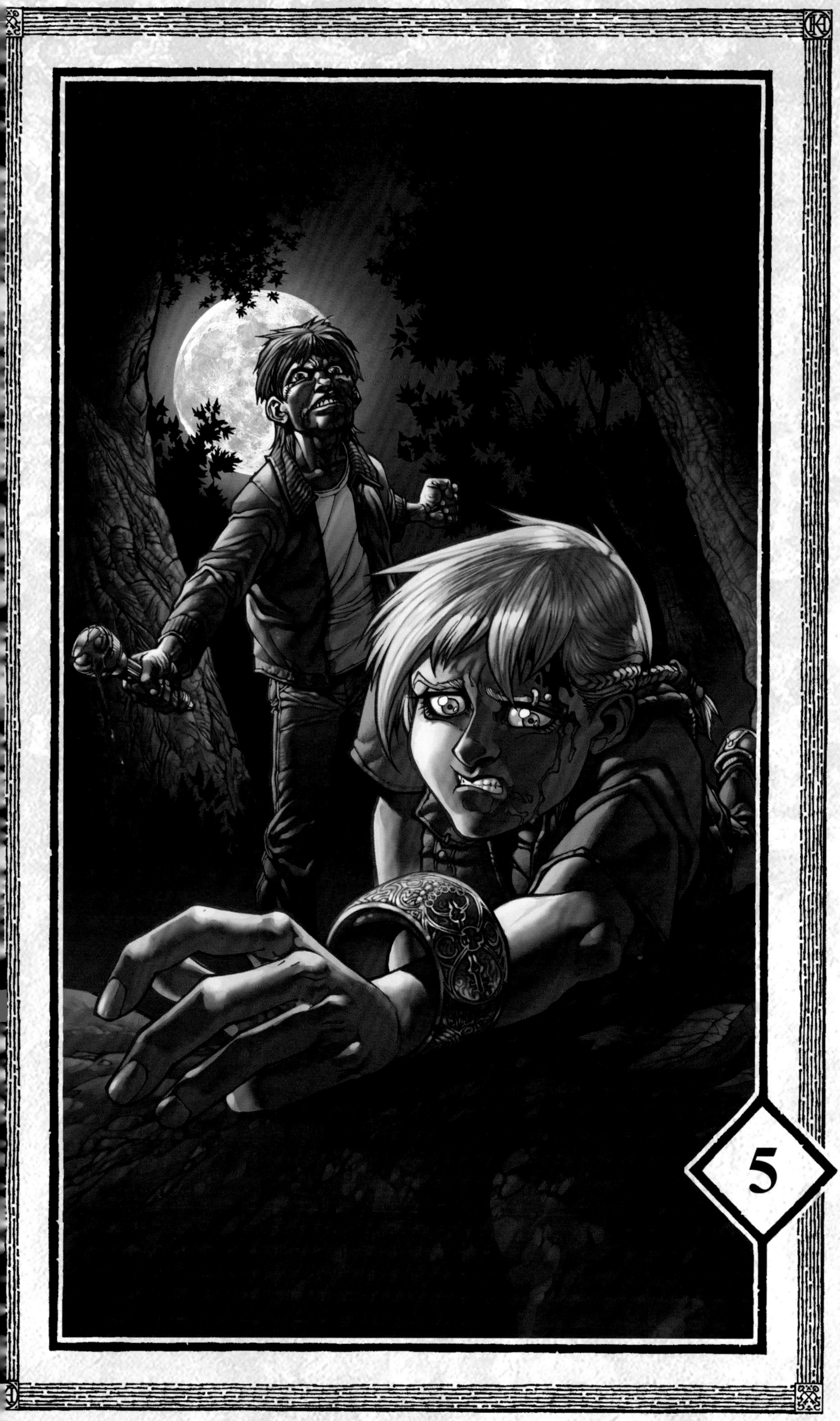

5

WELCOME TO LOVECRAFT
- FIVE -

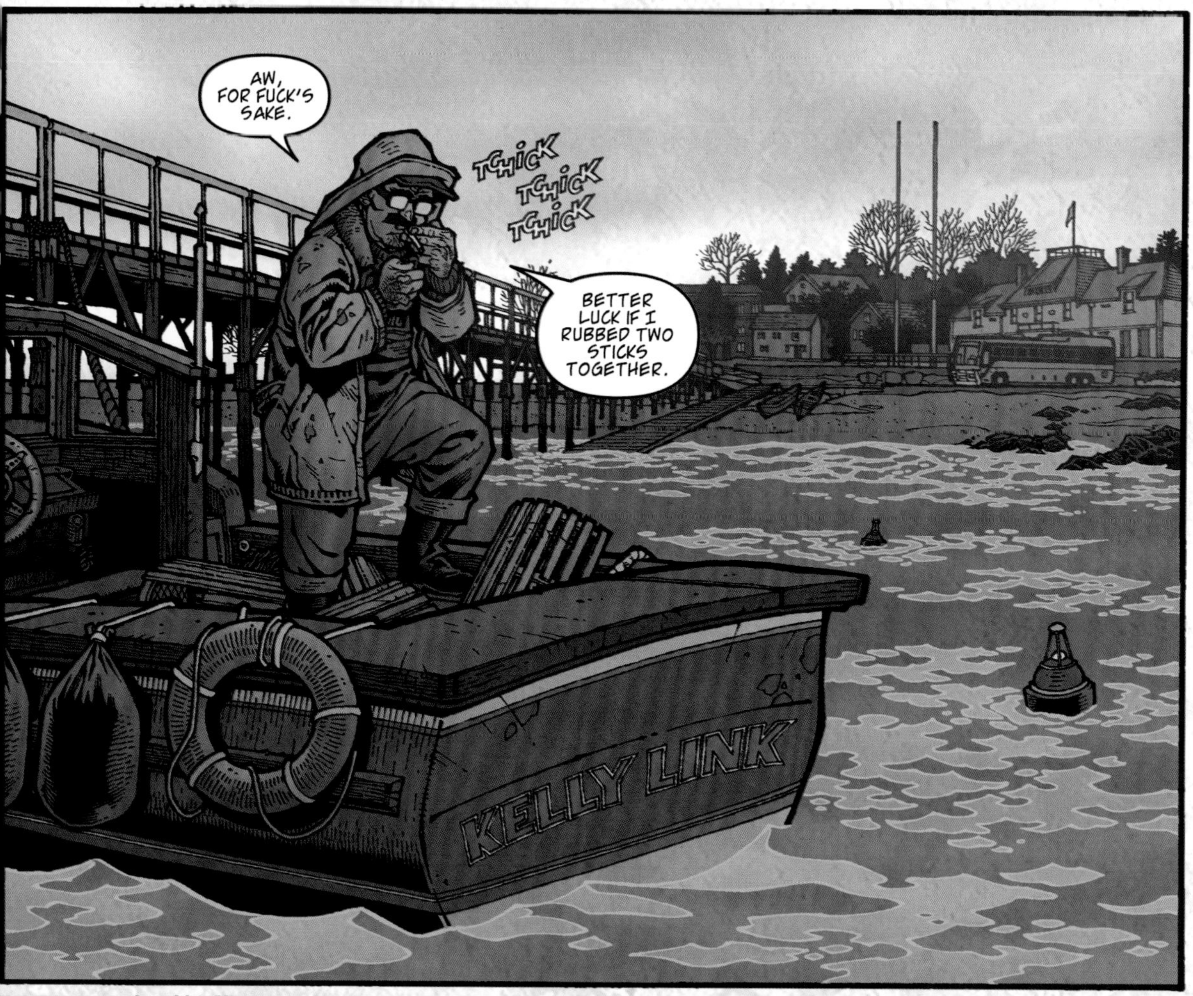
AW, FOR FUCK'S SAKE.
TCHICK TCHICK TCHICK
BETTER LUCK IF I RUBBED TWO STICKS TOGETHER.
KELLY LINK

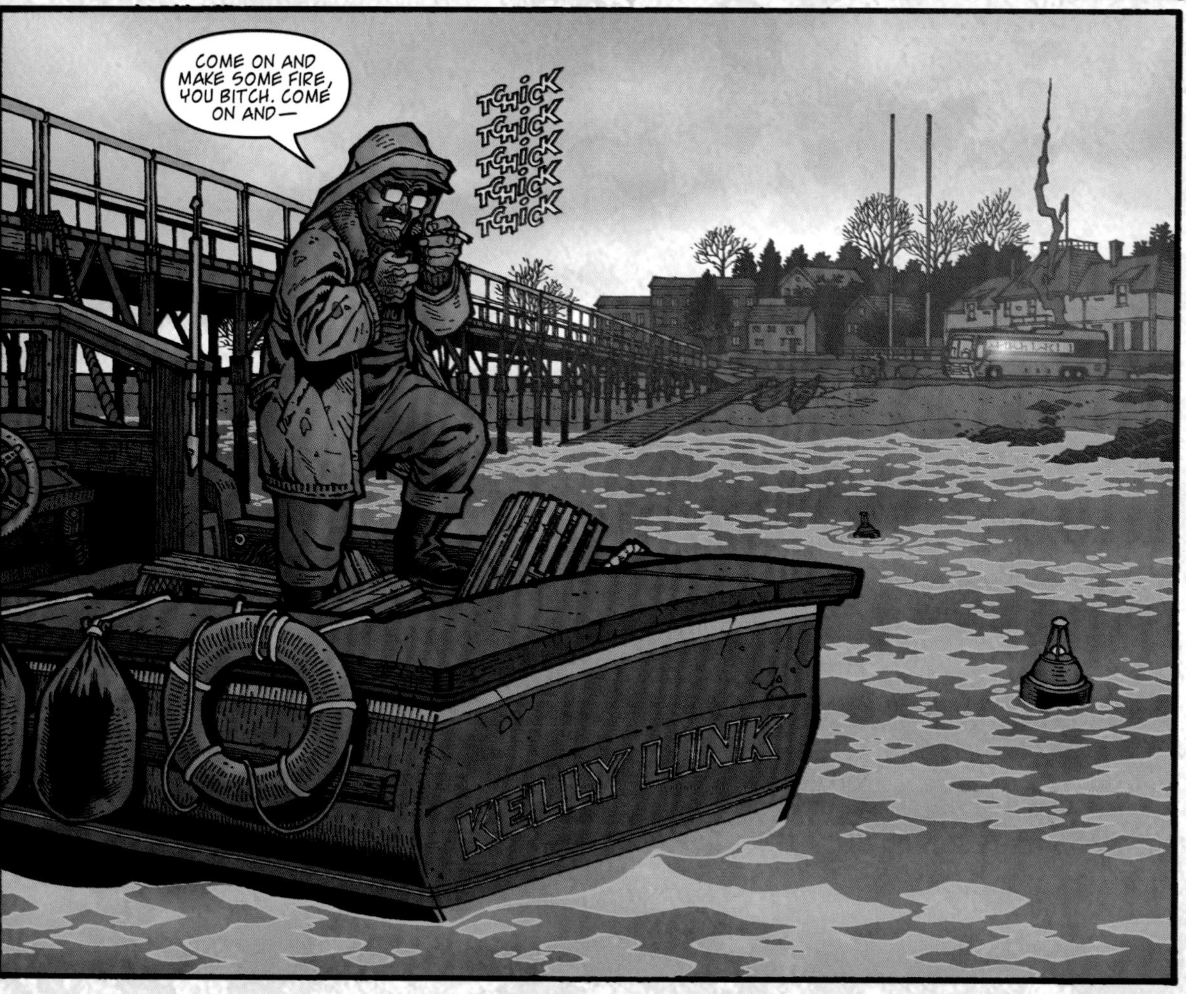
COME ON AND MAKE SOME FIRE, YOU BITCH. COME ON AND—
TCHICK TCHICK TCHICK TCHICK TCHICK
KELLY LINK

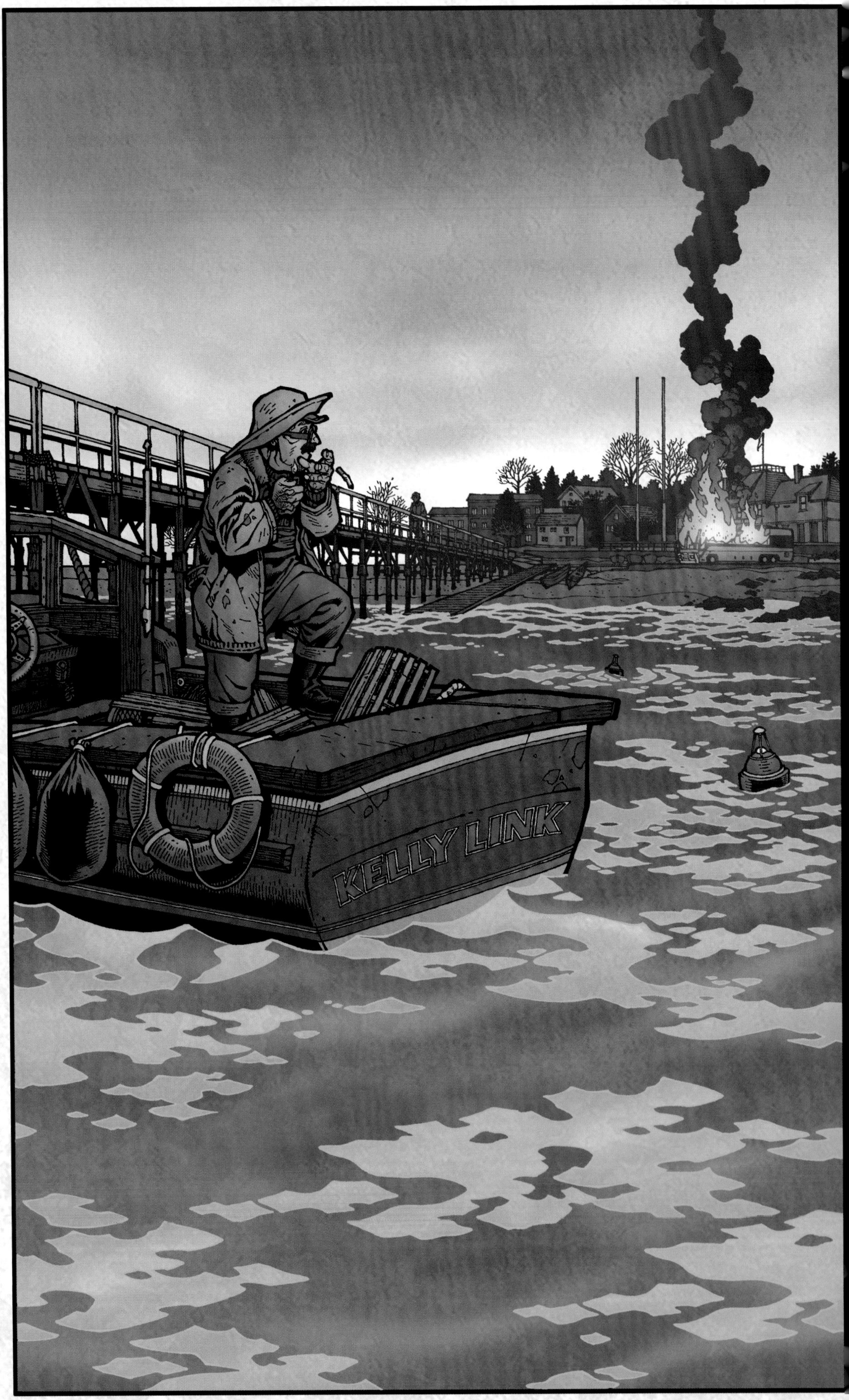
KELLY LINK

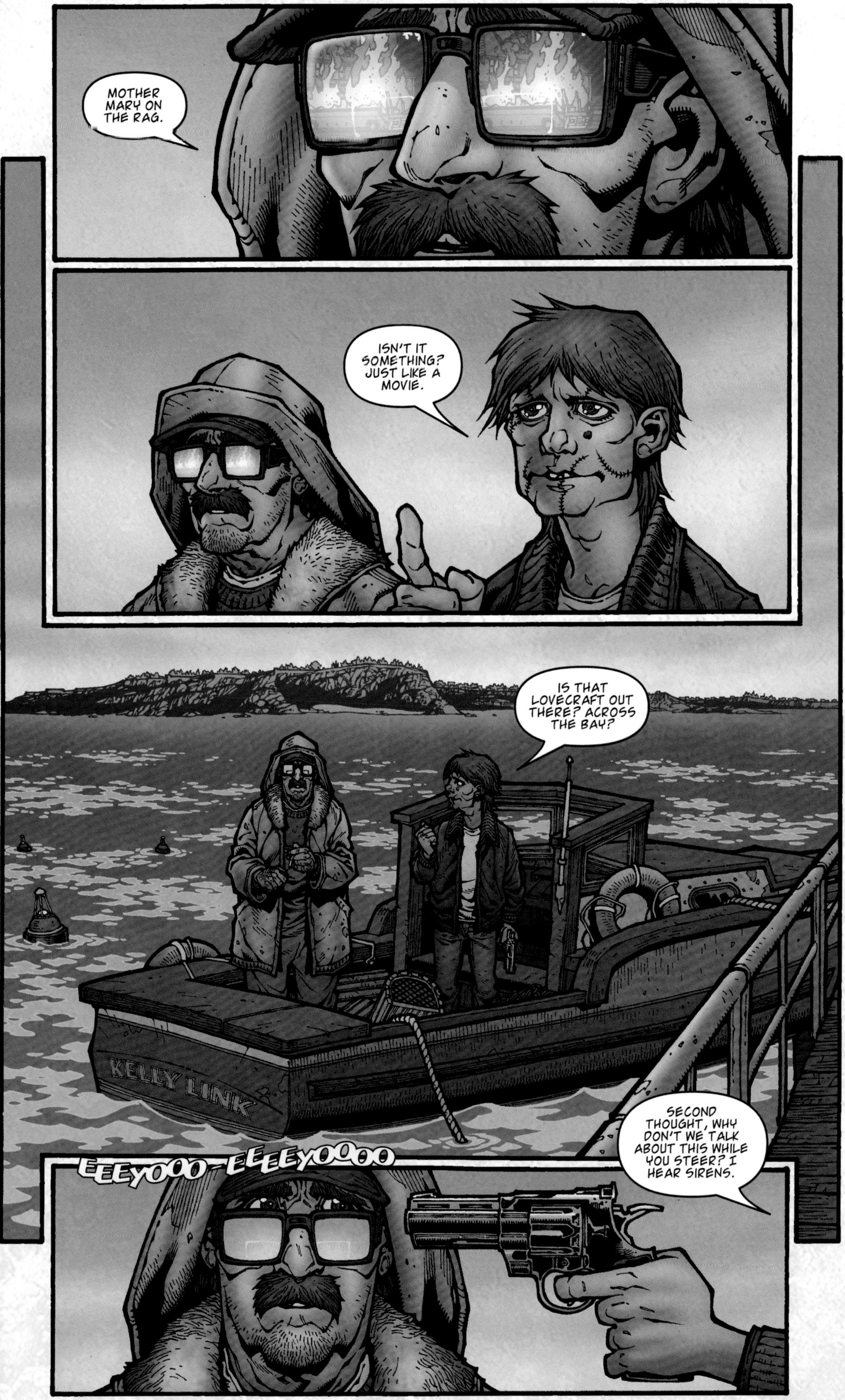
MOTHER MARY ON THE RAG.
ISN'T IT SOMETHING? JUST LIKE A MOVIE.
IS THAT LOVECRAFT OUT THERE? ACROSS THE BAY?
KELLY LINK
SECOND THOUGHT, WHY DON'T WE TALK ABOUT THIS WHILE YOU STEER? I HEAR SIRENS.
EEEYOOO-EEEEYOOOO

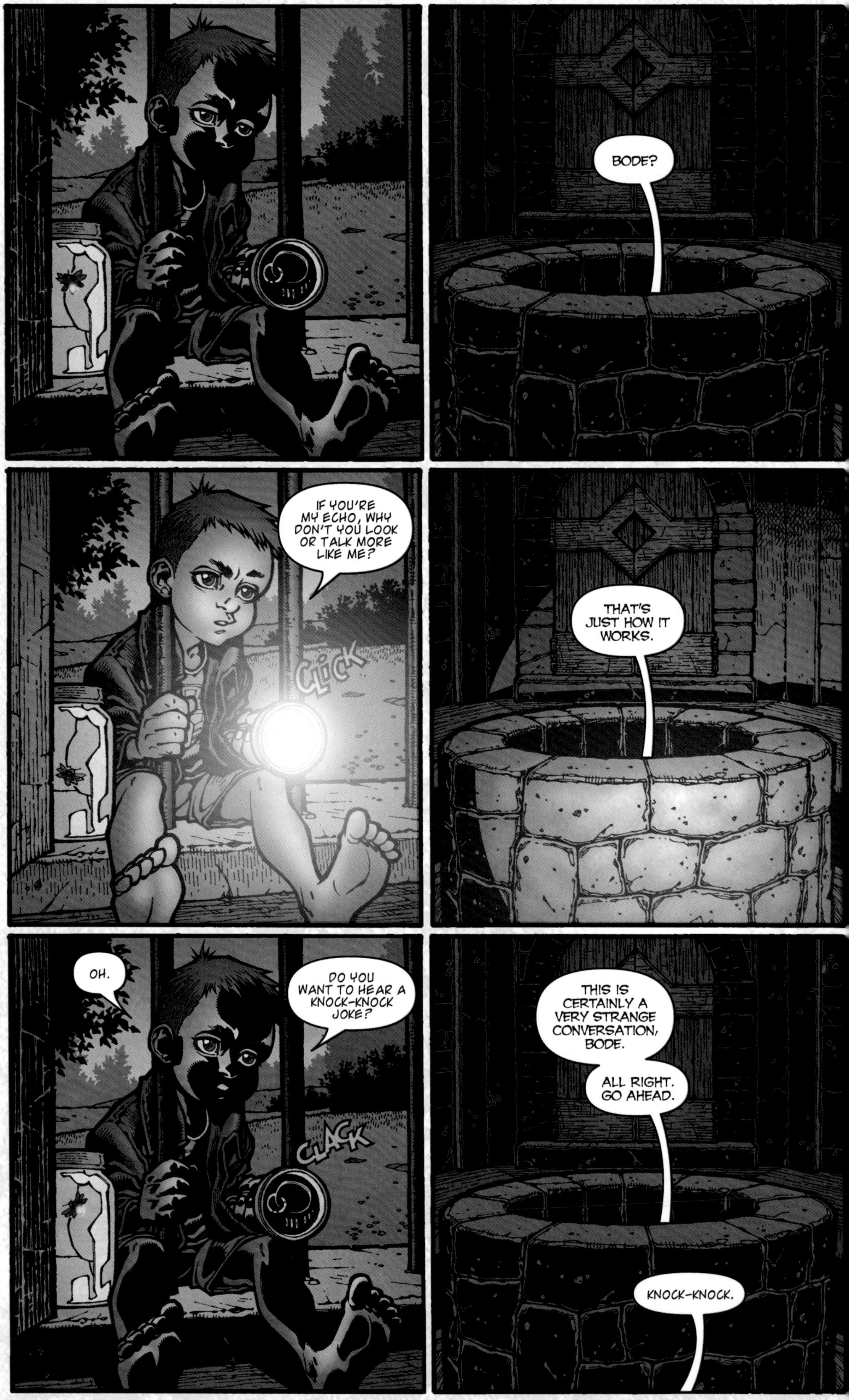
BODE?
IF YOU'RE MY ECHO, WHY DON'T YOU LOOK OR TALK MORE LIKE ME?
CLICK
THAT'S JUST HOW IT WORKS.
OH.
DO YOU WANT TO HEAR A KNOCK-KNOCK JOKE?
CLACK
THIS IS CERTAINLY A VERY STRANGE CONVERSATION, BODE.
ALL RIGHT. GO AHEAD.
KNOCK-KNOCK.

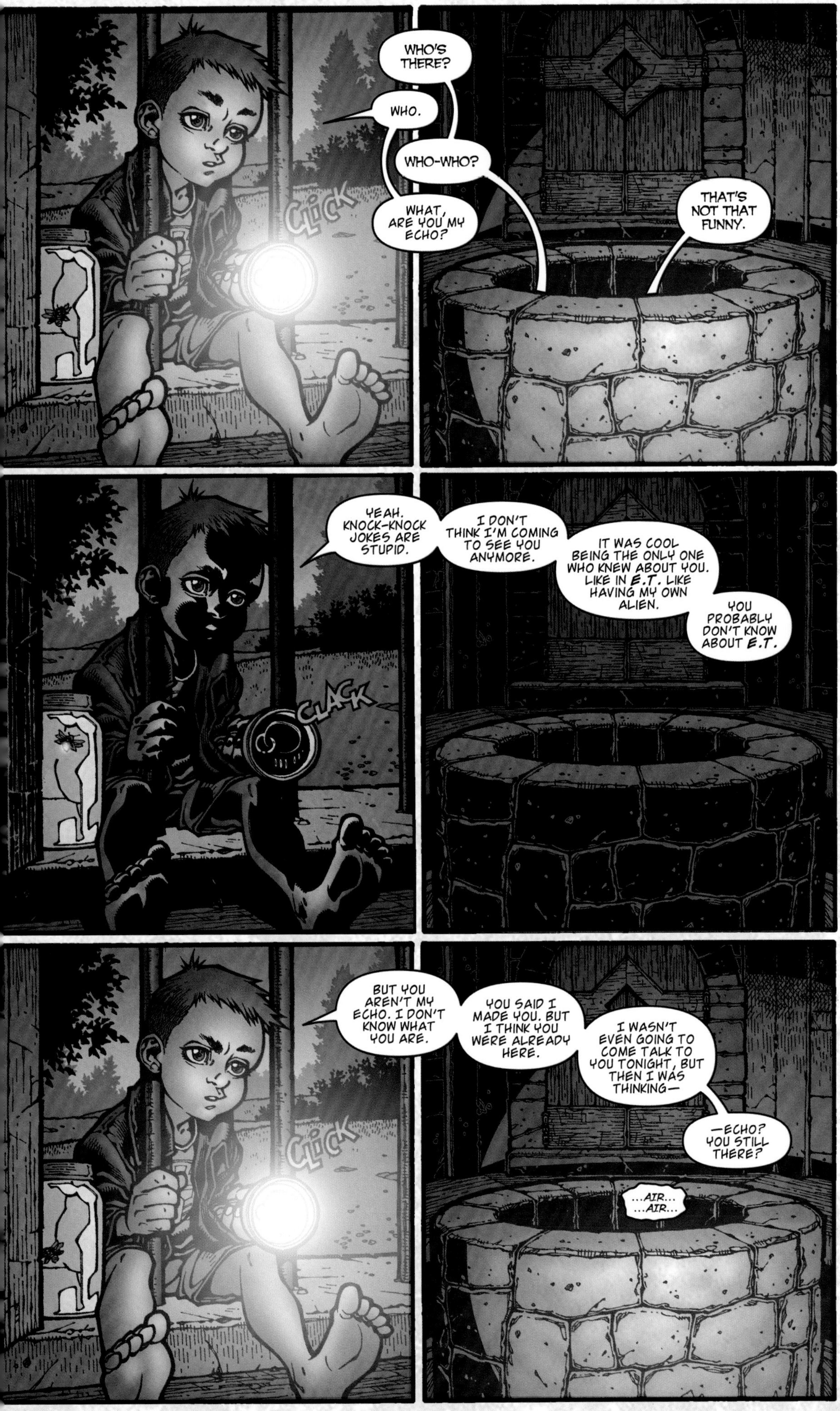
WHO'S THERE?
WHO.
WHO-WHO?
WHAT, ARE YOU MY ECHO?
CLICK
THAT'S NOT THAT FUNNY.
YEAH. KNOCK-KNOCK JOKES ARE STUPID.
I DON'T THINK I'M COMING TO SEE YOU ANYMORE.
IT WAS COOL BEING THE ONLY ONE WHO KNEW ABOUT YOU. LIKE IN E.T. LIKE HAVING MY OWN ALIEN.
YOU PROBABLY DON'T KNOW ABOUT E.T.
CLACK
BUT YOU AREN'T MY ECHO. I DON'T KNOW WHAT YOU ARE.
YOU SAID I MADE YOU. BUT I THINK YOU WERE ALREADY HERE.
I WASN'T EVEN GOING TO COME TALK TO YOU TONIGHT, BUT THEN I WAS THINKING—
CLICK
—ECHO? YOU STILL THERE?
...AIR... ...AIR...

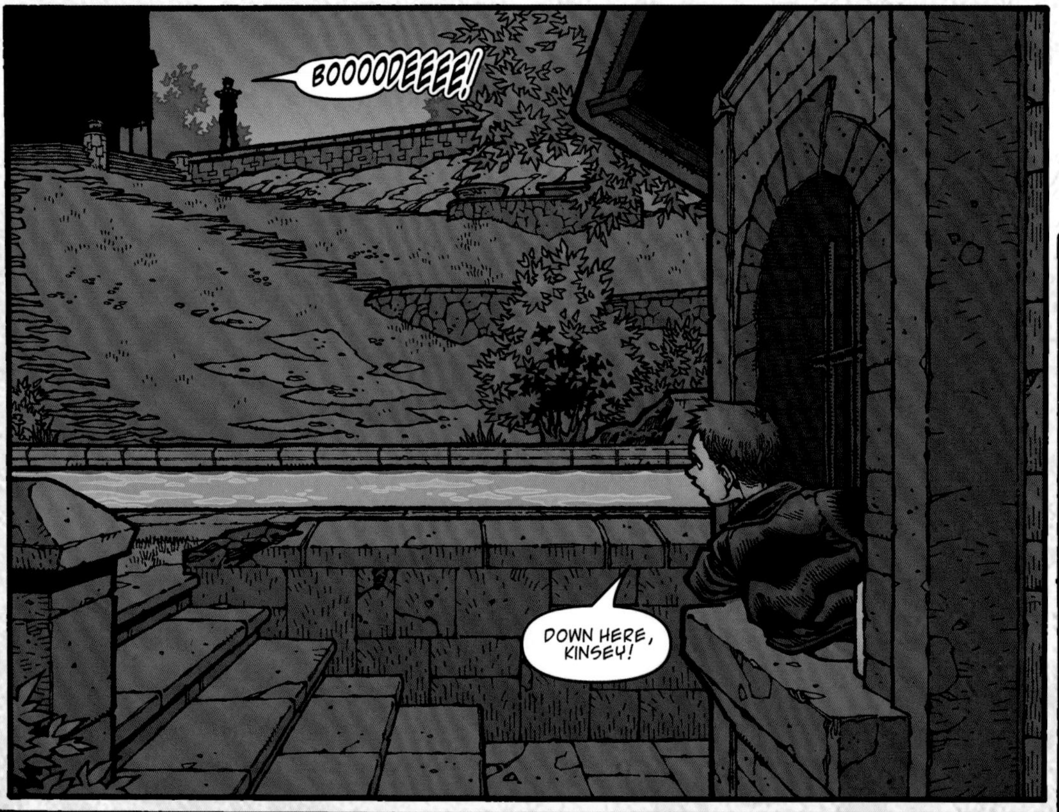
BOOOODEEEE!
DOWN HERE, KINSEY!
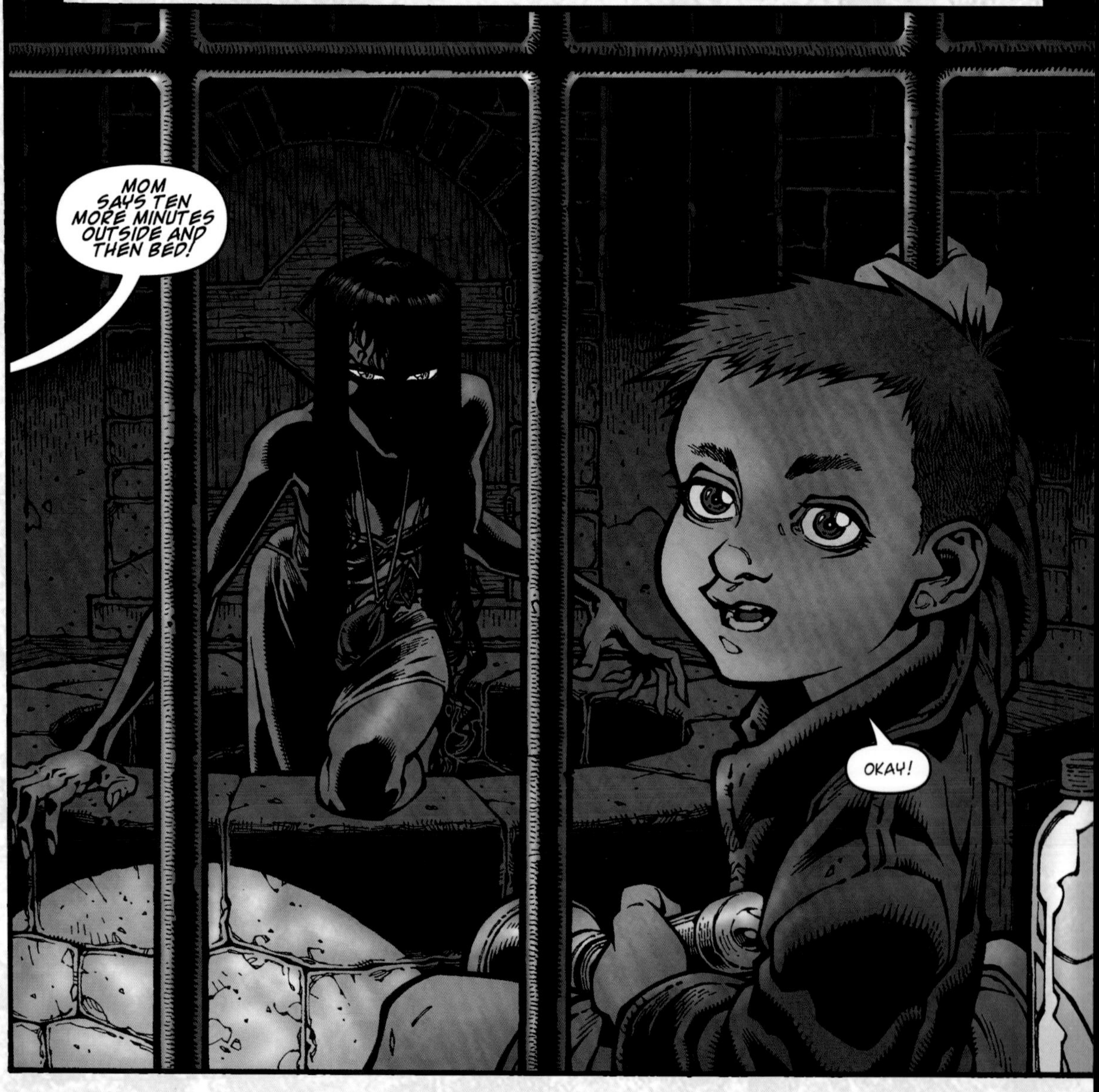
MOM SAYS TEN MORE MINUTES OUTSIDE AND THEN BED!
OKAY!

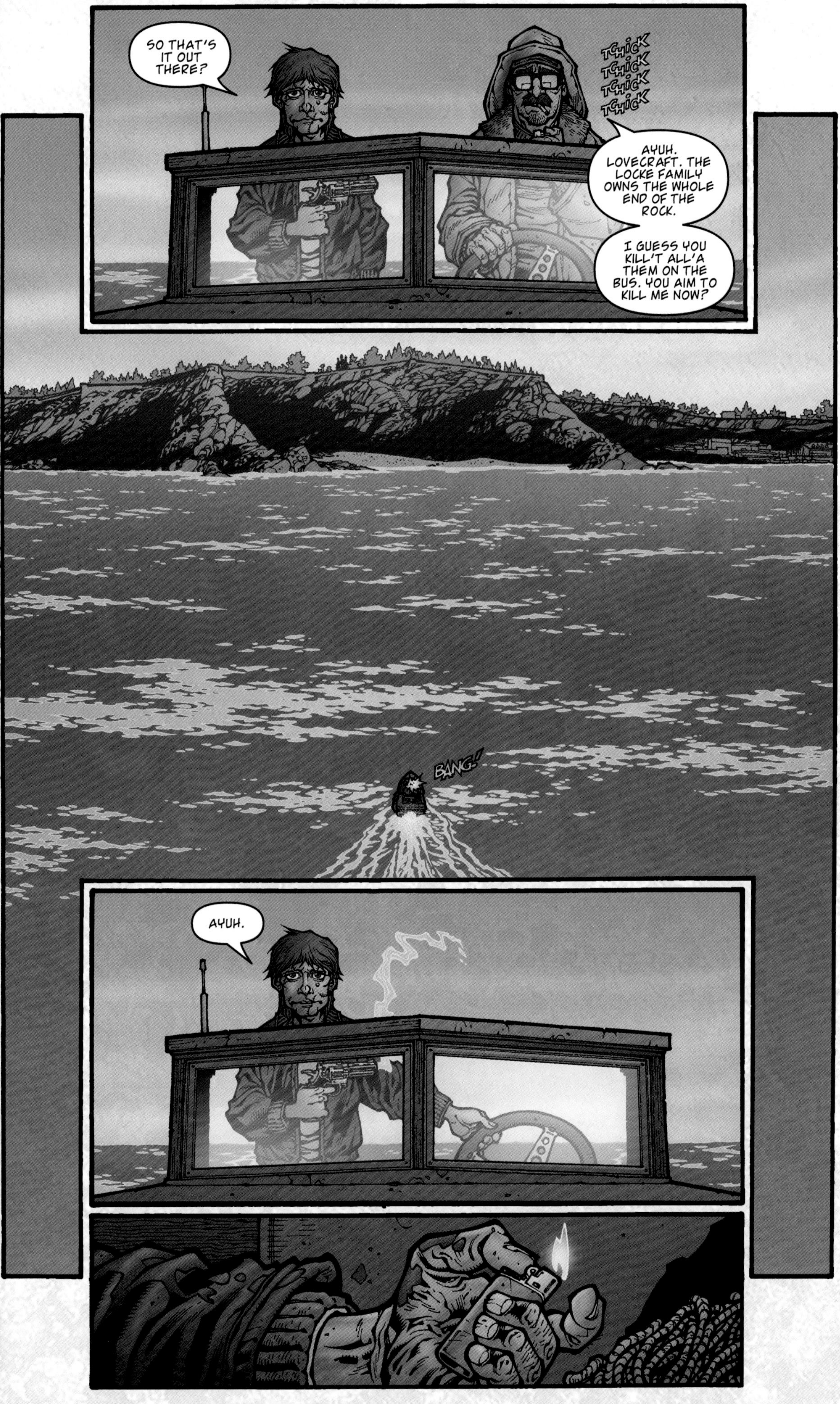
SO THAT'S IT OUT THERE?
TCHICK TCHICK TCHICK TCHICK
AYUH. LOVECRAFT. THE LOCKE FAMILY OWNS THE WHOLE END OF THE ROCK.
I GUESS YOU KILL'T ALL'A THEM ON THE BUS. YOU AIM TO KILL ME NOW?
BANG!
AYUH.

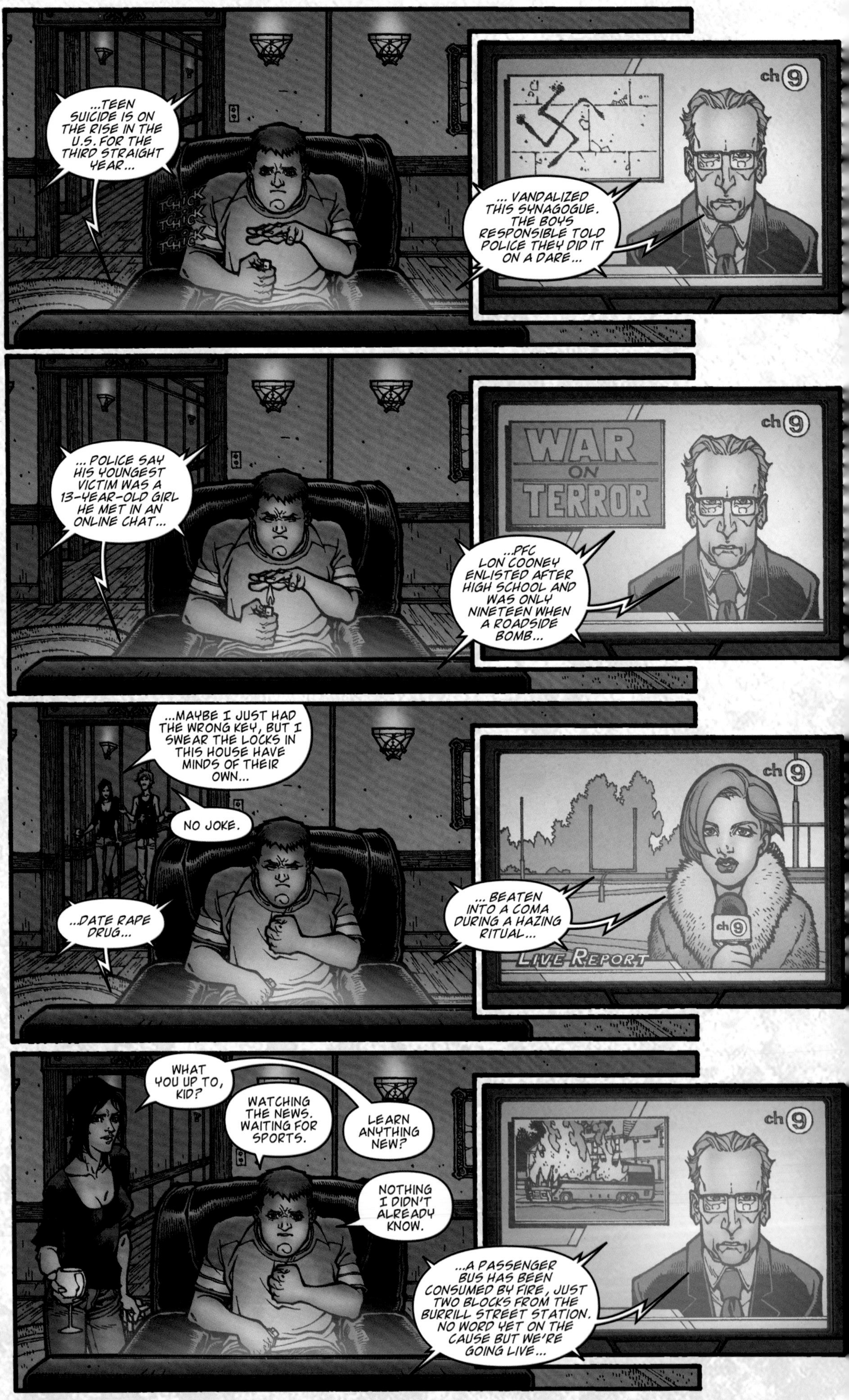
...TEEN SUICIDE IS ON THE RISE IN THE U.S. FOR THE THIRD STRAIGHT YEAR...
TCHICK TCHICK TCHICK
... VANDALIZED THIS SYNAGOGUE. THE BOYS RESPONSIBLE TOLD POLICE THEY DID IT ON A DARE...
ch 9
... POLICE SAY HIS YOUNGEST VICTIM WAS A 13-YEAR-OLD GIRL HE MET IN AN ONLINE CHAT...
WAR ON TERROR
...PFC LON COONEY ENLISTED AFTER HIGH SCHOOL AND WAS ONLY NINETEEN WHEN A ROADSIDE BOMB...
...MAYBE I JUST HAD THE WRONG KEY, BUT I SWEAR THE LOCKS IN THIS HOUSE HAVE MINDS OF THEIR OWN...
NO JOKE.
...DATE RAPE DRUG...
... BEATEN INTO A COMA DURING A HAZING RITUAL...
LIVE REPORT
WHAT YOU UP TO, KID?
WATCHING THE NEWS. WAITING FOR SPORTS.
LEARN ANYTHING NEW?
NOTHING I DIDN'T ALREADY KNOW.
...A PASSENGER BUS HAS BEEN CONSUMED BY FIRE, JUST TWO BLOCKS FROM THE BURRILL STREET STATION. NO WORD YET ON THE CAUSE BUT WE'RE GOING LIVE...

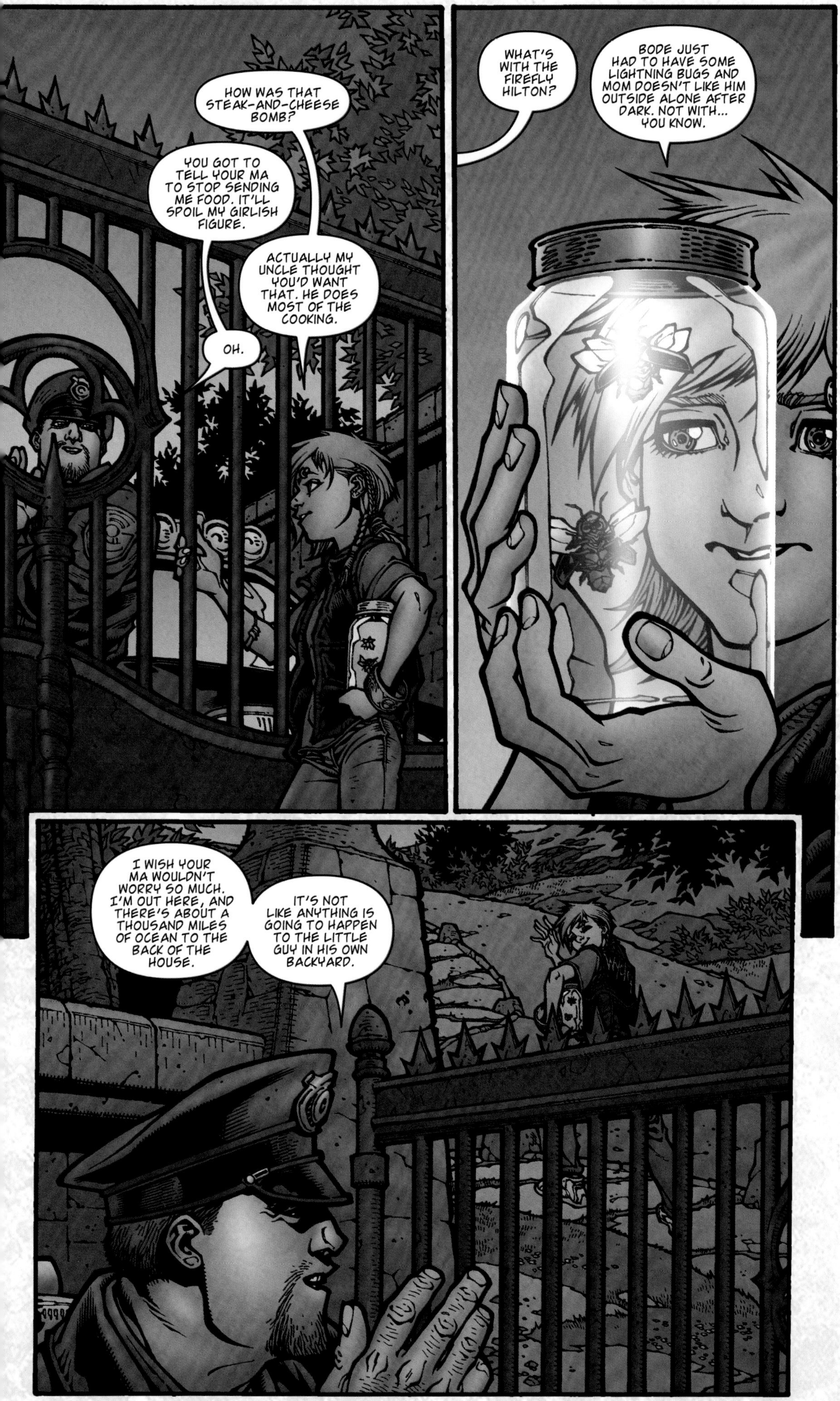
HOW WAS THAT STEAK-AND-CHEESE BOMB?
YOU GOT TO TELL YOUR MA TO STOP SENDING ME FOOD. IT'LL SPOIL MY GIRLISH FIGURE.
ACTUALLY MY UNCLE THOUGHT YOU'D WANT THAT. HE DOES MOST OF THE COOKING.
OH.
WHAT'S WITH THE FIREFLY HILTON?
BODE JUST HAD TO HAVE SOME LIGHTNING BUGS AND MOM DOESN'T LIKE HIM OUTSIDE ALONE AFTER DARK. NOT WITH... YOU KNOW.
I WISH YOUR MA WOULDN'T WORRY SO MUCH. I'M OUT HERE, AND THERE'S ABOUT A THOUSAND MILES OF OCEAN TO THE BACK OF THE HOUSE.
IT'S NOT LIKE ANYTHING IS GOING TO HAPPEN TO THE LITTLE GUY IN HIS OWN BACKYARD.

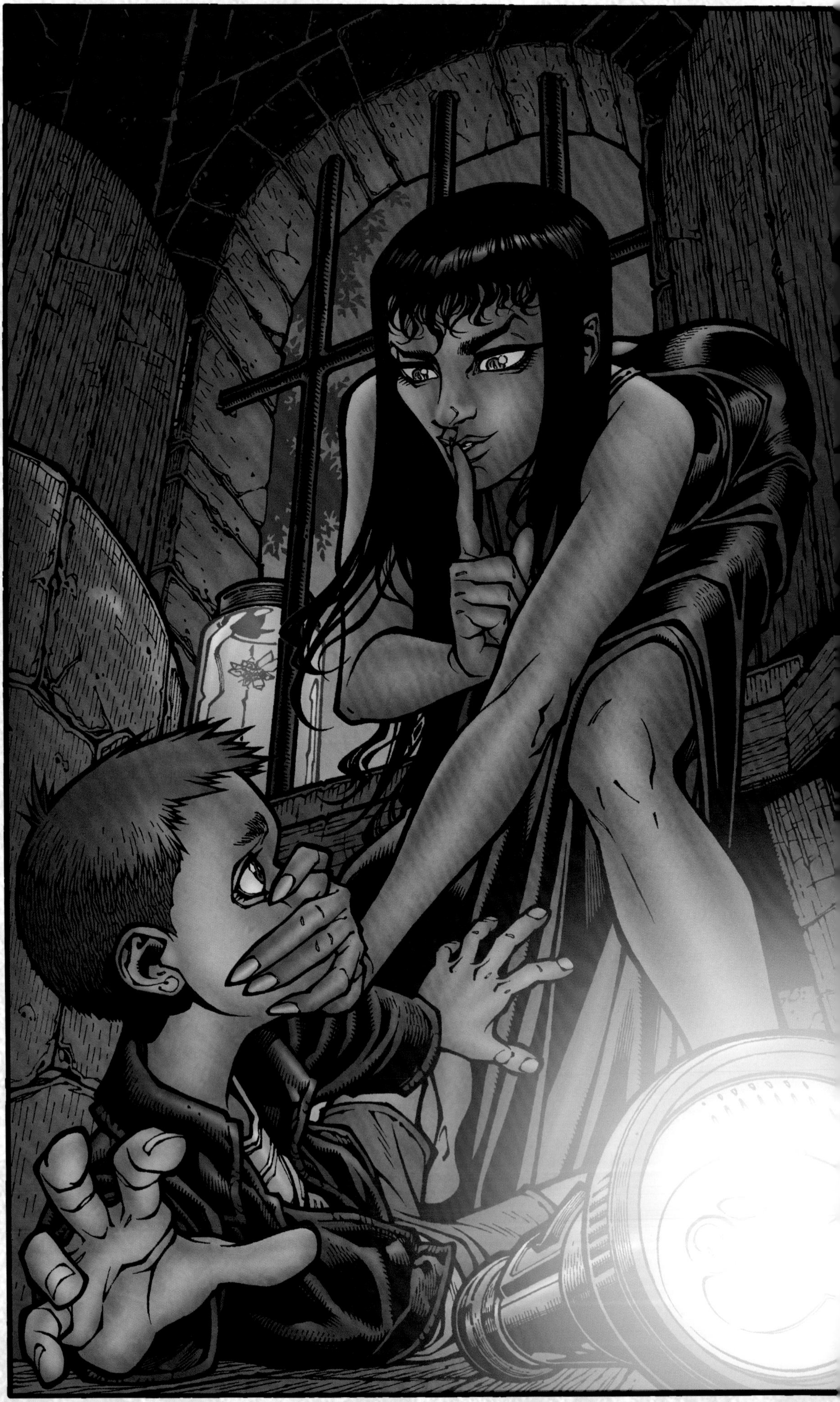

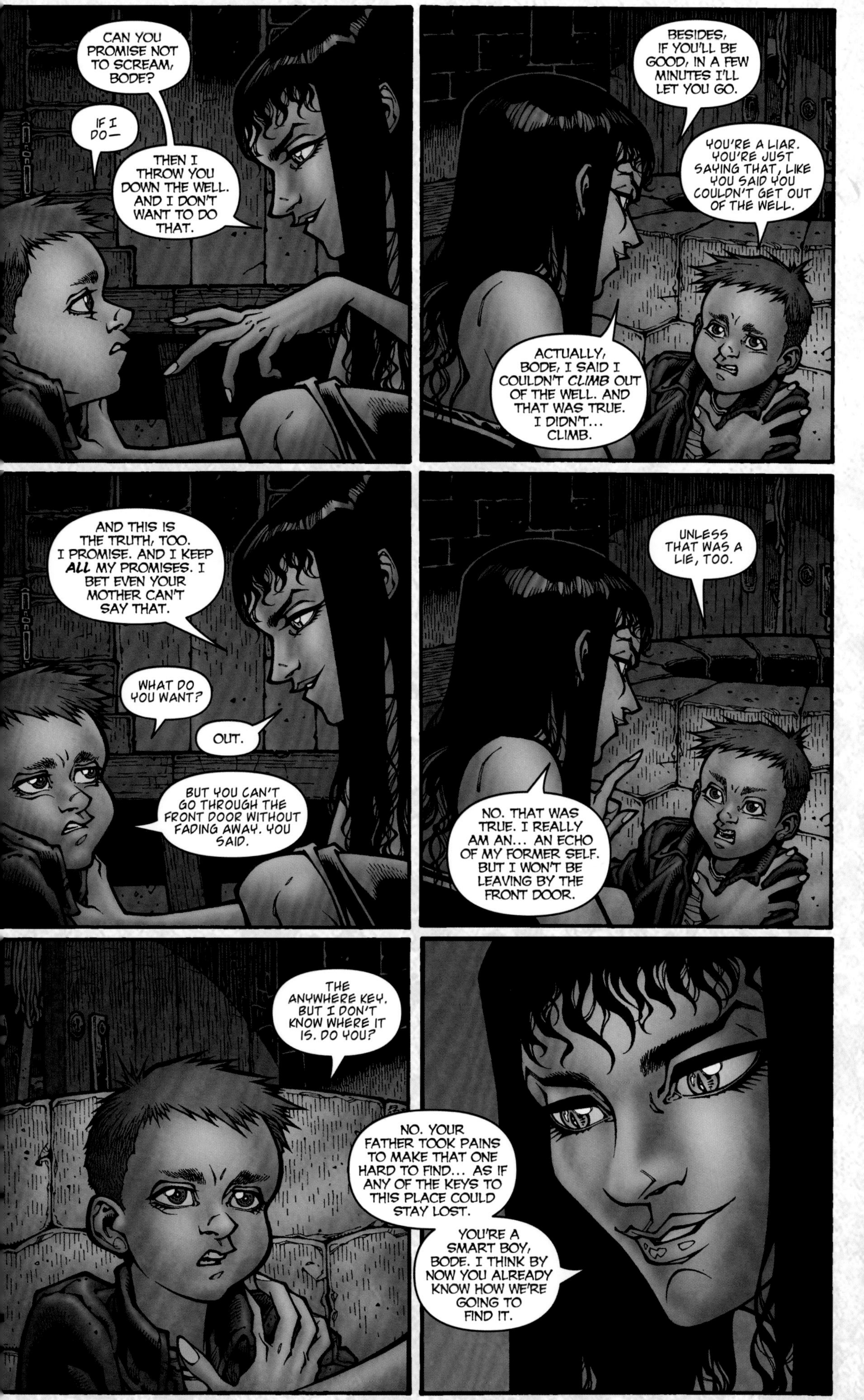
CAN YOU PROMISE NOT TO SCREAM, BODE?
IF I DO—
THEN I THROW YOU DOWN THE WELL. AND I DON'T WANT TO DO THAT.
BESIDES, IF YOU'LL BE GOOD, IN A FEW MINUTES I'LL LET YOU GO.
YOU'RE A LIAR. YOU'RE JUST SAYING THAT, LIKE YOU SAID YOU COULDN'T GET OUT OF THE WELL.
ACTUALLY, BODE, I SAID I COULDN'T CLIMB OUT OF THE WELL. AND THAT WAS TRUE. I DIDN'T... CLIMB.
AND THIS IS THE TRUTH, TOO. I PROMISE. AND I KEEP ALL MY PROMISES. I BET EVEN YOUR MOTHER CAN'T SAY THAT.
WHAT DO YOU WANT?
OUT.
BUT YOU CAN'T GO THROUGH THE FRONT DOOR WITHOUT FADING AWAY. YOU SAID.
UNLESS THAT WAS A LIE, TOO.
NO. THAT WAS TRUE. I REALLY AM AN... AN ECHO OF MY FORMER SELF. BUT I WON'T BE LEAVING BY THE FRONT DOOR.
THE ANYWHERE KEY. BUT I DON'T KNOW WHERE IT IS. DO YOU?
NO. YOUR FATHER TOOK PAINS TO MAKE THAT ONE HARD TO FIND... AS IF ANY OF THE KEYS TO THIS PLACE COULD STAY LOST.
YOU'RE A SMART BOY, BODE. I THINK BY NOW YOU ALREADY KNOW HOW WE'RE GOING TO FIND IT.

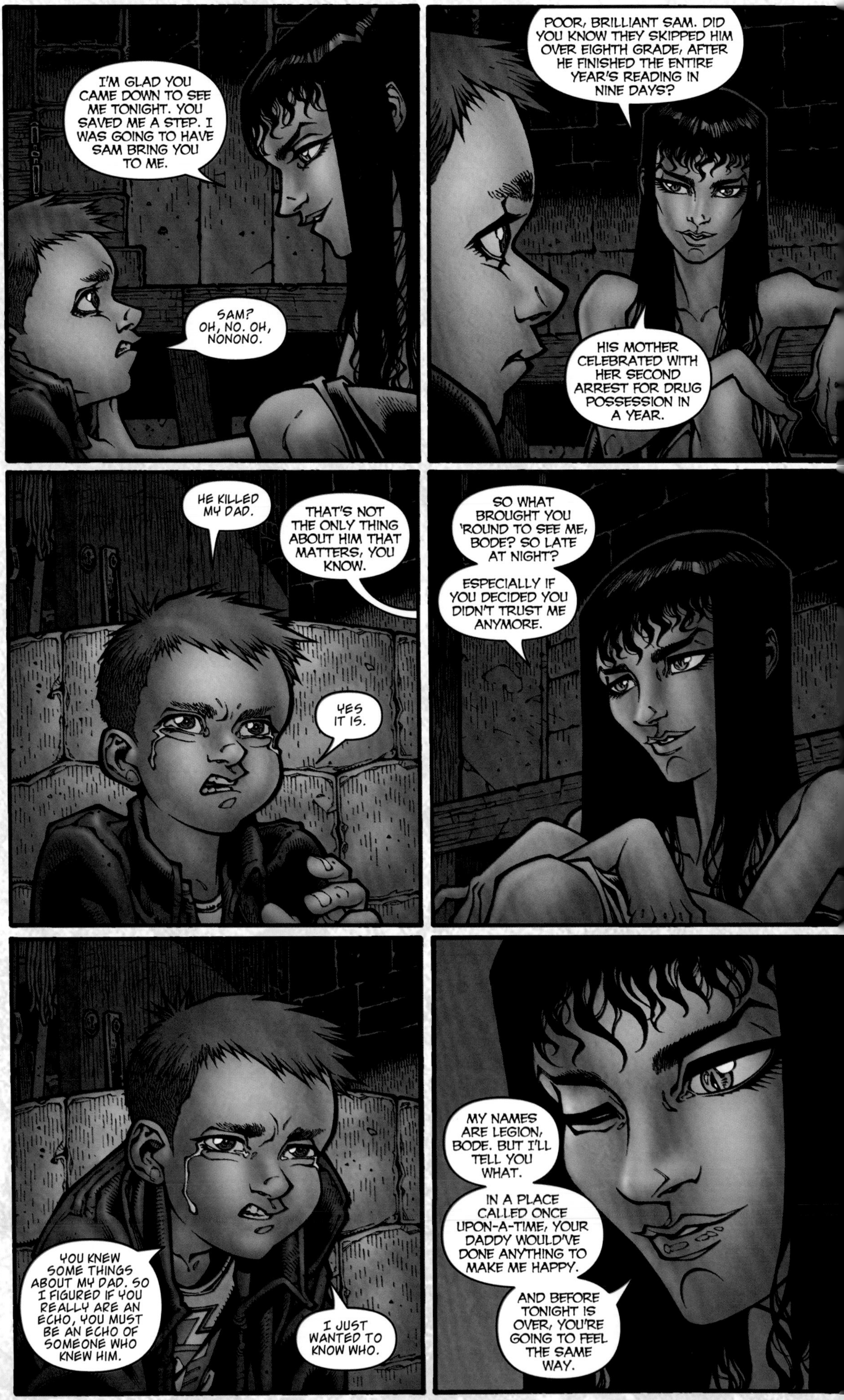
I'M GLAD YOU CAME DOWN TO SEE ME TONIGHT. YOU SAVED ME A STEP. I WAS GOING TO HAVE SAM BRING YOU TO ME.
SAM? OH, NO. OH, NONONO.
POOR, BRILLIANT SAM. DID YOU KNOW THEY SKIPPED HIM OVER EIGHTH GRADE, AFTER HE FINISHED THE ENTIRE YEAR'S READING IN NINE DAYS?
HIS MOTHER CELEBRATED WITH HER SECOND ARREST FOR DRUG POSSESSION IN A YEAR.
HE KILLED MY DAD.
THAT'S NOT THE ONLY THING ABOUT HIM THAT MATTERS, YOU KNOW.
YES IT IS.
SO WHAT BROUGHT YOU 'ROUND TO SEE ME, BODE? SO LATE AT NIGHT?
ESPECIALLY IF YOU DECIDED YOU DIDN'T TRUST ME ANYMORE.
YOU KNEW SOME THINGS ABOUT MY DAD. SO I FIGURED IF YOU REALLY ARE AN ECHO, YOU MUST BE AN ECHO OF SOMEONE WHO KNEW HIM.
I JUST WANTED TO KNOW WHO.
MY NAMES ARE LEGION, BODE. BUT I'LL TELL YOU WHAT.
IN A PLACE CALLED ONCE UPON-A-TIME, YOUR DADDY WOULD'VE DONE ANYTHING TO MAKE ME HAPPY.
AND BEFORE TONIGHT IS OVER, YOU'RE GOING TO FEEL THE SAME WAY.

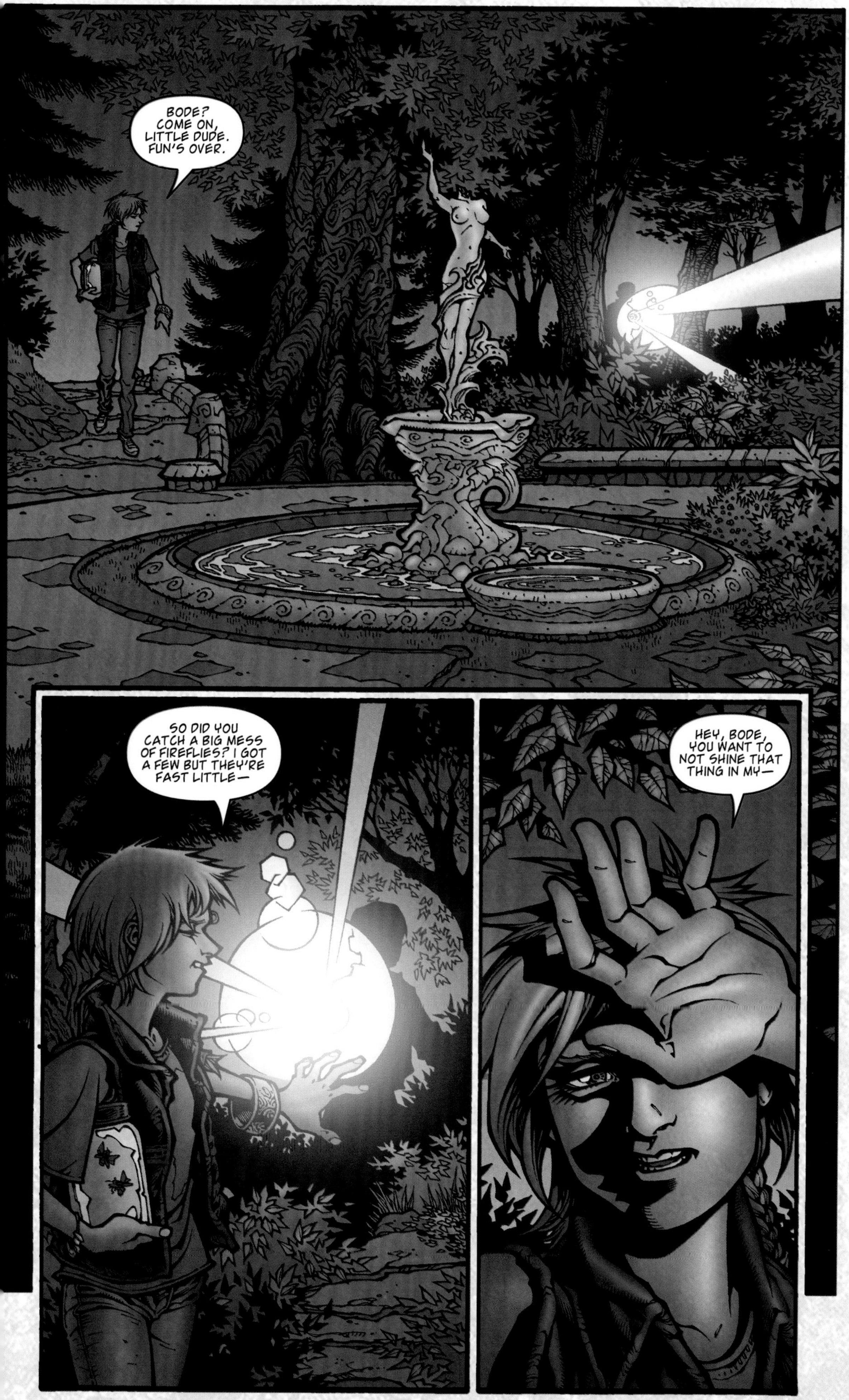
BODE? COME ON, LITTLE DUDE. FUN'S OVER.
SO DID YOU CATCH A BIG MESS OF FIREFLIES? I GOT A FEW BUT THEY'RE FAST LITTLE—
HEY, BODE, YOU WANT TO NOT SHINE THAT THING IN MY—

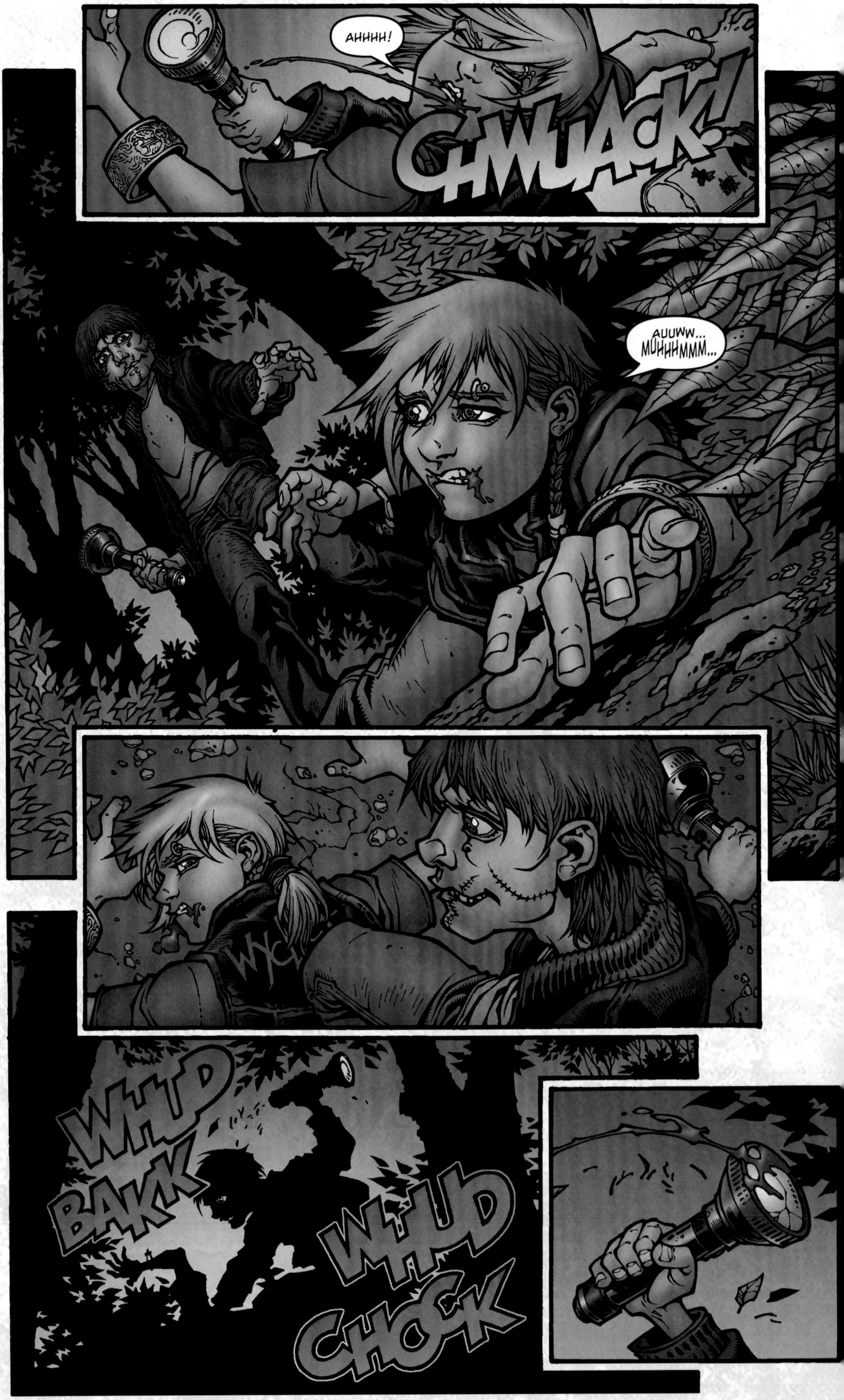
AHHHH!
CHWUACK!
AUUWW... MUHHHMMM...
WHUD
BAKK
WHUD
CHOCK

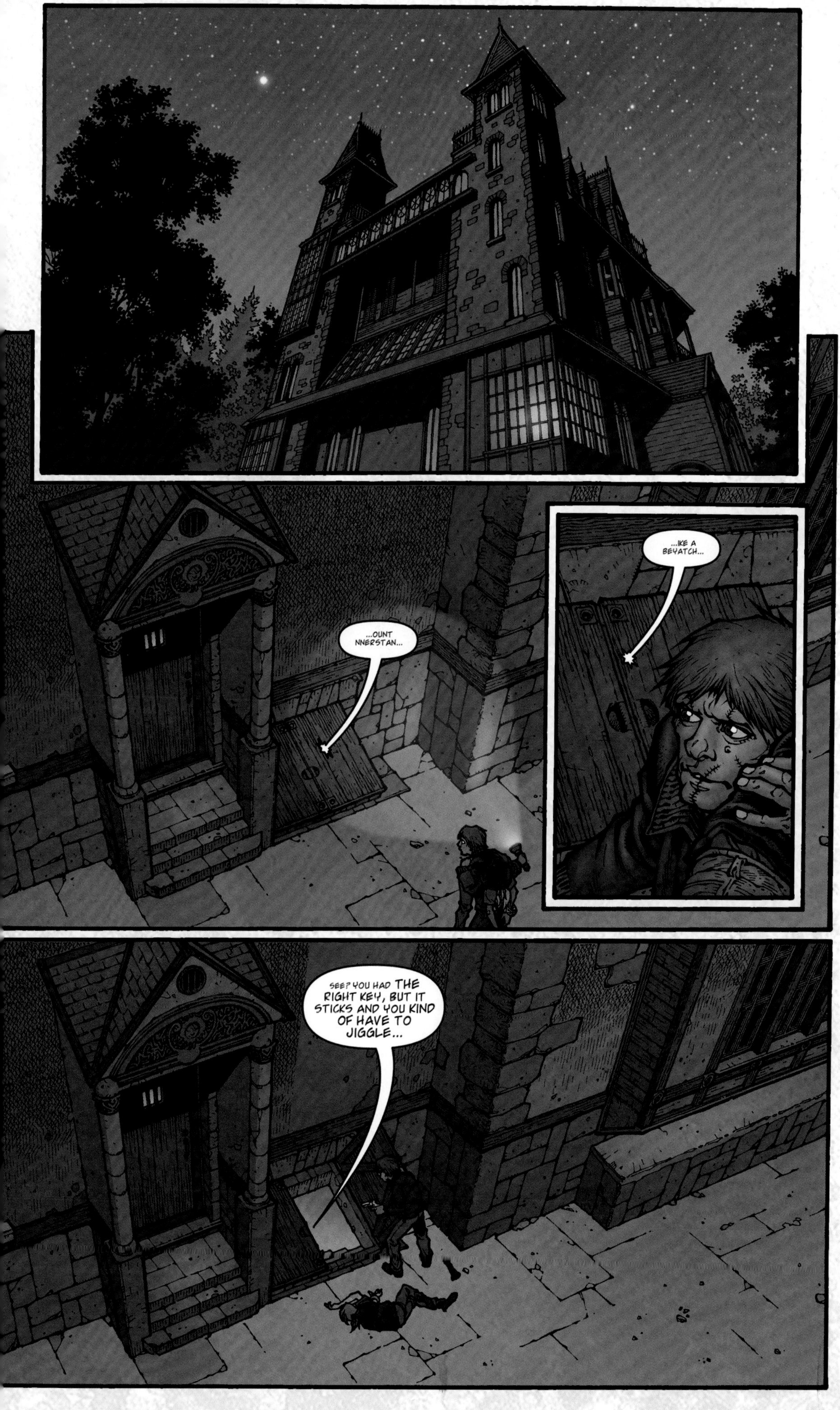
...OUNT NNERSTAN...
...IKE A BEYATCH...
SEE? YOU HAD THE RIGHT KEY, BUT IT STICKS AND YOU KIND OF HAVE TO JIGGLE...

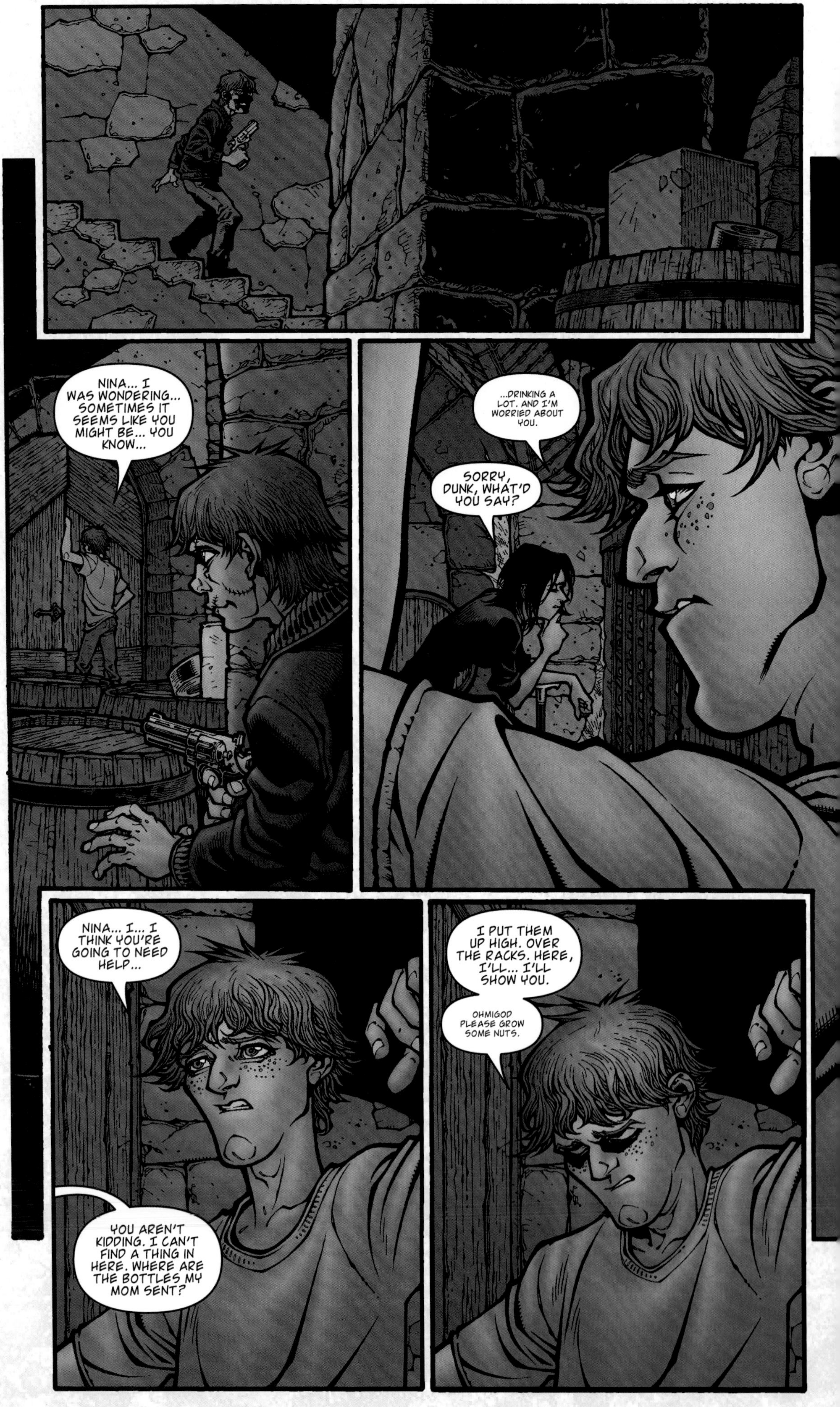
NINA... I WAS WONDERING... SOMETIMES IT SEEMS LIKE YOU MIGHT BE... YOU KNOW...
...DRINKING A LOT. AND I'M WORRIED ABOUT YOU.
SORRY, DUNK, WHAT'D YOU SAY?
NINA... I... I THINK YOU'RE GOING TO NEED HELP...
YOU AREN'T KIDDING. I CAN'T FIND A THING IN HERE. WHERE ARE THE BOTTLES MY MOM SENT?
I PUT THEM UP HIGH. OVER THE RACKS. HERE, I'LL... I'LL SHOW YOU.
OHMIGOD PLEASE GROW SOME NUTS.

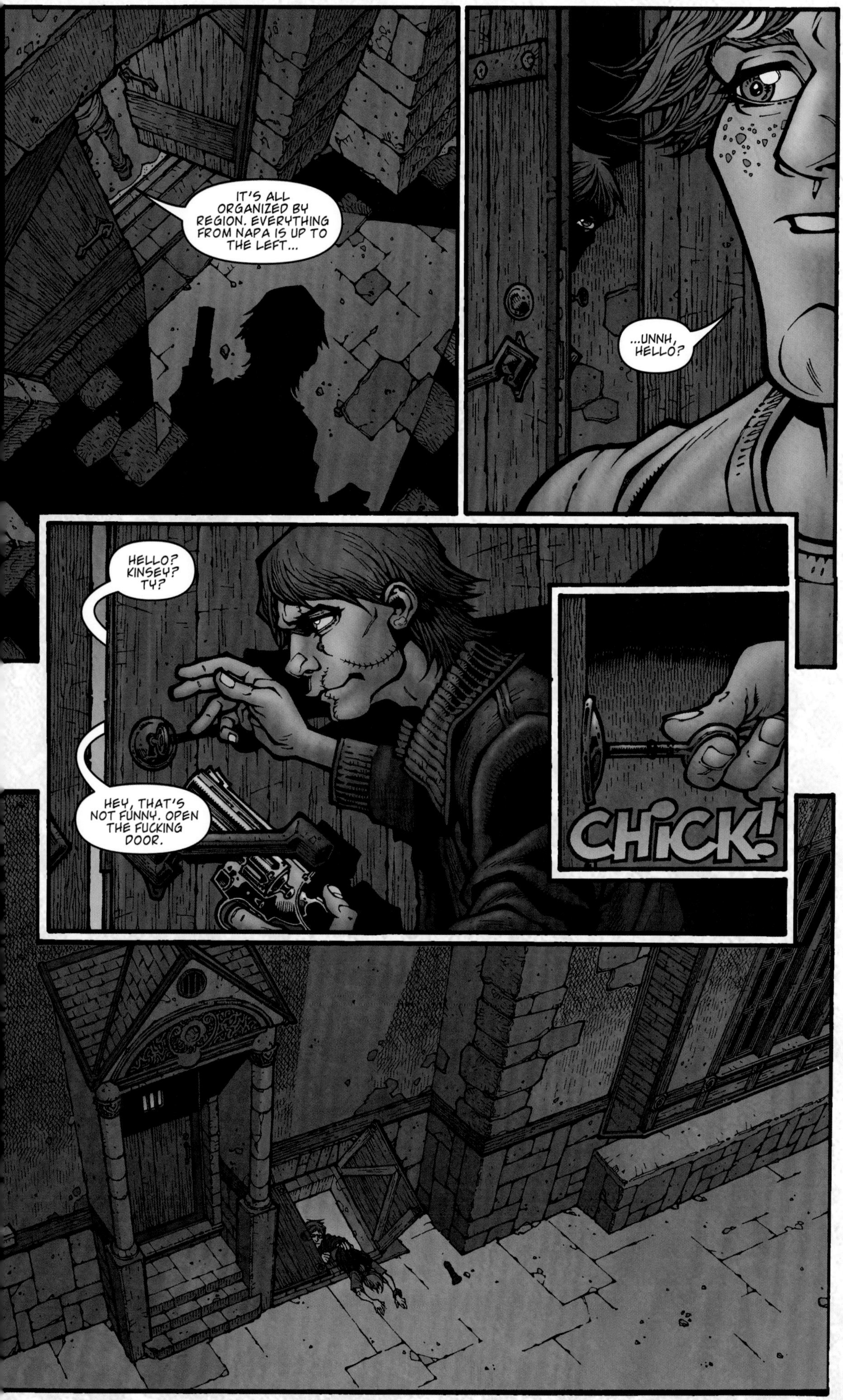
IT'S ALL ORGANIZED BY REGION. EVERYTHING FROM NAPA IS UP TO THE LEFT...
...UNNH, HELLO?
HELLO? KINSEY? TY?
HEY, THAT'S NOT FUNNY. OPEN THE FUCKING DOOR.
CHICK!

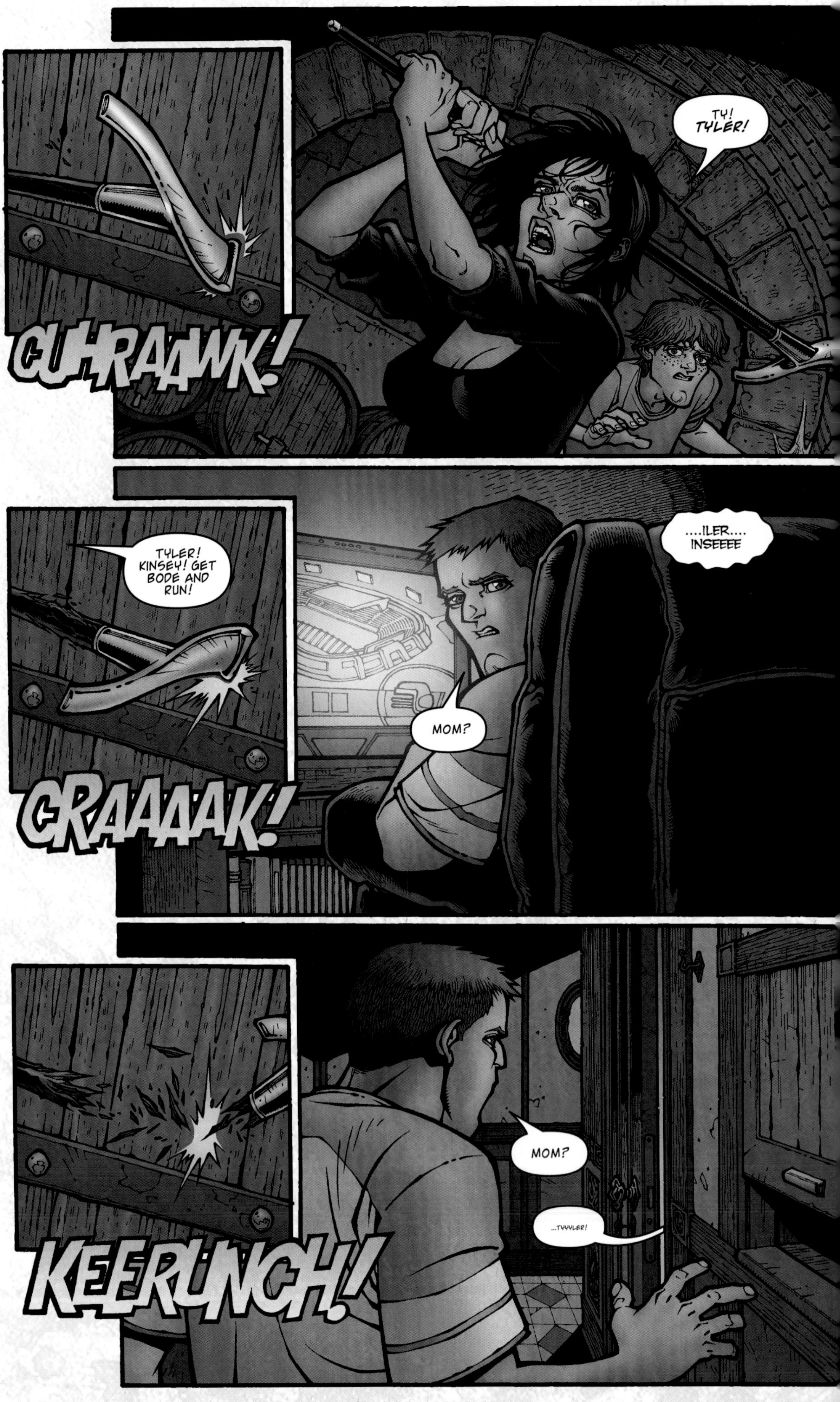
CUHRAAWK!
TY! TYLER!
TYLER! KINSEY! GET BODE AND RUN!
....ILER.... INSEEEE
MOM?
GRAAAAK!
MOM?
...TYYYLER!
KEERUNCH!

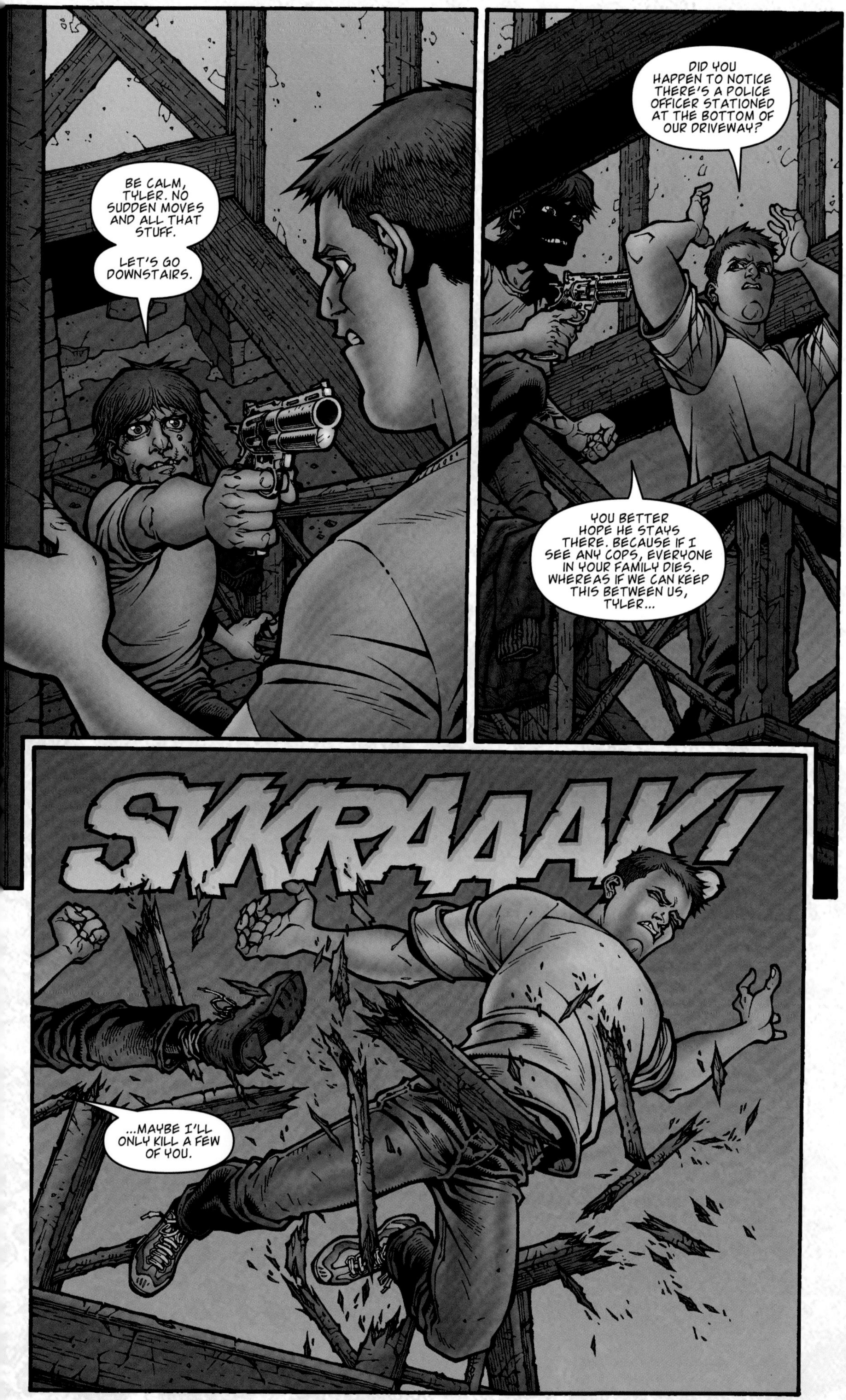
BE CALM, TYLER. NO SUDDEN MOVES AND ALL THAT STUFF.
LET'S GO DOWNSTAIRS.
DID YOU HAPPEN TO NOTICE THERE'S A POLICE OFFICER STATIONED AT THE BOTTOM OF OUR DRIVEWAY?
YOU BETTER HOPE HE STAYS THERE. BECAUSE IF I SEE ANY COPS, EVERYONE IN YOUR FAMILY DIES. WHEREAS IF WE CAN KEEP THIS BETWEEN US, TYLER...
SKRAAAK!
...MAYBE I'LL ONLY KILL A FEW OF YOU.

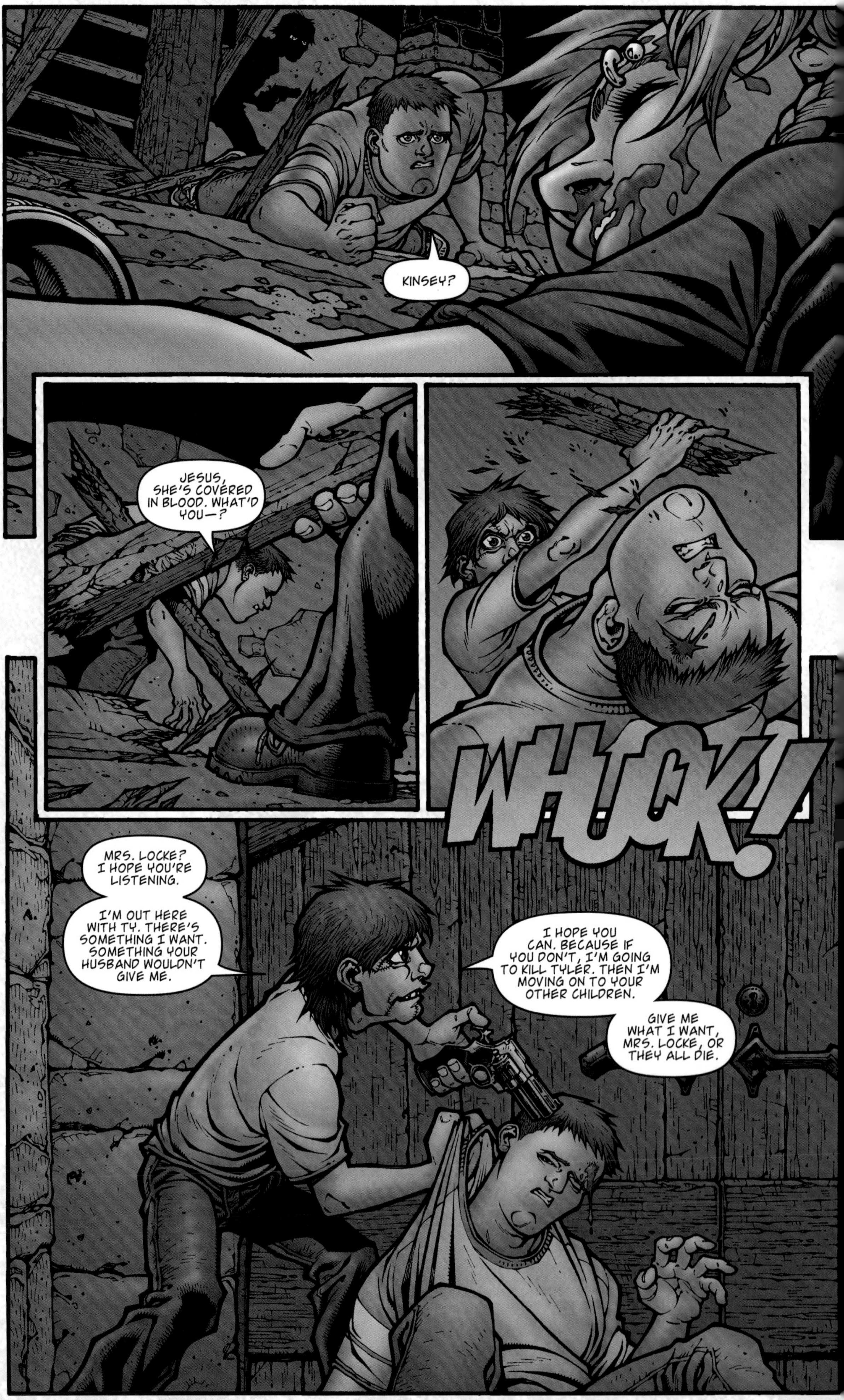
KINSEY?
JESUS, SHE'S COVERED IN BLOOD. WHAT'D YOU—?
WHUCK!
MRS. LOCKE? I HOPE YOU'RE LISTENING.
I'M OUT HERE WITH TY. THERE'S SOMETHING I WANT. SOMETHING YOUR HUSBAND WOULDN'T GIVE ME.
I HOPE YOU CAN. BECAUSE IF YOU DON'T, I'M GOING TO KILL TYLER. THEN I'M MOVING ON TO YOUR OTHER CHILDREN.
GIVE ME WHAT I WANT, MRS. LOCKE, OR THEY ALL DIE.

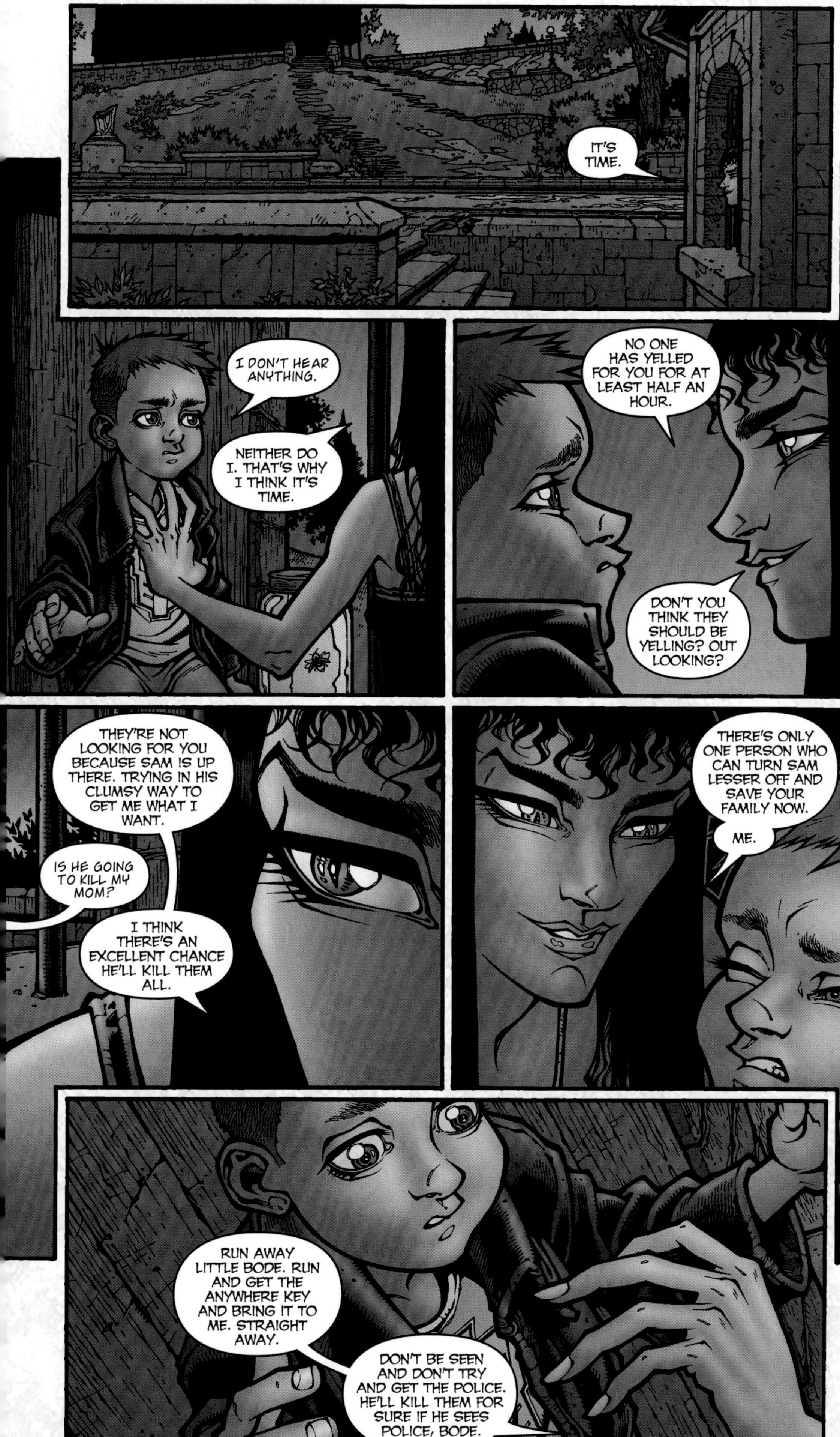
IT'S TIME.
I DON'T HEAR ANYTHING.
NEITHER DO I. THAT'S WHY I THINK IT'S TIME.
NO ONE HAS YELLED FOR YOU FOR AT LEAST HALF AN HOUR.
DON'T YOU THINK THEY SHOULD BE YELLING? OUT LOOKING?
THEY'RE NOT LOOKING FOR YOU BECAUSE SAM IS UP THERE. TRYING IN HIS CLUMSY WAY TO GET ME WHAT I WANT.
IS HE GOING TO KILL MY MOM?
I THINK THERE'S AN EXCELLENT CHANCE HE'LL KILL THEM ALL.
THERE'S ONLY ONE PERSON WHO CAN TURN SAM LESSER OFF AND SAVE YOUR FAMILY NOW.
ME.
RUN AWAY LITTLE BODE. RUN AND GET THE ANYWHERE KEY AND BRING IT TO ME. STRAIGHT AWAY.
DON'T BE SEEN AND DON'T TRY AND GET THE POLICE. HE'LL KILL THEM FOR SURE IF HE SEES POLICE, BODE.

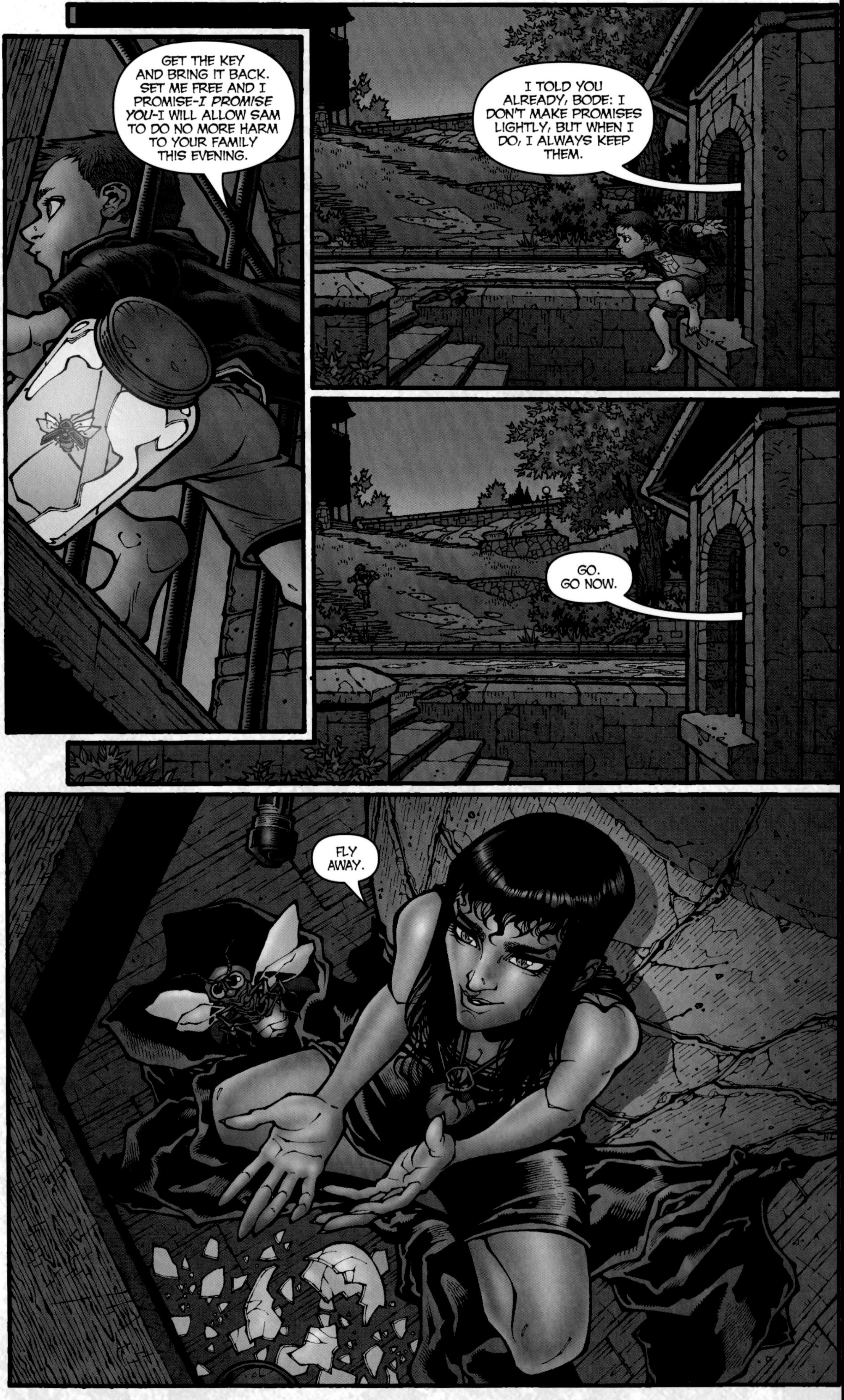
GET THE KEY AND BRING IT BACK. SET ME FREE AND I PROMISE-*I PROMISE YOU*-I WILL ALLOW SAM TO DO NO MORE HARM TO YOUR FAMILY THIS EVENING.
I TOLD YOU ALREADY, BODE: I DON'T MAKE PROMISES LIGHTLY, BUT WHEN I DO, I ALWAYS KEEP THEM.
GO. GO NOW.
FLY AWAY.

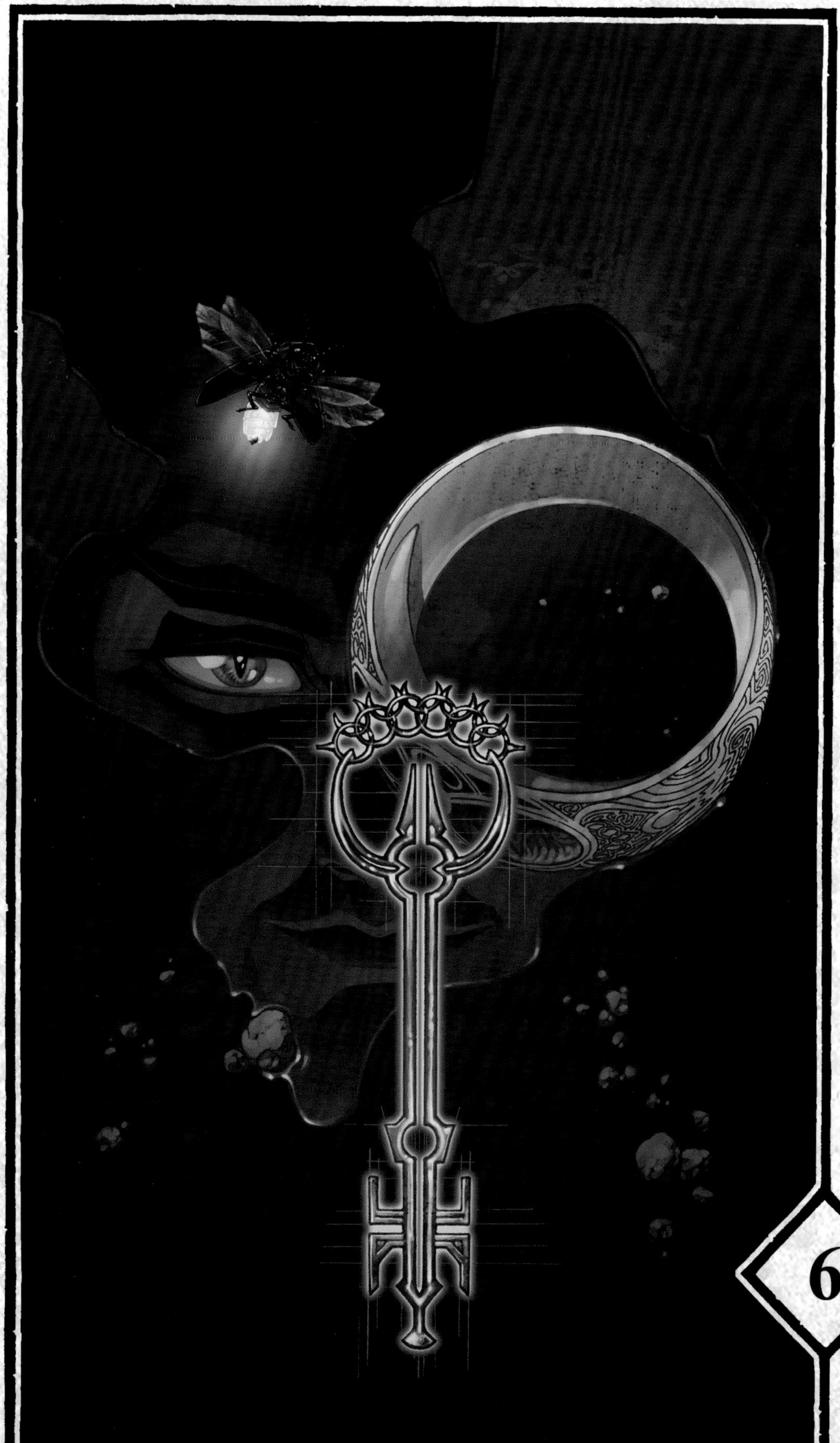

6

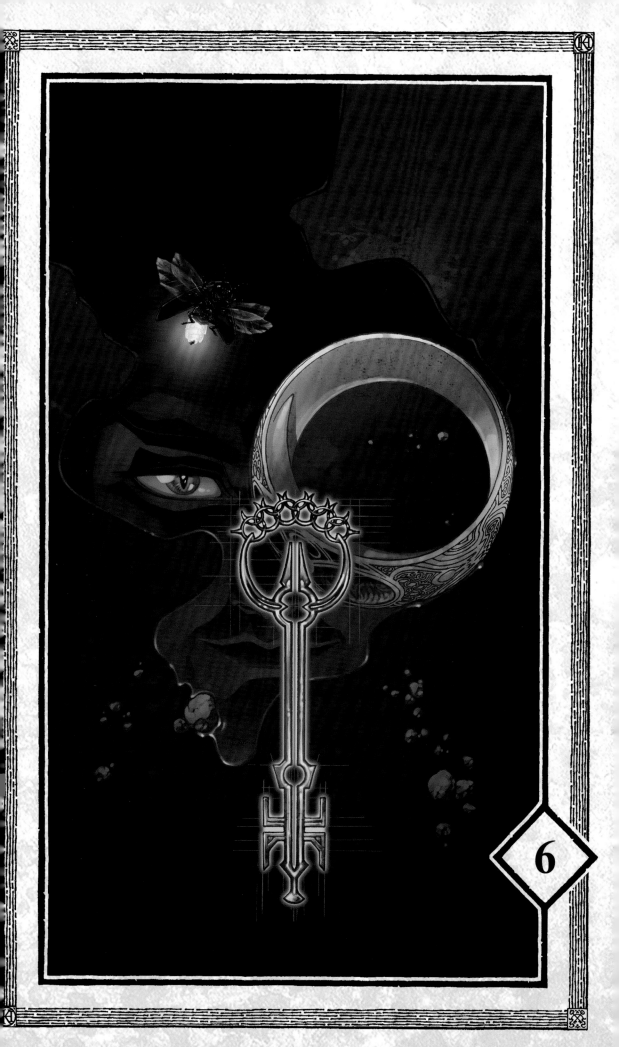

WELCOME TO LOVECRAFT
- SIX -

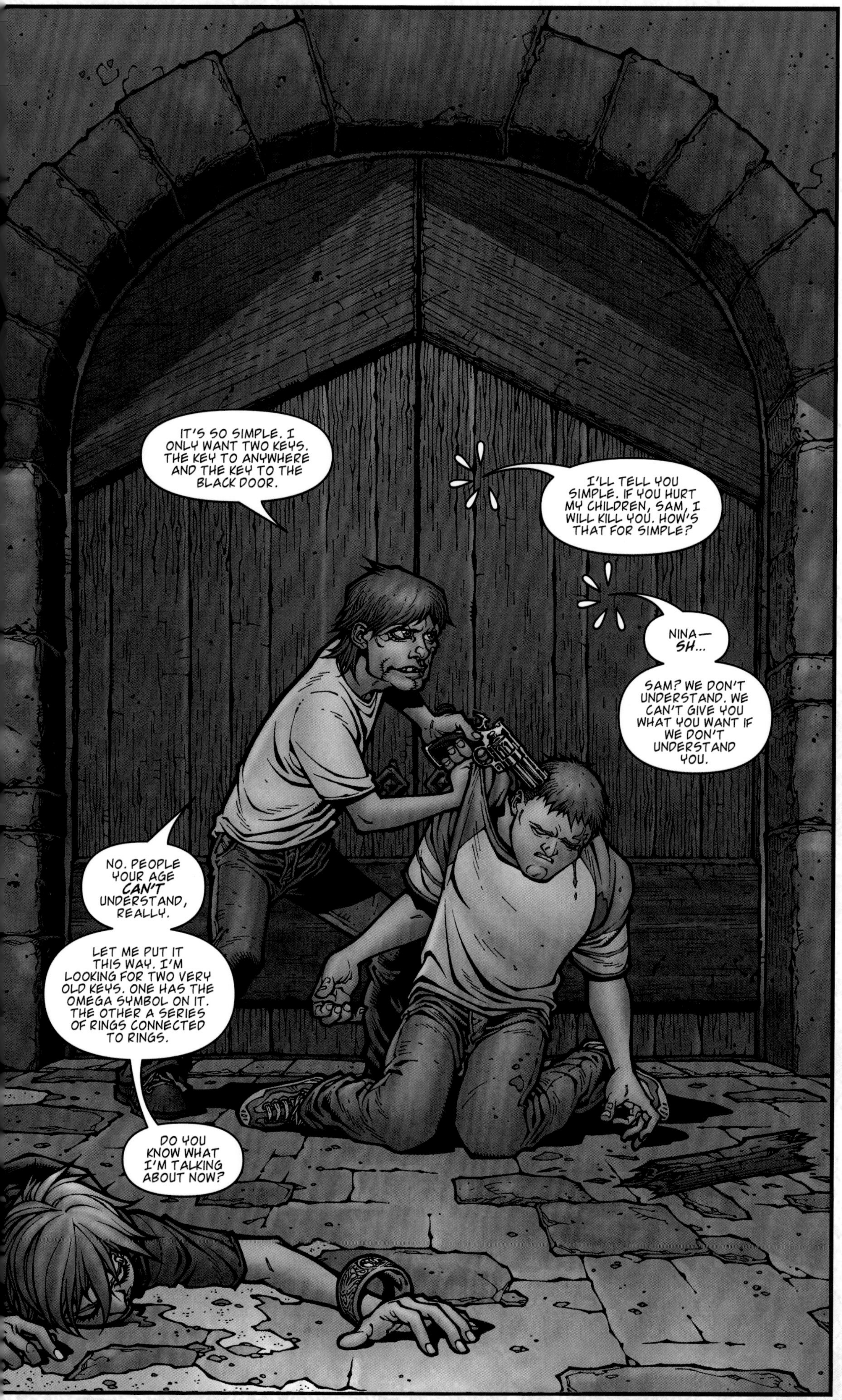
IT'S SO SIMPLE. I ONLY WANT TWO KEYS. THE KEY TO ANYWHERE AND THE KEY TO THE BLACK DOOR.
I'LL TELL YOU SIMPLE. IF YOU HURT MY CHILDREN, SAM, I WILL KILL YOU. HOW'S THAT FOR SIMPLE?
NINA— SH...
SAM? WE DON'T UNDERSTAND. WE CAN'T GIVE YOU WHAT YOU WANT IF WE DON'T UNDERSTAND YOU.
NO. PEOPLE YOUR AGE CAN'T UNDERSTAND, REALLY.
LET ME PUT IT THIS WAY. I'M LOOKING FOR TWO VERY OLD KEYS. ONE HAS THE OMEGA SYMBOL ON IT. THE OTHER A SERIES OF RINGS CONNECTED TO RINGS.
DO YOU KNOW WHAT I'M TALKING ABOUT NOW?

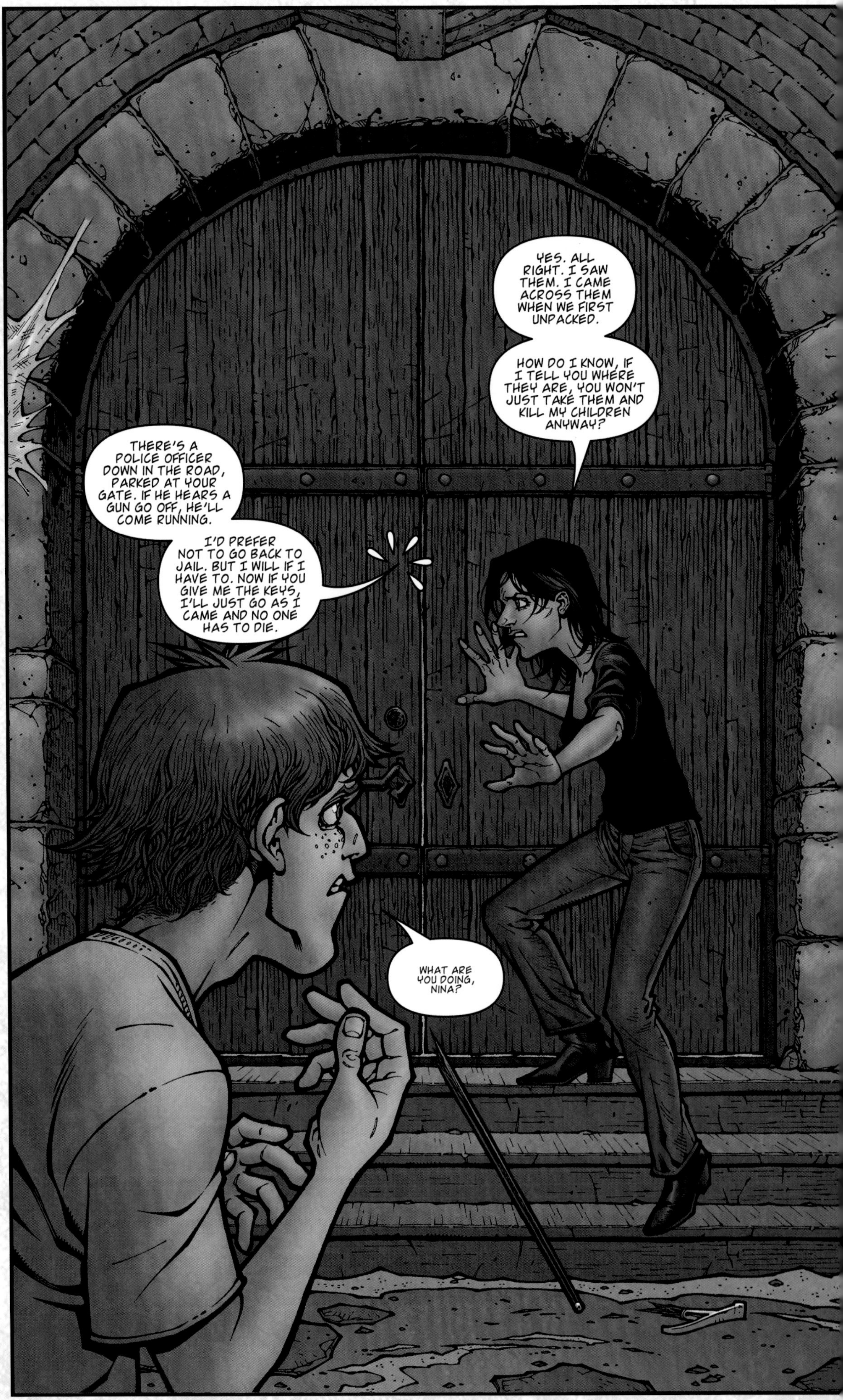
YES. ALL RIGHT. I SAW THEM. I CAME ACROSS THEM WHEN WE FIRST UNPACKED.
HOW DO I KNOW, IF I TELL YOU WHERE THEY ARE, YOU WON'T JUST TAKE THEM AND KILL MY CHILDREN ANYWAY?
THERE'S A POLICE OFFICER DOWN IN THE ROAD, PARKED AT YOUR GATE. IF HE HEARS A GUN GO OFF, HE'LL COME RUNNING.
I'D PREFER NOT TO GO BACK TO JAIL. BUT I WILL IF I HAVE TO. NOW IF YOU GIVE ME THE KEYS, I'LL JUST GO AS I CAME AND NO ONE HAS TO DIE.
WHAT ARE YOU DOING, NINA?

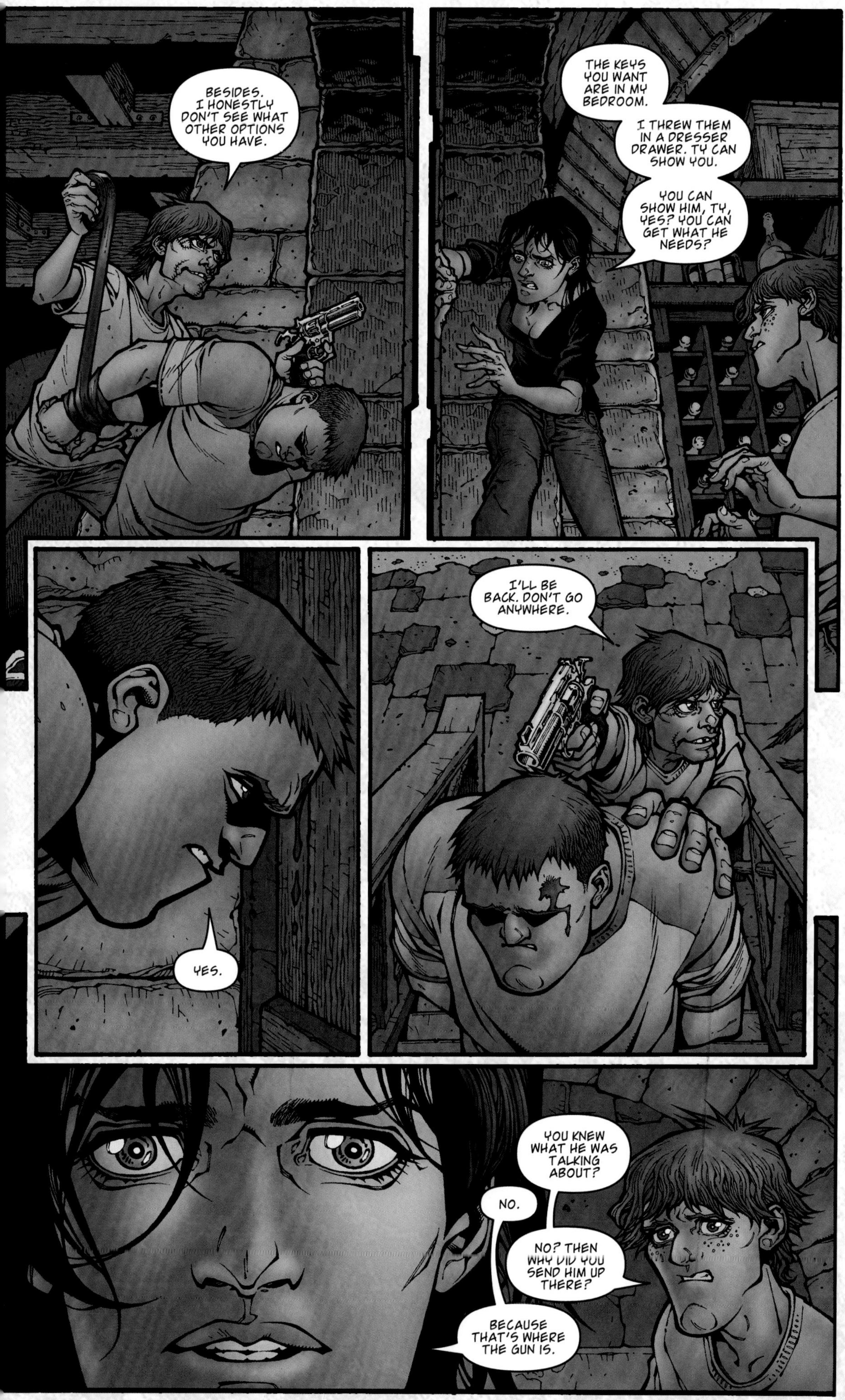
BESIDES. I HONESTLY DON'T SEE WHAT OTHER OPTIONS YOU HAVE.
THE KEYS YOU WANT ARE IN MY BEDROOM.
I THREW THEM IN A DRESSER DRAWER. TY CAN SHOW YOU.
YOU CAN SHOW HIM, TY, YES? YOU CAN GET WHAT HE NEEDS?
YES.
I'LL BE BACK. DON'T GO ANYWHERE.
YOU KNEW WHAT HE WAS TALKING ABOUT?
NO.
NO? THEN WHY DID YOU SEND HIM UP THERE?
BECAUSE THAT'S WHERE THE GUN IS.

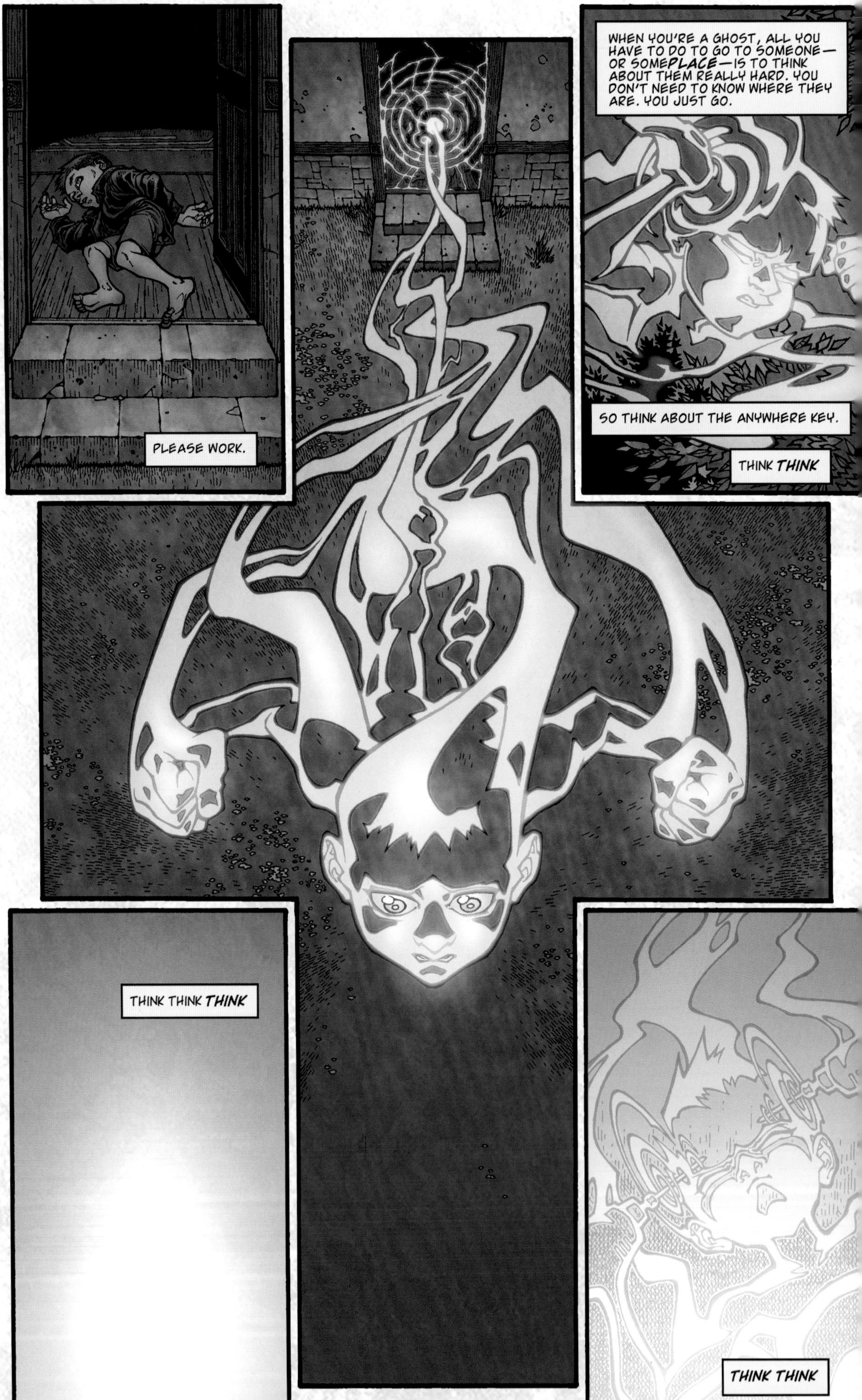
PLEASE WORK.
WHEN YOU'RE A GHOST, ALL YOU HAVE TO DO TO GO TO SOMEONE— OR SOME*PLACE*—IS TO THINK ABOUT THEM REALLY HARD. YOU DON'T NEED TO KNOW WHERE THEY ARE. YOU JUST GO.
SO THINK ABOUT THE ANYWHERE KEY.
THINK *THINK*
THINK THINK *THINK*
THINK THINK

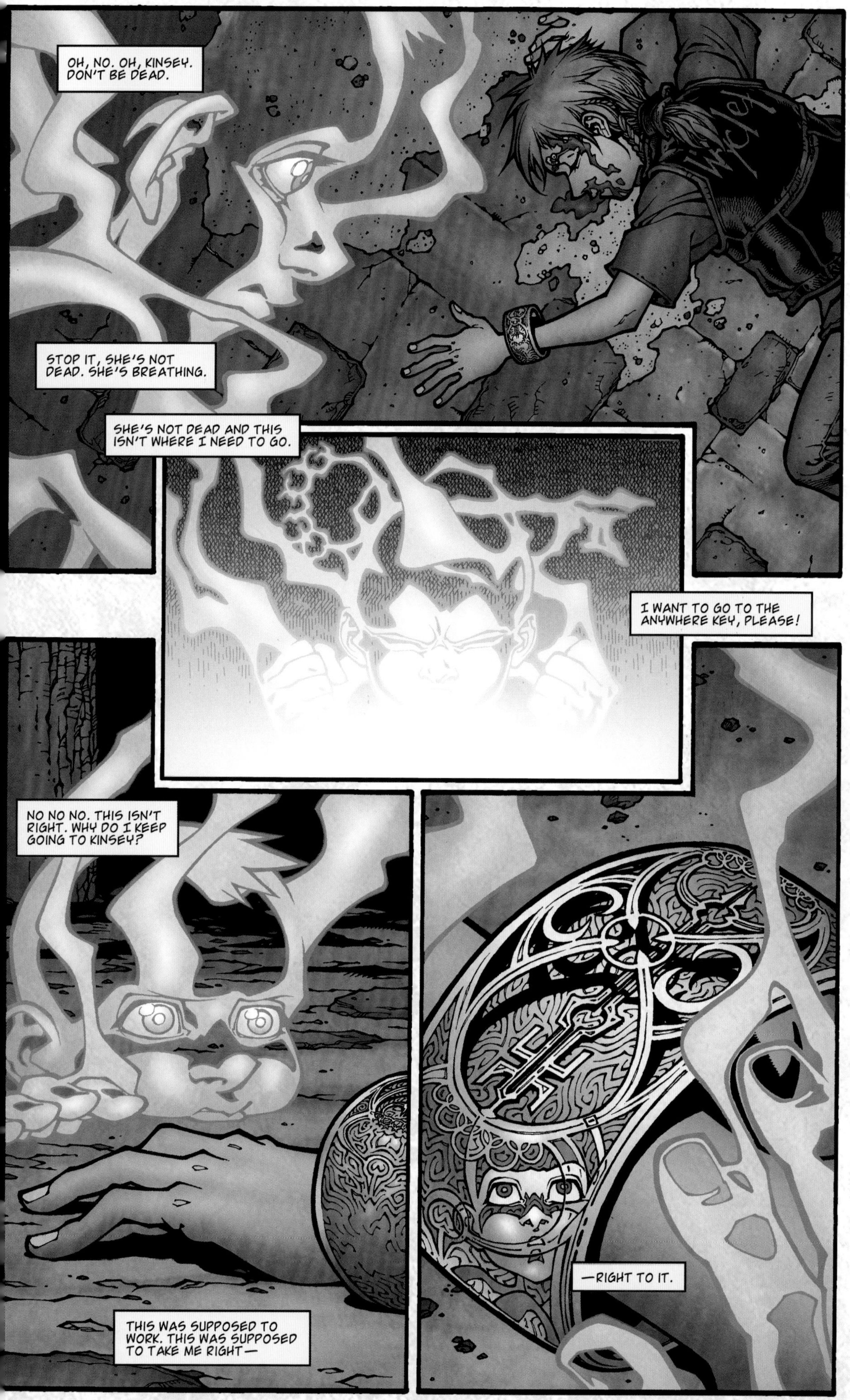

OH, NO. OH, KINSEY. DON'T BE DEAD.
STOP IT, SHE'S NOT DEAD. SHE'S BREATHING.
SHE'S NOT DEAD AND THIS ISN'T WHERE I NEED TO GO.
I WANT TO GO TO THE ANYWHERE KEY, PLEASE!
NO NO NO. THIS ISN'T RIGHT. WHY DO I KEEP GOING TO KINSEY?
THIS WAS SUPPOSED TO WORK. THIS WAS SUPPOSED TO TAKE ME RIGHT—
—RIGHT TO IT.

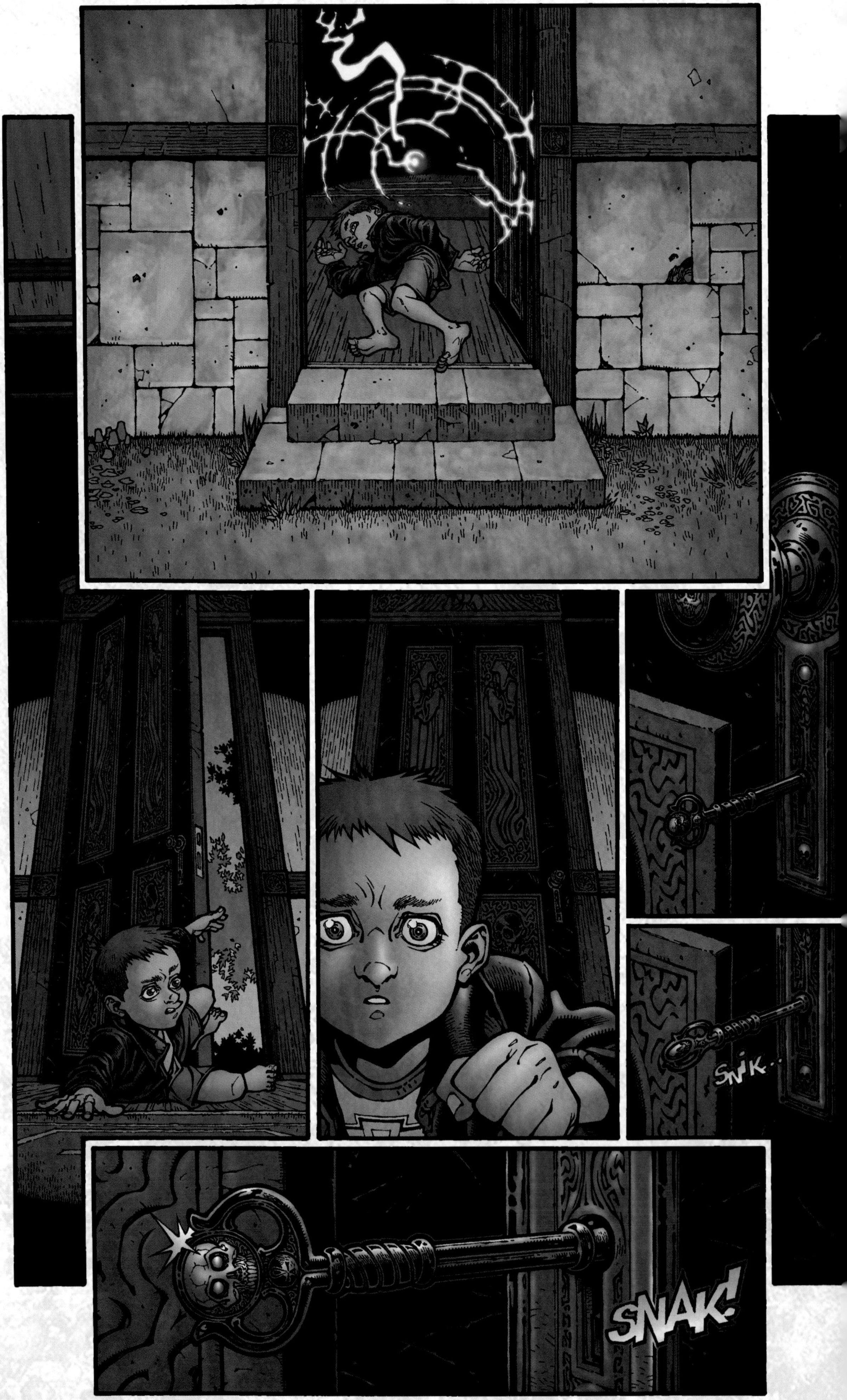
SNIK...
SNAK!

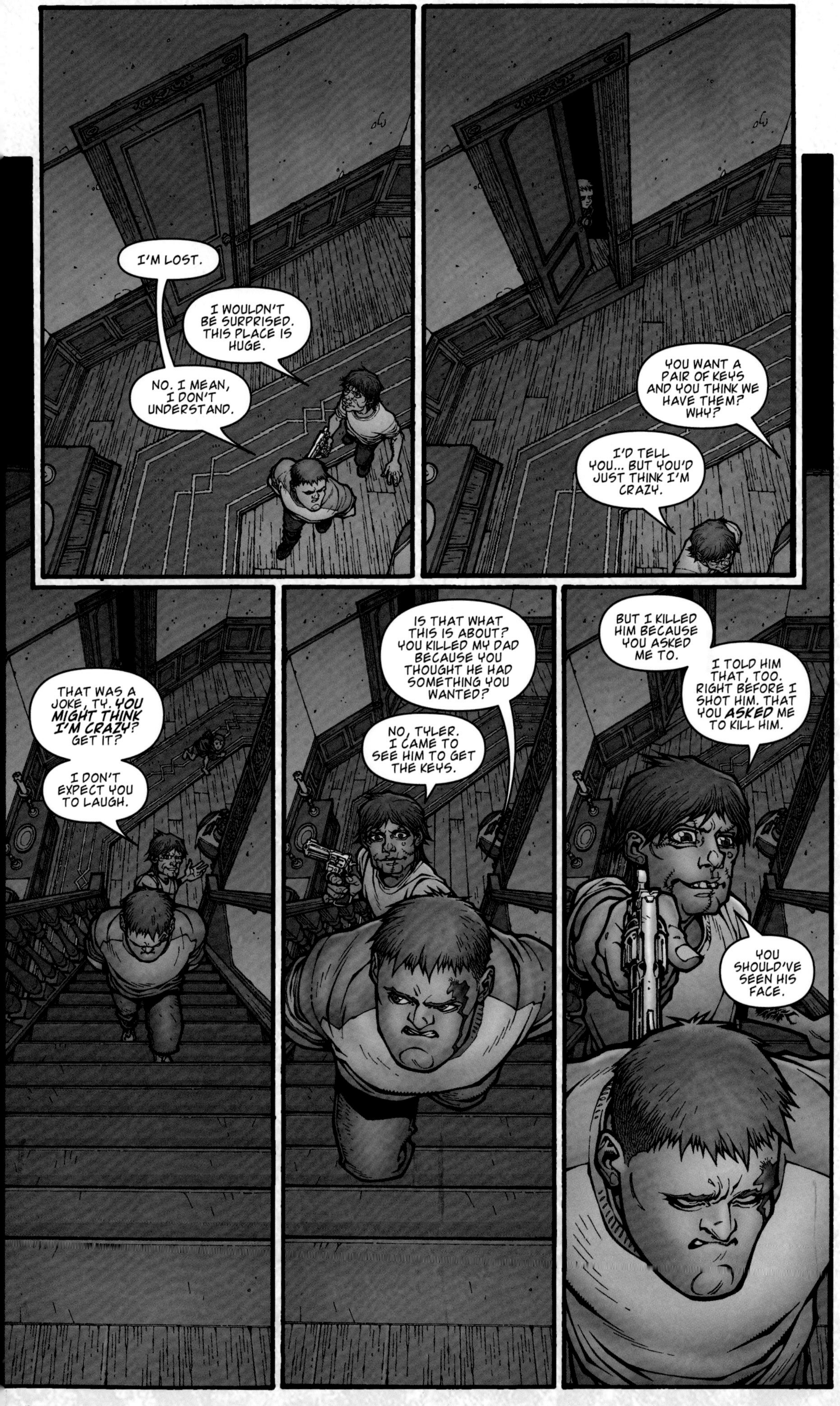
I'M LOST.
I WOULDN'T BE SURPRISED. THIS PLACE IS HUGE.
NO. I MEAN, I DON'T UNDERSTAND.
YOU WANT A PAIR OF KEYS AND YOU THINK WE HAVE THEM? WHY?
I'D TELL YOU... BUT YOU'D JUST THINK I'M CRAZY.
THAT WAS A JOKE, TY. *YOU MIGHT THINK I'M CRAZY*? GET IT?
I DON'T EXPECT YOU TO LAUGH.
IS THAT WHAT THIS IS ABOUT? YOU KILLED MY DAD BECAUSE YOU THOUGHT HE HAD SOMETHING YOU WANTED?
NO, TYLER. I CAME TO SEE HIM TO GET THE KEYS.
BUT I KILLED HIM BECAUSE YOU ASKED ME TO.
I TOLD HIM THAT, TOO. RIGHT BEFORE I SHOT HIM. THAT YOU *ASKED* ME TO KILL HIM.
YOU SHOULD'VE SEEN HIS FACE.

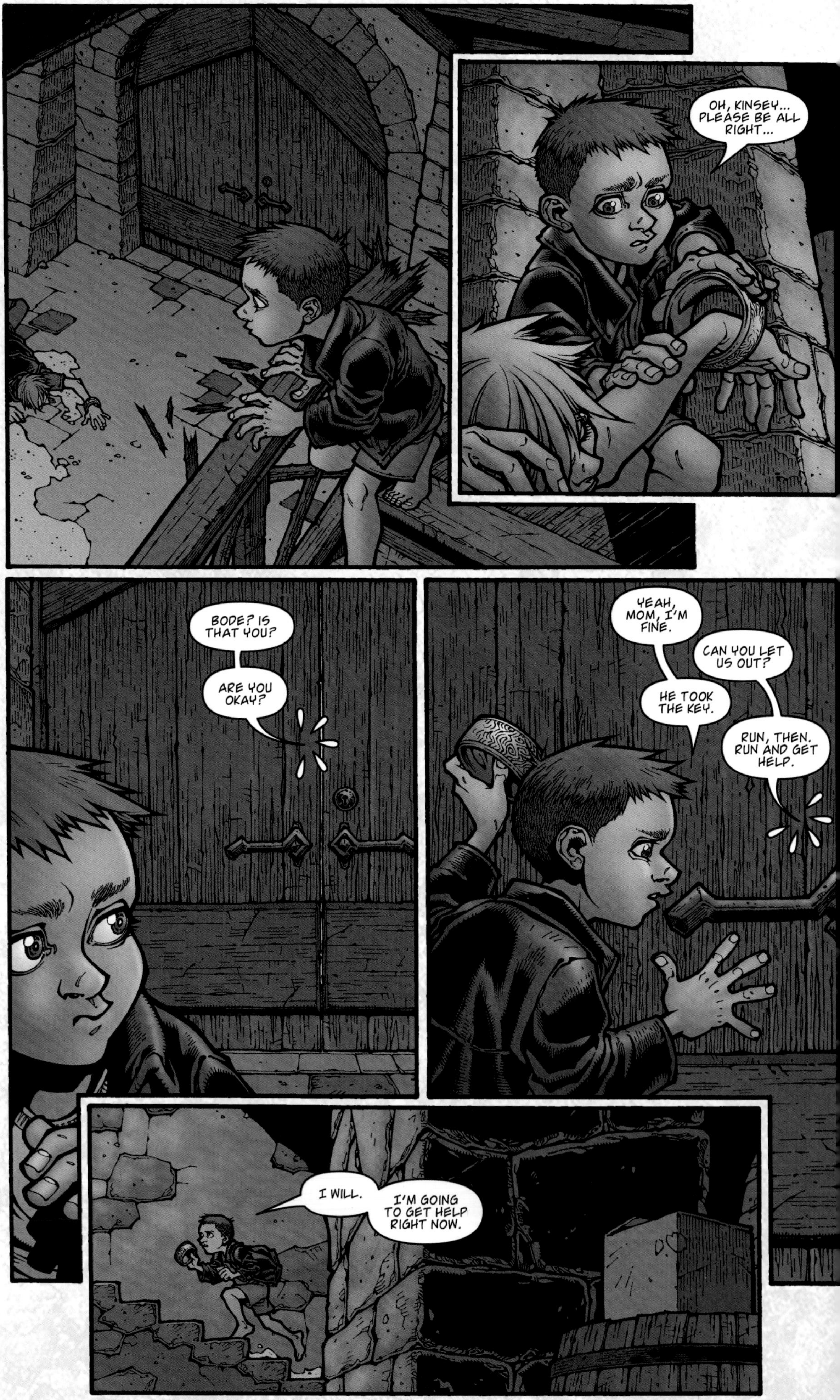

OH, KINSEY... PLEASE BE ALL RIGHT...
BODE? IS THAT YOU?
ARE YOU OKAY?
YEAH, MOM, I'M FINE.
HE TOOK THE KEY.
CAN YOU LET US OUT?
RUN, THEN. RUN AND GET HELP.
I WILL.
I'M GOING TO GET HELP RIGHT NOW.

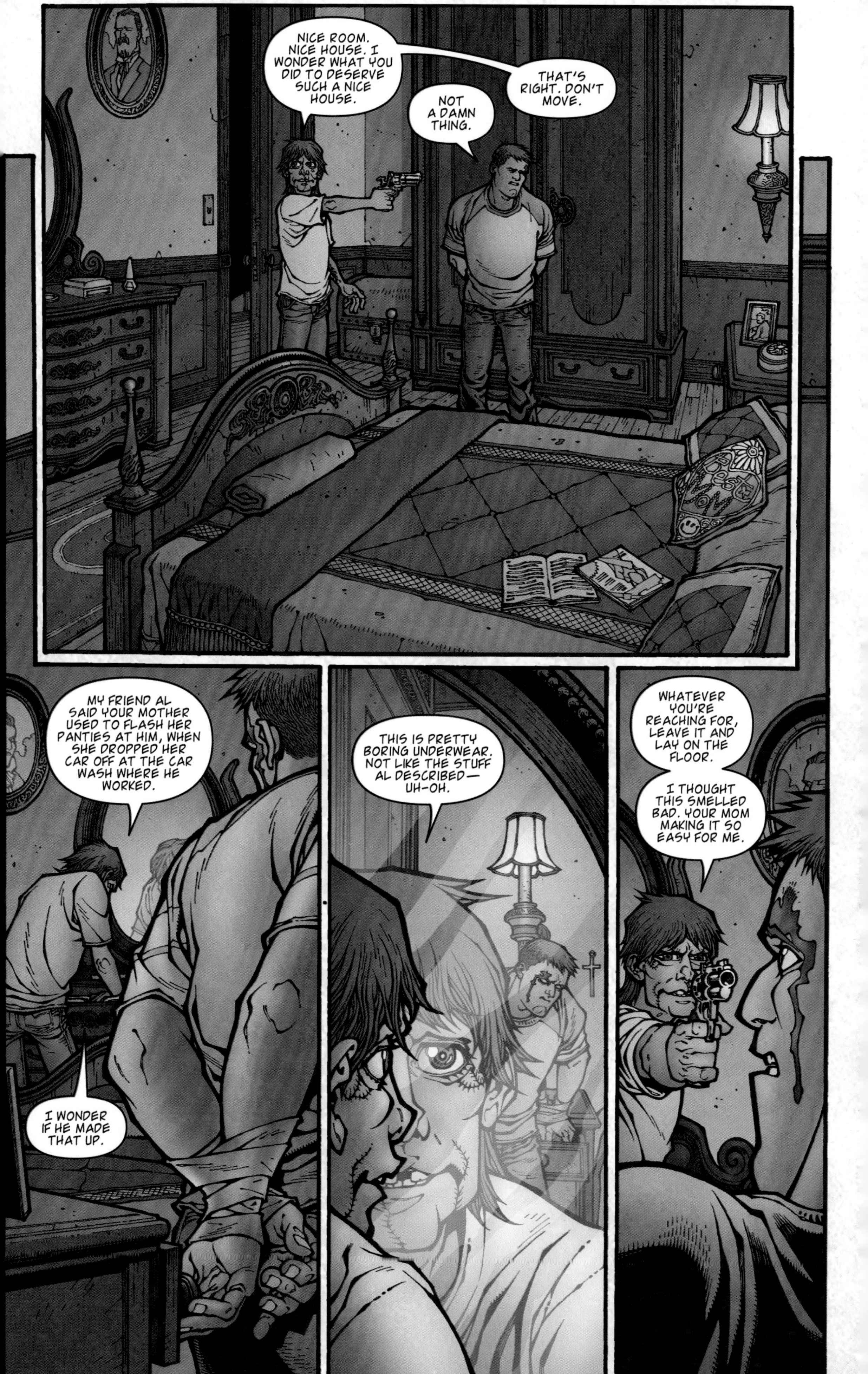
NICE ROOM. NICE HOUSE. I WONDER WHAT YOU DID TO DESERVE SUCH A NICE HOUSE.
NOT A DAMN THING.
THAT'S RIGHT. DON'T MOVE.
MY FRIEND AL SAID YOUR MOTHER USED TO FLASH HER PANTIES AT HIM, WHEN SHE DROPPED HER CAR OFF AT THE CAR WASH WHERE HE WORKED.
I WONDER IF HE MADE THAT UP.
THIS IS PRETTY BORING UNDERWEAR. NOT LIKE THE STUFF AL DESCRIBED— UH-OH.
WHATEVER YOU'RE REACHING FOR, LEAVE IT AND LAY ON THE FLOOR.
I THOUGHT THIS SMELLED BAD. YOUR MOM MAKING IT SO EASY FOR ME.

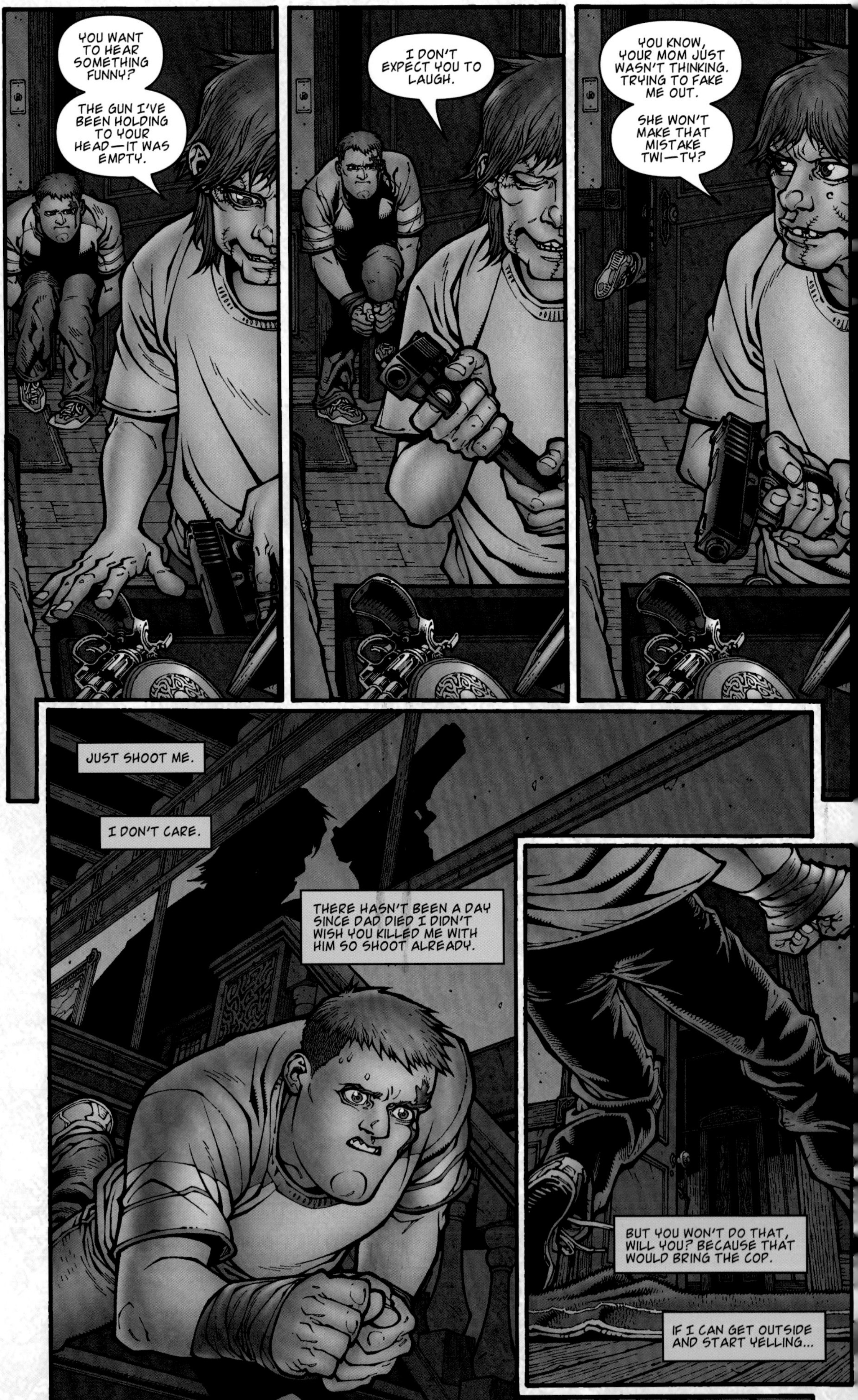
YOU WANT TO HEAR SOMETHING FUNNY?
THE GUN I'VE BEEN HOLDING TO YOUR HEAD—IT WAS EMPTY.
I DON'T EXPECT YOU TO LAUGH.
YOU KNOW, YOUR MOM JUST WASN'T THINKING. TRYING TO FAKE ME OUT.
SHE WON'T MAKE THAT MISTAKE TWI—TY?
JUST SHOOT ME.
I DON'T CARE.
THERE HASN'T BEEN A DAY SINCE DAD DIED I DIDN'T WISH YOU KILLED ME WITH HIM SO SHOOT ALREADY.
BUT YOU WON'T DO THAT, WILL YOU? BECAUSE THAT WOULD BRING THE COP.
IF I CAN GET OUTSIDE AND START YELLING...

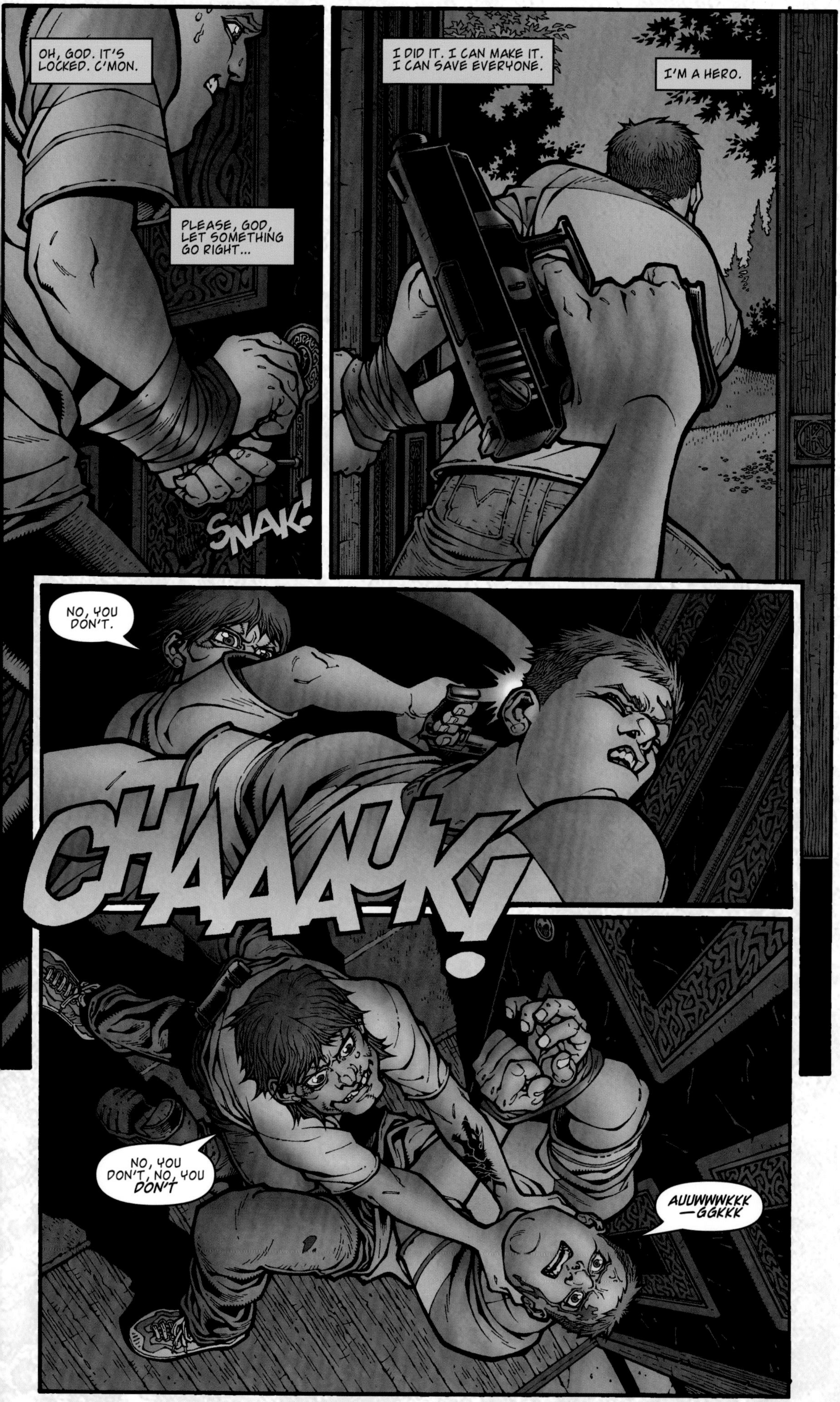
OH, GOD. IT'S LOCKED. C'MON.
PLEASE, GOD, LET SOMETHING GO RIGHT...
SNAK!
I DID IT. I CAN MAKE IT. I CAN SAVE EVERYONE.
I'M A HERO.
NO, YOU DON'T.
CHAAAUK!
NO, YOU DON'T, NO, YOU DON'T
AUUWWWKKK —GGKKK

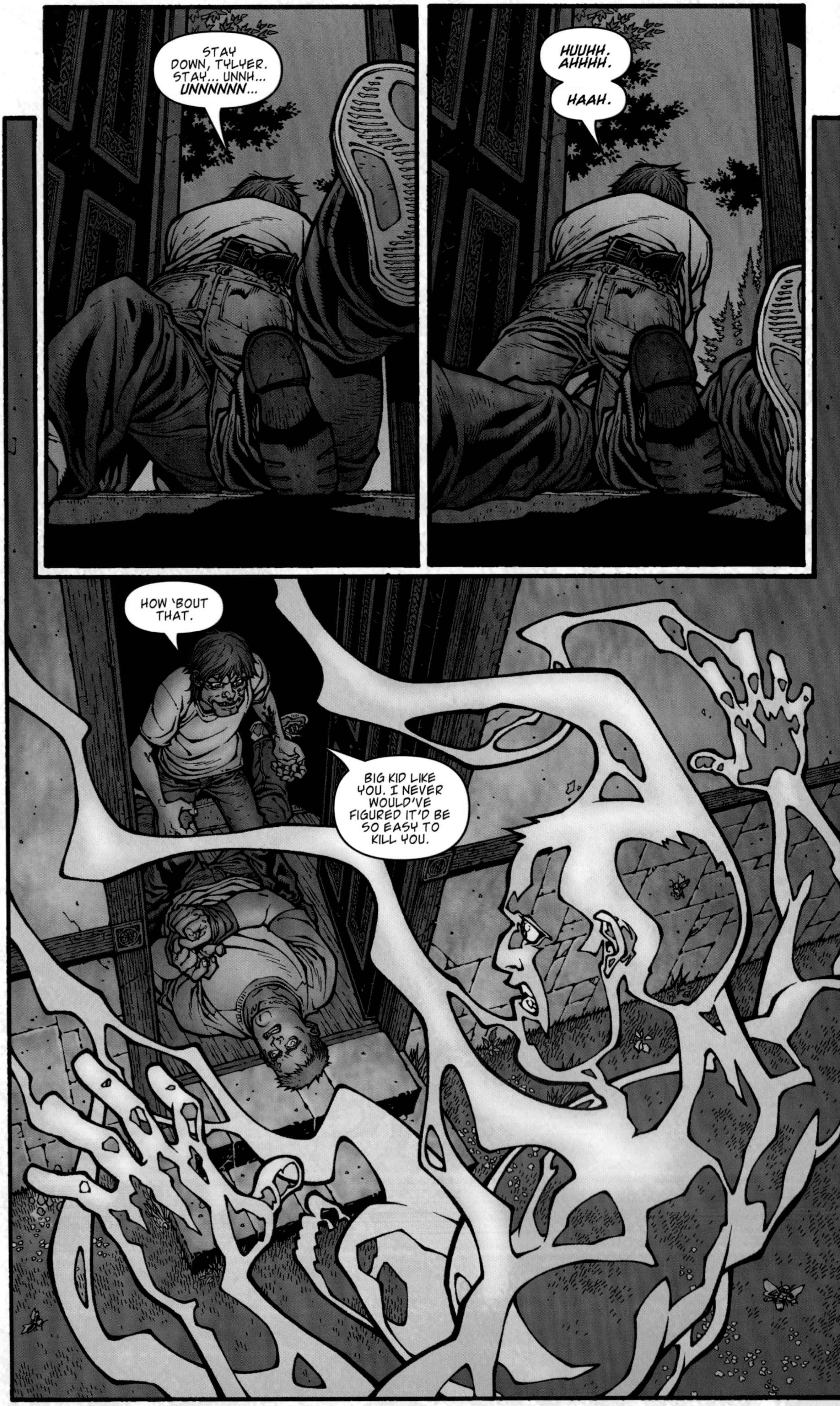
STAY DOWN, TYLYER. STAY... UNNH... UNNNNNN...
HUUHH. AHHHH.
HAAH.
HOW 'BOUT THAT.
BIG KID LIKE YOU. I NEVER WOULD'VE FIGURED IT'D BE SO EASY TO KILL YOU.

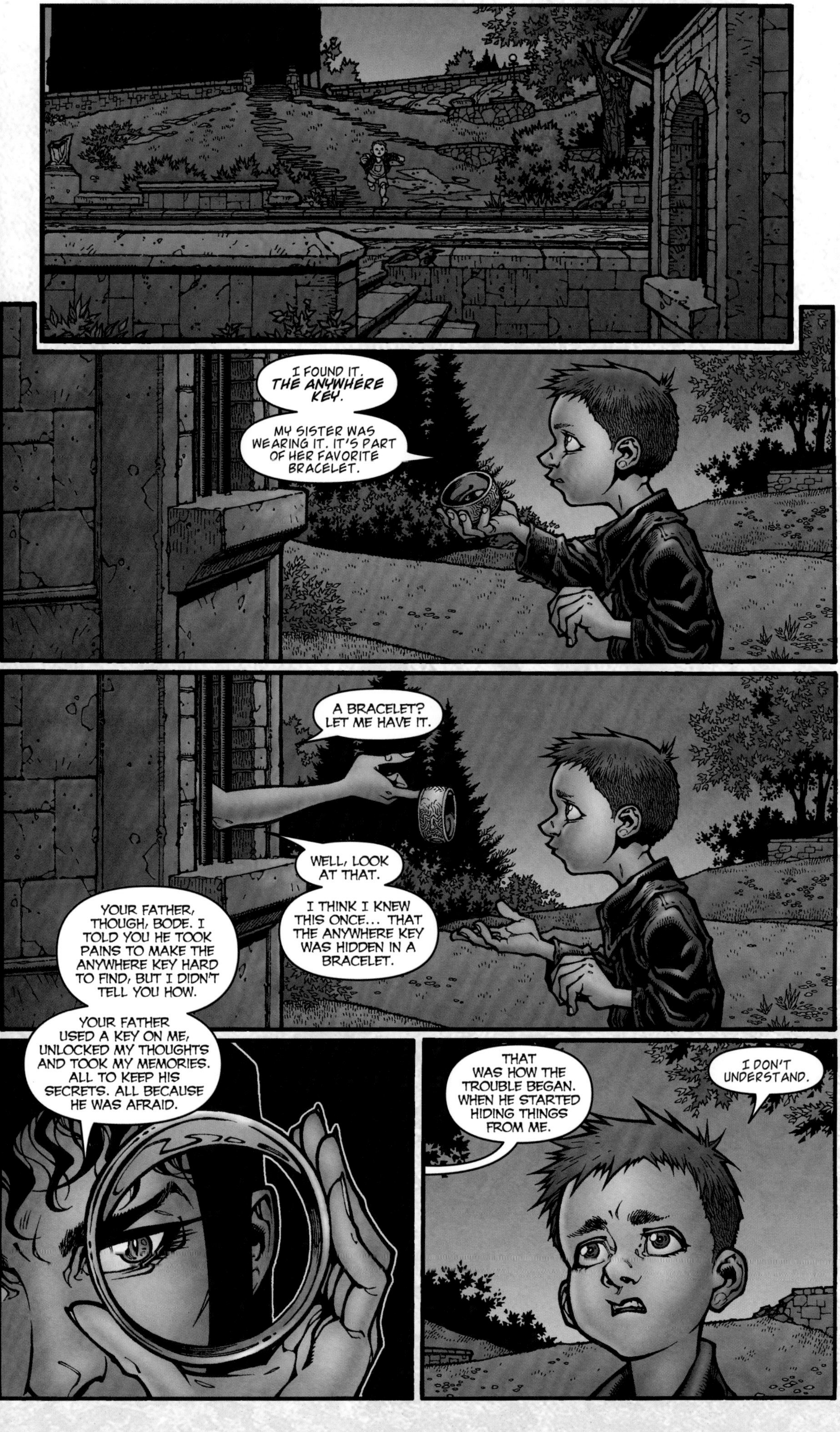
I FOUND IT. THE ANYWHERE KEY.
MY SISTER WAS WEARING IT. IT'S PART OF HER FAVORITE BRACELET.
A BRACELET? LET ME HAVE IT.
WELL, LOOK AT THAT.
I THINK I KNEW THIS ONCE... THAT THE ANYWHERE KEY WAS HIDDEN IN A BRACELET.
YOUR FATHER, THOUGH, BODE. I TOLD YOU HE TOOK PAINS TO MAKE THE ANYWHERE KEY HARD TO FIND, BUT I DIDN'T TELL YOU HOW.
YOUR FATHER USED A KEY ON ME, UNLOCKED MY THOUGHTS AND TOOK MY MEMORIES. ALL TO KEEP HIS SECRETS. ALL BECAUSE HE WAS AFRAID.
THAT WAS HOW THE TROUBLE BEGAN. WHEN HE STARTED HIDING THINGS FROM ME.
I DON'T UNDERSTAND.

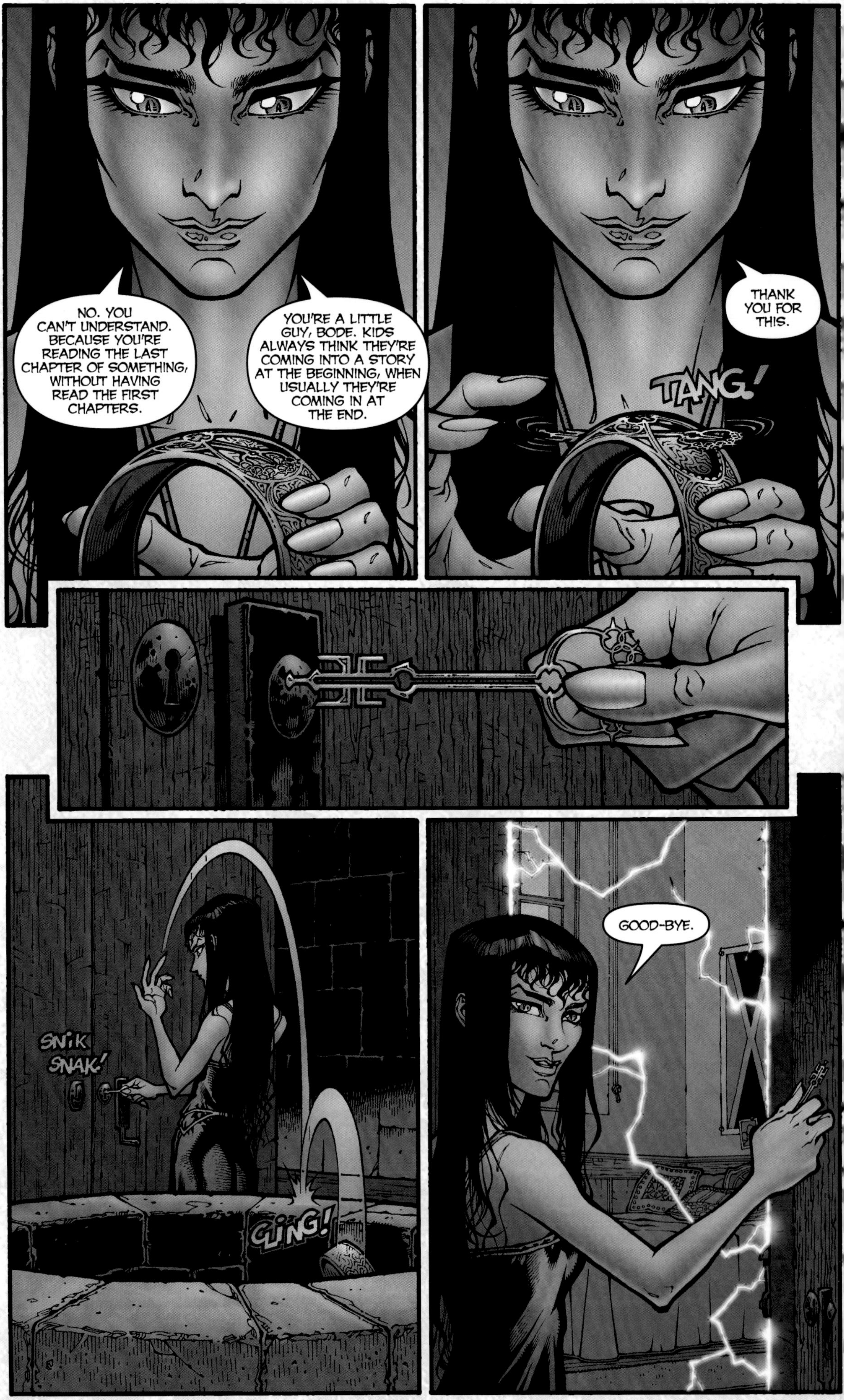
NO. YOU CAN'T UNDERSTAND. BECAUSE YOU'RE READING THE LAST CHAPTER OF SOMETHING, WITHOUT HAVING READ THE FIRST CHAPTERS.
YOU'RE A LITTLE GUY, BODE. KIDS ALWAYS THINK THEY'RE COMING INTO A STORY AT THE BEGINNING, WHEN USUALLY THEY'RE COMING IN AT THE END.
THANK YOU FOR THIS.
TANG!
SNIK SNAK!
CLING!
GOOD-BYE.

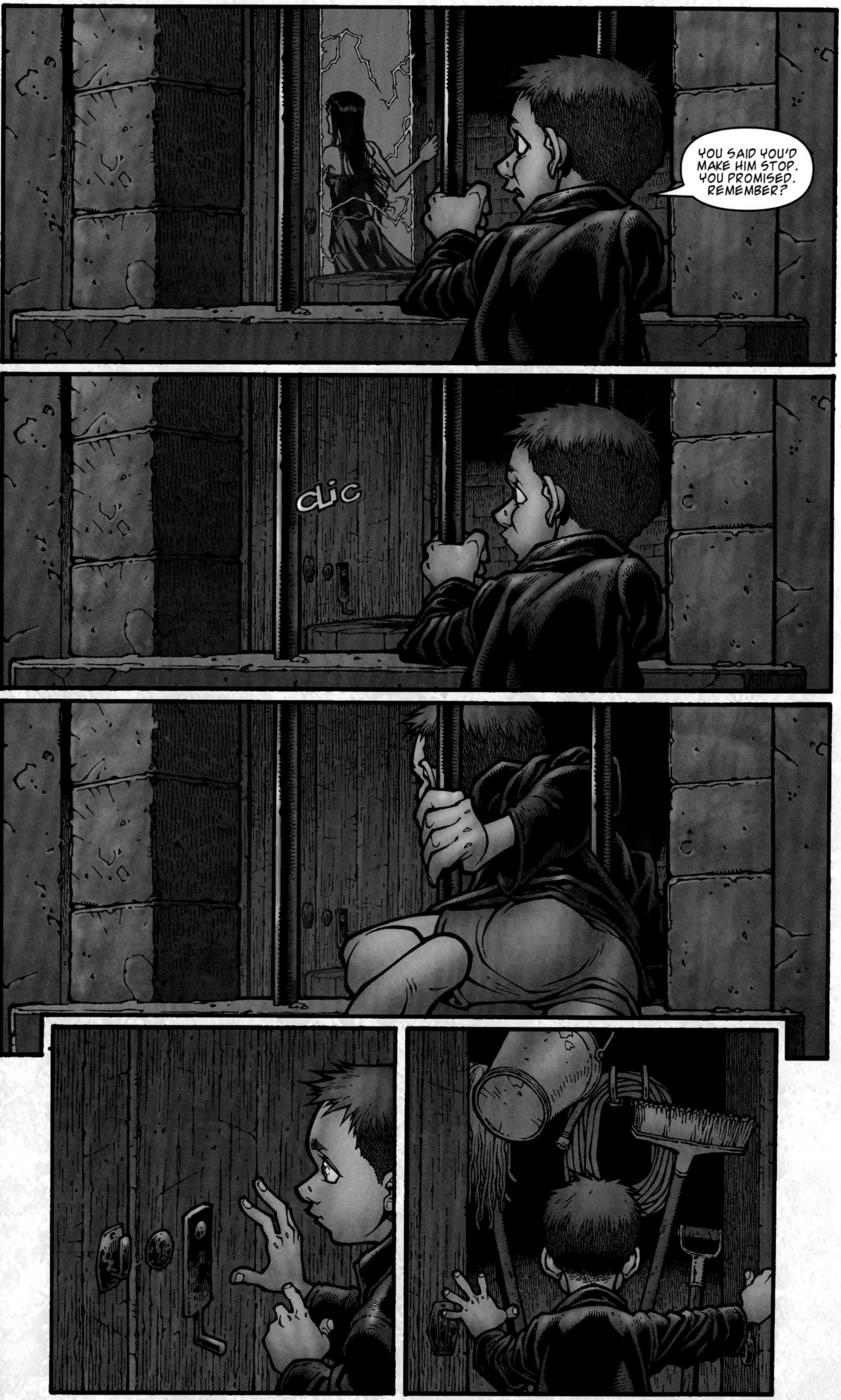
YOU SAID YOU'D MAKE HIM STOP. YOU PROMISED. REMEMBER?
CLIC

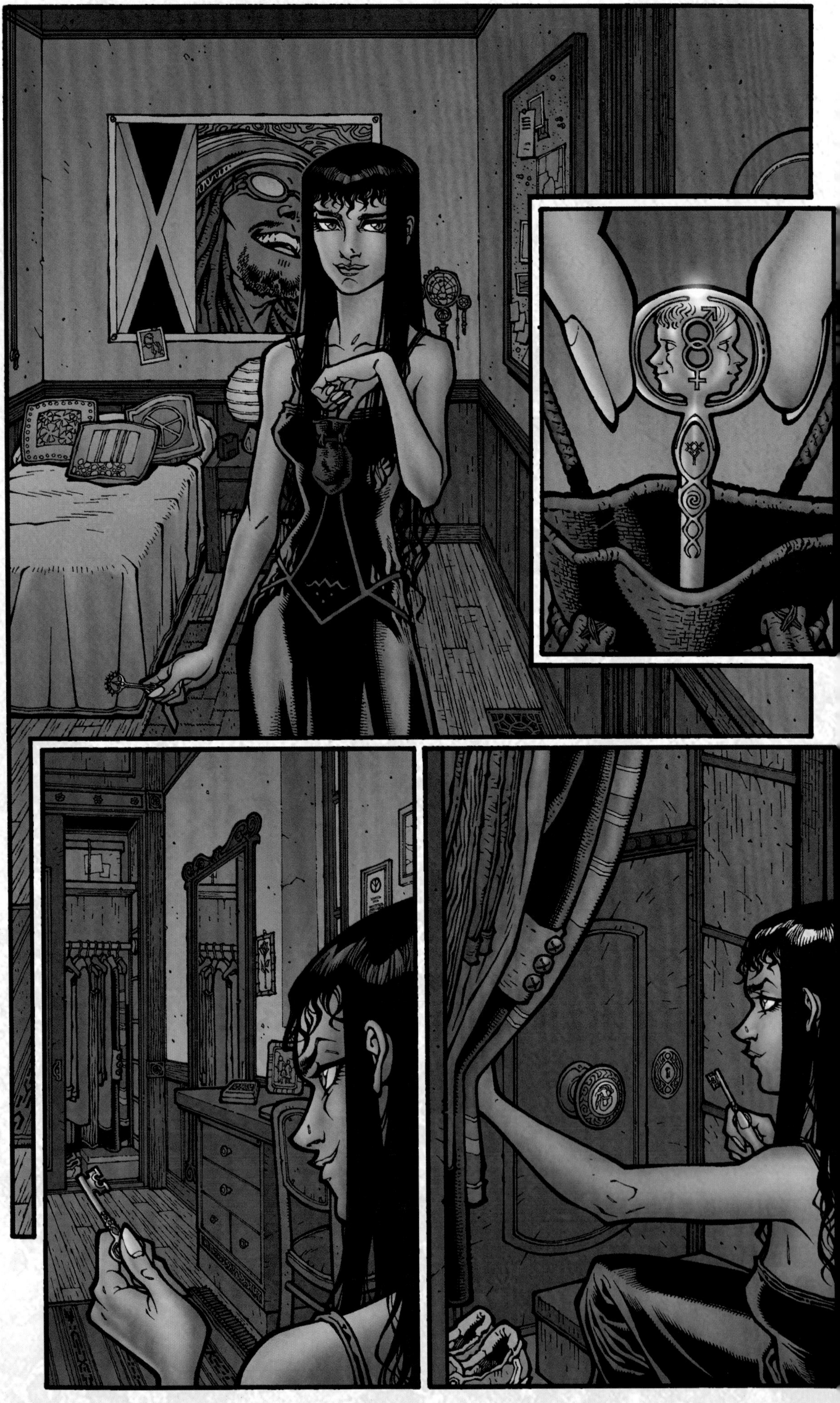

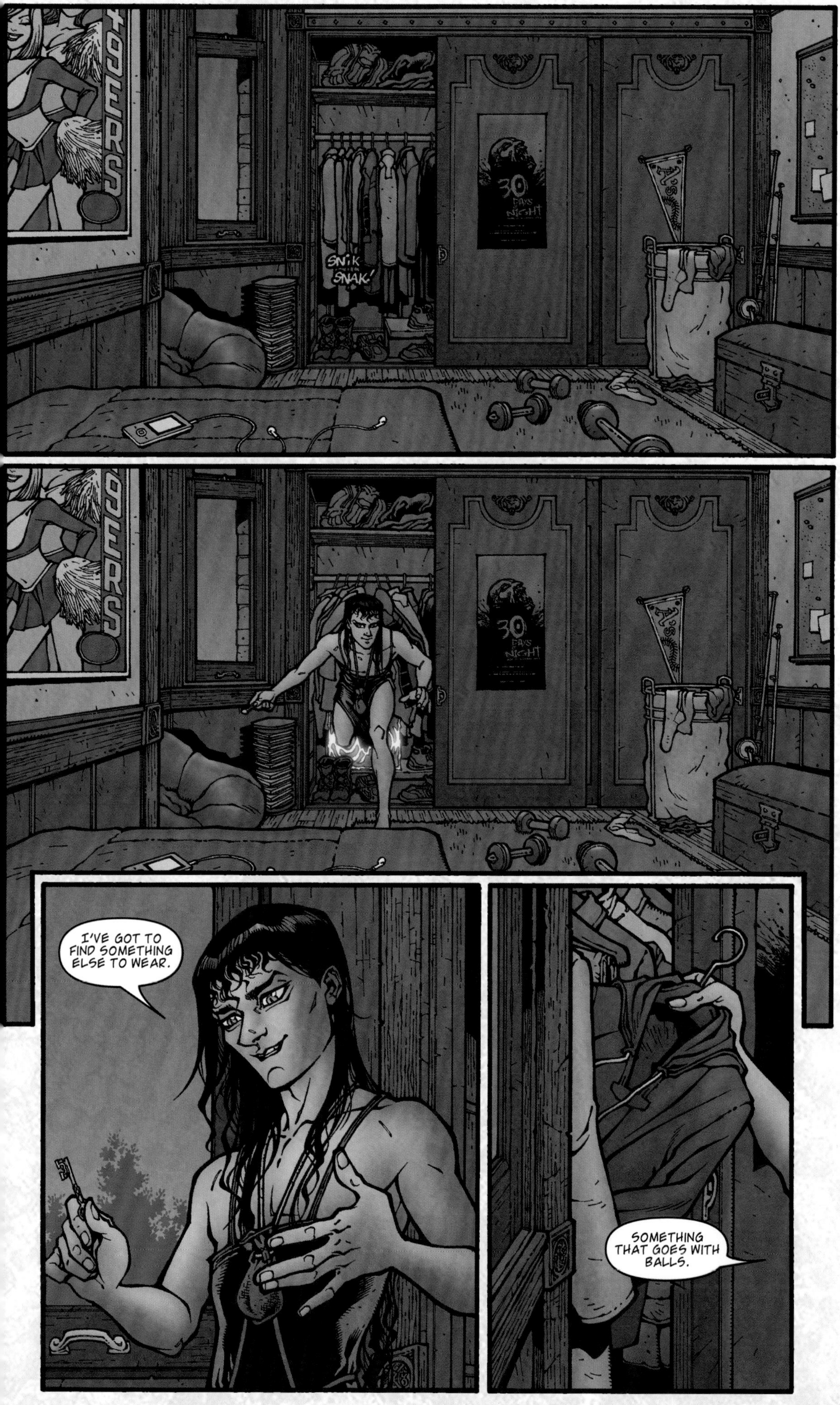

SNIK SNAK!
30 DAYS NIGHT
49ERS
I'VE GOT TO FIND SOMETHING ELSE TO WEAR.
SOMETHING THAT GOES WITH BALLS.

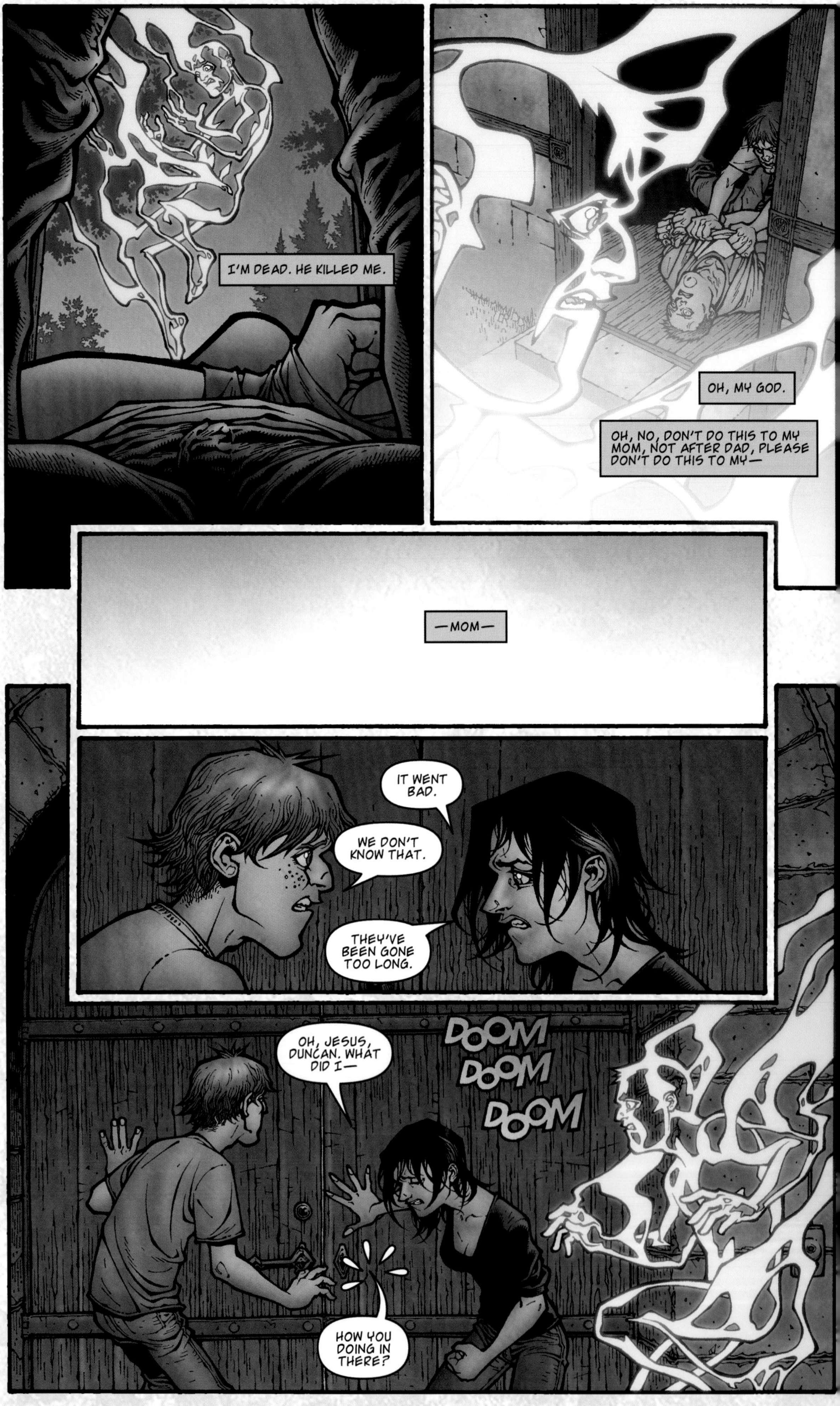
I'M DEAD. HE KILLED ME.
OH, MY GOD.
OH, NO, DON'T DO THIS TO MY MOM, NOT AFTER DAD, PLEASE DON'T DO THIS TO MY—
—MOM—
IT WENT BAD.
WE DON'T KNOW THAT.
THEY'VE BEEN GONE TOO LONG.
OH, JESUS, DUNCAN. WHAT DID I—
DOOM DOOM DOOM
HOW YOU DOING IN THERE?

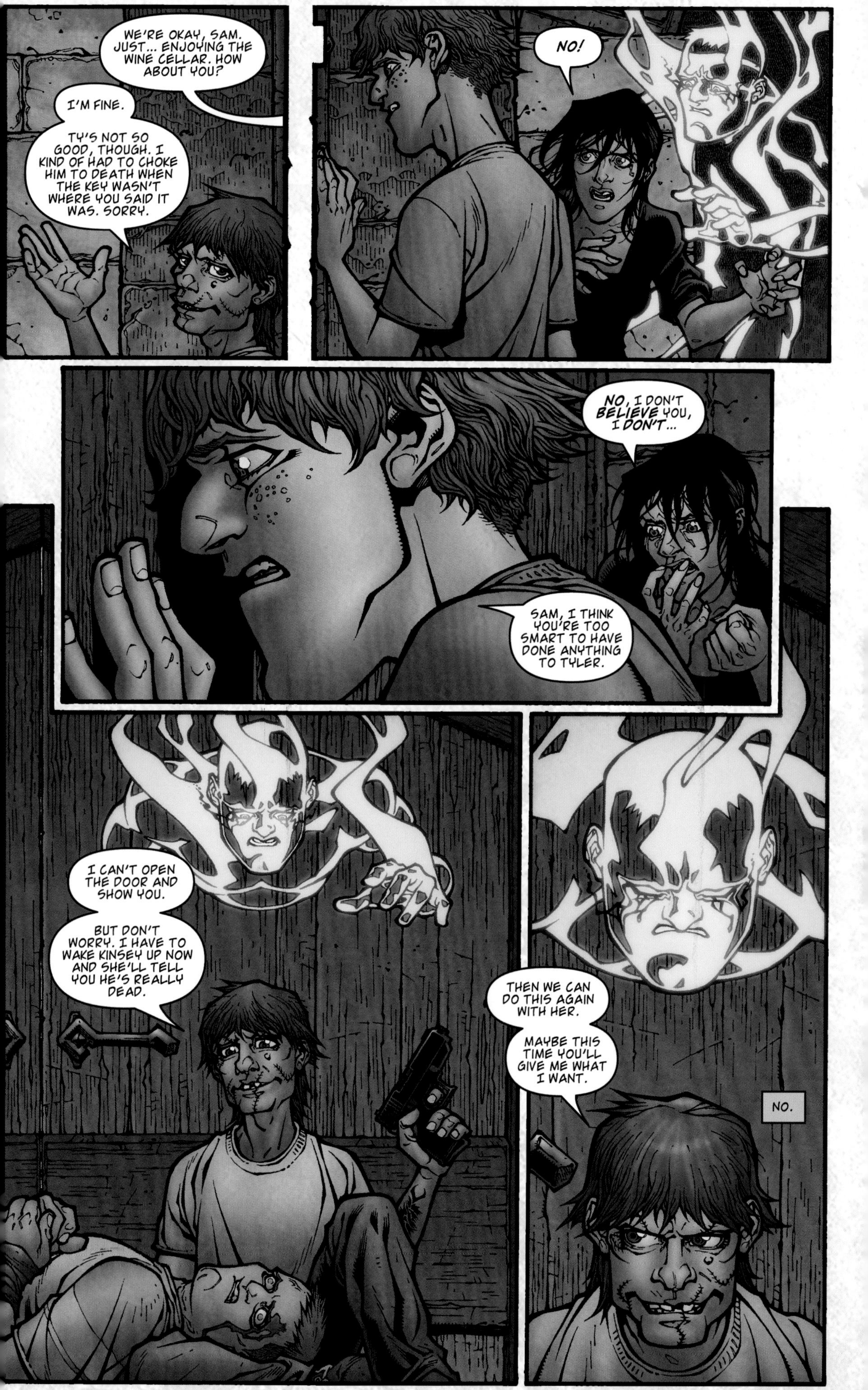
WE'RE OKAY, SAM. JUST... ENJOYING THE WINE CELLAR. HOW ABOUT YOU?
I'M FINE.
TY'S NOT SO GOOD, THOUGH. I KIND OF HAD TO CHOKE HIM TO DEATH WHEN THE KEY WASN'T WHERE YOU SAID IT WAS. SORRY.
NO!
NO, I DON'T BELIEVE YOU, I DON'T...
SAM, I THINK YOU'RE TOO SMART TO HAVE DONE ANYTHING TO TYLER.
I CAN'T OPEN THE DOOR AND SHOW YOU.
BUT DON'T WORRY. I HAVE TO WAKE KINSEY UP NOW AND SHE'LL TELL YOU HE'S REALLY DEAD.
THEN WE CAN DO THIS AGAIN WITH HER.
MAYBE THIS TIME YOU'LL GIVE ME WHAT I WANT.
NO.

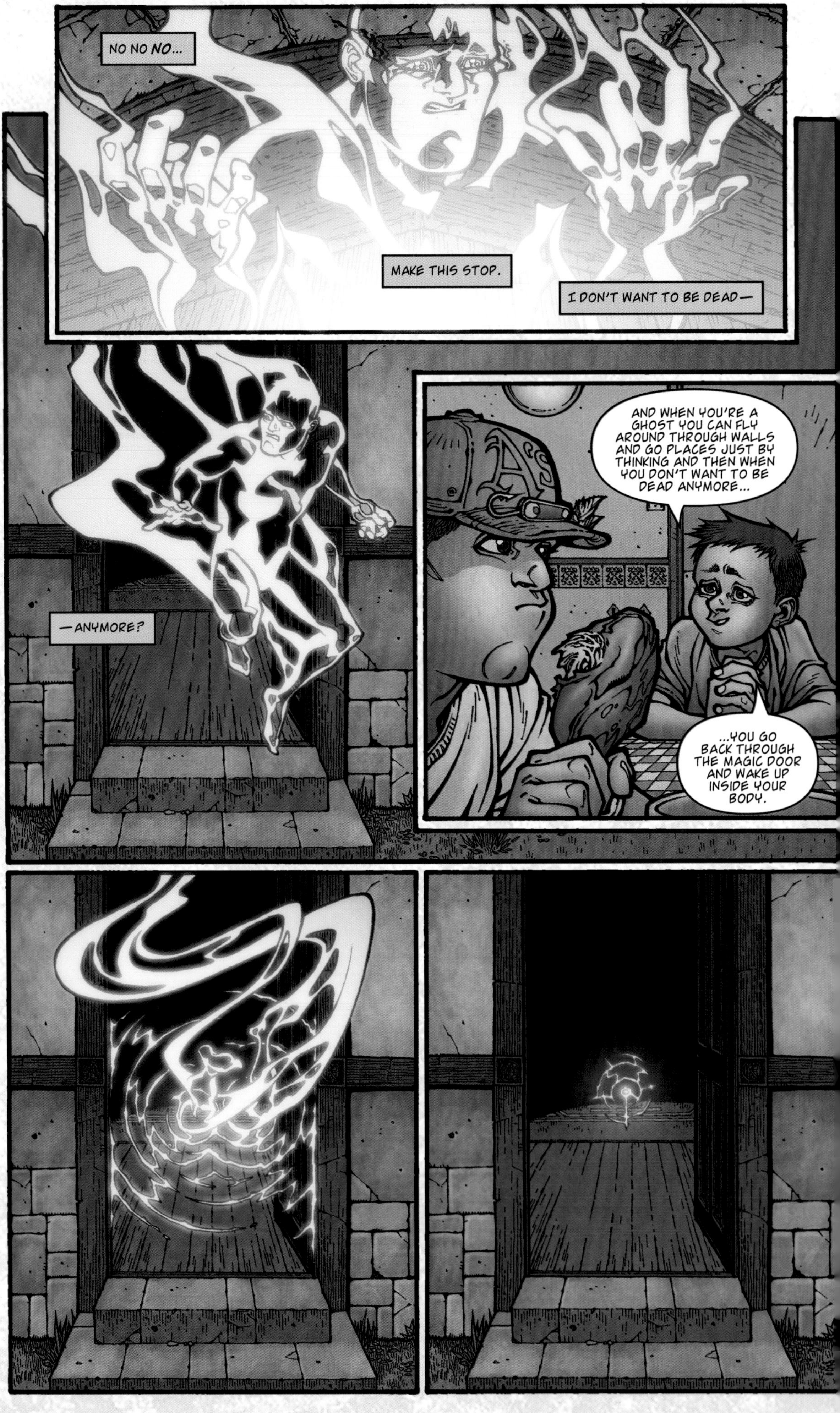
NO NO NO...
MAKE THIS STOP.
I DON'T WANT TO BE DEAD—
—ANYMORE?
AND WHEN YOU'RE A GHOST YOU CAN FLY AROUND THROUGH WALLS AND GO PLACES JUST BY THINKING AND THEN WHEN YOU DON'T WANT TO BE DEAD ANYMORE...
...YOU GO BACK THROUGH THE MAGIC DOOR AND WAKE UP INSIDE YOUR BODY.

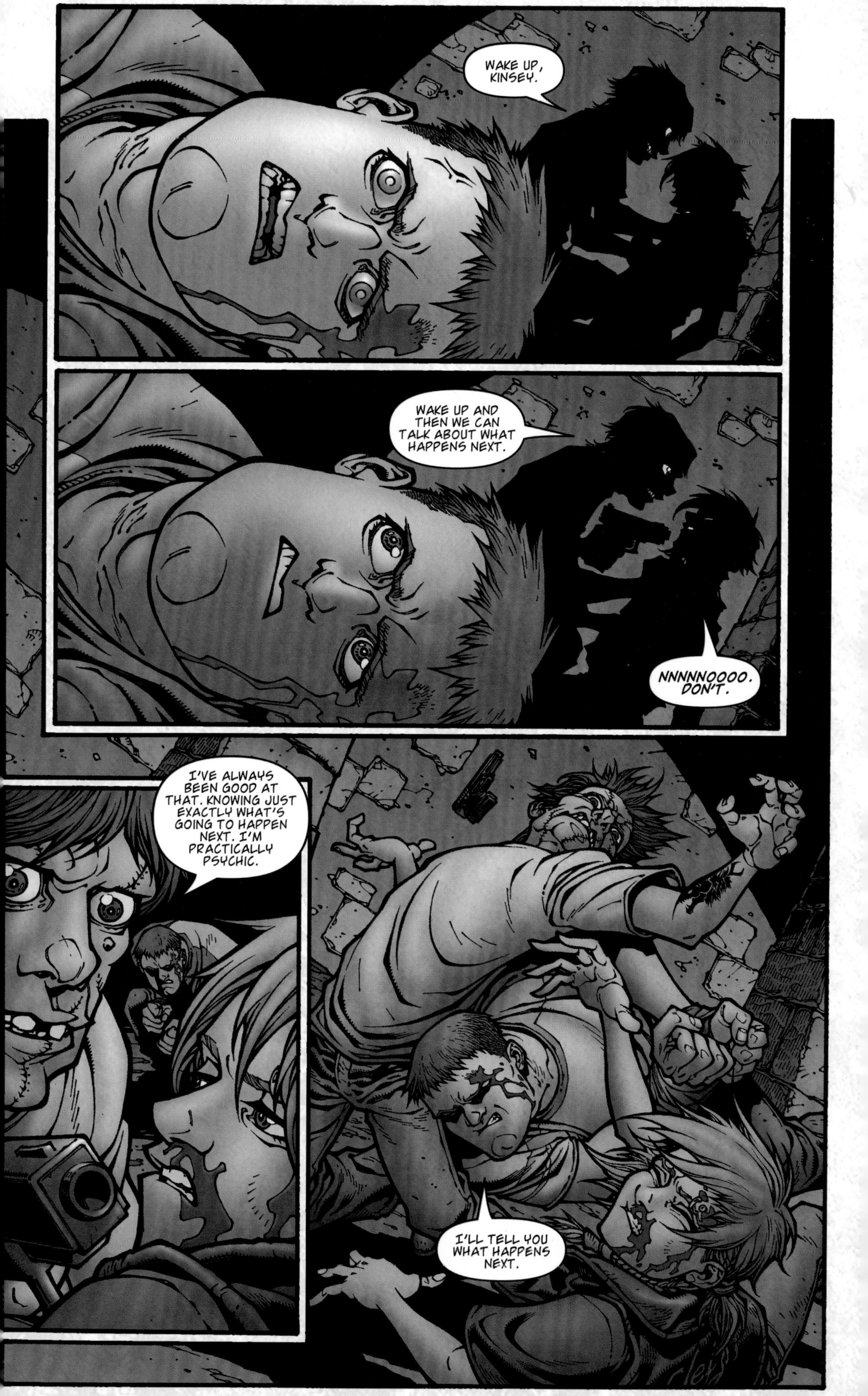
WAKE UP, KINSEY.
WAKE UP AND THEN WE CAN TALK ABOUT WHAT HAPPENS NEXT.
NNNNNOOOO. DON'T.
I'VE ALWAYS BEEN GOOD AT THAT. KNOWING JUST EXACTLY WHAT'S GOING TO HAPPEN NEXT. I'M PRACTICALLY PSYCHIC.
I'LL TELL YOU WHAT HAPPENS NEXT.

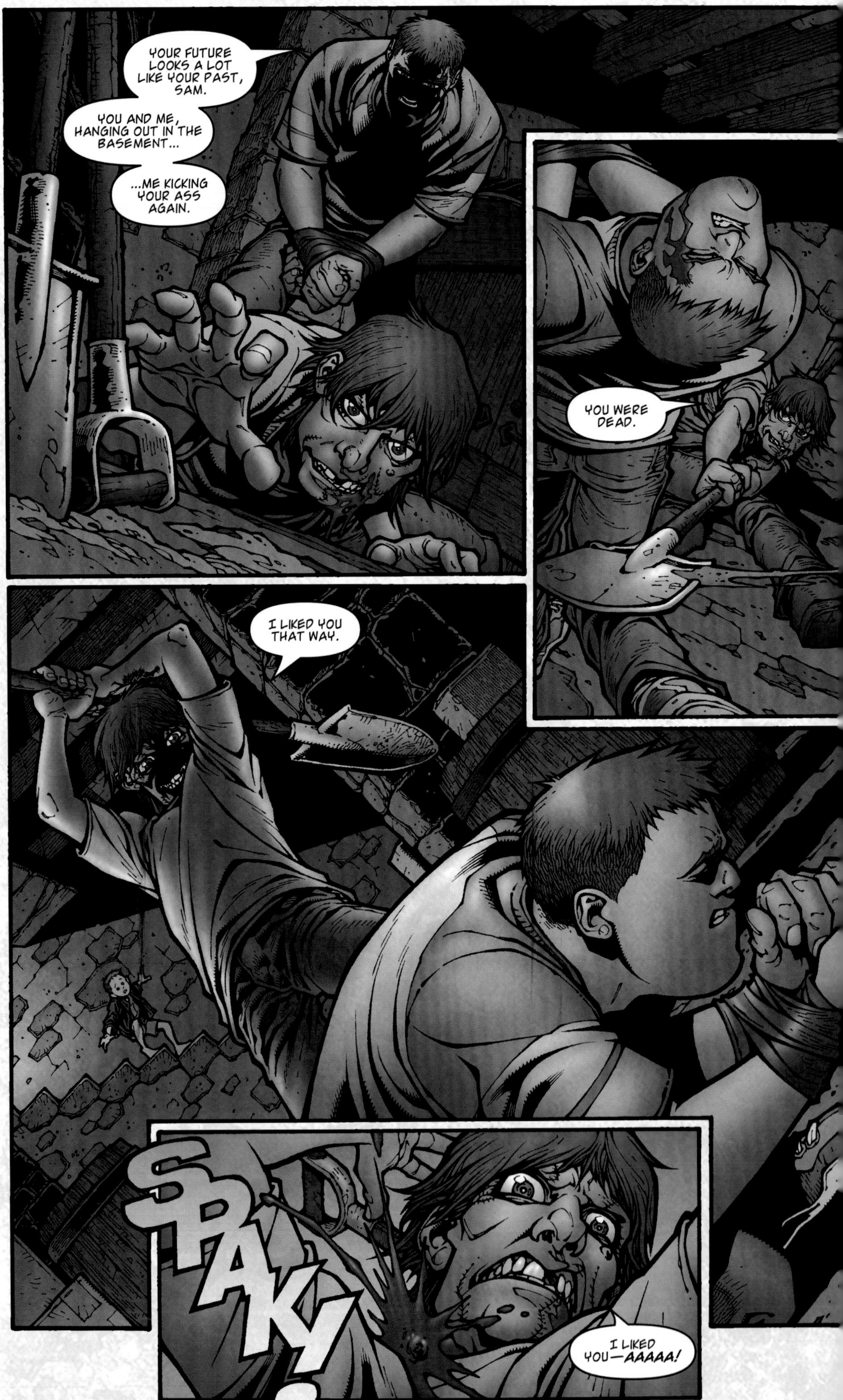
YOUR FUTURE LOOKS A LOT LIKE YOUR PAST, SAM.
YOU AND ME, HANGING OUT IN THE BASEMENT...
...ME KICKING YOUR ASS AGAIN.
YOU WERE DEAD.
I LIKED YOU THAT WAY.
SPAK!
I LIKED YOU—AAAAA!

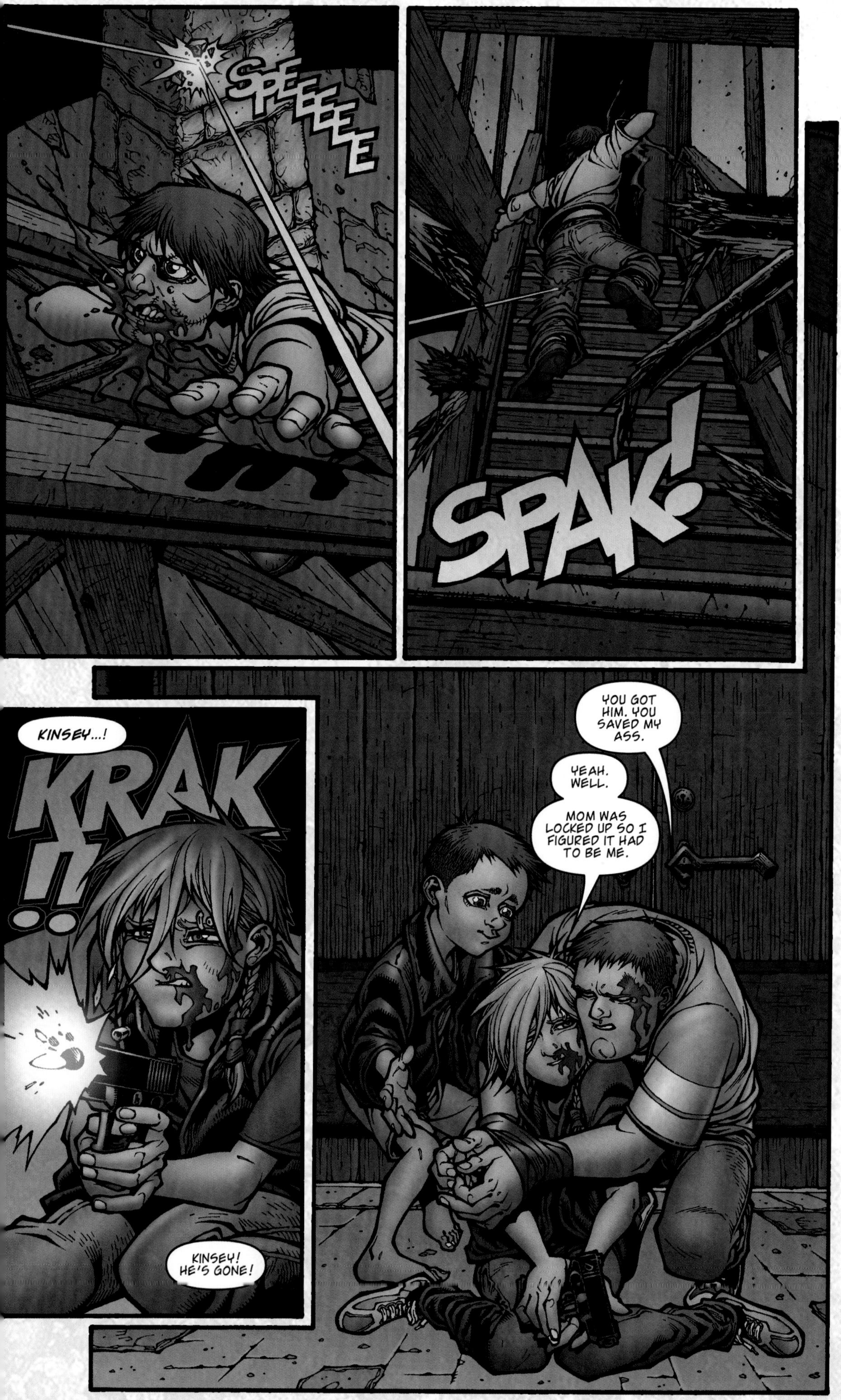

SPEEEEEE
SPAK!
KINSEY...!
KRAKK!!
KINSEY! HE'S GONE!
YOU GOT HIM. YOU SAVED MY ASS.
YEAH. WELL.
MOM WAS LOCKED UP SO I FIGURED IT HAD TO BE ME.

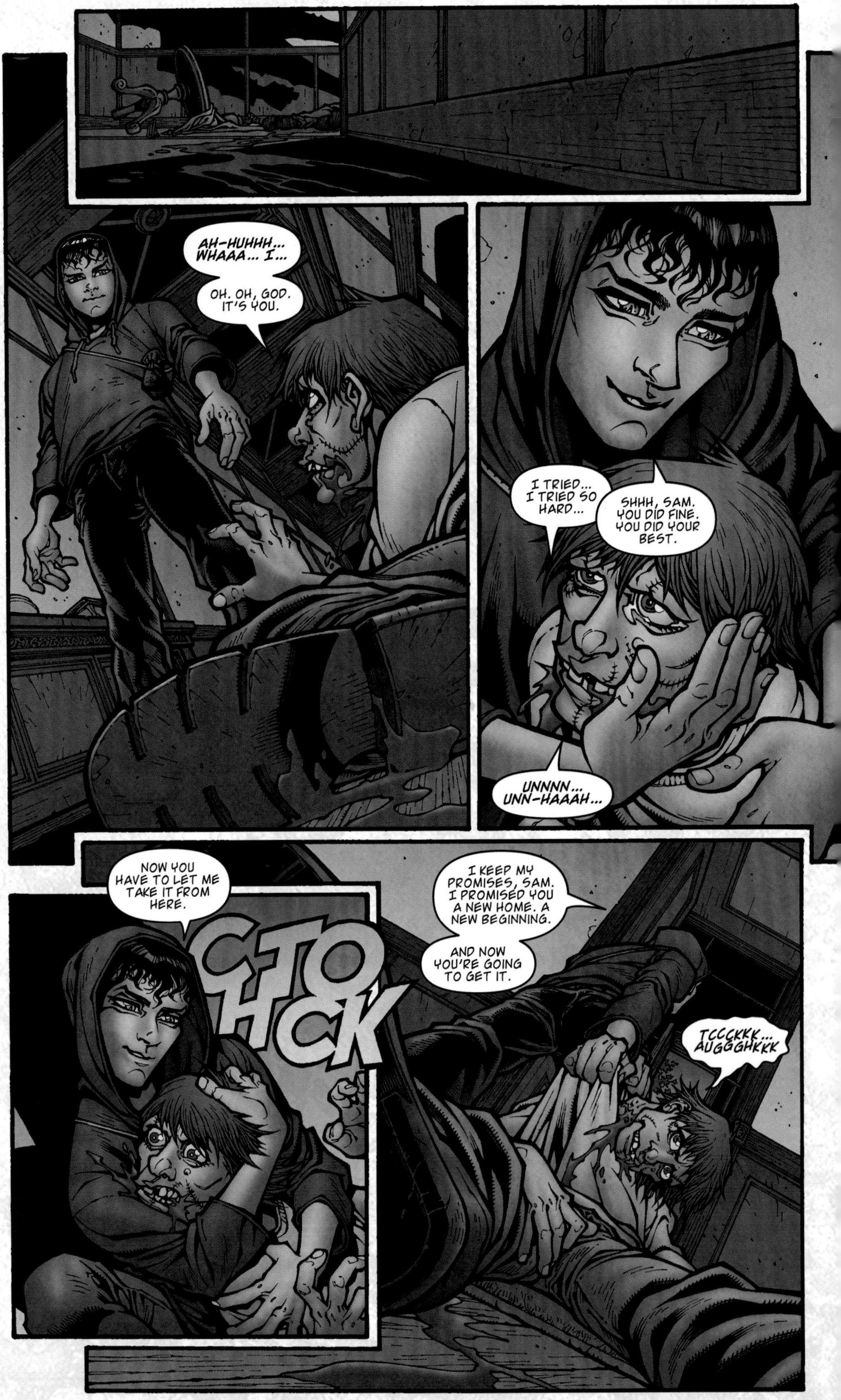
AH-HUHHH... WHAAA... I...
OH. OH, GOD. IT'S YOU.
I TRIED... I TRIED SO HARD...
SHHH, SAM. YOU DID FINE. YOU DID YOUR BEST.
UNNNN... UNN-HAAAH...
NOW YOU HAVE TO LET ME TAKE IT FROM HERE.
CTO
HCK
I KEEP MY PROMISES, SAM. I PROMISED YOU A NEW HOME. A NEW BEGINNING.
AND NOW YOU'RE GOING TO GET IT.
TCCCKKK... AUGGGHKKK

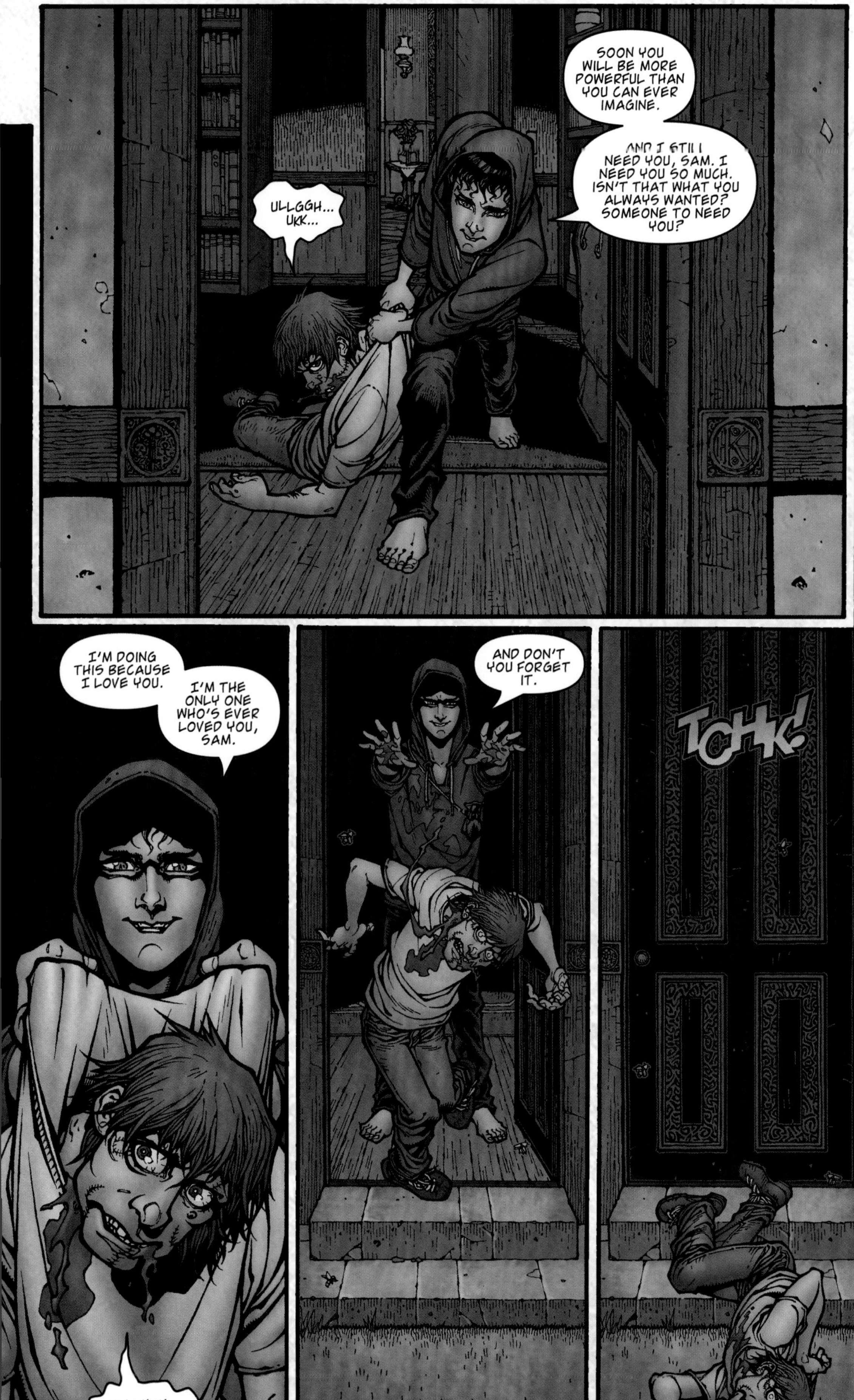
SOON YOU WILL BE MORE POWERFUL THAN YOU CAN EVER IMAGINE.
AND I STILL NEED YOU, SAM. I NEED YOU SO MUCH. ISN'T THAT WHAT YOU ALWAYS WANTED? SOMEONE TO NEED YOU?
ULLGGH... UKK...
I'M DOING THIS BECAUSE I LOVE YOU.
I'M THE ONLY ONE WHO'S EVER LOVED YOU, SAM.
PLLLUGH... NUUHKK...
AND DON'T YOU FORGET IT.
TCHK!

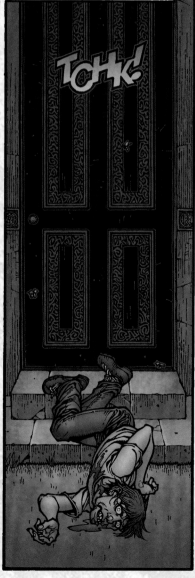

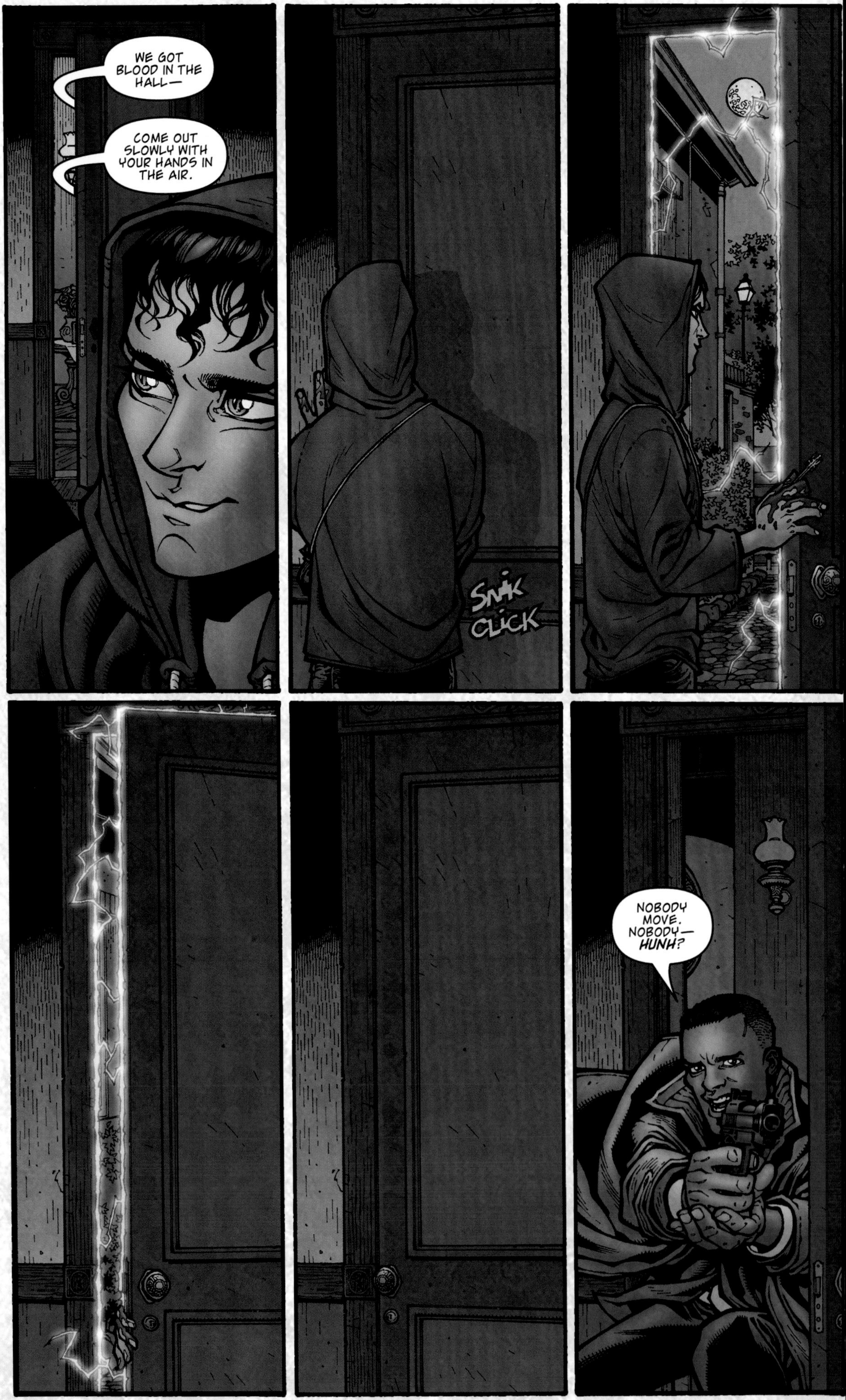
WE GOT BLOOD IN THE HALL—
COME OUT SLOWLY WITH YOUR HANDS IN THE AIR.
SNIK
CLICK
NOBODY MOVE. NOBODY— HUNH?

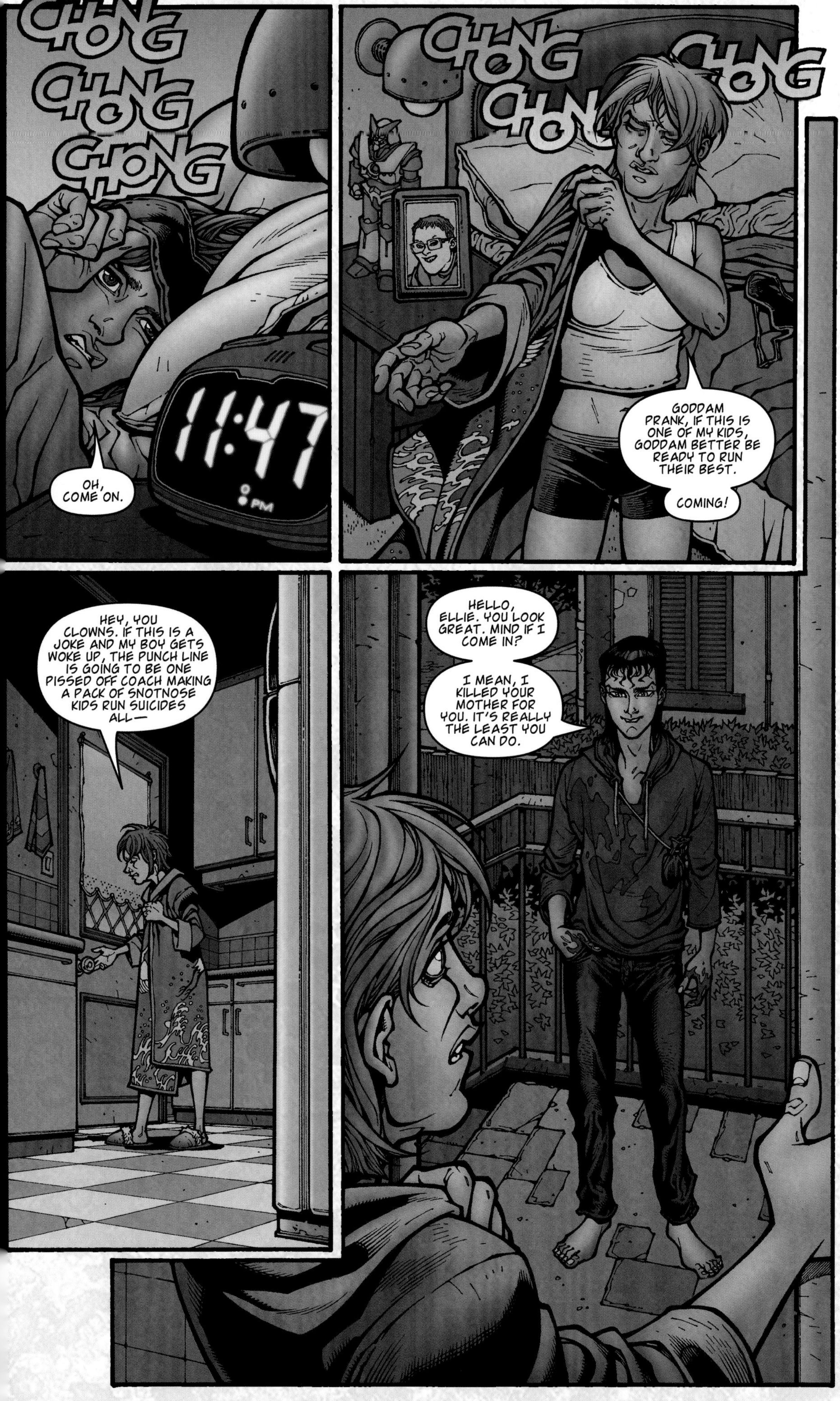
CHONG CHONG CHONG
OH, COME ON.
11:47 PM
CHONG CHONG CHONG
GODDAM PRANK, IF THIS IS ONE OF MY KIDS, GODDAM BETTER BE READY TO RUN THEIR BEST.
COMING!
HEY, YOU CLOWNS. IF THIS IS A JOKE AND MY BOY GETS WOKE UP, THE PUNCH LINE IS GOING TO BE ONE PISSED OFF COACH MAKING A PACK OF SNOTNOSE KIDS RUN SUICIDES ALL—
HELLO, ELLIE. YOU LOOK GREAT. MIND IF I COME IN?
I MEAN, I KILLED YOUR MOTHER FOR YOU. IT'S REALLY THE LEAST YOU CAN DO.

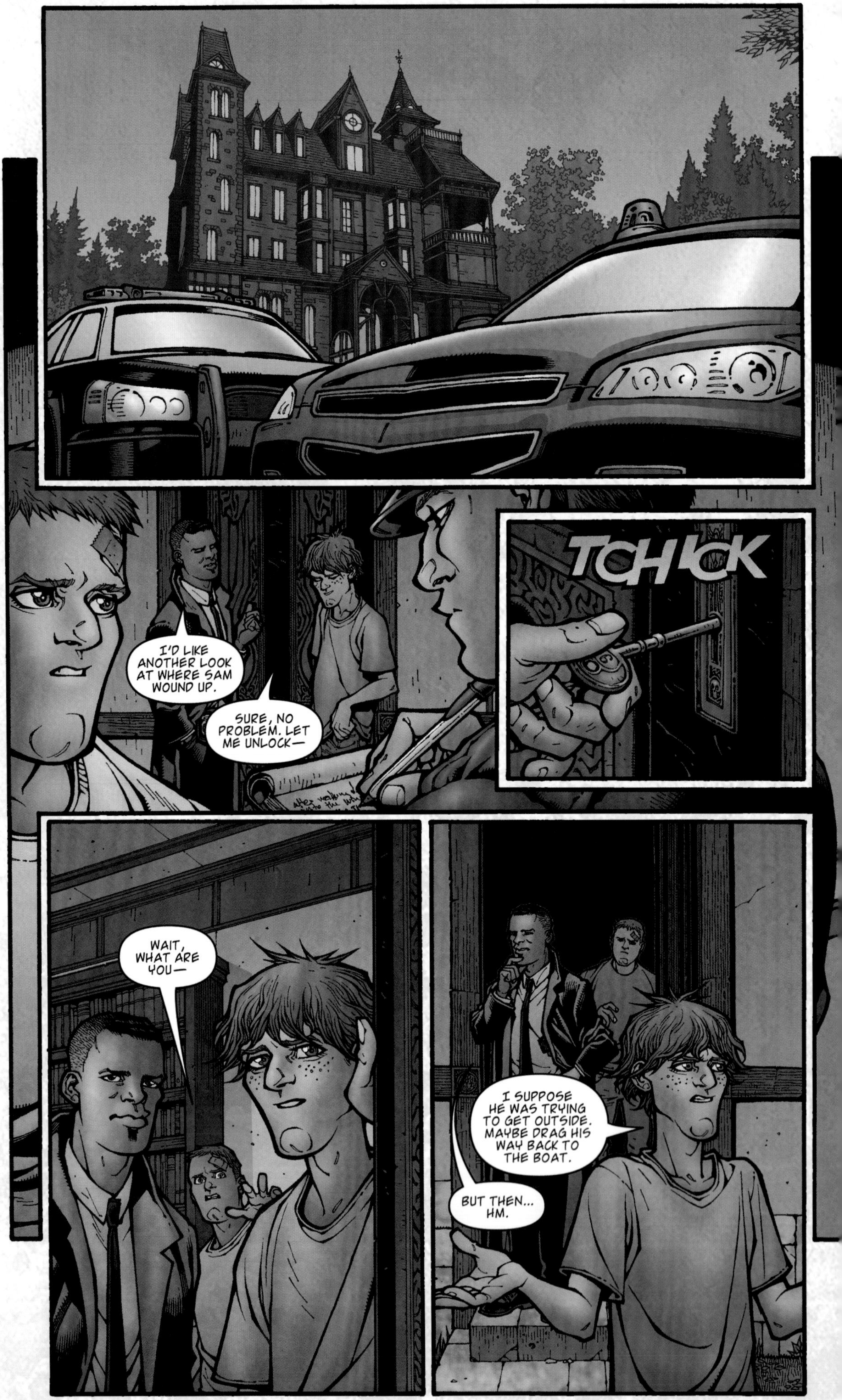
I'D LIKE ANOTHER LOOK AT WHERE SAM WOUND UP.
SURE, NO PROBLEM. LET ME UNLOCK—
TCHICK
WAIT, WHAT ARE YOU—
I SUPPOSE HE WAS TRYING TO GET OUTSIDE. MAYBE DRAG HIS WAY BACK TO THE BOAT.
BUT THEN... HM.

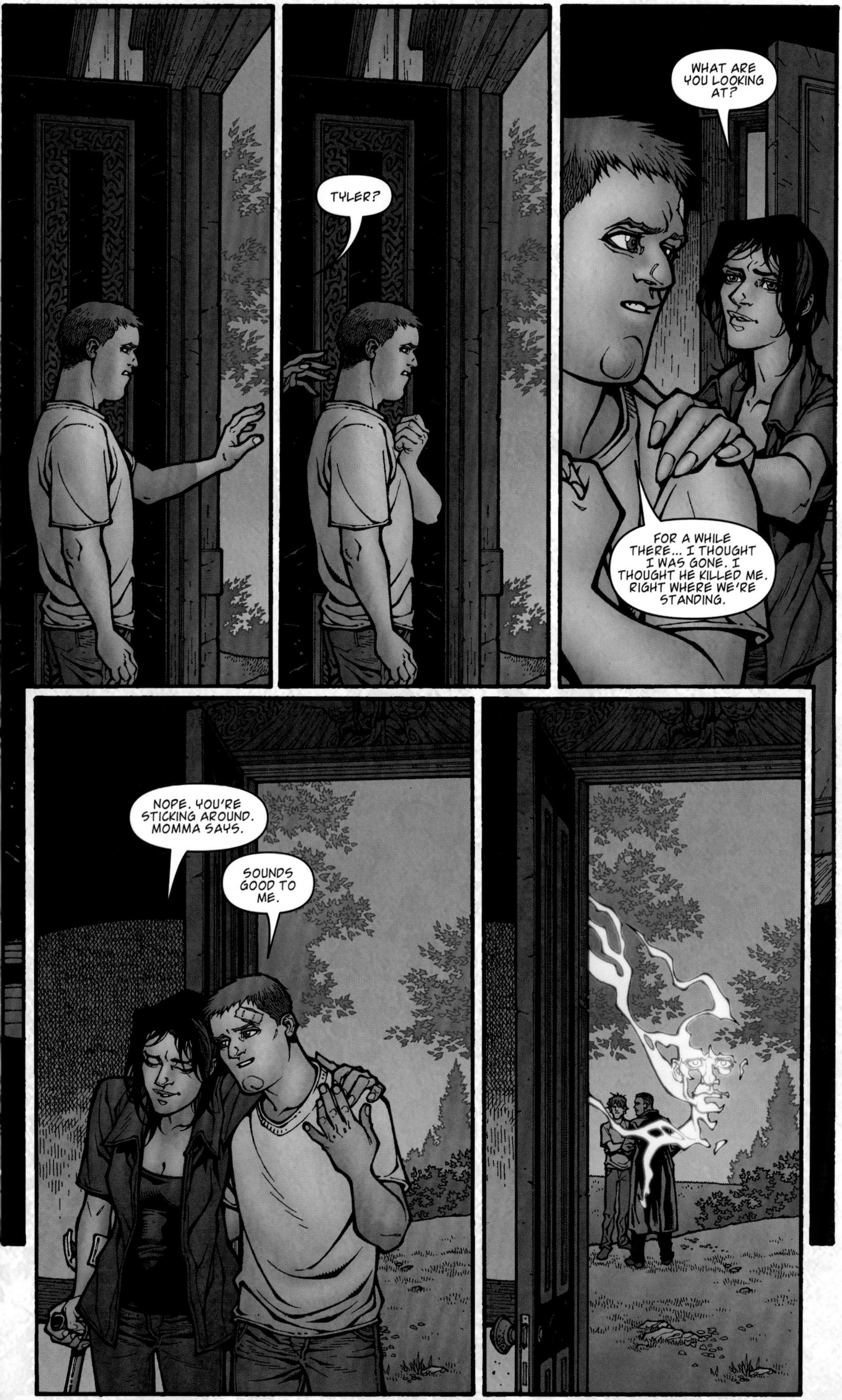

TYLER?
WHAT ARE YOU LOOKING AT?
FOR A WHILE THERE... I THOUGHT I WAS GONE. I THOUGHT HE KILLED ME. RIGHT WHERE WE'RE STANDING.
NOPE. YOU'RE STICKING AROUND. MOMMA SAYS.
SOUNDS GOOD TO ME.

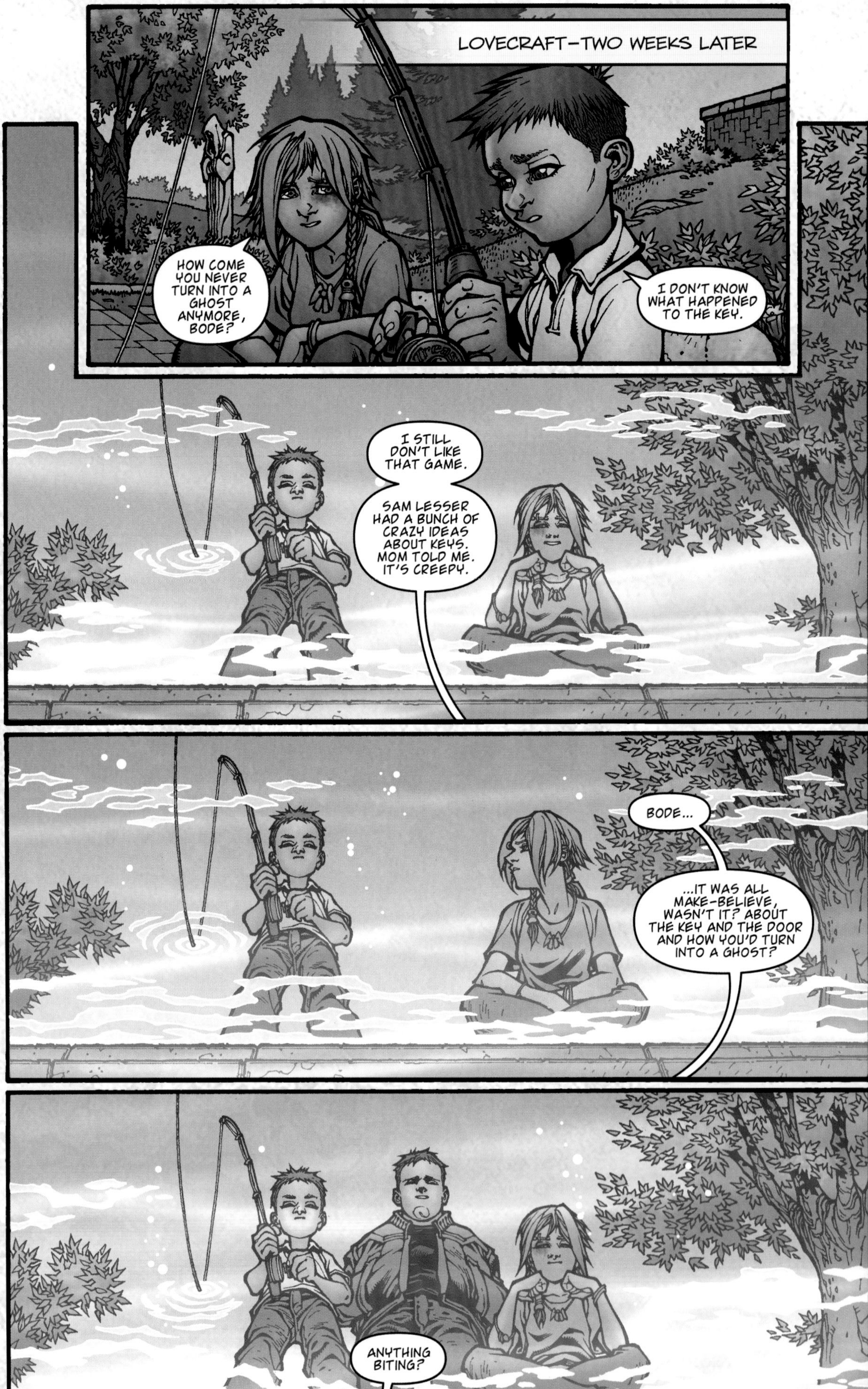
LOVECRAFT—TWO WEEKS LATER
HOW COME YOU NEVER TURN INTO A GHOST ANYMORE, BODE?
I DON'T KNOW WHAT HAPPENED TO THE KEY.
I STILL DON'T LIKE THAT GAME.
SAM LESSER HAD A BUNCH OF CRAZY IDEAS ABOUT KEYS. MOM TOLD ME. IT'S CREEPY.
BODE...
...IT WAS ALL MAKE-BELIEVE, WASN'T IT? ABOUT THE KEY AND THE DOOR AND HOW YOU'D TURN INTO A GHOST?
ANYTHING BITING?

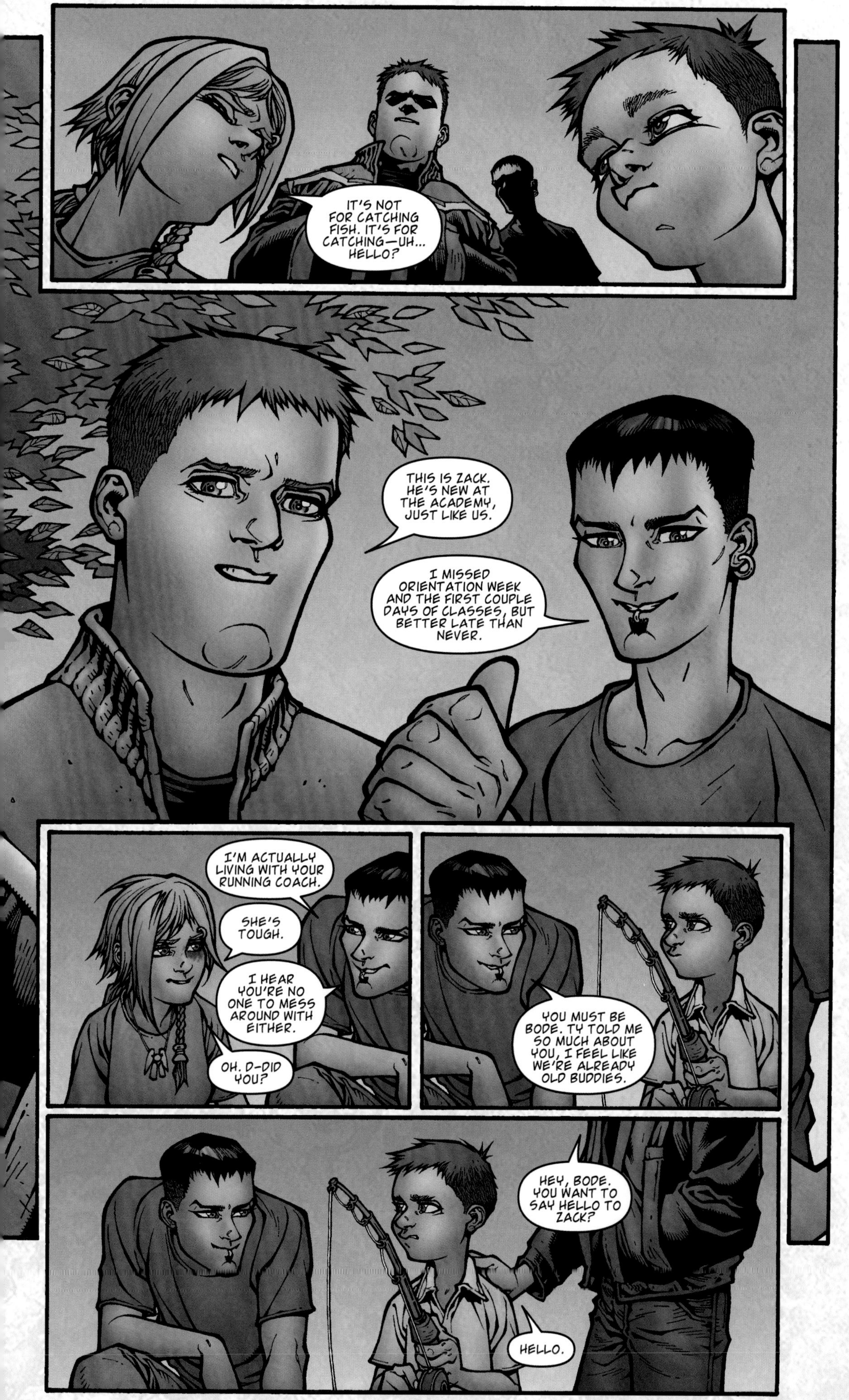
IT'S NOT FOR CATCHING FISH. IT'S FOR CATCHING—UH... HELLO?
THIS IS ZACK. HE'S NEW AT THE ACADEMY, JUST LIKE US.
I MISSED ORIENTATION WEEK AND THE FIRST COUPLE DAYS OF CLASSES, BUT BETTER LATE THAN NEVER.
I'M ACTUALLY LIVING WITH YOUR RUNNING COACH.
SHE'S TOUGH.
I HEAR YOU'RE NO ONE TO MESS AROUND WITH EITHER.
OH. D-DID YOU?
YOU MUST BE BODE. TY TOLD ME SO MUCH ABOUT YOU, I FEEL LIKE WE'RE ALREADY OLD BUDDIES.
HEY, BODE. YOU WANT TO SAY HELLO TO ZACK?
HELLO.

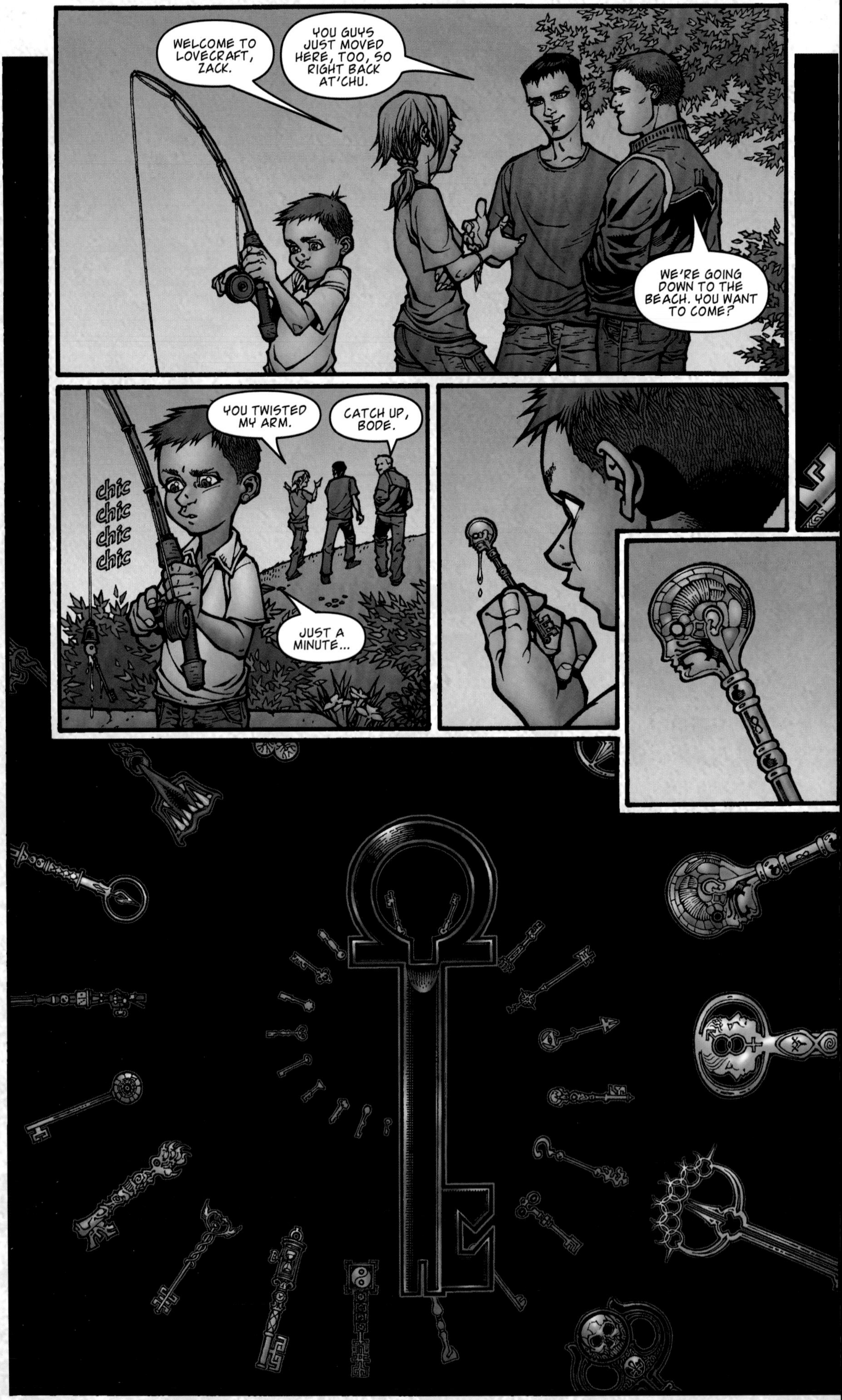
WELCOME TO LOVECRAFT, ZACK.
YOU GUYS JUST MOVED HERE, TOO, SO RIGHT BACK AT'CHU.
WE'RE GOING DOWN TO THE BEACH. YOU WANT TO COME?
YOU TWISTED MY ARM.
CATCH UP, BODE.
chic
chic
chic
chic
JUST A MINUTE...

LOCKE & KEY

- Book Two -

HEAD GAMES

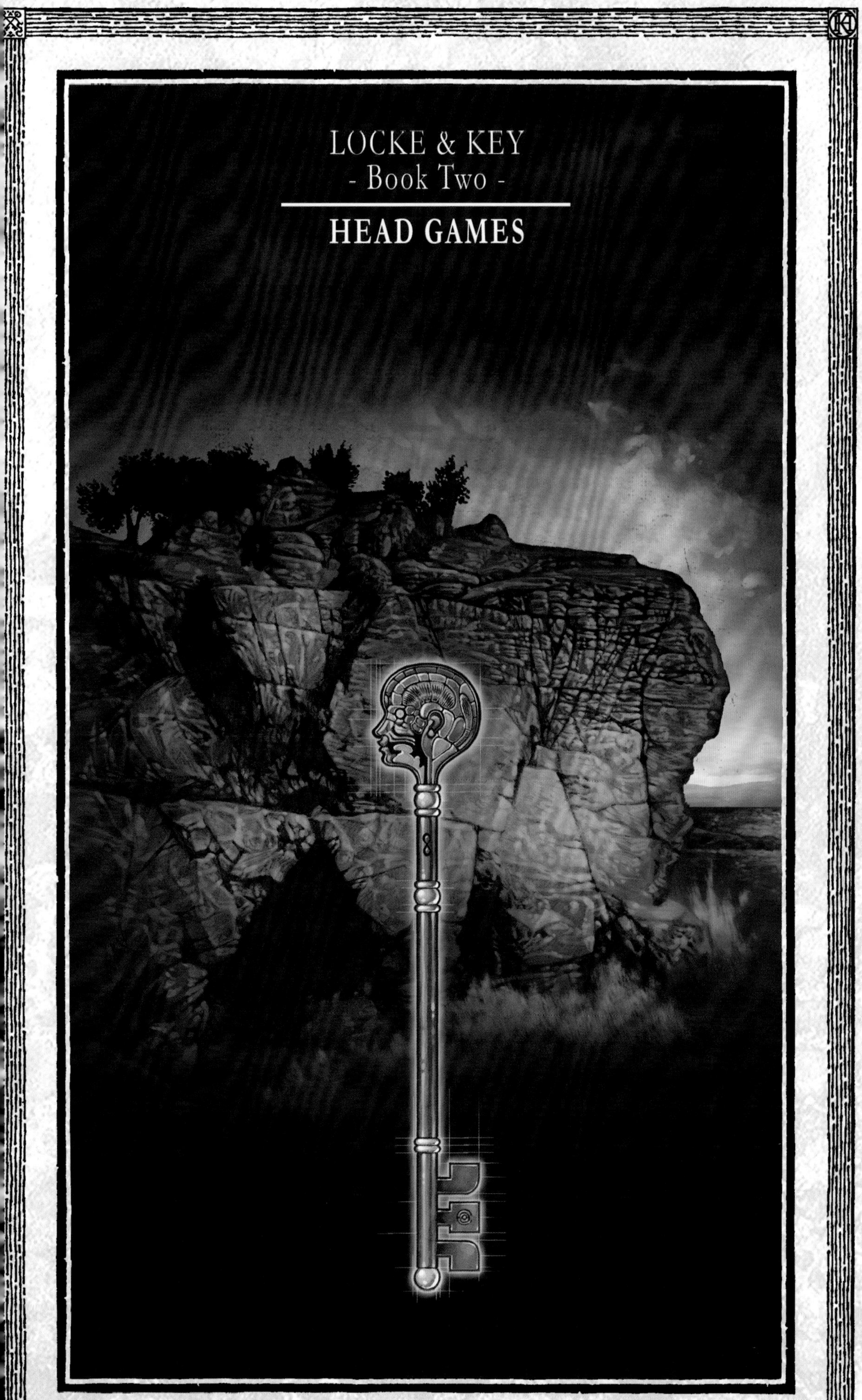

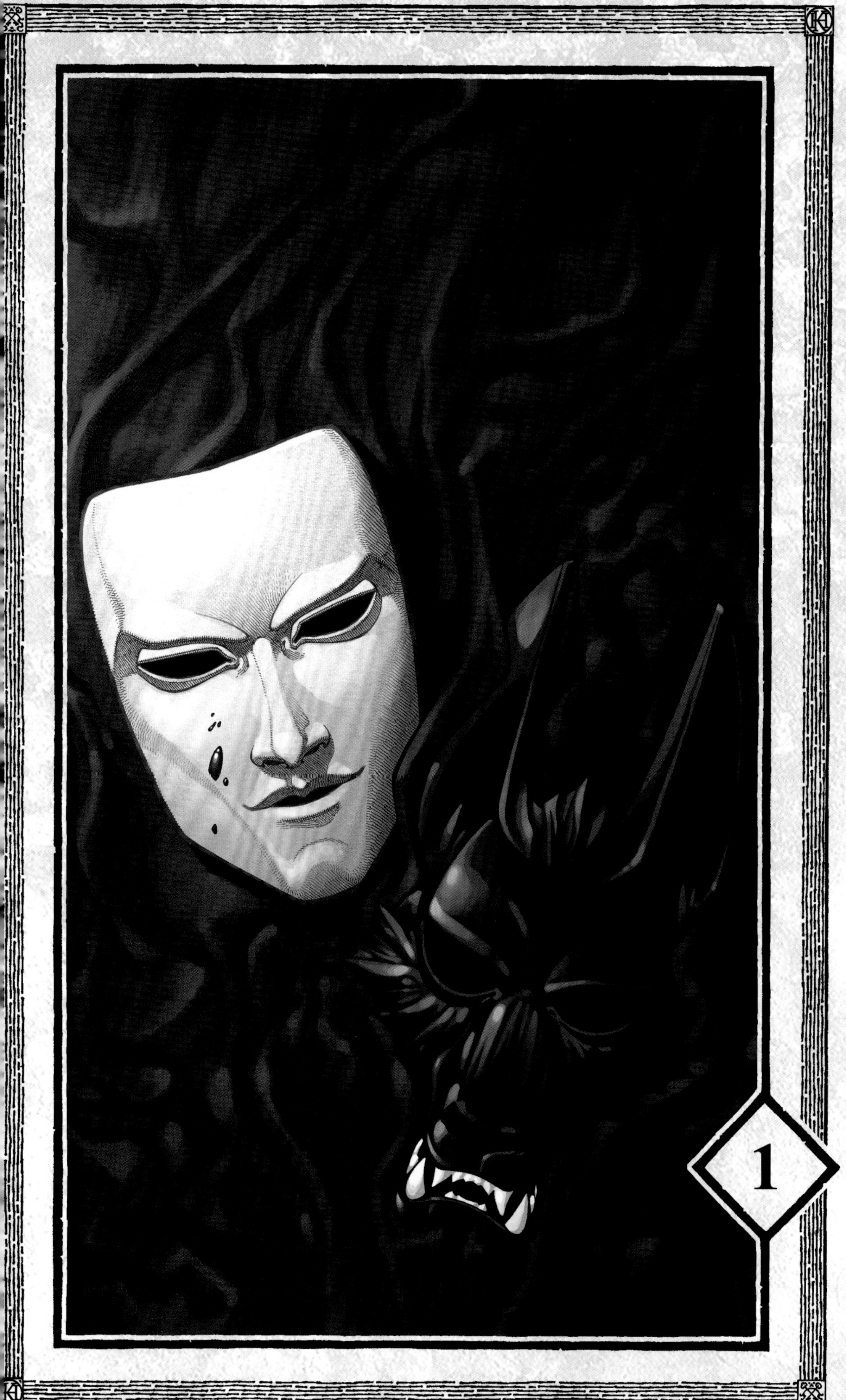
1

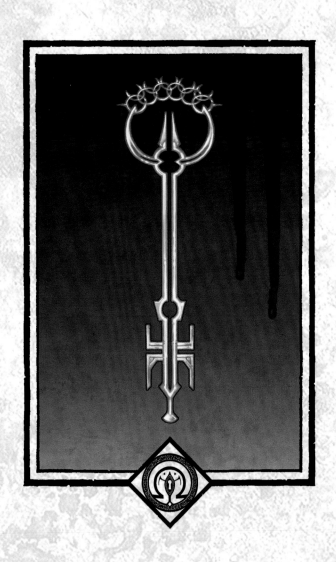

HEAD GAMES

- PROLOGUE: 21st CENTURY GHOST -

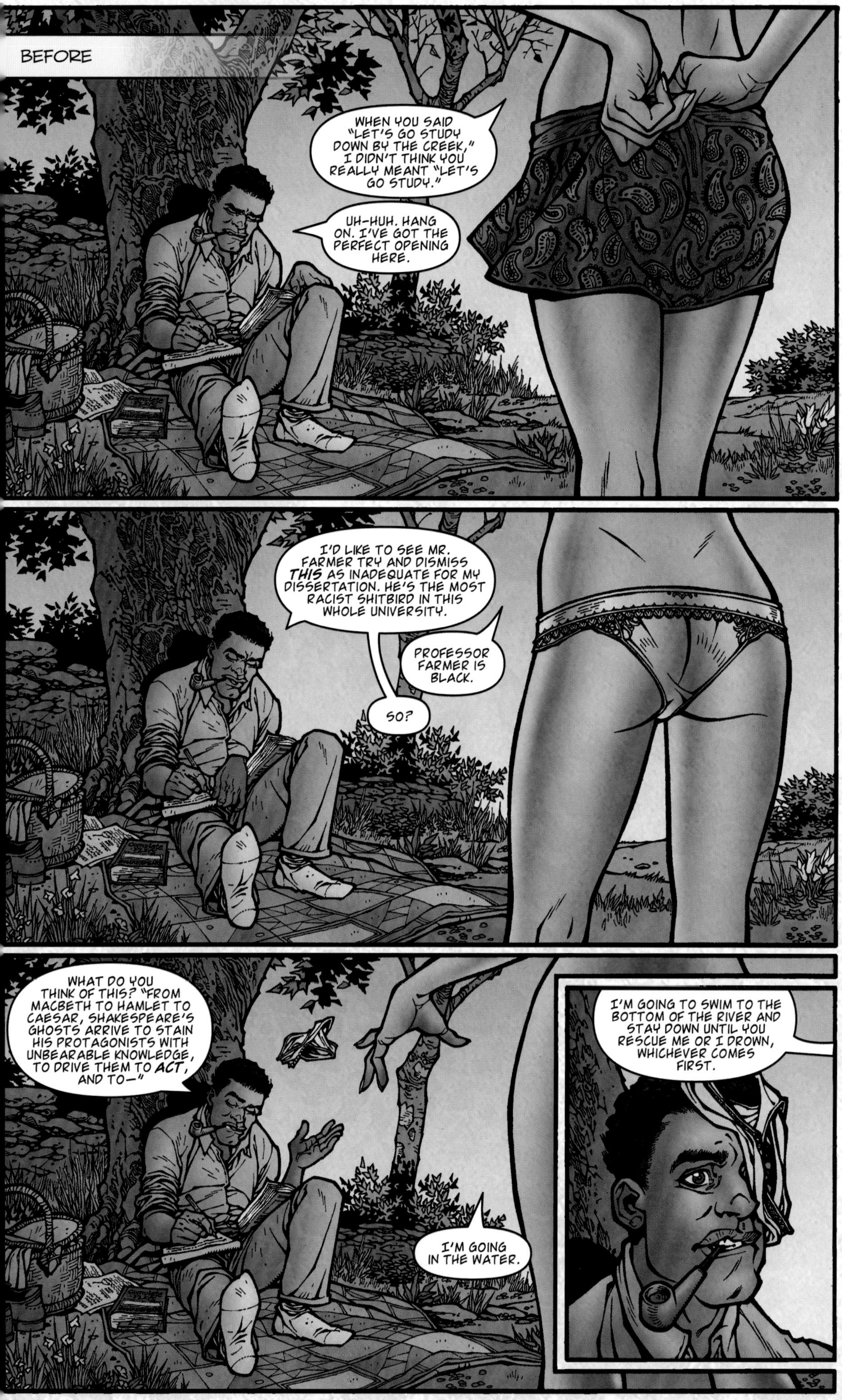

BEFORE
WHEN YOU SAID "LET'S GO STUDY DOWN BY THE CREEK," I DIDN'T THINK YOU REALLY MEANT "LET'S GO STUDY."
UH-HUH. HANG ON. I'VE GOT THE PERFECT OPENING HERE.
I'D LIKE TO SEE MR. FARMER TRY AND DISMISS *THIS* AS INADEQUATE FOR MY DISSERTATION. HE'S THE MOST RACIST SHITBIRD IN THIS WHOLE UNIVERSITY.
PROFESSOR FARMER IS BLACK.
SO?
WHAT DO YOU THINK OF THIS? "FROM MACBETH TO HAMLET TO CAESAR, SHAKESPEARE'S GHOSTS ARRIVE TO STAIN HIS PROTAGONISTS WITH UNBEARABLE KNOWLEDGE, TO DRIVE THEM TO *ACT*, AND TO—"
I'M GOING IN THE WATER.
I'M GOING TO SWIM TO THE BOTTOM OF THE RIVER AND STAY DOWN UNTIL YOU RESCUE ME OR I DROWN, WHICHEVER COMES FIRST.

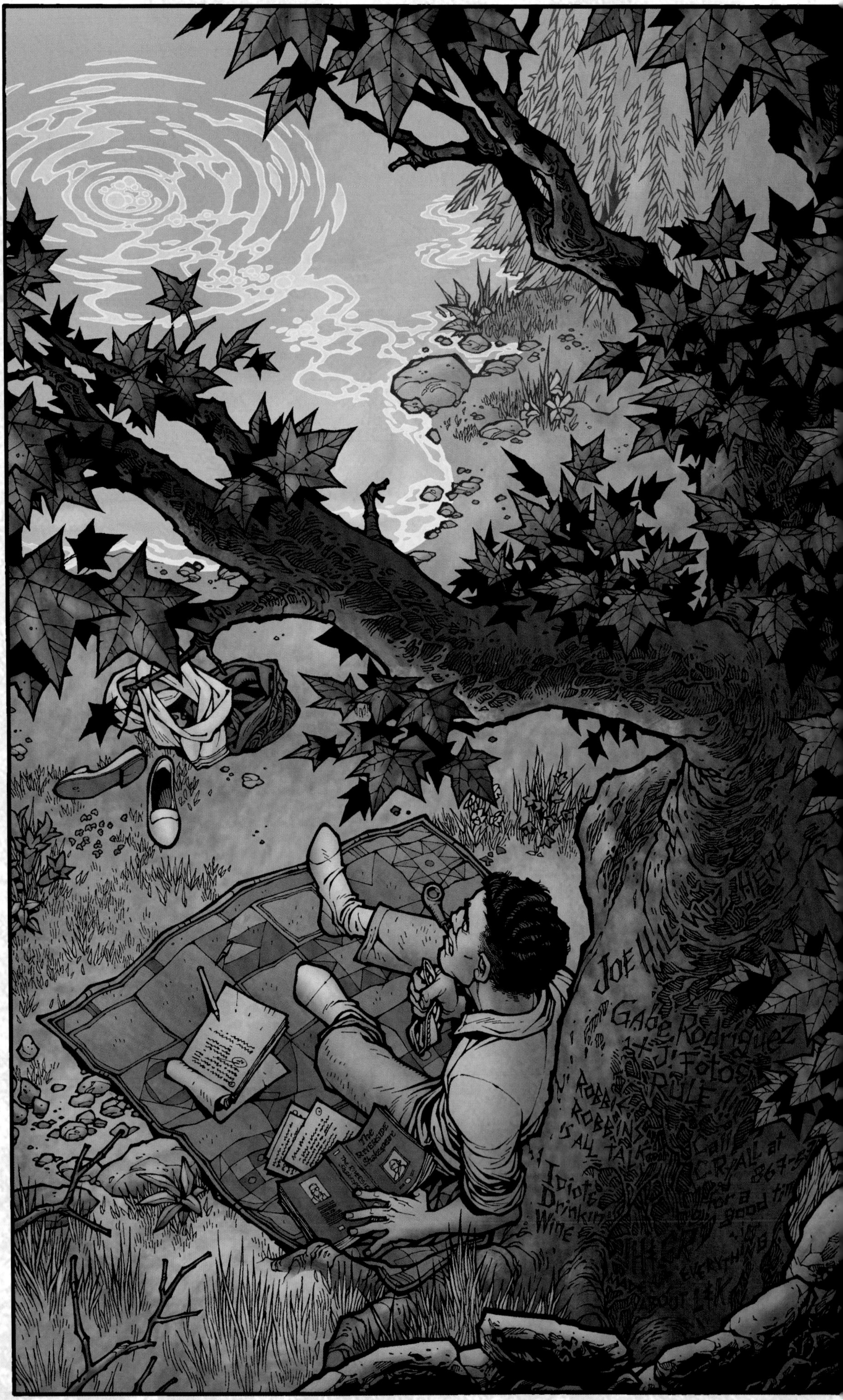
JOE HILL WAS HERE
Gabe Rodriguez
J. Fotos
RULE
ROBBIE ROBBINS IS ALL TALK
Call C. RYALL at 867-5
for a good ti
Idiots Drinkin Wine
The Riverside Shakespeare

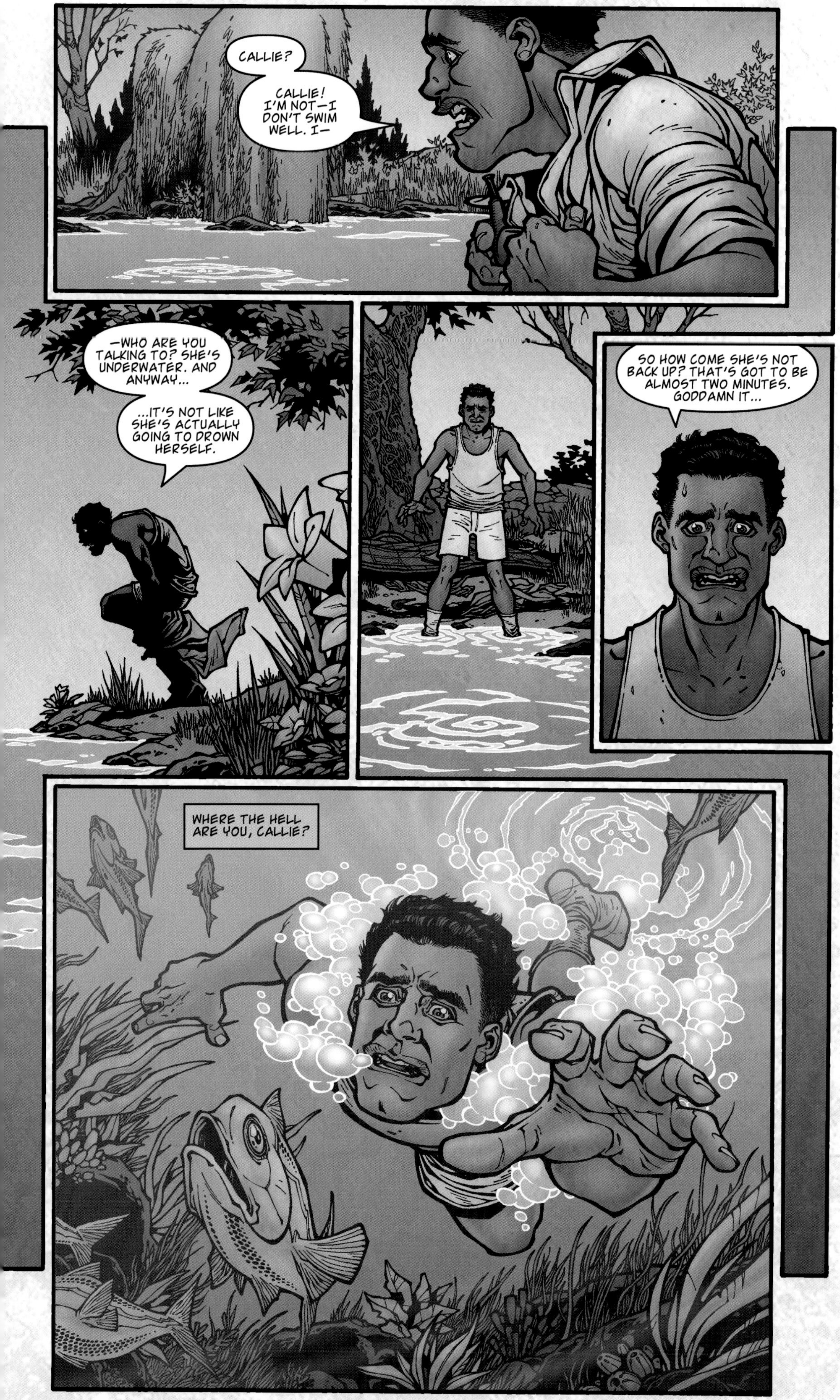
CALLIE?
CALLIE! I'M NOT—I DON'T SWIM WELL. I—
—WHO ARE YOU TALKING TO? SHE'S UNDERWATER. AND ANYWAY...
...IT'S NOT LIKE SHE'S ACTUALLY GOING TO DROWN HERSELF.
SO HOW COME SHE'S NOT BACK UP? THAT'S GOT TO BE ALMOST TWO MINUTES. GODDAMN IT...
WHERE THE HELL ARE YOU, CALLIE?

WHERE DID YOU GO?

LOVECRAFT, MASSACHUSETTS. NOW.

I WOULD'VE RETIRED BY NOW IF YOU DIDN'T DIE ON ME. THE PLAN WAS TO BOTH GET OUT AT THE SAME TIME.

GO TO AMALFI, WHERE WE WENT FOR OUR TENTH.

THE GHOST CODE
Joseph Elmore Ridgeway III

I ALWAYS THOUGHT WE'D HAVE TIME FOR ITALY.

MEMORY-
GHOSTS: *Inaction is a* CHOICE

STAY, ILLUSION! IF THOU HAST ANY SOUND OR USE OF VOICE, SPEAK TO ME!

BUT I LIKE HAVING YOU NEAR. I CAN CLOSE MY EYES AND IMAGINE YOU'RE WAITING FOR ME IN THE FACULTY LOUNGE AND IN A MOMENT WE'LL HAVE OUR MORNING COFFEE TOGETHER.

FACULTY LOUNGE

I SHOULD'VE GOT OUT A WHILE AGO BUT I CAN'T LEAVE. YOU WORKED HERE, TOO. THIS WAS OUR PLACE.

SOME PEOPLE WOULD'VE WANTED TO GET AWAY. TOO MANY GHOSTS.

BESIDES, HOW OFTEN DID I SAY I WOULD LOVE, JUST ONCE IN MY LIFE, TO SEE A REAL, HONEST-TO-GOD...

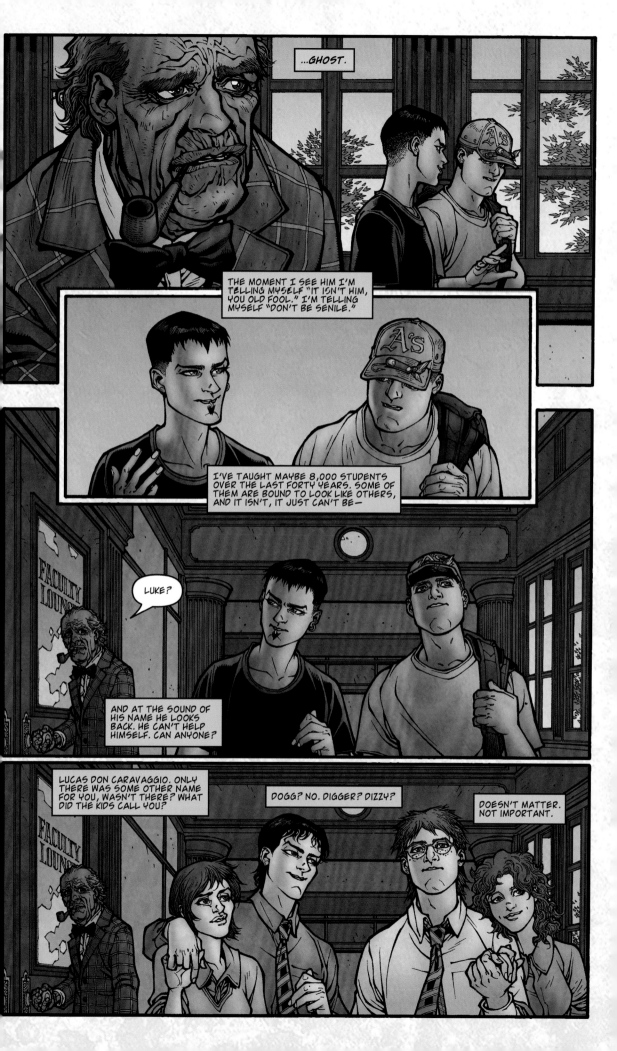

...GHOST.

THE MOMENT I SEE HIM I'M TELLING MYSELF "IT ISN'T HIM, YOU OLD FOOL." I'M TELLING MYSELF "DON'T BE SENILE."

I'VE TAUGHT MAYBE 8,000 STUDENTS OVER THE LAST FORTY YEARS. SOME OF THEM ARE BOUND TO LOOK LIKE OTHERS, AND IT ISN'T, IT JUST CAN'T BE—

LUKE?

AND AT THE SOUND OF HIS NAME HE LOOKS BACK. HE CAN'T HELP HIMSELF. CAN ANYONE?

LUCAS DON CARAVAGGIO. ONLY THERE WAS SOME OTHER NAME FOR YOU, WASN'T THERE? WHAT DID THE KIDS CALL YOU?

DOGG? NO. DIGGER? DIZZY?

DOESN'T MATTER. NOT IMPORTANT.

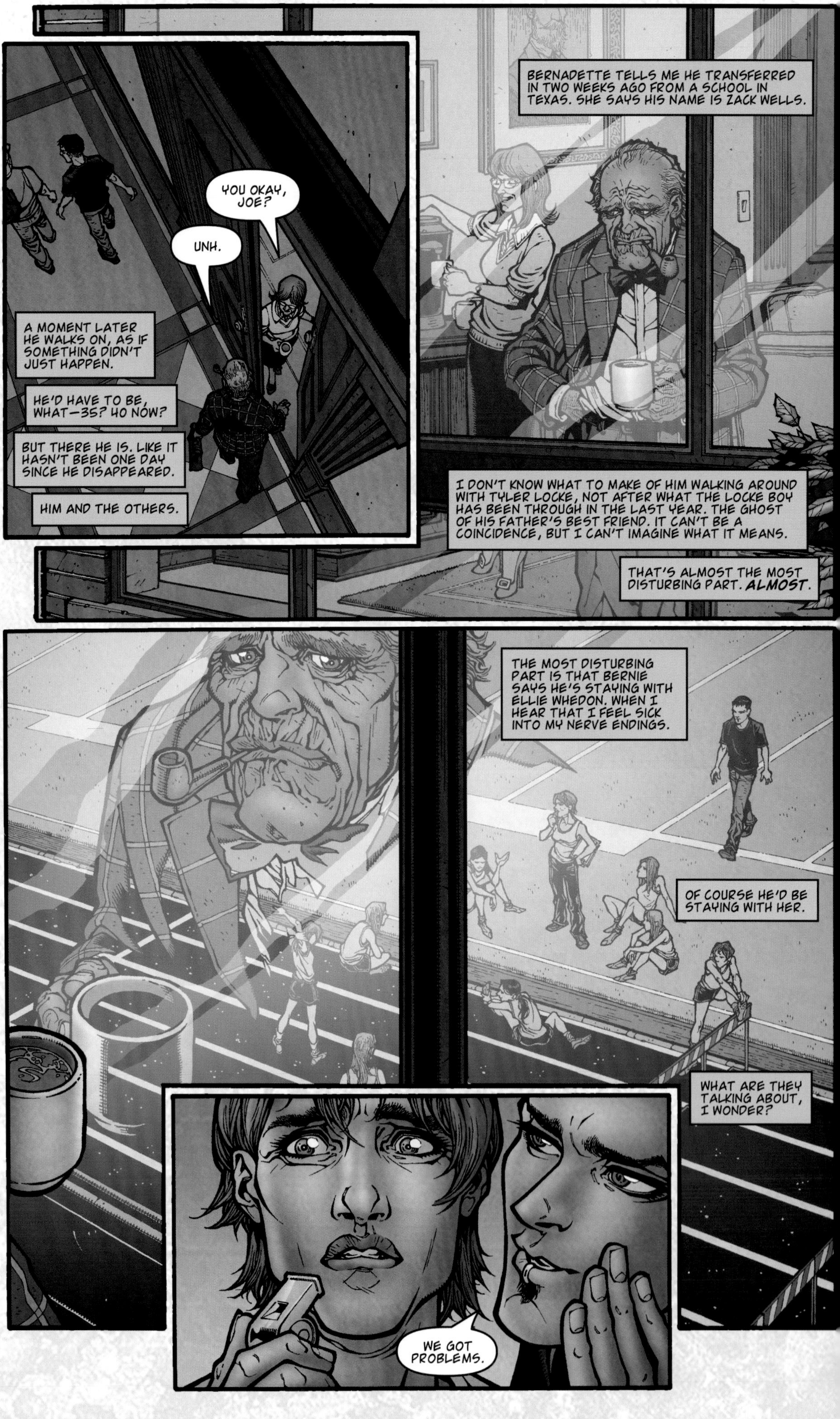
YOU OKAY, JOE?
UNH.
A MOMENT LATER HE WALKS ON, AS IF SOMETHING DIDN'T JUST HAPPEN.
HE'D HAVE TO BE, WHAT—35? 40 NOW?
BUT THERE HE IS. LIKE IT HASN'T BEEN ONE DAY SINCE HE DISAPPEARED.
HIM AND THE OTHERS.
BERNADETTE TELLS ME HE TRANSFERRED IN TWO WEEKS AGO FROM A SCHOOL IN TEXAS. SHE SAYS HIS NAME IS ZACK WELLS.
I DON'T KNOW WHAT TO MAKE OF HIM WALKING AROUND WITH TYLER LOCKE, NOT AFTER WHAT THE LOCKE BOY HAS BEEN THROUGH IN THE LAST YEAR. THE GHOST OF HIS FATHER'S BEST FRIEND. IT CAN'T BE A COINCIDENCE, BUT I CAN'T IMAGINE WHAT IT MEANS.
THAT'S ALMOST THE MOST DISTURBING PART. ALMOST.
THE MOST DISTURBING PART IS THAT BERNIE SAYS HE'S STAYING WITH ELLIE WHEDON. WHEN I HEAR THAT I FEEL SICK INTO MY NERVE ENDINGS.
OF COURSE HE'D BE STAYING WITH HER.
WHAT ARE THEY TALKING ABOUT, I WONDER?
WE GOT PROBLEMS.

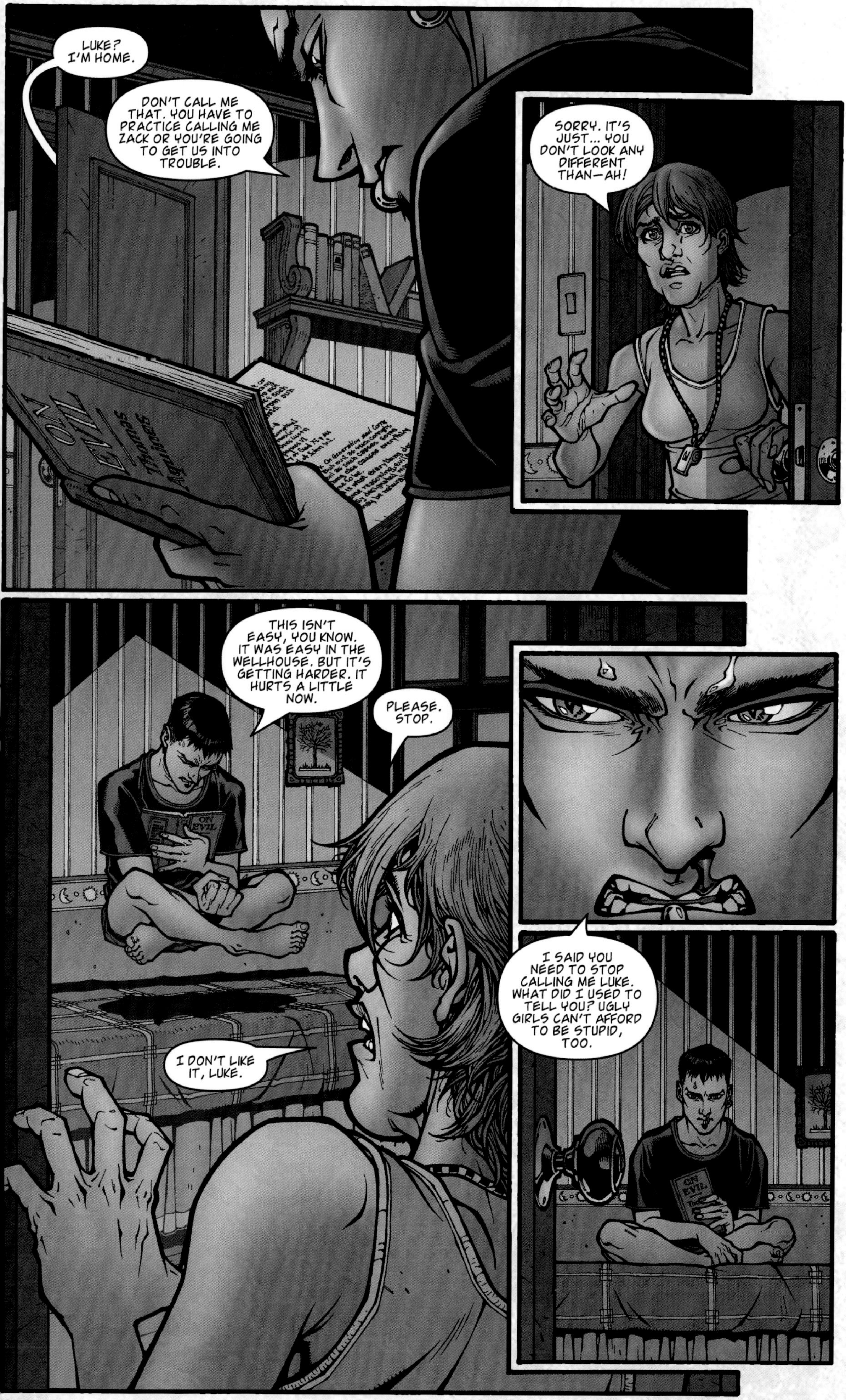
LUKE? I'M HOME.
DON'T CALL ME THAT. YOU HAVE TO PRACTICE CALLING ME ZACK OR YOU'RE GOING TO GET US INTO TROUBLE.
SORRY. IT'S JUST... YOU DON'T LOOK ANY DIFFERENT THAN—AH!
ON EVIL
THIS ISN'T EASY, YOU KNOW. IT WAS EASY IN THE WELLHOUSE. BUT IT'S GETTING HARDER. IT HURTS A LITTLE NOW.
PLEASE. STOP.
I DON'T LIKE IT, LUKE.
I SAID YOU NEED TO STOP CALLING ME LUKE. WHAT DID I USED TO TELL YOU? UGLY GIRLS CAN'T AFFORD TO BE STUPID, TOO.

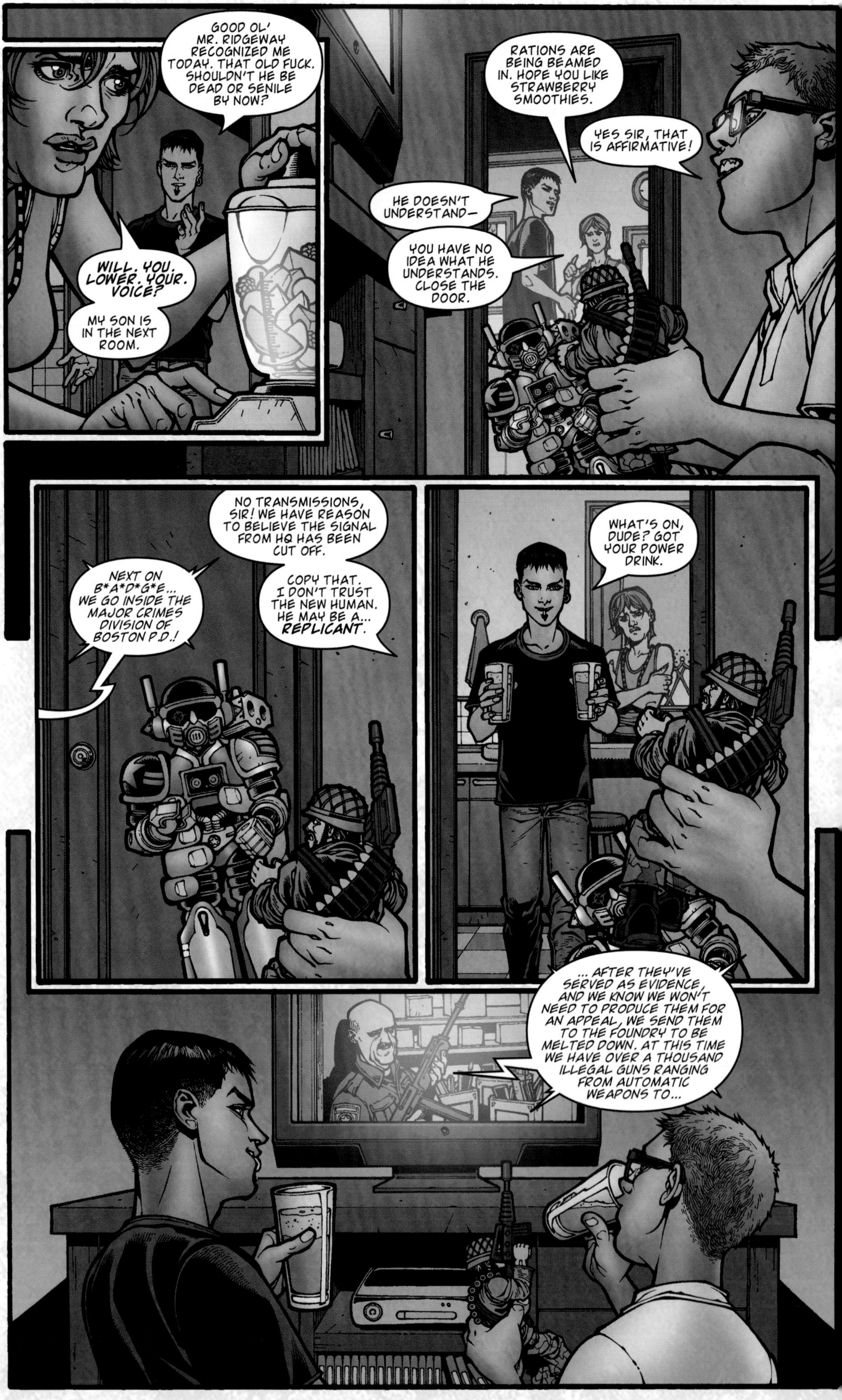

GOOD OL' MR. RIDGEWAY RECOGNIZED ME TODAY. THAT OLD FUCK. SHOULDN'T HE BE DEAD OR SENILE BY NOW?
WILL. YOU. LOWER. YOUR. VOICE?
MY SON IS IN THE NEXT ROOM.
RATIONS ARE BEING BEAMED IN. HOPE YOU LIKE STRAWBERRY SMOOTHIES.
YES SIR, THAT IS AFFIRMATIVE!
HE DOESN'T UNDERSTAND—
YOU HAVE NO IDEA WHAT HE UNDERSTANDS. CLOSE THE DOOR.
NO TRANSMISSIONS, SIR! WE HAVE REASON TO BELIEVE THE SIGNAL FROM HQ HAS BEEN CUT OFF.
NEXT ON B*A*D*G*E... WE GO INSIDE THE MAJOR CRIMES DIVISION OF BOSTON P.D.!
COPY THAT. I DON'T TRUST THE NEW HUMAN. HE MAY BE A... REPLICANT.
WHAT'S ON, DUDE? GOT YOUR POWER DRINK.
... AFTER THEY'VE SERVED AS EVIDENCE, AND WE KNOW WE WON'T NEED TO PRODUCE THEM FOR AN APPEAL, WE SEND THEM TO THE FOUNDRY TO BE MELTED DOWN. AT THIS TIME WE HAVE OVER A THOUSAND ILLEGAL GUNS RANGING FROM AUTOMATIC WEAPONS TO...

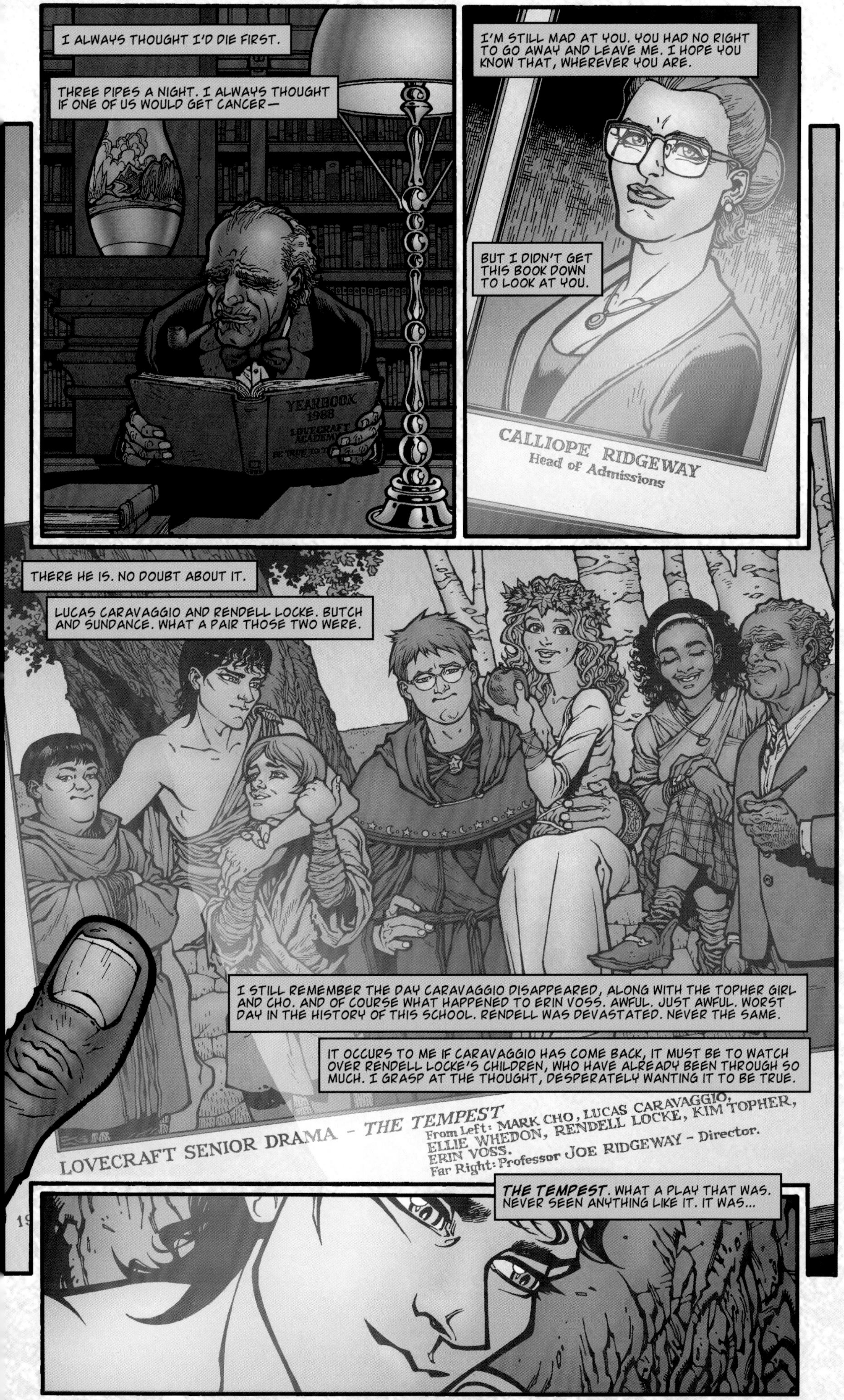
I ALWAYS THOUGHT I'D DIE FIRST.
THREE PIPES A NIGHT. I ALWAYS THOUGHT IF ONE OF US WOULD GET CANCER—
YEARBOOK 1988 LOVECRAFT ACADEMY
I'M STILL MAD AT YOU. YOU HAD NO RIGHT TO GO AWAY AND LEAVE ME. I HOPE YOU KNOW THAT, WHEREVER YOU ARE.
BUT I DIDN'T GET THIS BOOK DOWN TO LOOK AT YOU.
CALLIOPE RIDGEWAY
Head of Admissions
THERE HE IS. NO DOUBT ABOUT IT.
LUCAS CARAVAGGIO AND RENDELL LOCKE. BUTCH AND SUNDANCE. WHAT A PAIR THOSE TWO WERE.
I STILL REMEMBER THE DAY CARAVAGGIO DISAPPEARED, ALONG WITH THE TOPHER GIRL AND CHO. AND OF COURSE WHAT HAPPENED TO ERIN VOSS. AWFUL. JUST AWFUL. WORST DAY IN THE HISTORY OF THIS SCHOOL. RENDELL WAS DEVASTATED. NEVER THE SAME.
IT OCCURS TO ME IF CARAVAGGIO HAS COME BACK, IT MUST BE TO WATCH OVER RENDELL LOCKE'S CHILDREN, WHO HAVE ALREADY BEEN THROUGH SO MUCH. I GRASP AT THE THOUGHT, DESPERATELY WANTING IT TO BE TRUE.
LOVECRAFT SENIOR DRAMA - THE TEMPEST
From Left: MARK CHO, LUCAS CARAVAGGIO, ELLIE WHEDON, RENDELL LOCKE, KIM TOPHER, ERIN VOSS.
Far Right: Professor JOE RIDGEWAY - Director.
THE TEMPEST. WHAT A PLAY THAT WAS. NEVER SEEN ANYTHING LIKE IT. IT WAS...

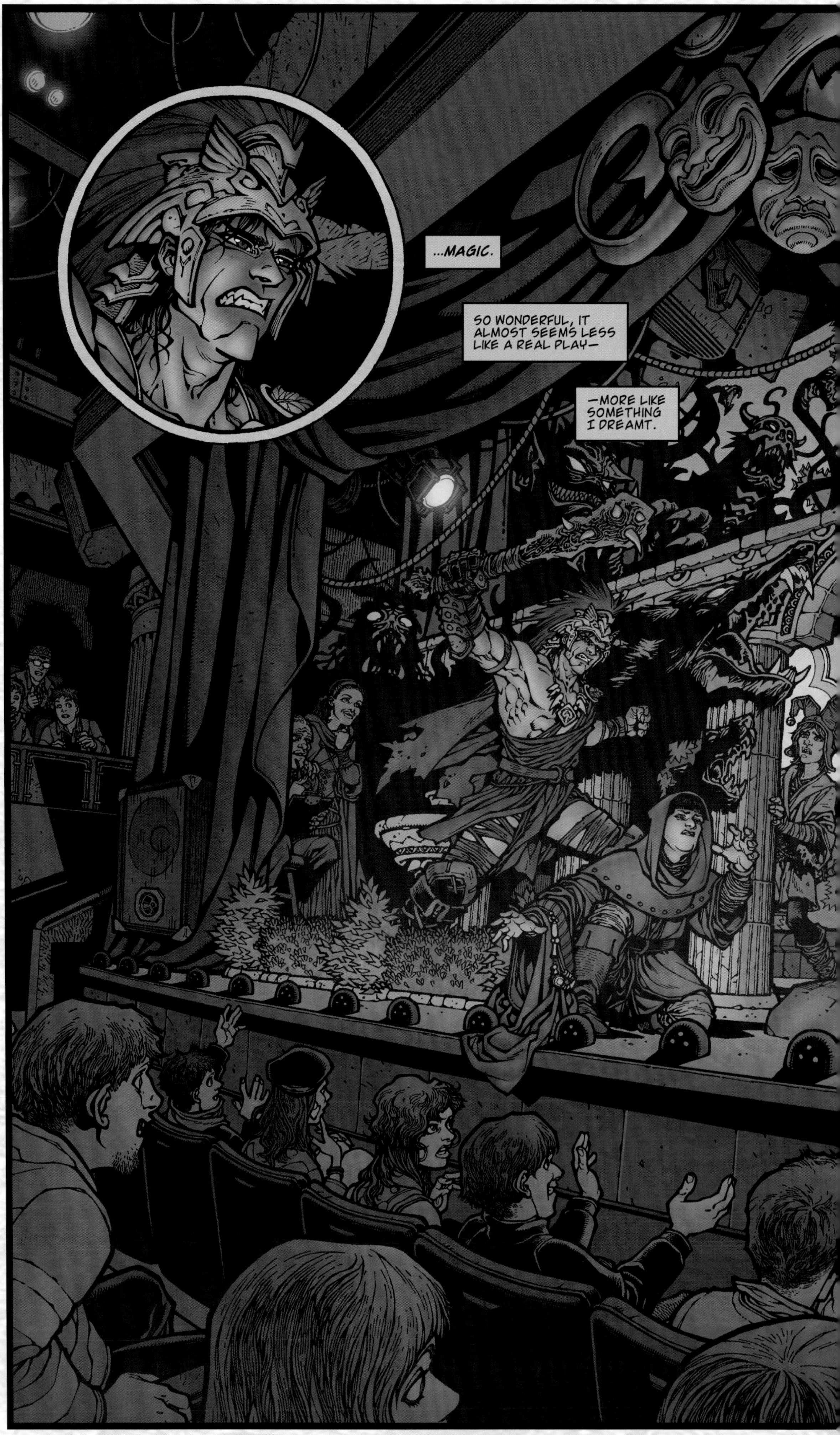
...MAGIC.
SO WONDERFUL, IT ALMOST SEEMS LESS LIKE A REAL PLAY—
—MORE LIKE SOMETHING I DREAMT.

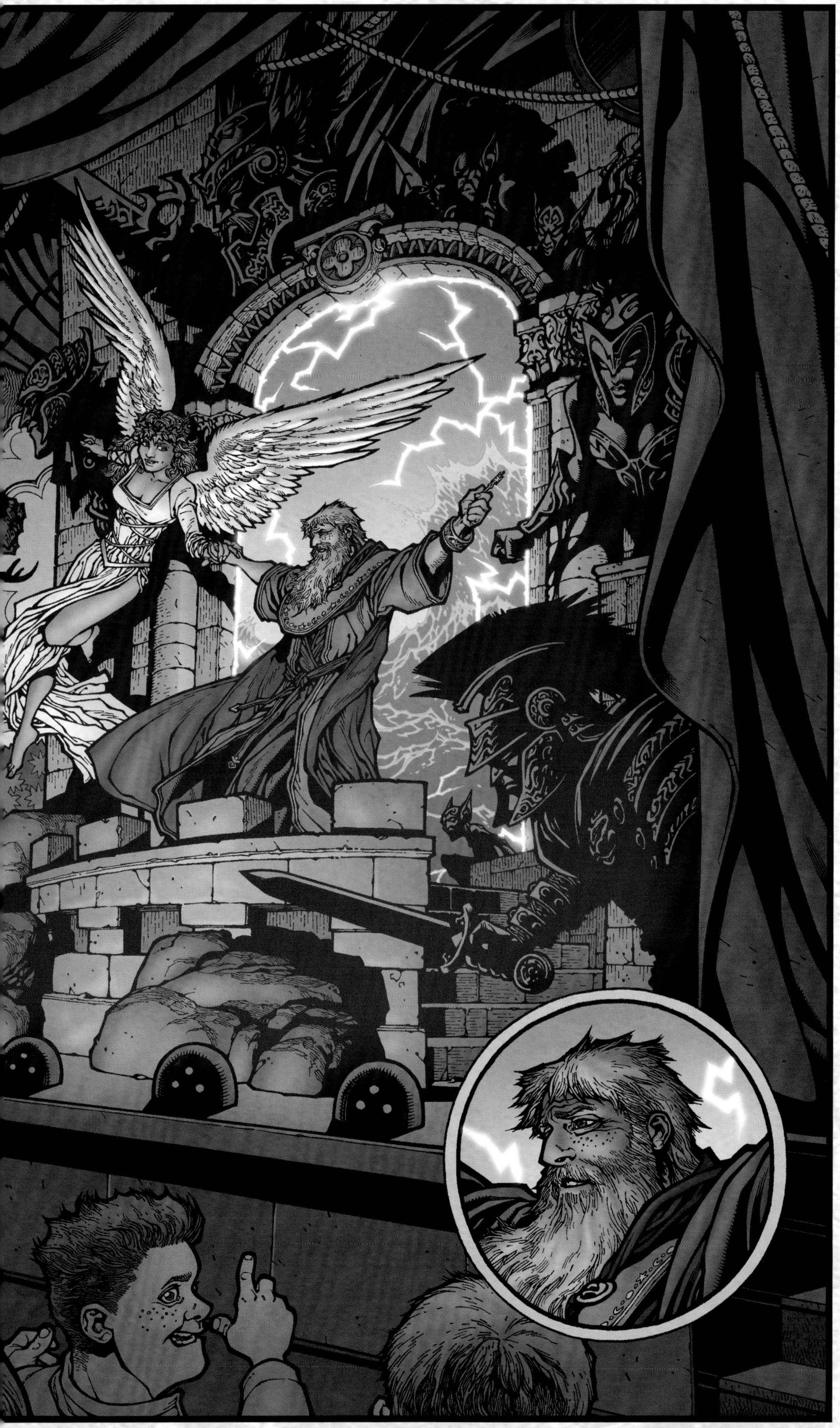

MR. RIDGEWAY.

IT'S NEARLY FIRST PERIOD. YOU HAVE A LESSON TO TEACH.

I BELIEVE I HAVE ONE TO TEACH RIGHT NOW.

OH, HA-HA.

WE TALKED ABOUT WHAT IT WOULD BE LIKE, FOR ONE OF US TO LOSE THE OTHER.

BUT THAT'S NOT HOW IT WORKS. YOU DON'T LOSE ANYONE. YOU AREN'T LOST. I CLOSE MY EYES AND THERE YOU ARE.

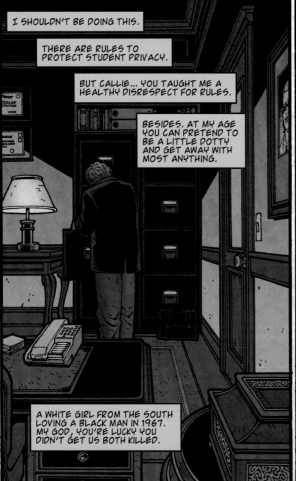

I SHOULDN'T BE DOING THIS.

THERE ARE RULES TO PROTECT STUDENT PRIVACY.

BUT CALLIE... YOU TAUGHT ME A HEALTHY DISRESPECT FOR RULES.

BESIDES. AT MY AGE YOU CAN PRETEND TO BE A LITTLE DOTTY AND GET AWAY WITH MOST ANYTHING.

A WHITE GIRL FROM THE SOUTH LOVING A BLACK MAN IN 1967. MY GOD, YOU'RE LUCKY YOU DIDN'T GET US BOTH KILLED.

SAYS HERE HE WAS ON THE DEAN'S LIST FOR ACADEMIC ACHIEVEMENT AND CAPTAIN OF THEIR FENCING TEAM. WASN'T LUCAS CARAVAGGIO ALSO... BUT THAT DOESN'T PROVE ANYTHING.

THEN THERE'S A PERSONAL NOTE FROM ELLIE, IDENTIFYING HIM AS A COUSIN AND EXPLAINING HE'LL BE STAYING WITH HER. I DIDN'T KNOW YOU HAD KIN OUT WEST, ELLIE.

THERE'S A NUMBER FOR THE SCHOOL HE TRANSFERRED OUT OF IN TEXAS. A PART OF ME DOESN'T WANT TO CALL. A PART OF ME IS AFRAID TO... AFRAID OF WHAT I MIGHT FIND OUT.

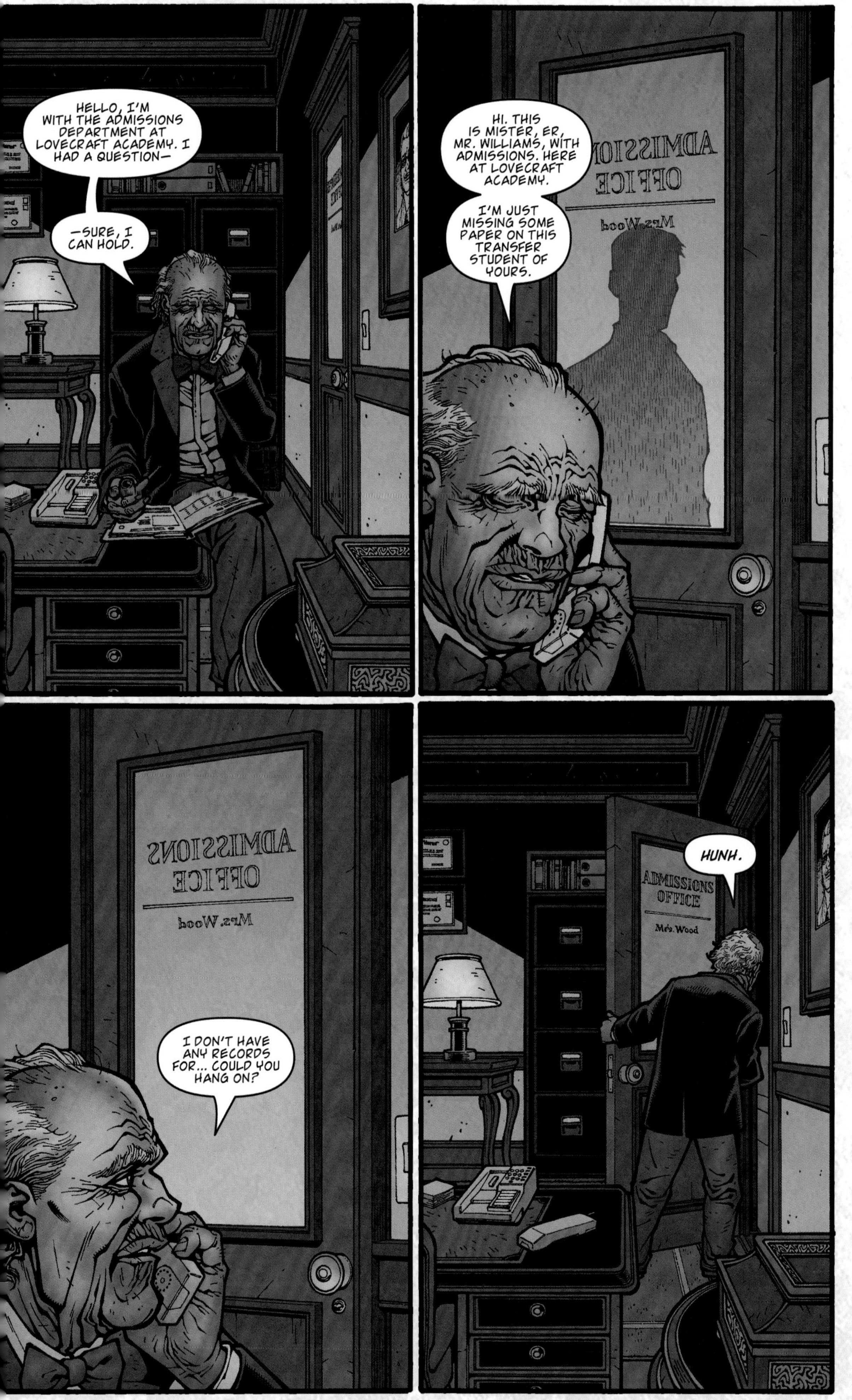
HELLO, I'M WITH THE ADMISSIONS DEPARTMENT AT LOVECRAFT ACADEMY. I HAD A QUESTION—
—SURE, I CAN HOLD.
HI. THIS IS MISTER, ER, MR. WILLIAMS, WITH ADMISSIONS. HERE AT LOVECRAFT ACADEMY.
I'M JUST MISSING SOME PAPER ON THIS TRANSFER STUDENT OF YOURS.
I DON'T HAVE ANY RECORDS FOR... COULD YOU HANG ON?
ADMISSIONS OFFICE
Mrs. Wood
HUNH.

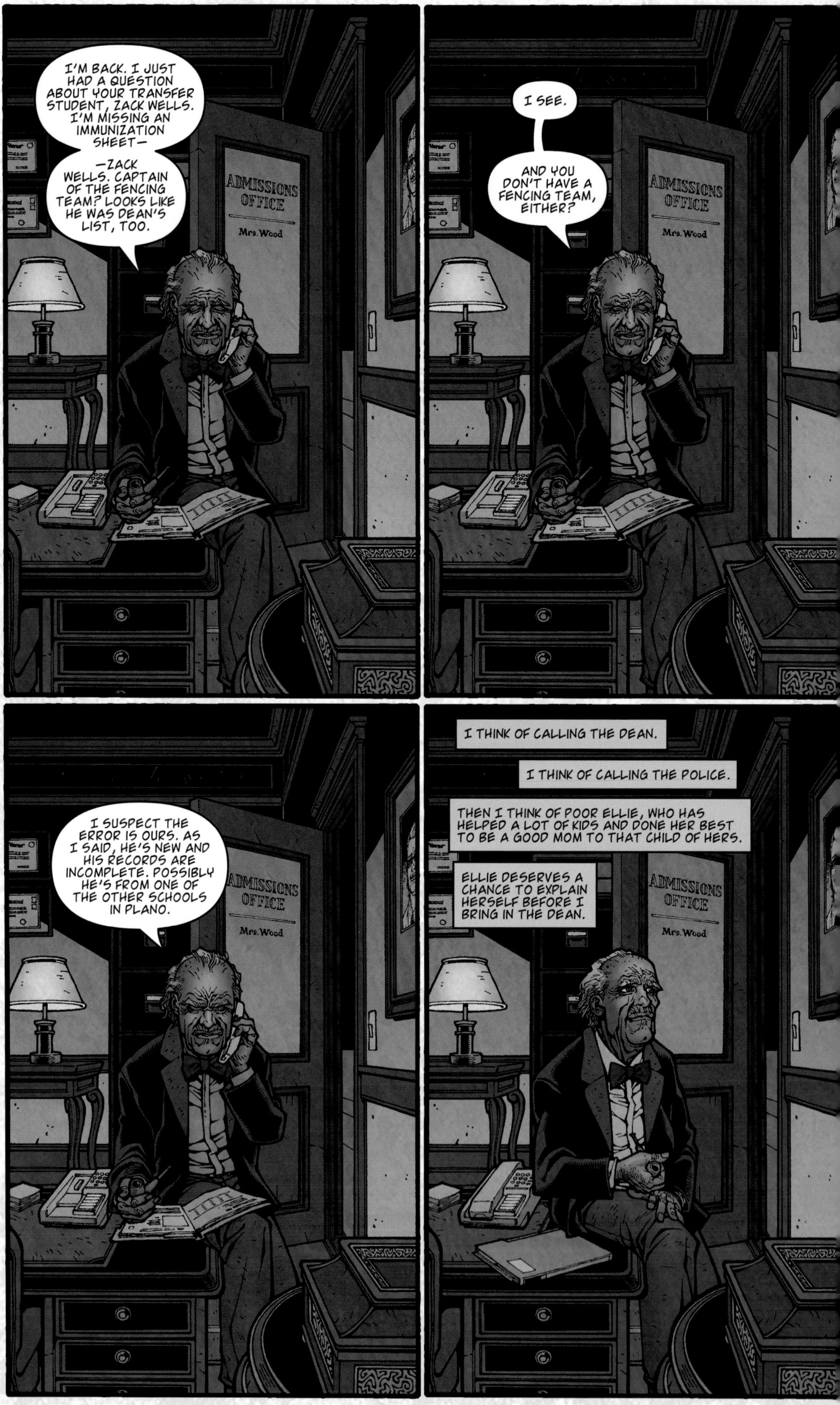

I'M BACK. I JUST HAD A QUESTION ABOUT YOUR TRANSFER STUDENT, ZACK WELLS. I'M MISSING AN IMMUNIZATION SHEET—
—ZACK WELLS. CAPTAIN OF THE FENCING TEAM? LOOKS LIKE HE WAS DEAN'S LIST, TOO.
ADMISSIONS OFFICE
Mrs. Wood
I SEE.
AND YOU DON'T HAVE A FENCING TEAM, EITHER?
I SUSPECT THE ERROR IS OURS. AS I SAID, HE'S NEW AND HIS RECORDS ARE INCOMPLETE. POSSIBLY HE'S FROM ONE OF THE OTHER SCHOOLS IN PLANO.
I THINK OF CALLING THE DEAN.
I THINK OF CALLING THE POLICE.
THEN I THINK OF POOR ELLIE, WHO HAS HELPED A LOT OF KIDS AND DONE HER BEST TO BE A GOOD MOM TO THAT CHILD OF HERS.
ELLIE DESERVES A CHANCE TO EXPLAIN HERSELF BEFORE I BRING IN THE DEAN.

ELLIE WHEDON LOVED LUCAS CARAVAGGIO AND NOW HE'S BACK FROM THE DEAD...

...ALWAYS ASSUMING HE REALLY DIED, AND I THINK THAT'S A SAFE ASSUMPTION. AND SHE'S READY TO RISK HER JOB AND MORE FOR HIM.

CALLIOPE RIDGEWAY
Director Of Admissions
1979 - 2004

~

You Are Missed

WOULD I DO ANY DIFFERENT IF IT MEANT HAVING YOU BACK?

HELL, NO.

ADMISSIONS OFFICE

Mrs. Wood

I'D DIE TO HAVE YOU BACK. KILL TO HAVE YOU BACK, FOR THAT MATTER.

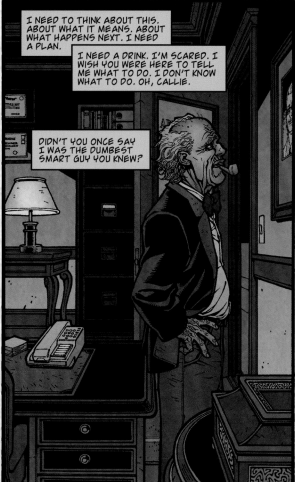

I NEED TO THINK ABOUT THIS. ABOUT WHAT IT MEANS. ABOUT WHAT HAPPENS NEXT. I NEED A PLAN.

I NEED A DRINK. I'M SCARED. I WISH YOU WERE HERE TO TELL ME WHAT TO DO. I DON'T KNOW WHAT TO DO. OH, CALLIE.

DIDN'T YOU ONCE SAY I WAS THE DUMBEST SMART GUY YOU KNEW?

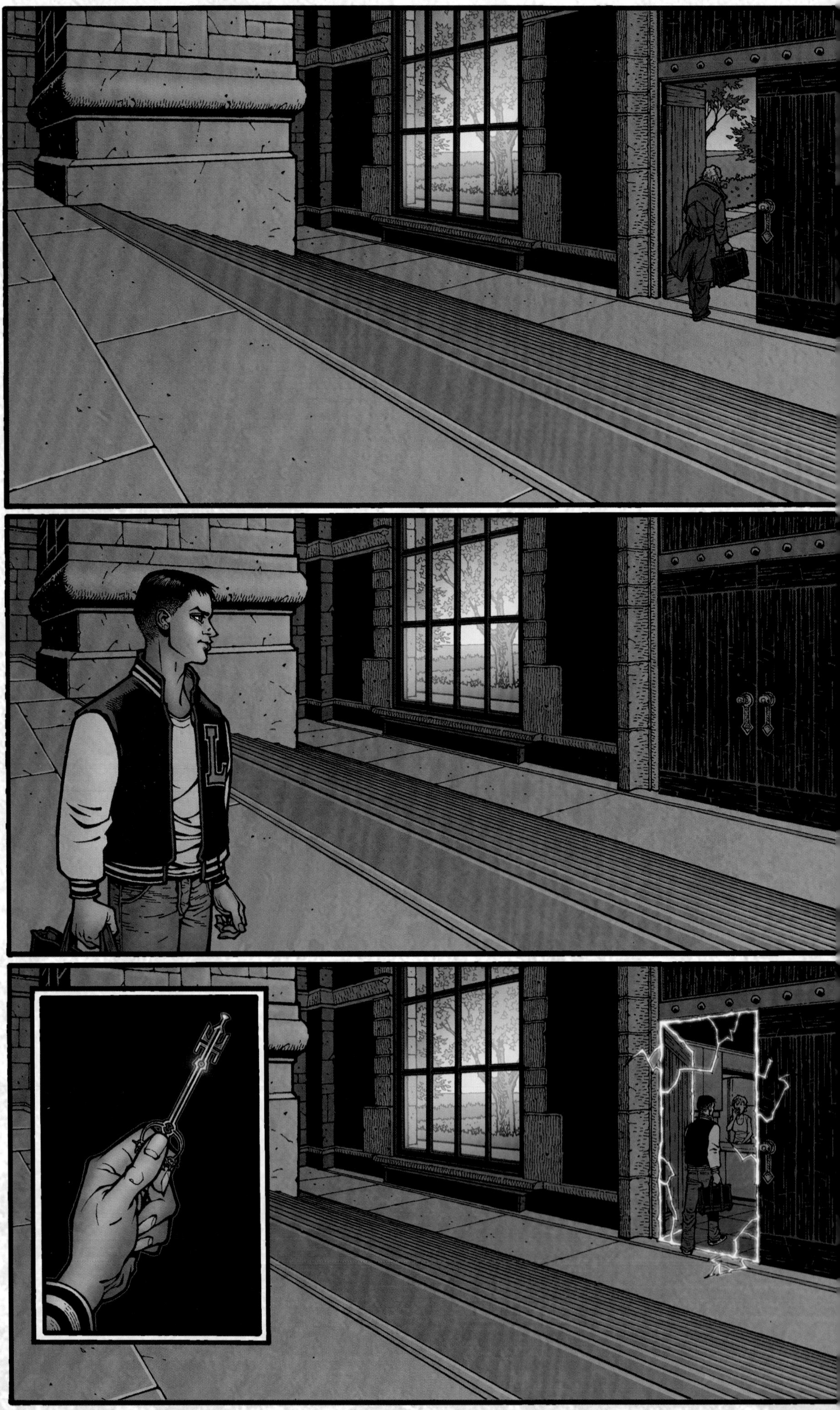

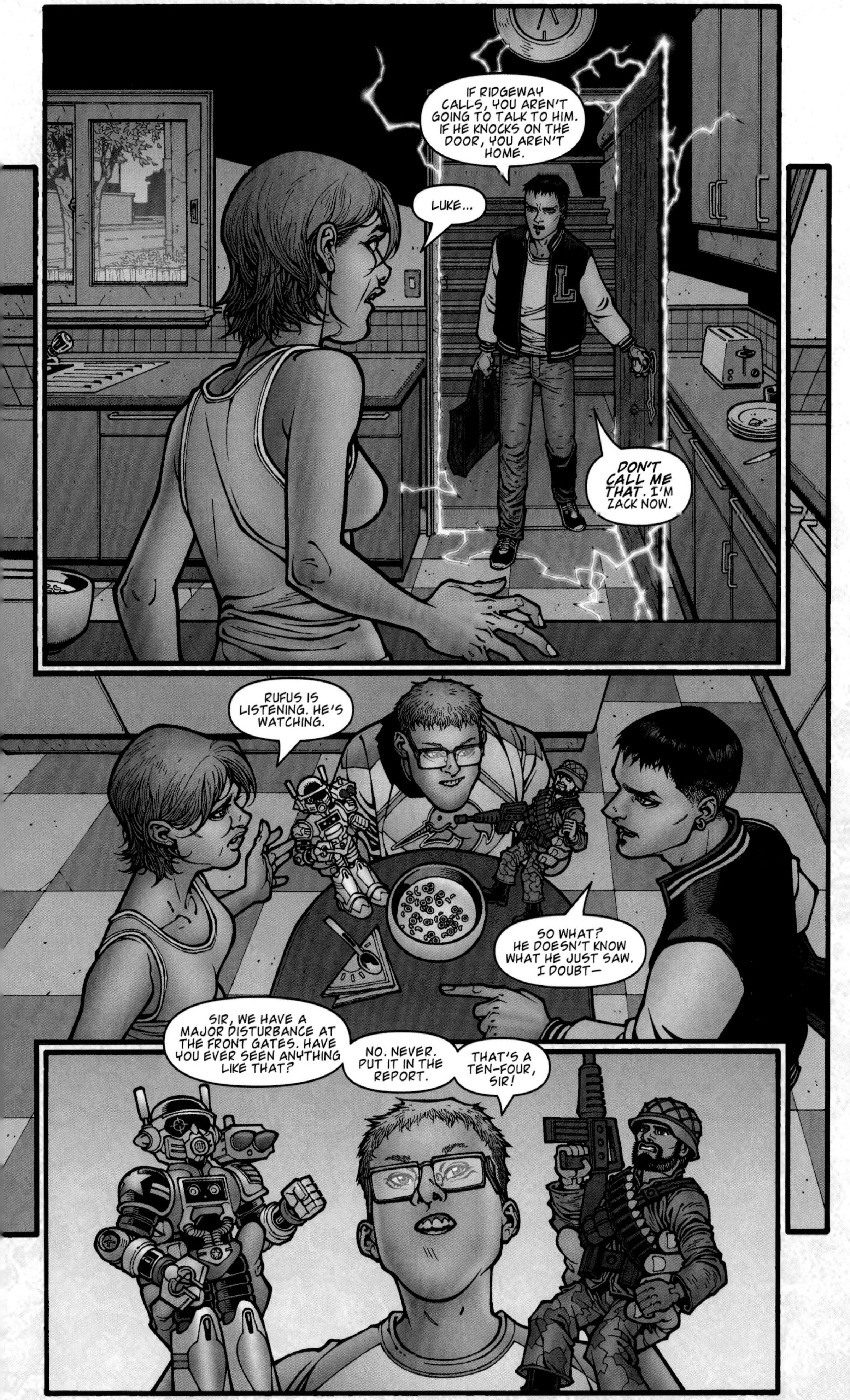
IF RIDGEWAY CALLS, YOU AREN'T GOING TO TALK TO HIM. IF HE KNOCKS ON THE DOOR, YOU AREN'T HOME.
LUKE...
DON'T CALL ME THAT. I'M ZACK NOW.
RUFUS IS LISTENING. HE'S WATCHING.
SO WHAT? HE DOESN'T KNOW WHAT HE JUST SAW. I DOUBT—
SIR, WE HAVE A MAJOR DISTURBANCE AT THE FRONT GATES. HAVE YOU EVER SEEN ANYTHING LIKE THAT?
NO. NEVER. PUT IT IN THE REPORT.
THAT'S A TEN-FOUR, SIR!

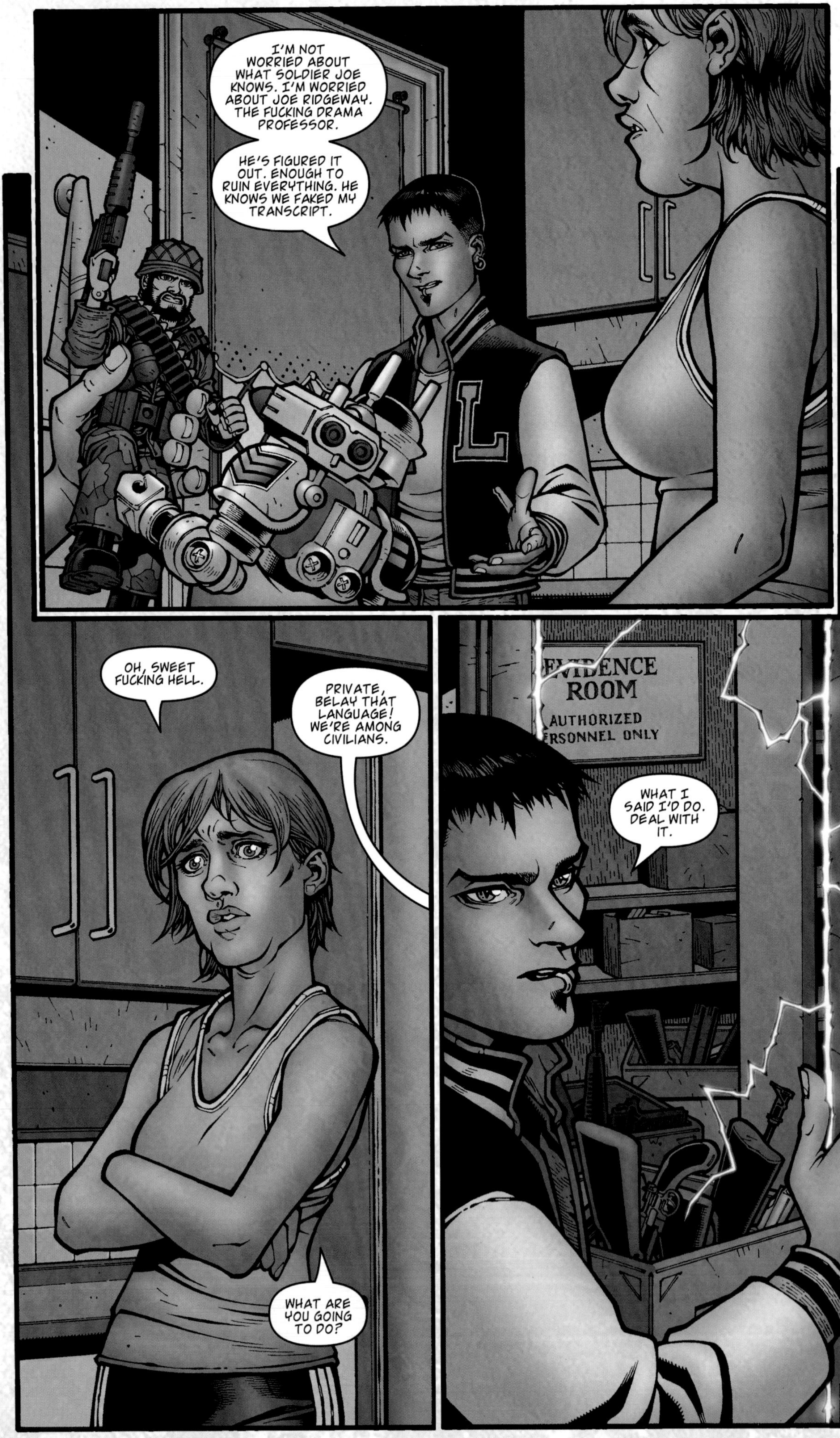
I'M NOT WORRIED ABOUT WHAT SOLDIER JOE KNOWS. I'M WORRIED ABOUT JOE RIDGEWAY. THE FUCKING DRAMA PROFESSOR.
HE'S FIGURED IT OUT. ENOUGH TO RUIN EVERYTHING. HE KNOWS WE FAKED MY TRANSCRIPT.
OH, SWEET FUCKING HELL.
PRIVATE, BELAY THAT LANGUAGE! WE'RE AMONG CIVILIANS.
WHAT ARE YOU GOING TO DO?
EVIDENCE ROOM
AUTHORIZED
RSONNEL ONLY
WHAT I SAID I'D DO. DEAL WITH IT.

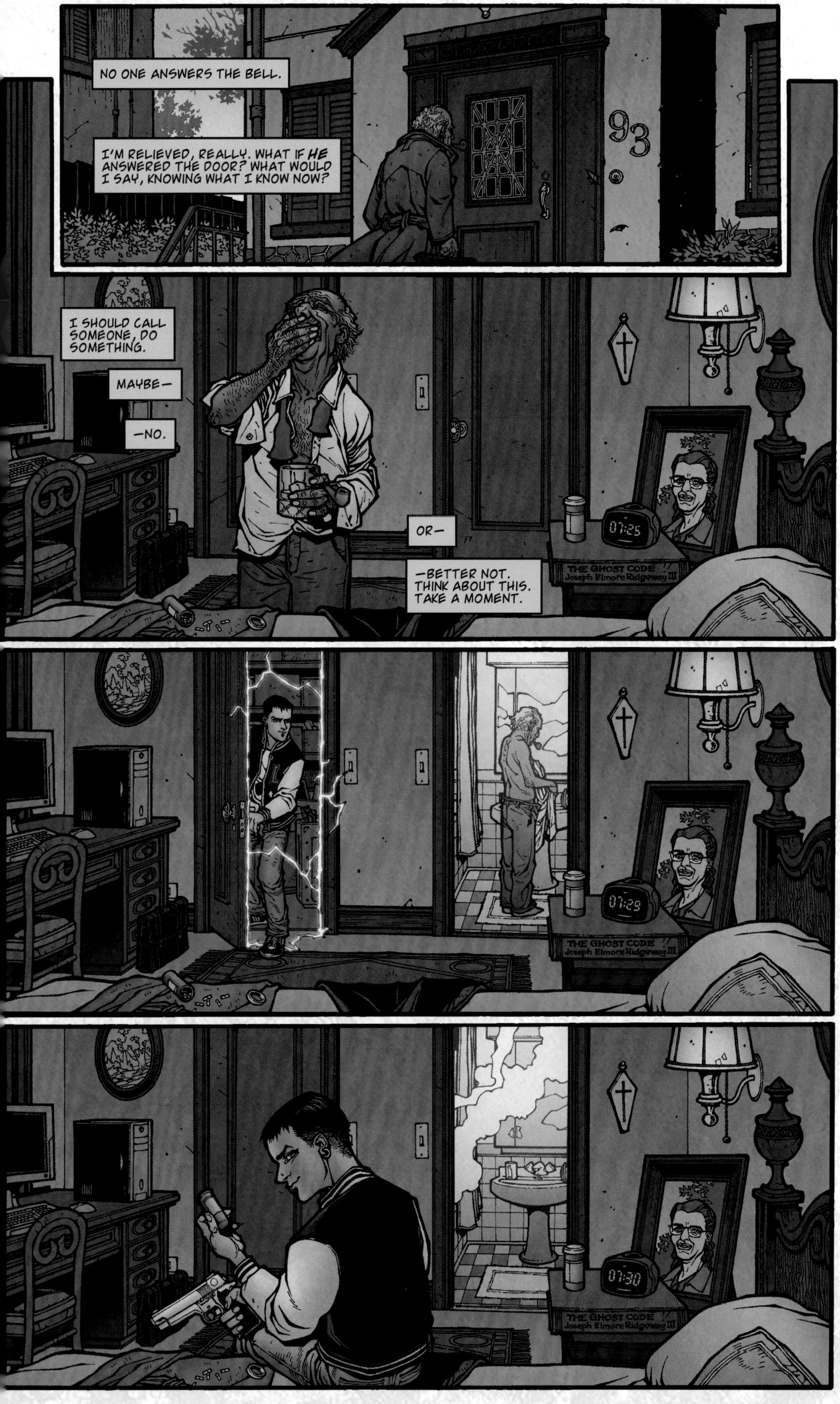
NO ONE ANSWERS THE BELL.
I'M RELIEVED, REALLY. WHAT IF HE ANSWERED THE DOOR? WHAT WOULD I SAY, KNOWING WHAT I KNOW NOW?
93
I SHOULD CALL SOMEONE, DO SOMETHING.
MAYBE—
—NO.
OR—
—BETTER NOT. THINK ABOUT THIS. TAKE A MOMENT.
07:25
THE GHOST CODE Joseph Elmore Ridgeway III
07:29
THE GHOST CODE Joseph Elmore Ridgeway III
07:30
THE GHOST CODE Joseph Elmore Ridgeway III

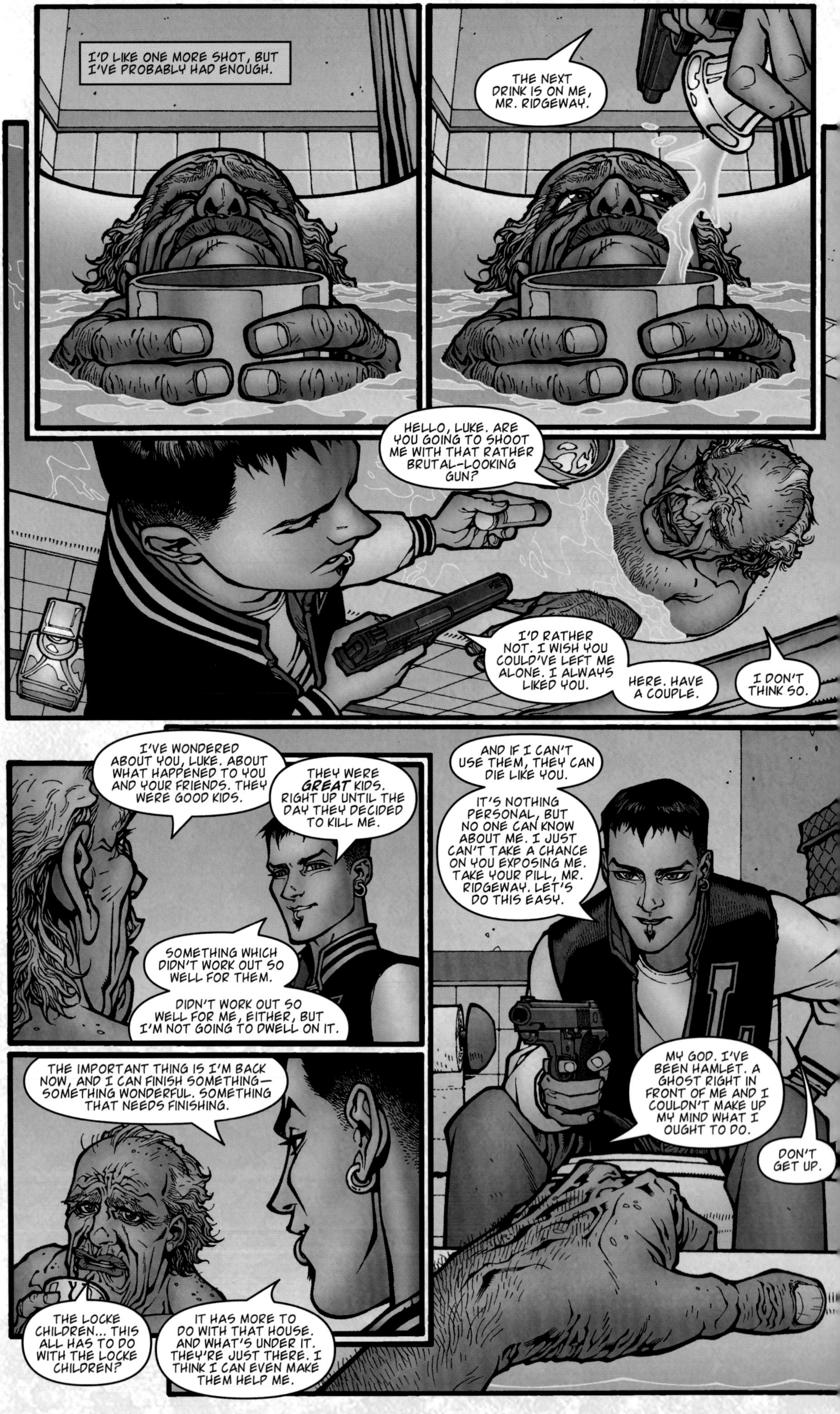
I'D LIKE ONE MORE SHOT, BUT I'VE PROBABLY HAD ENOUGH.
THE NEXT DRINK IS ON ME, MR. RIDGEWAY.
HELLO, LUKE. ARE YOU GOING TO SHOOT ME WITH THAT RATHER BRUTAL-LOOKING GUN?
I'D RATHER NOT. I WISH YOU COULD'VE LEFT ME ALONE. I ALWAYS LIKED YOU.
HERE. HAVE A COUPLE.
I DON'T THINK SO.
I'VE WONDERED ABOUT YOU, LUKE. ABOUT WHAT HAPPENED TO YOU AND YOUR FRIENDS. THEY WERE GOOD KIDS.
THEY WERE GREAT KIDS. RIGHT UP UNTIL THE DAY THEY DECIDED TO KILL ME.
SOMETHING WHICH DIDN'T WORK OUT SO WELL FOR THEM.
DIDN'T WORK OUT SO WELL FOR ME, EITHER, BUT I'M NOT GOING TO DWELL ON IT.
THE IMPORTANT THING IS I'M BACK NOW, AND I CAN FINISH SOMETHING— SOMETHING WONDERFUL. SOMETHING THAT NEEDS FINISHING.
THE LOCKE CHILDREN... THIS ALL HAS TO DO WITH THE LOCKE CHILDREN?
IT HAS MORE TO DO WITH THAT HOUSE. AND WHAT'S UNDER IT. THEY'RE JUST THERE. I THINK I CAN EVEN MAKE THEM HELP ME.
AND IF I CAN'T USE THEM, THEY CAN DIE LIKE YOU.
IT'S NOTHING PERSONAL, BUT NO ONE CAN KNOW ABOUT ME. I JUST CAN'T TAKE A CHANCE ON YOU EXPOSING ME. TAKE YOUR PILL, MR. RIDGEWAY. LET'S DO THIS EASY.
MY GOD. I'VE BEEN HAMLET. A GHOST RIGHT IN FRONT OF ME AND I COULDN'T MAKE UP MY MIND WHAT I OUGHT TO DO.
DON'T GET UP.

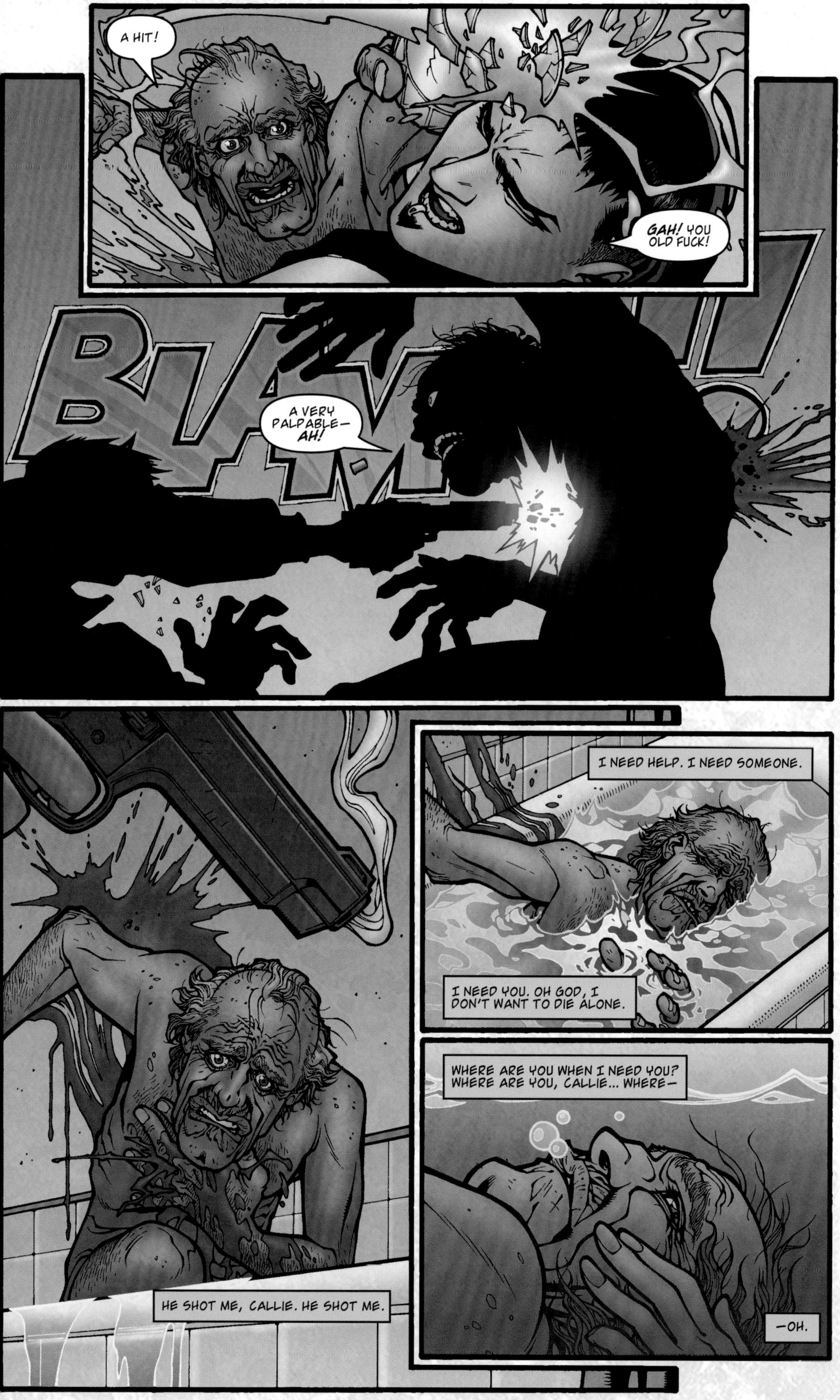
A HIT!
GAH! YOU OLD FUCK!
A VERY PALPABLE— AH!
I NEED HELP. I NEED SOMEONE.
I NEED YOU. OH GOD, I DON'T WANT TO DIE ALONE.
HE SHOT ME, CALLIE. HE SHOT ME.
WHERE ARE YOU WHEN I NEED YOU? WHERE ARE YOU, CALLIE... WHERE—
—OH.

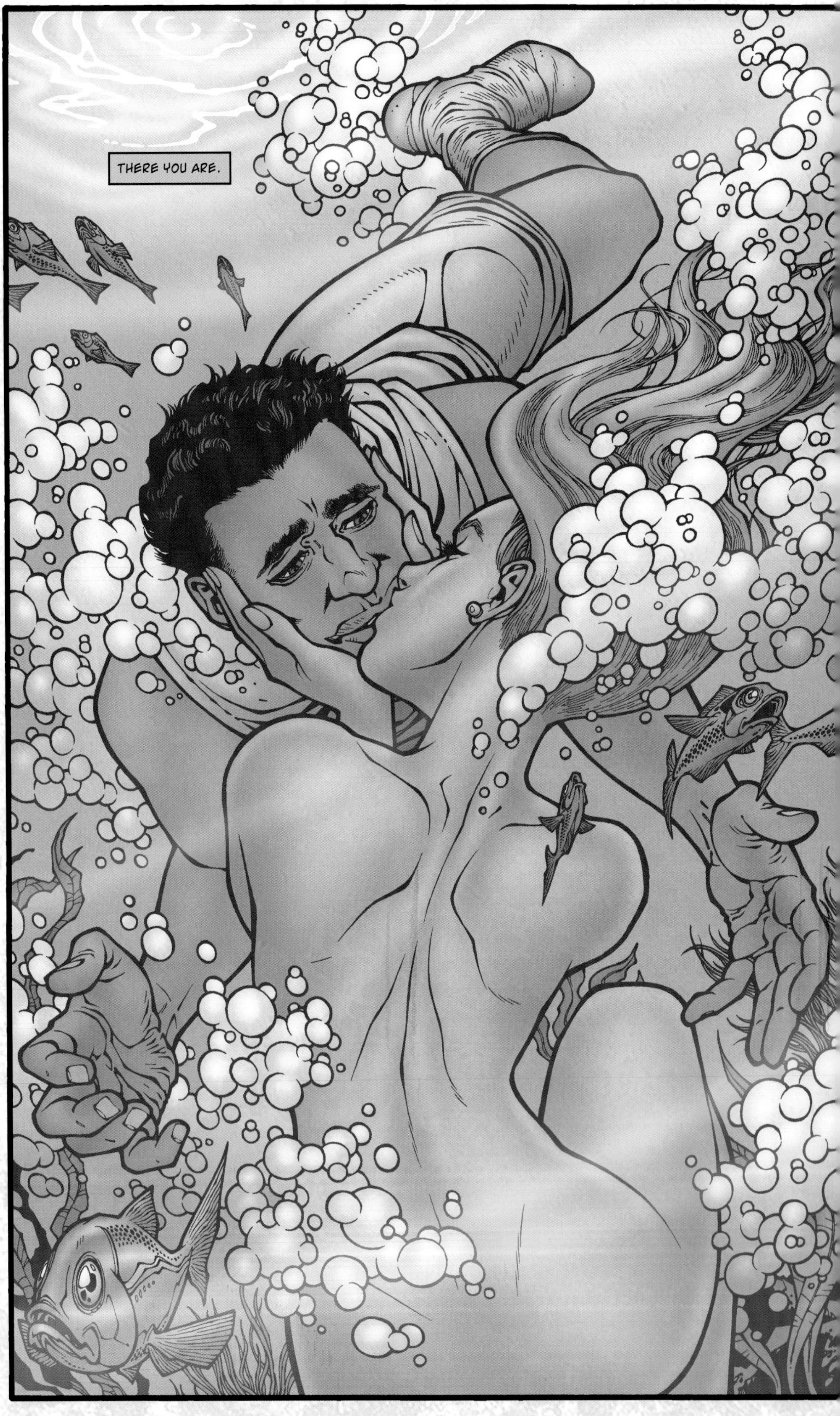
THERE YOU ARE.

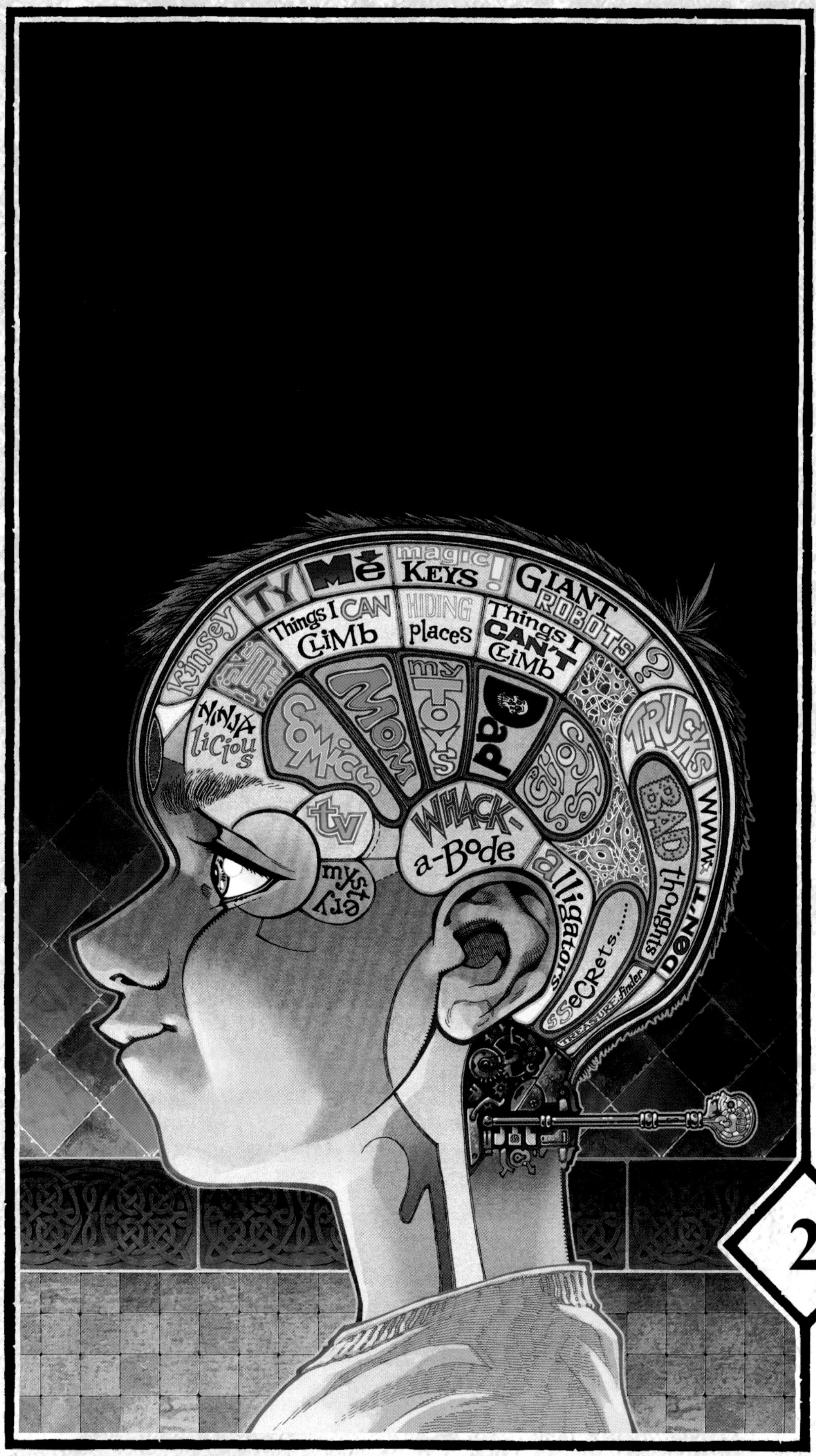
Kinsey
TY
Me
magic
KEYS
!
GIANT
ROBOTS
?
Things I CAN CLiMb
HIDING places
Things I CAN'T CLiMb
NINJA licious
Comics
Mom
my TOYS
Dad
Ghosts
TRUCKS
BAD thoughts
www
DON'T
tv
WHACK-a-Bode
alligators
mystery
secrets.....
TREASURE finder

2

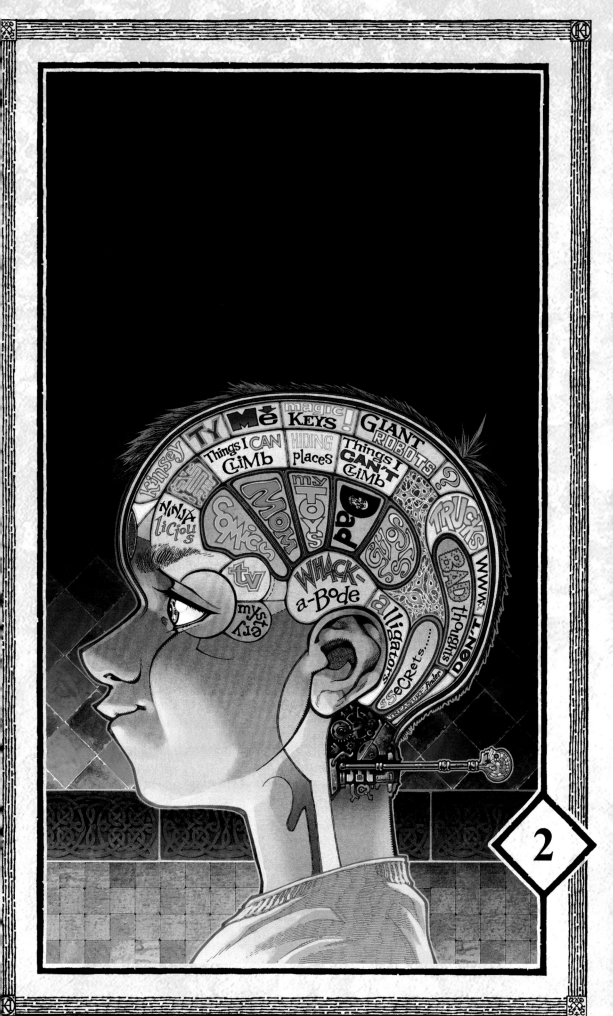

HEAD GAMES

- HEAD GAMES: Parts I-IV -

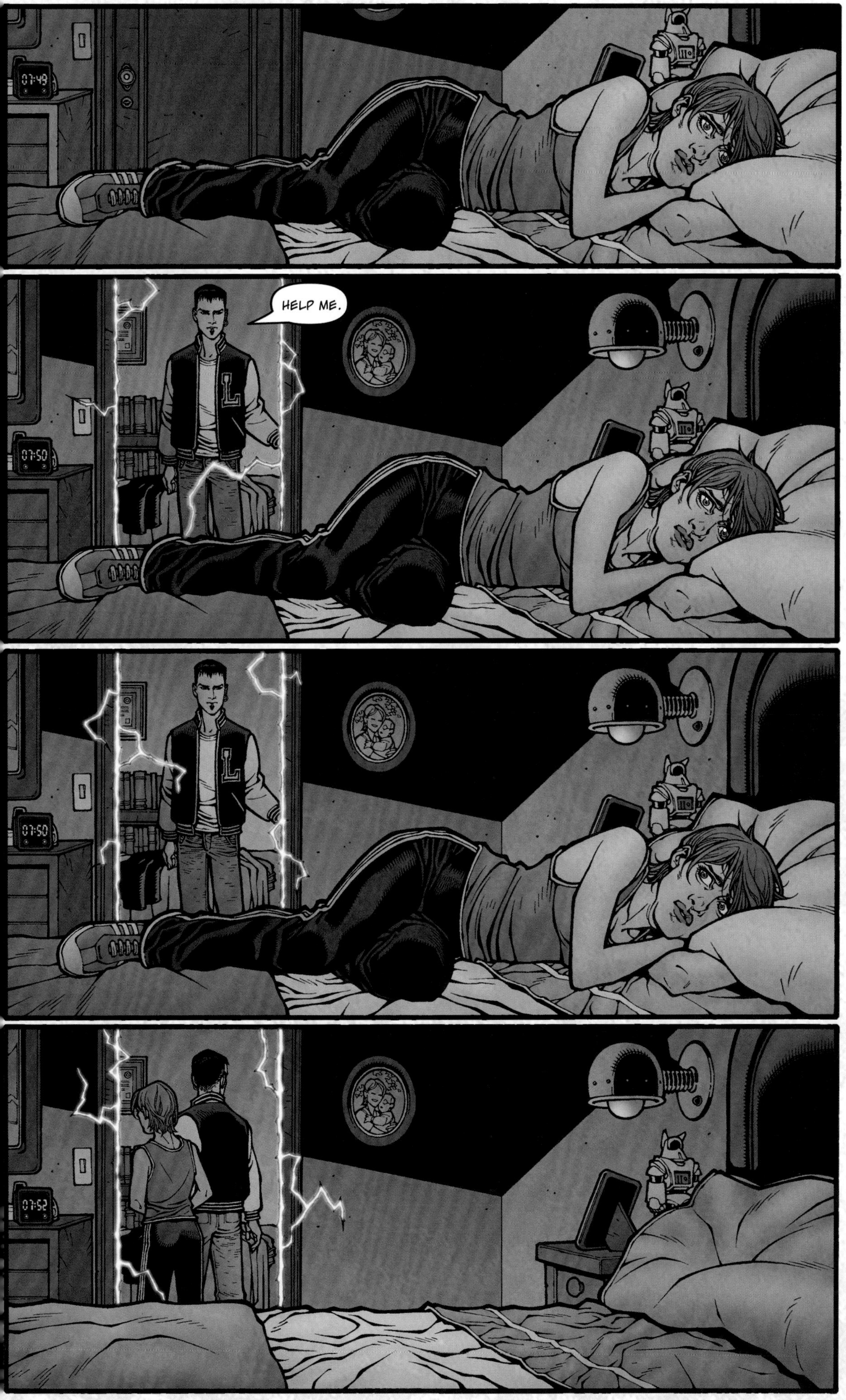
07:49
07:50
HELP ME.
07:50
07:52

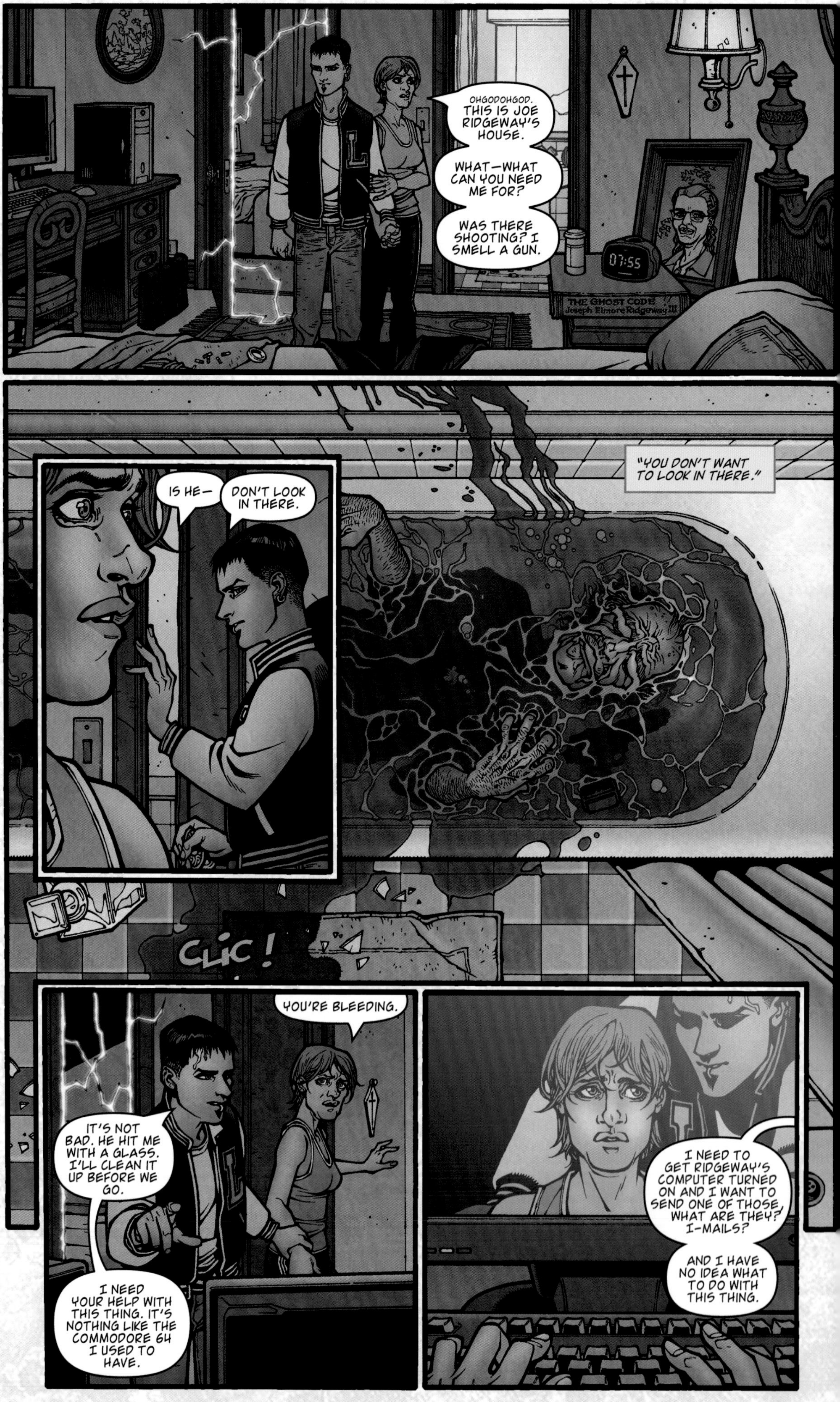
OHGODOHGOD. THIS IS JOE RIDGEWAY'S HOUSE.
WHAT—WHAT CAN YOU NEED ME FOR?
WAS THERE SHOOTING? I SMELL A GUN.
07:55
THE GHOST CODE Joseph Elmore Ridgeway III
"YOU DON'T WANT TO LOOK IN THERE."
IS HE—
DON'T LOOK IN THERE.
CLIC!
YOU'RE BLEEDING.
IT'S NOT BAD. HE HIT ME WITH A GLASS. I'LL CLEAN IT UP BEFORE WE GO.
I NEED YOUR HELP WITH THIS THING. IT'S NOTHING LIKE THE COMMODORE 64 I USED TO HAVE.
I NEED TO GET RIDGEWAY'S COMPUTER TURNED ON AND I WANT TO SEND ONE OF THOSE, WHAT ARE THEY? I-MAILS?
AND I HAVE NO IDEA WHAT TO DO WITH THIS THING.

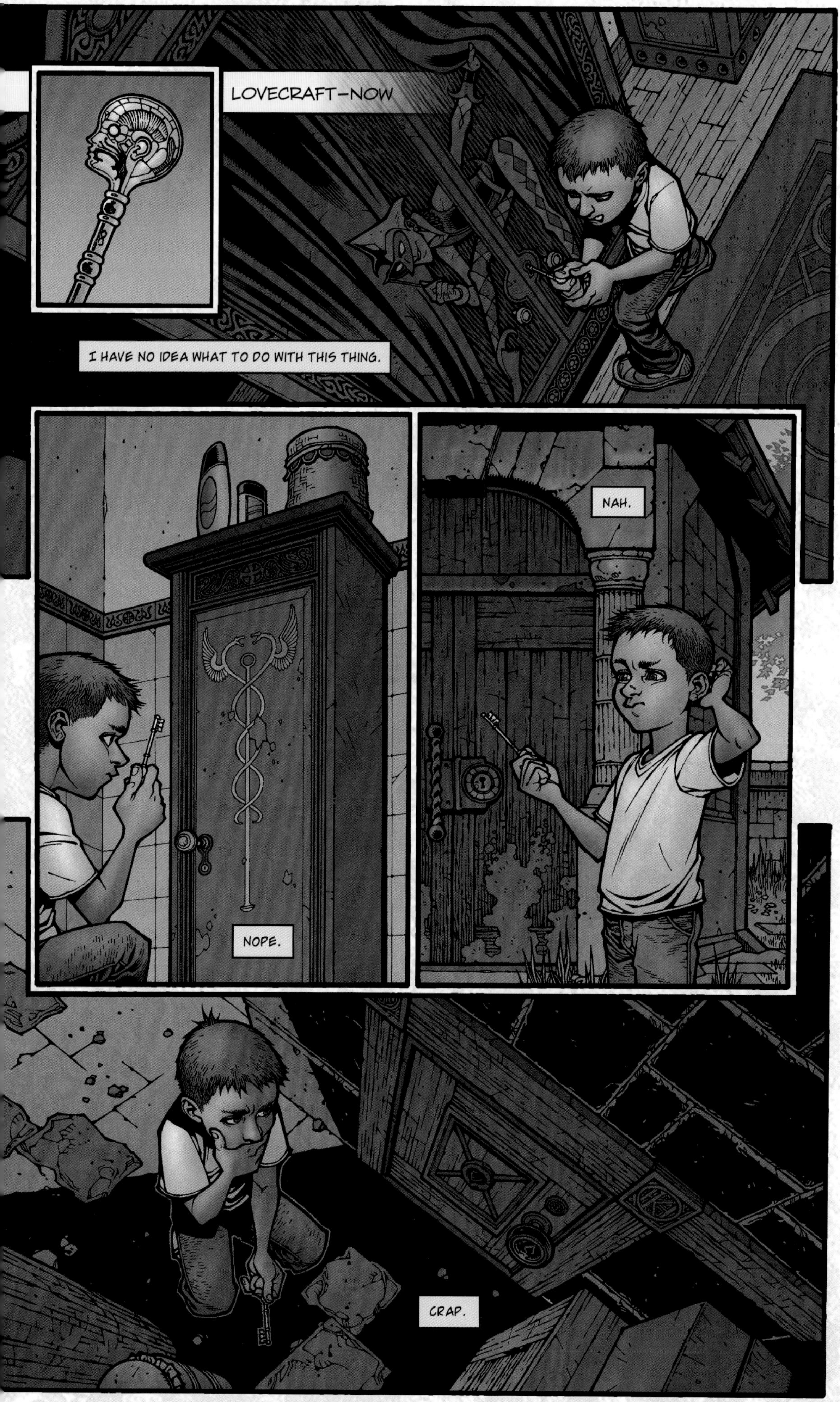
LOVECRAFT—NOW
I HAVE NO IDEA WHAT TO DO WITH THIS THING.
NOPE.
NAH.
CRAP.

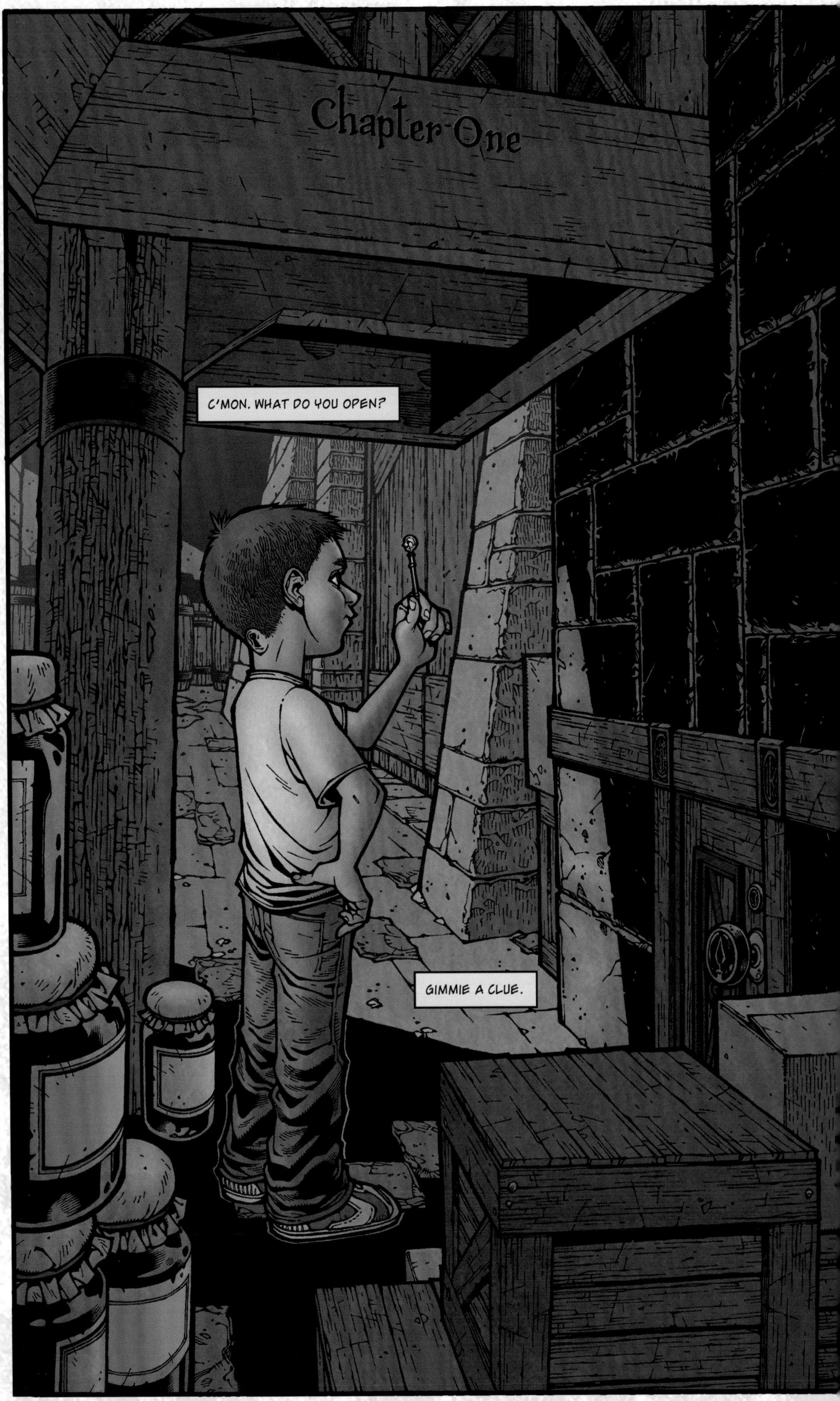
Chapter One
C'MON. WHAT DO YOU OPEN?
GIMMIE A CLUE.

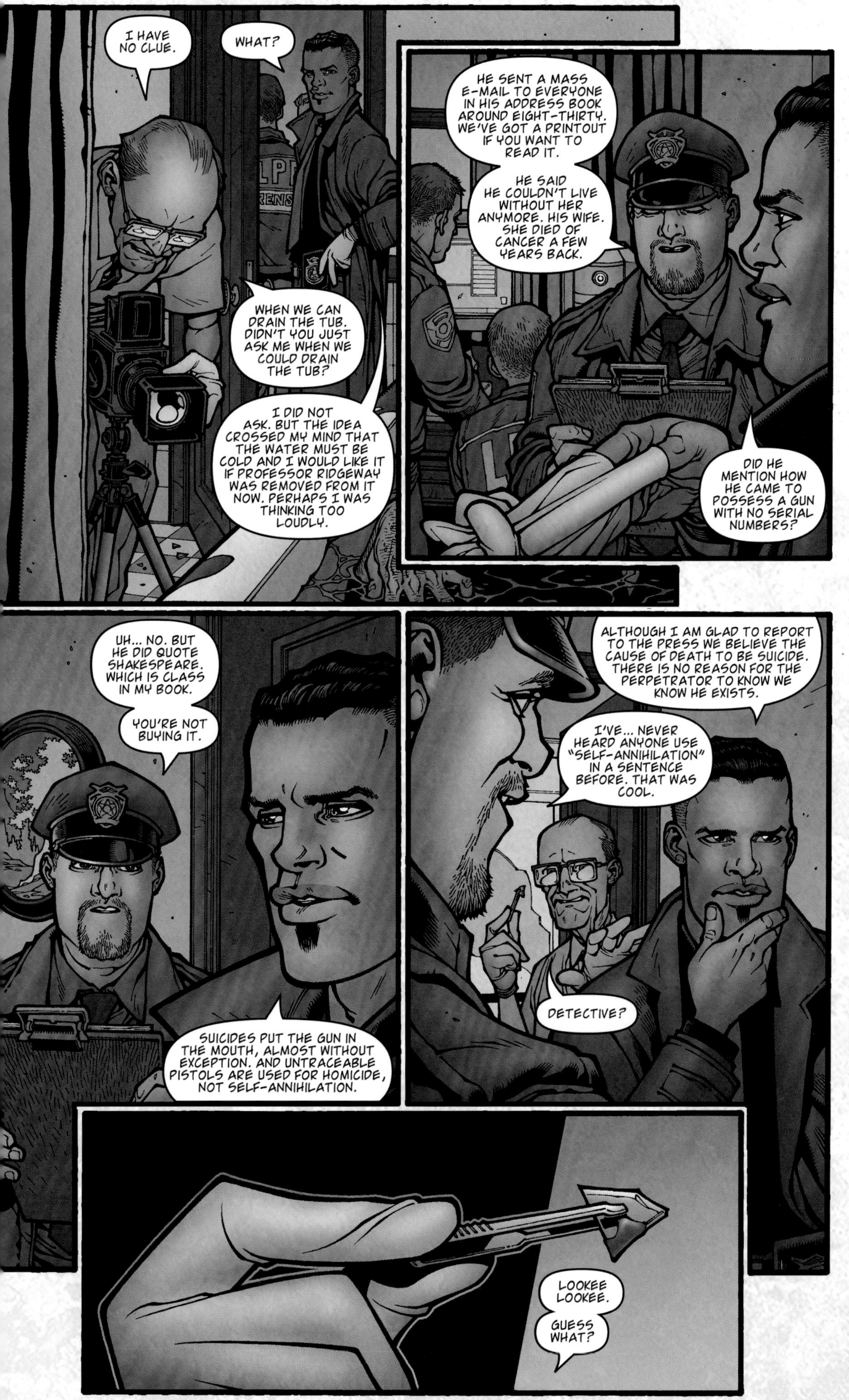
I HAVE NO CLUE.
WHAT?
WHEN WE CAN DRAIN THE TUB. DIDN'T YOU JUST ASK ME WHEN WE COULD DRAIN THE TUB?
I DID NOT ASK. BUT THE IDEA CROSSED MY MIND THAT THE WATER MUST BE COLD AND I WOULD LIKE IT IF PROFESSOR RIDGEWAY WAS REMOVED FROM IT NOW. PERHAPS I WAS THINKING TOO LOUDLY.
HE SENT A MASS E-MAIL TO EVERYONE IN HIS ADDRESS BOOK AROUND EIGHT-THIRTY. WE'VE GOT A PRINTOUT IF YOU WANT TO READ IT.
HE SAID HE COULDN'T LIVE WITHOUT HER ANYMORE. HIS WIFE. SHE DIED OF CANCER A FEW YEARS BACK.
DID HE MENTION HOW HE CAME TO POSSESS A GUN WITH NO SERIAL NUMBERS?
UH... NO. BUT HE DID QUOTE SHAKESPEARE. WHICH IS CLASS IN MY BOOK.
YOU'RE NOT BUYING IT.
SUICIDES PUT THE GUN IN THE MOUTH, ALMOST WITHOUT EXCEPTION. AND UNTRACEABLE PISTOLS ARE USED FOR HOMICIDE, NOT SELF-ANNIHILATION.
ALTHOUGH I AM GLAD TO REPORT TO THE PRESS WE BELIEVE THE CAUSE OF DEATH TO BE SUICIDE. THERE IS NO REASON FOR THE PERPETRATOR TO KNOW WE KNOW HE EXISTS.
I'VE... NEVER HEARD ANYONE USE "SELF-ANNIHILATION" IN A SENTENCE BEFORE. THAT WAS COOL.
DETECTIVE?
LOOKEE LOOKEE.
GUESS WHAT?

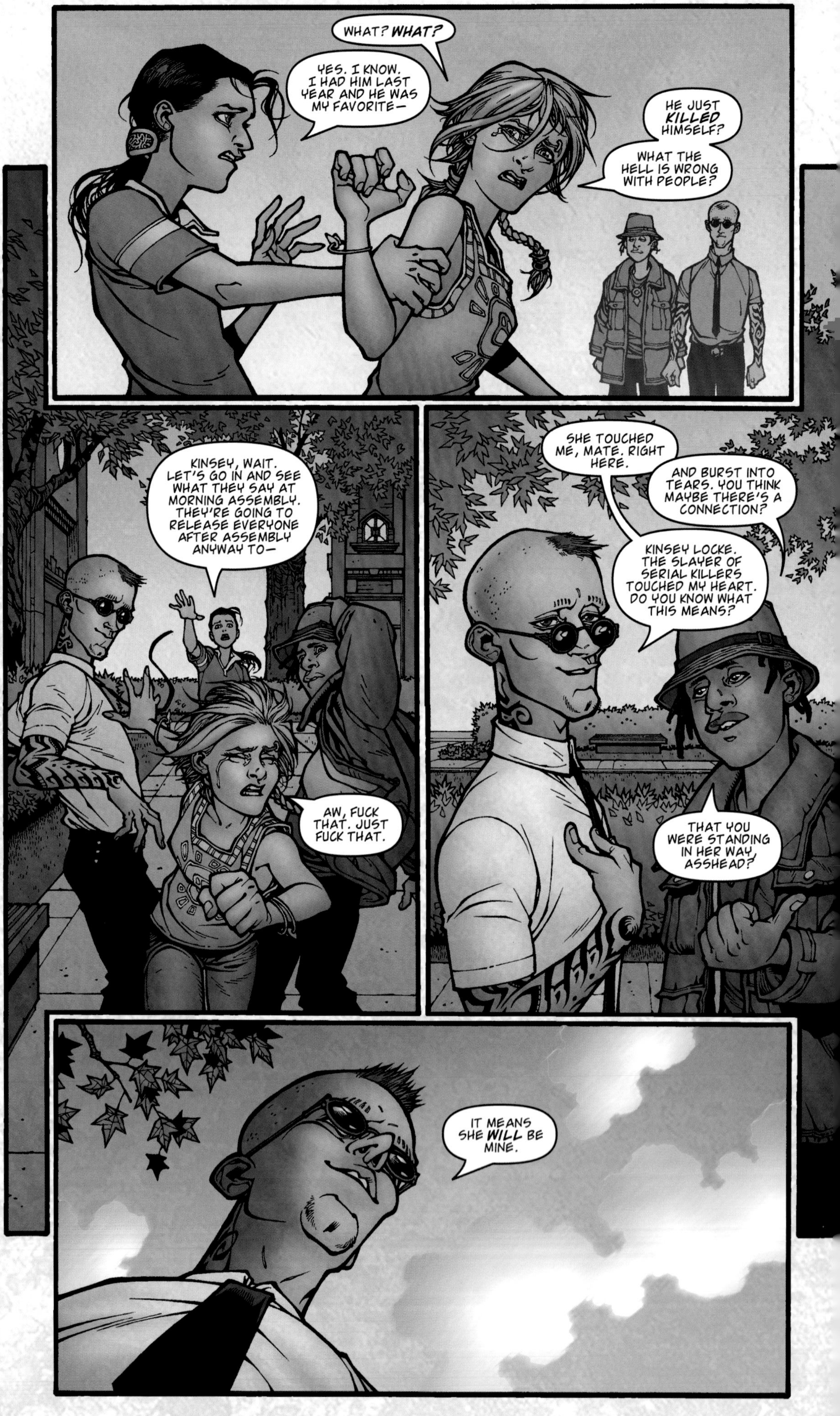
WHAT? **WHAT?**
YES. I KNOW. I HAD HIM LAST YEAR AND HE WAS MY FAVORITE—
HE JUST **KILLED** HIMSELF?
WHAT THE HELL IS WRONG WITH PEOPLE?
KINSEY, WAIT. LET'S GO IN AND SEE WHAT THEY SAY AT MORNING ASSEMBLY. THEY'RE GOING TO RELEASE EVERYONE AFTER ASSEMBLY ANYWAY TO—
AW, FUCK THAT. JUST FUCK THAT.
SHE TOUCHED ME, MATE. RIGHT HERE.
AND BURST INTO TEARS. YOU THINK MAYBE THERE'S A CONNECTION?
KINSEY LOCKE. THE SLAYER OF SERIAL KILLERS TOUCHED MY HEART. DO YOU KNOW WHAT THIS MEANS?
THAT YOU WERE STANDING IN HER WAY, ASSHEAD?
IT MEANS SHE **WILL** BE MINE.

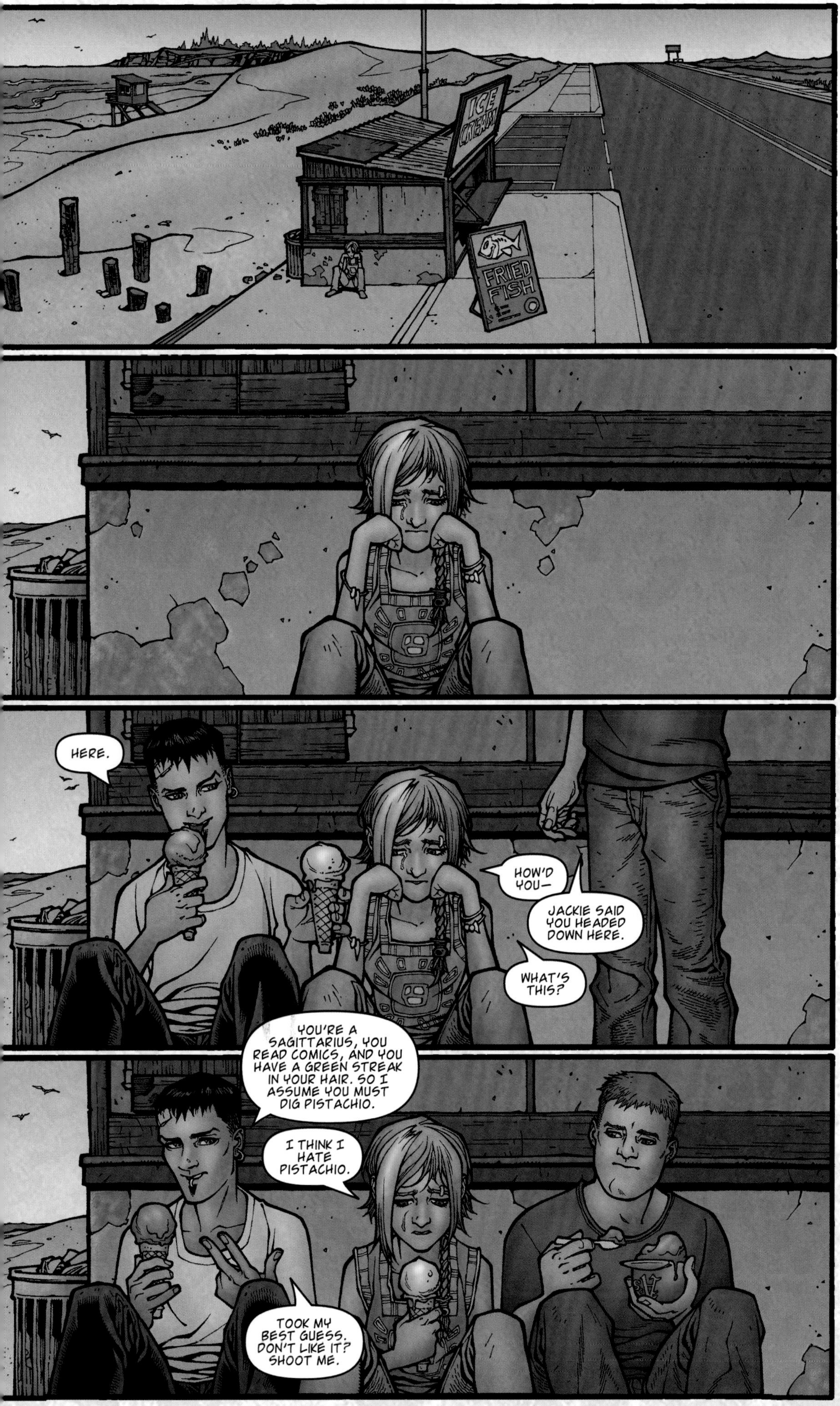
ICE CREAM
FRIED FISH
HERE.
HOW'D YOU—
JACKIE SAID YOU HEADED DOWN HERE.
WHAT'S THIS?
YOU'RE A SAGITTARIUS, YOU READ COMICS, AND YOU HAVE A GREEN STREAK IN YOUR HAIR. SO I ASSUME YOU MUST DIG PISTACHIO.
I THINK I HATE PISTACHIO.
TOOK MY BEST GUESS. DON'T LIKE IT? SHOOT ME.

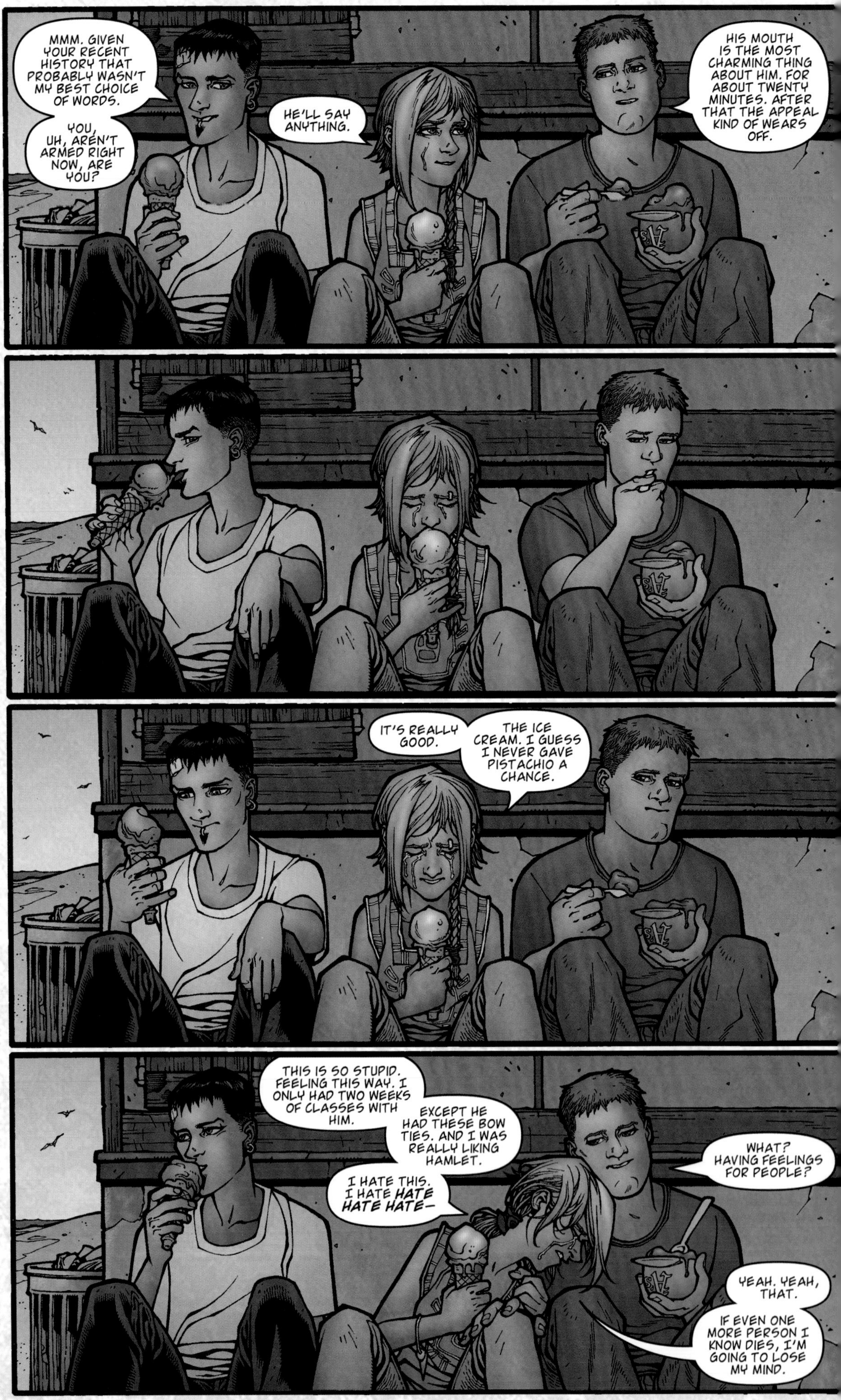
MMM. GIVEN YOUR RECENT HISTORY THAT PROBABLY WASN'T MY BEST CHOICE OF WORDS.
YOU, UH, AREN'T ARMED RIGHT NOW, ARE YOU?
HE'LL SAY ANYTHING.
HIS MOUTH IS THE MOST CHARMING THING ABOUT HIM. FOR ABOUT TWENTY MINUTES. AFTER THAT THE APPEAL KIND OF WEARS OFF.
IT'S REALLY GOOD.
THE ICE CREAM. I GUESS I NEVER GAVE PISTACHIO A CHANCE.
THIS IS SO STUPID. FEELING THIS WAY. I ONLY HAD TWO WEEKS OF CLASSES WITH HIM.
EXCEPT HE HAD THESE BOW TIES. AND I WAS REALLY LIKING HAMLET.
I HATE THIS. I HATE ***HATE HATE HATE***—
WHAT? HAVING FEELINGS FOR PEOPLE?
YEAH. YEAH, THAT.
IF EVEN ONE MORE PERSON I KNOW DIES, I'M GOING TO LOSE MY MIND.

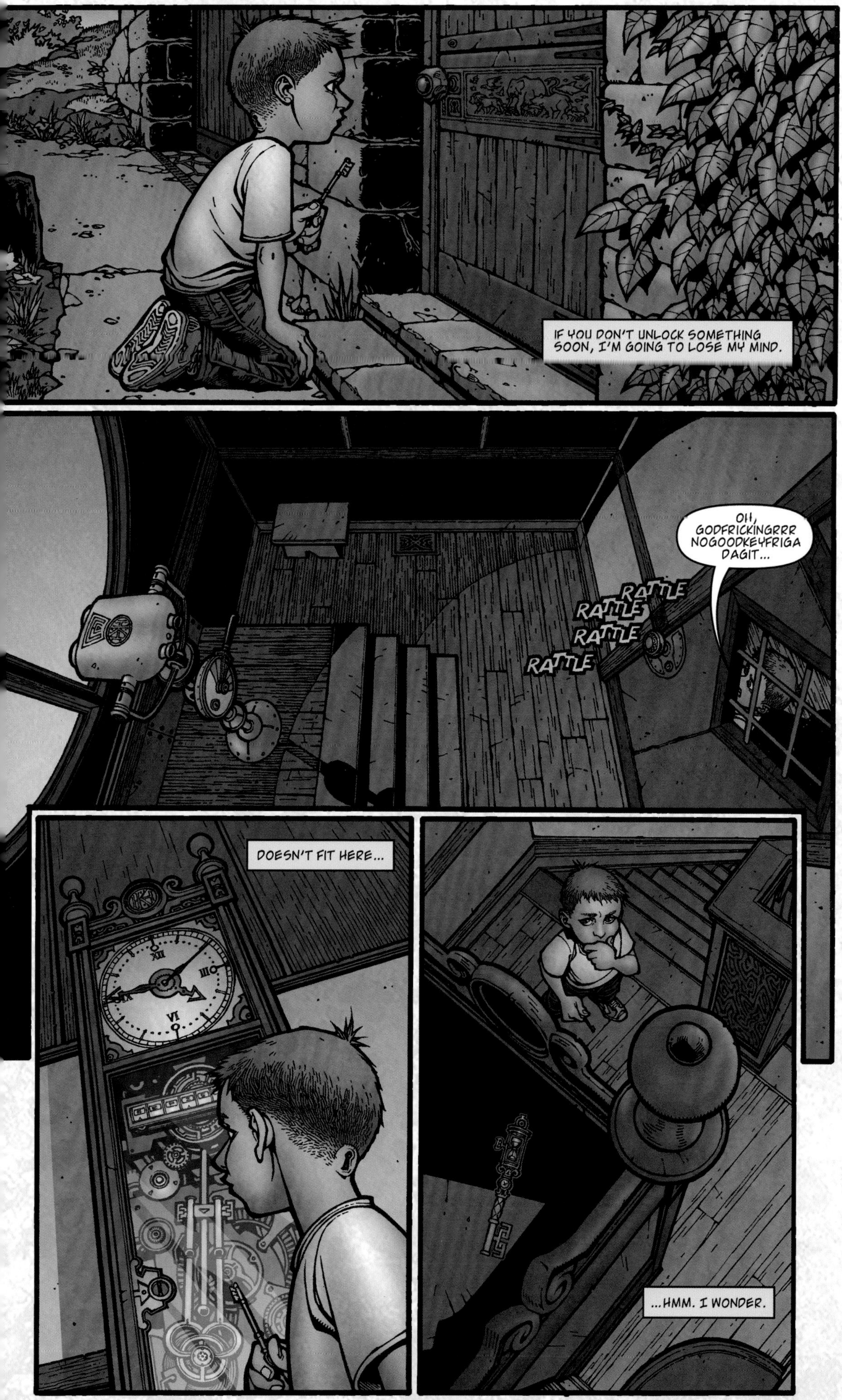
IF YOU DON'T UNLOCK SOMETHING SOON, I'M GOING TO LOSE MY MIND.
OH, GODFRICKINGRRR NOGOODKEYFRIGA DAGIT...
RATTLE RATTLE RATTLE RATTLE
DOESN'T FIT HERE...
...HMM. I WONDER.

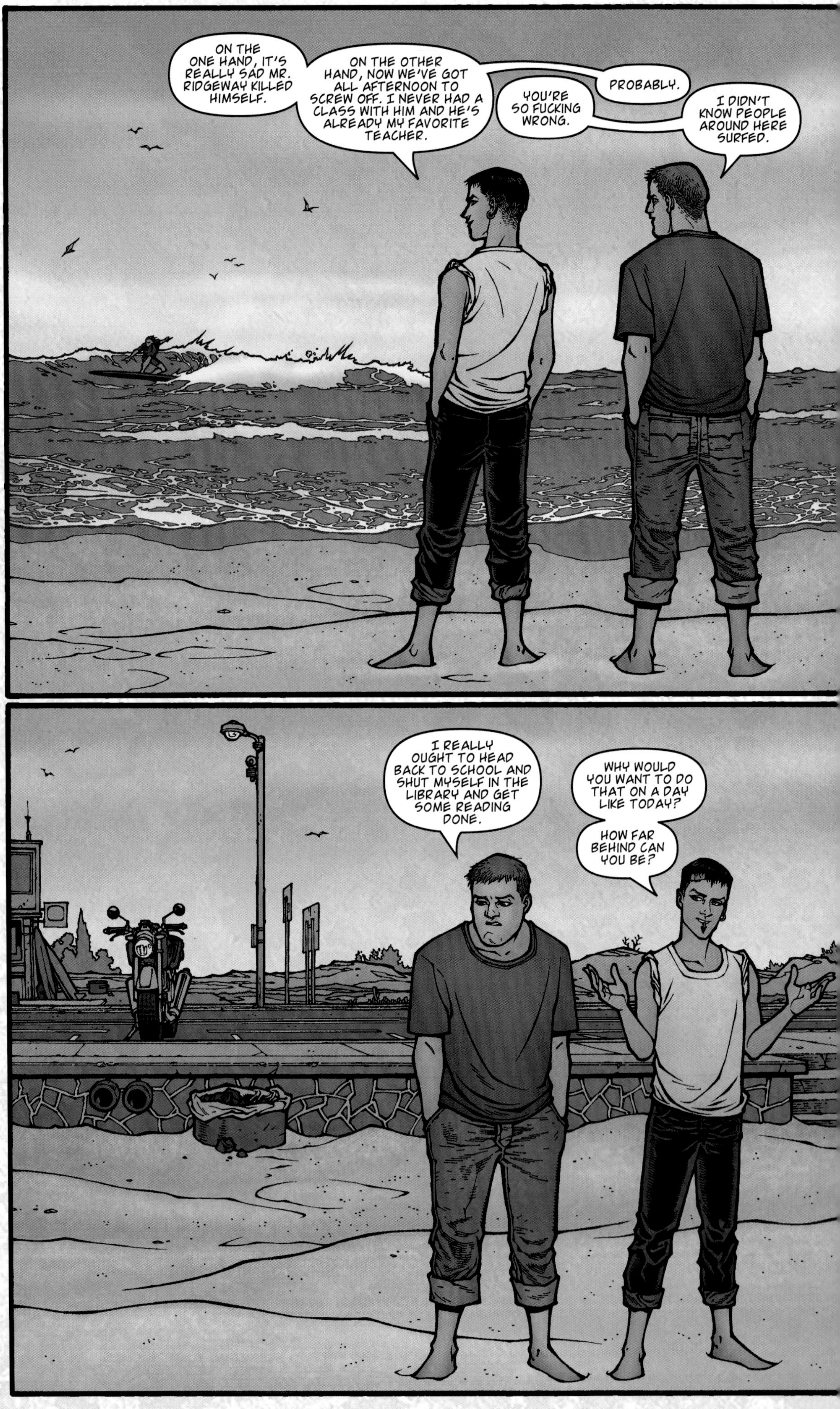
ON THE ONE HAND, IT'S REALLY SAD MR. RIDGEWAY KILLED HIMSELF.
ON THE OTHER HAND, NOW WE'VE GOT ALL AFTERNOON TO SCREW OFF. I NEVER HAD A CLASS WITH HIM AND HE'S ALREADY MY FAVORITE TEACHER.
PROBABLY.
YOU'RE SO FUCKING WRONG.
I DIDN'T KNOW PEOPLE AROUND HERE SURFED.
I REALLY OUGHT TO HEAD BACK TO SCHOOL AND SHUT MYSELF IN THE LIBRARY AND GET SOME READING DONE.
WHY WOULD YOU WANT TO DO THAT ON A DAY LIKE TODAY?
HOW FAR BEHIND CAN YOU BE?

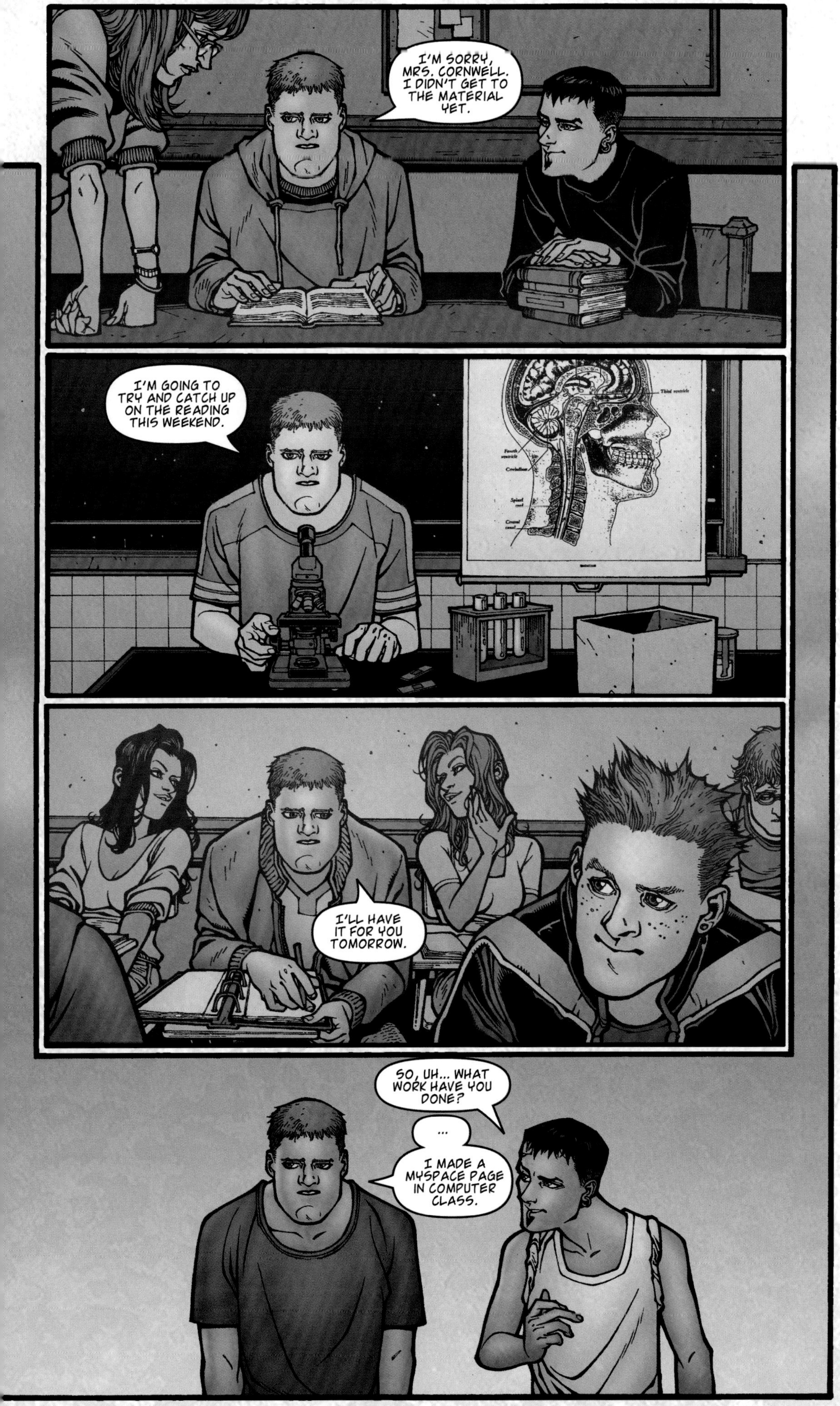
I'M SORRY, MRS. CORNWELL. I DIDN'T GET TO THE MATERIAL YET.
I'M GOING TO TRY AND CATCH UP ON THE READING THIS WEEKEND.
I'LL HAVE IT FOR YOU TOMORROW.
SO, UH... WHAT WORK HAVE YOU DONE?
...
I MADE A MYSPACE PAGE IN COMPUTER CLASS.

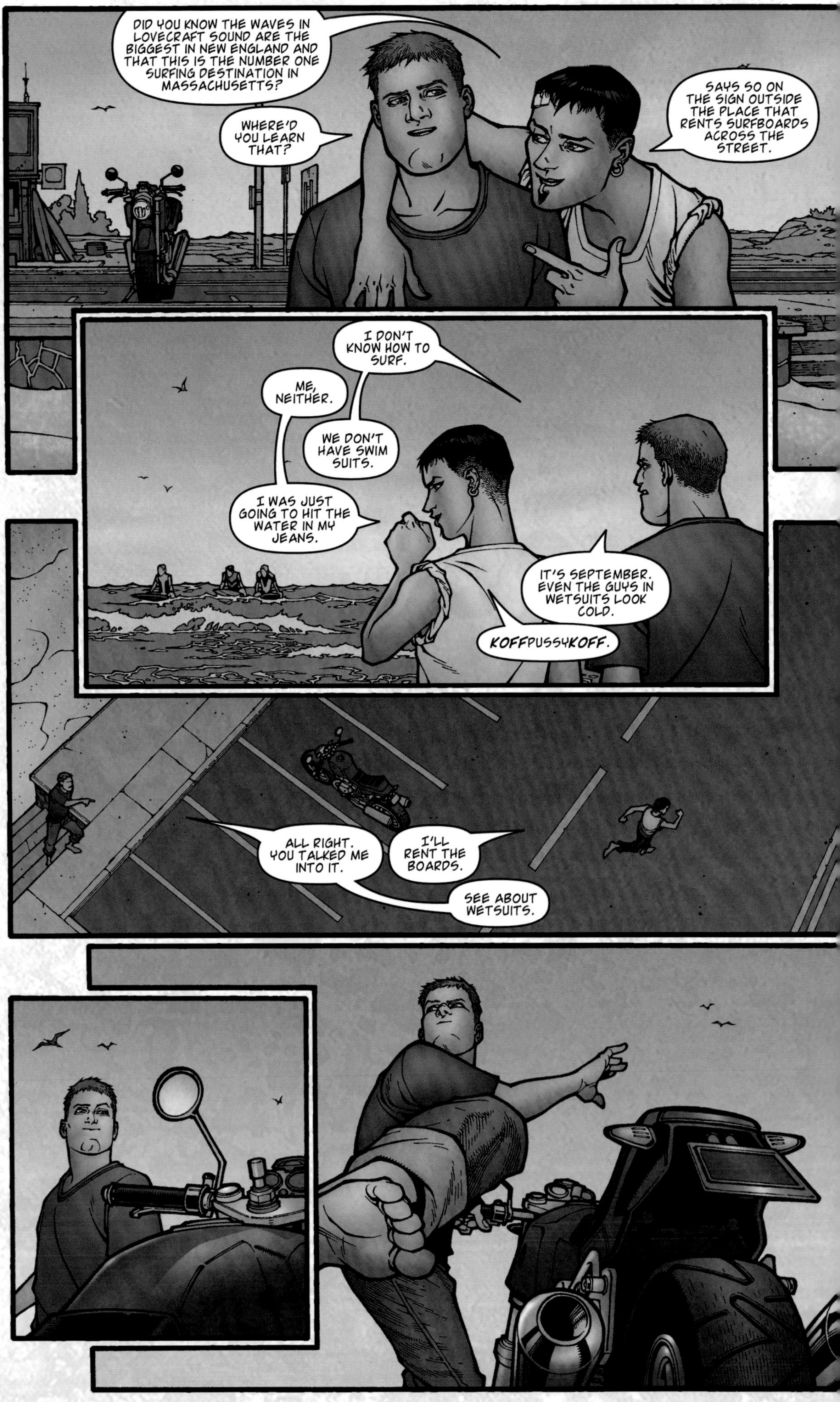
DID YOU KNOW THE WAVES IN LOVECRAFT SOUND ARE THE BIGGEST IN NEW ENGLAND AND THAT THIS IS THE NUMBER ONE SURFING DESTINATION IN MASSACHUSETTS?
WHERE'D YOU LEARN THAT?
SAYS SO ON THE SIGN OUTSIDE THE PLACE THAT RENTS SURFBOARDS ACROSS THE STREET.
I DON'T KNOW HOW TO SURF.
ME, NEITHER.
WE DON'T HAVE SWIM SUITS.
I WAS JUST GOING TO HIT THE WATER IN MY JEANS.
IT'S SEPTEMBER. EVEN THE GUYS IN WETSUITS LOOK COLD.
KOFFPUSSYKOFF.
ALL RIGHT. YOU TALKED ME INTO IT.
I'LL RENT THE BOARDS.
SEE ABOUT WETSUITS.

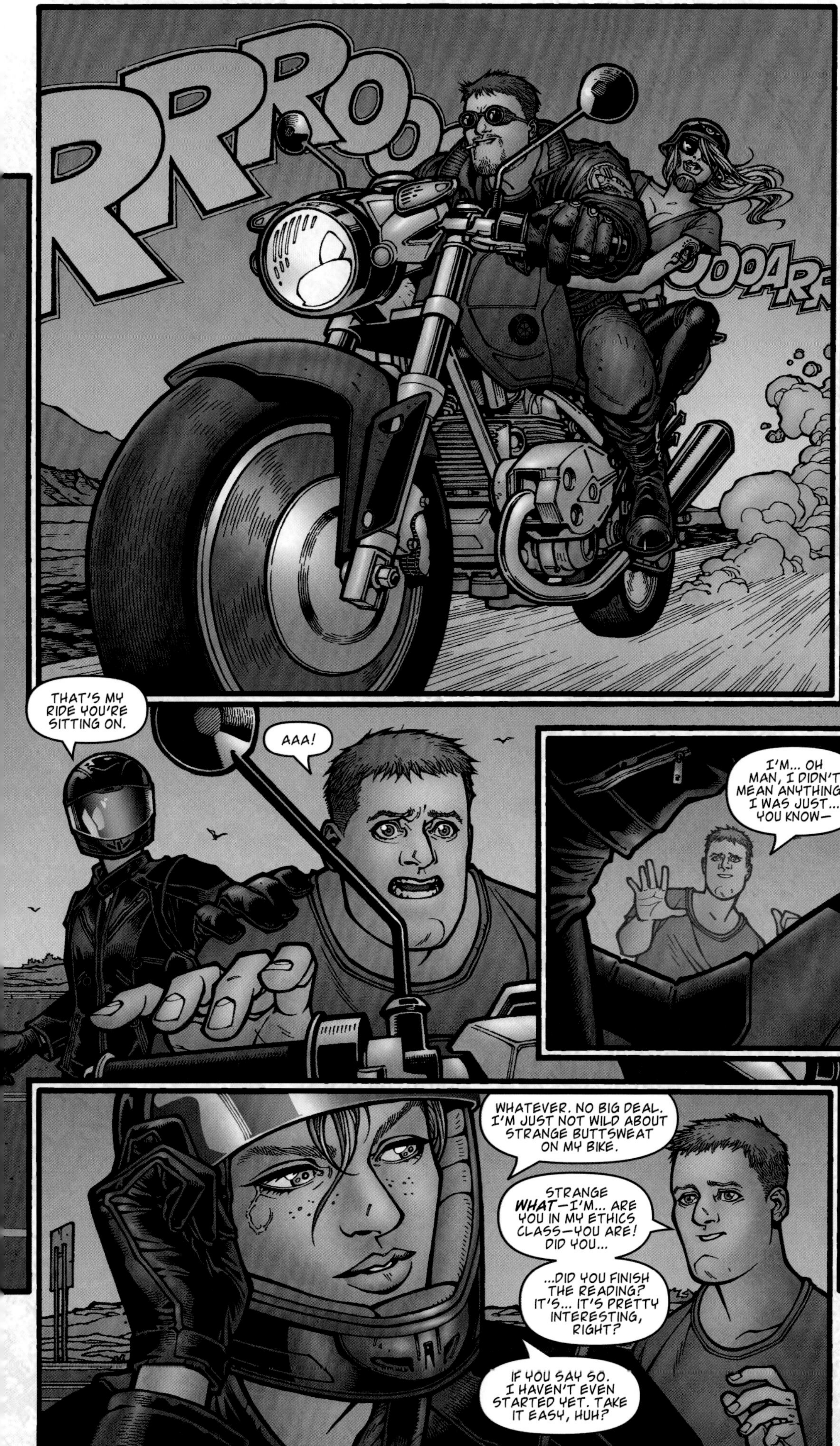
RRROOO
OOOARR
THAT'S MY RIDE YOU'RE SITTING ON.
AAA!
I'M... OH MAN, I DIDN'T MEAN ANYTHING... I WAS JUST... YOU KNOW—
WHATEVER. NO BIG DEAL. I'M JUST NOT WILD ABOUT STRANGE BUTTSWEAT ON MY BIKE.
STRANGE *WHAT*—I'M... ARE YOU IN MY ETHICS CLASS—YOU ARE! DID YOU...
...DID YOU FINISH THE READING? IT'S... IT'S PRETTY INTERESTING, RIGHT?
IF YOU SAY SO. I HAVEN'T EVEN STARTED YET. TAKE IT EASY, HUH?

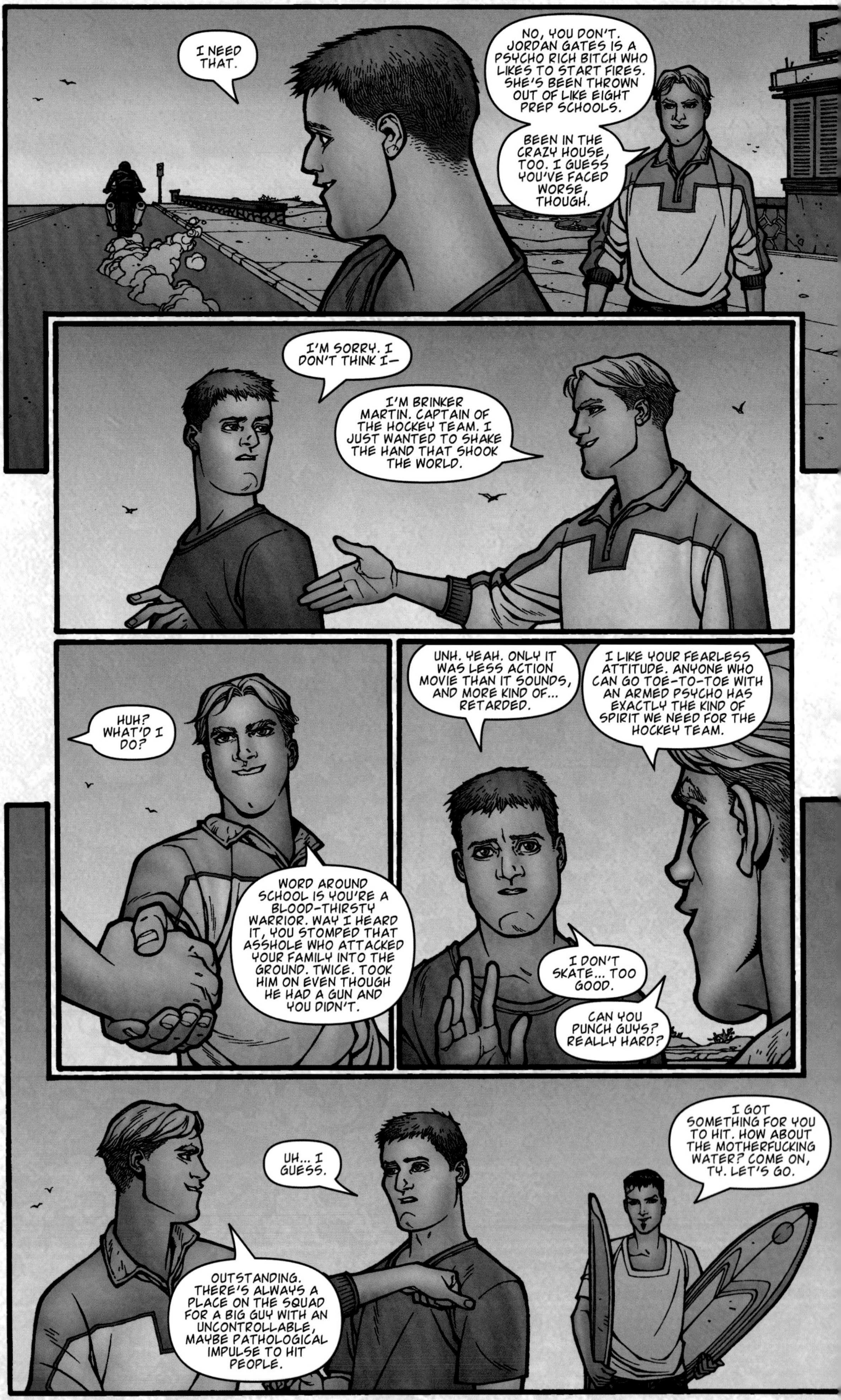
I NEED THAT.
NO, YOU DON'T. JORDAN GATES IS A PSYCHO RICH BITCH WHO LIKES TO START FIRES. SHE'S BEEN THROWN OUT OF LIKE EIGHT PREP SCHOOLS.
BEEN IN THE CRAZY HOUSE, TOO. I GUESS YOU'VE FACED WORSE, THOUGH.
I'M SORRY. I DON'T THINK I—
I'M BRINKER MARTIN. CAPTAIN OF THE HOCKEY TEAM. I JUST WANTED TO SHAKE THE HAND THAT SHOOK THE WORLD.
HUH? WHAT'D I DO?
WORD AROUND SCHOOL IS YOU'RE A BLOOD-THIRSTY WARRIOR. WAY I HEARD IT, YOU STOMPED THAT ASSHOLE WHO ATTACKED YOUR FAMILY INTO THE GROUND. TWICE. TOOK HIM ON EVEN THOUGH HE HAD A GUN AND YOU DIDN'T.
UNH. YEAH. ONLY IT WAS LESS ACTION MOVIE THAN IT SOUNDS, AND MORE KIND OF... RETARDED.
I LIKE YOUR FEARLESS ATTITUDE. ANYONE WHO CAN GO TOE-TO-TOE WITH AN ARMED PSYCHO HAS EXACTLY THE KIND OF SPIRIT WE NEED FOR THE HOCKEY TEAM.
I DON'T SKATE... TOO GOOD.
CAN YOU PUNCH GUYS? REALLY HARD?
UH... I GUESS.
OUTSTANDING. THERE'S ALWAYS A PLACE ON THE SQUAD FOR A BIG GUY WITH AN UNCONTROLLABLE, MAYBE PATHOLOGICAL IMPULSE TO HIT PEOPLE.
I GOT SOMETHING FOR YOU TO HIT. HOW ABOUT THE MOTHERFUCKING WATER? COME ON, TY. LET'S GO.

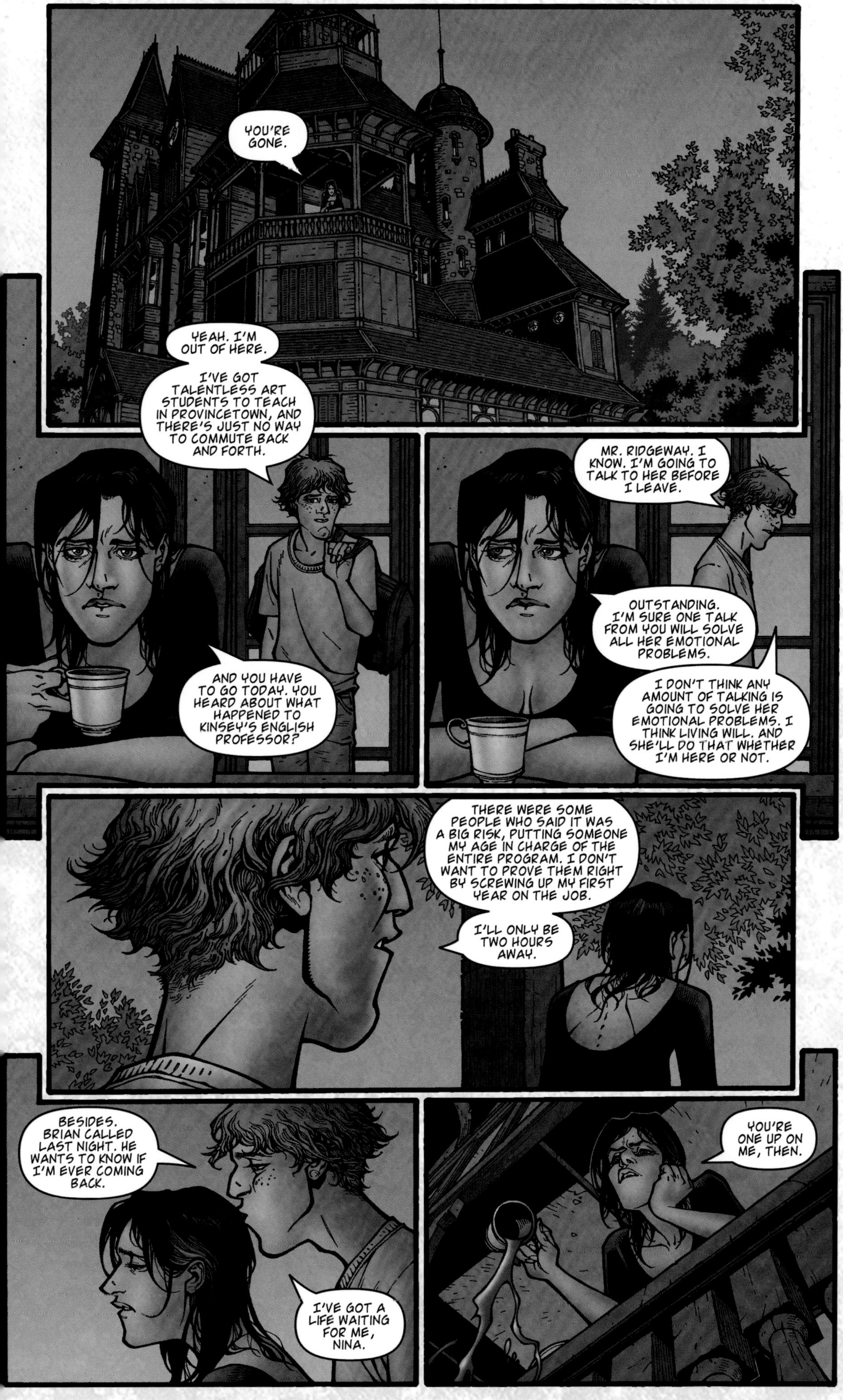
YOU'RE GONE.
YEAH. I'M OUT OF HERE.
I'VE GOT TALENTLESS ART STUDENTS TO TEACH IN PROVINCETOWN, AND THERE'S JUST NO WAY TO COMMUTE BACK AND FORTH.
AND YOU HAVE TO GO TODAY. YOU HEARD ABOUT WHAT HAPPENED TO KINSEY'S ENGLISH PROFESSOR?
MR. RIDGEWAY. I KNOW. I'M GOING TO TALK TO HER BEFORE I LEAVE.
OUTSTANDING. I'M SURE ONE TALK FROM YOU WILL SOLVE ALL HER EMOTIONAL PROBLEMS.
I DON'T THINK ANY AMOUNT OF TALKING IS GOING TO SOLVE HER EMOTIONAL PROBLEMS. I THINK LIVING WILL. AND SHE'LL DO THAT WHETHER I'M HERE OR NOT.
THERE WERE SOME PEOPLE WHO SAID IT WAS A BIG RISK, PUTTING SOMEONE MY AGE IN CHARGE OF THE ENTIRE PROGRAM. I DON'T WANT TO PROVE THEM RIGHT BY SCREWING UP MY FIRST YEAR ON THE JOB.
I'LL ONLY BE TWO HOURS AWAY.
BESIDES. BRIAN CALLED LAST NIGHT. HE WANTS TO KNOW IF I'M EVER COMING BACK.
I'VE GOT A LIFE WAITING FOR ME, NINA.
YOU'RE ONE UP ON ME, THEN.

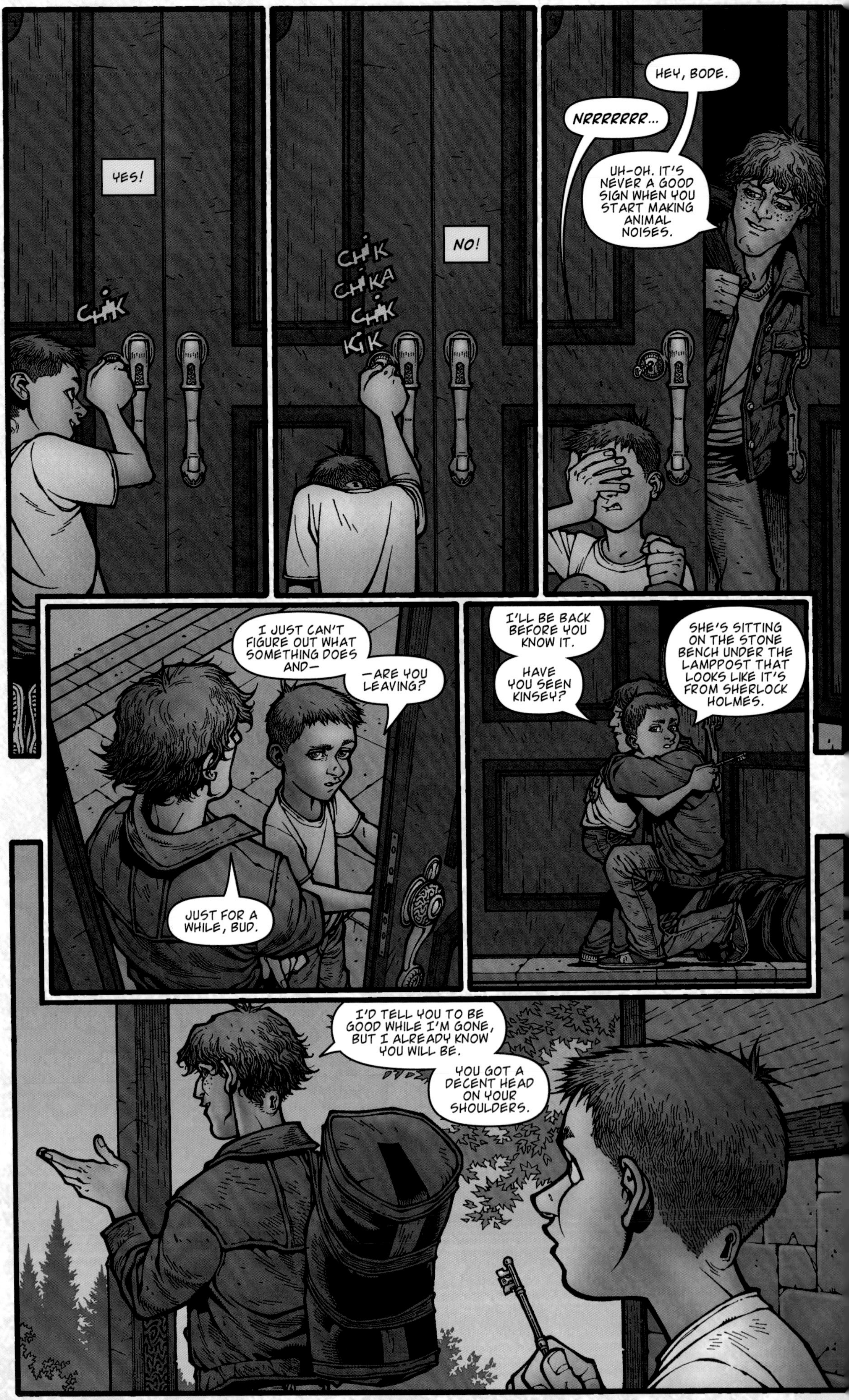
YES!
CHIK
CHIK
CHIKA
CHIK
KIK
NO!
HEY, BODE.
NRRRRRRR...
UH-OH. IT'S NEVER A GOOD SIGN WHEN YOU START MAKING ANIMAL NOISES.
I JUST CAN'T FIGURE OUT WHAT SOMETHING DOES AND—
—ARE YOU LEAVING?
JUST FOR A WHILE, BUD.
I'LL BE BACK BEFORE YOU KNOW IT.
HAVE YOU SEEN KINSEY?
SHE'S SITTING ON THE STONE BENCH UNDER THE LAMPPOST THAT LOOKS LIKE IT'S FROM SHERLOCK HOLMES.
I'D TELL YOU TO BE GOOD WHILE I'M GONE, BUT I ALREADY KNOW YOU WILL BE.
YOU GOT A DECENT HEAD ON YOUR SHOULDERS.

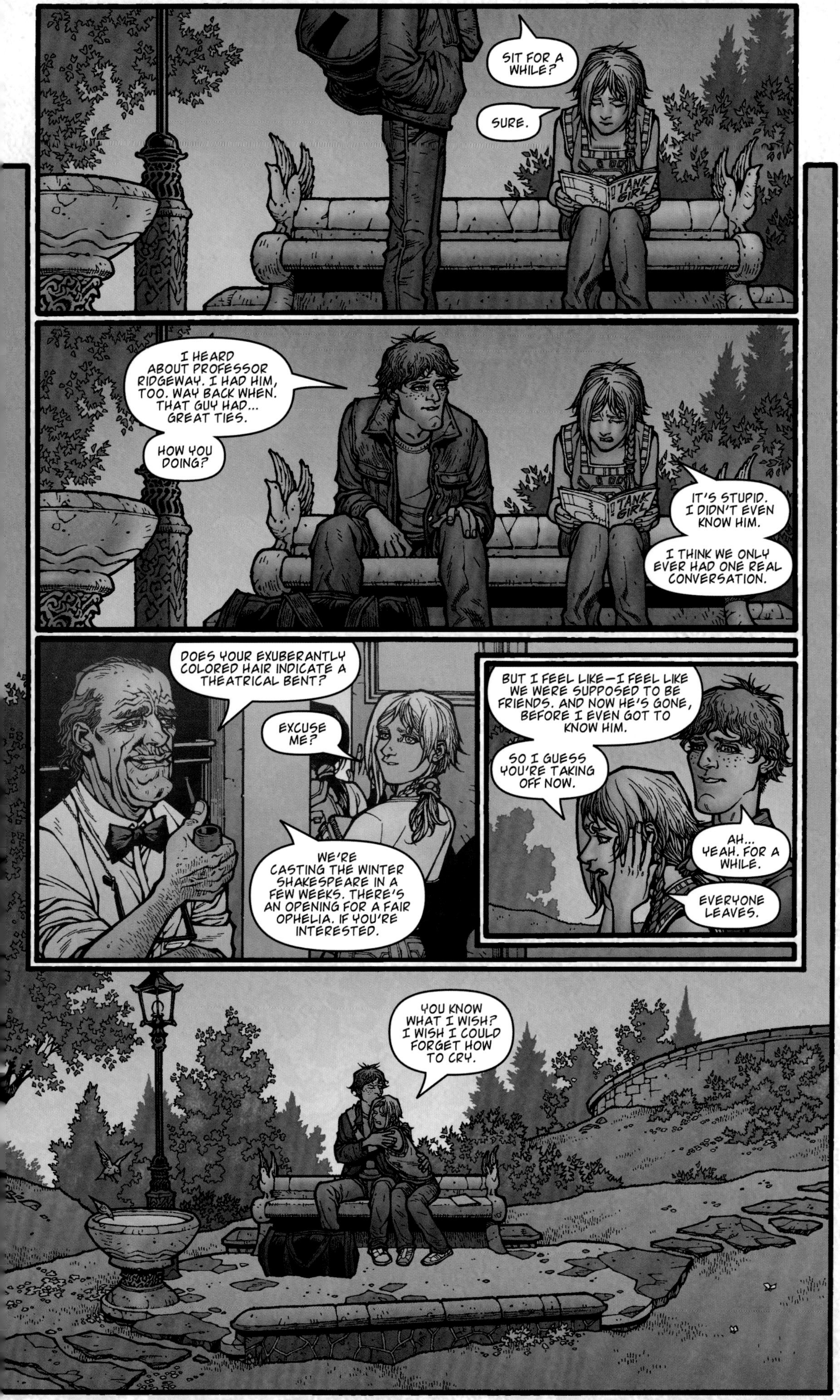
SIT FOR A WHILE?
SURE.
TANK GIRL
I HEARD ABOUT PROFESSOR RIDGEWAY. I HAD HIM, TOO. WAY BACK WHEN. THAT GUY HAD... GREAT TIES.
HOW YOU DOING?
TANK GIRL
IT'S STUPID. I DIDN'T EVEN KNOW HIM.
I THINK WE ONLY EVER HAD ONE REAL CONVERSATION.
DOES YOUR EXUBERANTLY COLORED HAIR INDICATE A THEATRICAL BENT?
EXCUSE ME?
WE'RE CASTING THE WINTER SHAKESPEARE IN A FEW WEEKS. THERE'S AN OPENING FOR A FAIR OPHELIA. IF YOU'RE INTERESTED.
BUT I FEEL LIKE—I FEEL LIKE WE WERE SUPPOSED TO BE FRIENDS. AND NOW HE'S GONE, BEFORE I EVEN GOT TO KNOW HIM.
SO I GUESS YOU'RE TAKING OFF NOW.
AH... YEAH. FOR A WHILE.
EVERYONE LEAVES.
YOU KNOW WHAT I WISH? I WISH I COULD FORGET HOW TO CRY.

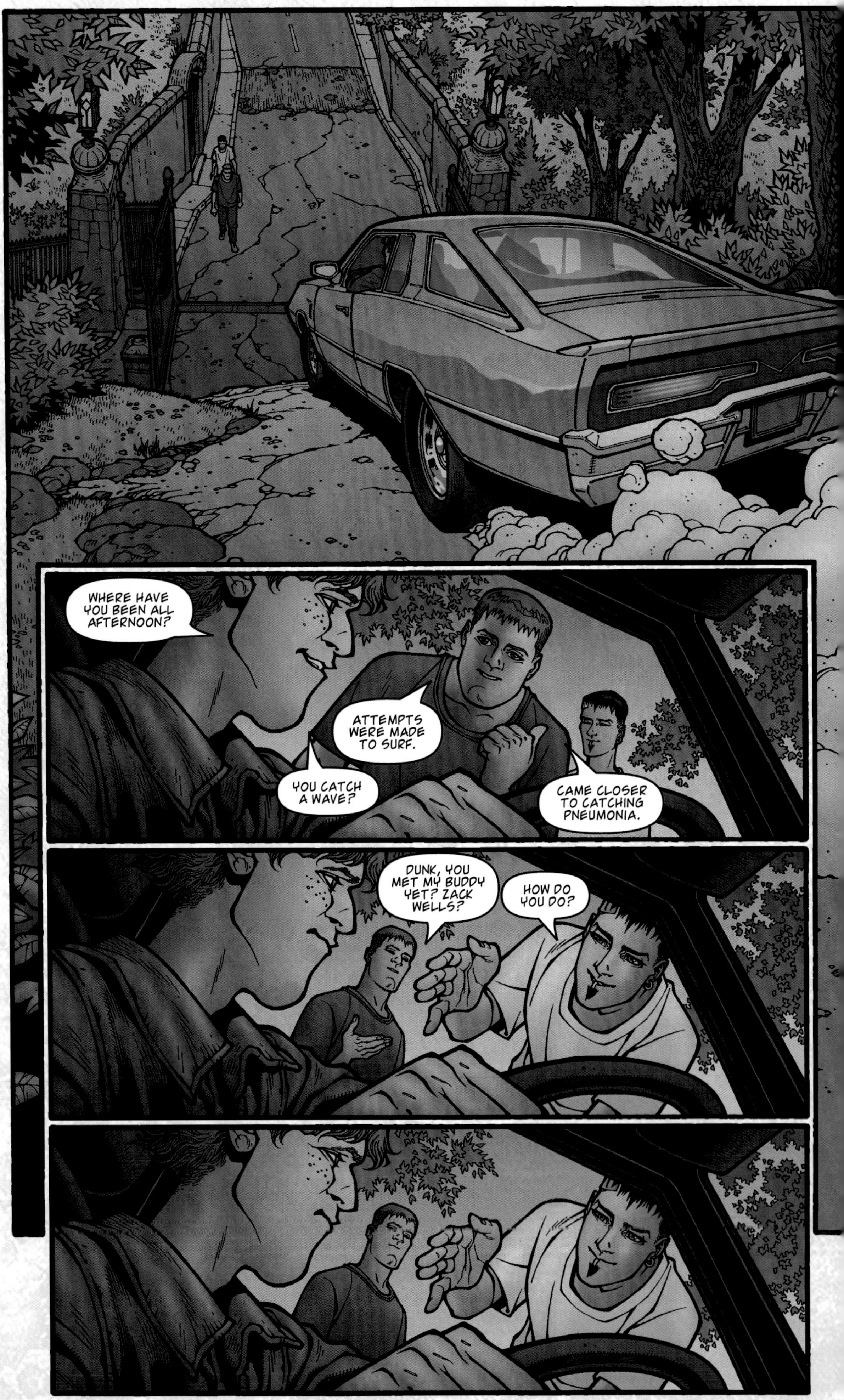
WHERE HAVE YOU BEEN ALL AFTERNOON?
ATTEMPTS WERE MADE TO SURF.
YOU CATCH A WAVE?
CAME CLOSER TO CATCHING PNEUMONIA.
DUNK, YOU MET MY BUDDY YET? ZACK WELLS?
HOW DO YOU DO?

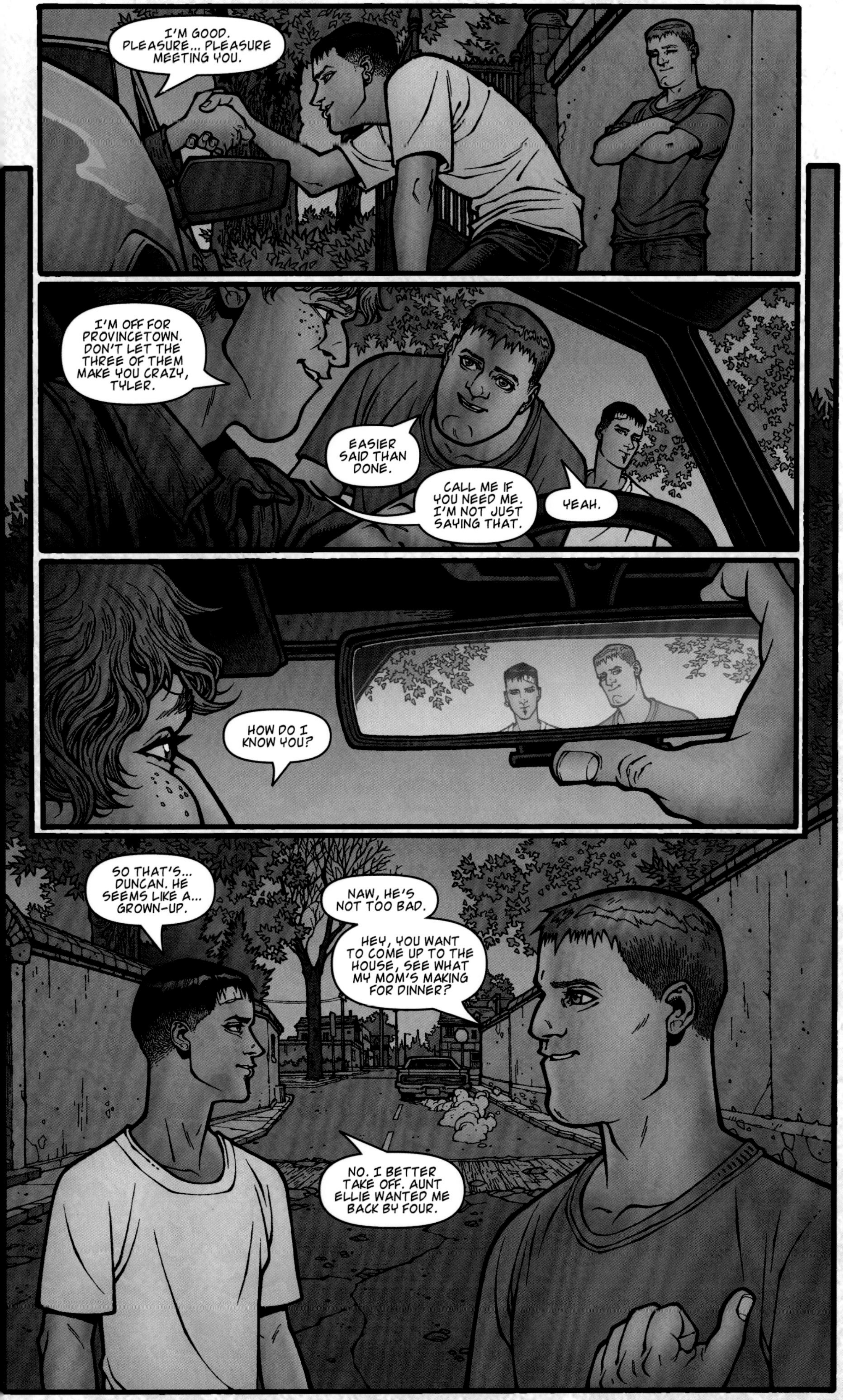
I'M GOOD. PLEASURE... PLEASURE MEETING YOU.
I'M OFF FOR PROVINCETOWN. DON'T LET THE THREE OF THEM MAKE YOU CRAZY, TYLER.
EASIER SAID THAN DONE.
CALL ME IF YOU NEED ME. I'M NOT JUST SAYING THAT.
YEAH.
HOW DO I KNOW YOU?
SO THAT'S... DUNCAN. HE SEEMS LIKE A... GROWN-UP.
NAW, HE'S NOT TOO BAD.
HEY, YOU WANT TO COME UP TO THE HOUSE, SEE WHAT MY MOM'S MAKING FOR DINNER?
NO. I BETTER TAKE OFF. AUNT ELLIE WANTED ME BACK BY FOUR.

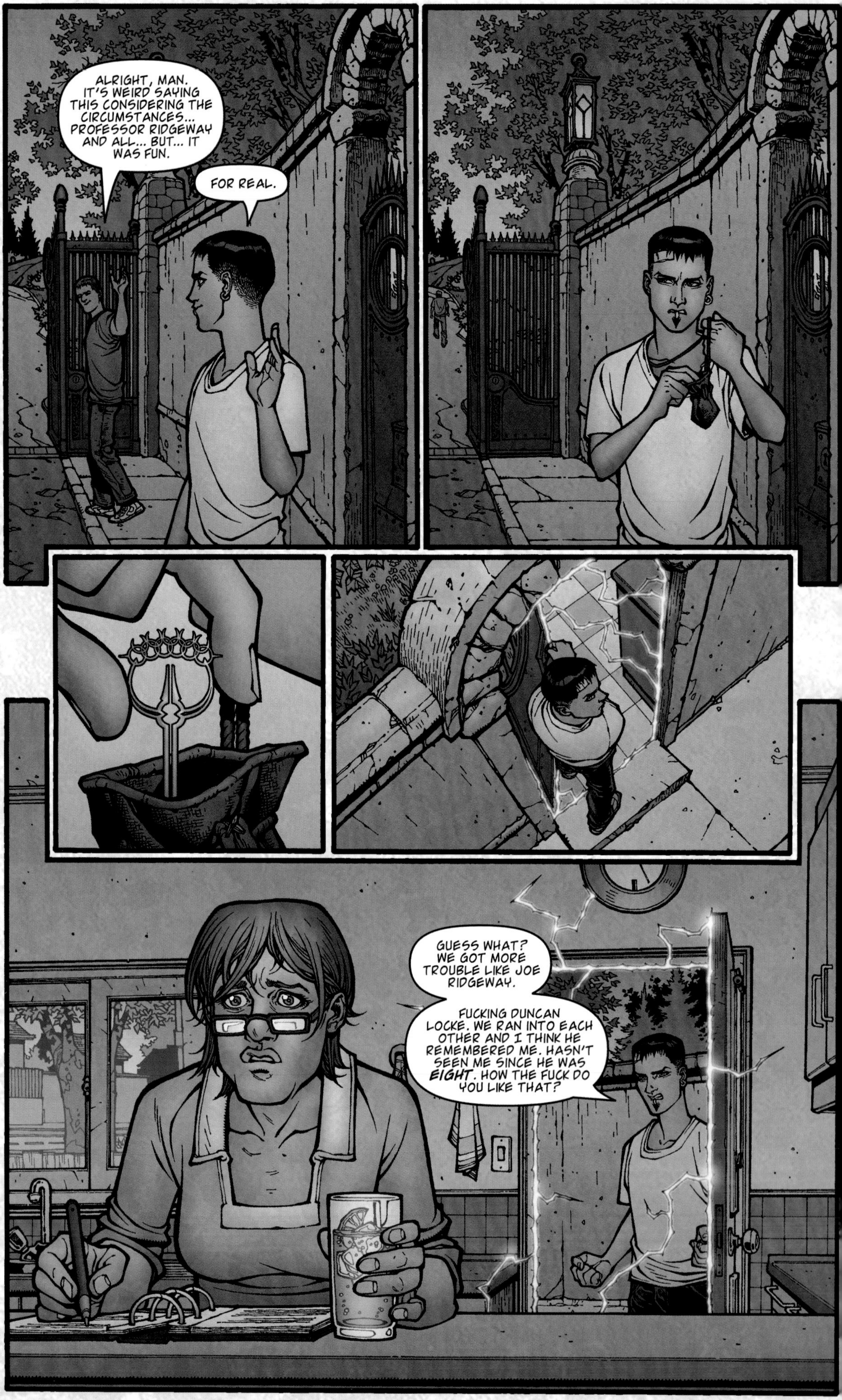
ALRIGHT, MAN. IT'S WEIRD SAYING THIS CONSIDERING THE CIRCUMSTANCES... PROFESSOR RIDGEWAY AND ALL... BUT... IT WAS FUN.
FOR REAL.
GUESS WHAT? WE GOT MORE TROUBLE LIKE JOE RIDGEWAY.
FUCKING DUNCAN LOCKE. WE RAN INTO EACH OTHER AND I THINK HE REMEMBERED ME. HASN'T SEEN ME SINCE HE WAS *EIGHT*. HOW THE FUCK DO YOU LIKE THAT?

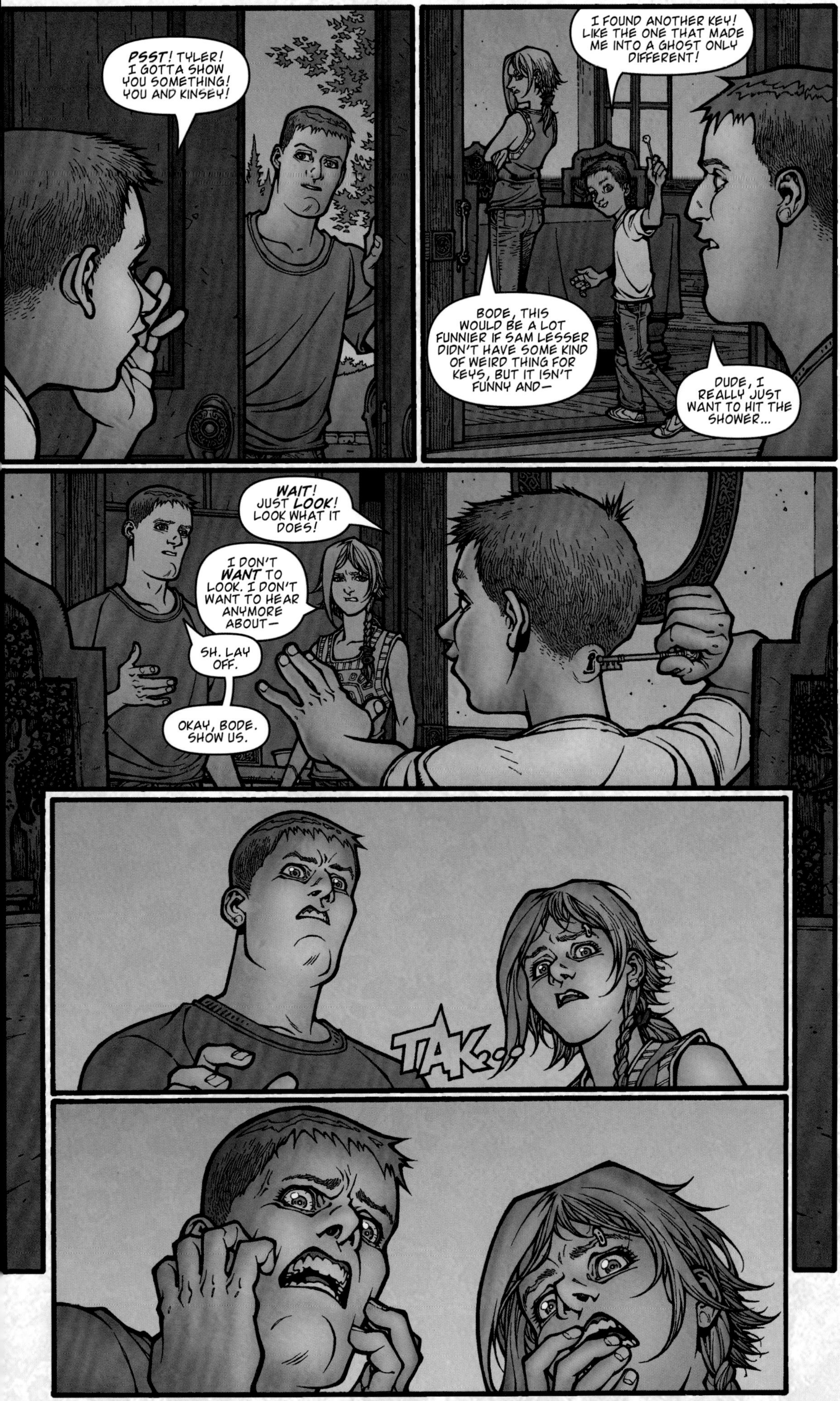
PSST! TYLER! I GOTTA SHOW YOU SOMETHING! YOU AND KINSEY!
I FOUND ANOTHER KEY! LIKE THE ONE THAT MADE ME INTO A GHOST ONLY DIFFERENT!
BODE, THIS WOULD BE A LOT FUNNIER IF SAM LESSER DIDN'T HAVE SOME KIND OF WEIRD THING FOR KEYS, BUT IT ISN'T FUNNY AND—
DUDE, I REALLY JUST WANT TO HIT THE SHOWER...
WAIT! JUST LOOK! LOOK WHAT IT DOES!
I DON'T WANT TO LOOK. I DON'T WANT TO HEAR ANYMORE ABOUT—
SH. LAY OFF.
OKAY, BODE. SHOW US.
TAK...

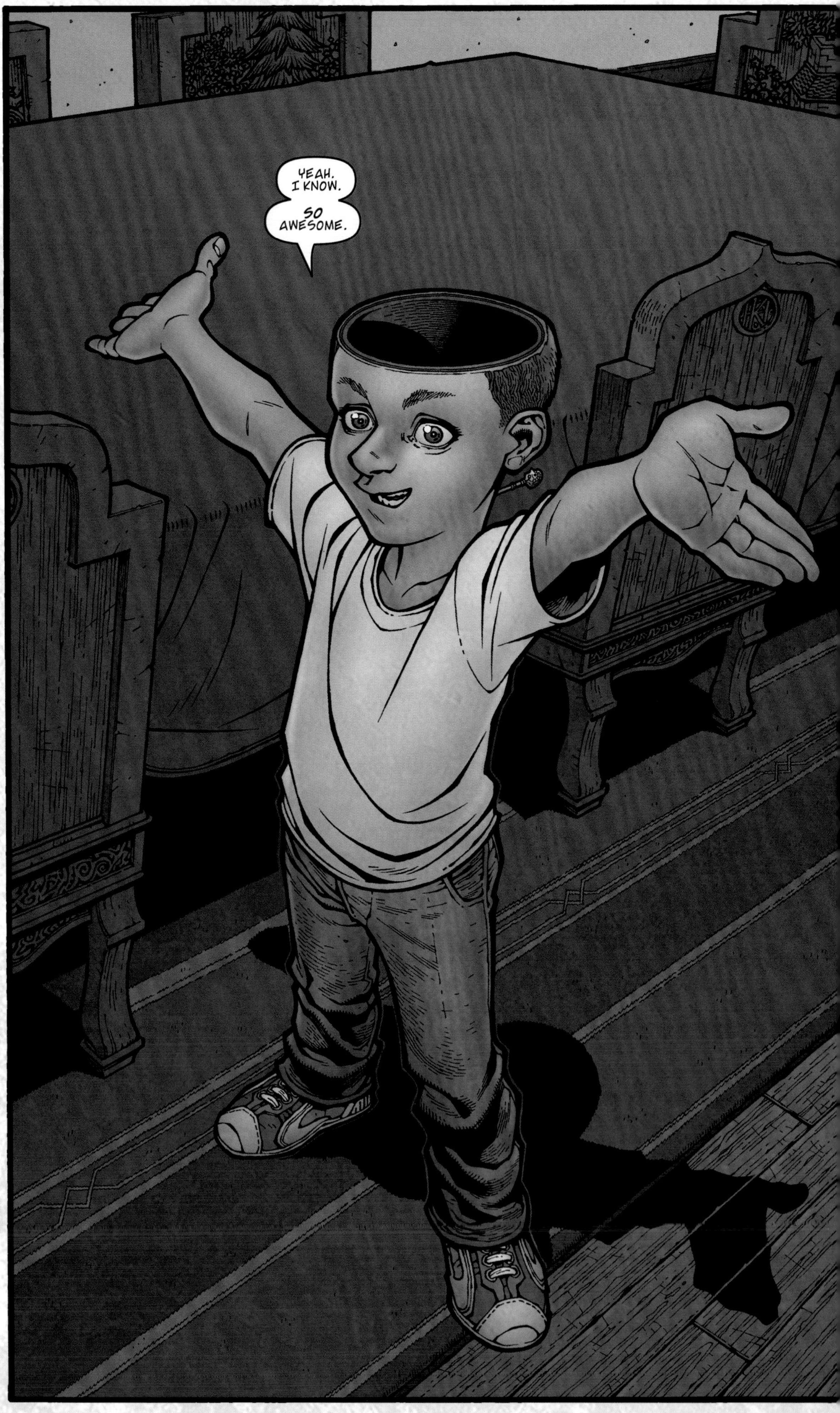
YEAH. I KNOW.
SO AWESOME.

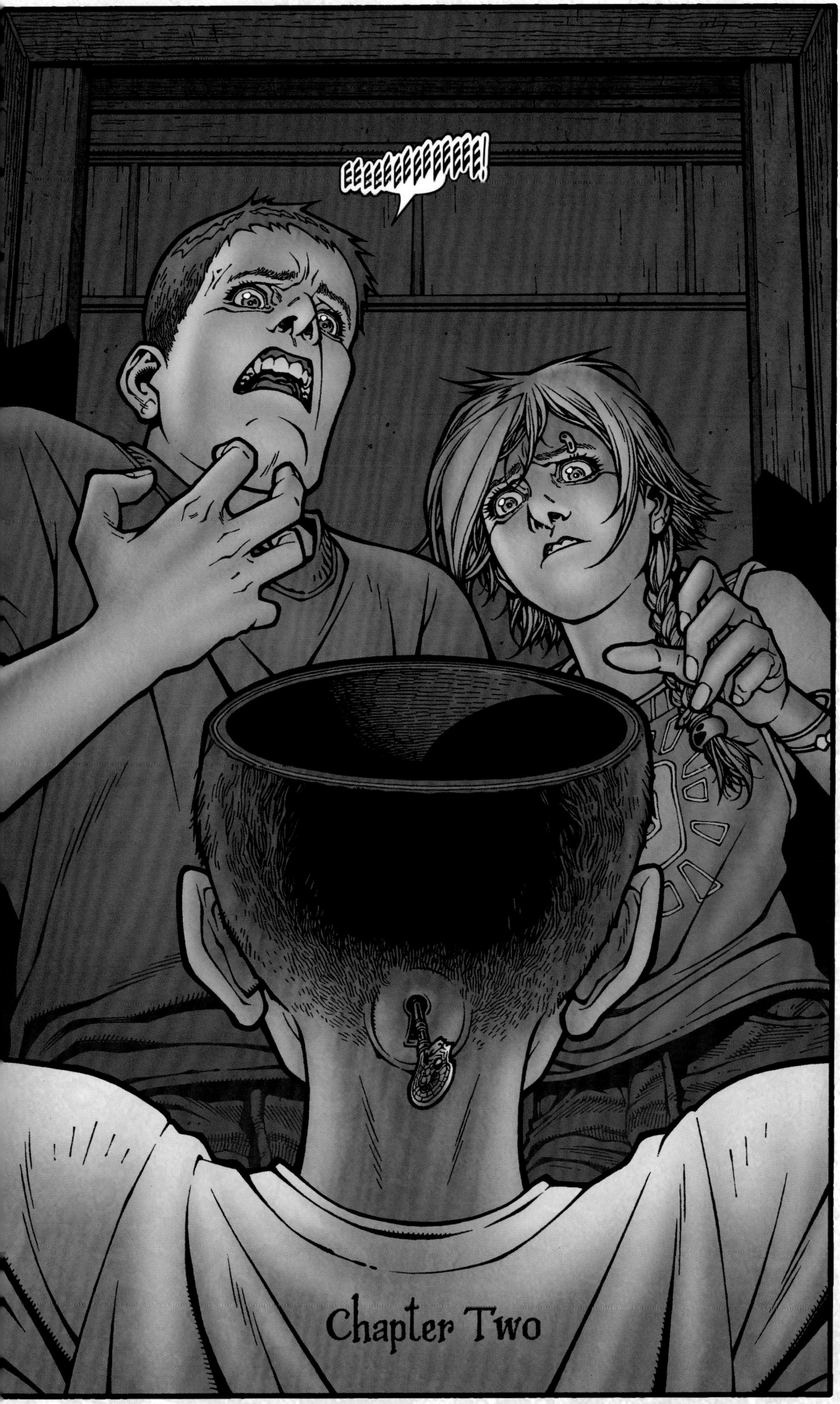
EEEEEEEEEEEEEEEE!
Chapter Two

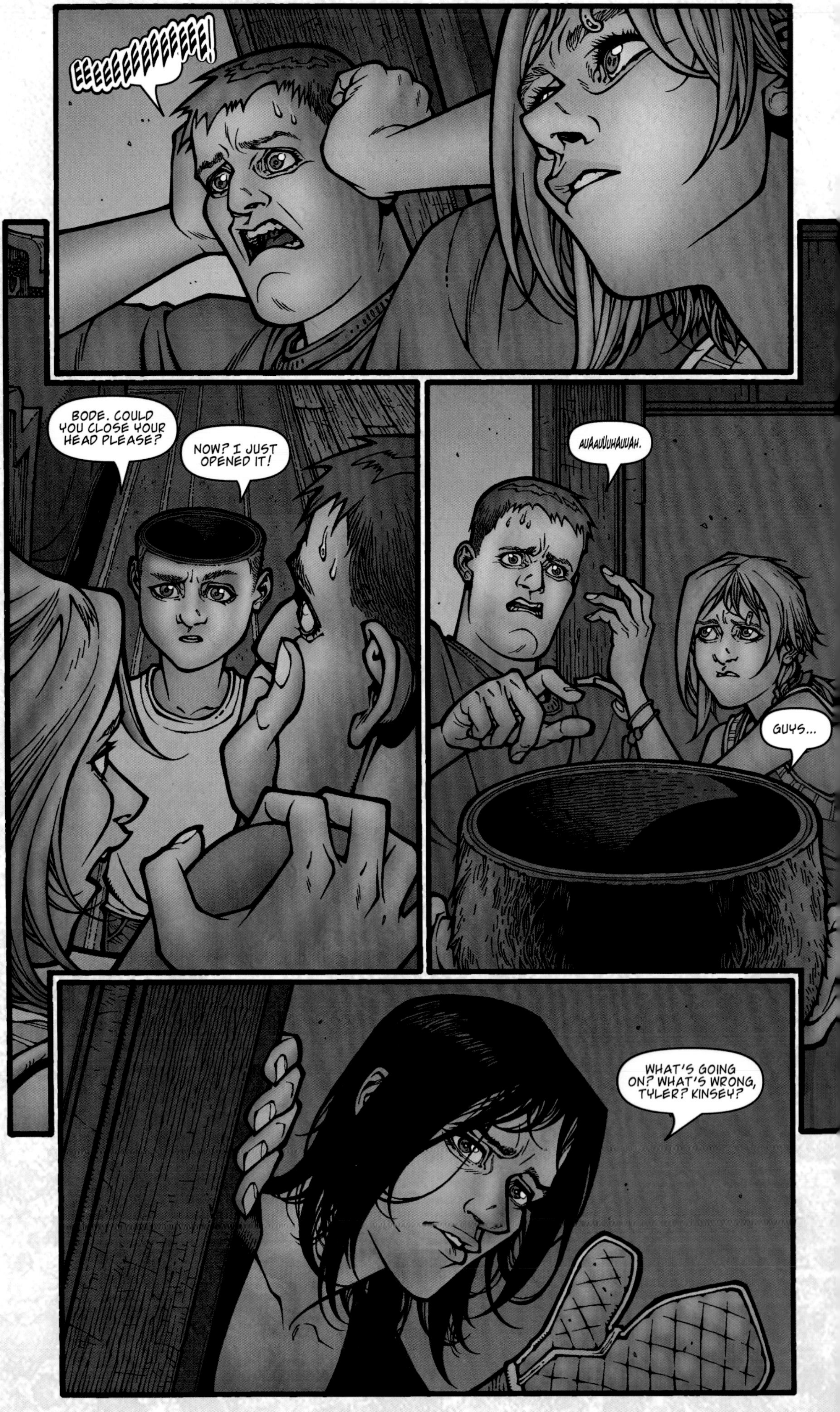
EEEEEEEEEEEEEEE!
BODE. COULD YOU CLOSE YOUR HEAD PLEASE?
NOW? I JUST OPENED IT!
AUAAUUUHAUUAH.
GUYS...
WHAT'S GOING ON? WHAT'S WRONG, TYLER? KINSEY?

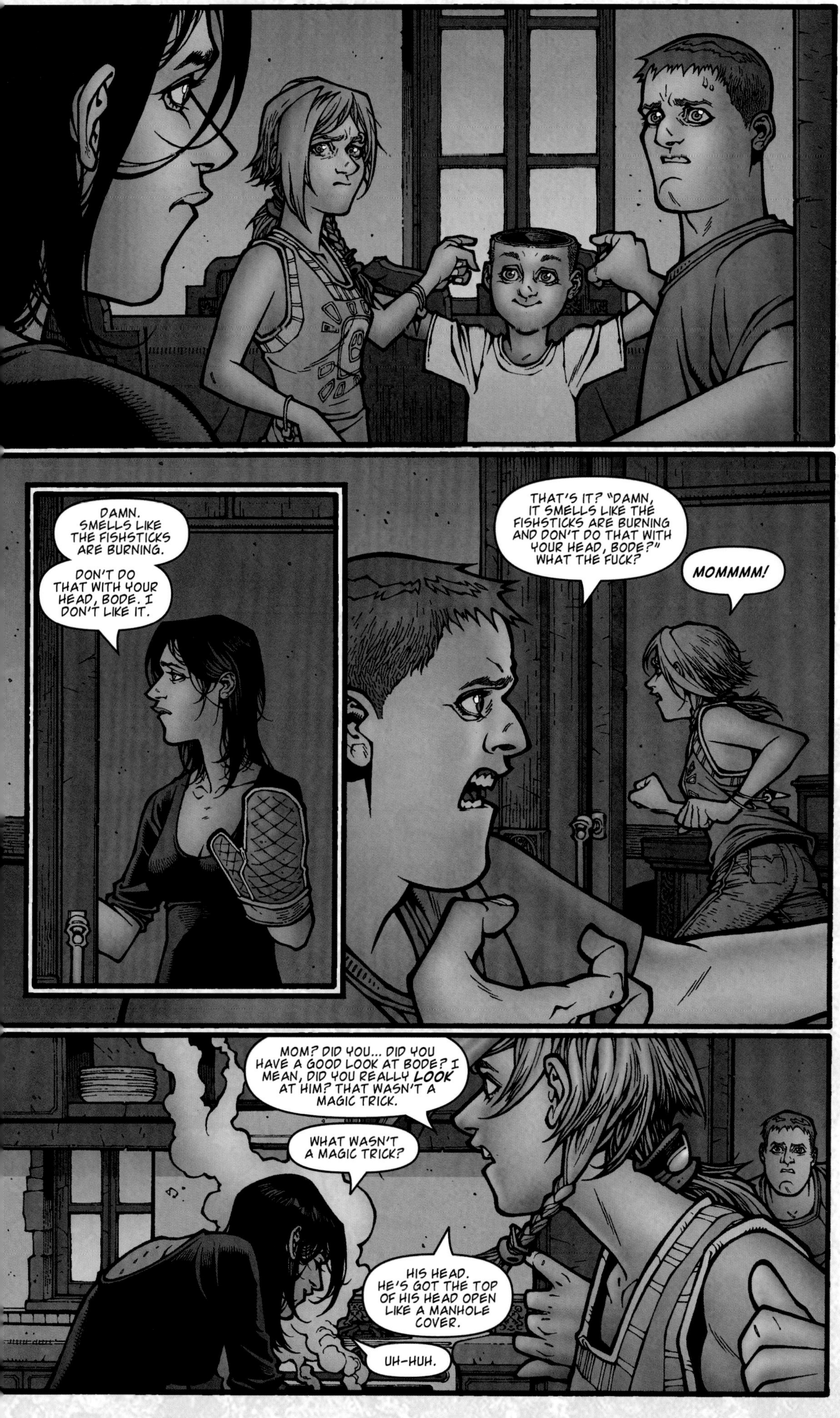
DAMN. SMELLS LIKE THE FISHSTICKS ARE BURNING.
DON'T DO THAT WITH YOUR HEAD, BODE. I DON'T LIKE IT.
THAT'S IT? "DAMN, IT SMELLS LIKE THE FISHSTICKS ARE BURNING AND DON'T DO THAT WITH YOUR HEAD, BODE?" WHAT THE FUCK?
MOMMMM!
MOM? DID YOU... DID YOU HAVE A GOOD LOOK AT BODE? I MEAN, DID YOU REALLY LOOK AT HIM? THAT WASN'T A MAGIC TRICK.
WHAT WASN'T A MAGIC TRICK?
HIS HEAD. HE'S GOT THE TOP OF HIS HEAD OPEN LIKE A MANHOLE COVER.
UH-HUH.

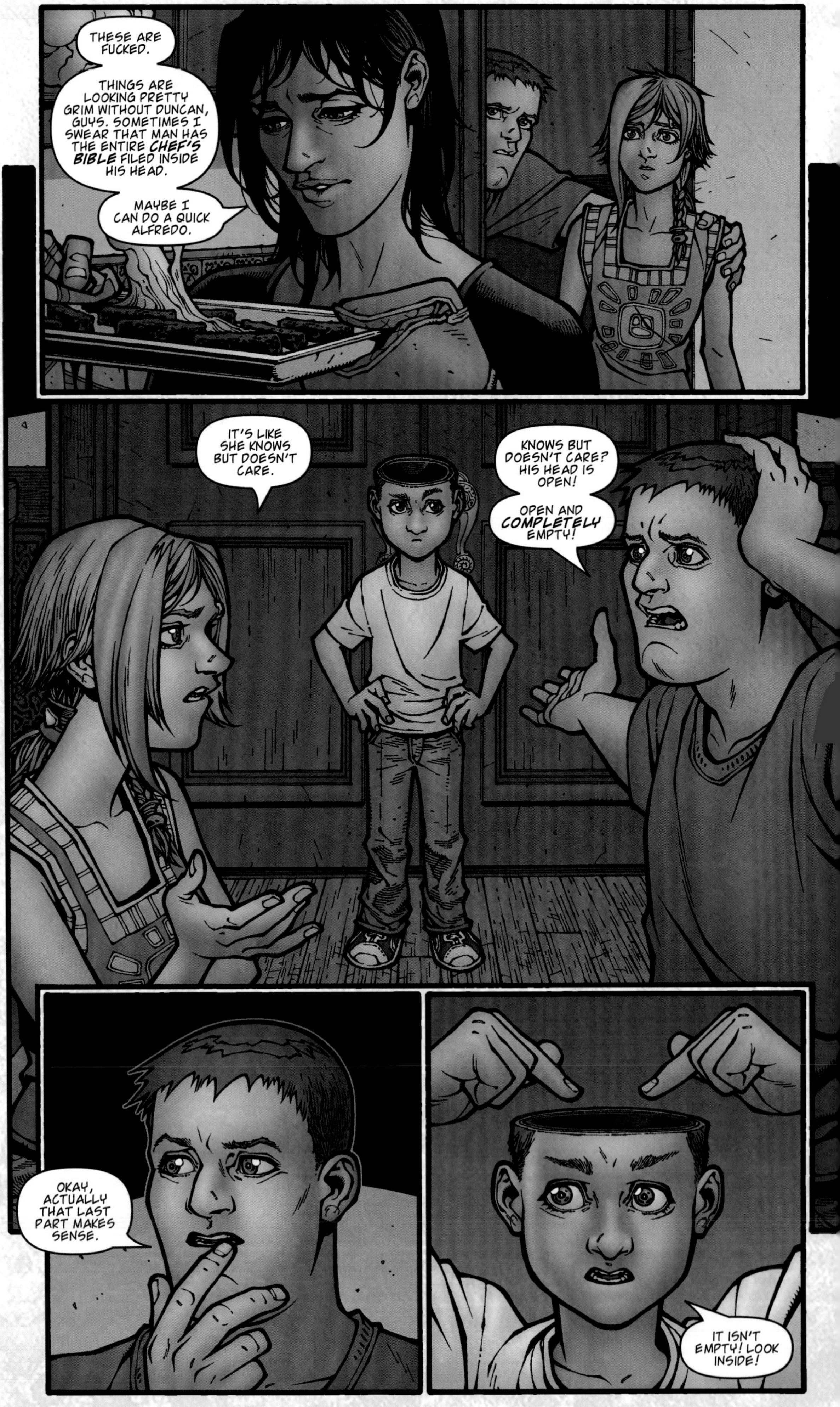
THESE ARE FUCKED.
THINGS ARE LOOKING PRETTY GRIM WITHOUT DUNCAN, GUYS. SOMETIMES I SWEAR THAT MAN HAS THE ENTIRE CHEF'S BIBLE FILED INSIDE HIS HEAD.
MAYBE I CAN DO A QUICK ALFREDO.
IT'S LIKE SHE KNOWS BUT DOESN'T CARE.
KNOWS BUT DOESN'T CARE? HIS HEAD IS OPEN!
OPEN AND COMPLETELY EMPTY!
OKAY, ACTUALLY THAT LAST PART MAKES SENSE.
IT ISN'T EMPTY! LOOK INSIDE!

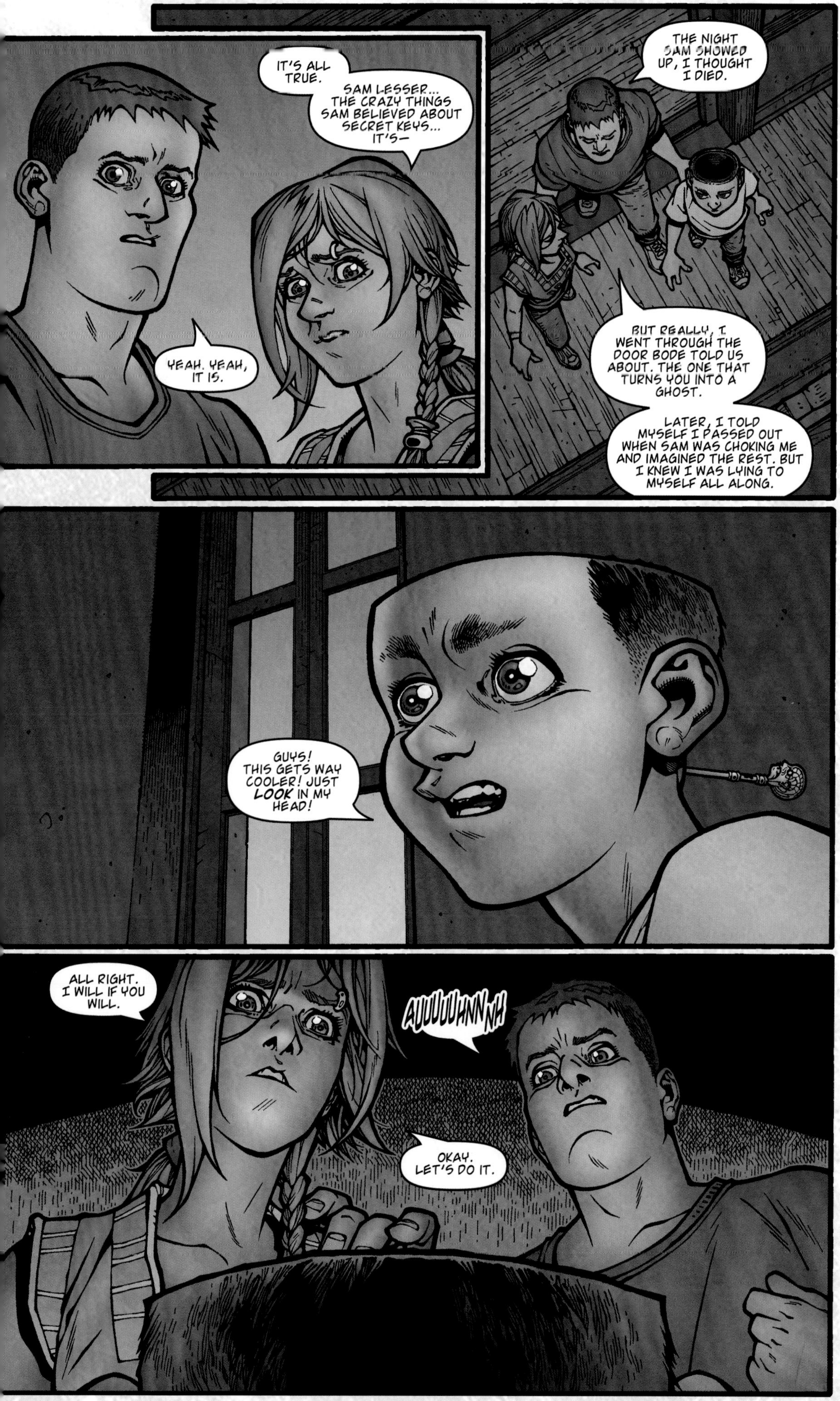
IT'S ALL TRUE.
SAM LESSER... THE CRAZY THINGS SAM BELIEVED ABOUT SECRET KEYS... IT'S—
YEAH. YEAH, IT IS.
THE NIGHT SAM SHOWED UP, I THOUGHT I DIED.
BUT REALLY, I WENT THROUGH THE DOOR BODE TOLD US ABOUT. THE ONE THAT TURNS YOU INTO A GHOST.
LATER, I TOLD MYSELF I PASSED OUT WHEN SAM WAS CHOKING ME AND IMAGINED THE REST. BUT I KNEW I WAS LYING TO MYSELF ALL ALONG.
GUYS! THIS GETS WAY COOLER! JUST LOOK IN MY HEAD!
ALL RIGHT. I WILL IF YOU WILL.
AUUUUHNNNH
OKAY. LET'S DO IT.

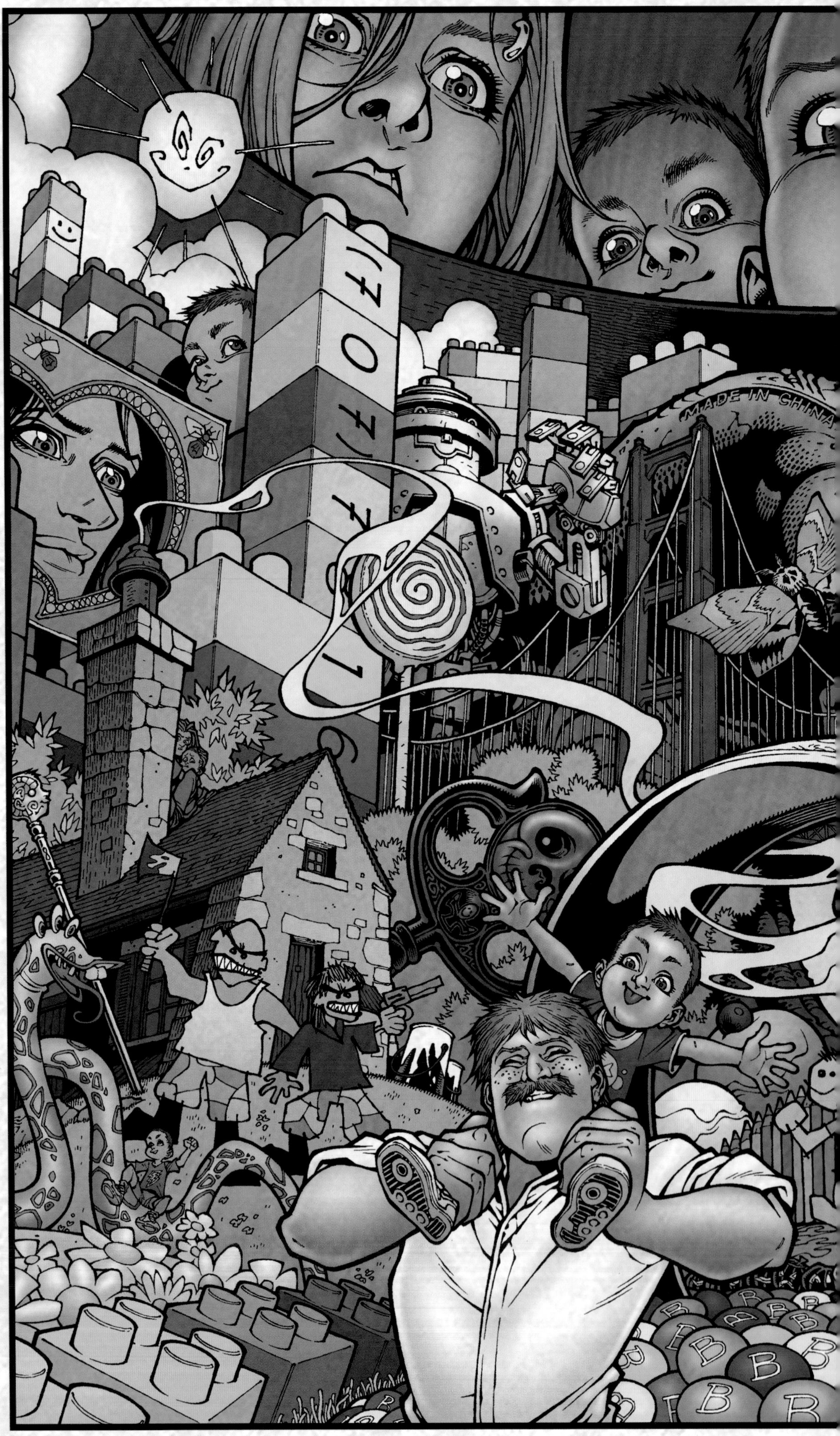
MADE IN CHINA

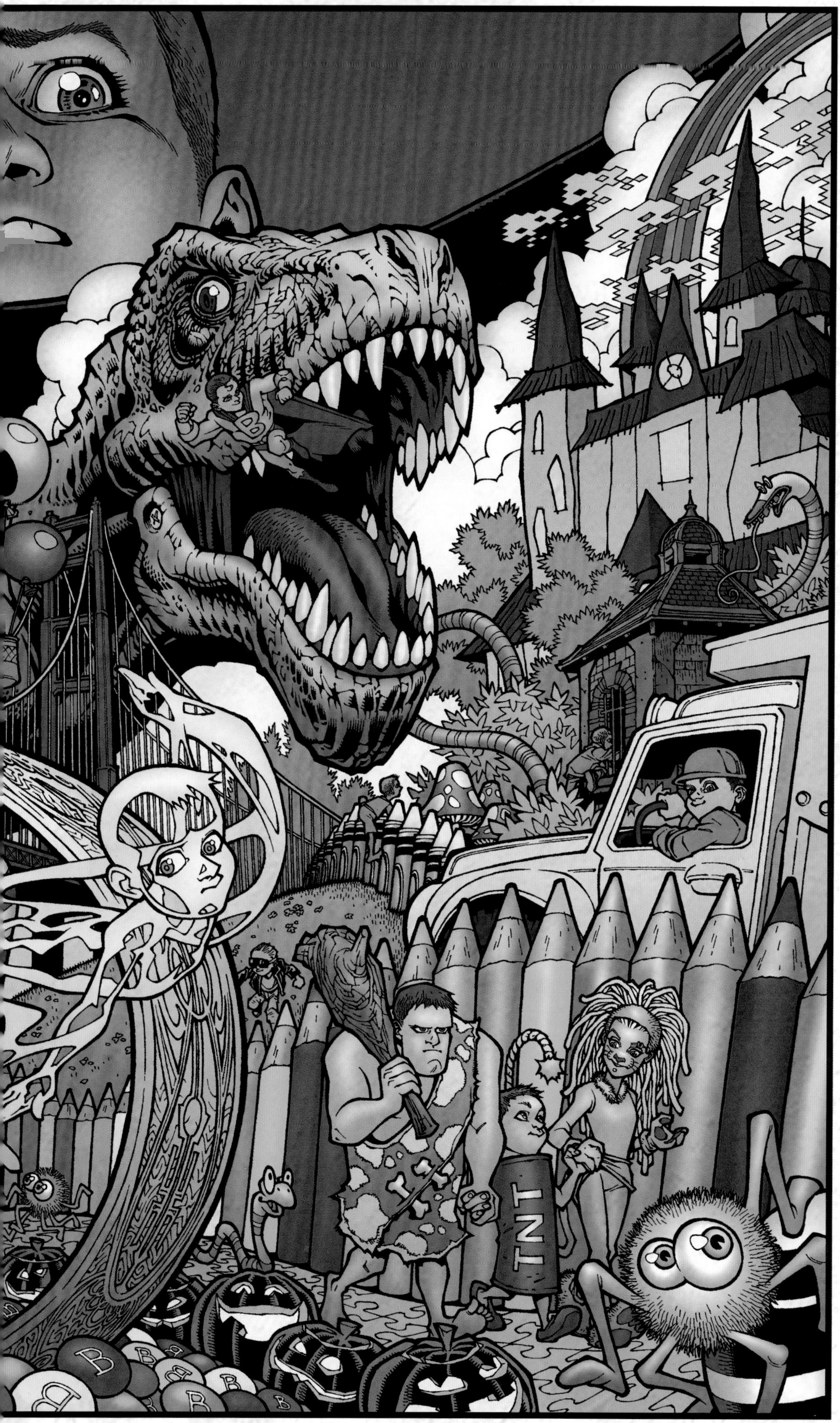
TNT

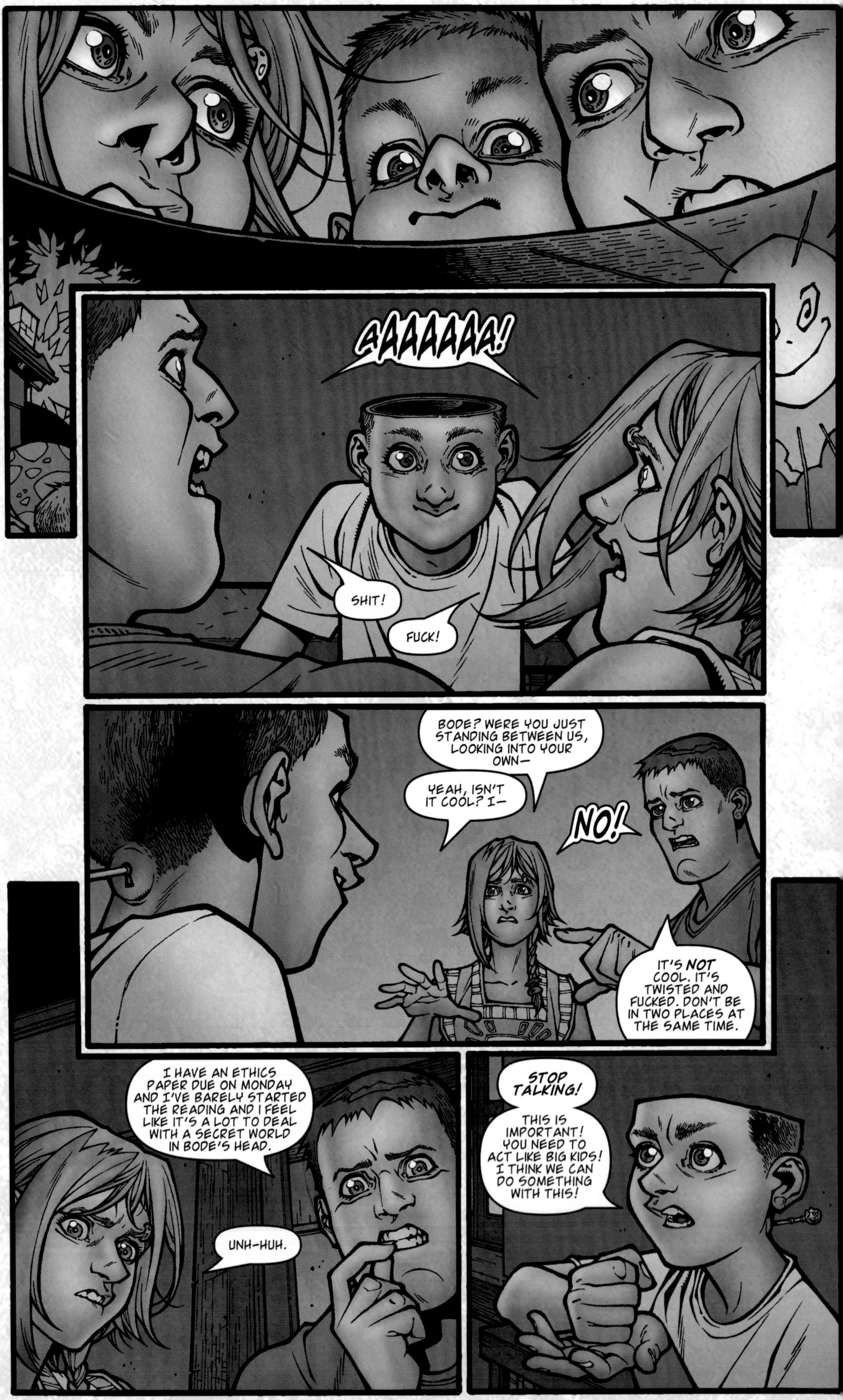
AAAAAAA!
SHIT!
FUCK!
BODE? WERE YOU JUST STANDING BETWEEN US, LOOKING INTO YOUR OWN—
YEAH, ISN'T IT COOL? I—
NO!
IT'S NOT COOL. IT'S TWISTED AND FUCKED. DON'T BE IN TWO PLACES AT THE SAME TIME.
I HAVE AN ETHICS PAPER DUE ON MONDAY AND I'VE BARELY STARTED THE READING AND I FEEL LIKE IT'S A LOT TO DEAL WITH A SECRET WORLD IN BODE'S HEAD.
UNH-HUH.
STOP TALKING!
THIS IS IMPORTANT! YOU NEED TO ACT LIKE BIG KIDS! I THINK WE CAN DO SOMETHING WITH THIS!

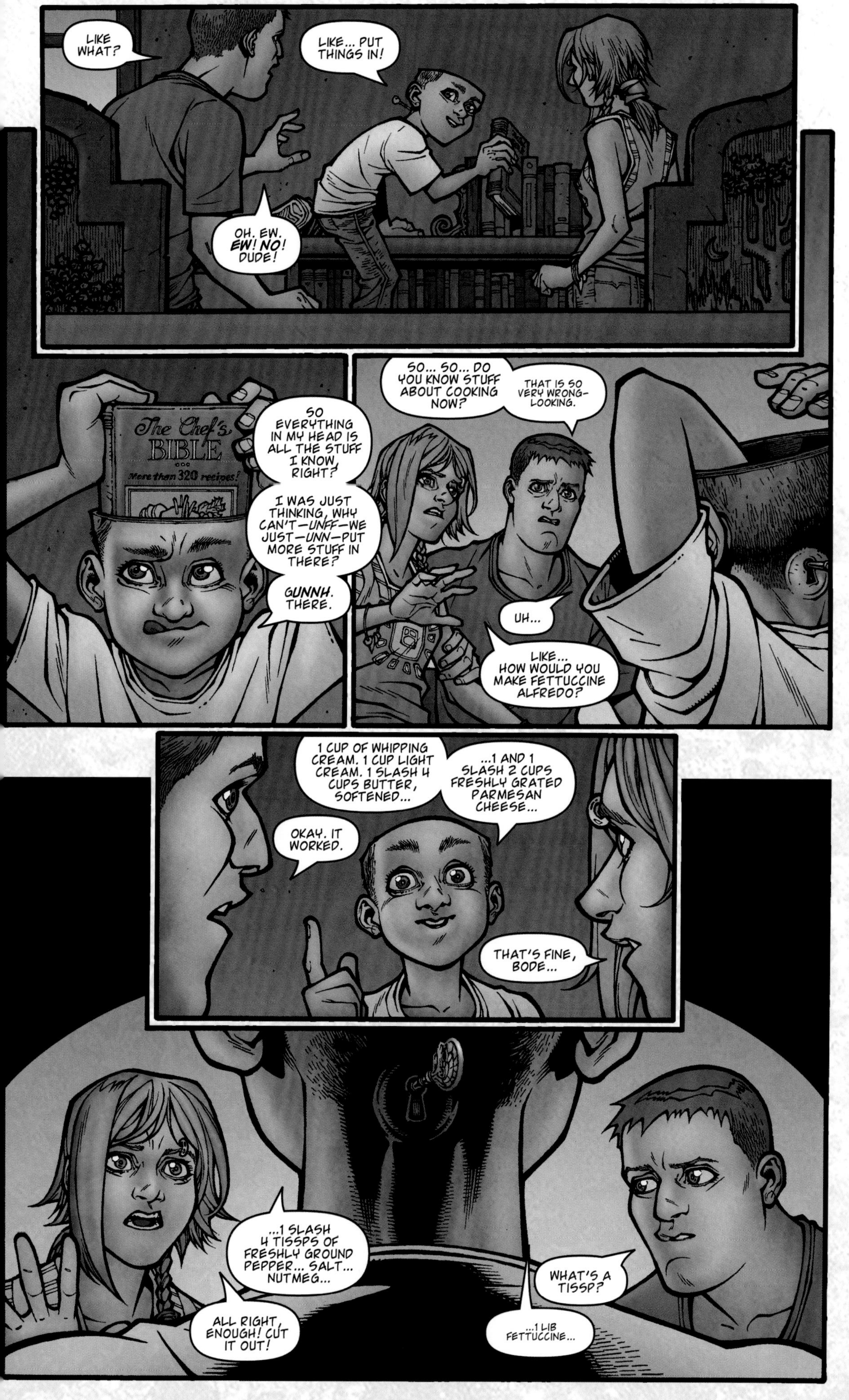
LIKE WHAT?
LIKE... PUT THINGS IN!
OH. EW. EW! NO! DUDE!
The Chef's BIBLE
More than 320 recipes!
SO EVERYTHING IN MY HEAD IS ALL THE STUFF I KNOW, RIGHT?
I WAS JUST THINKING, WHY CAN'T—UNFF—WE JUST—UNN—PUT MORE STUFF IN THERE?
GUNNH. THERE.
SO... SO... DO YOU KNOW STUFF ABOUT COOKING NOW?
THAT IS SO VERY WRONG-LOOKING.
UH...
LIKE... HOW WOULD YOU MAKE FETTUCCINE ALFREDO?
1 CUP OF WHIPPING CREAM. 1 CUP LIGHT CREAM. 1 SLASH 4 CUPS BUTTER, SOFTENED...
...1 AND 1 SLASH 2 CUPS FRESHLY GRATED PARMESAN CHEESE...
OKAY. IT WORKED.
THAT'S FINE, BODE...
...1 SLASH 4 TISSPS OF FRESHLY GROUND PEPPER... SALT... NUTMEG...
ALL RIGHT, ENOUGH! CUT IT OUT!
WHAT'S A TISSP?
...1 LIB FETTUCCINE...

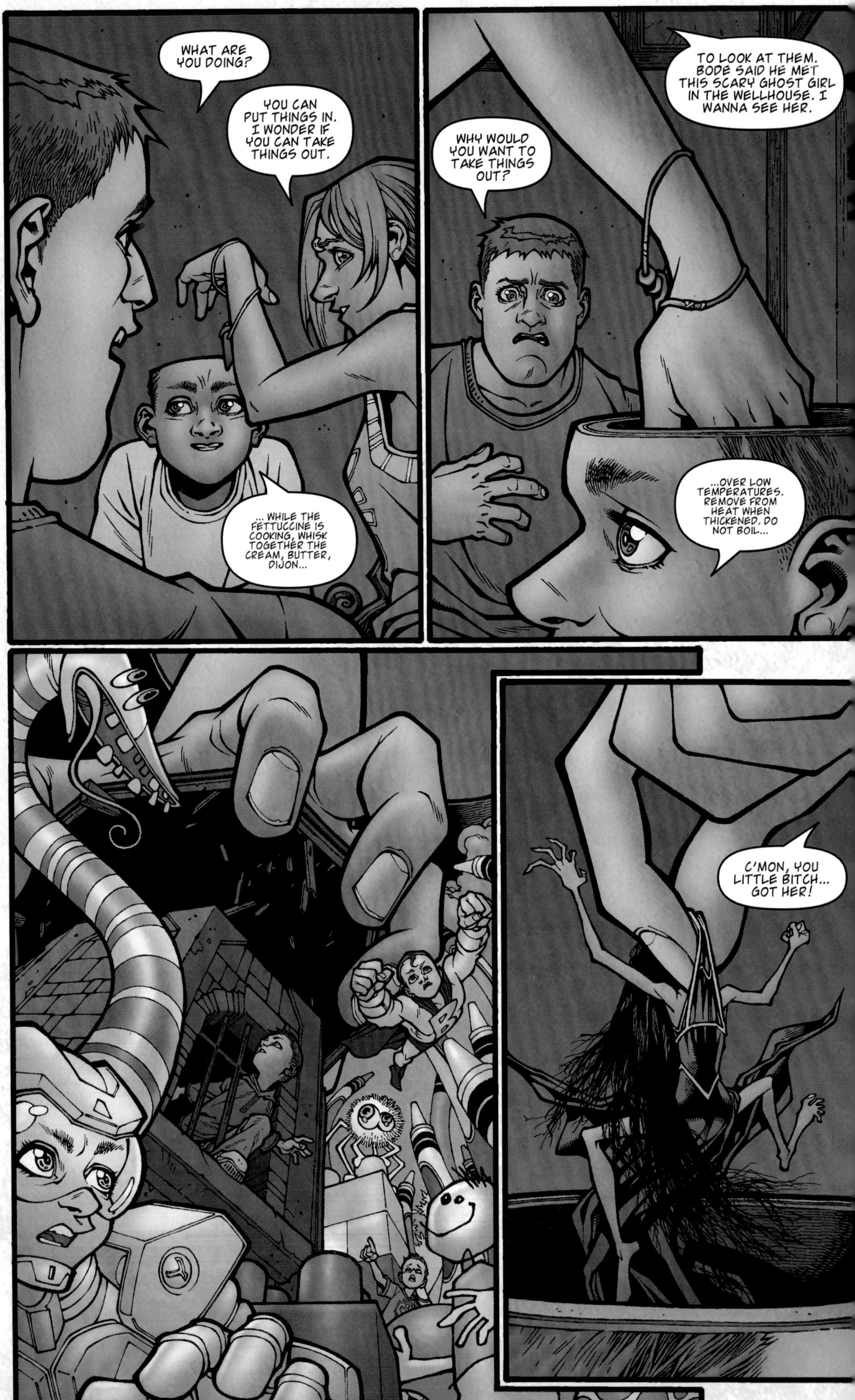
WHAT ARE YOU DOING?
YOU CAN PUT THINGS IN. I WONDER IF YOU CAN TAKE THINGS OUT.
... WHILE THE FETTUCCINE IS COOKING, WHISK TOGETHER THE CREAM, BUTTER, DIJON...
WHY WOULD YOU WANT TO TAKE THINGS OUT?
TO LOOK AT THEM. BODE SAID HE MET THIS SCARY GHOST GIRL IN THE WELLHOUSE. I WANNA SEE HER.
...OVER LOW TEMPERATURES. REMOVE FROM HEAT WHEN THICKENED. DO NOT BOIL...
C'MON, YOU LITTLE BITCH... GOT HER!

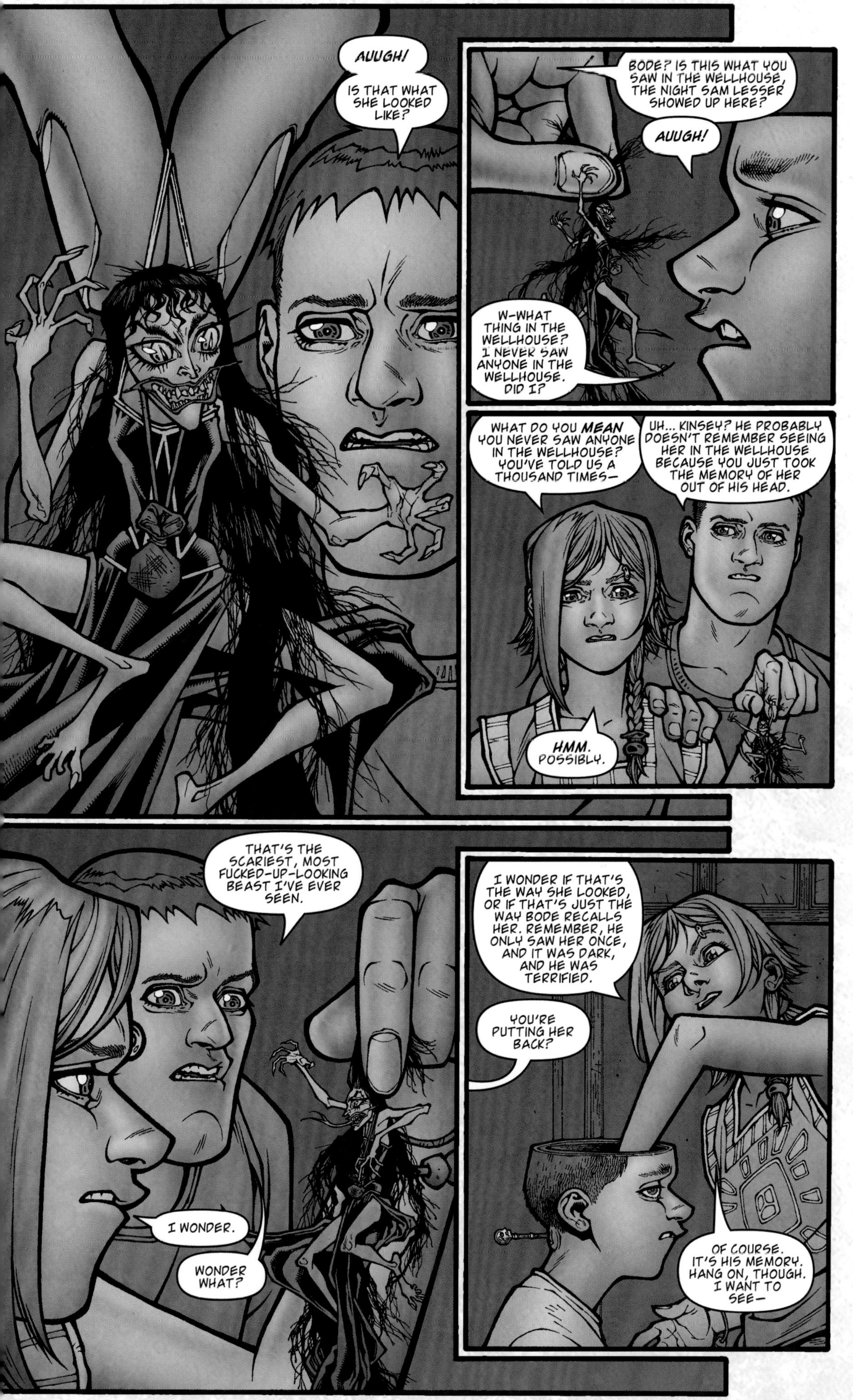
AUUGH!
IS THAT WHAT SHE LOOKED LIKE?
BODE? IS THIS WHAT YOU SAW IN THE WELLHOUSE, THE NIGHT SAM LESSER SHOWED UP HERE?
AUUGH!
W-WHAT THING IN THE WELLHOUSE? I NEVER SAW ANYONE IN THE WELLHOUSE. DID I?
WHAT DO YOU MEAN YOU NEVER SAW ANYONE IN THE WELLHOUSE? YOU'VE TOLD US A THOUSAND TIMES—
UH... KINSEY? HE PROBABLY DOESN'T REMEMBER SEEING HER IN THE WELLHOUSE BECAUSE YOU JUST TOOK THE MEMORY OF HER OUT OF HIS HEAD.
HMM. POSSIBLY.
THAT'S THE SCARIEST, MOST FUCKED-UP-LOOKING BEAST I'VE EVER SEEN.
I WONDER.
WONDER WHAT?
I WONDER IF THAT'S THE WAY SHE LOOKED, OR IF THAT'S JUST THE WAY BODE RECALLS HER. REMEMBER, HE ONLY SAW HER ONCE, AND IT WAS DARK, AND HE WAS TERRIFIED.
YOU'RE PUTTING HER BACK?
OF COURSE. IT'S HIS MEMORY. HANG ON, THOUGH. I WANT TO SEE—

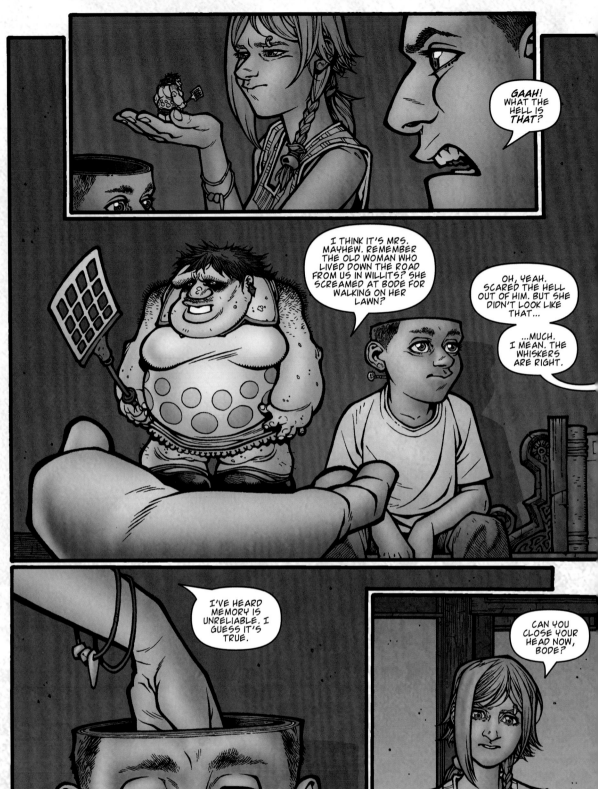

GAAH! WHAT THE HELL IS *THAT?*

I THINK IT'S MRS. MAYHEW. REMEMBER THE OLD WOMAN WHO LIVED DOWN THE ROAD FROM US IN WILLITS? SHE SCREAMED AT BODE FOR WALKING ON HER LAWN?

OH, YEAH. SCARED THE HELL OUT OF HIM. BUT SHE DIDN'T LOOK LIKE THAT...

...MUCH. I MEAN. THE WHISKERS ARE RIGHT.

I'VE HEARD MEMORY IS UNRELIABLE. I GUESS IT'S TRUE.

CAN YOU CLOSE YOUR HEAD NOW, BODE?

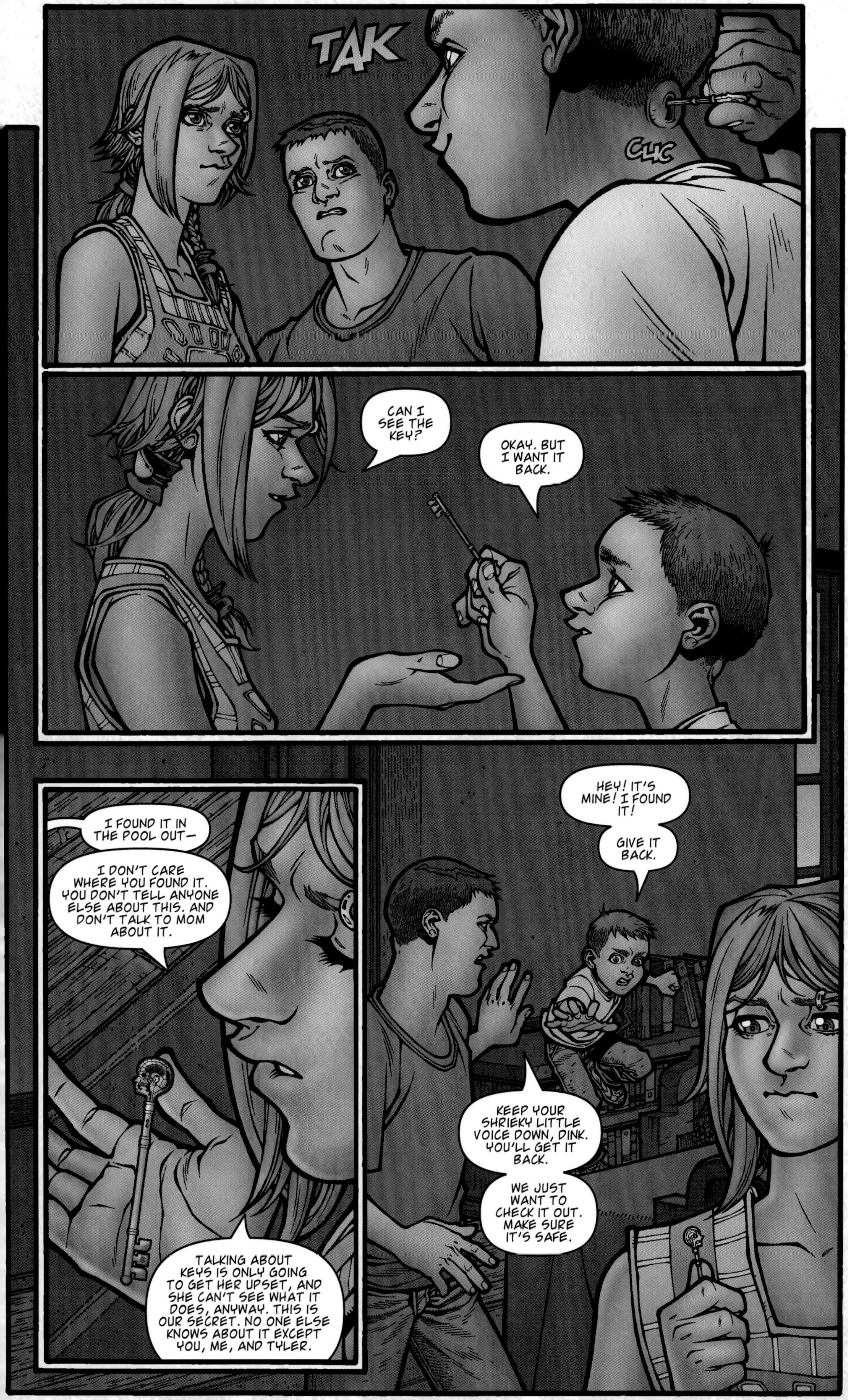
TAK
CLIC
CAN I SEE THE KEY?
OKAY. BUT I WANT IT BACK.
I FOUND IT IN THE POOL OUT—
I DON'T CARE WHERE YOU FOUND IT. YOU DON'T TELL ANYONE ELSE ABOUT THIS. AND DON'T TALK TO MOM ABOUT IT.
TALKING ABOUT KEYS IS ONLY GOING TO GET HER UPSET, AND SHE CAN'T SEE WHAT IT DOES, ANYWAY. THIS IS OUR SECRET. NO ONE ELSE KNOWS ABOUT IT EXCEPT YOU, ME, AND TYLER.
HEY! IT'S MINE! I FOUND IT!
GIVE IT BACK.
KEEP YOUR SHRIEKY LITTLE VOICE DOWN, DINK. YOU'LL GET IT BACK.
WE JUST WANT TO CHECK IT OUT. MAKE SURE IT'S SAFE.

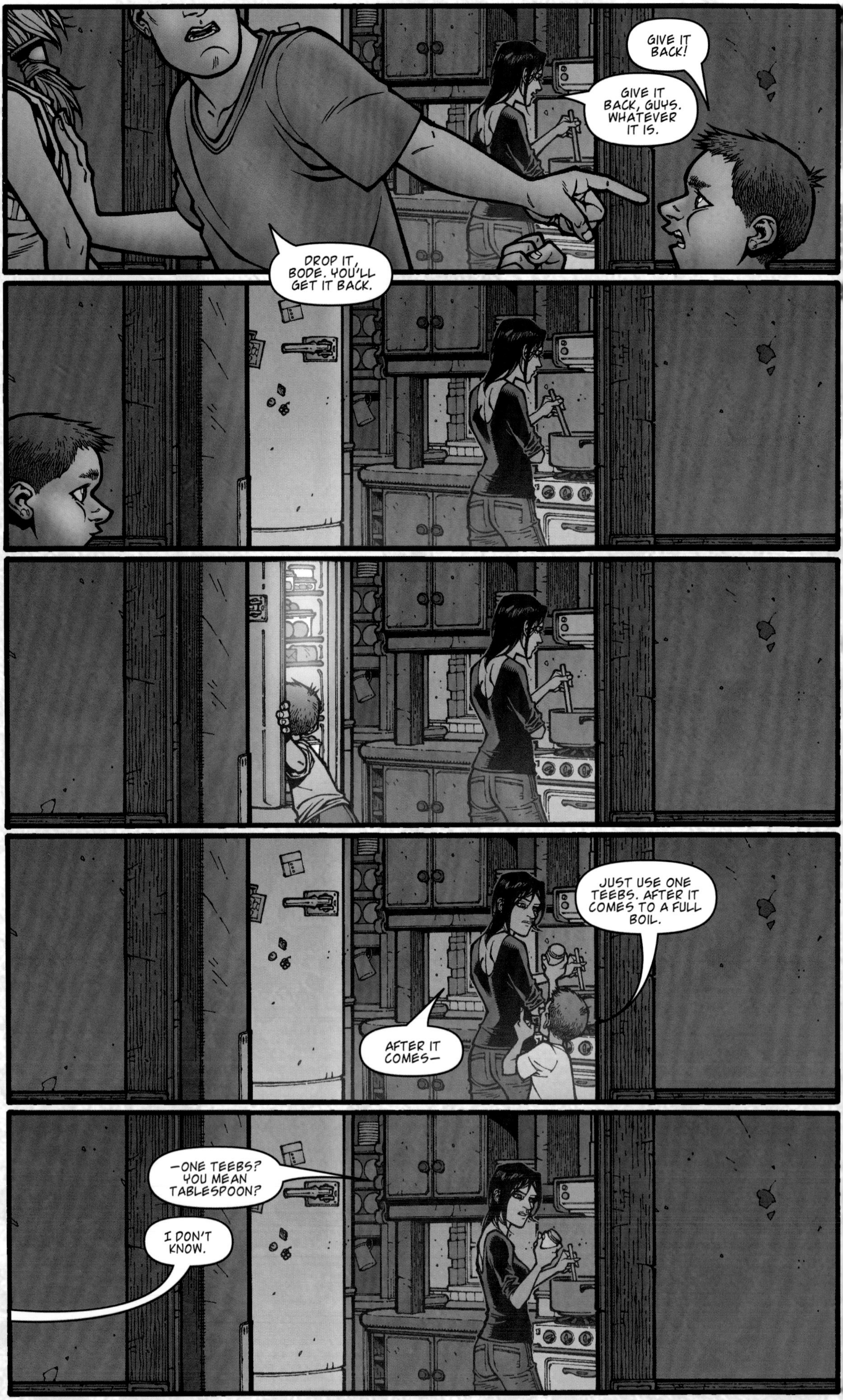
GIVE IT BACK!
GIVE IT BACK, GUYS. WHATEVER IT IS.
DROP IT, BODE. YOU'LL GET IT BACK.
JUST USE ONE TEEBS. AFTER IT COMES TO A FULL BOIL.
AFTER IT COMES—
—ONE TEEBS? YOU MEAN TABLESPOON?
I DON'T KNOW.

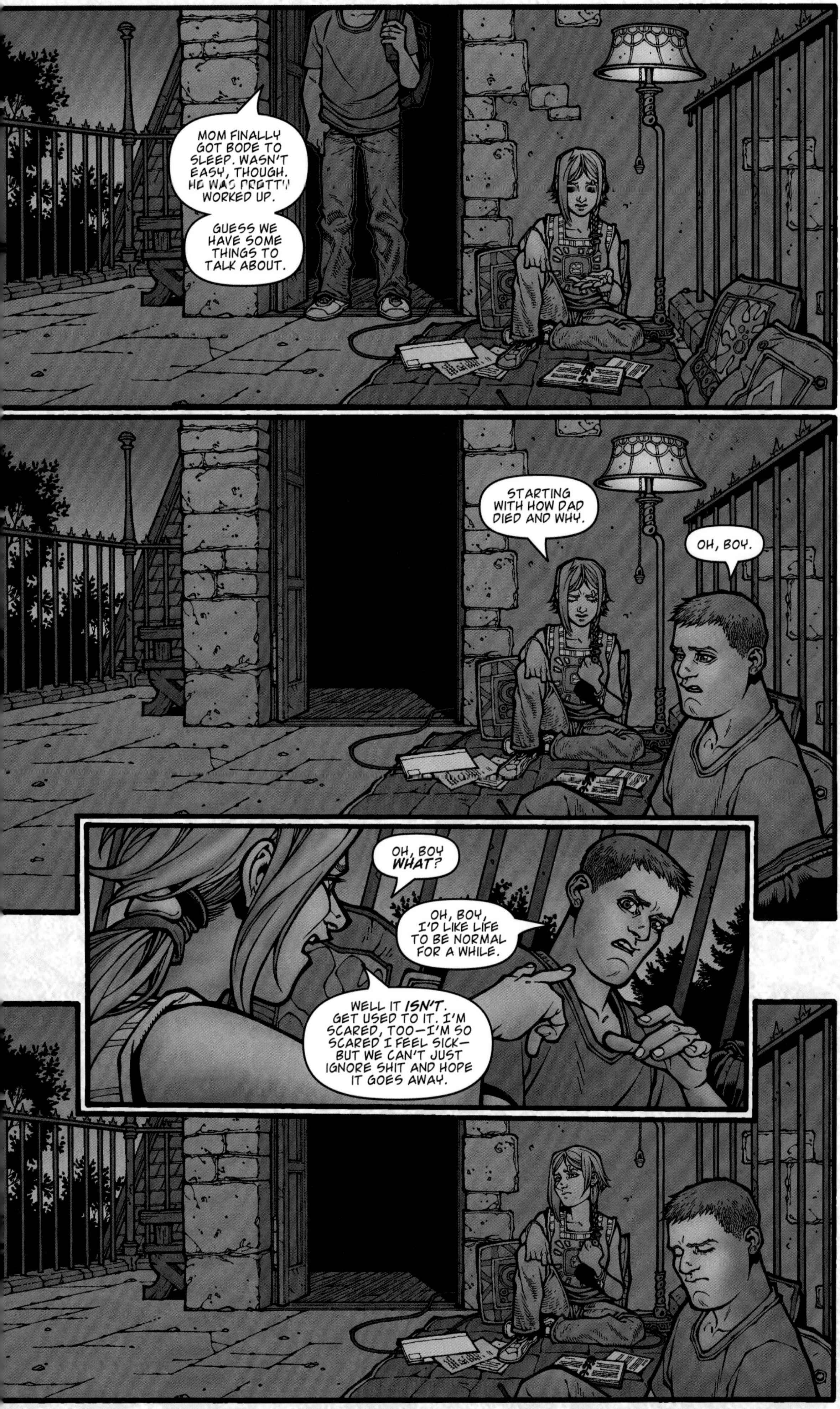

MOM FINALLY GOT BODE TO SLEEP. WASN'T EASY, THOUGH. HE WAS PRETTY WORKED UP.
GUESS WE HAVE SOME THINGS TO TALK ABOUT.
STARTING WITH HOW DAD DIED AND WHY.
OH, BOY.
OH, BOY *WHAT*?
OH, BOY, I'D LIKE LIFE TO BE NORMAL FOR A WHILE.
WELL IT *ISN'T*. GET USED TO IT. I'M SCARED, TOO—I'M SO SCARED I FEEL SICK—BUT WE CAN'T JUST IGNORE SHIT AND HOPE IT GOES AWAY.

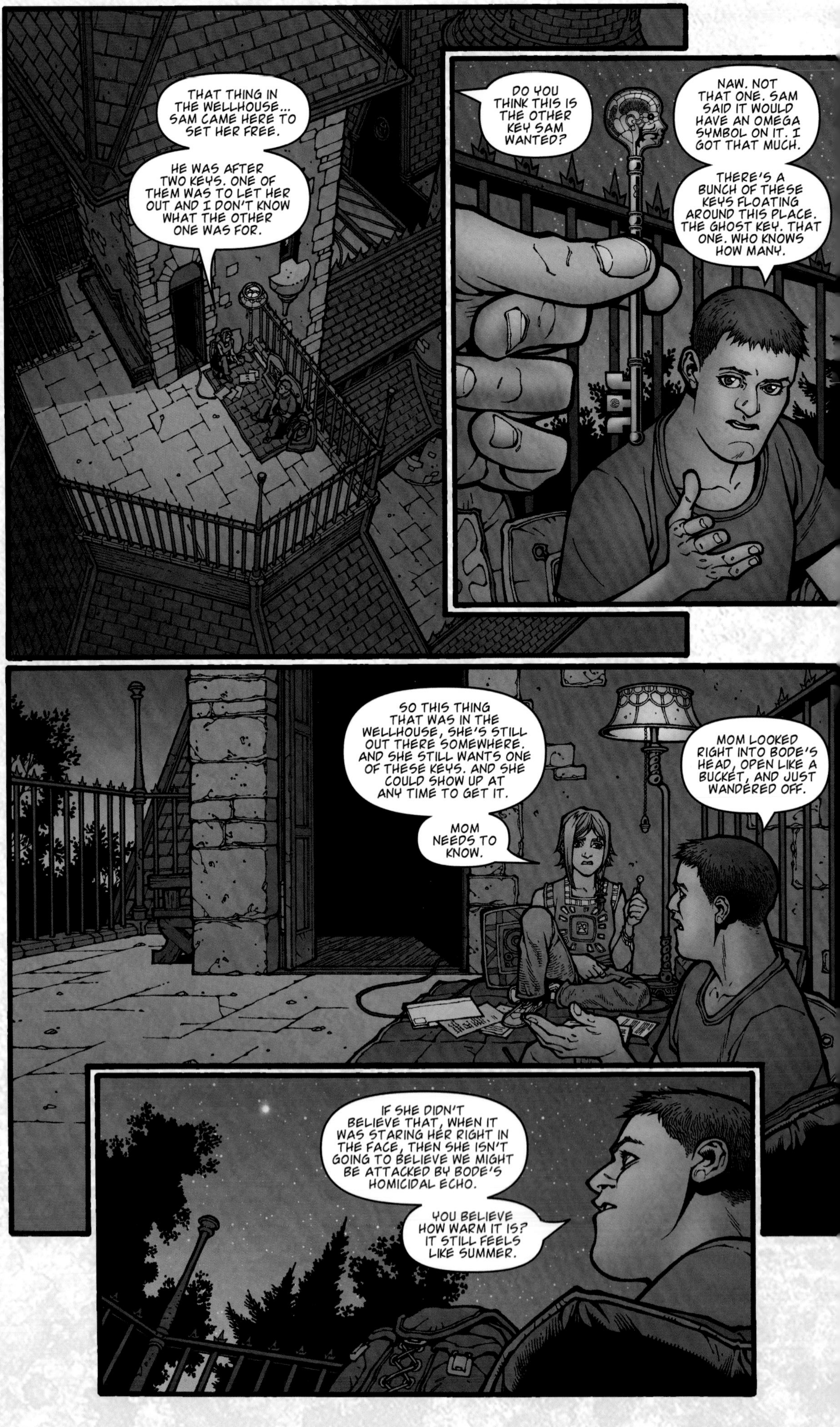
THAT THING IN THE WELLHOUSE... SAM CAME HERE TO SET HER FREE.
HE WAS AFTER TWO KEYS. ONE OF THEM WAS TO LET HER OUT AND I DON'T KNOW WHAT THE OTHER ONE WAS FOR.
DO YOU THINK THIS IS THE OTHER KEY SAM WANTED?
NAW. NOT THAT ONE. SAM SAID IT WOULD HAVE AN OMEGA SYMBOL ON IT. I GOT THAT MUCH.
THERE'S A BUNCH OF THESE KEYS FLOATING AROUND THIS PLACE. THE GHOST KEY. THAT ONE. WHO KNOWS HOW MANY.
SO THIS THING THAT WAS IN THE WELLHOUSE, SHE'S STILL OUT THERE SOMEWHERE. AND SHE STILL WANTS ONE OF THESE KEYS. AND SHE COULD SHOW UP AT ANY TIME TO GET IT.
MOM NEEDS TO KNOW.
MOM LOOKED RIGHT INTO BODE'S HEAD, OPEN LIKE A BUCKET, AND JUST WANDERED OFF.
IF SHE DIDN'T BELIEVE THAT, WHEN IT WAS STARING HER RIGHT IN THE FACE, THEN SHE ISN'T GOING TO BELIEVE WE MIGHT BE ATTACKED BY BODE'S HOMICIDAL ECHO.
YOU BELIEVE HOW WARM IT IS? IT STILL FEELS LIKE SUMMER.

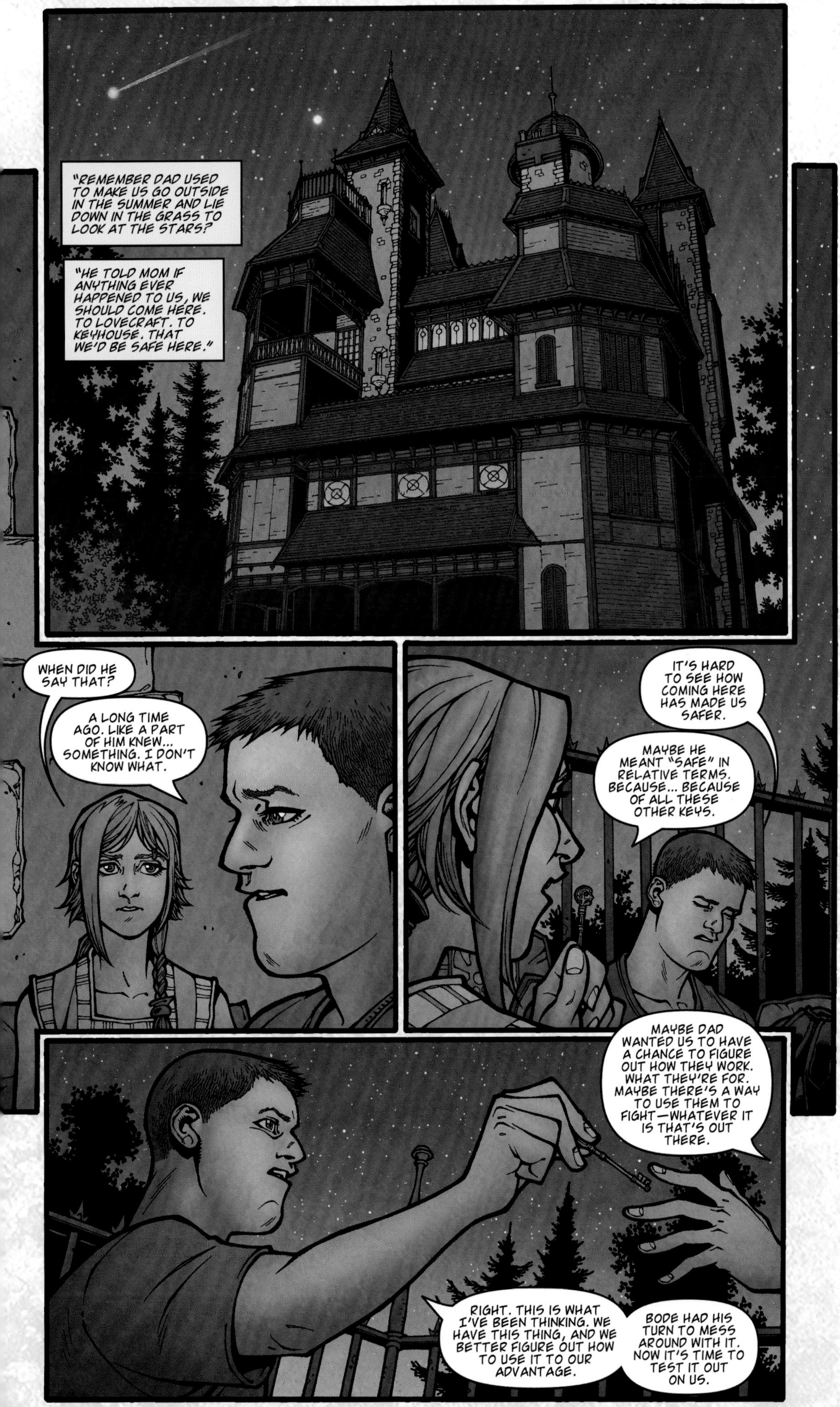
"REMEMBER DAD USED TO MAKE US GO OUTSIDE IN THE SUMMER AND LIE DOWN IN THE GRASS TO LOOK AT THE STARS?
"HE TOLD MOM IF ANYTHING EVER HAPPENED TO US, WE SHOULD COME HERE. TO LOVECRAFT. TO KEYHOUSE. THAT WE'D BE SAFE HERE."
WHEN DID HE SAY THAT?
A LONG TIME AGO. LIKE A PART OF HIM KNEW... SOMETHING. I DON'T KNOW WHAT.
IT'S HARD TO SEE HOW COMING HERE HAS MADE US SAFER.
MAYBE HE MEANT "SAFE" IN RELATIVE TERMS. BECAUSE... BECAUSE OF ALL THESE OTHER KEYS.
MAYBE DAD WANTED US TO HAVE A CHANCE TO FIGURE OUT HOW THEY WORK. WHAT THEY'RE FOR. MAYBE THERE'S A WAY TO USE THEM TO FIGHT—WHATEVER IT IS THAT'S OUT THERE.
RIGHT. THIS IS WHAT I'VE BEEN THINKING. WE HAVE THIS THING, AND WE BETTER FIGURE OUT HOW TO USE IT TO OUR ADVANTAGE.
BODE HAD HIS TURN TO MESS AROUND WITH IT. NOW IT'S TIME TO TEST IT OUT ON US.

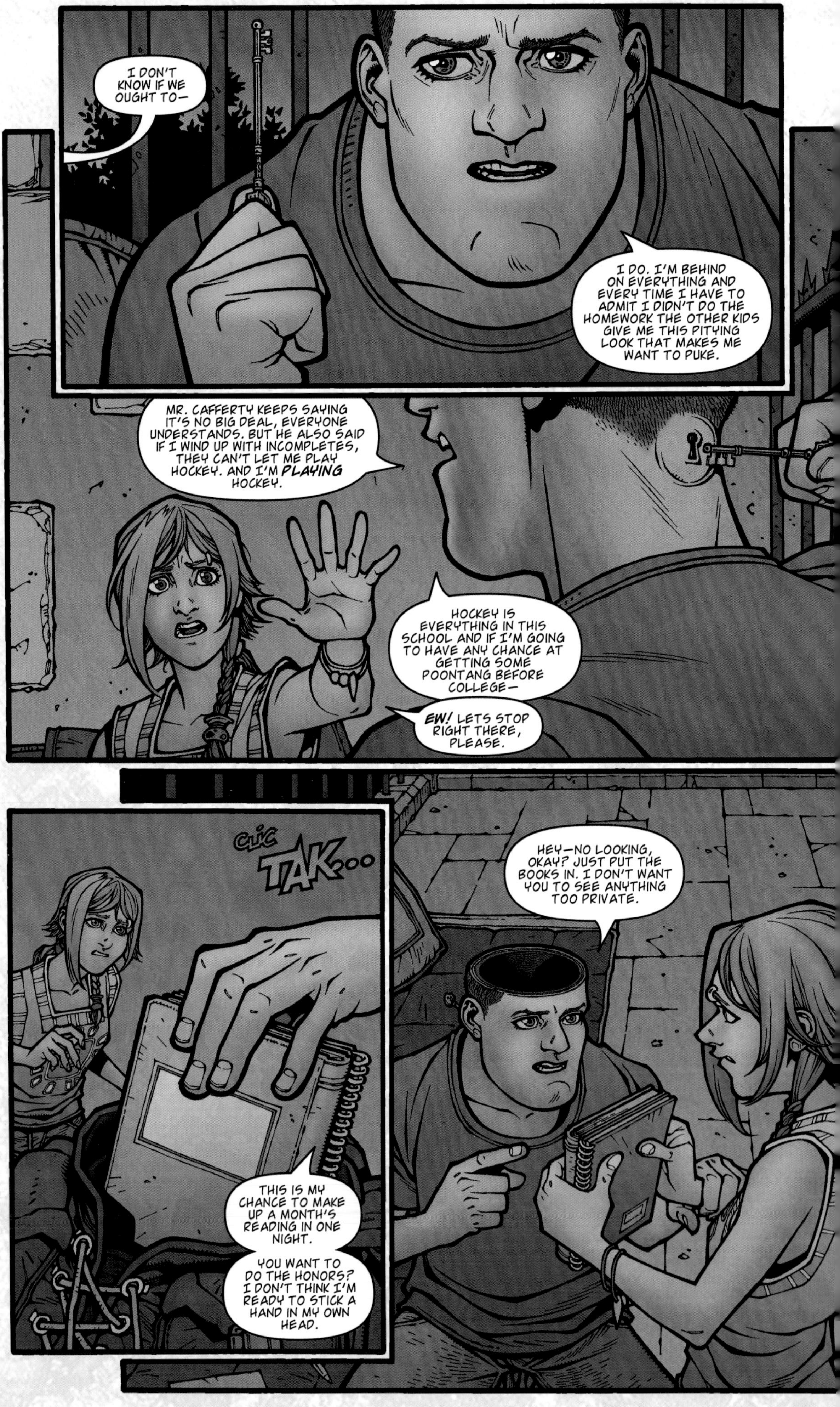
I DON'T KNOW IF WE OUGHT TO—
I DO. I'M BEHIND ON EVERYTHING AND EVERY TIME I HAVE TO ADMIT I DIDN'T DO THE HOMEWORK THE OTHER KIDS GIVE ME THIS PITYING LOOK THAT MAKES ME WANT TO PUKE.
MR. CAFFERTY KEEPS SAYING IT'S NO BIG DEAL, EVERYONE UNDERSTANDS. BUT HE ALSO SAID IF I WIND UP WITH INCOMPLETES, THEY CAN'T LET ME PLAY HOCKEY. AND I'M PLAYING HOCKEY.
HOCKEY IS EVERYTHING IN THIS SCHOOL AND IF I'M GOING TO HAVE ANY CHANCE AT GETTING SOME POONTANG BEFORE COLLEGE—
EW! LETS STOP RIGHT THERE, PLEASE.
CLIC
TAK...
THIS IS MY CHANCE TO MAKE UP A MONTH'S READING IN ONE NIGHT.
YOU WANT TO DO THE HONORS? I DON'T THINK I'M READY TO STICK A HAND IN MY OWN HEAD.
HEY—NO LOOKING, OKAY? JUST PUT THE BOOKS IN. I DON'T WANT YOU TO SEE ANYTHING TOO PRIVATE.

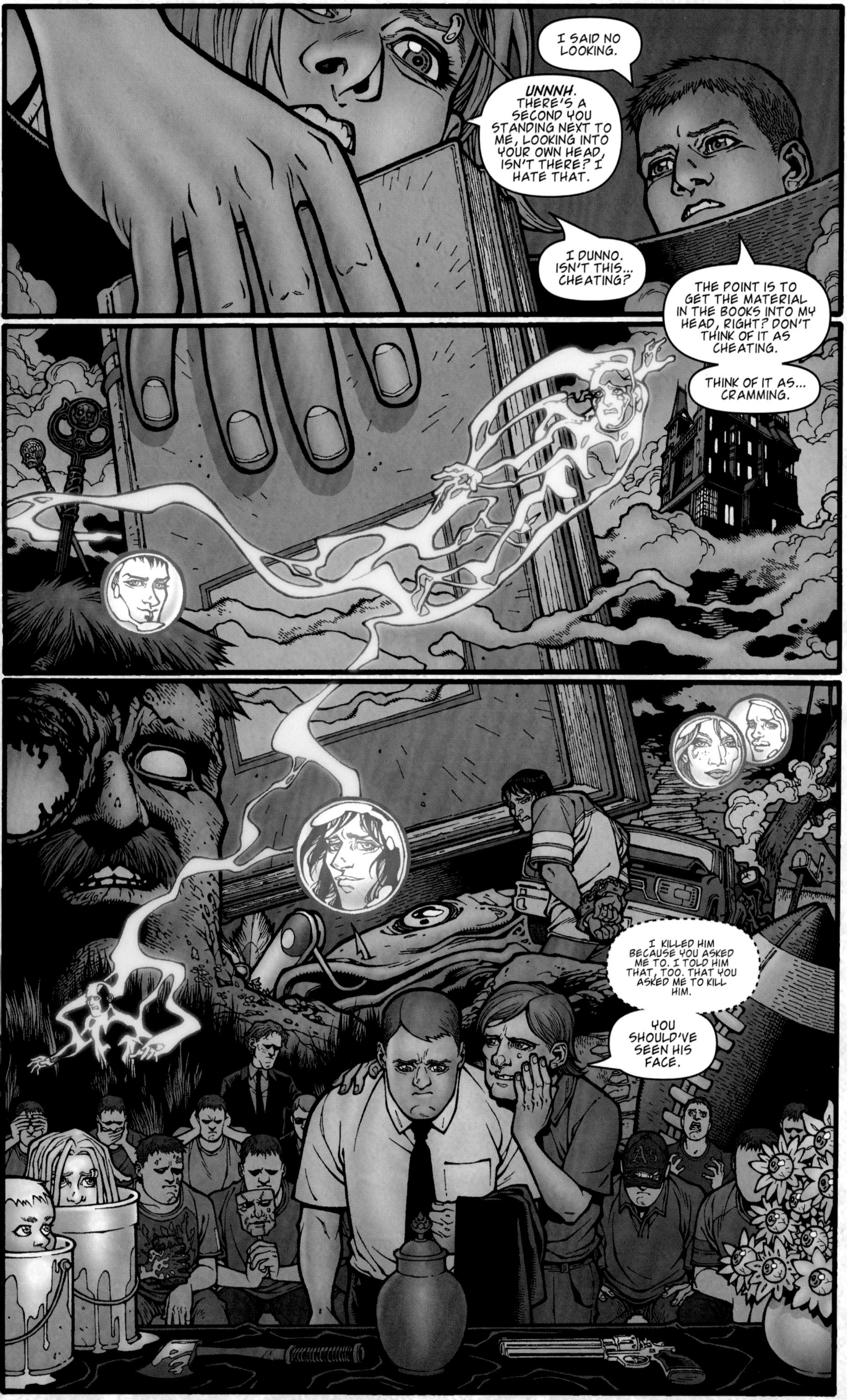
I SAID NO LOOKING.
UNNNH. THERE'S A SECOND YOU STANDING NEXT TO ME, LOOKING INTO YOUR OWN HEAD, ISN'T THERE? I HATE THAT.
I DUNNO. ISN'T THIS... CHEATING?
THE POINT IS TO GET THE MATERIAL IN THE BOOKS INTO MY HEAD, RIGHT? DON'T THINK OF IT AS CHEATING.
THINK OF IT AS... CRAMMING.
I KILLED HIM BECAUSE YOU ASKED ME TO. I TOLD HIM THAT, TOO. THAT YOU ASKED ME TO KILL HIM.
YOU SHOULD'VE SEEN HIS FACE.

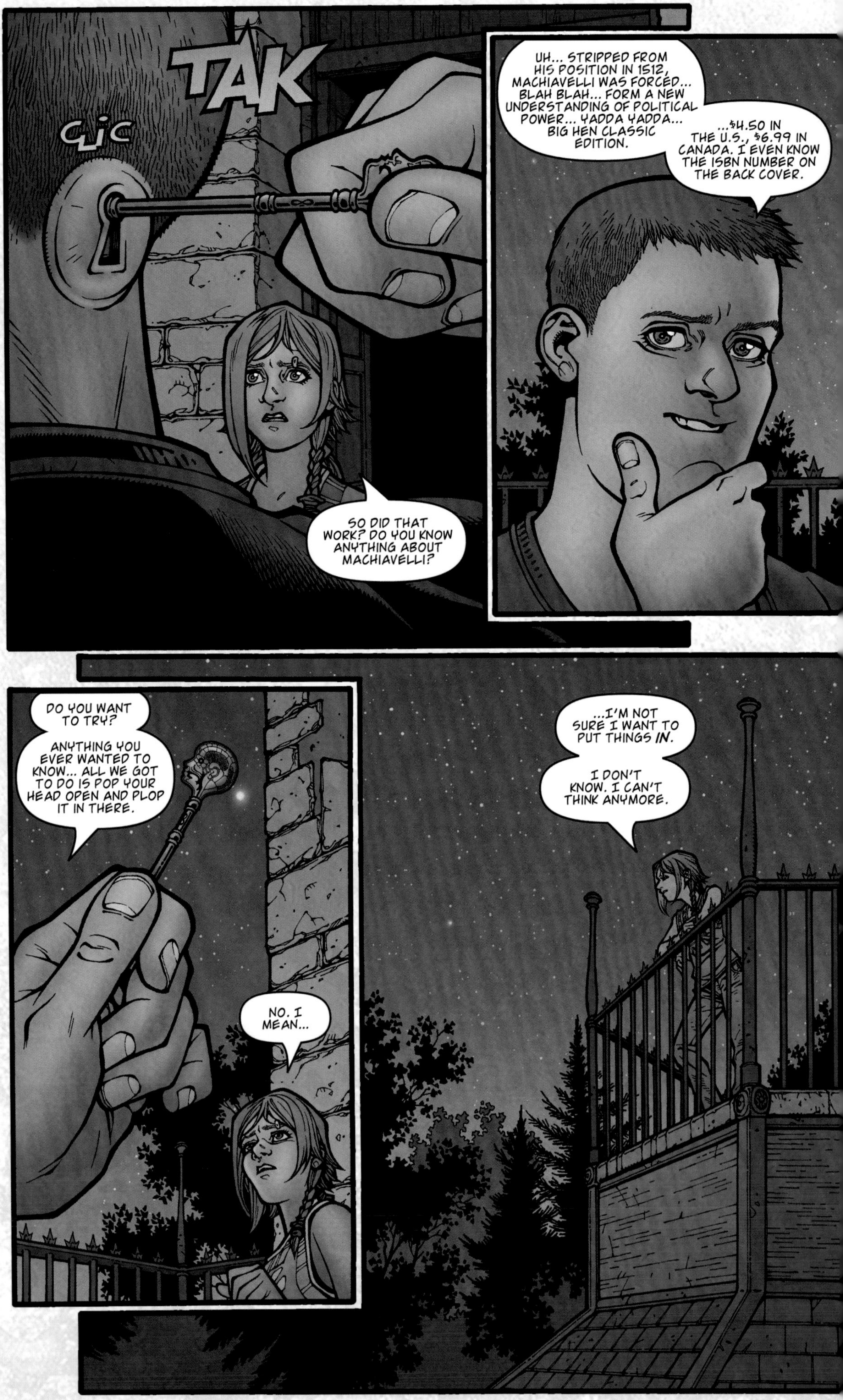
TAK
CLIC
SO DID THAT WORK? DO YOU KNOW ANYTHING ABOUT MACHIAVELLI?
UH... STRIPPED FROM HIS POSITION IN 1512, MACHIAVELLI WAS FORCED... BLAH BLAH... FORM A NEW UNDERSTANDING OF POLITICAL POWER... YADDA YADDA... BIG HEN CLASSIC EDITION.
...$4.50 IN THE U.S., $6.99 IN CANADA. I EVEN KNOW THE ISBN NUMBER ON THE BACK COVER.
DO YOU WANT TO TRY?
ANYTHING YOU EVER WANTED TO KNOW... ALL WE GOT TO DO IS POP YOUR HEAD OPEN AND PLOP IT IN THERE.
NO. I MEAN...
...I'M NOT SURE I WANT TO PUT THINGS IN.
I DON'T KNOW. I CAN'T THINK ANYMORE.

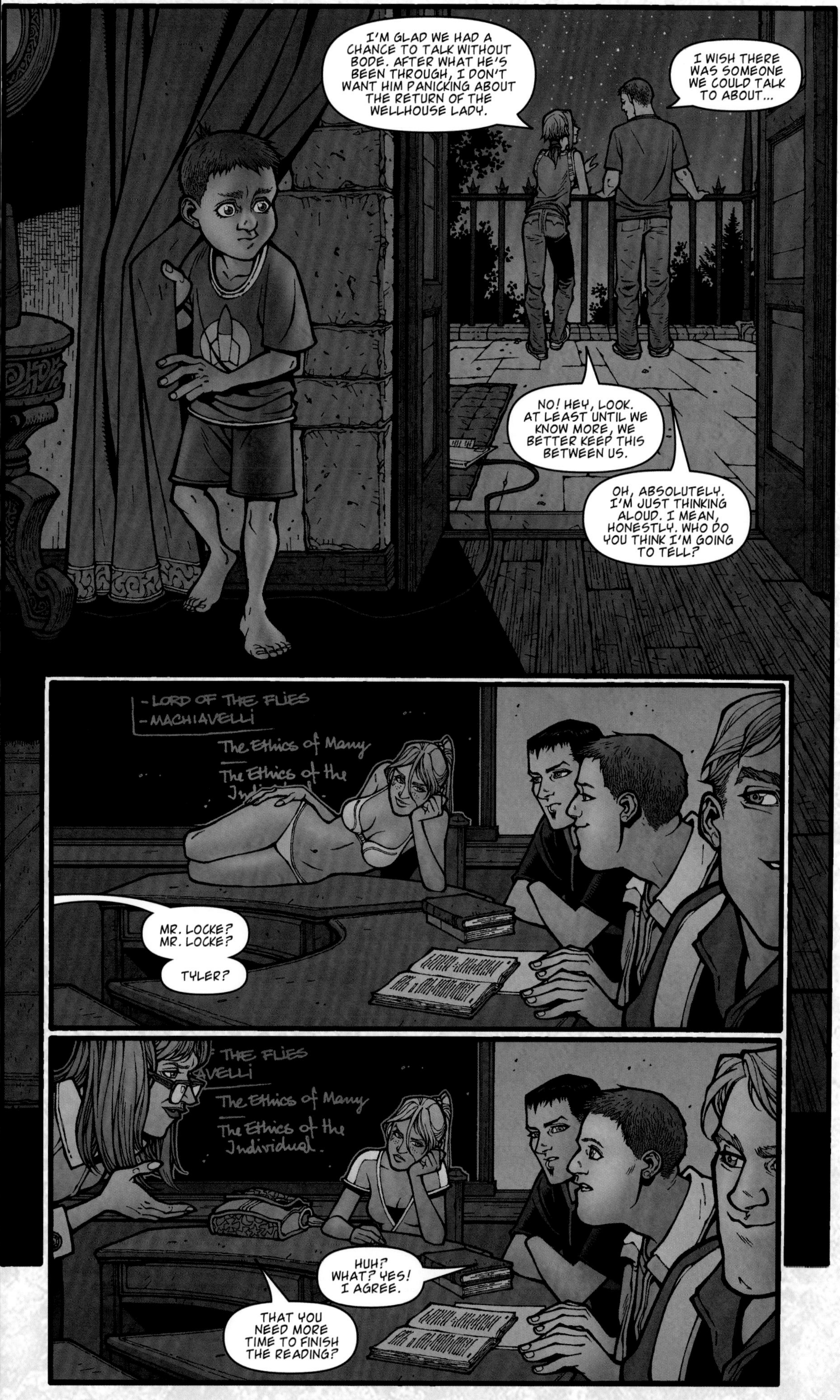
I'M GLAD WE HAD A CHANCE TO TALK WITHOUT BODE. AFTER WHAT HE'S BEEN THROUGH, I DON'T WANT HIM PANICKING ABOUT THE RETURN OF THE WELLHOUSE LADY.
I WISH THERE WAS SOMEONE WE COULD TALK TO ABOUT...
NO! HEY, LOOK. AT LEAST UNTIL WE KNOW MORE, WE BETTER KEEP THIS BETWEEN US.
OH, ABSOLUTELY. I'M JUST THINKING ALOUD. I MEAN, HONESTLY. WHO DO YOU THINK I'M GOING TO TELL?
- LORD OF THE FLIES
- MACHIAVELLI
The Ethics of Many
The Ethics of the Individual
MR. LOCKE? MR. LOCKE?
TYLER?
HUH? WHAT? YES! I AGREE.
THAT YOU NEED MORE TIME TO FINISH THE READING?

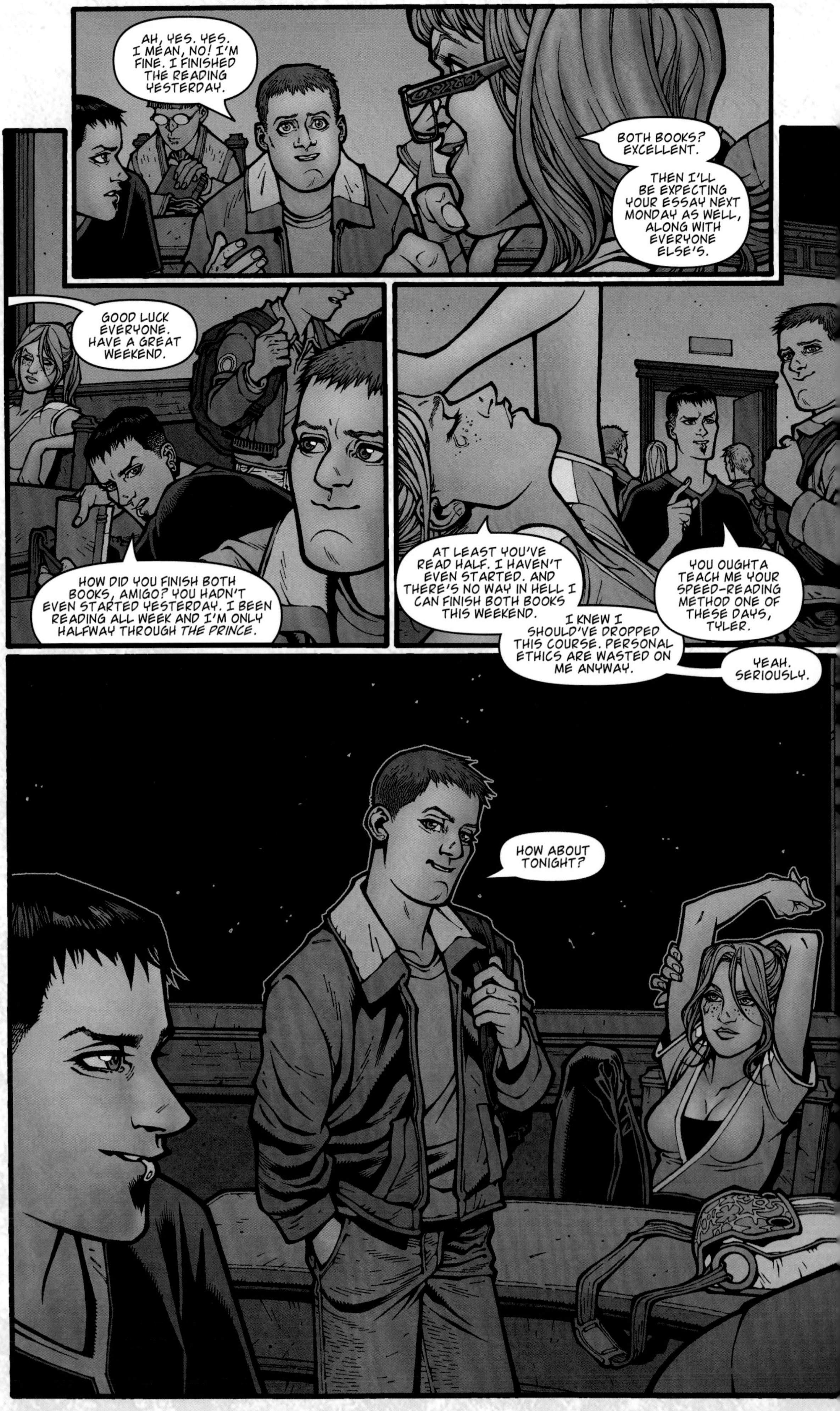
AH, YES. YES. I MEAN, NO! I'M FINE. I FINISHED THE READING YESTERDAY.
BOTH BOOKS? EXCELLENT.
THEN I'LL BE EXPECTING YOUR ESSAY NEXT MONDAY AS WELL, ALONG WITH EVERYONE ELSE'S.
GOOD LUCK EVERYONE. HAVE A GREAT WEEKEND.
HOW DID YOU FINISH BOTH BOOKS, AMIGO? YOU HADN'T EVEN STARTED YESTERDAY. I BEEN READING ALL WEEK AND I'M ONLY HALFWAY THROUGH *THE PRINCE*.
AT LEAST YOU'VE READ HALF. I HAVEN'T EVEN STARTED. AND THERE'S NO WAY IN HELL I CAN FINISH BOTH BOOKS THIS WEEKEND.
I KNEW I SHOULD'VE DROPPED THIS COURSE. PERSONAL ETHICS ARE WASTED ON ME ANYWAY.
YOU OUGHTA TEACH ME YOUR SPEED-READING METHOD ONE OF THESE DAYS, TYLER.
YEAH. SERIOUSLY.
HOW ABOUT TONIGHT?

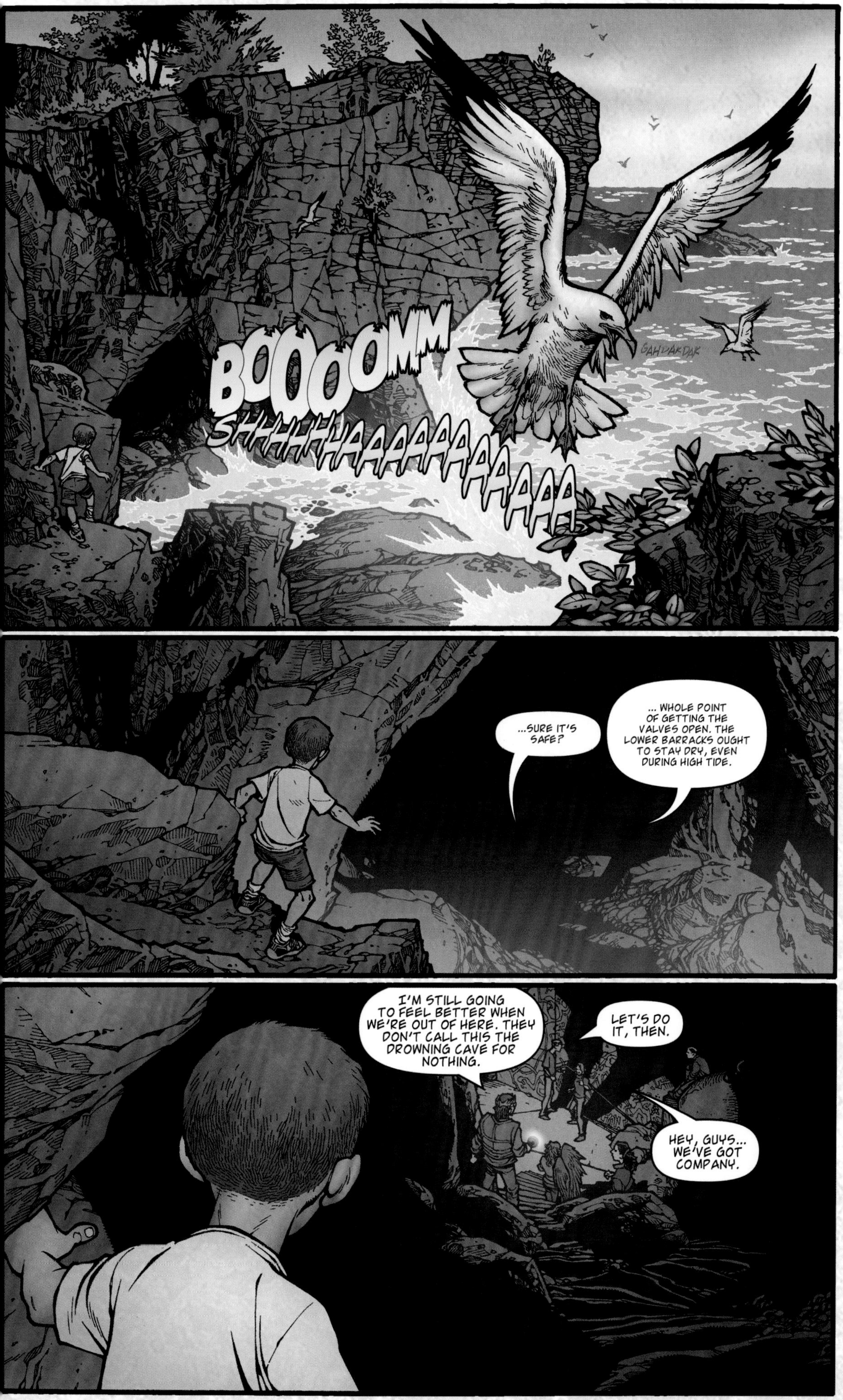
BOOOOMM
SHHHHAAAAAAAAAAAA
GAHDAKDAK
...SURE IT'S SAFE?
... WHOLE POINT OF GETTING THE VALVES OPEN. THE LOWER BARRACKS OUGHT TO STAY DRY, EVEN DURING HIGH TIDE.
I'M STILL GOING TO FEEL BETTER WHEN WE'RE OUT OF HERE. THEY DON'T CALL THIS THE DROWNING CAVE FOR NOTHING.
LET'S DO IT, THEN.
HEY, GUYS... WE'VE GOT COMPANY.

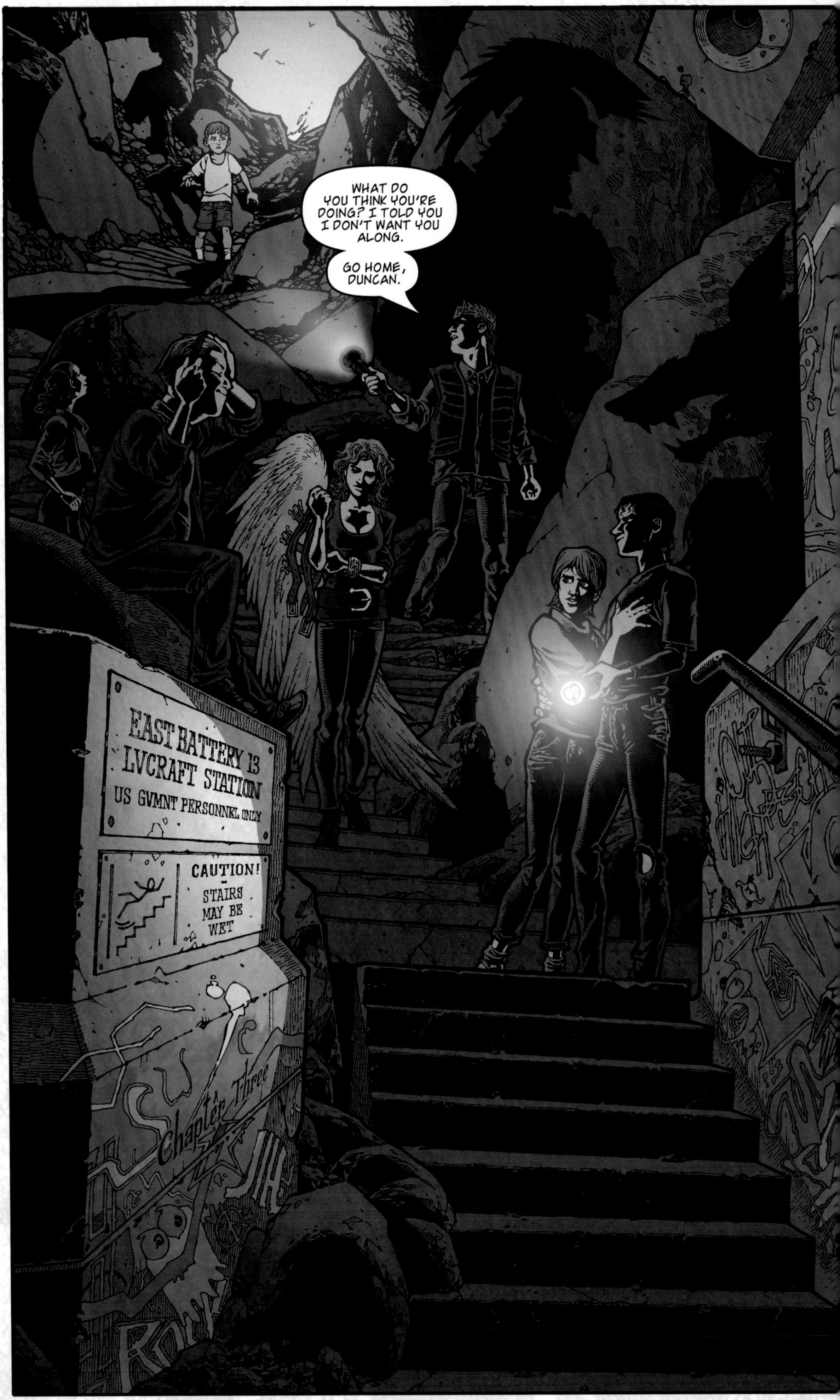
WHAT DO YOU THINK YOU'RE DOING? I TOLD YOU I DON'T WANT YOU ALONG.
GO HOME, DUNCAN.
EAST BATTERY 13
LVCRAFT STATION
US GVMNT PERSONNEL ONLY
CAUTION! STAIRS MAY BE WET
Chapter Three

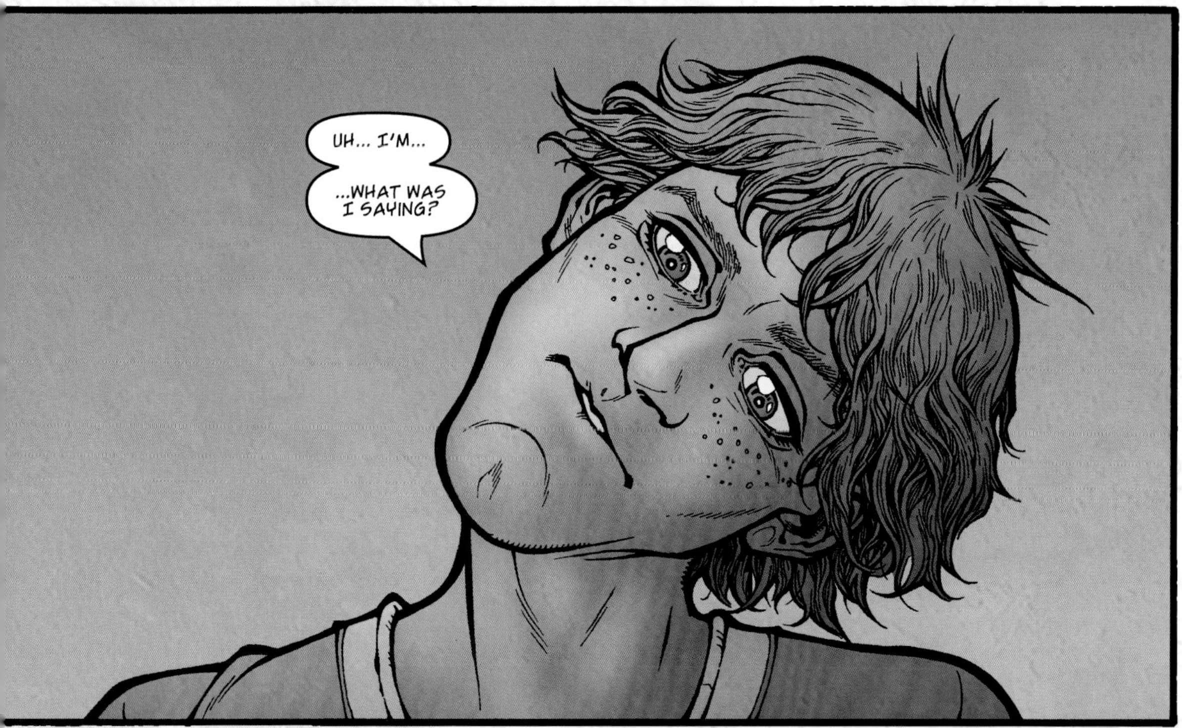
UH... I'M...
...WHAT WAS I SAYING?

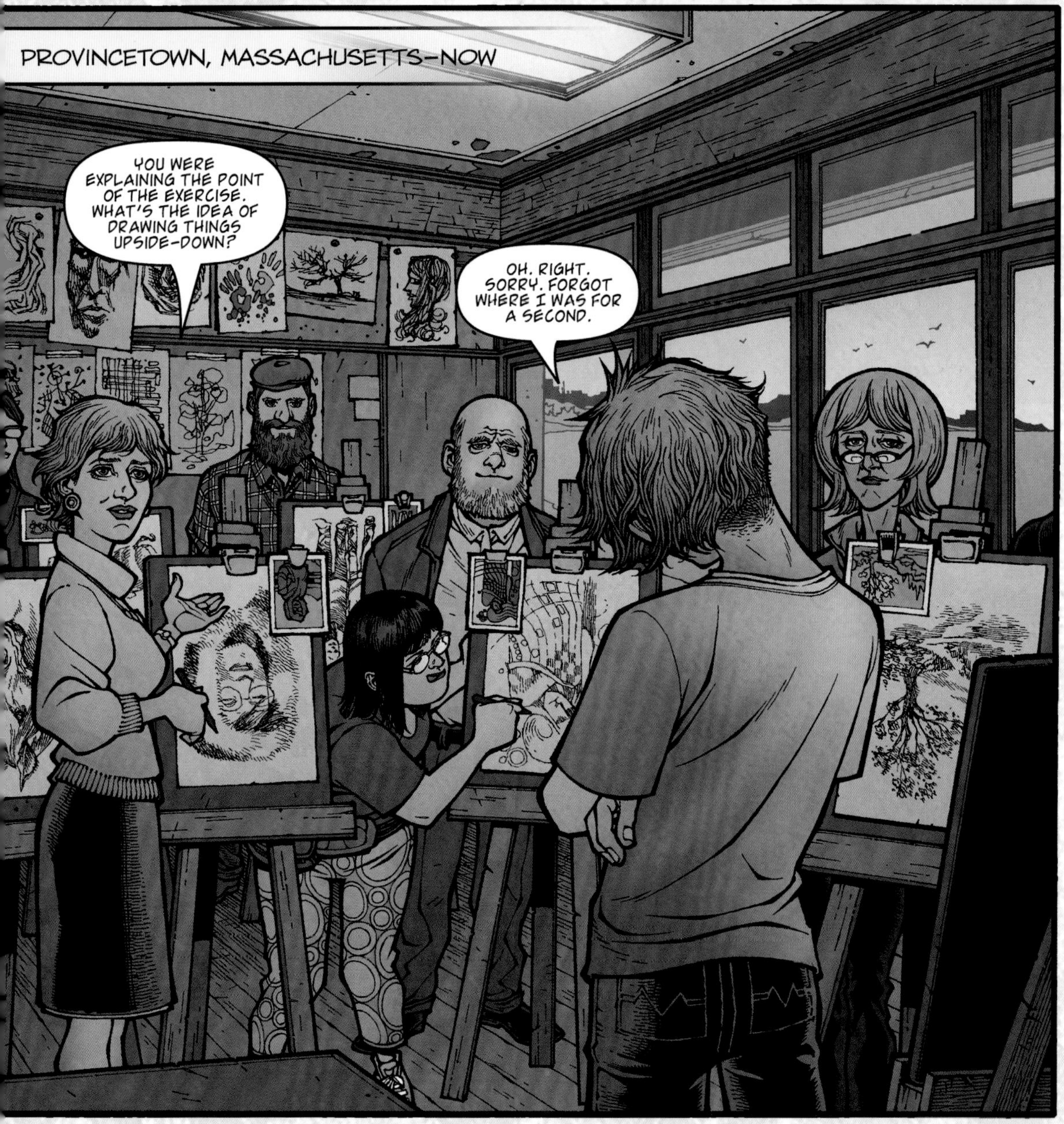
PROVINCETOWN, MASSACHUSETTS–NOW
YOU WERE EXPLAINING THE POINT OF THE EXERCISE. WHAT'S THE IDEA OF DRAWING THINGS UPSIDE-DOWN?
OH. RIGHT. SORRY. FORGOT WHERE I WAS FOR A SECOND.

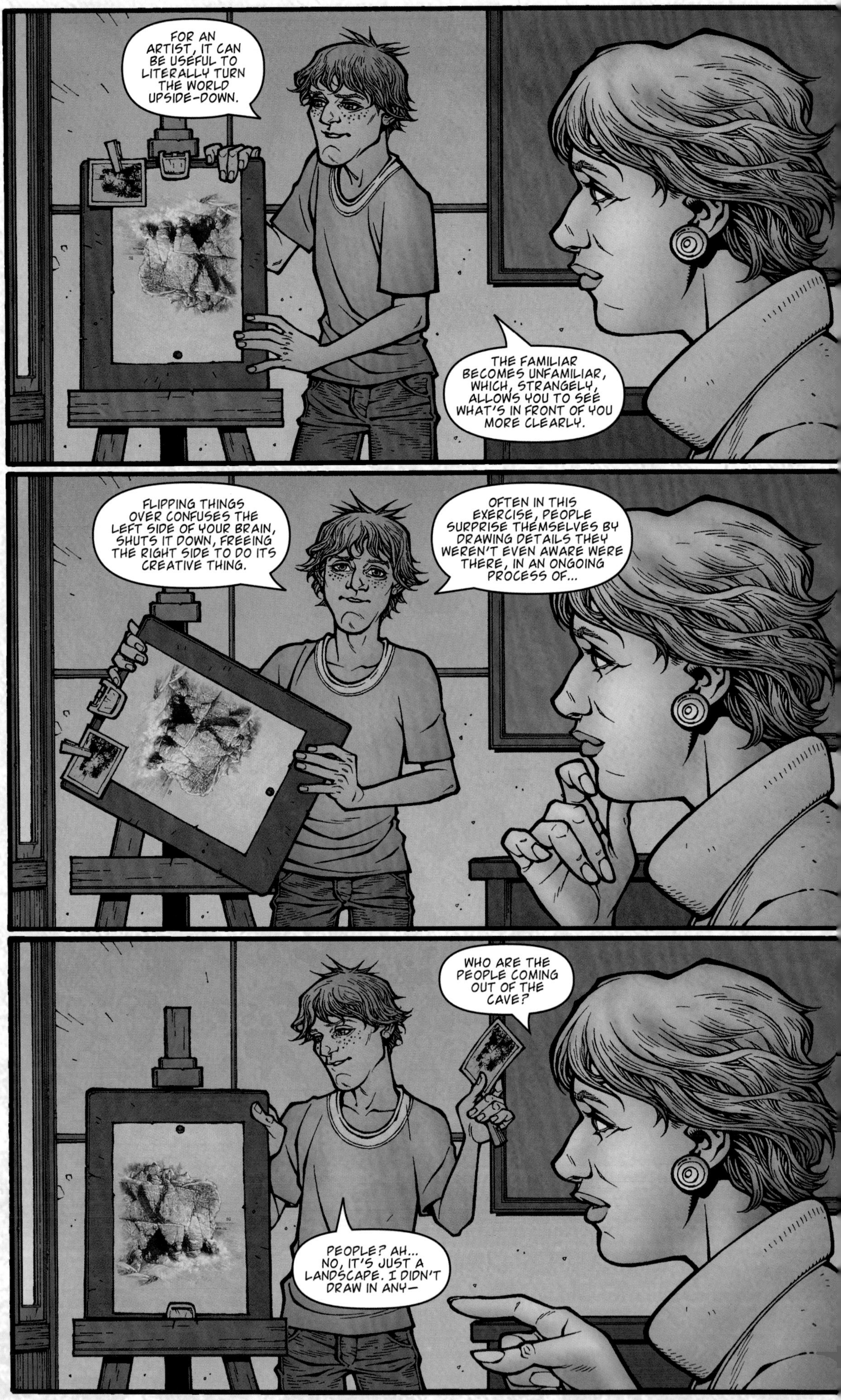
FOR AN ARTIST, IT CAN BE USEFUL TO LITERALLY TURN THE WORLD UPSIDE-DOWN.
THE FAMILIAR BECOMES UNFAMILIAR, WHICH, STRANGELY, ALLOWS YOU TO SEE WHAT'S IN FRONT OF YOU MORE CLEARLY.
FLIPPING THINGS OVER CONFUSES THE LEFT SIDE OF YOUR BRAIN, SHUTS IT DOWN, FREEING THE RIGHT SIDE TO DO ITS CREATIVE THING.
OFTEN IN THIS EXERCISE, PEOPLE SURPRISE THEMSELVES BY DRAWING DETAILS THEY WEREN'T EVEN AWARE WERE THERE, IN AN ONGOING PROCESS OF...
WHO ARE THE PEOPLE COMING OUT OF THE CAVE?
PEOPLE? AH... NO, IT'S JUST A LANDSCAPE. I DIDN'T DRAW IN ANY—

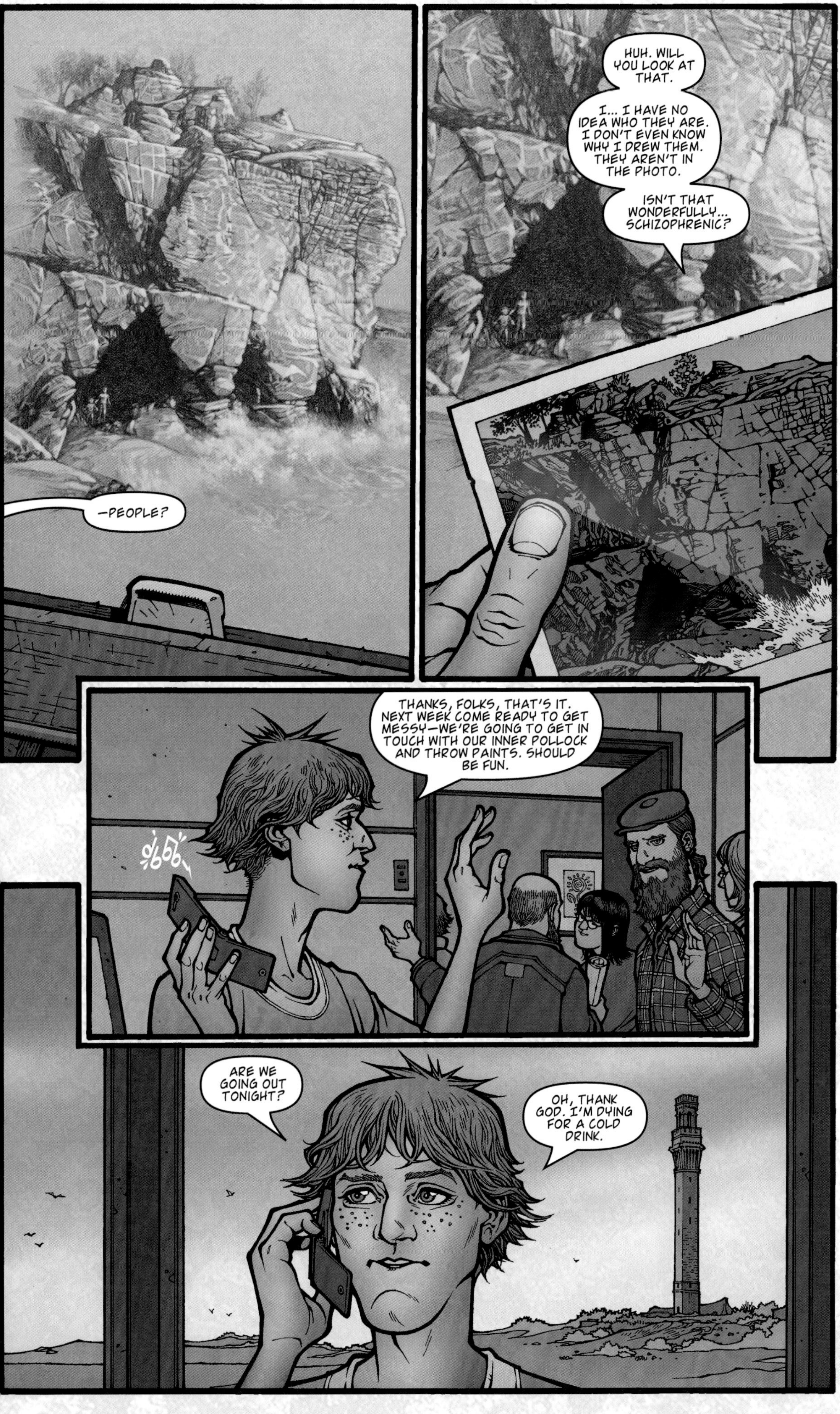

—PEOPLE?
HUH. WILL YOU LOOK AT THAT.
I... I HAVE NO IDEA WHO THEY ARE. I DON'T EVEN KNOW WHY I DREW THEM. THEY AREN'T IN THE PHOTO.
ISN'T THAT WONDERFULLY... SCHIZOPHRENIC?
THANKS, FOLKS, THAT'S IT. NEXT WEEK COME READY TO GET MESSY—WE'RE GOING TO GET IN TOUCH WITH OUR INNER POLLOCK AND THROW PAINTS. SHOULD BE FUN.
ARE WE GOING OUT TONIGHT?
OH, THANK GOD. I'M DYING FOR A COLD DRINK.

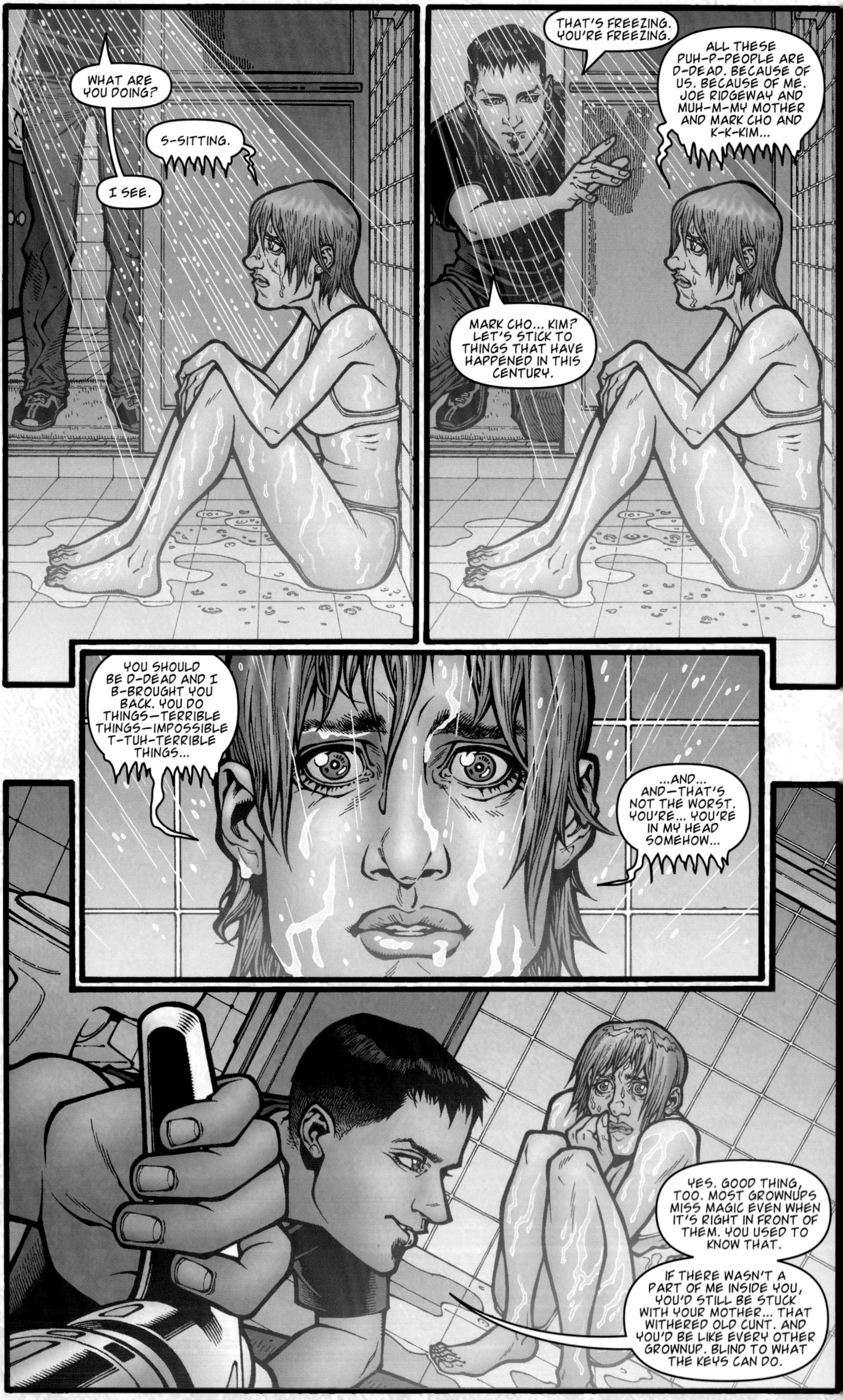
WHAT ARE YOU DOING?
S-SITTING.
I SEE.
THAT'S FREEZING. YOU'RE FREEZING.
ALL THESE PUH-P-PEOPLE ARE D-DEAD. BECAUSE OF US. BECAUSE OF ME. JOE RIDGEWAY AND MUH-M-MY MOTHER AND MARK CHO AND K-K-KIM...
MARK CHO... KIM? LET'S STICK TO THINGS THAT HAVE HAPPENED IN THIS CENTURY.
YOU SHOULD BE D-DEAD AND I B-BROUGHT YOU BACK. YOU DO THINGS—TERRIBLE THINGS—IMPOSSIBLE T-TUH-TERRIBLE THINGS...
...AND... AND—THAT'S NOT THE WORST. YOU'RE... YOU'RE IN MY HEAD SOMEHOW...
YES. GOOD THING, TOO. MOST GROWNUPS MISS MAGIC EVEN WHEN IT'S RIGHT IN FRONT OF THEM. YOU USED TO KNOW THAT.
IF THERE WASN'T A PART OF ME INSIDE YOU, YOU'D STILL BE STUCK WITH YOUR MOTHER... THAT WITHERED OLD CUNT. AND YOU'D BE LIKE EVERY OTHER GROWNUP. BLIND TO WHAT THE KEYS CAN DO.

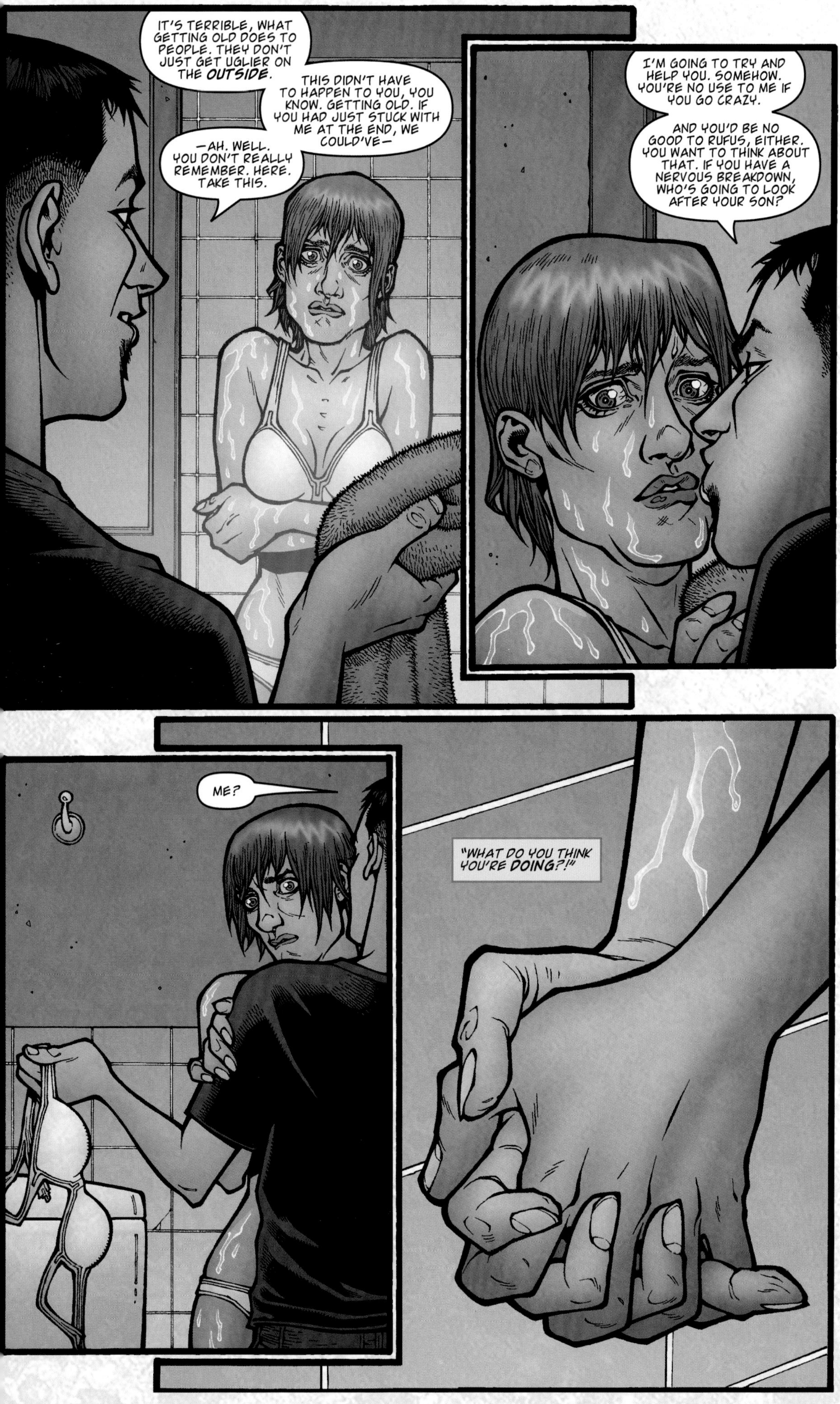
IT'S TERRIBLE, WHAT GETTING OLD DOES TO PEOPLE. THEY DON'T JUST GET UGLIER ON THE OUTSIDE.
THIS DIDN'T HAVE TO HAPPEN TO YOU, YOU KNOW. GETTING OLD. IF YOU HAD JUST STUCK WITH ME AT THE END, WE COULD'VE—
—AH. WELL. YOU DON'T REALLY REMEMBER. HERE. TAKE THIS.
I'M GOING TO TRY AND HELP YOU. SOMEHOW. YOU'RE NO USE TO ME IF YOU GO CRAZY.
AND YOU'D BE NO GOOD TO RUFUS, EITHER. YOU WANT TO THINK ABOUT THAT. IF YOU HAVE A NERVOUS BREAKDOWN, WHO'S GOING TO LOOK AFTER YOUR SON?
ME?
"WHAT DO YOU THINK YOU'RE DOING?!"

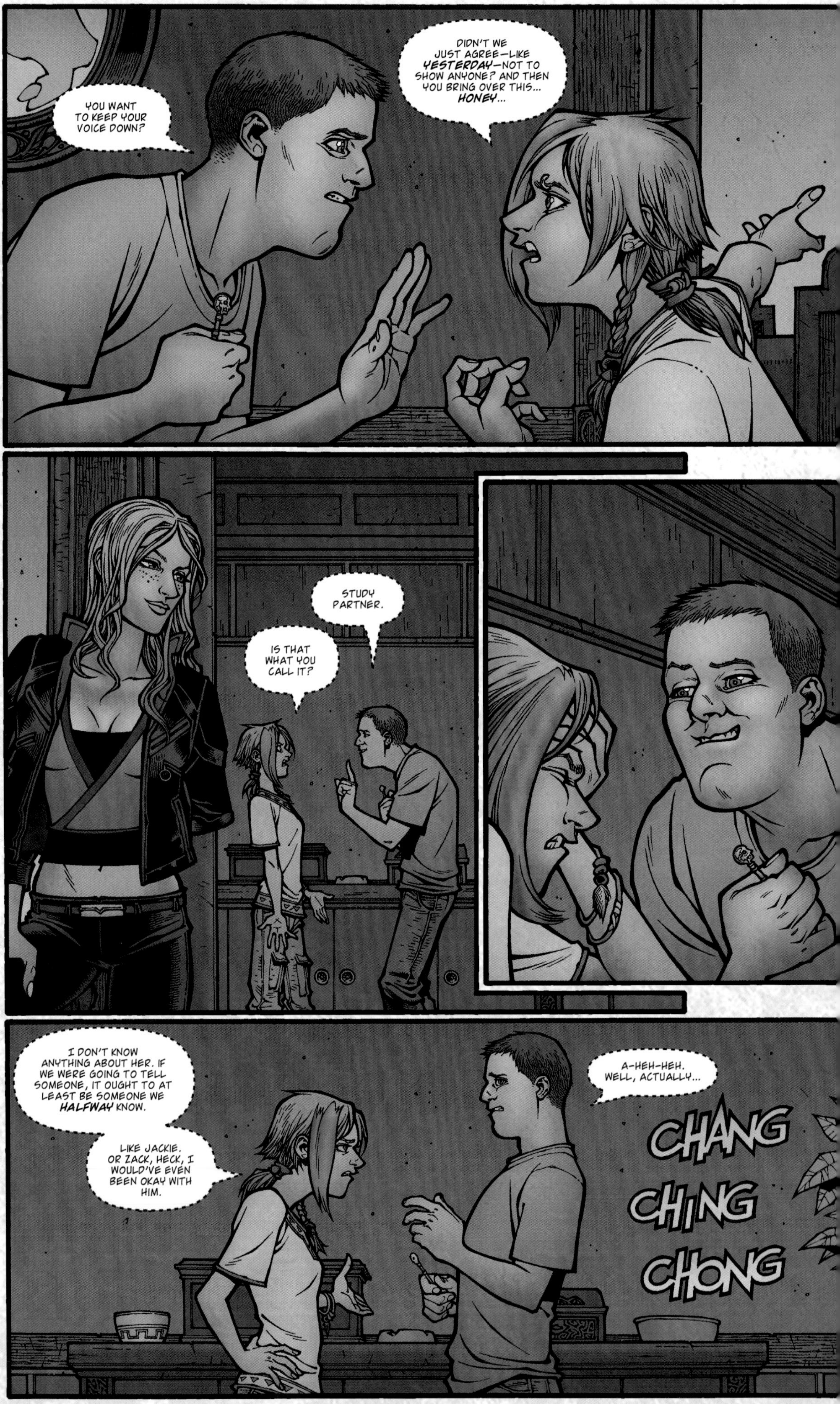
YOU WANT TO KEEP YOUR VOICE DOWN?
DIDN'T WE JUST AGREE—LIKE YESTERDAY—NOT TO SHOW ANYONE? AND THEN YOU BRING OVER THIS... HONEY...
STUDY PARTNER.
IS THAT WHAT YOU CALL IT?
I DON'T KNOW ANYTHING ABOUT HER. IF WE WERE GOING TO TELL SOMEONE, IT OUGHT TO AT LEAST BE SOMEONE WE HALFWAY KNOW.
LIKE JACKIE. OR ZACK, HECK, I WOULD'VE EVEN BEEN OKAY WITH HIM.
A-HEH-HEH. WELL, ACTUALLY...
CHANG
CHING
CHONG

WHAT TOOK YOU SO LONG? IT'S LATE.

AUNT ELLIE SHOVED A BUNCH OF HOT CHERRY PIE IN MY FACE AND WOULDN'T LET ME GO UNTIL I ATE MYSELF SICK. WOMAN CAN COOK.

OKAY FOR YOU TO SPEND THE NIGHT?

SURE. I HAVE THAT LADY UNDER MY POWERS.

SO WHAT'S THIS AMAZING THING YOU JUST HAD TO SHOW US ON A FRIDAY NIGHT AND HOW'S IT GOING TO HELP US GET A'S?

IT'S, UH, IT'S PRETTY INTENSE. PROBABLY THE MOST INTENSE THING EITHER OF YOU HAVE EVER SEEN.

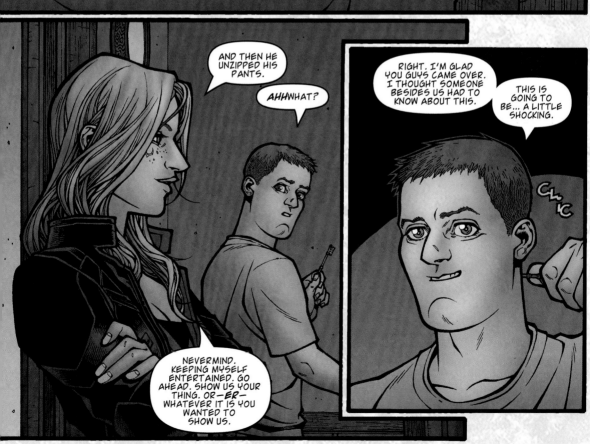

AND THEN HE UNZIPPED HIS PANTS.

AHH WHAT?

RIGHT. I'M GLAD YOU GUYS CAME OVER. I THOUGHT SOMEONE BESIDES US HAD TO KNOW ABOUT THIS.

THIS IS GOING TO BE... A LITTLE SHOCKING.

NEVERMIND. KEEPING MYSELF ENTERTAINED. GO AHEAD. SHOW US YOUR THING. OR—ER—WHATEVER IT IS YOU WANTED TO SHOW US.

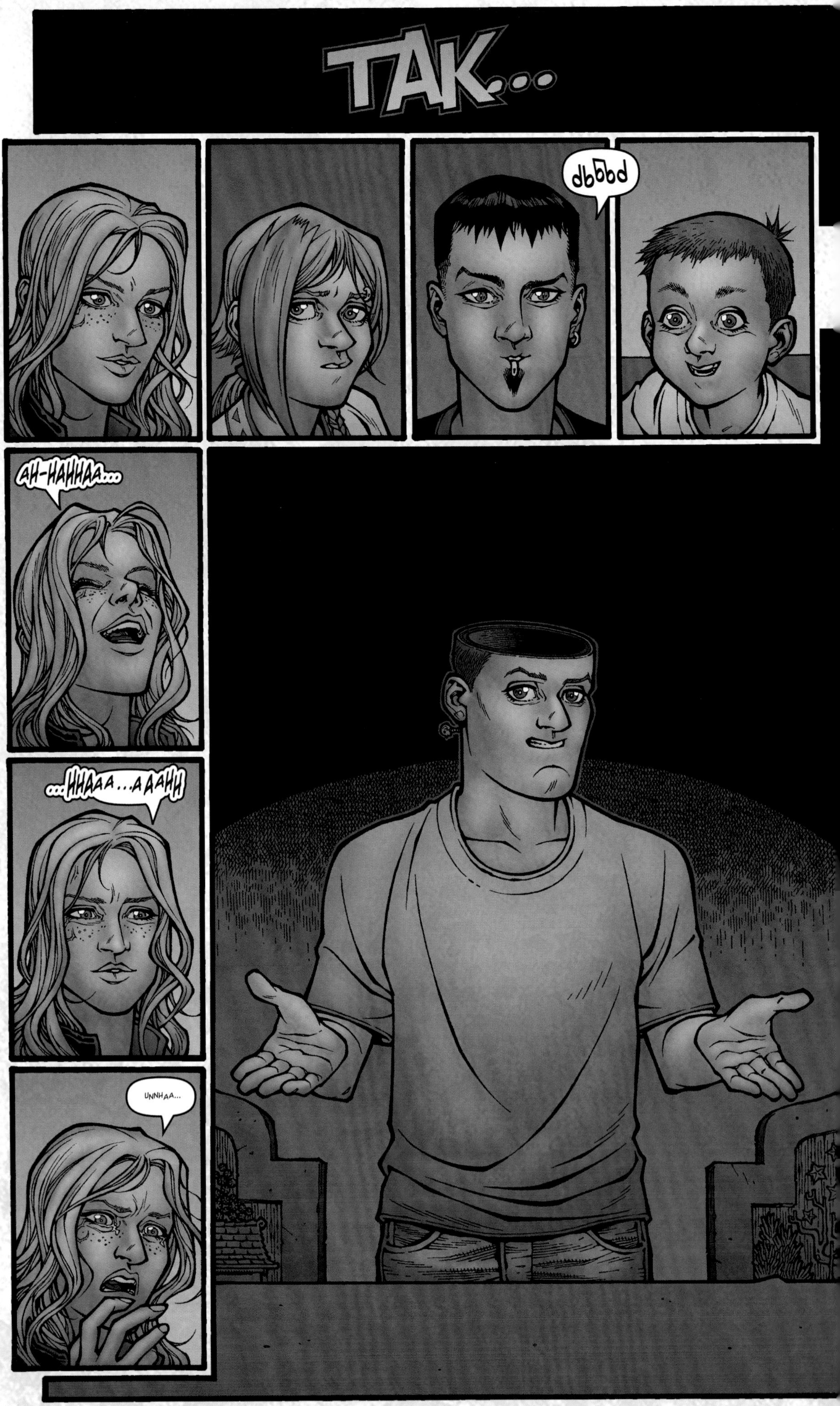
TAK...
AH-HAHHAA...
...HHAAA...AAAHH
UNNHAA...

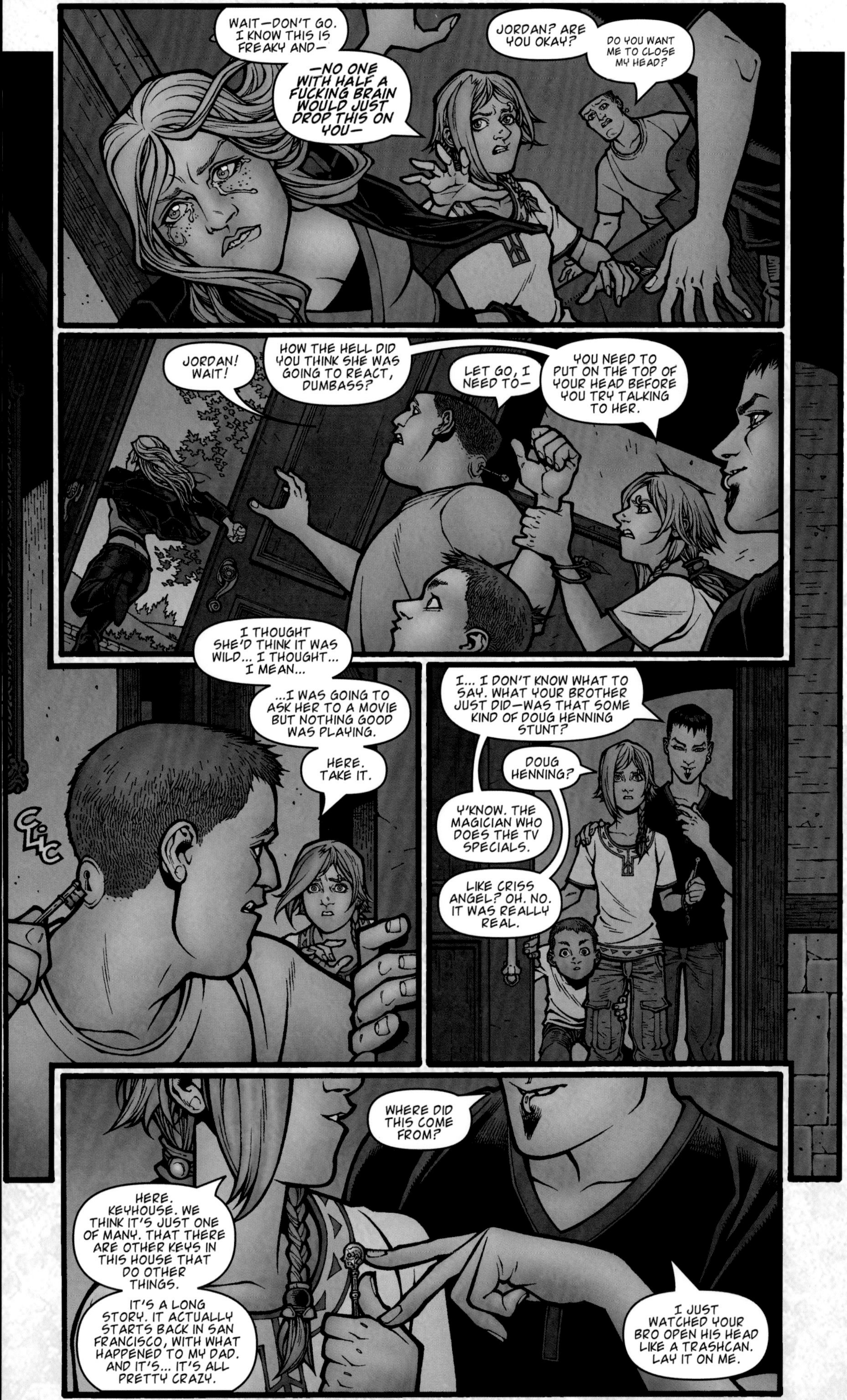
WAIT—DON'T GO. I KNOW THIS IS FREAKY AND—
—NO ONE WITH HALF A FUCKING BRAIN WOULD JUST DROP THIS ON YOU—
JORDAN? ARE YOU OKAY?
DO YOU WANT ME TO CLOSE MY HEAD?
JORDAN! WAIT!
HOW THE HELL DID YOU THINK SHE WAS GOING TO REACT, DUMBASS?
LET GO, I NEED TO—
YOU NEED TO PUT ON THE TOP OF YOUR HEAD BEFORE YOU TRY TALKING TO HER.
I THOUGHT SHE'D THINK IT WAS WILD... I THOUGHT... I MEAN...
...I WAS GOING TO ASK HER TO A MOVIE BUT NOTHING GOOD WAS PLAYING.
HERE. TAKE IT.
CLIC
I... I DON'T KNOW WHAT TO SAY. WHAT YOUR BROTHER JUST DID—WAS THAT SOME KIND OF DOUG HENNING STUNT?
DOUG HENNING?
Y'KNOW. THE MAGICIAN WHO DOES THE TV SPECIALS.
LIKE CRISS ANGEL? OH. NO. IT WAS REALLY REAL.
WHERE DID THIS COME FROM?
HERE. KEYHOUSE. WE THINK IT'S JUST ONE OF MANY. THAT THERE ARE OTHER KEYS IN THIS HOUSE THAT DO OTHER THINGS.
IT'S A LONG STORY. IT ACTUALLY STARTS BACK IN SAN FRANCISCO, WITH WHAT HAPPENED TO MY DAD. AND IT'S... IT'S ALL PRETTY CRAZY.
I JUST WATCHED YOUR BRO OPEN HIS HEAD LIKE A TRASHCAN. LAY IT ON ME.

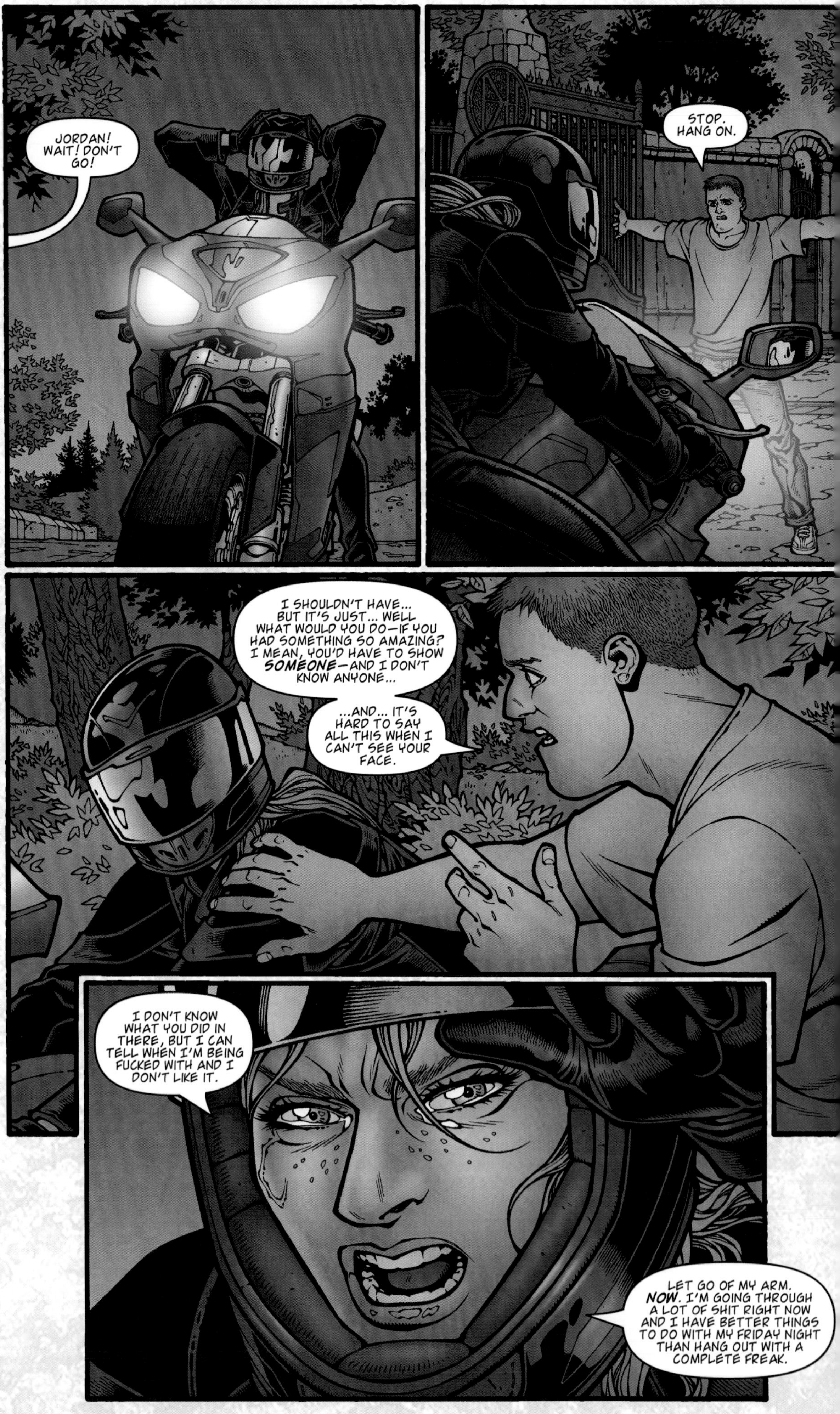
JORDAN! WAIT! DON'T GO!
STOP. HANG ON.
I SHOULDN'T HAVE... BUT IT'S JUST... WELL WHAT WOULD YOU DO—IF YOU HAD SOMETHING SO AMAZING? I MEAN, YOU'D HAVE TO SHOW **SOMEONE**—AND I DON'T KNOW ANYONE...
...AND... IT'S HARD TO SAY ALL THIS WHEN I CAN'T SEE YOUR FACE.
I DON'T KNOW WHAT YOU DID IN THERE, BUT I CAN TELL WHEN I'M BEING FUCKED WITH AND I DON'T LIKE IT.
LET GO OF MY ARM. **NOW.** I'M GOING THROUGH A LOT OF SHIT RIGHT NOW AND I HAVE BETTER THINGS TO DO WITH MY FRIDAY NIGHT THAN HANG OUT WITH A COMPLETE FREAK.

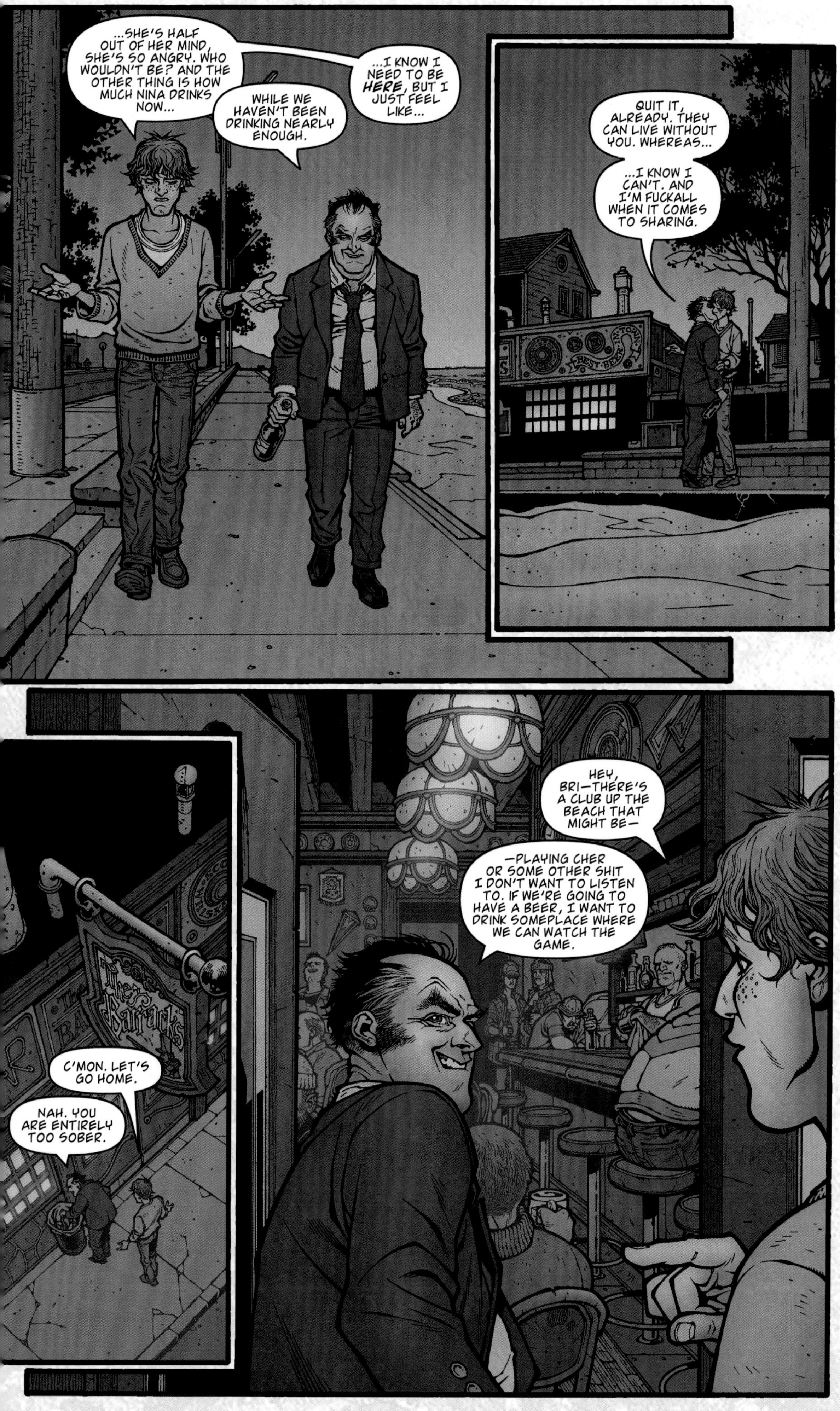
...SHE'S HALF OUT OF HER MIND, SHE'S SO ANGRY. WHO WOULDN'T BE? AND THE OTHER THING IS HOW MUCH NINA DRINKS NOW...
WHILE WE HAVEN'T BEEN DRINKING NEARLY ENOUGH.
...I KNOW I NEED TO BE *HERE*, BUT I JUST FEEL LIKE...
QUIT IT, ALREADY. THEY CAN LIVE WITHOUT YOU. WHEREAS...
...I KNOW I CAN'T. AND I'M FUCKALL WHEN IT COMES TO SHARING.
The Barracks
C'MON. LET'S GO HOME.
NAH. YOU ARE ENTIRELY TOO SOBER.
HEY, BRI—THERE'S A CLUB UP THE BEACH THAT MIGHT BE—
—PLAYING CHER OR SOME OTHER SHIT I DON'T WANT TO LISTEN TO. IF WE'RE GOING TO HAVE A BEER, I WANT TO DRINK SOMEPLACE WHERE WE CAN WATCH THE GAME.

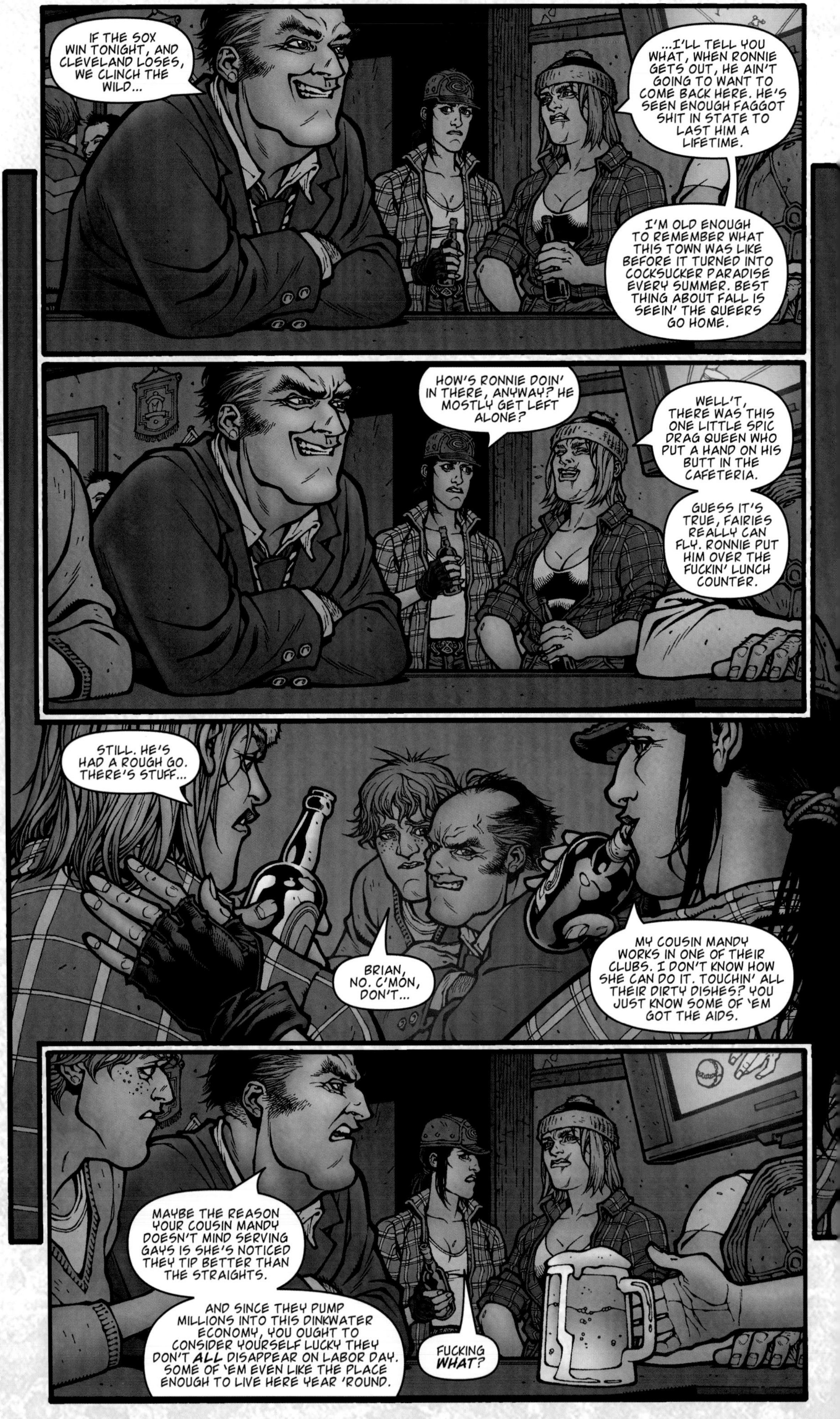
IF THE SOX WIN TONIGHT, AND CLEVELAND LOSES, WE CLINCH THE WILD...
...I'LL TELL YOU WHAT, WHEN RONNIE GETS OUT, HE AIN'T GOING TO WANT TO COME BACK HERE. HE'S SEEN ENOUGH FAGGOT SHIT IN STATE TO LAST HIM A LIFETIME.
I'M OLD ENOUGH TO REMEMBER WHAT THIS TOWN WAS LIKE BEFORE IT TURNED INTO COCKSUCKER PARADISE EVERY SUMMER. BEST THING ABOUT FALL IS SEEIN' THE QUEERS GO HOME.
HOW'S RONNIE DOIN' IN THERE, ANYWAY? HE MOSTLY GET LEFT ALONE?
WELL'T, THERE WAS THIS ONE LITTLE SPIC DRAG QUEEN WHO PUT A HAND ON HIS BUTT IN THE CAFETERIA.
GUESS IT'S TRUE, FAIRIES REALLY CAN FLY. RONNIE PUT HIM OVER THE FUCKIN' LUNCH COUNTER.
STILL. HE'S HAD A ROUGH GO. THERE'S STUFF...
BRIAN, NO. C'MON, DON'T...
MY COUSIN MANDY WORKS IN ONE OF THEIR CLUBS. I DON'T KNOW HOW SHE CAN DO IT. TOUCHIN' ALL THEIR DIRTY DISHES? YOU JUST KNOW SOME OF 'EM GOT THE AIDS.
MAYBE THE REASON YOUR COUSIN MANDY DOESN'T MIND SERVING GAYS IS SHE'S NOTICED THEY TIP BETTER THAN THE STRAIGHTS.
AND SINCE THEY PUMP MILLIONS INTO THIS DINKWATER ECONOMY, YOU OUGHT TO CONSIDER YOURSELF LUCKY THEY DON'T ALL DISAPPEAR ON LABOR DAY. SOME OF 'EM EVEN LIKE THE PLACE ENOUGH TO LIVE HERE YEAR 'ROUND.
FUCKING WHAT?

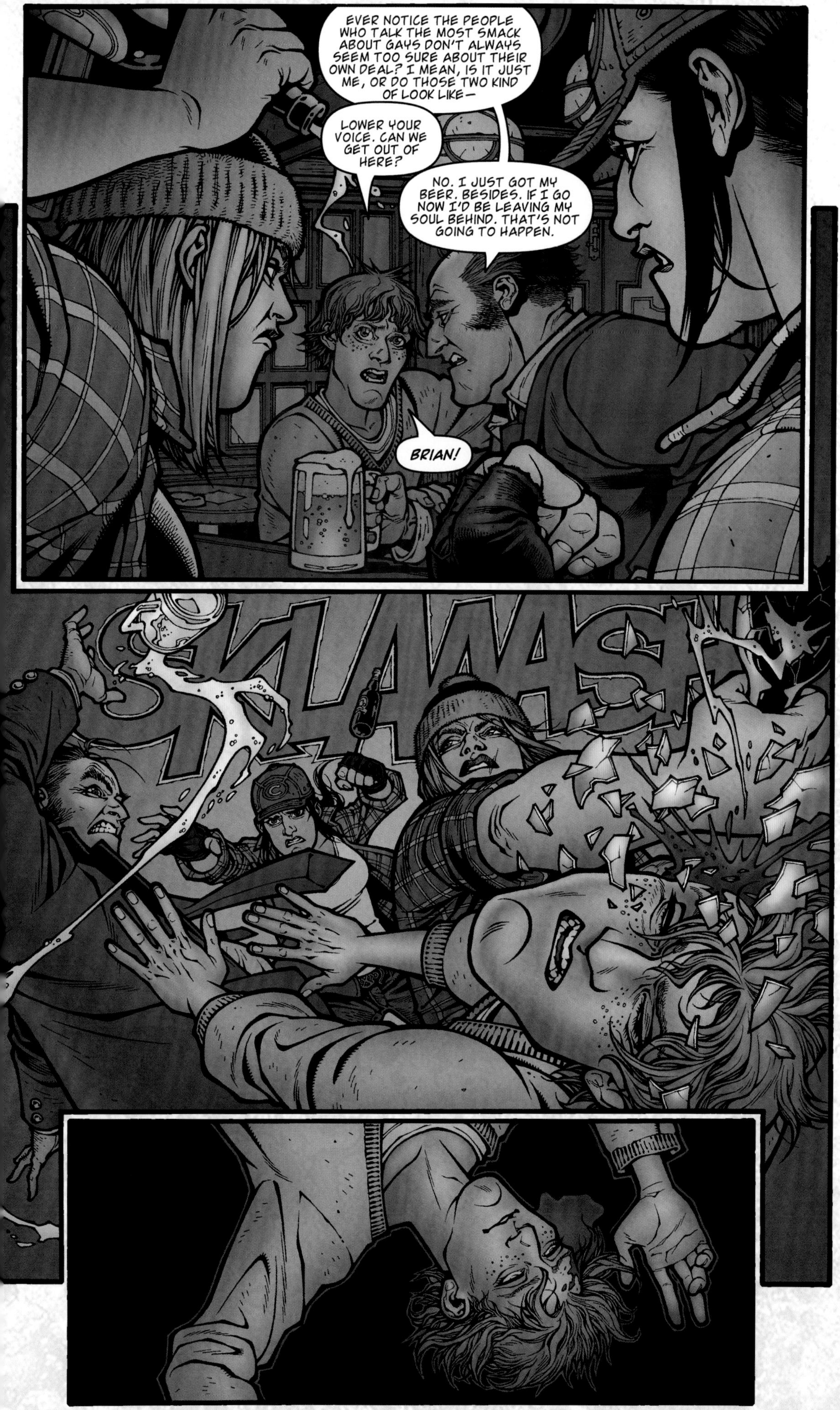
EVER NOTICE THE PEOPLE WHO TALK THE MOST SMACK ABOUT GAYS DON'T ALWAYS SEEM TOO SURE ABOUT THEIR OWN DEAL? I MEAN, IS IT JUST ME, OR DO THOSE TWO KIND OF LOOK LIKE—
LOWER YOUR VOICE. CAN WE GET OUT OF HERE?
NO. I JUST GOT MY BEER. BESIDES. IF I GO NOW I'D BE LEAVING MY SOUL BEHIND. THAT'S NOT GOING TO HAPPEN.
BRIAN!

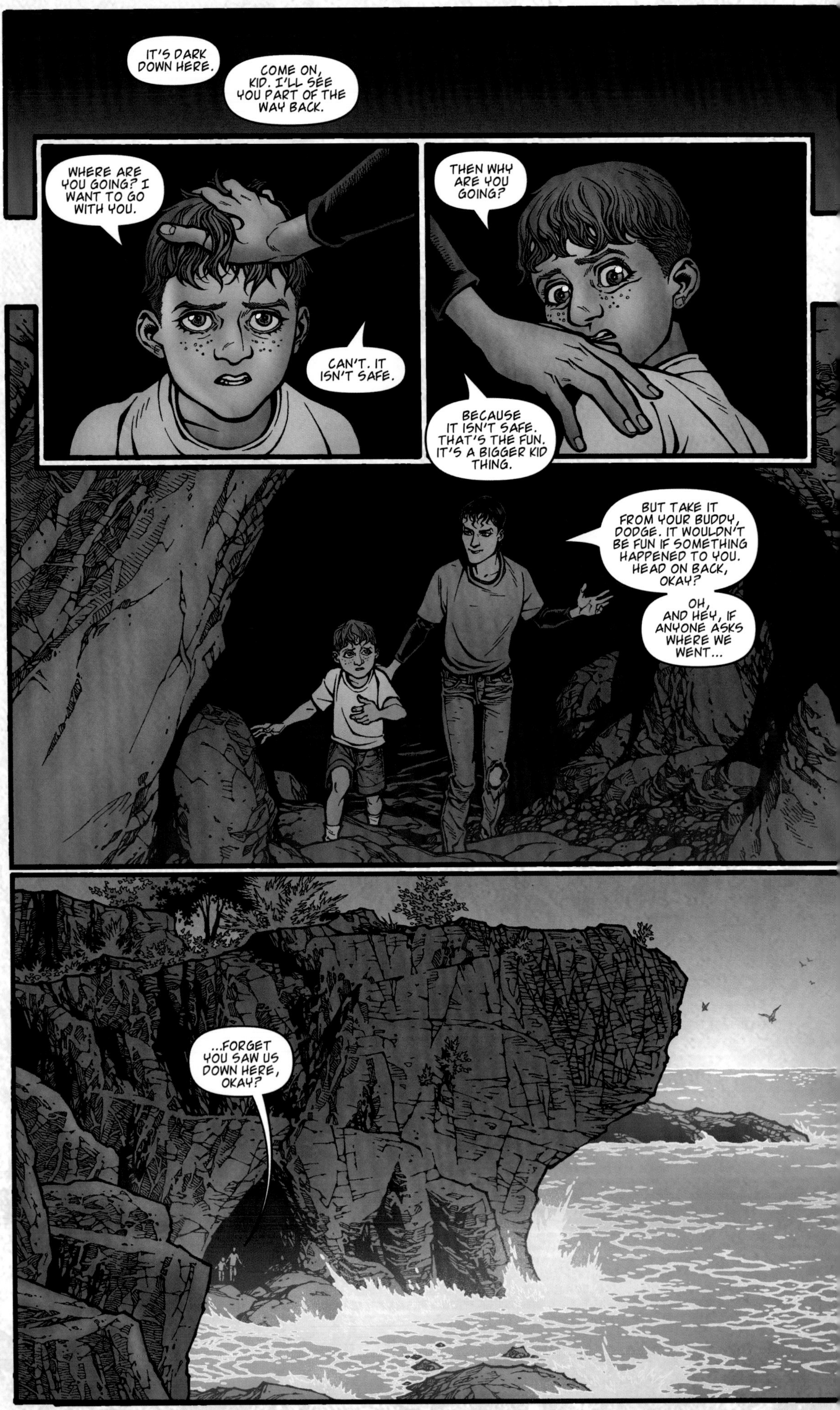
IT'S DARK DOWN HERE.
COME ON, KID. I'LL SEE YOU PART OF THE WAY BACK.
WHERE ARE YOU GOING? I WANT TO GO WITH YOU.
CAN'T. IT ISN'T SAFE.
THEN WHY ARE YOU GOING?
BECAUSE IT ISN'T SAFE. THAT'S THE FUN. IT'S A BIGGER KID THING.
BUT TAKE IT FROM YOUR BUDDY, DODGE. IT WOULDN'T BE FUN IF SOMETHING HAPPENED TO YOU. HEAD ON BACK, OKAY?
OH, AND HEY, IF ANYONE ASKS WHERE WE WENT...
...FORGET YOU SAW US DOWN HERE, OKAY?

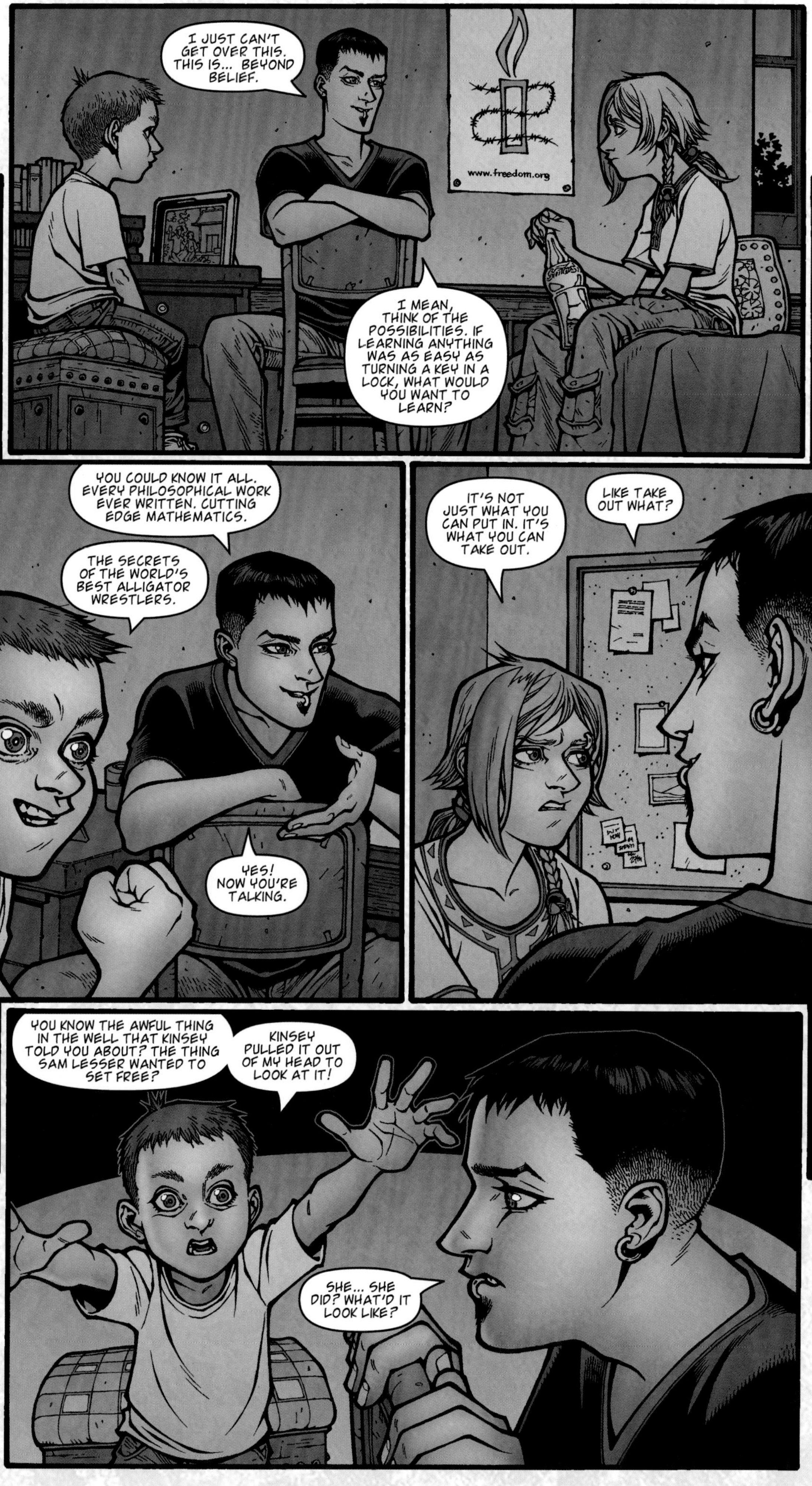
I JUST CAN'T GET OVER THIS. THIS IS... BEYOND BELIEF.
www.freedom.org
I MEAN, THINK OF THE POSSIBILITIES. IF LEARNING ANYTHING WAS AS EASY AS TURNING A KEY IN A LOCK, WHAT WOULD YOU WANT TO LEARN?
YOU COULD KNOW IT ALL. EVERY PHILOSOPHICAL WORK EVER WRITTEN. CUTTING EDGE MATHEMATICS.
THE SECRETS OF THE WORLD'S BEST ALLIGATOR WRESTLERS.
YES! NOW YOU'RE TALKING.
IT'S NOT JUST WHAT YOU CAN PUT IN. IT'S WHAT YOU CAN TAKE OUT.
LIKE TAKE OUT WHAT?
YOU KNOW THE AWFUL THING IN THE WELL THAT KINSEY TOLD YOU ABOUT? THE THING SAM LESSER WANTED TO SET FREE?
KINSEY PULLED IT OUT OF MY HEAD TO LOOK AT IT!
SHE... SHE DID? WHAT'D IT LOOK LIKE?

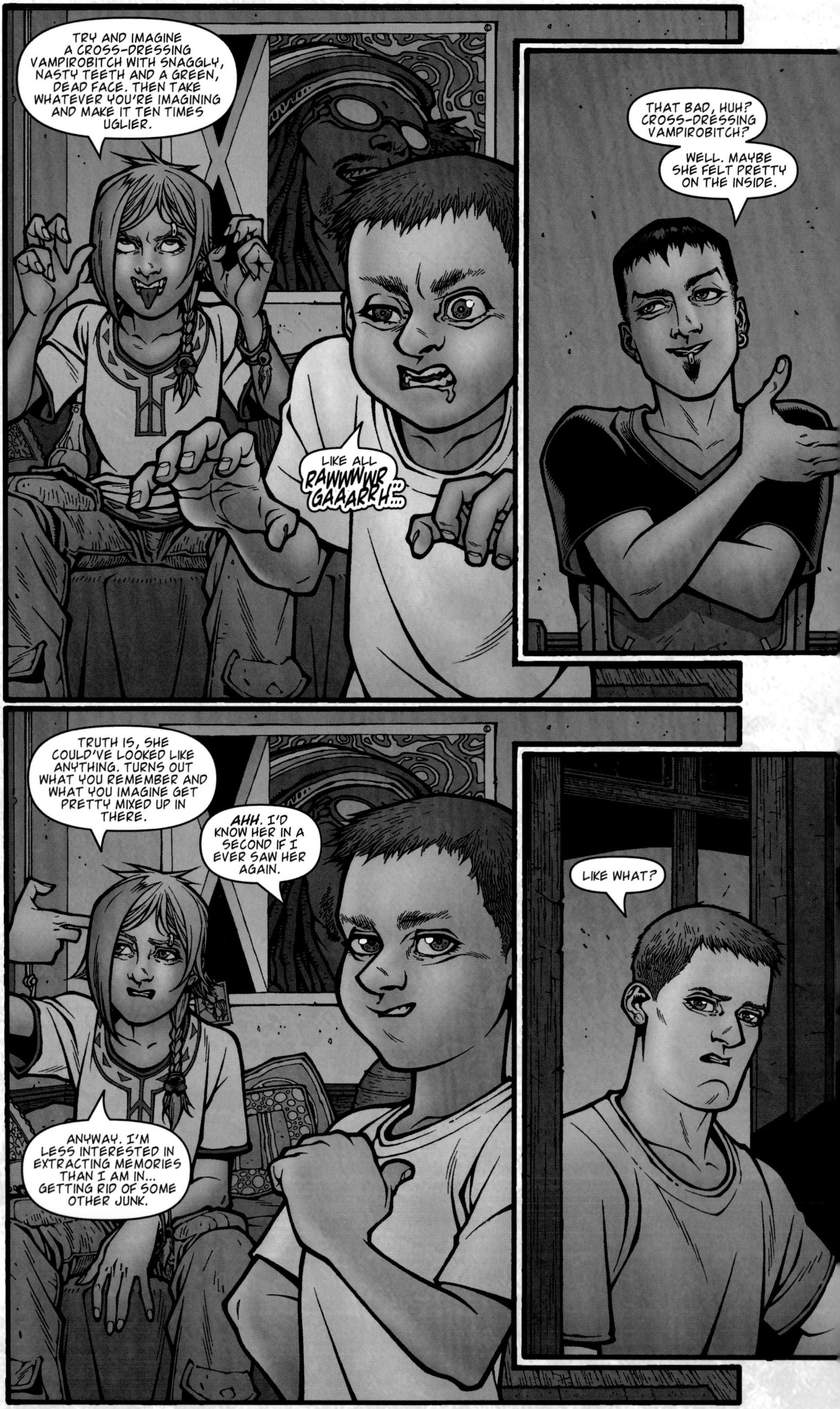
TRY AND IMAGINE A CROSS-DRESSING VAMPIROBITCH WITH SNAGGLY, NASTY TEETH AND A GREEN, DEAD FACE. THEN TAKE WHATEVER YOU'RE IMAGINING AND MAKE IT TEN TIMES UGLIER.
LIKE ALL RAWWWWR... GAAARRH...
THAT BAD, HUH? CROSS-DRESSING VAMPIROBITCH?
WELL. MAYBE SHE FELT PRETTY ON THE INSIDE.
TRUTH IS, SHE COULD'VE LOOKED LIKE ANYTHING. TURNS OUT WHAT YOU REMEMBER AND WHAT YOU IMAGINE GET PRETTY MIXED UP IN THERE.
AHH. I'D KNOW HER IN A SECOND IF I EVER SAW HER AGAIN.
LIKE WHAT?
ANYWAY. I'M LESS INTERESTED IN EXTRACTING MEMORIES THAN I AM IN... GETTING RID OF SOME OTHER JUNK.

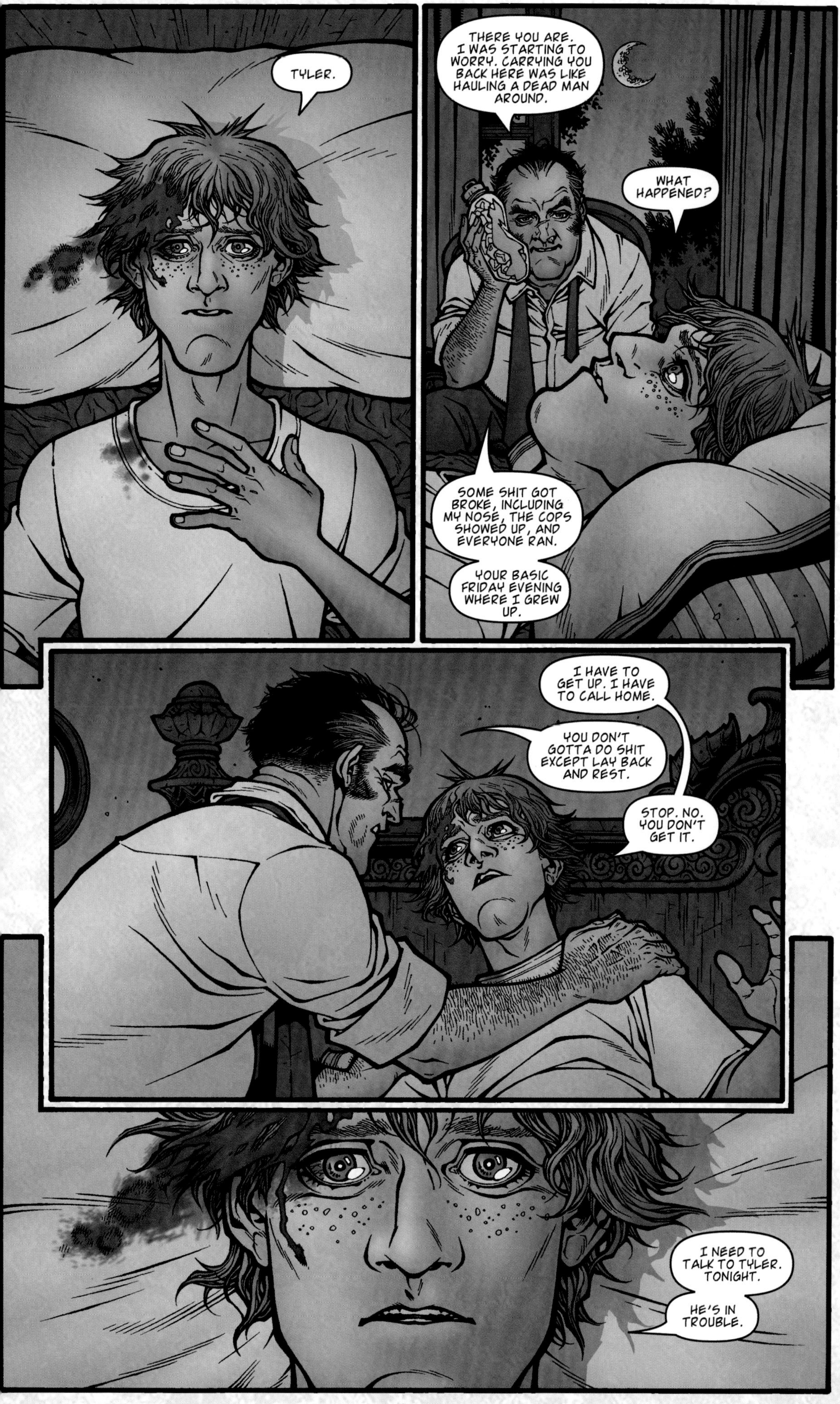
TYLER.
THERE YOU ARE. I WAS STARTING TO WORRY. CARRYING YOU BACK HERE WAS LIKE HAULING A DEAD MAN AROUND.
WHAT HAPPENED?
SOME SHIT GOT BROKE, INCLUDING MY NOSE, THE COPS SHOWED UP, AND EVERYONE RAN.
YOUR BASIC FRIDAY EVENING WHERE I GREW UP.
I HAVE TO GET UP. I HAVE TO CALL HOME.
YOU DON'T GOTTA DO SHIT EXCEPT LAY BACK AND REST.
STOP. NO. YOU DON'T GET IT.
I NEED TO TALK TO TYLER. TONIGHT.
HE'S IN TROUBLE.

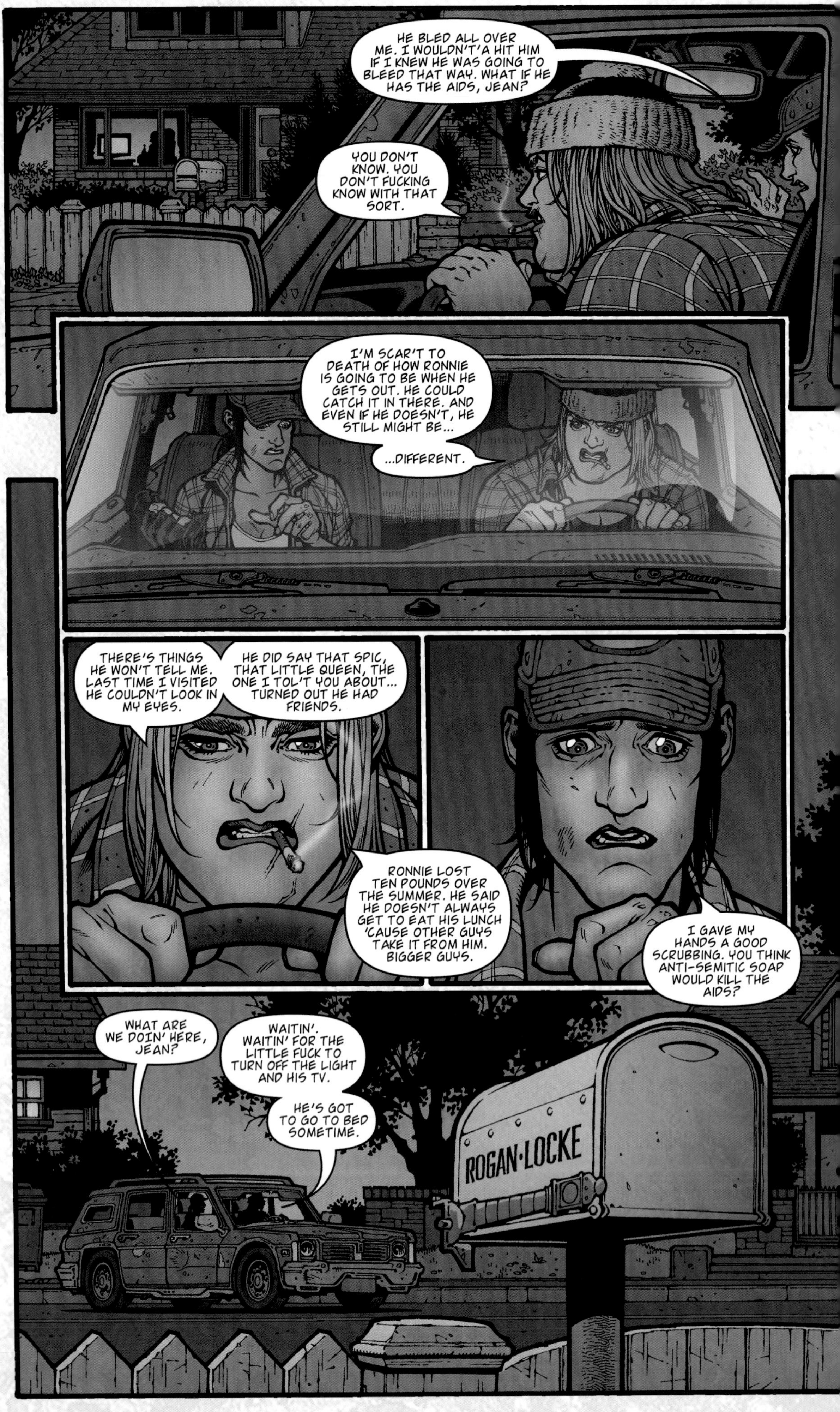
HE BLED ALL OVER ME. I WOULDN'T'A HIT HIM IF I KNEW HE WAS GOING TO BLEED THAT WAY. WHAT IF HE HAS THE AIDS, JEAN?
YOU DON'T KNOW. YOU DON'T FUCKING KNOW WITH THAT SORT.
I'M SCAR'T TO DEATH OF HOW RONNIE IS GOING TO BE WHEN HE GETS OUT. HE COULD CATCH IT IN THERE. AND EVEN IF HE DOESN'T, HE STILL MIGHT BE...
...DIFFERENT.
THERE'S THINGS HE WON'T TELL ME. LAST TIME I VISITED HE COULDN'T LOOK IN MY EYES.
HE DID SAY THAT SPIC, THAT LITTLE QUEEN, THE ONE I TOL'T YOU ABOUT... TURNED OUT HE HAD FRIENDS.
RONNIE LOST TEN POUNDS OVER THE SUMMER. HE SAID HE DOESN'T ALWAYS GET TO EAT HIS LUNCH 'CAUSE OTHER GUYS TAKE IT FROM HIM. BIGGER GUYS.
I GAVE MY HANDS A GOOD SCRUBBING. YOU THINK ANTI-SEMITIC SOAP WOULD KILL THE AIDS?
WHAT ARE WE DOIN' HERE, JEAN?
WAITIN'. WAITIN' FOR THE LITTLE FUCK TO TURN OFF THE LIGHT AND HIS TV.
HE'S GOT TO GO TO BED SOMETIME.
ROGAN·LOCKE

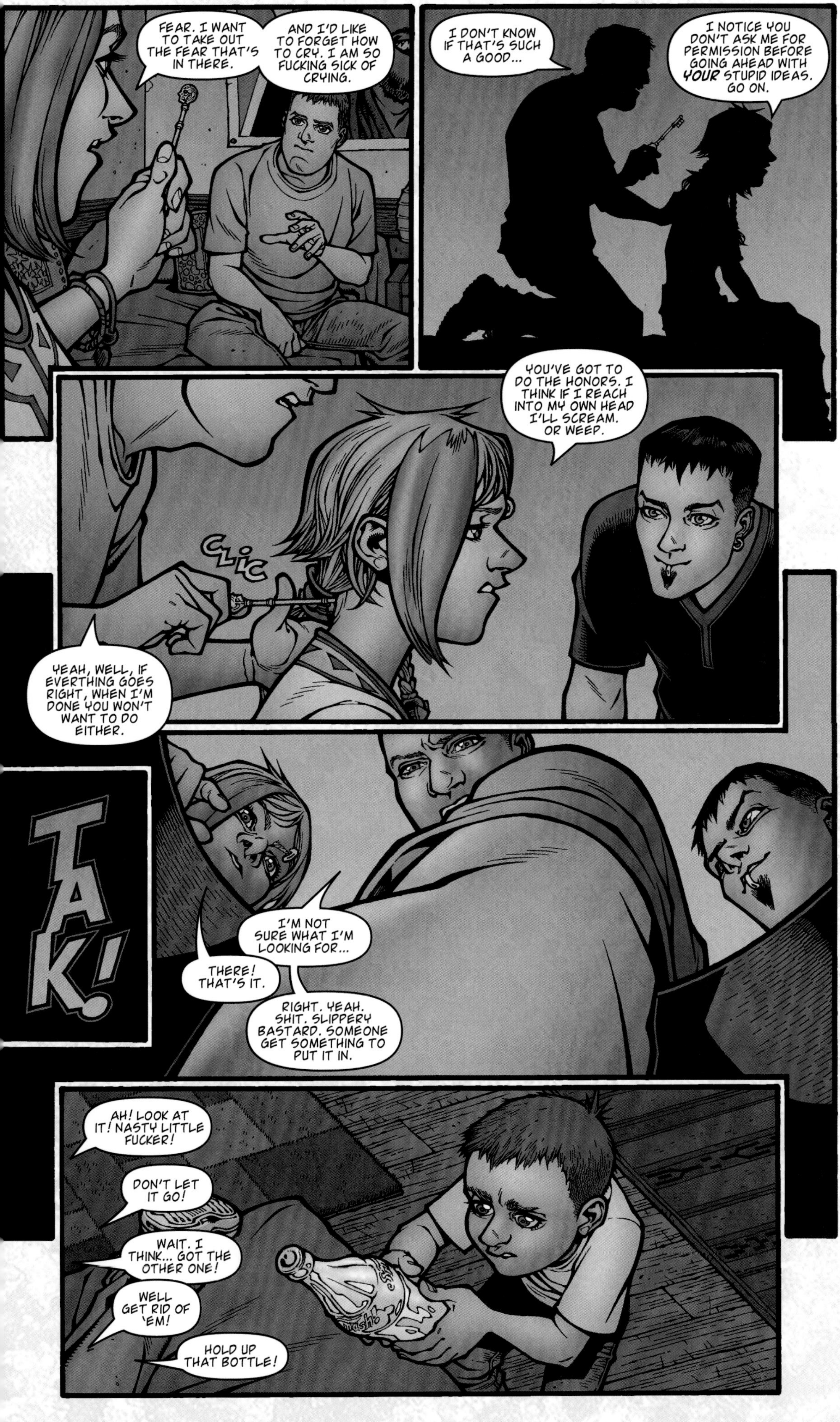
FEAR. I WANT TO TAKE OUT THE FEAR THAT'S IN THERE.
AND I'D LIKE TO FORGET HOW TO CRY. I AM SO FUCKING SICK OF CRYING.
I DON'T KNOW IF THAT'S SUCH A GOOD...
I NOTICE YOU DON'T ASK ME FOR PERMISSION BEFORE GOING AHEAD WITH YOUR STUPID IDEAS. GO ON.
YOU'VE GOT TO DO THE HONORS. I THINK IF I REACH INTO MY OWN HEAD I'LL SCREAM. OR WEEP.
CLIC
YEAH, WELL, IF EVERTHING GOES RIGHT, WHEN I'M DONE YOU WON'T WANT TO DO EITHER.
TAK!
I'M NOT SURE WHAT I'M LOOKING FOR...
THERE! THAT'S IT.
RIGHT. YEAH. SHIT. SLIPPERY BASTARD. SOMEONE GET SOMETHING TO PUT IT IN.
AH! LOOK AT IT! NASTY LITTLE FUCKER!
DON'T LET IT GO!
WAIT. I THINK... GOT THE OTHER ONE!
WELL GET RID OF 'EM!
HOLD UP THAT BOTTLE!

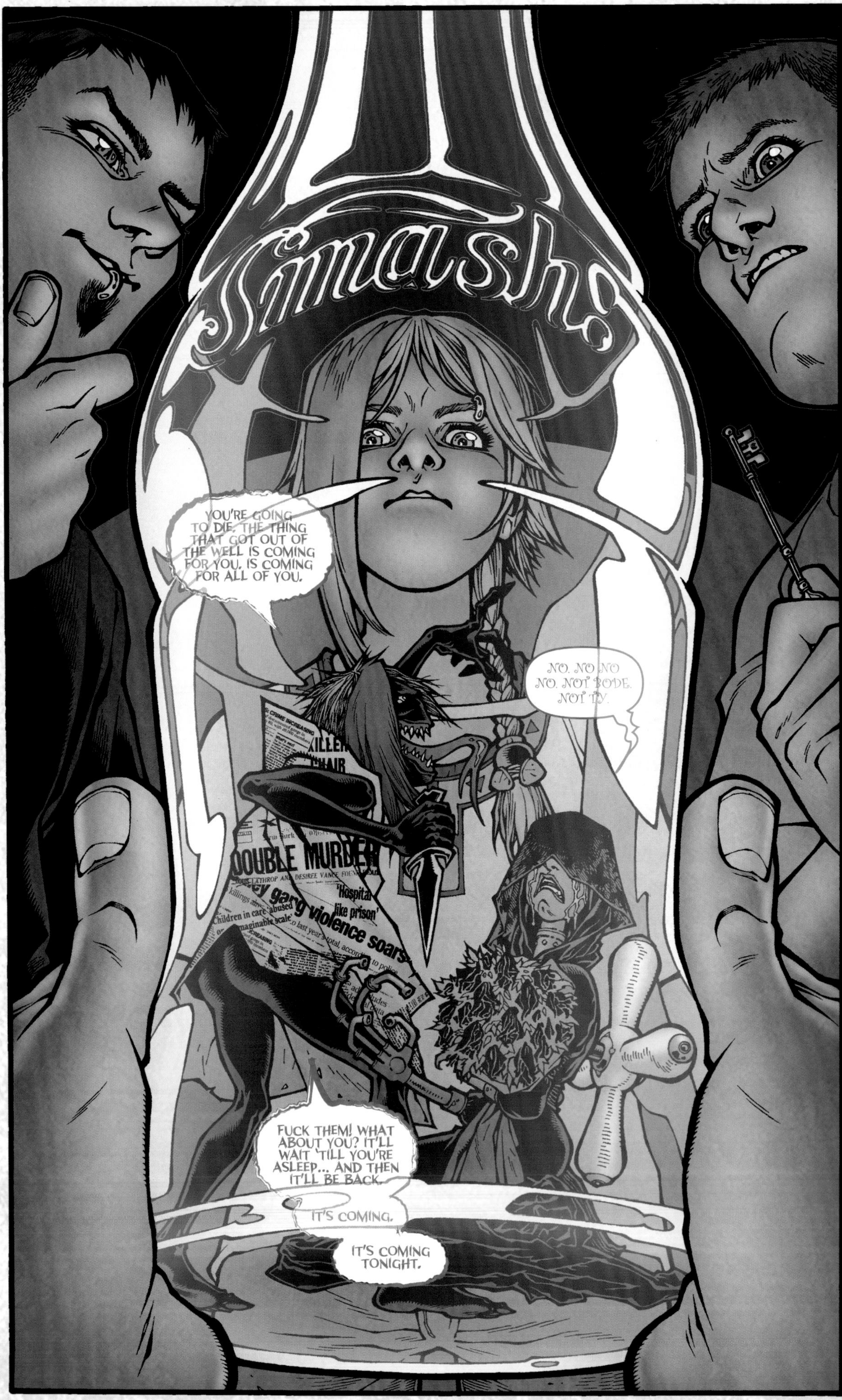
YOU'RE GOING TO DIE. THE THING THAT GOT OUT OF THE WELL IS COMING FOR YOU. IS COMING FOR ALL OF YOU.
NO. NO NO NO. NOT BODE. NOT TY.
CRIME INCREASING
DOUBLE MURDER
'Hospital like prison'
Children in care 'abused'
violence
FUCK THEM! WHAT ABOUT YOU? IT'LL WAIT 'TILL YOU'RE ASLEEP... AND THEN IT'LL BE BACK.
IT'S COMING.
IT'S COMING TONIGHT.

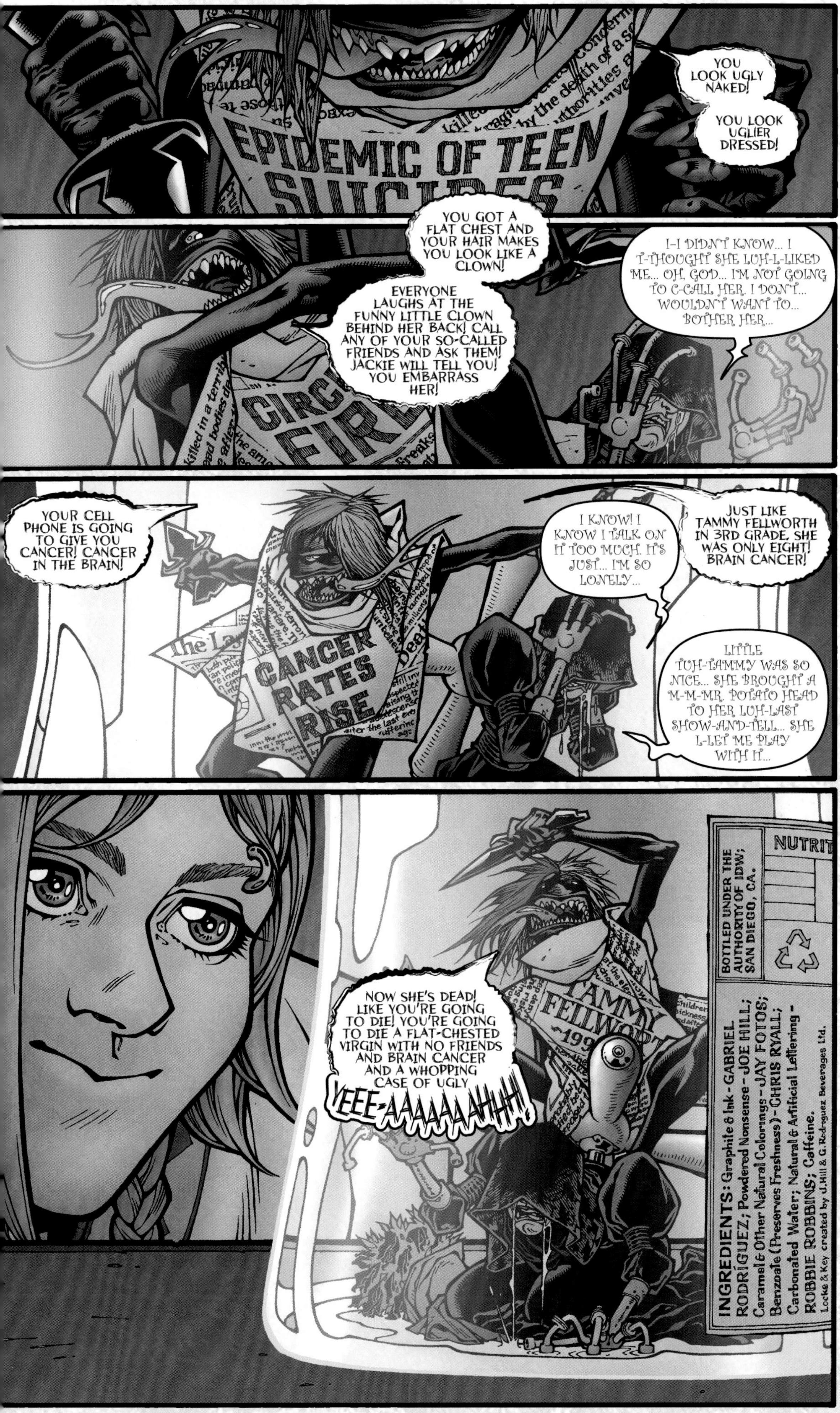
EPIDEMIC OF TEEN
YOU LOOK UGLY NAKED!
YOU LOOK UGLIER DRESSED!
YOU GOT A FLAT CHEST AND YOUR HAIR MAKES YOU LOOK LIKE A CLOWN!
EVERYONE LAUGHS AT THE FUNNY LITTLE CLOWN BEHIND HER BACK! CALL ANY OF YOUR SO-CALLED FRIENDS AND ASK THEM! JACKIE WILL TELL YOU! YOU EMBARRASS HER!
I-I DIDN'T KNOW... I T-THOUGHT SHE LUH-L-LIKED ME... OH, GOD... I'M NOT GOING TO C-CALL HER. I DON'T... WOULDN'T WANT TO... BOTHER HER...
YOUR CELL PHONE IS GOING TO GIVE YOU CANCER! CANCER IN THE BRAIN!
CANCER RATES RISE
I KNOW! I KNOW I TALK ON IT TOO MUCH. IT'S JUST... I'M SO LONELY...
JUST LIKE TAMMY FELLWORTH IN 3RD GRADE. SHE WAS ONLY EIGHT! BRAIN CANCER!
LITTLE TUH-TAMMY WAS SO NICE... SHE BROUGHT A M-M-MR. POTATO HEAD TO HER LUH-LAST SHOW-AND-TELL... SHE L-LET ME PLAY WITH IT...
NOW SHE'S DEAD! LIKE YOU'RE GOING TO DIE! YOU'RE GOING TO DIE A FLAT-CHESTED VIRGIN WITH NO FRIENDS AND BRAIN CANCER AND A WHOPPING CASE OF UGLY
YEEE-AAAAAAAHHH!
BOTTLED UNDER THE AUTHORITY OF IDW; SAN DIEGO, CA.
NUTRIT
INGREDIENTS: Graphite & Ink - GABRIEL RODRÍGUEZ; Powdered Nonsense - JOE HILL; Caramel & Other Natural Colorings - JAY FOTOS; Benzoate (Preserves Freshness) - CHRIS RYALL; Carbonated Water; Natural & Artificial Lettering - ROBBIE ROBBINS; Caffeine.
Locke & Key created by J. Hill & G. Rodriguez Beverages Ltd.

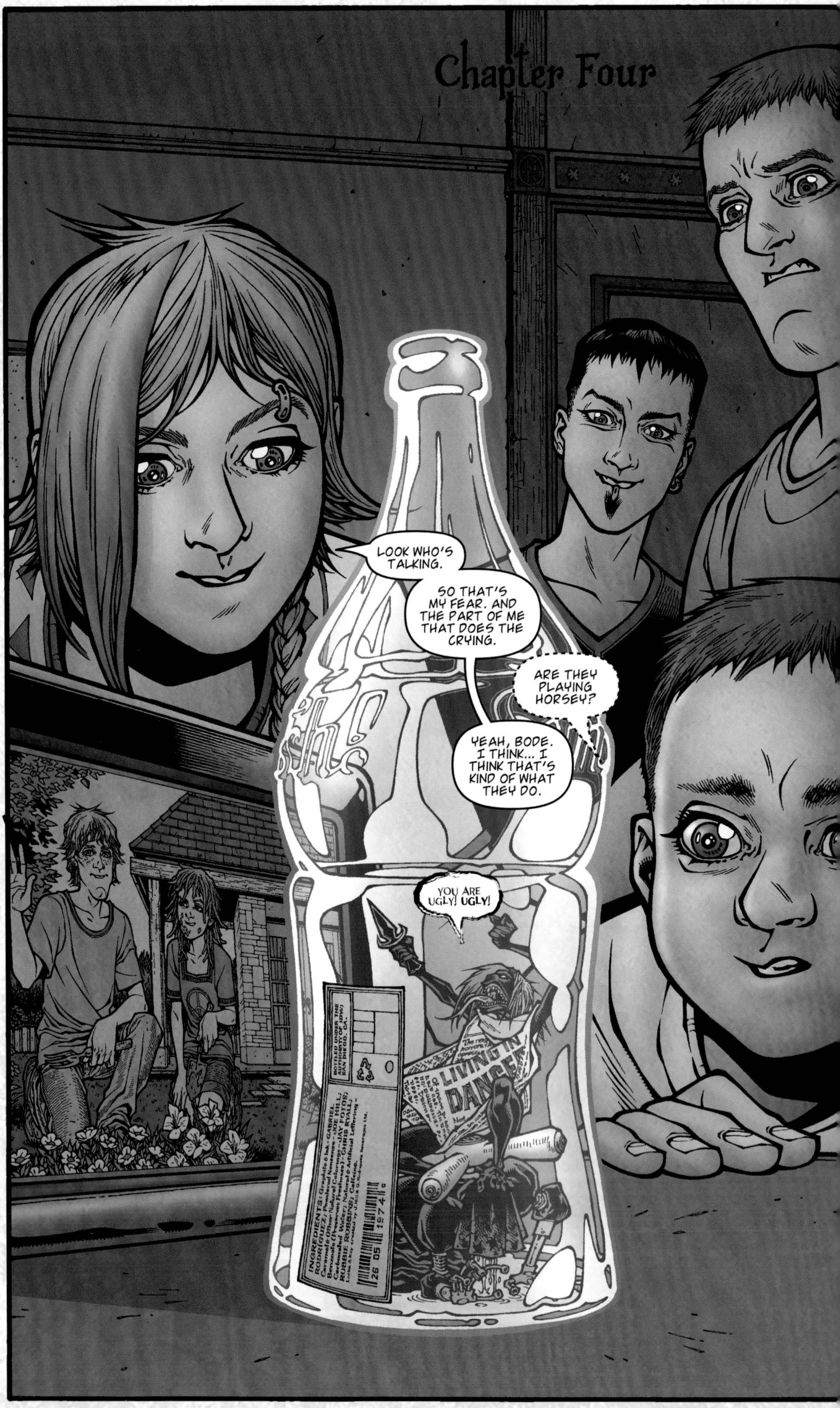
Chapter Four
LOOK WHO'S TALKING.
SO THAT'S MY FEAR. AND THE PART OF ME THAT DOES THE CRYING.
ARE THEY PLAYING HORSEY?
YEAH, BODE. I THINK... I THINK THAT'S KIND OF WHAT THEY DO.
YOU ARE UGLY! UGLY!
BOTTLED UNDER THE AUTHORITY OF IDW; SAN DIEGO, CA.
INGREDIENTS: Graphite & Ink - GABRIEL RODRÍGUEZ; Powdered Nonsense - JOE HILL; Caramel & Other Natural Colorings - JAY FOTOS; Benzoate (Preserves Freshness) - CHRIS RYALL; Carbonated Water; Natural & Artificial Lettering - ROBBIE ROBBINS; Caffeine.
Locke & Key created by J. Hill & G. Rodríguez
26 05 1974 G
LIVING IN

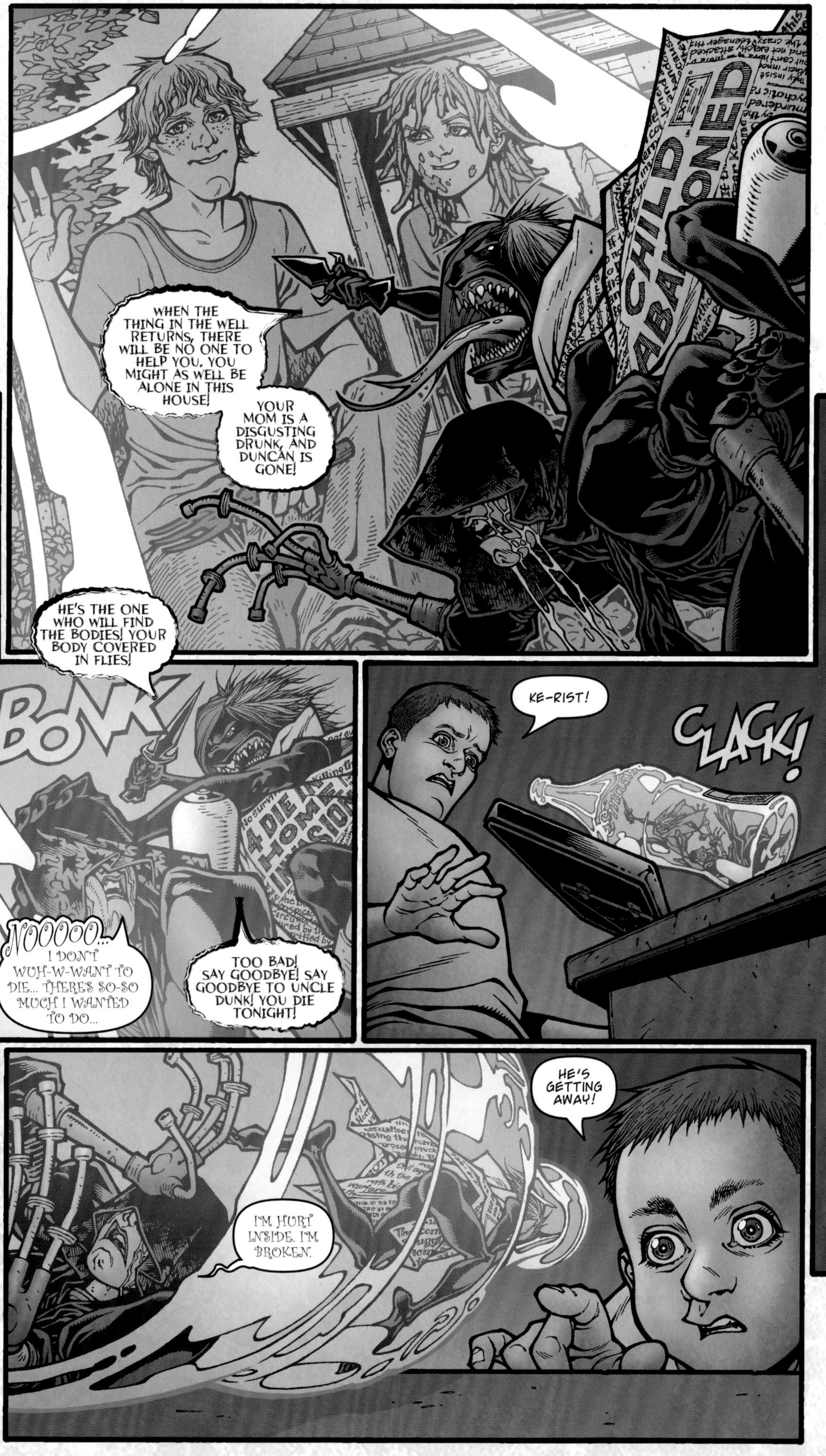
WHEN THE THING IN THE WELL RETURNS, THERE WILL BE NO ONE TO HELP YOU. YOU MIGHT AS WELL BE ALONE IN THIS HOUSE!
YOUR MOM IS A DISGUSTING DRUNK, AND DUNCAN IS GONE!
CHILD ABANDONED
HE'S THE ONE WHO WILL FIND THE BODIES! YOUR BODY COVERED IN FLIES!
BONK
4 DIE IN HOME INVASION
NOOOOO... I DON'T WUH-W-WANT TO DIE... THERE'S SO-SO MUCH I WANTED TO DO...
TOO BAD! SAY GOODBYE! SAY GOODBYE TO UNCLE DUNK! YOU DIE TONIGHT!
KE-RIST!
CLAGK!
HE'S GETTING AWAY!
I'M HURT INSIDE. I'M BROKEN.

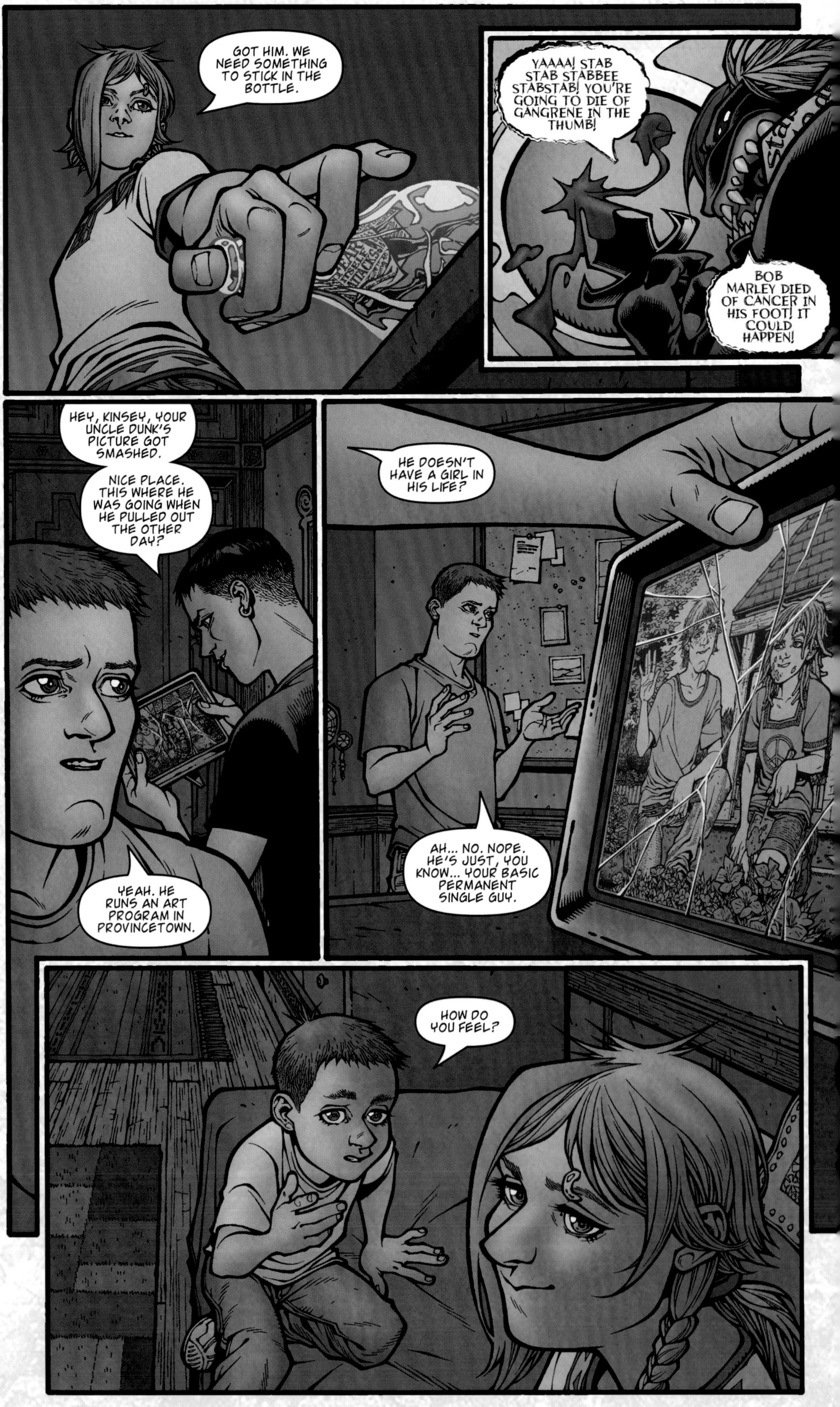
GOT HIM. WE NEED SOMETHING TO STICK IN THE BOTTLE.
YAAAA! STAB STAB STABBEE STABSTAB! YOU'RE GOING TO DIE OF GANGRENE IN THE THUMB!
BOB MARLEY DIED OF CANCER IN HIS FOOT! IT COULD HAPPEN!
HEY, KINSEY, YOUR UNCLE DUNK'S PICTURE GOT SMASHED.
NICE PLACE. THIS WHERE HE WAS GOING WHEN HE PULLED OUT THE OTHER DAY?
YEAH. HE RUNS AN ART PROGRAM IN PROVINCETOWN.
HE DOESN'T HAVE A GIRL IN HIS LIFE?
AH... NO. NOPE. HE'S JUST, YOU KNOW... YOUR BASIC PERMANENT SINGLE GUY.
HOW DO YOU FEEL?

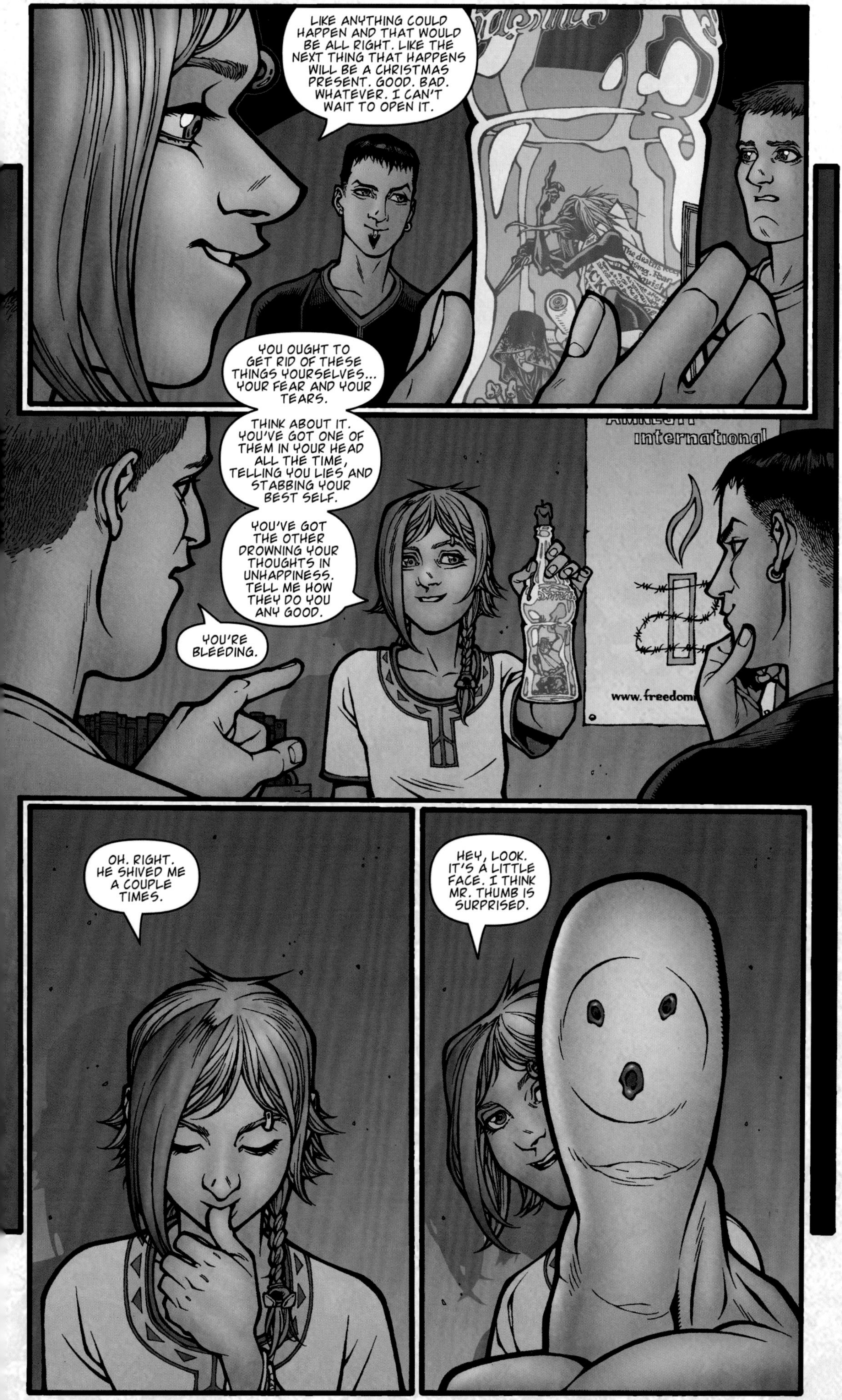
LIKE ANYTHING COULD HAPPEN AND THAT WOULD BE ALL RIGHT. LIKE THE NEXT THING THAT HAPPENS WILL BE A CHRISTMAS PRESENT. GOOD. BAD. WHATEVER. I CAN'T WAIT TO OPEN IT.
YOU OUGHT TO GET RID OF THESE THINGS YOURSELVES... YOUR FEAR AND YOUR TEARS.
THINK ABOUT IT. YOU'VE GOT ONE OF THEM IN YOUR HEAD ALL THE TIME, TELLING YOU LIES AND STABBING YOUR BEST SELF.
YOU'VE GOT THE OTHER DROWNING YOUR THOUGHTS IN UNHAPPINESS. TELL ME HOW THEY DO YOU ANY GOOD.
international
www.freedom
YOU'RE BLEEDING.
OH. RIGHT. HE SHIVED ME A COUPLE TIMES.
HEY, LOOK. IT'S A LITTLE FACE. I THINK MR. THUMB IS SURPRISED.

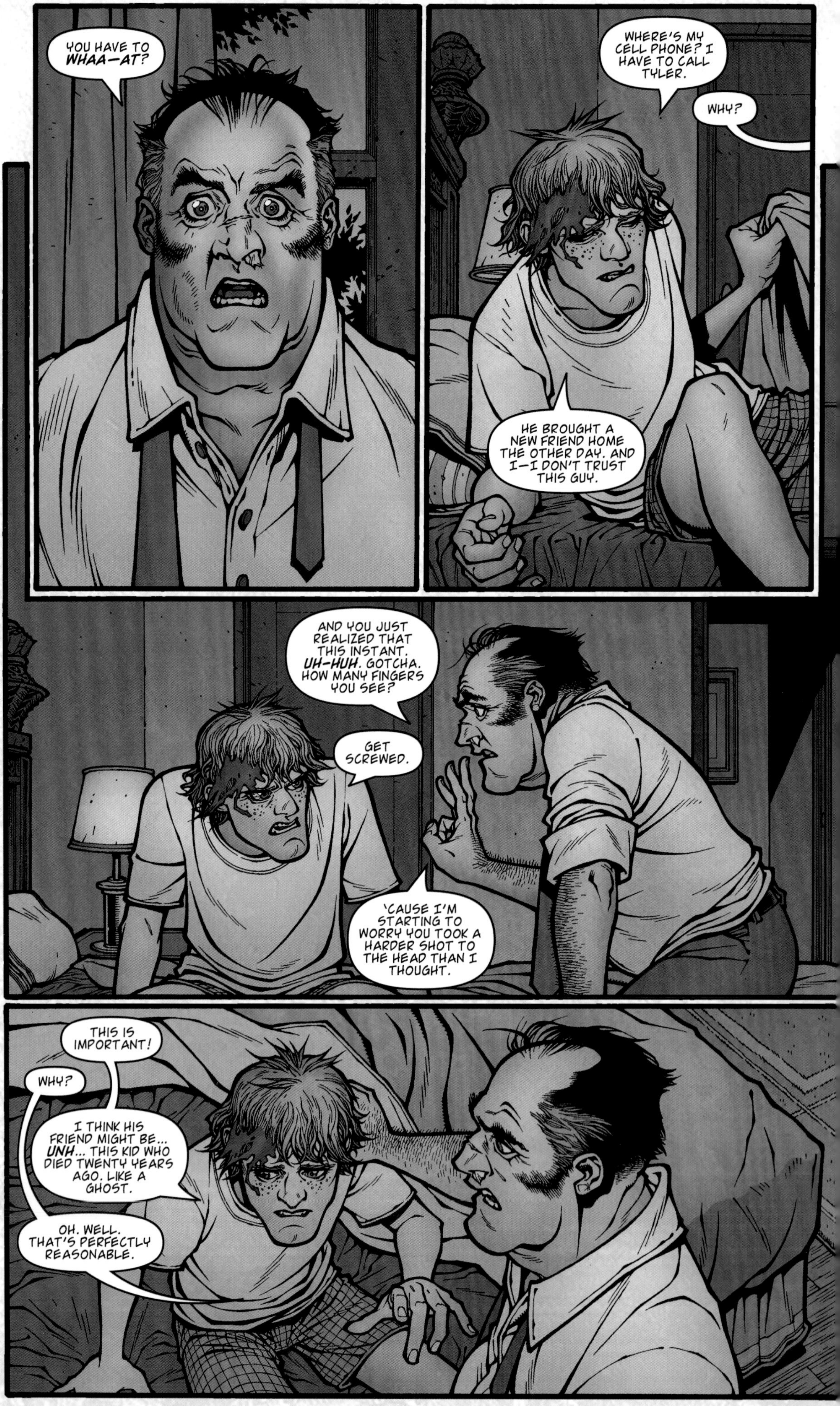
YOU HAVE TO *WHAA—AT*?
WHERE'S MY CELL PHONE? I HAVE TO CALL TYLER.
WHY?
HE BROUGHT A NEW FRIEND HOME THE OTHER DAY. AND I—I DON'T TRUST THIS GUY.
AND YOU JUST REALIZED THAT THIS INSTANT. *UH-HUH*. GOTCHA. HOW MANY FINGERS YOU SEE?
GET SCREWED.
'CAUSE I'M STARTING TO WORRY YOU TOOK A HARDER SHOT TO THE HEAD THAN I THOUGHT.
THIS IS IMPORTANT!
WHY?
I THINK HIS FRIEND MIGHT BE... *UNH*... THIS KID WHO DIED TWENTY YEARS AGO. LIKE A GHOST.
OH. WELL. THAT'S PERFECTLY REASONABLE.

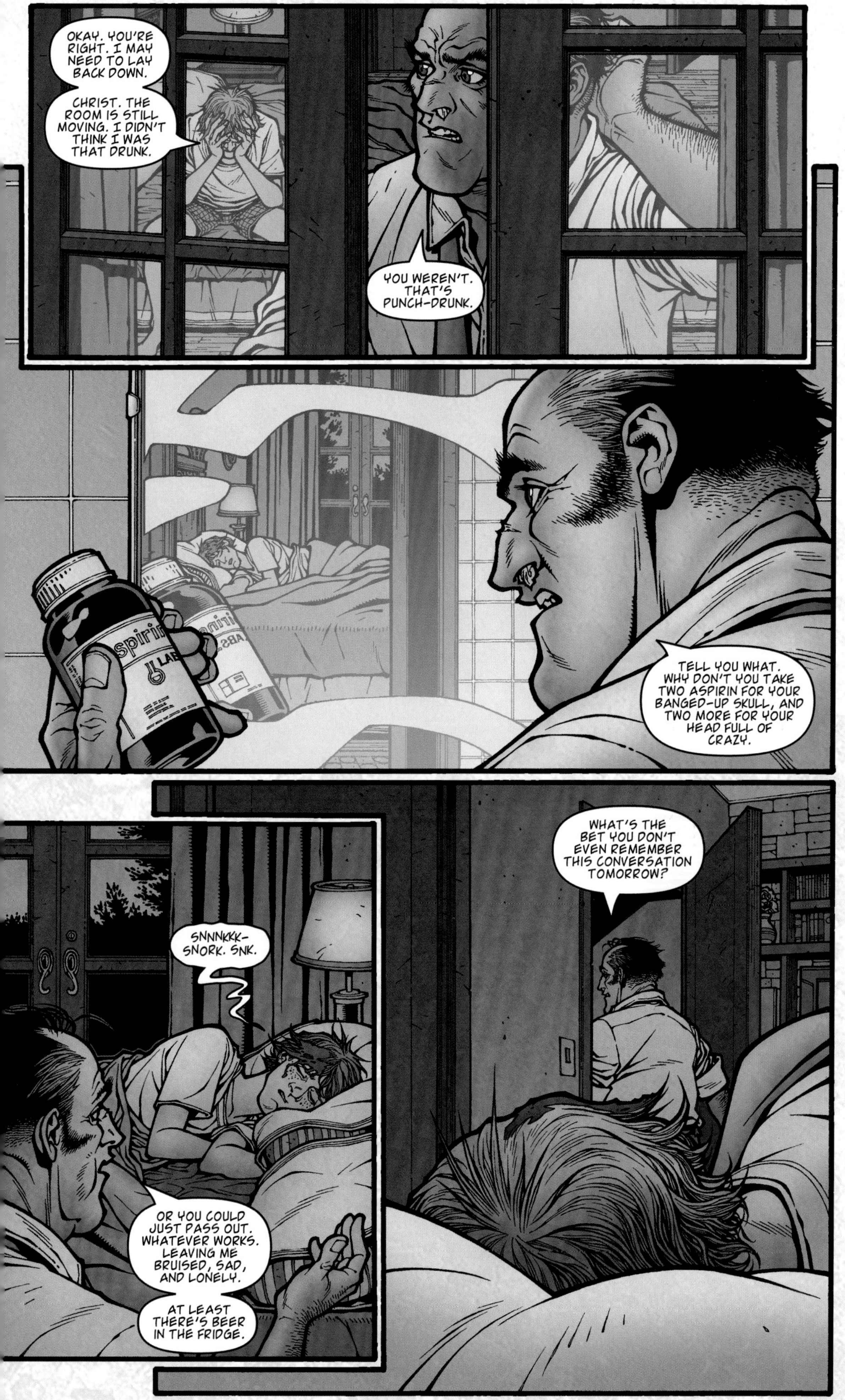
OKAY. YOU'RE RIGHT. I MAY NEED TO LAY BACK DOWN.
CHRIST. THE ROOM IS STILL MOVING. I DIDN'T THINK I WAS THAT DRUNK.
YOU WEREN'T. THAT'S PUNCH-DRUNK.
TELL YOU WHAT. WHY DON'T YOU TAKE TWO ASPIRIN FOR YOUR BANGED-UP SKULL, AND TWO MORE FOR YOUR HEAD FULL OF CRAZY.
SNNNKKK-SNORK. SNK.
OR YOU COULD JUST PASS OUT. WHATEVER WORKS. LEAVING ME BRUISED, SAD, AND LONELY.
AT LEAST THERE'S BEER IN THE FRIDGE.
WHAT'S THE BET YOU DON'T EVEN REMEMBER THIS CONVERSATION TOMORROW?

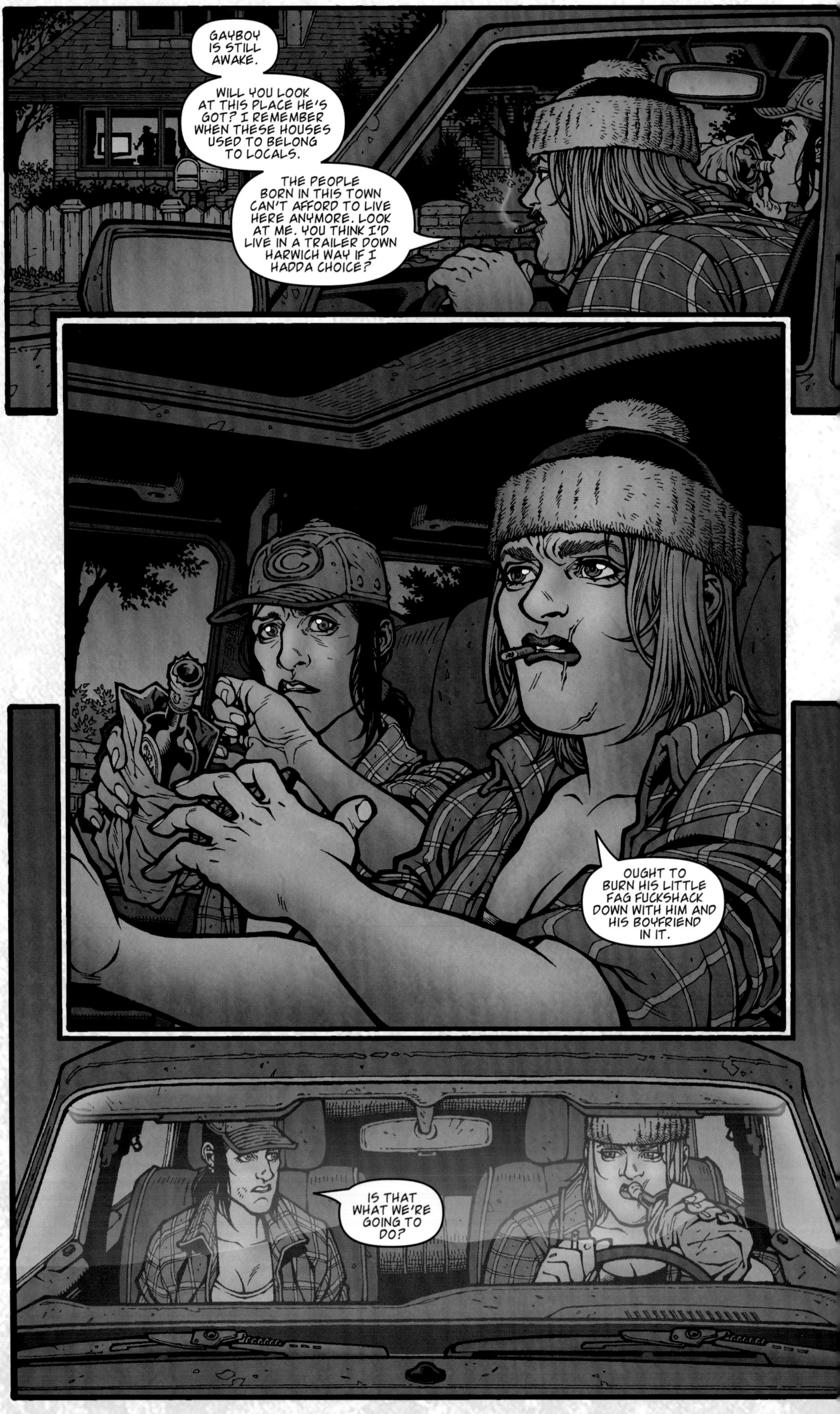
GAYBOY IS STILL AWAKE.
WILL YOU LOOK AT THIS PLACE HE'S GOT? I REMEMBER WHEN THESE HOUSES USED TO BELONG TO LOCALS.
THE PEOPLE BORN IN THIS TOWN CAN'T AFFORD TO LIVE HERE ANYMORE. LOOK AT ME. YOU THINK I'D LIVE IN A TRAILER DOWN HARWICH WAY IF I HADDA CHOICE?
OUGHT TO BURN HIS LITTLE FAG FUCKSHACK DOWN WITH HIM AND HIS BOYFRIEND IN IT.
IS THAT WHAT WE'RE GOING TO DO?

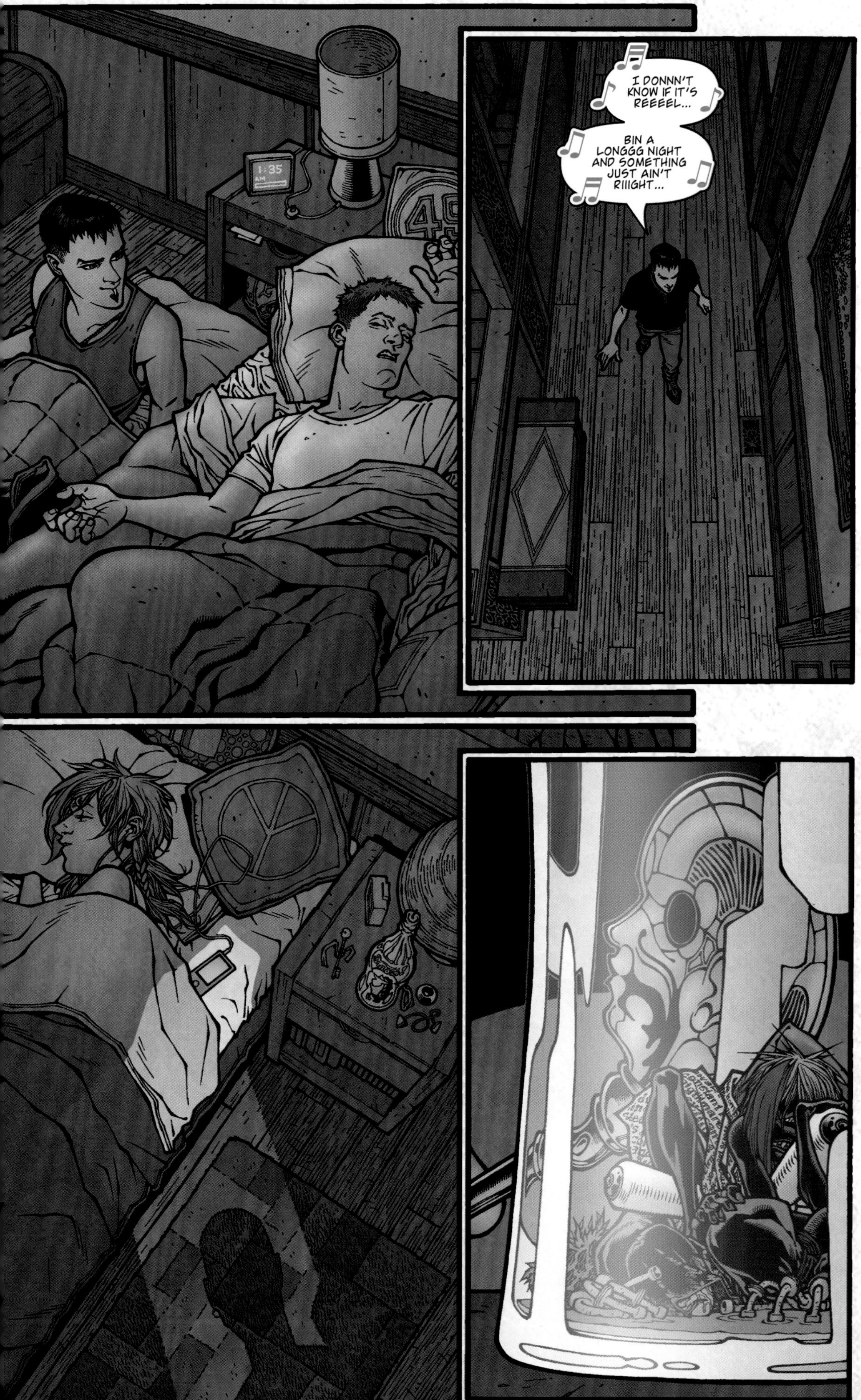
I DONNN'T KNOW IF IT'S REEEEL...
BIN A LONGGG NIGHT AND SOMETHING JUST AIN'T RIIIGHT...

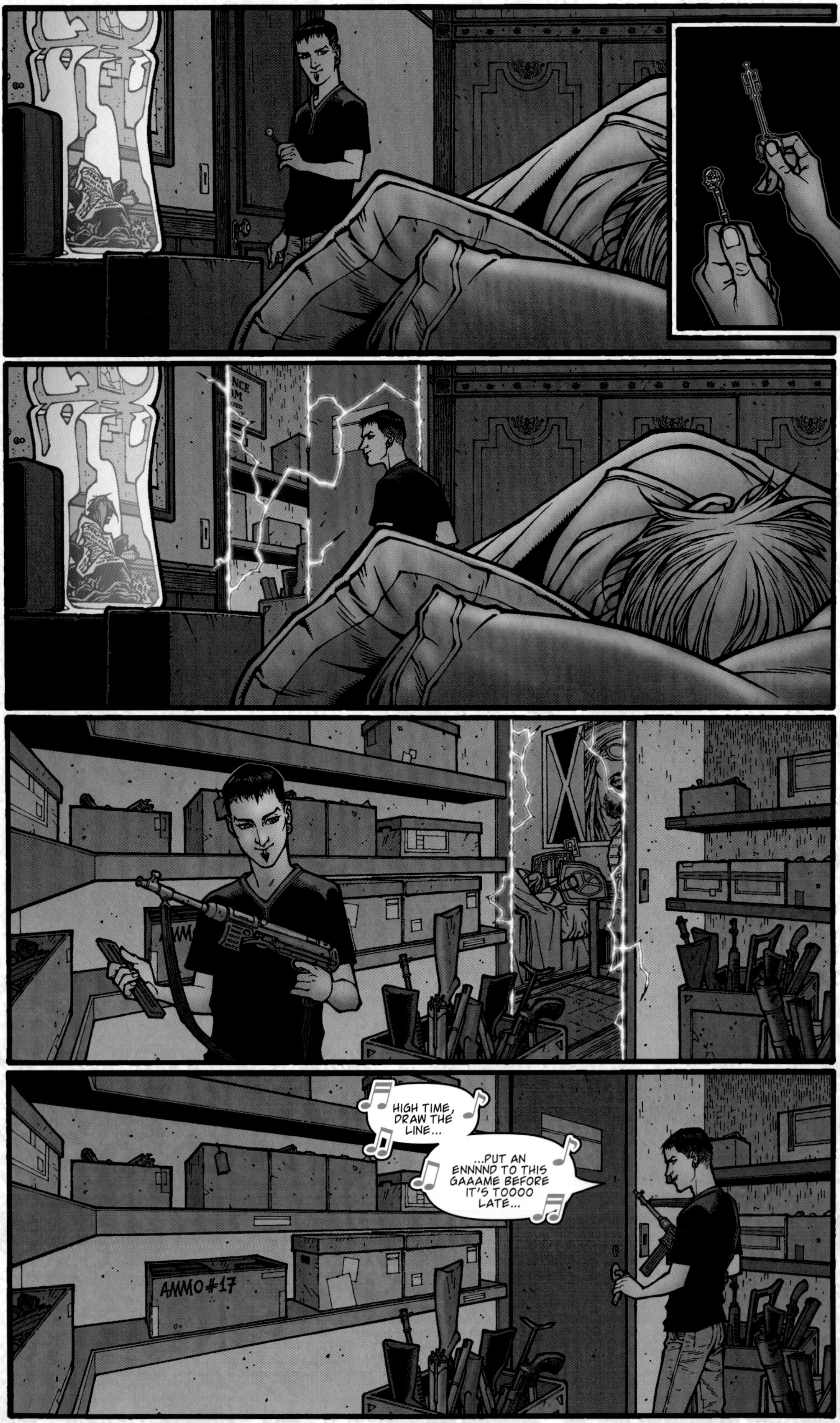

AMMO
AMMO #17
HIGH TIME, DRAW THE LINE...
...PUT AN ENNNND TO THIS GAAAME BEFORE IT'S TOOOO LATE...

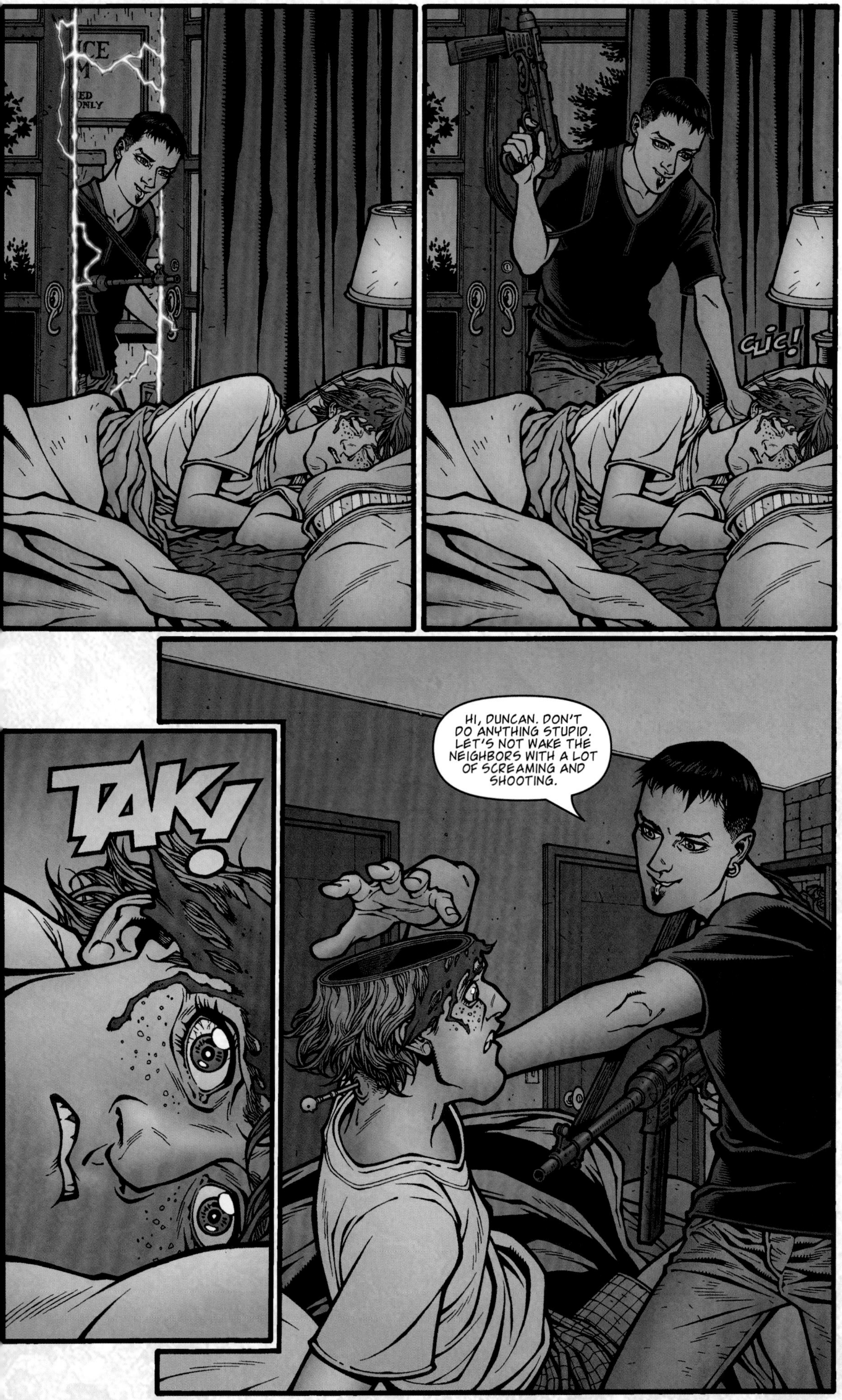
CLIC!
TAK!
HI, DUNCAN. DON'T DO ANYTHING STUPID. LET'S NOT WAKE THE NEIGHBORS WITH A LOT OF SCREAMING AND SHOOTING.

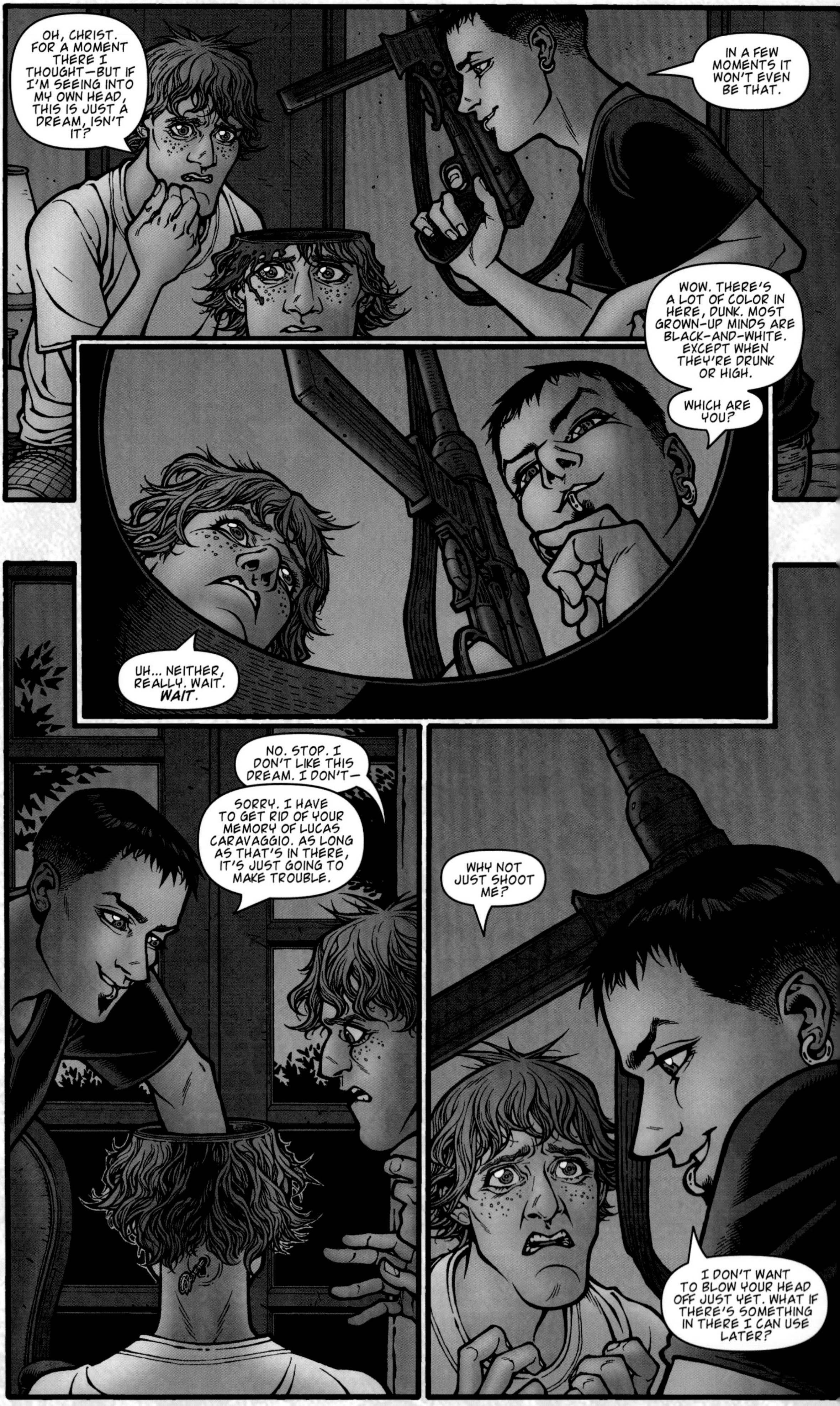
OH, CHRIST. FOR A MOMENT THERE I THOUGHT—BUT IF I'M SEEING INTO MY OWN HEAD, THIS IS JUST A DREAM, ISN'T IT?
IN A FEW MOMENTS IT WON'T EVEN BE THAT.
WOW. THERE'S A LOT OF COLOR IN HERE, DUNK. MOST GROWN-UP MINDS ARE BLACK-AND-WHITE. EXCEPT WHEN THEY'RE DRUNK OR HIGH.
WHICH ARE YOU?
UH... NEITHER, REALLY. WAIT. WAIT.
NO. STOP. I DON'T LIKE THIS DREAM. I DON'T—
SORRY. I HAVE TO GET RID OF YOUR MEMORY OF LUCAS CARAVAGGIO. AS LONG AS THAT'S IN THERE, IT'S JUST GOING TO MAKE TROUBLE.
WHY NOT JUST SHOOT ME?
I DON'T WANT TO BLOW YOUR HEAD OFF JUST YET. WHAT IF THERE'S SOMETHING IN THERE I CAN USE LATER?

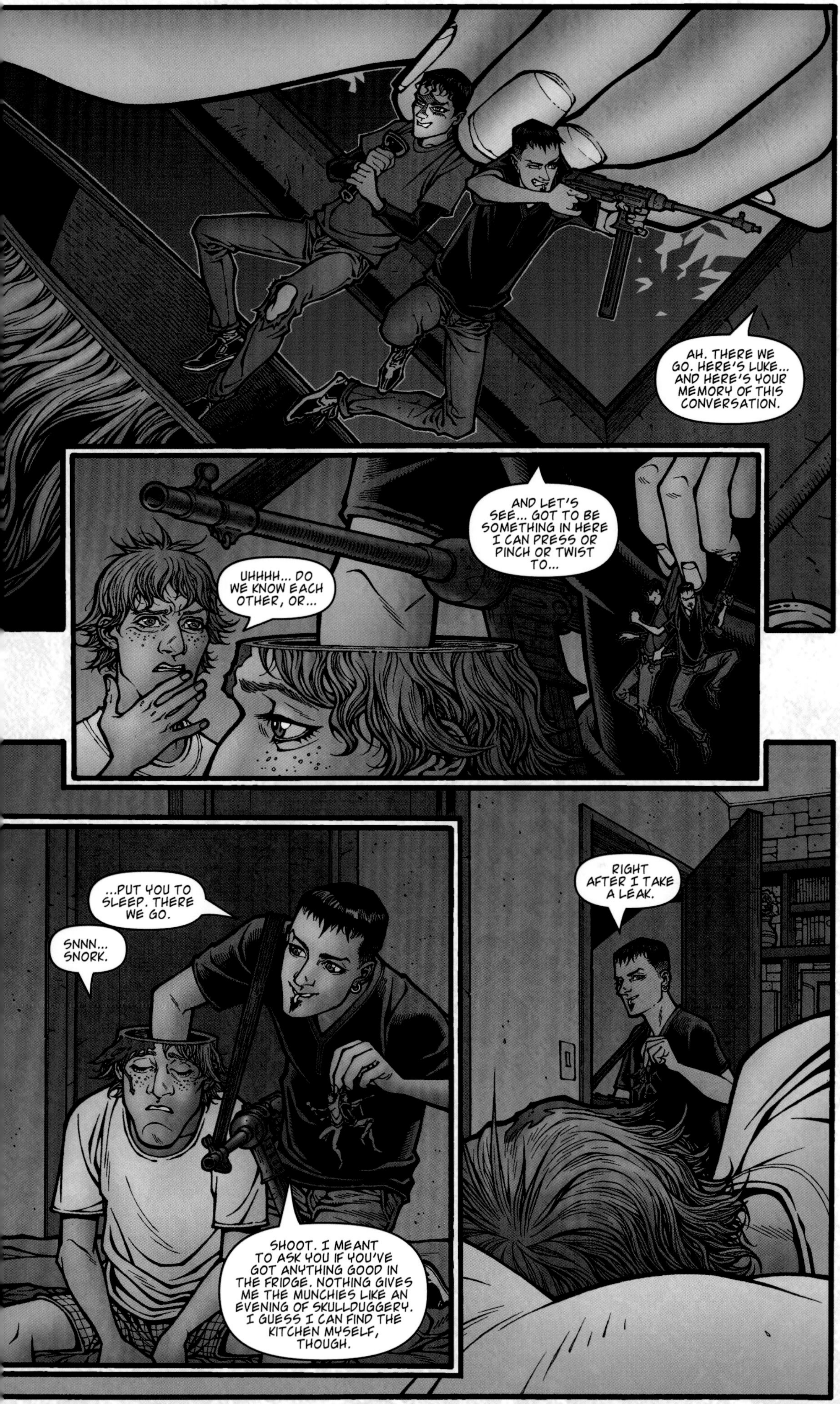
AH. THERE WE GO. HERE'S LUKE... AND HERE'S YOUR MEMORY OF THIS CONVERSATION.
UHHHH... DO WE KNOW EACH OTHER, OR...
AND LET'S SEE... GOT TO BE SOMETHING IN HERE I CAN PRESS OR PINCH OR TWIST TO...
...PUT YOU TO SLEEP. THERE WE GO.
SNNN... SNORK.
SHOOT. I MEANT TO ASK YOU IF YOU'VE GOT ANYTHING GOOD IN THE FRIDGE. NOTHING GIVES ME THE MUNCHIES LIKE AN EVENING OF SKULLDUGGERY. I GUESS I CAN FIND THE KITCHEN MYSELF, THOUGH.
RIGHT AFTER I TAKE A LEAK.

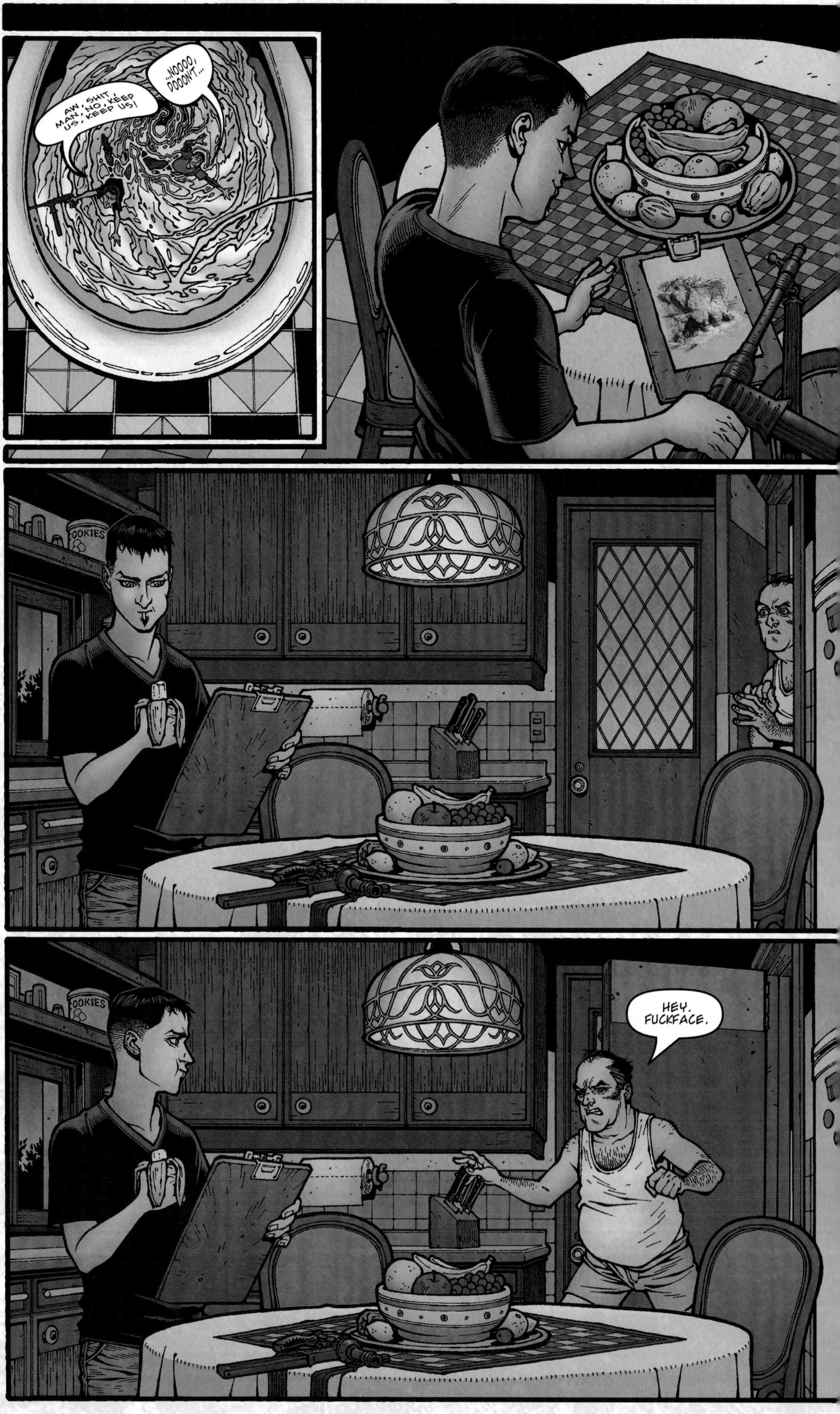
AW, SHIT, MAN, NO, KEEP US, KEEP US!
...NOOOO, DOOON'T...
COOKIES
COOKIES
HEY. FUCKFACE.

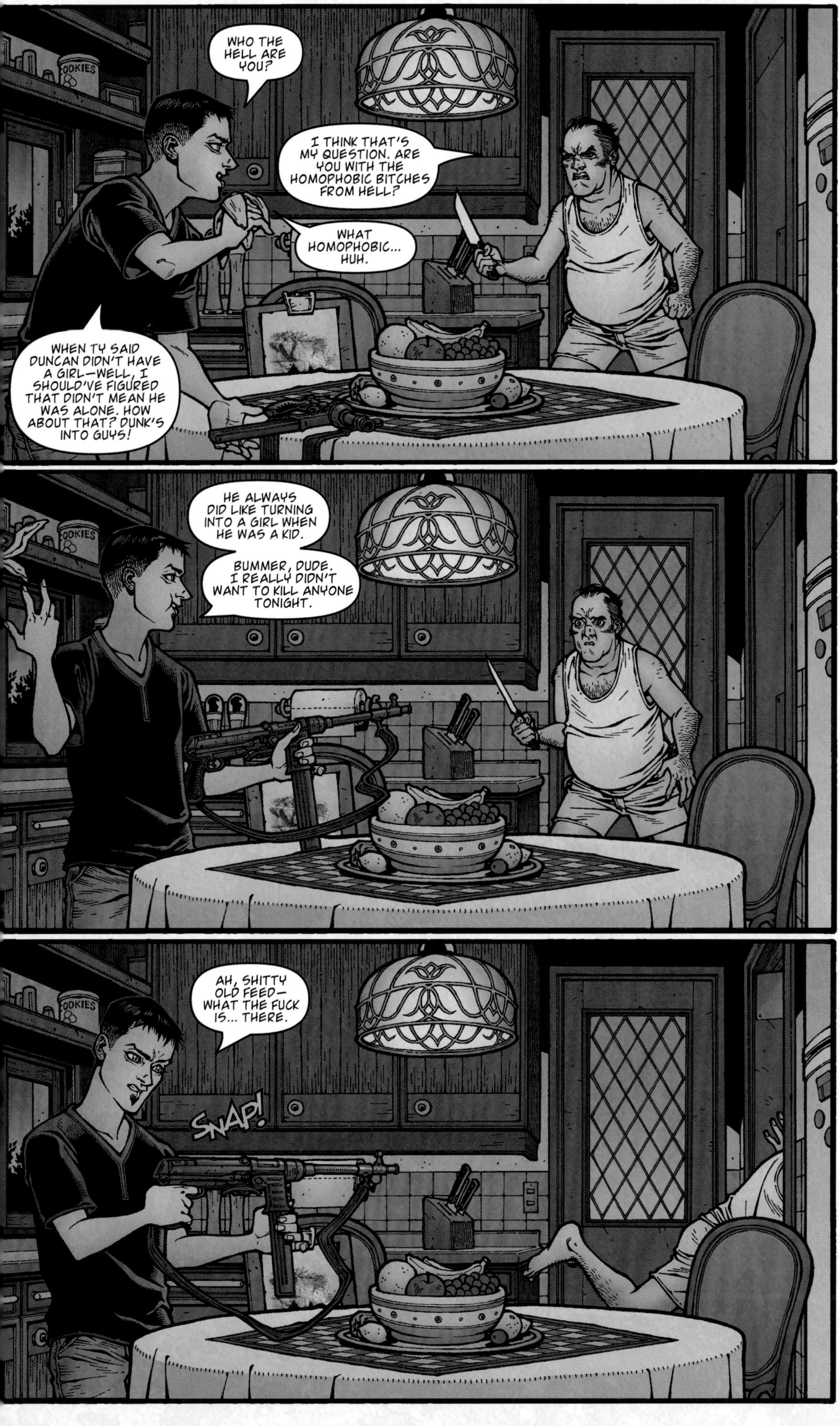
WHO THE HELL ARE YOU?
I THINK THAT'S MY QUESTION. ARE YOU WITH THE HOMOPHOBIC BITCHES FROM HELL?
WHAT HOMOPHOBIC... HUH.
WHEN TY SAID DUNCAN DIDN'T HAVE A GIRL—WELL, I SHOULD'VE FIGURED THAT DIDN'T MEAN HE WAS ALONE. HOW ABOUT THAT? DUNK'S INTO GUYS!
HE ALWAYS DID LIKE TURNING INTO A GIRL WHEN HE WAS A KID.
BUMMER, DUDE. I REALLY DIDN'T WANT TO KILL ANYONE TONIGHT.
AH, SHITTY OLD FEED—WHAT THE FUCK IS... THERE.
SNAP!

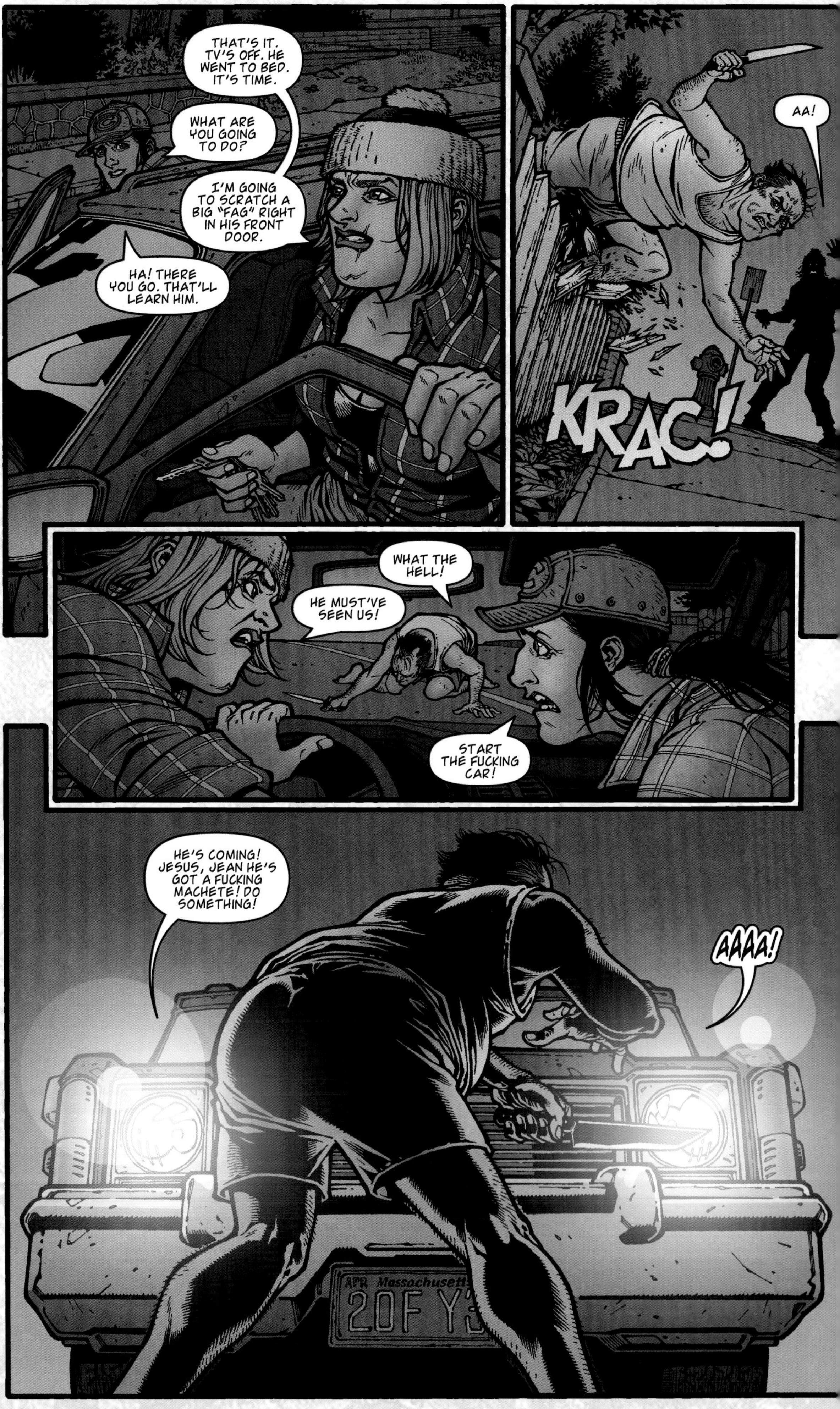
THAT'S IT. TV'S OFF. HE WENT TO BED. IT'S TIME.
WHAT ARE YOU GOING TO DO?
I'M GOING TO SCRATCH A BIG "FAG" RIGHT IN HIS FRONT DOOR.
HA! THERE YOU GO. THAT'LL LEARN HIM.
AA!
KRAC!
WHAT THE HELL!
HE MUST'VE SEEN US!
START THE FUCKING CAR!
HE'S COMING! JESUS, JEAN HE'S GOT A FUCKING MACHETE! DO SOMETHING!
AAAA!
APR Massachusetts
20F Y3

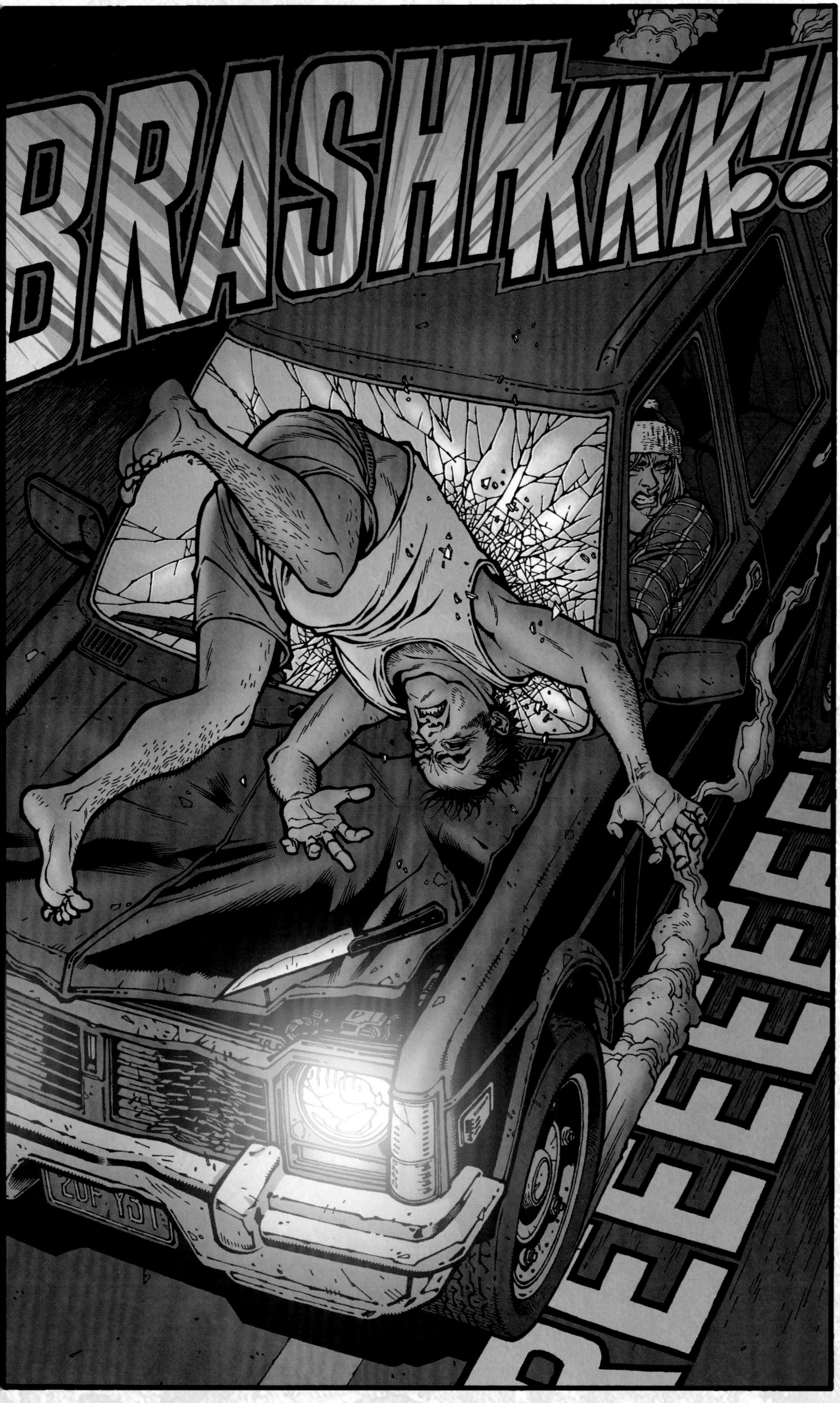
BRASHKKK!!

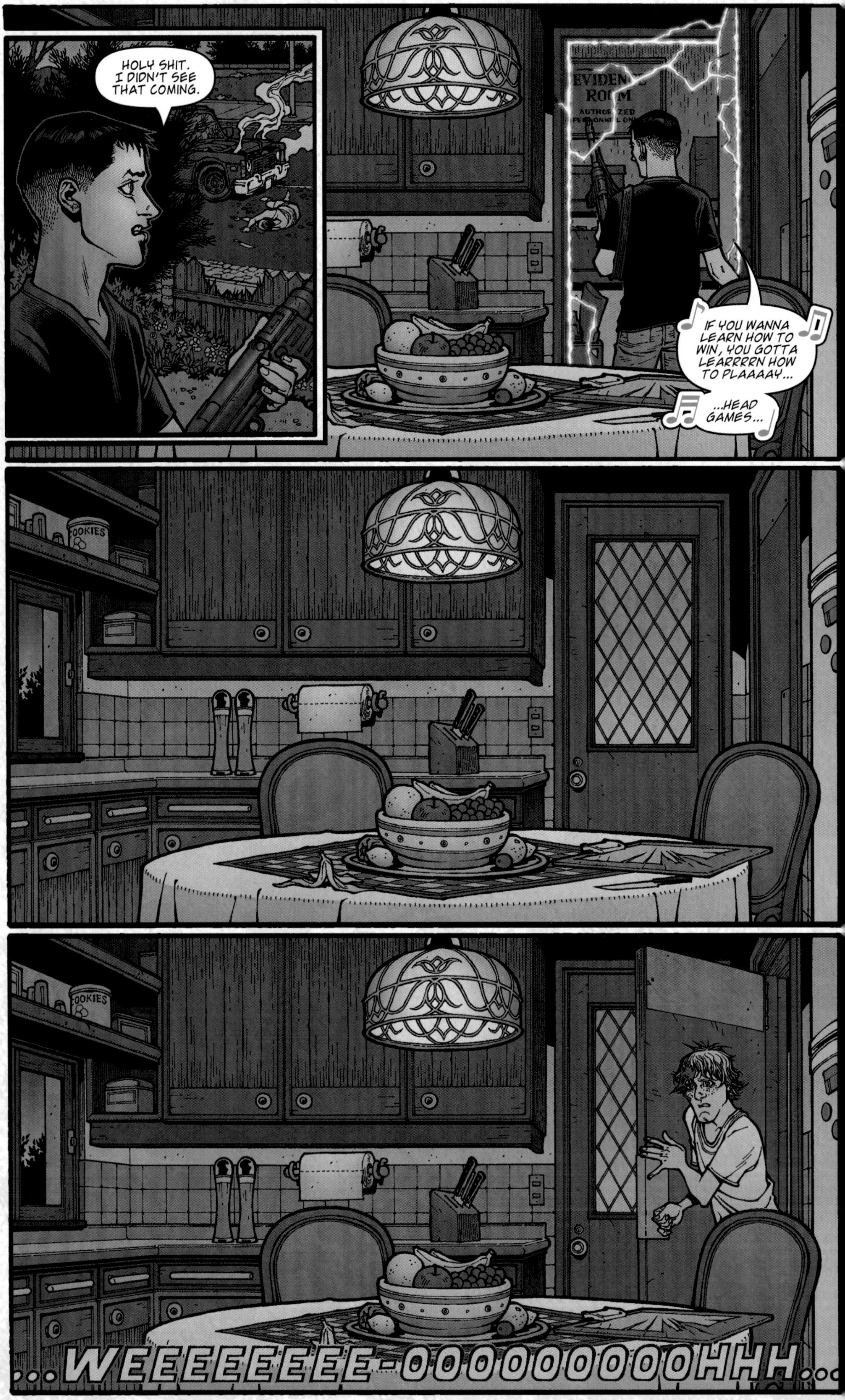
HOLY SHIT. I DIDN'T SEE THAT COMING.
EVIDENCE ROOM
IF YOU WANNA LEARN HOW TO WIN, YOU GOTTA LEARRRRN HOW TO PLAAAAY...
...HEAD GAMES...
COOKIES
...WEEEEEEEEE-OOOOOOOOOOHHH...

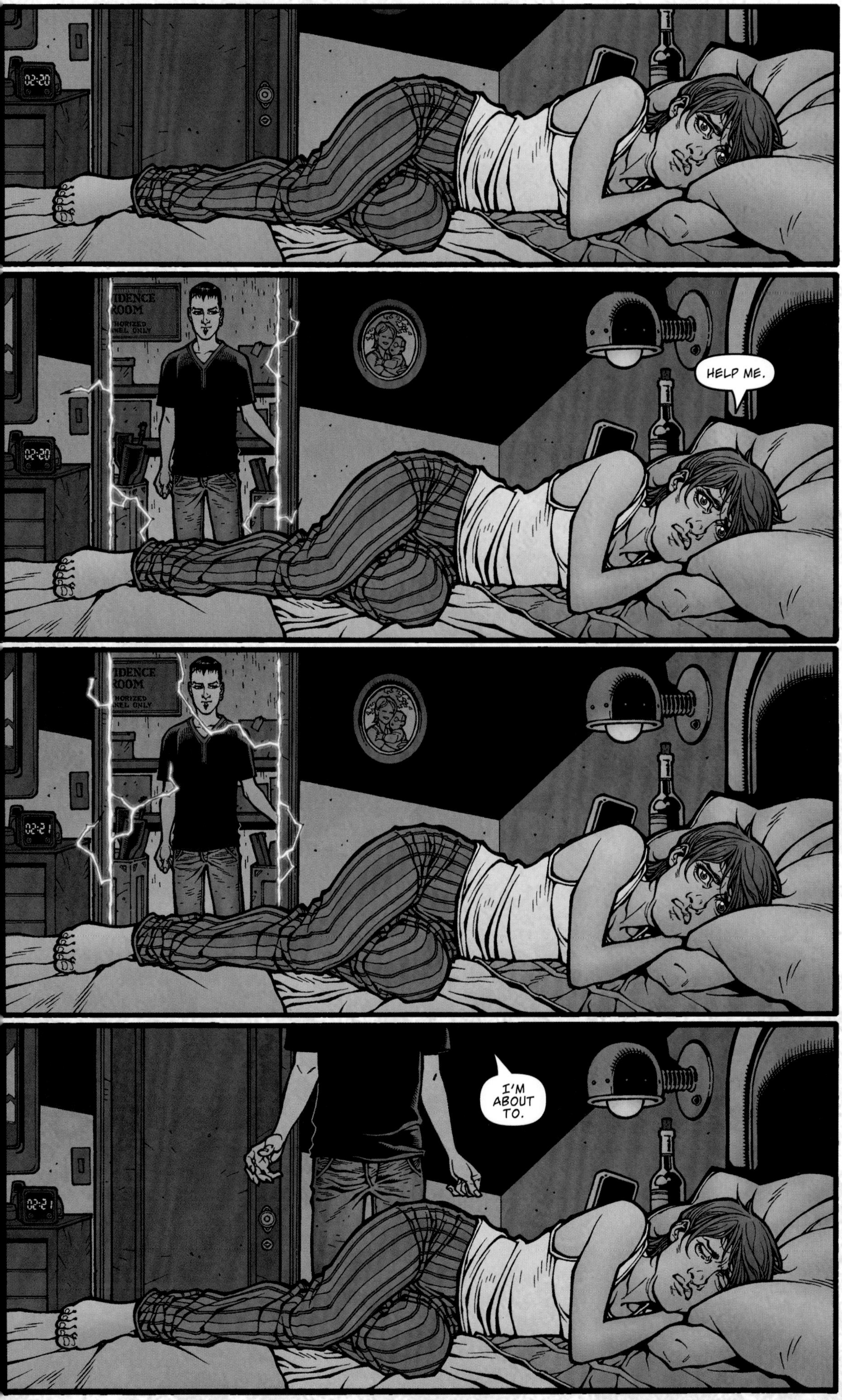
02:20
02:20
HELP ME.
02:21
02:21
I'M ABOUT TO.

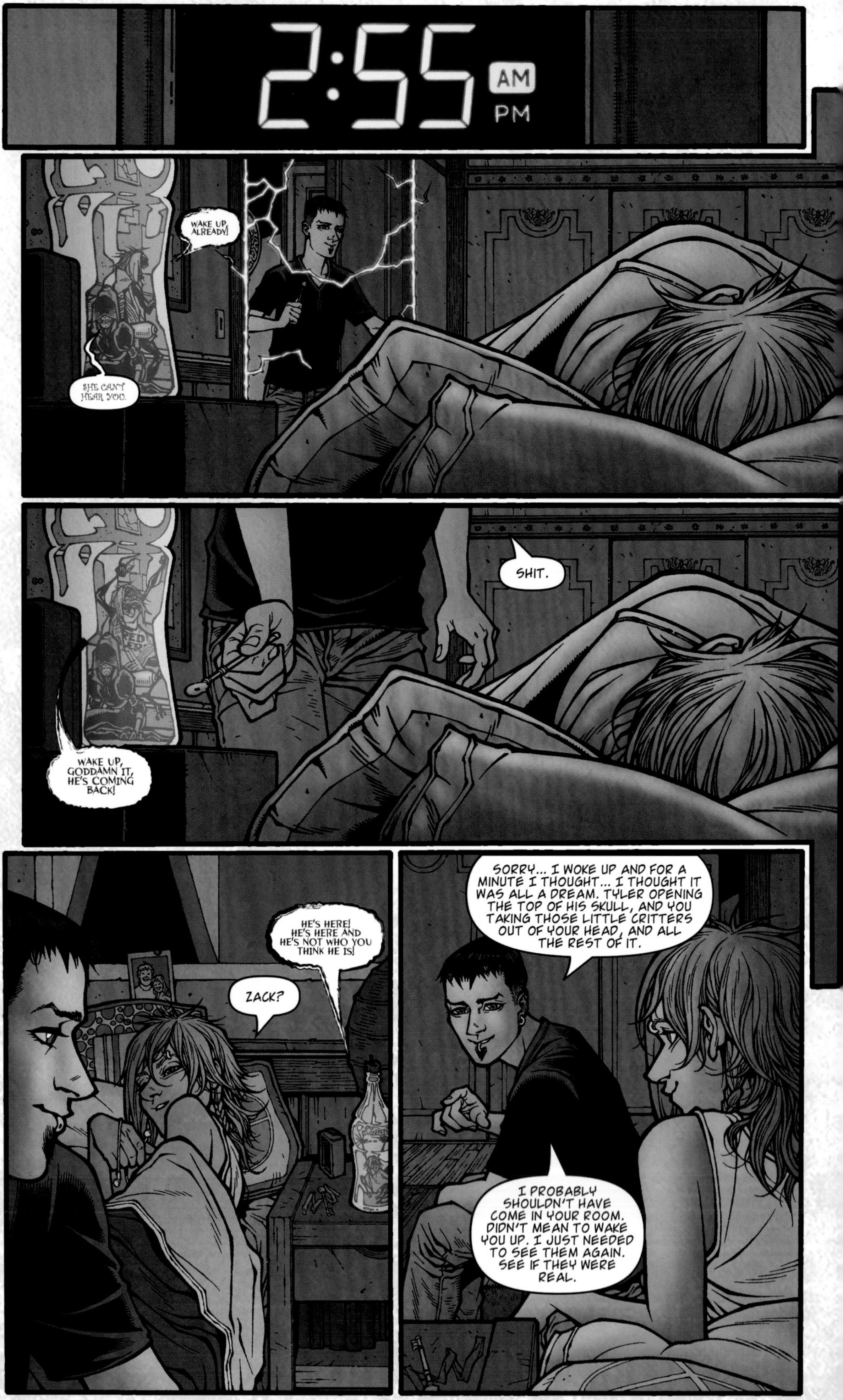
2:55 AM PM
WAKE UP ALREADY!
SHE CAN'T HEAR YOU.
SHIT.
WAKE UP, GODDAMN IT, HE'S COMING BACK!
HE'S HERE! HE'S HERE AND HE'S NOT WHO YOU THINK HE IS!
ZACK?
SORRY... I WOKE UP AND FOR A MINUTE I THOUGHT... I THOUGHT IT WAS ALL A DREAM. TYLER OPENING THE TOP OF HIS SKULL, AND YOU TAKING THOSE LITTLE CRITTERS OUT OF YOUR HEAD, AND ALL THE REST OF IT.
I PROBABLY SHOULDN'T HAVE COME IN YOUR ROOM. DIDN'T MEAN TO WAKE YOU UP. I JUST NEEDED TO SEE THEM AGAIN. SEE IF THEY WERE REAL.

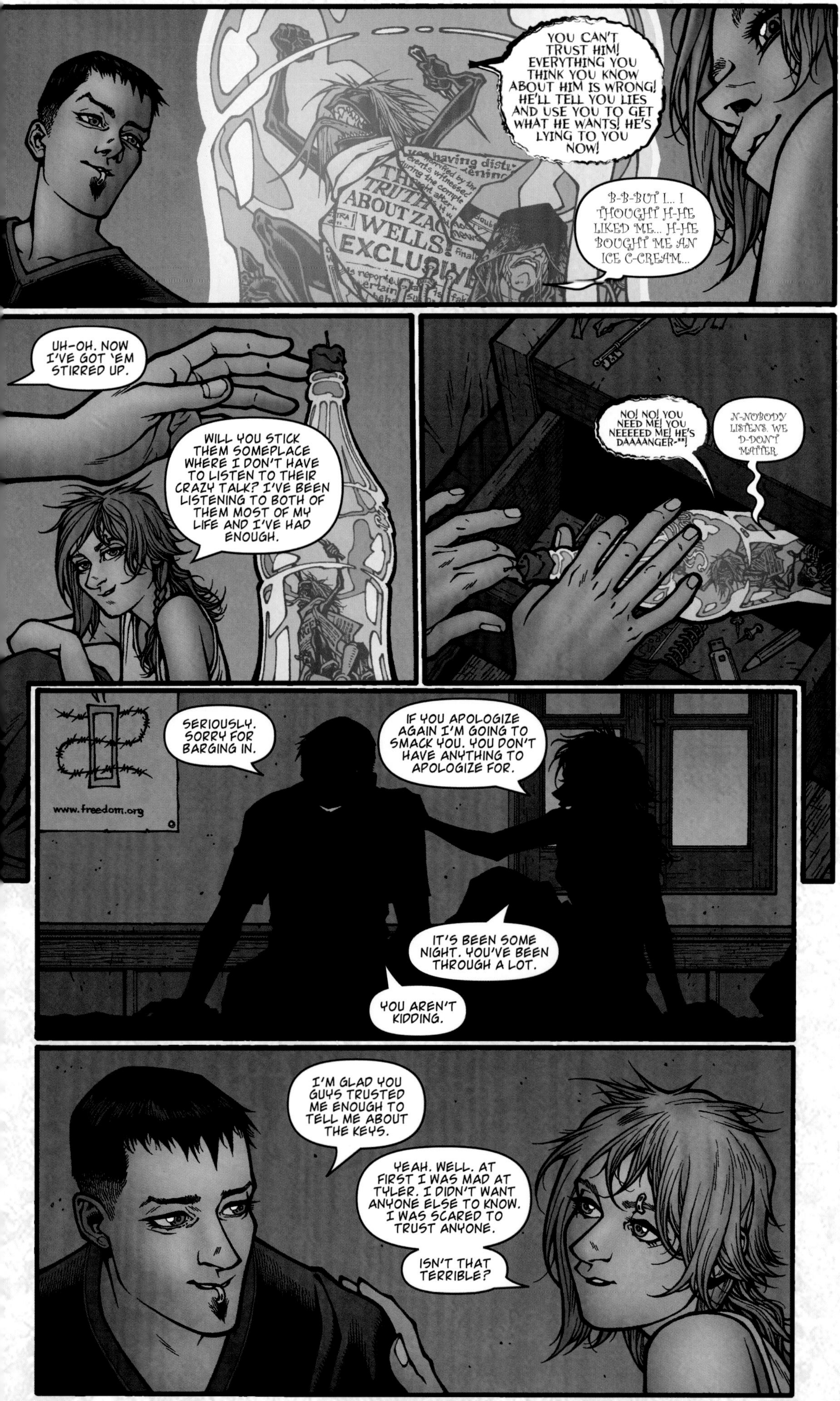
YOU CAN'T TRUST HIM! EVERYTHING YOU THINK YOU KNOW ABOUT HIM IS WRONG! HE'LL TELL YOU LIES AND USE YOU TO GET WHAT HE WANTS! HE'S LYING TO YOU NOW!
B-B-BUT I... I THOUGHT H-HE LIKED ME... H-HE BOUGHT ME AN ICE C-CREAM...
UH-OH. NOW I'VE GOT 'EM STIRRED UP.
WILL YOU STICK THEM SOMEPLACE WHERE I DON'T HAVE TO LISTEN TO THEIR CRAZY TALK? I'VE BEEN LISTENING TO BOTH OF THEM MOST OF MY LIFE AND I'VE HAD ENOUGH.
NO! NO! YOU NEED ME! YOU NEEEEED ME! HE'S DAAAANGER-**!
N-NOBODY LISTENS. WE D-DON'T MATTER.
www.freedom.org
SERIOUSLY. SORRY FOR BARGING IN.
IF YOU APOLOGIZE AGAIN I'M GOING TO SMACK YOU. YOU DON'T HAVE ANYTHING TO APOLOGIZE FOR.
IT'S BEEN SOME NIGHT. YOU'VE BEEN THROUGH A LOT.
YOU AREN'T KIDDING.
I'M GLAD YOU GUYS TRUSTED ME ENOUGH TO TELL ME ABOUT THE KEYS.
YEAH. WELL. AT FIRST I WAS MAD AT TYLER. I DIDN'T WANT ANYONE ELSE TO KNOW. I WAS SCARED TO TRUST ANYONE.
ISN'T THAT TERRIBLE?

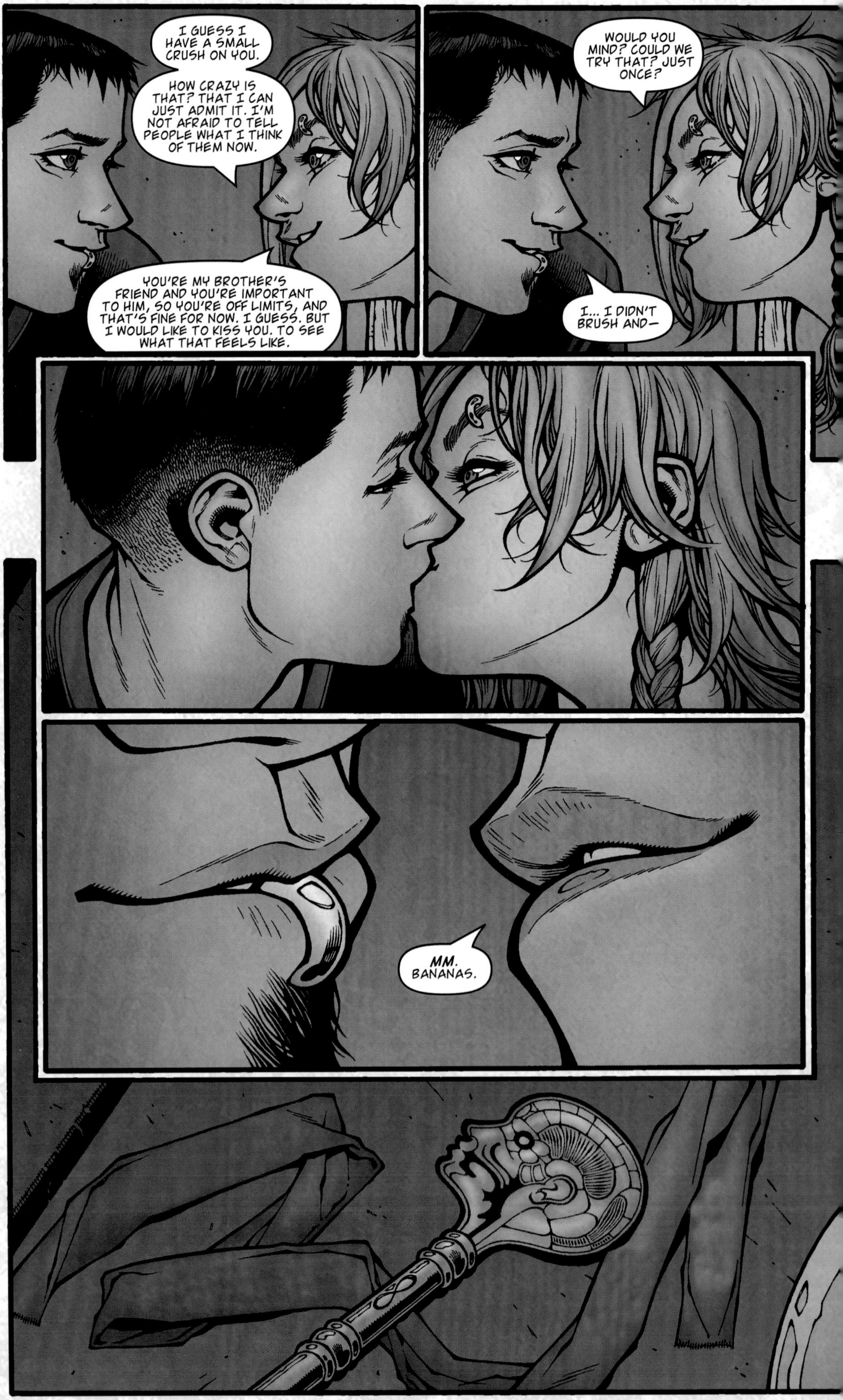
I GUESS I HAVE A SMALL CRUSH ON YOU.
HOW CRAZY IS THAT? THAT I CAN JUST ADMIT IT. I'M NOT AFRAID TO TELL PEOPLE WHAT I THINK OF THEM NOW.
YOU'RE MY BROTHER'S FRIEND AND YOU'RE IMPORTANT TO HIM, SO YOU'RE OFF LIMITS, AND THAT'S FINE FOR NOW. I GUESS. BUT I WOULD LIKE TO KISS YOU. TO SEE WHAT THAT FEELS LIKE.
WOULD YOU MIND? COULD WE TRY THAT? JUST ONCE?
I... I DIDN'T BRUSH AND—
MM. BANANAS.

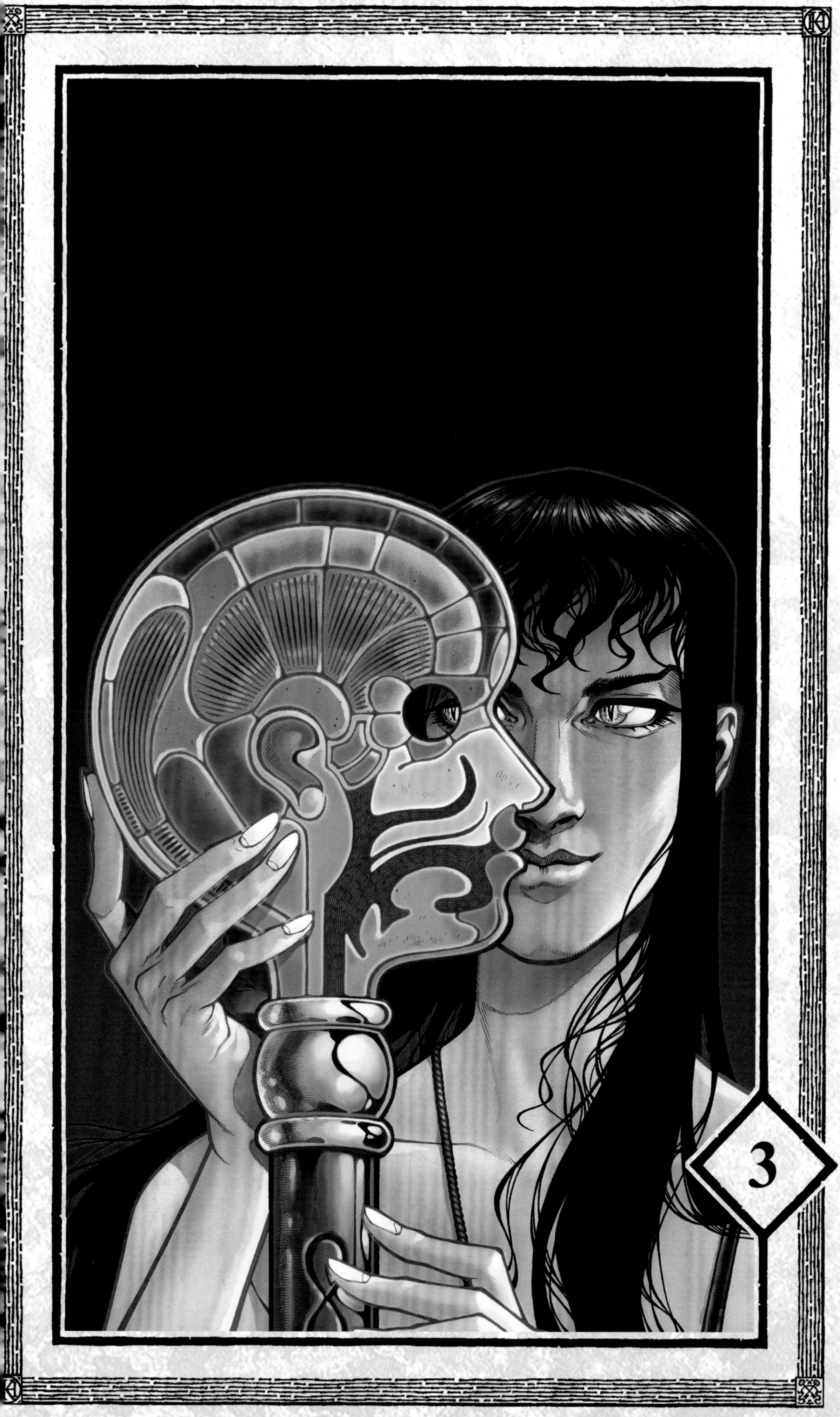
3

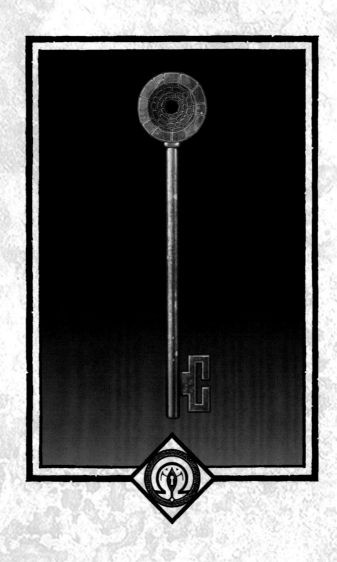

HEAD GAMES
- EPILOGUE: ARMY OF ONE -

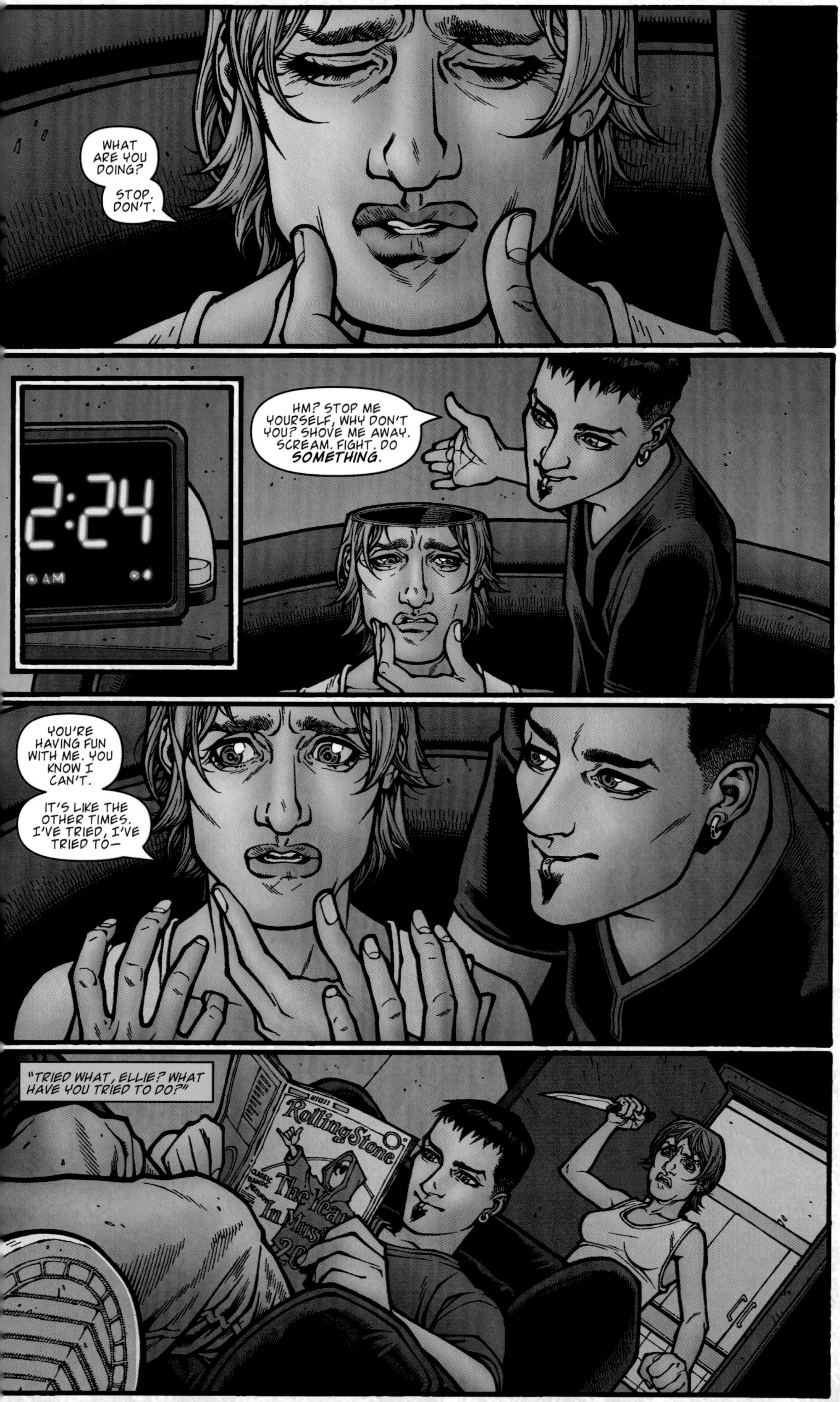
WHAT ARE YOU DOING?
STOP. DON'T.
2:24
AM
HM? STOP ME YOURSELF, WHY DON'T YOU? SHOVE ME AWAY. SCREAM. FIGHT. DO SOMETHING.
YOU'RE HAVING FUN WITH ME. YOU KNOW I CAN'T.
IT'S LIKE THE OTHER TIMES. I'VE TRIED, I'VE TRIED TO—
"TRIED WHAT, ELLIE? WHAT HAVE YOU TRIED TO DO?"
Rolling Stone
The Year In Music

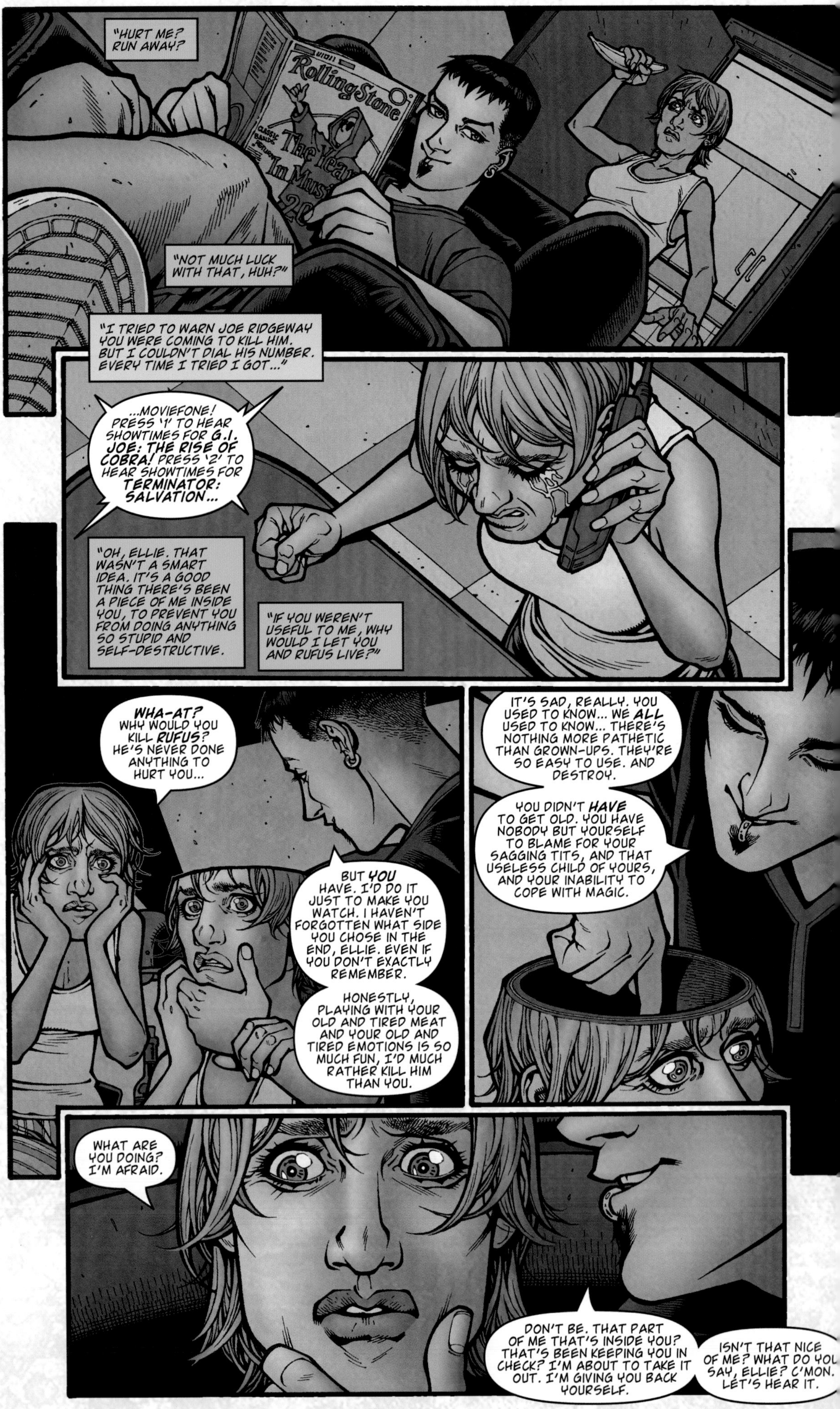
"HURT ME? RUN AWAY?
"NOT MUCH LUCK WITH THAT, HUH?"
"I TRIED TO WARN JOE RIDGEWAY YOU WERE COMING TO KILL HIM. BUT I COULDN'T DIAL HIS NUMBER. EVERY TIME I TRIED I GOT..."
...MOVIEFONE! PRESS '1' TO HEAR SHOWTIMES FOR G.I. JOE: THE RISE OF COBRA! PRESS '2' TO HEAR SHOWTIMES FOR TERMINATOR: SALVATION...
"OH, ELLIE. THAT WASN'T A SMART IDEA. IT'S A GOOD THING THERE'S BEEN A PIECE OF ME INSIDE YOU, TO PREVENT YOU FROM DOING ANYTHING SO STUPID AND SELF-DESTRUCTIVE.
"IF YOU WEREN'T USEFUL TO ME, WHY WOULD I LET YOU AND RUFUS LIVE?"
WHA-AT? WHY WOULD YOU KILL RUFUS? HE'S NEVER DONE ANYTHING TO HURT YOU...
BUT YOU HAVE. I'D DO IT JUST TO MAKE YOU WATCH. I HAVEN'T FORGOTTEN WHAT SIDE YOU CHOSE IN THE END, ELLIE. EVEN IF YOU DON'T EXACTLY REMEMBER.
HONESTLY, PLAYING WITH YOUR OLD AND TIRED MEAT AND YOUR OLD AND TIRED EMOTIONS IS SO MUCH FUN, I'D MUCH RATHER KILL HIM THAN YOU.
IT'S SAD, REALLY. YOU USED TO KNOW... WE ALL USED TO KNOW... THERE'S NOTHING MORE PATHETIC THAN GROWN-UPS. THEY'RE SO EASY TO USE. AND DESTROY.
YOU DIDN'T HAVE TO GET OLD. YOU HAVE NOBODY BUT YOURSELF TO BLAME FOR YOUR SAGGING TITS, AND THAT USELESS CHILD OF YOURS, AND YOUR INABILITY TO COPE WITH MAGIC.
WHAT ARE YOU DOING? I'M AFRAID.
DON'T BE. THAT PART OF ME THAT'S INSIDE YOU? THAT'S BEEN KEEPING YOU IN CHECK? I'M ABOUT TO TAKE IT OUT. I'M GIVING YOU BACK YOURSELF.
ISN'T THAT NICE OF ME? WHAT DO YOU SAY, ELLIE? C'MON. LET'S HEAR IT.

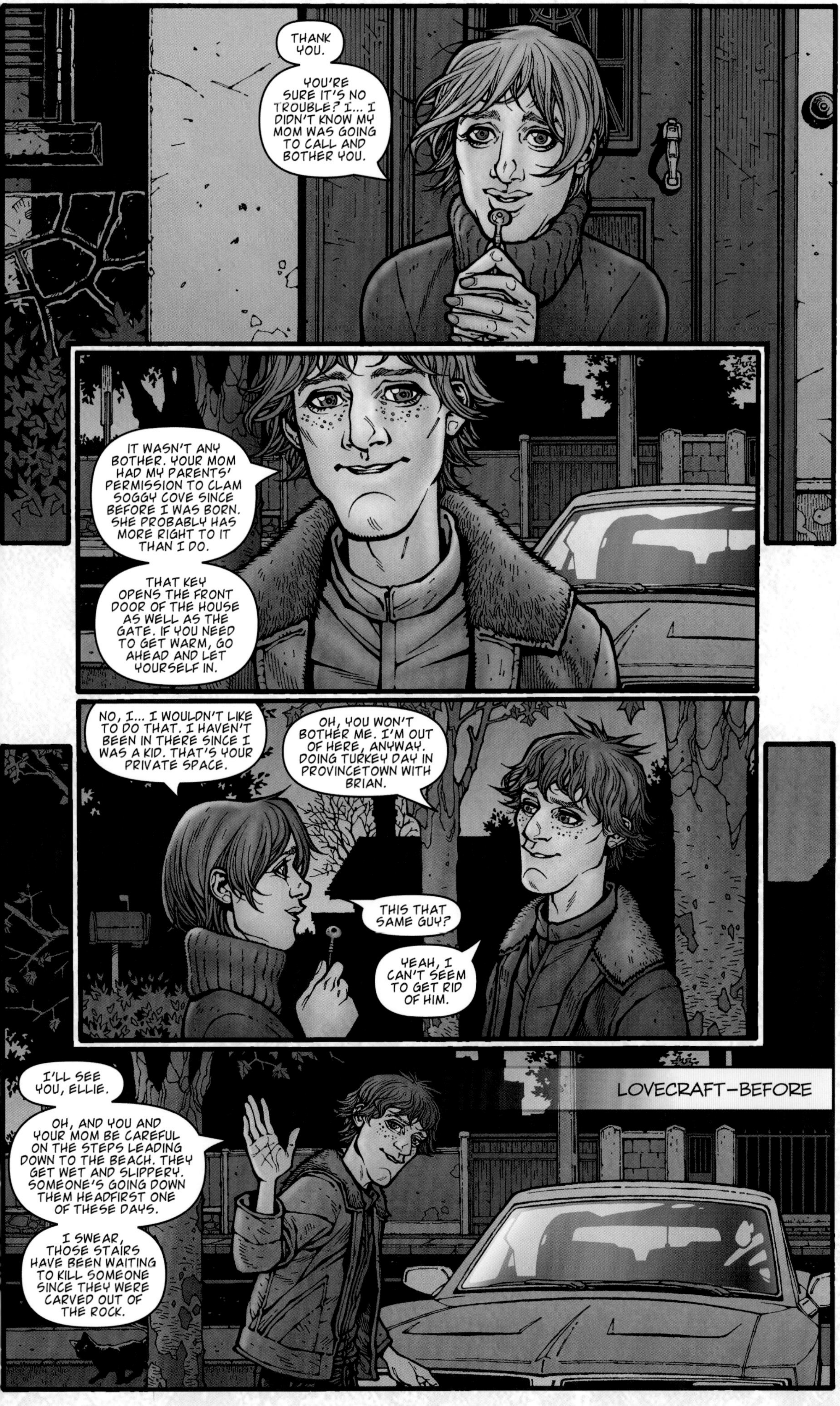
THANK YOU.
YOU'RE SURE IT'S NO TROUBLE? I... I DIDN'T KNOW MY MOM WAS GOING TO CALL AND BOTHER YOU.
IT WASN'T ANY BOTHER. YOUR MOM HAD MY PARENTS' PERMISSION TO CLAM SOGGY COVE SINCE BEFORE I WAS BORN. SHE PROBABLY HAS MORE RIGHT TO IT THAN I DO.
THAT KEY OPENS THE FRONT DOOR OF THE HOUSE AS WELL AS THE GATE. IF YOU NEED TO GET WARM, GO AHEAD AND LET YOURSELF IN.
NO, I... I WOULDN'T LIKE TO DO THAT. I HAVEN'T BEEN IN THERE SINCE I WAS A KID. THAT'S YOUR PRIVATE SPACE.
OH, YOU WON'T BOTHER ME. I'M OUT OF HERE, ANYWAY. DOING TURKEY DAY IN PROVINCETOWN WITH BRIAN.
THIS THAT SAME GUY?
YEAH, I CAN'T SEEM TO GET RID OF HIM.
I'LL SEE YOU, ELLIE.
LOVECRAFT–BEFORE
OH, AND YOU AND YOUR MOM BE CAREFUL ON THE STEPS LEADING DOWN TO THE BEACH. THEY GET WET AND SLIPPERY. SOMEONE'S GOING DOWN THEM HEADFIRST ONE OF THESE DAYS.
I SWEAR, THOSE STAIRS HAVE BEEN WAITING TO KILL SOMEONE SINCE THEY WERE CARVED OUT OF THE ROCK.

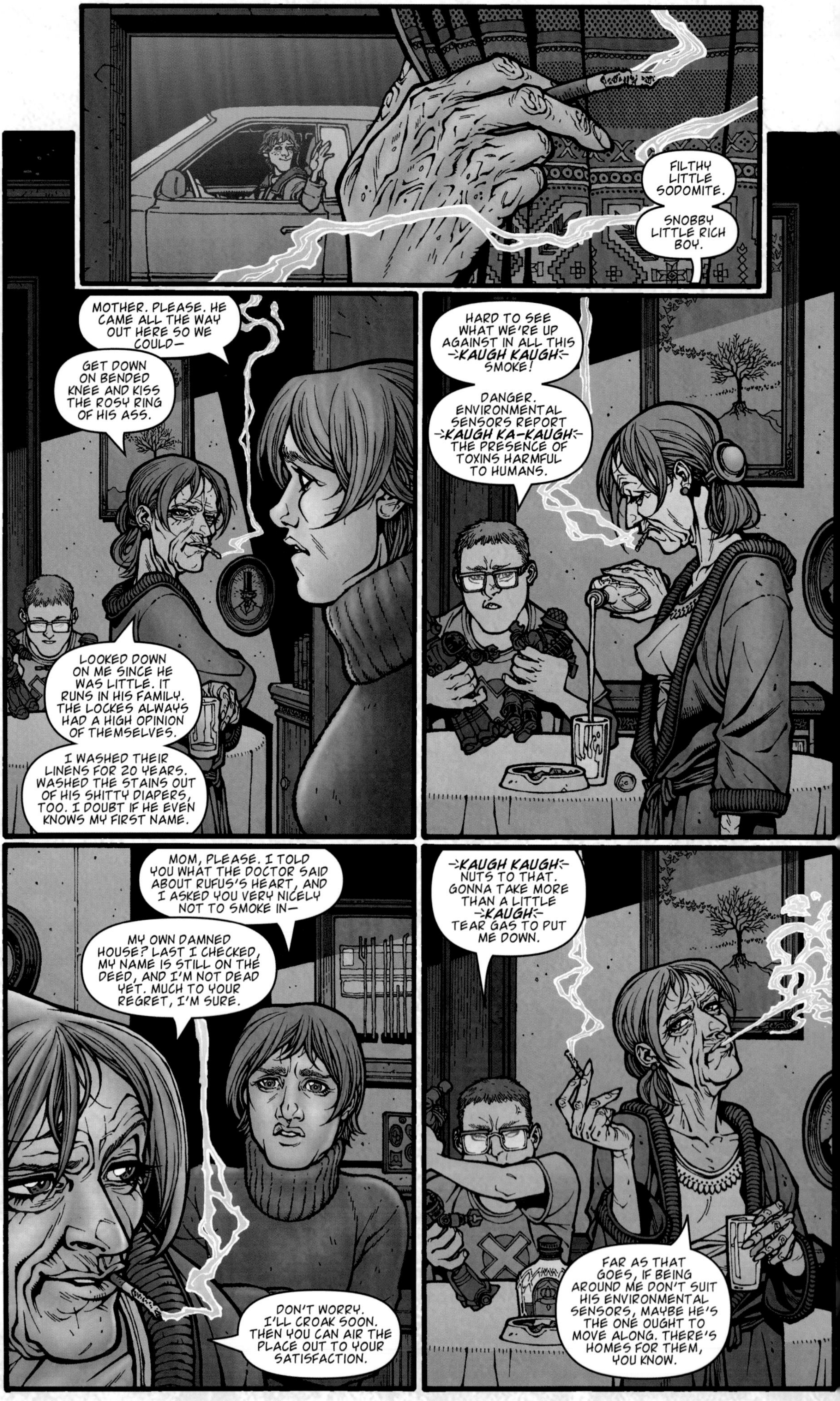
FILTHY LITTLE SODOMITE.
SNOBBY LITTLE RICH BOY.
MOTHER. PLEASE. HE CAME ALL THE WAY OUT HERE SO WE COULD—
GET DOWN ON BENDED KNEE AND KISS THE ROSY RING OF HIS ASS.
LOOKED DOWN ON ME SINCE HE WAS LITTLE. IT RUNS IN HIS FAMILY. THE LOCKES ALWAYS HAD A HIGH OPINION OF THEMSELVES.
I WASHED THEIR LINENS FOR 20 YEARS. WASHED THE STAINS OUT OF HIS SHITTY DIAPERS, TOO. I DOUBT IF HE EVEN KNOWS MY FIRST NAME.
HARD TO SEE WHAT WE'RE UP AGAINST IN ALL THIS -KAUGH KAUGH- SMOKE!
DANGER. ENVIRONMENTAL SENSORS REPORT -KAUGH KA-KAUGH- THE PRESENCE OF TOXINS HARMFUL TO HUMANS.
MOM, PLEASE. I TOLD YOU WHAT THE DOCTOR SAID ABOUT RUFUS'S HEART, AND I ASKED YOU VERY NICELY NOT TO SMOKE IN—
MY OWN DAMNED HOUSE? LAST I CHECKED, MY NAME IS STILL ON THE DEED, AND I'M NOT DEAD YET. MUCH TO YOUR REGRET, I'M SURE.
DON'T WORRY. I'LL CROAK SOON. THEN YOU CAN AIR THE PLACE OUT TO YOUR SATISFACTION.
-KAUGH KAUGH- NUTS TO THAT. GONNA TAKE MORE THAN A LITTLE -KAUGH- TEAR GAS TO PUT ME DOWN.
FAR AS THAT GOES, IF BEING AROUND ME DON'T SUIT HIS ENVIRONMENTAL SENSORS, MAYBE HE'S THE ONE OUGHT TO MOVE ALONG. THERE'S HOMES FOR THEM, YOU KNOW.

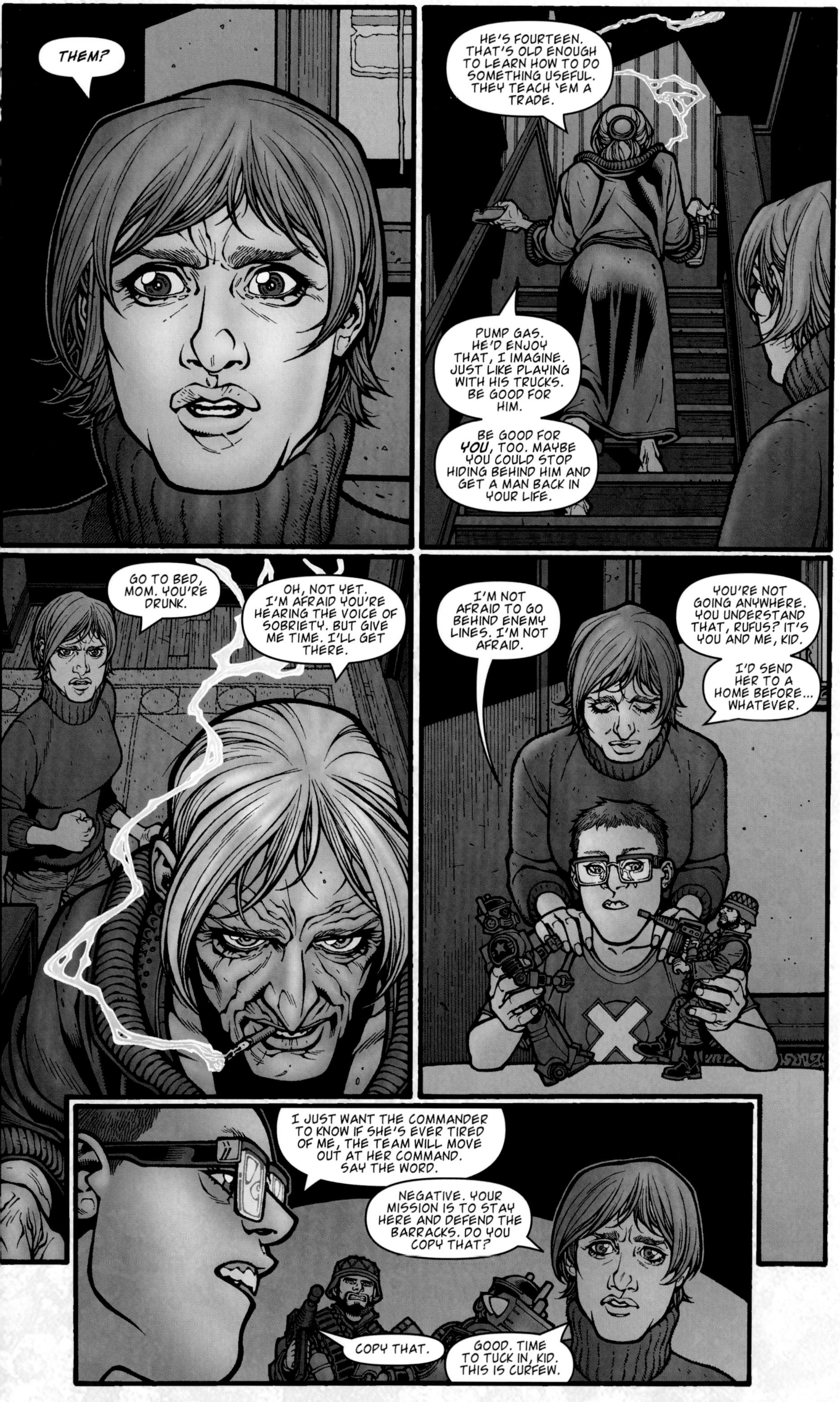
THEM?
HE'S FOURTEEN. THAT'S OLD ENOUGH TO LEARN HOW TO DO SOMETHING USEFUL. THEY TEACH 'EM A TRADE.
PUMP GAS. HE'D ENJOY THAT, I IMAGINE. JUST LIKE PLAYING WITH HIS TRUCKS. BE GOOD FOR HIM.
BE GOOD FOR YOU, TOO. MAYBE YOU COULD STOP HIDING BEHIND HIM AND GET A MAN BACK IN YOUR LIFE.
GO TO BED, MOM. YOU'RE DRUNK.
OH, NOT YET. I'M AFRAID YOU'RE HEARING THE VOICE OF SOBRIETY. BUT GIVE ME TIME. I'LL GET THERE.
I'M NOT AFRAID TO GO BEHIND ENEMY LINES. I'M NOT AFRAID.
YOU'RE NOT GOING ANYWHERE. YOU UNDERSTAND THAT, RUFUS? IT'S YOU AND ME, KID.
I'D SEND HER TO A HOME BEFORE... WHATEVER.
I JUST WANT THE COMMANDER TO KNOW IF SHE'S EVER TIRED OF ME, THE TEAM WILL MOVE OUT AT HER COMMAND. SAY THE WORD.
NEGATIVE. YOUR MISSION IS TO STAY HERE AND DEFEND THE BARRACKS. DO YOU COPY THAT?
COPY THAT.
GOOD. TIME TO TUCK IN, KID. THIS IS CURFEW.

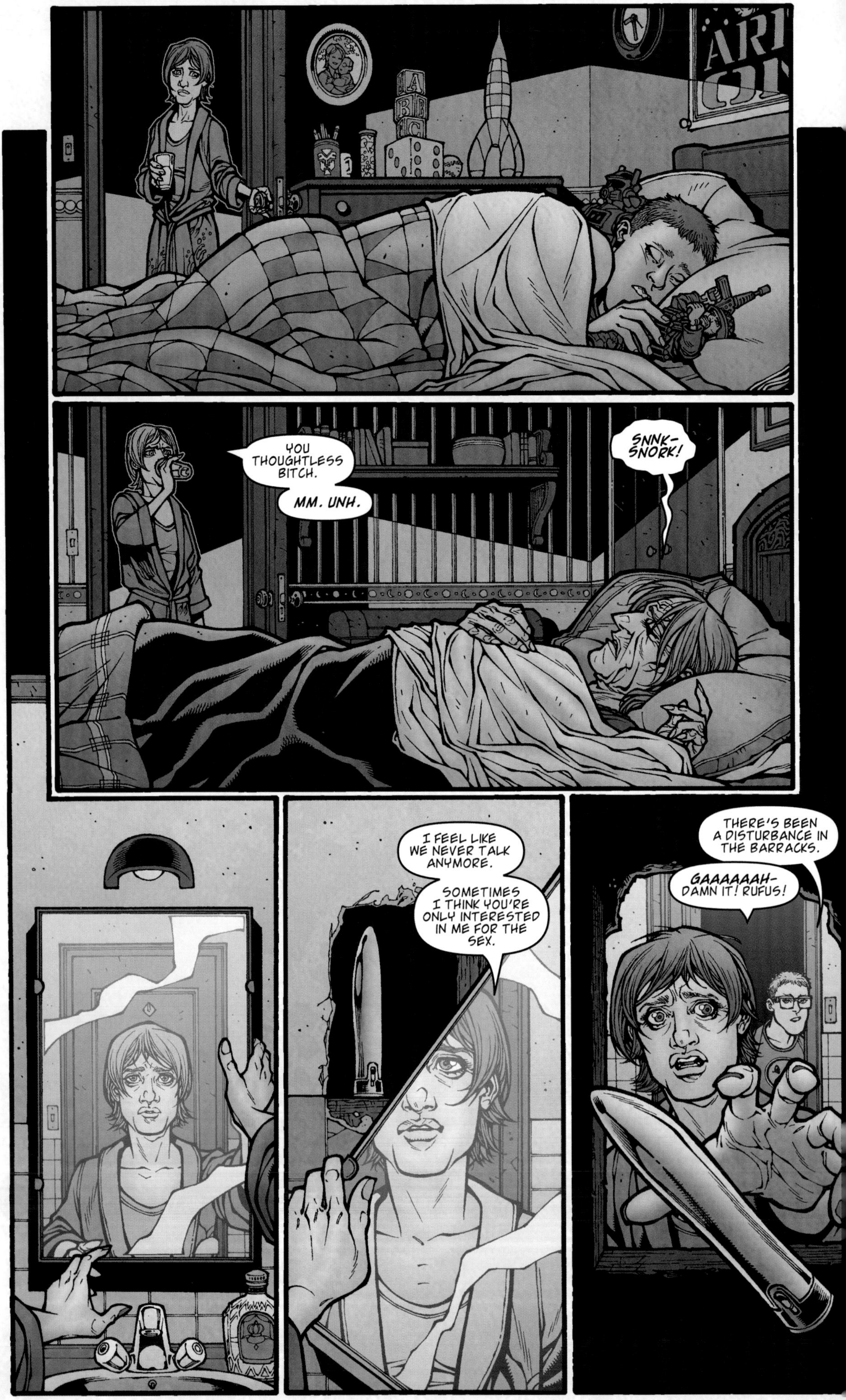

YOU THOUGHTLESS BITCH.
MM. UNH.
SNNK-SNORK!
I FEEL LIKE WE NEVER TALK ANYMORE.
SOMETIMES I THINK YOU'RE ONLY INTERESTED IN ME FOR THE SEX.
THERE'S BEEN A DISTURBANCE IN THE BARRACKS.
GAAAAAAH-DAMN IT! RUFUS!

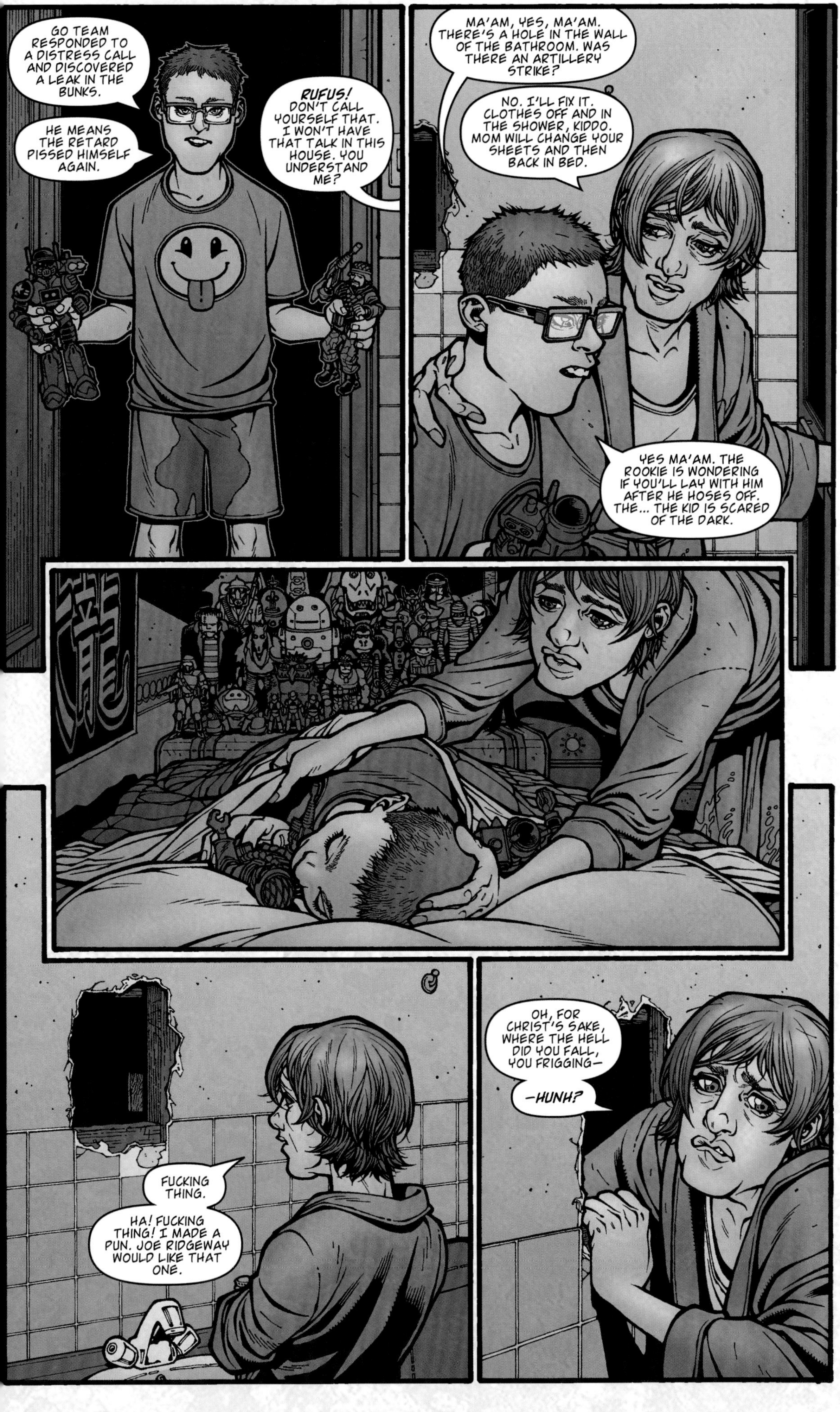

GO TEAM RESPONDED TO A DISTRESS CALL AND DISCOVERED A LEAK IN THE BUNKS.
HE MEANS THE RETARD PISSED HIMSELF AGAIN.
RUFUS! DON'T CALL YOURSELF THAT. I WON'T HAVE THAT TALK IN THIS HOUSE. YOU UNDERSTAND ME?
MA'AM, YES, MA'AM. THERE'S A HOLE IN THE WALL OF THE BATHROOM. WAS THERE AN ARTILLERY STRIKE?
NO. I'LL FIX IT. CLOTHES OFF AND IN THE SHOWER, KIDDO. MOM WILL CHANGE YOUR SHEETS AND THEN BACK IN BED.
YES MA'AM. THE ROOKIE IS WONDERING IF YOU'LL LAY WITH HIM AFTER HE HOSES OFF. THE... THE KID IS SCARED OF THE DARK.
FUCKING THING.
HA! FUCKING THING! I MADE A PUN. JOE RIDGEWAY WOULD LIKE THAT ONE.
OH, FOR CHRIST'S SAKE, WHERE THE HELL DID YOU FALL, YOU FRIGGING—
—HUNH?

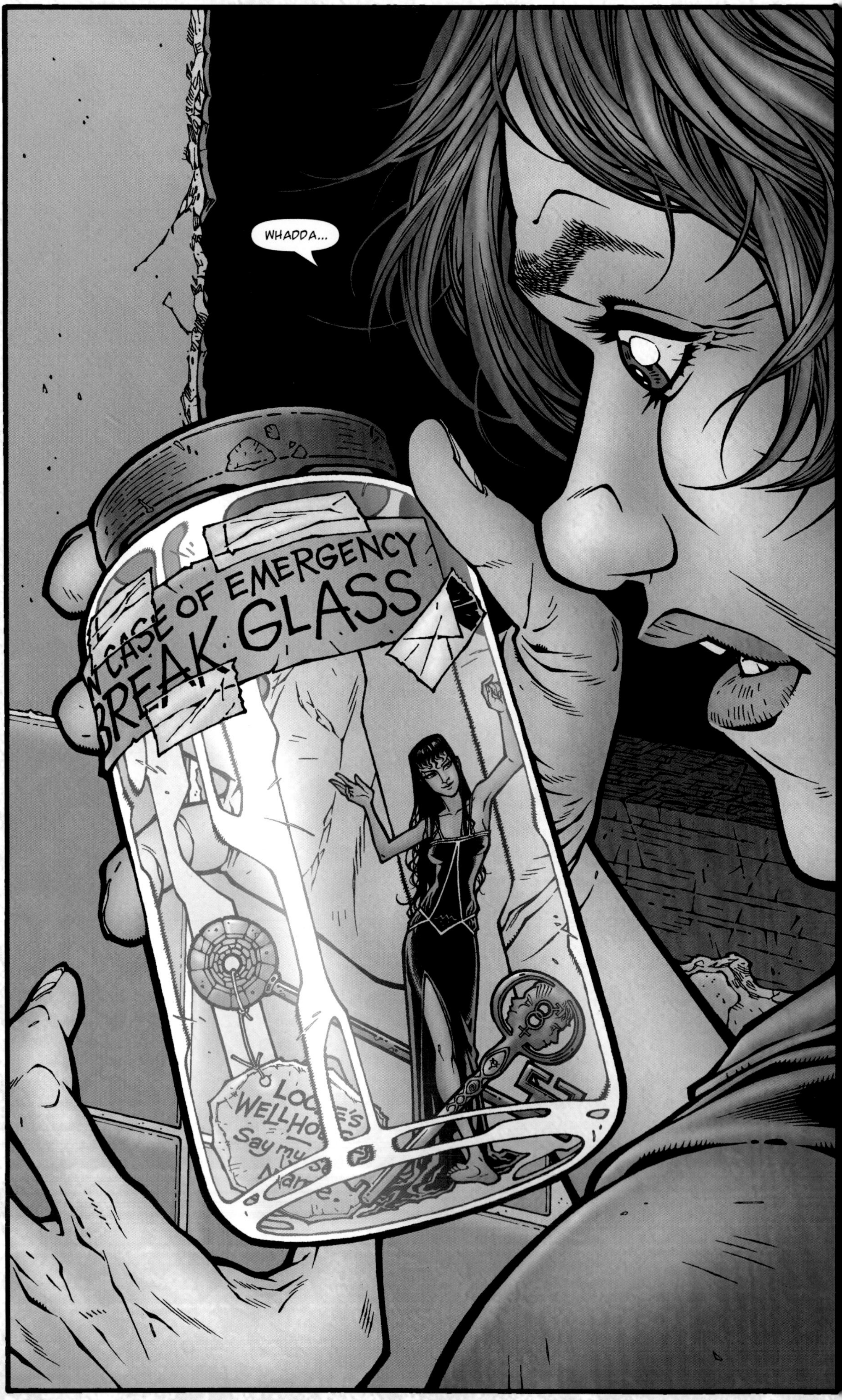
WHADDA...
CASE OF EMERGENCY
BREAK GLASS
LOC
WELLHO
Say my

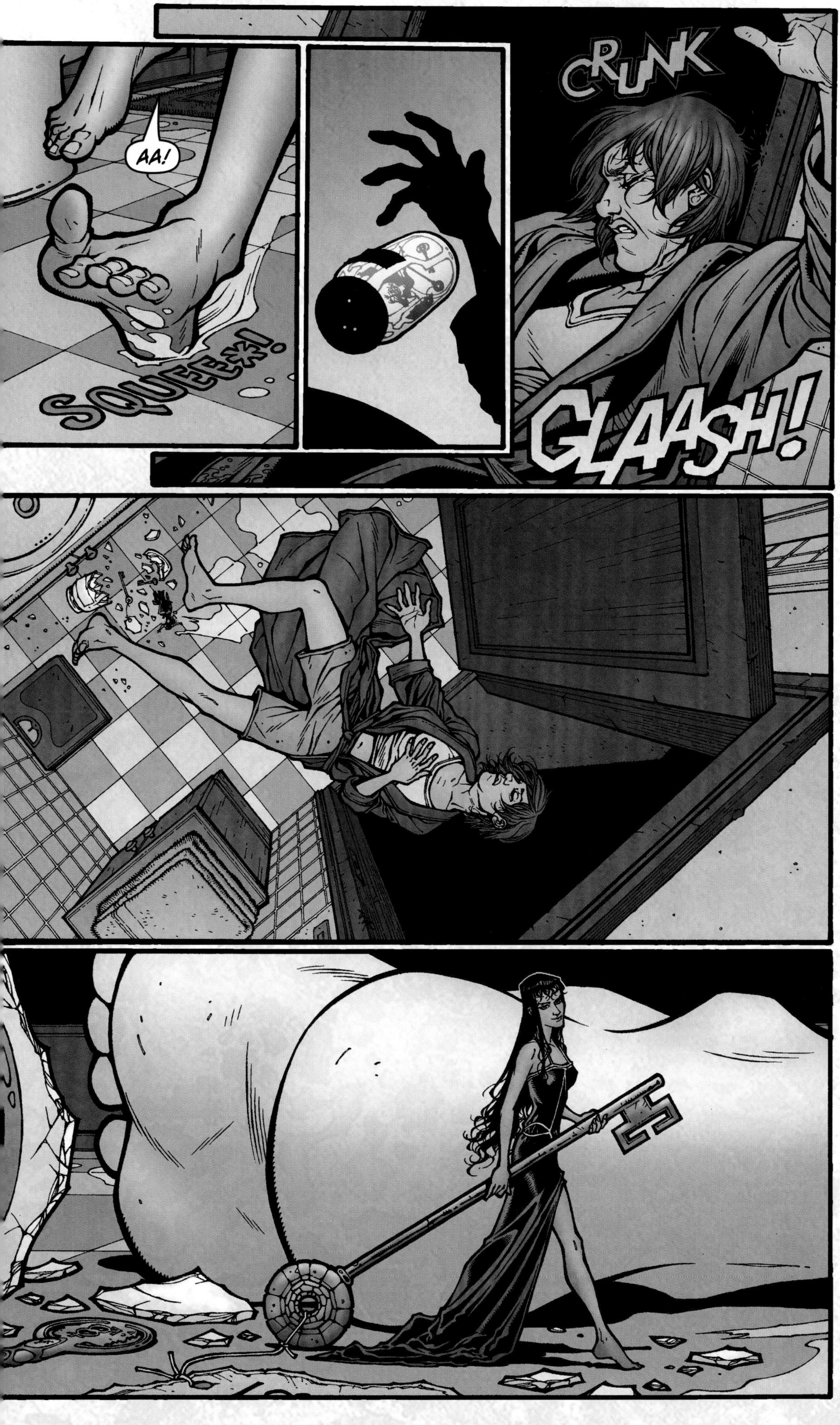
AA!
SQUEEK!
CRUNK
GLAASH!

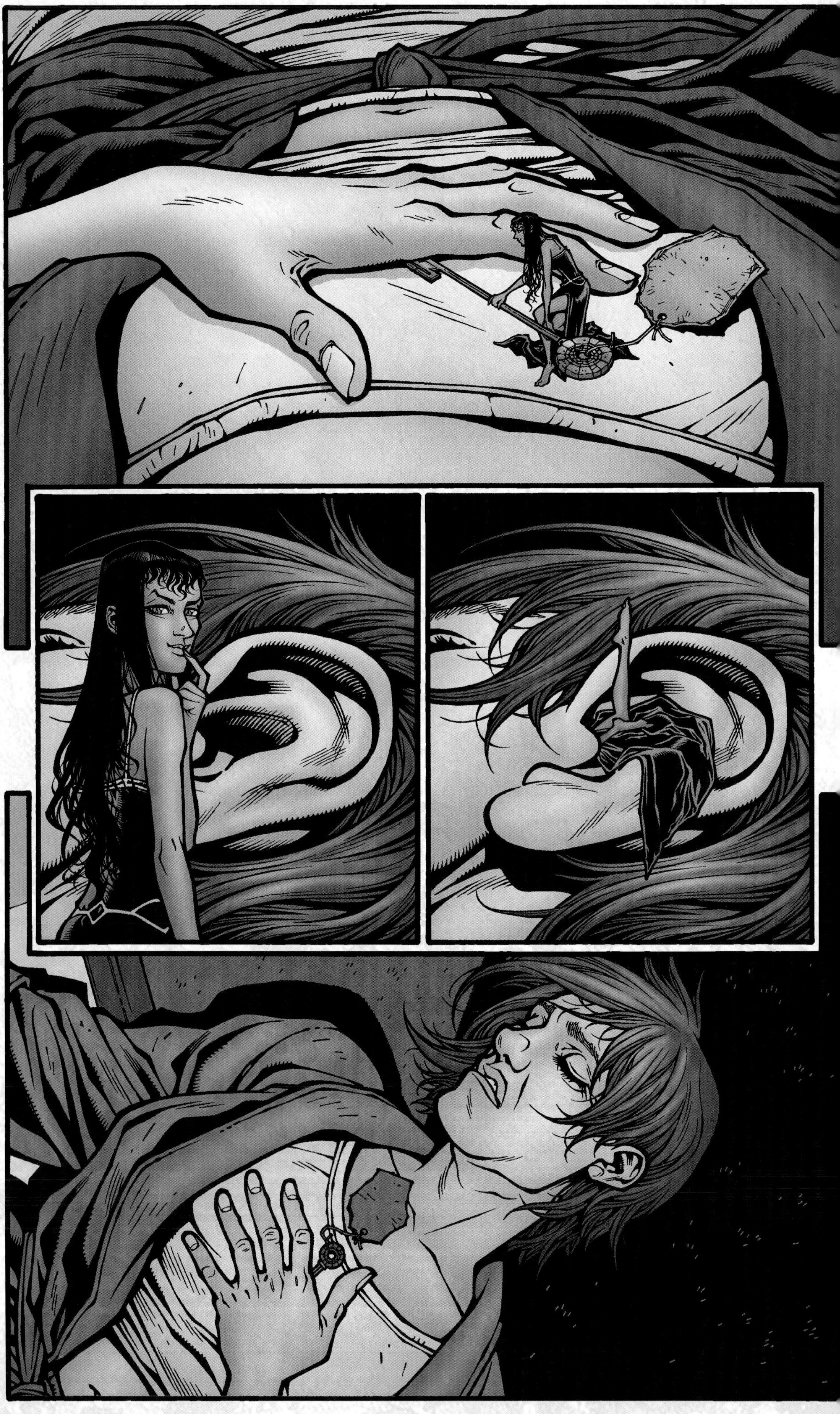

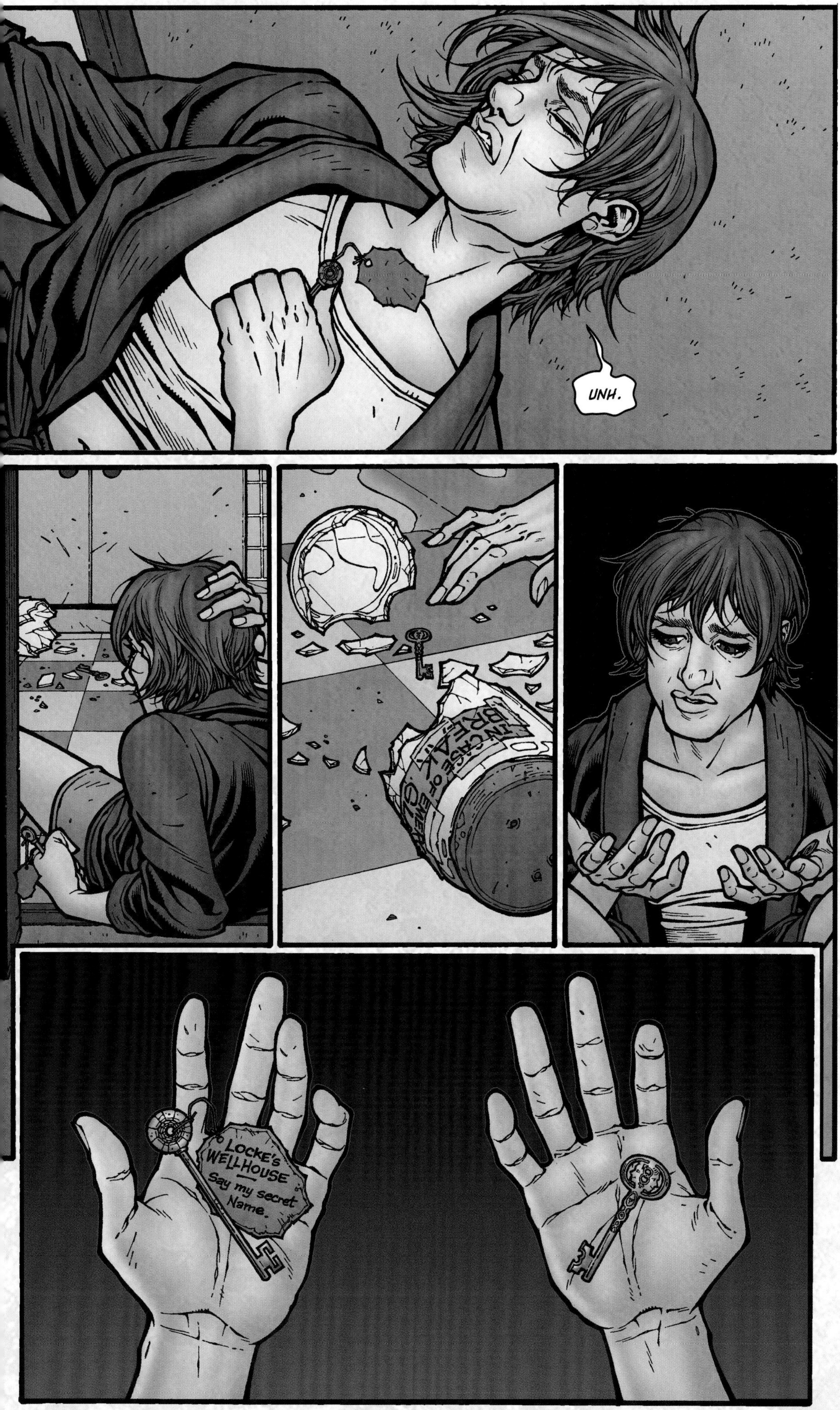
UNH.
Locke's
WELLHOUSE
Say my secret
Name.

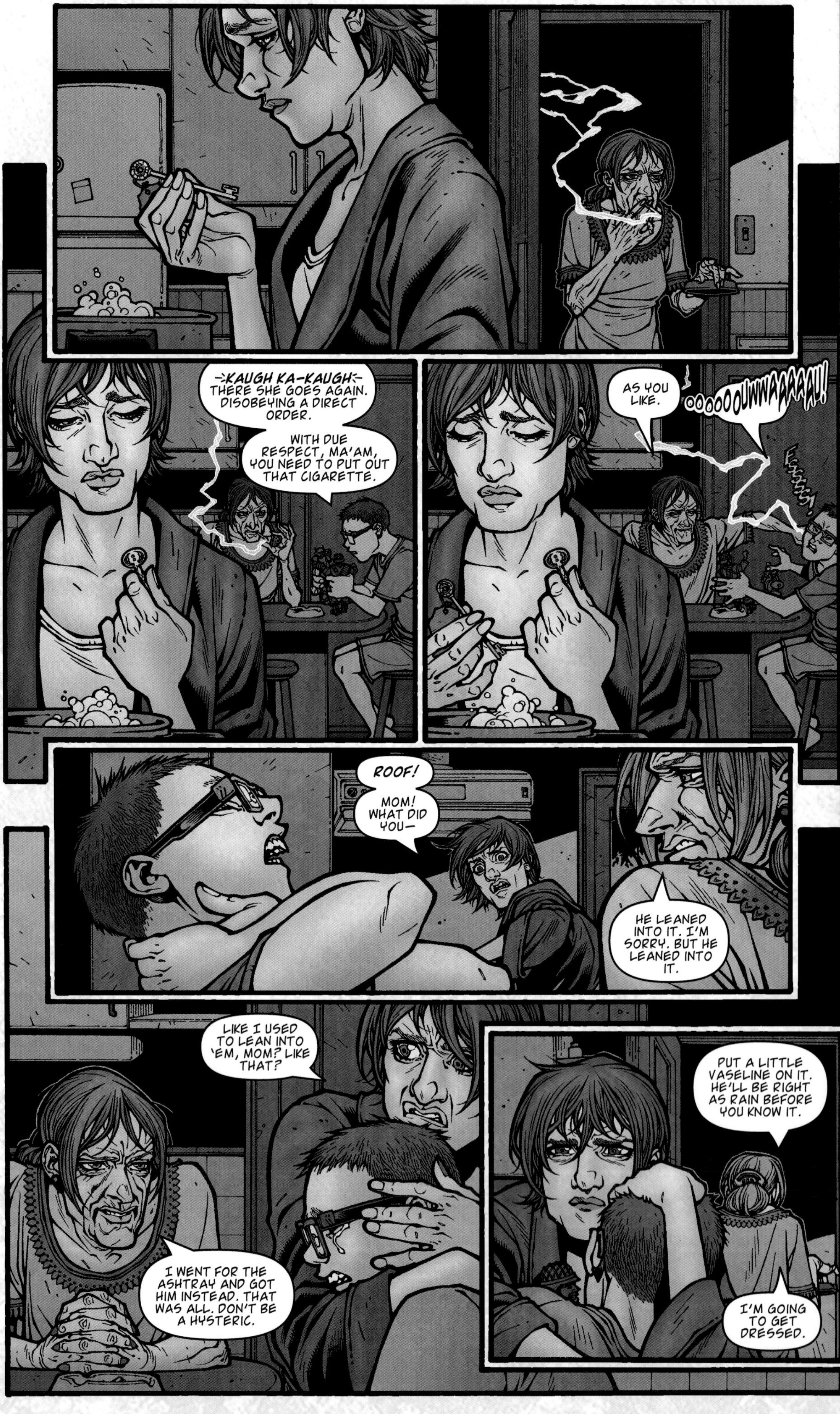

-KAUGH KA-KAUGH- THERE SHE GOES AGAIN. DISOBEYING A DIRECT ORDER.
WITH DUE RESPECT, MA'AM, YOU NEED TO PUT OUT THAT CIGARETTE.
AS YOU LIKE.
OOOOOOUWWAAAAAU!
ROOF!
MOM! WHAT DID YOU—
HE LEANED INTO IT. I'M SORRY. BUT HE LEANED INTO IT.
LIKE I USED TO LEAN INTO 'EM, MOM? LIKE THAT?
I WENT FOR THE ASHTRAY AND GOT HIM INSTEAD. THAT WAS ALL. DON'T BE A HYSTERIC.
PUT A LITTLE VASELINE ON IT. HE'LL BE RIGHT AS RAIN BEFORE YOU KNOW IT.
I'M GOING TO GET DRESSED.

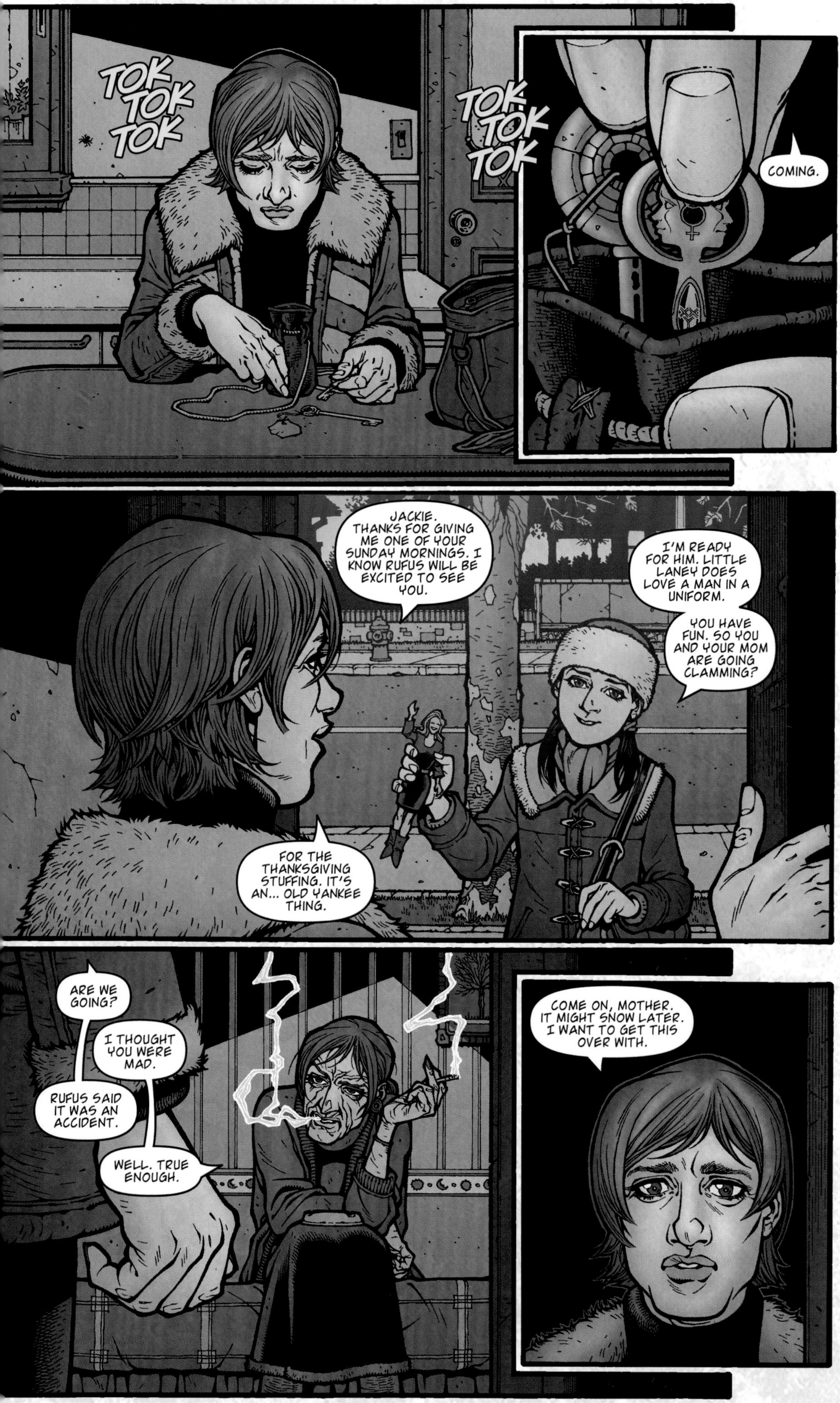
TOK TOK TOK
TOK TOK TOK
COMING.
JACKIE. THANKS FOR GIVING ME ONE OF YOUR SUNDAY MORNINGS. I KNOW RUFUS WILL BE EXCITED TO SEE YOU.
I'M READY FOR HIM. LITTLE LANEY DOES LOVE A MAN IN A UNIFORM.
YOU HAVE FUN. SO YOU AND YOUR MOM ARE GOING CLAMMING?
FOR THE THANKSGIVING STUFFING. IT'S AN... OLD YANKEE THING.
ARE WE GOING?
I THOUGHT YOU WERE MAD.
RUFUS SAID IT WAS AN ACCIDENT.
WELL. TRUE ENOUGH.
COME ON, MOTHER. IT MIGHT SNOW LATER. I WANT TO GET THIS OVER WITH.

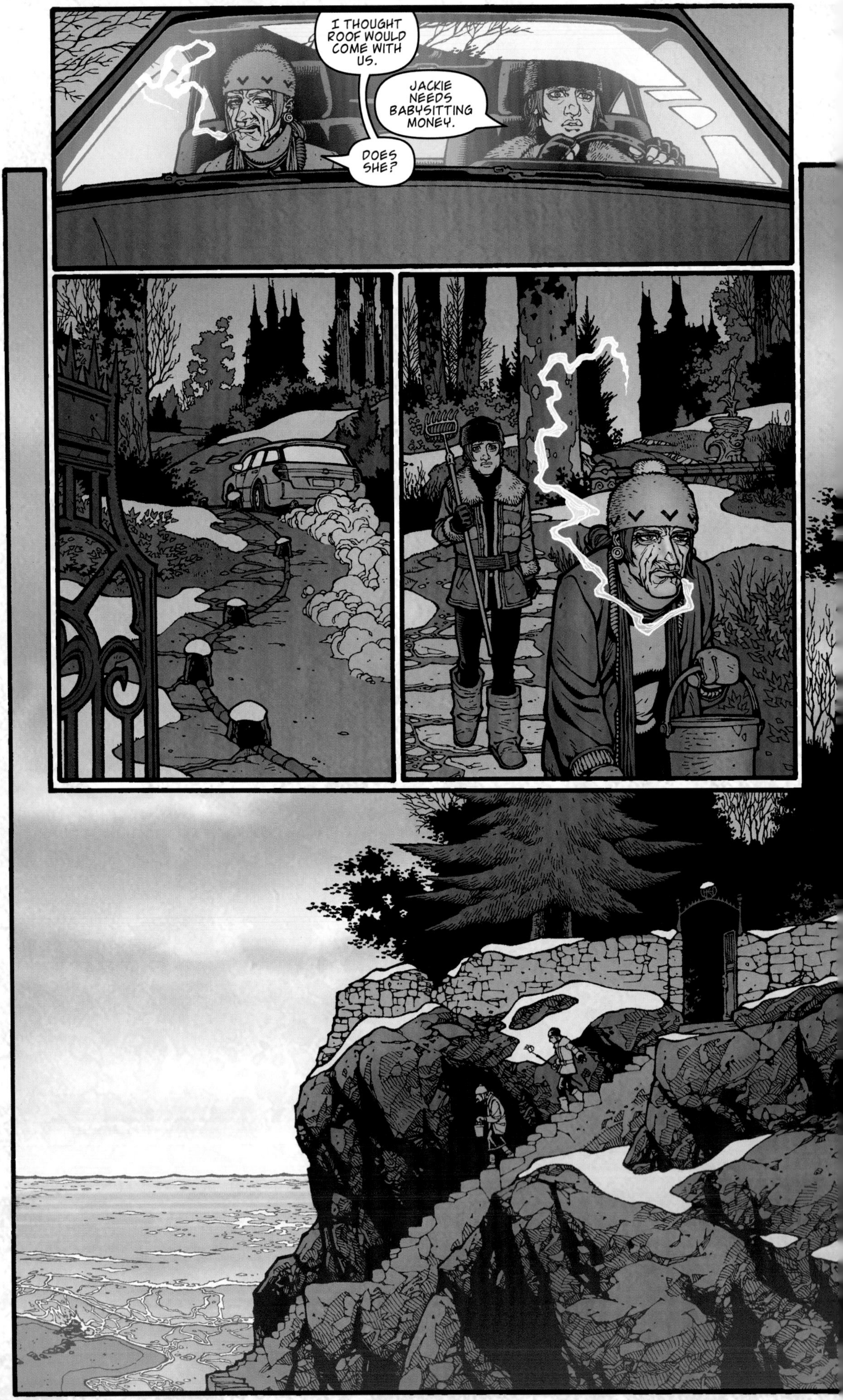
I THOUGHT ROOF WOULD COME WITH US.
JACKIE NEEDS BABYSITTING MONEY.
DOES SHE?

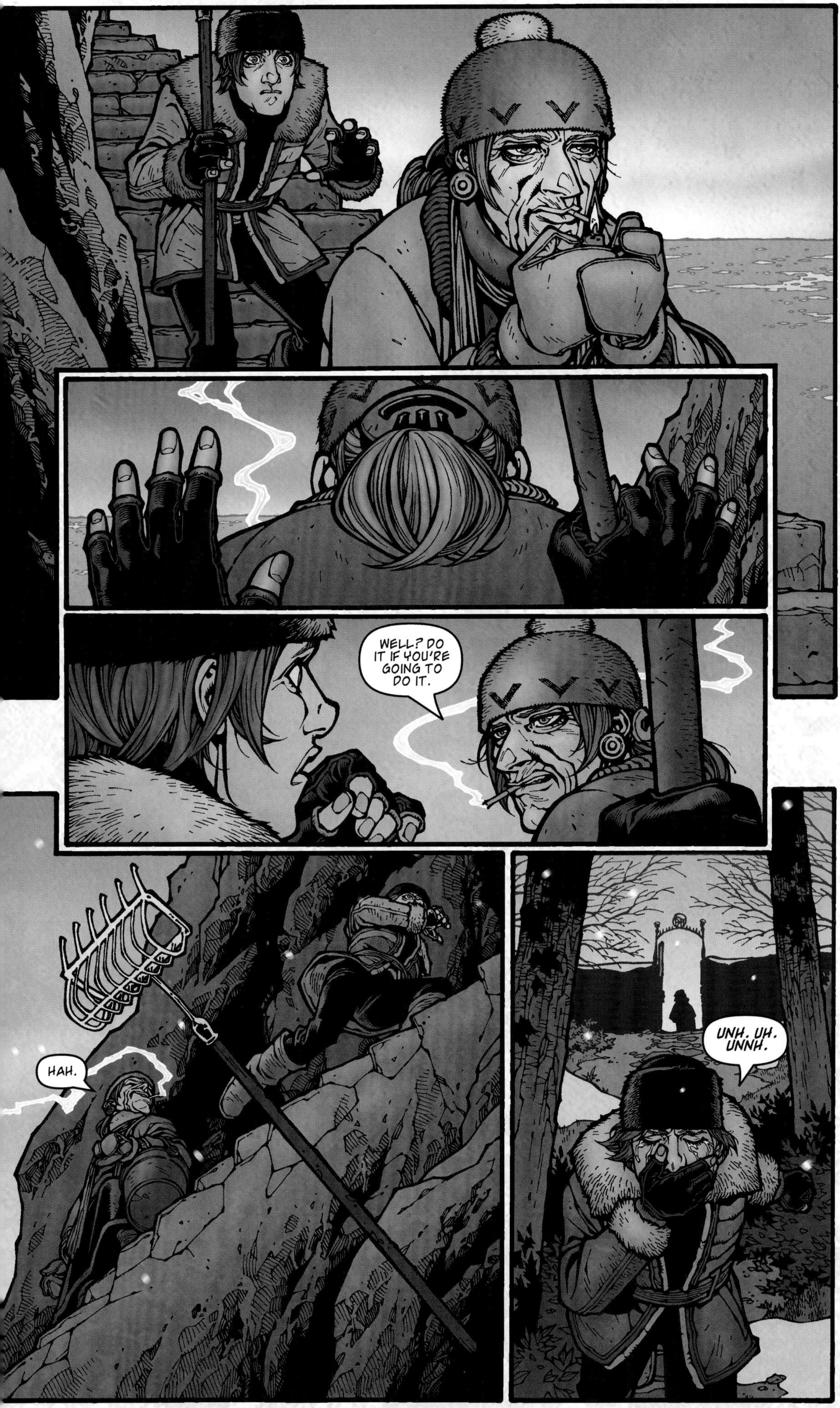
WELL? DO IT IF YOU'RE GOING TO DO IT.
HAH.
UNH. UH. UNNH.

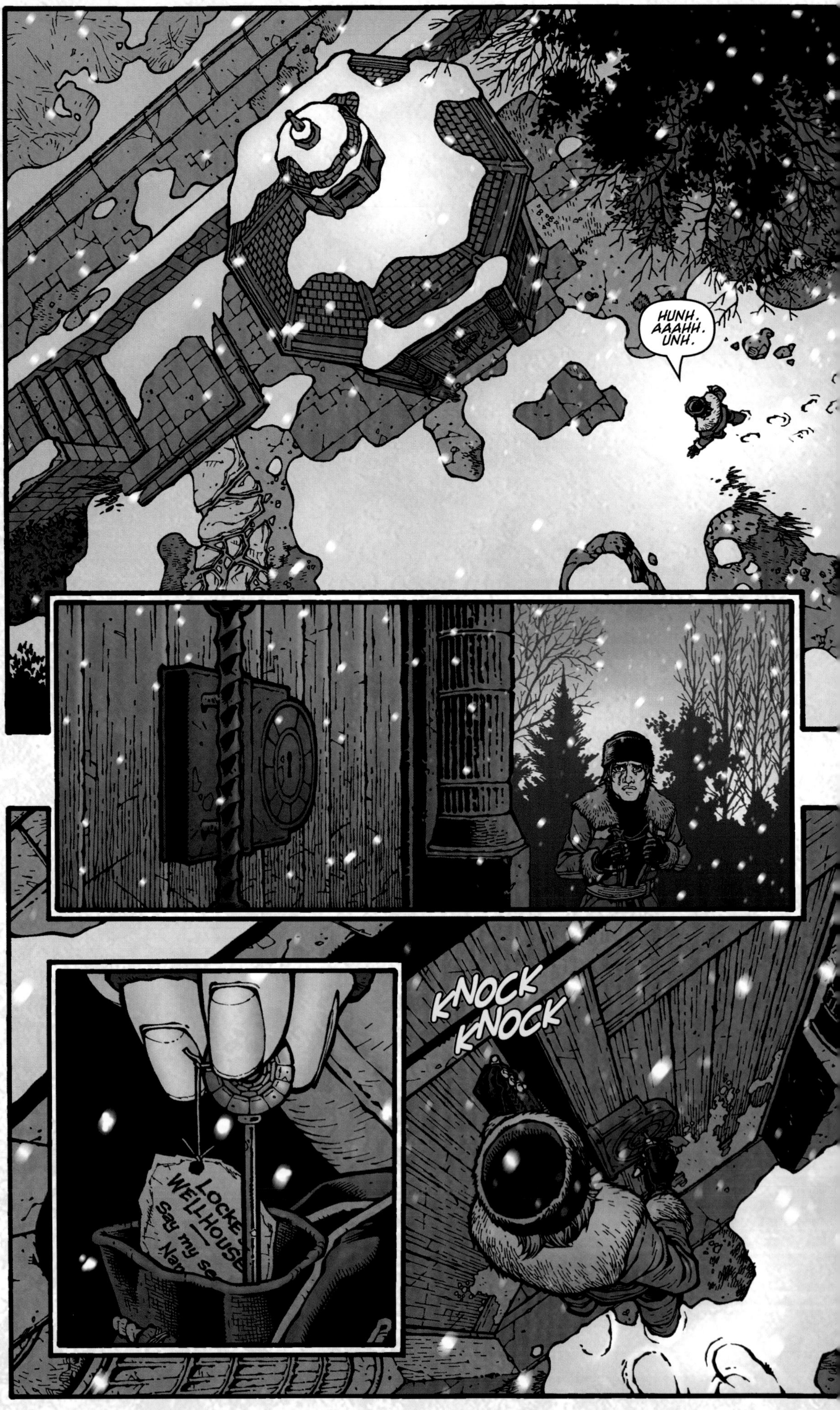
HUNH. AAAHH. UNH.
KNOCK KNOCK
LOCKE
WELLHOUSE
Say my

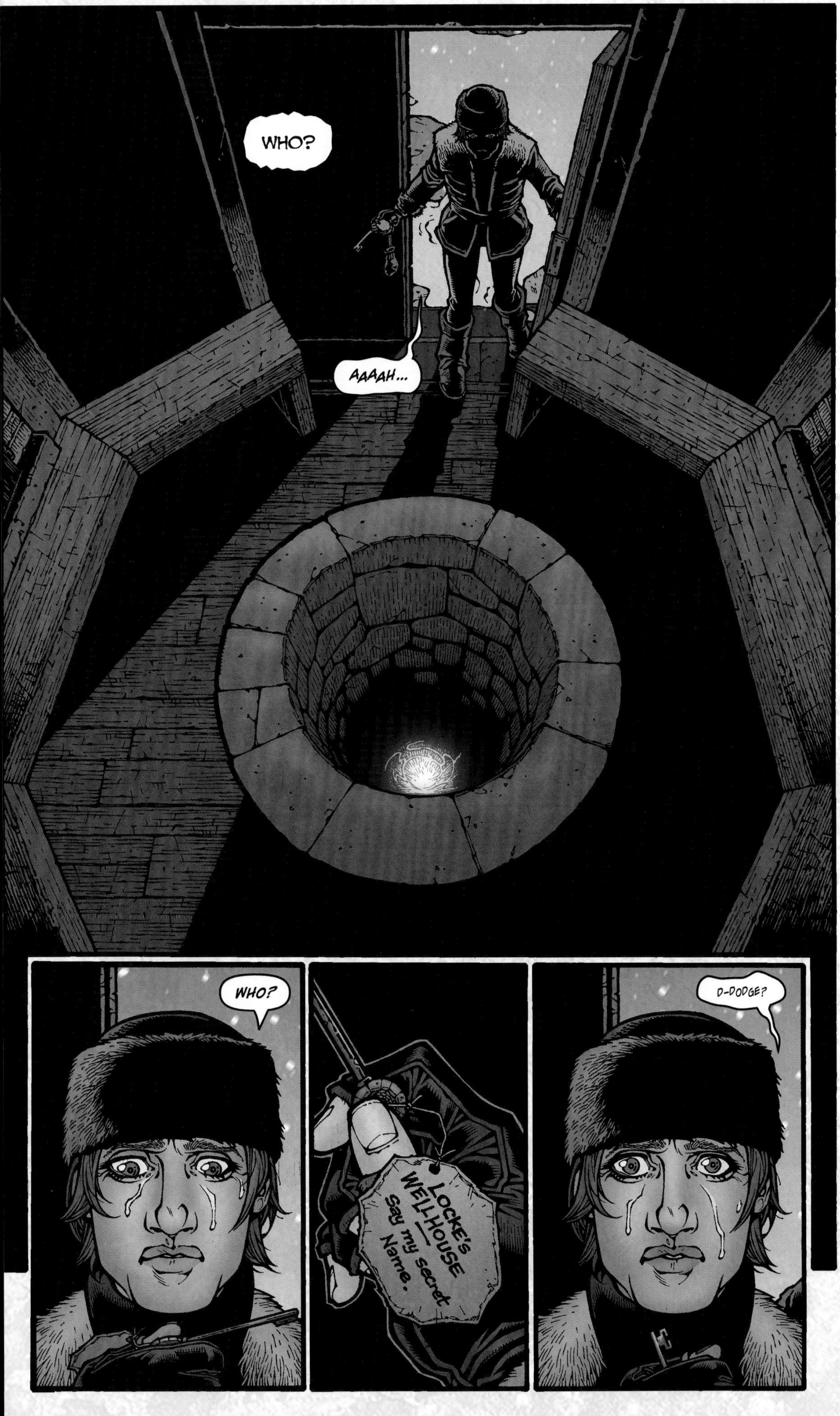
WHO?
AAAAH...
WHO?
LOCKE'S WELLHOUSE
Say my secret Name.
D-DODGE?

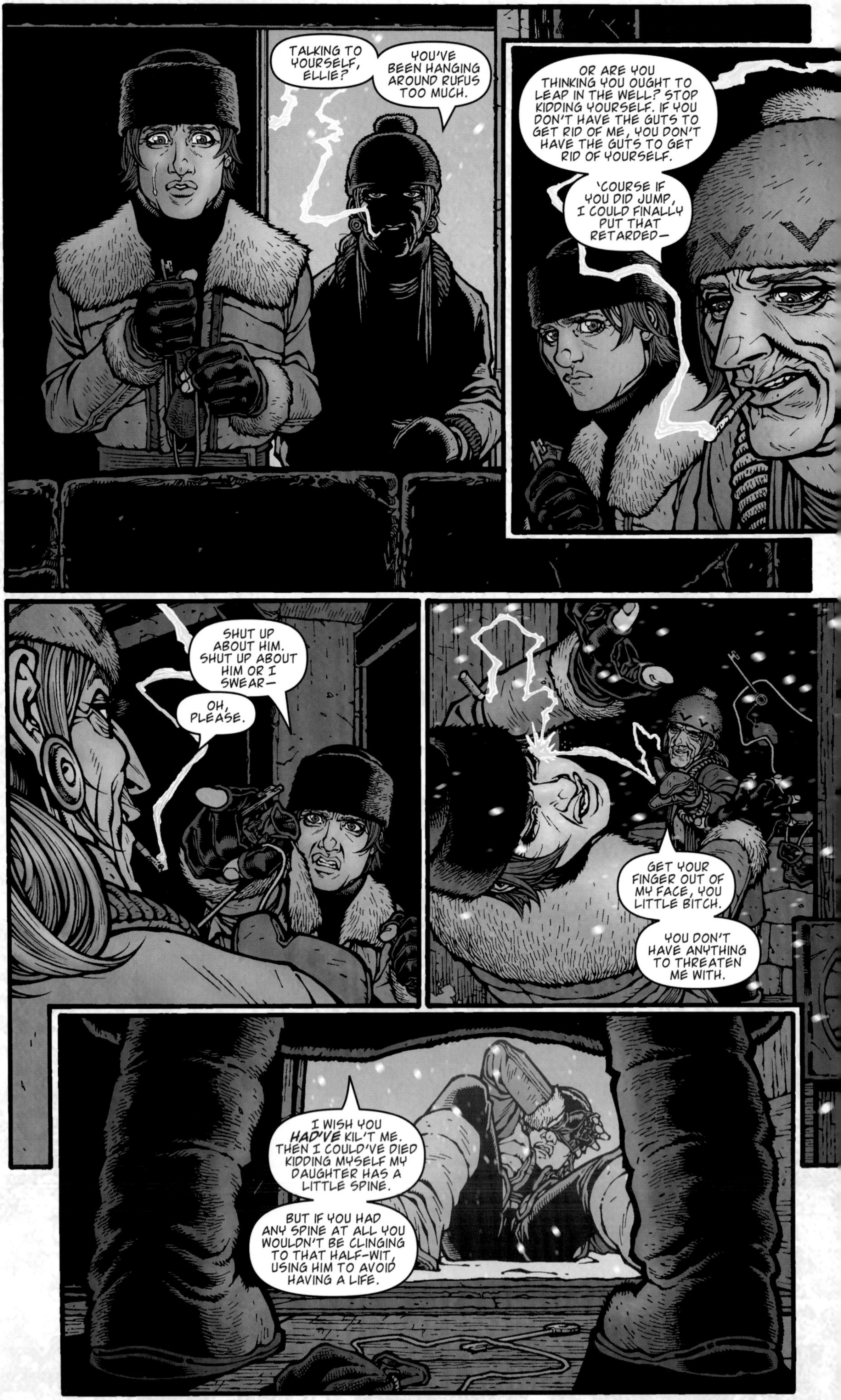

TALKING TO YOURSELF, ELLIE?
YOU'VE BEEN HANGING AROUND RUFUS TOO MUCH.
OR ARE YOU THINKING YOU OUGHT TO LEAP IN THE WELL? STOP KIDDING YOURSELF. IF YOU DON'T HAVE THE GUTS TO GET RID OF ME, YOU DON'T HAVE THE GUTS TO GET RID OF YOURSELF.
'COURSE IF YOU DID JUMP, I COULD FINALLY PUT THAT RETARDED—
SHUT UP ABOUT HIM. SHUT UP ABOUT HIM OR I SWEAR—
OH, PLEASE.
GET YOUR FINGER OUT OF MY FACE, YOU LITTLE BITCH.
YOU DON'T HAVE ANYTHING TO THREATEN ME WITH.
I WISH YOU *HAD'VE* KIL'T ME. THEN I COULD'VE DIED KIDDING MYSELF MY DAUGHTER HAS A LITTLE SPINE.
BUT IF YOU HAD ANY SPINE AT ALL YOU WOULDN'T BE CLINGING TO THAT HALF-WIT, USING HIM TO AVOID HAVING A LIFE.

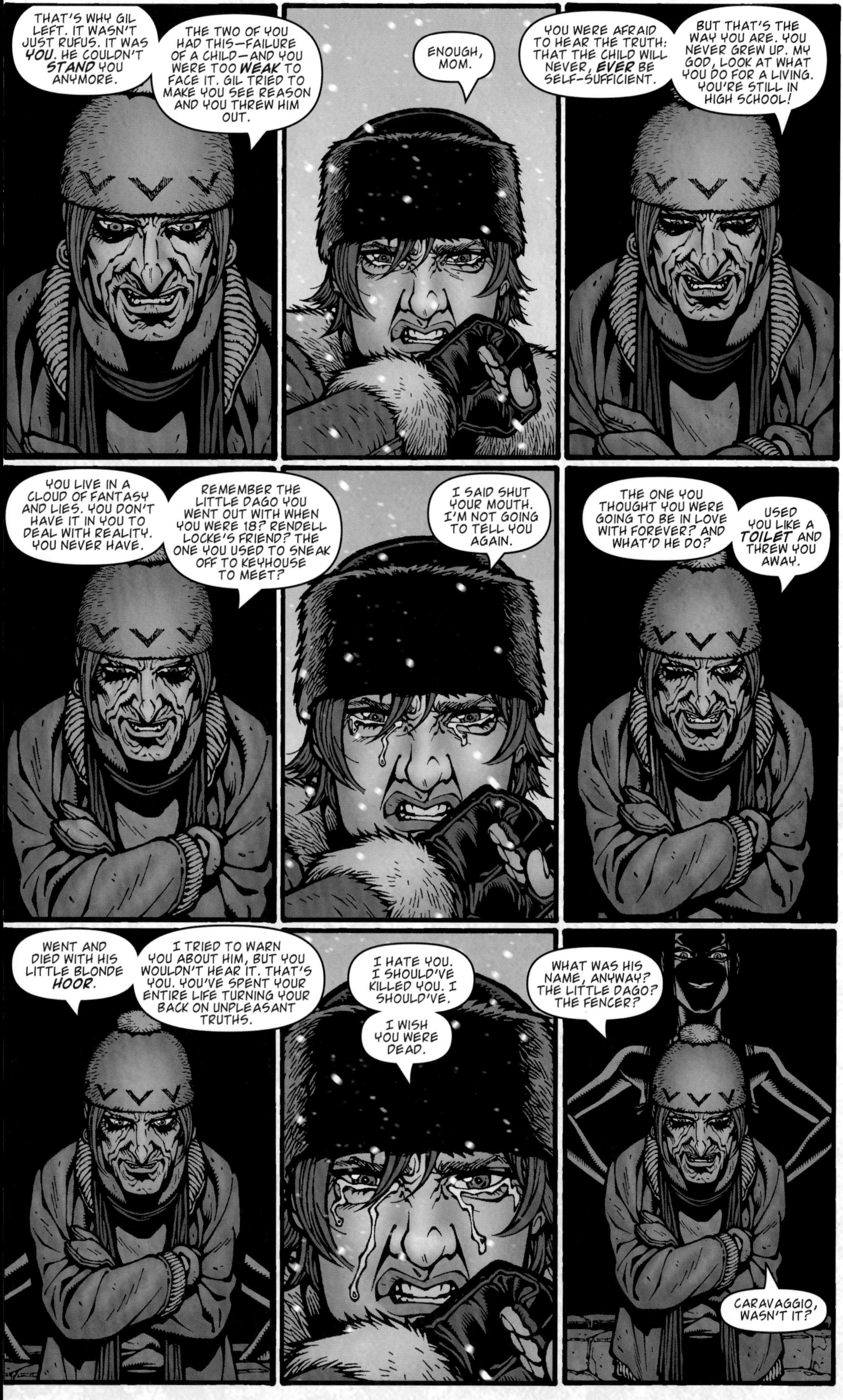
THAT'S WHY GIL LEFT. IT WASN'T JUST RUFUS. IT WAS YOU. HE COULDN'T STAND YOU ANYMORE.
THE TWO OF YOU HAD THIS—FAILURE OF A CHILD—AND YOU WERE TOO WEAK TO FACE IT. GIL TRIED TO MAKE YOU SEE REASON AND YOU THREW HIM OUT.
ENOUGH, MOM.
YOU WERE AFRAID TO HEAR THE TRUTH: THAT THE CHILD WILL NEVER, EVER BE SELF-SUFFICIENT.
BUT THAT'S THE WAY YOU ARE. YOU NEVER GREW UP. MY GOD, LOOK AT WHAT YOU DO FOR A LIVING. YOU'RE STILL IN HIGH SCHOOL!
YOU LIVE IN A CLOUD OF FANTASY AND LIES. YOU DON'T HAVE IT IN YOU TO DEAL WITH REALITY. YOU NEVER HAVE.
REMEMBER THE LITTLE DAGO YOU WENT OUT WITH WHEN YOU WERE 18? RENDELL LOCKE'S FRIEND? THE ONE YOU USED TO SNEAK OFF TO KEYHOUSE TO MEET?
I SAID SHUT YOUR MOUTH. I'M NOT GOING TO TELL YOU AGAIN.
THE ONE YOU THOUGHT YOU WERE GOING TO BE IN LOVE WITH FOREVER? AND WHAT'D HE DO?
USED YOU LIKE A TOILET AND THREW YOU AWAY.
WENT AND DIED WITH HIS LITTLE BLONDE HOOR.
I TRIED TO WARN YOU ABOUT HIM, BUT YOU WOULDN'T HEAR IT. THAT'S YOU. YOU'VE SPENT YOUR ENTIRE LIFE TURNING YOUR BACK ON UNPLEASANT TRUTHS.
I HATE YOU. I SHOULD'VE KILLED YOU. I SHOULD'VE.
I WISH YOU WERE DEAD.
WHAT WAS HIS NAME, ANYWAY? THE LITTLE DAGO? THE FENCER?
CARAVAGGIO, WASN'T IT?

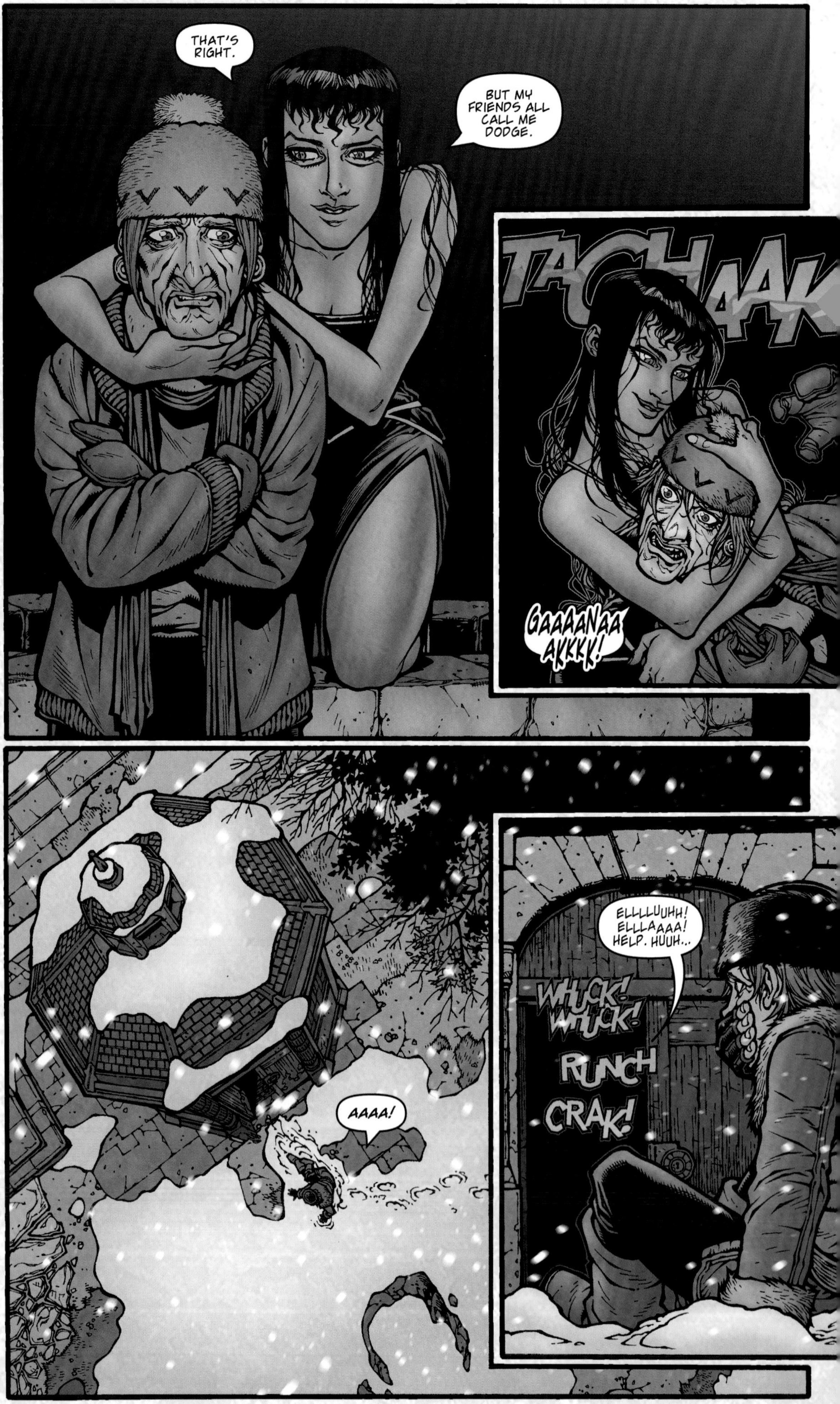
THAT'S RIGHT.
BUT MY FRIENDS ALL CALL ME DODGE.
TACHAAK
GAAAANAA AKKKK!
AAAA!
ELLLLUUHH! ELLLAAAA! HELP. HUUH...
WHUCK! WHUCK!
RUNCH
CRAK!

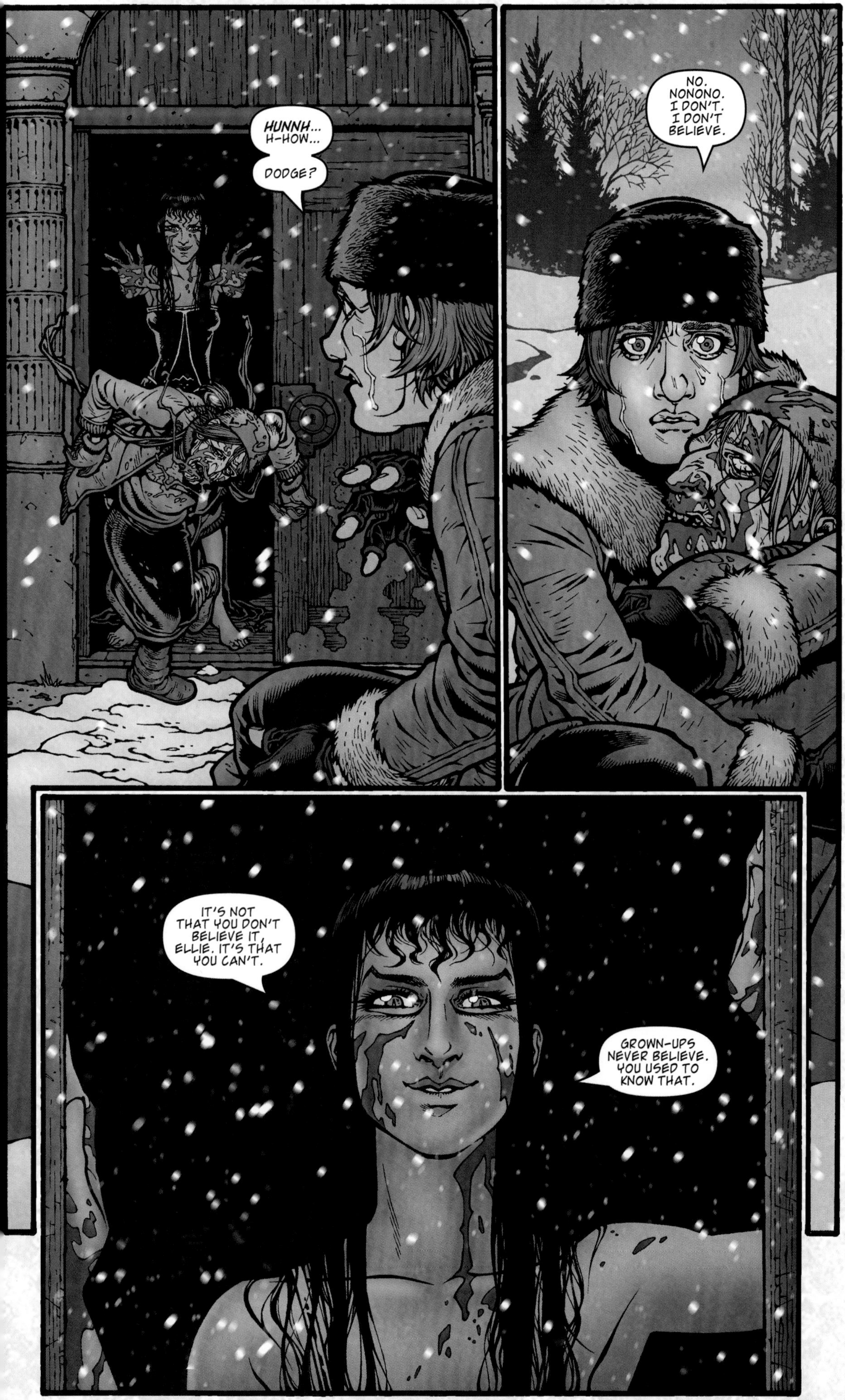
HUNNH... H-HOW...
DODGE?
NO. NONONO. I DON'T. I DON'T BELIEVE.
IT'S NOT THAT YOU DON'T BELIEVE IT, ELLIE. IT'S THAT YOU CAN'T.
GROWN-UPS NEVER BELIEVE. YOU USED TO KNOW THAT.

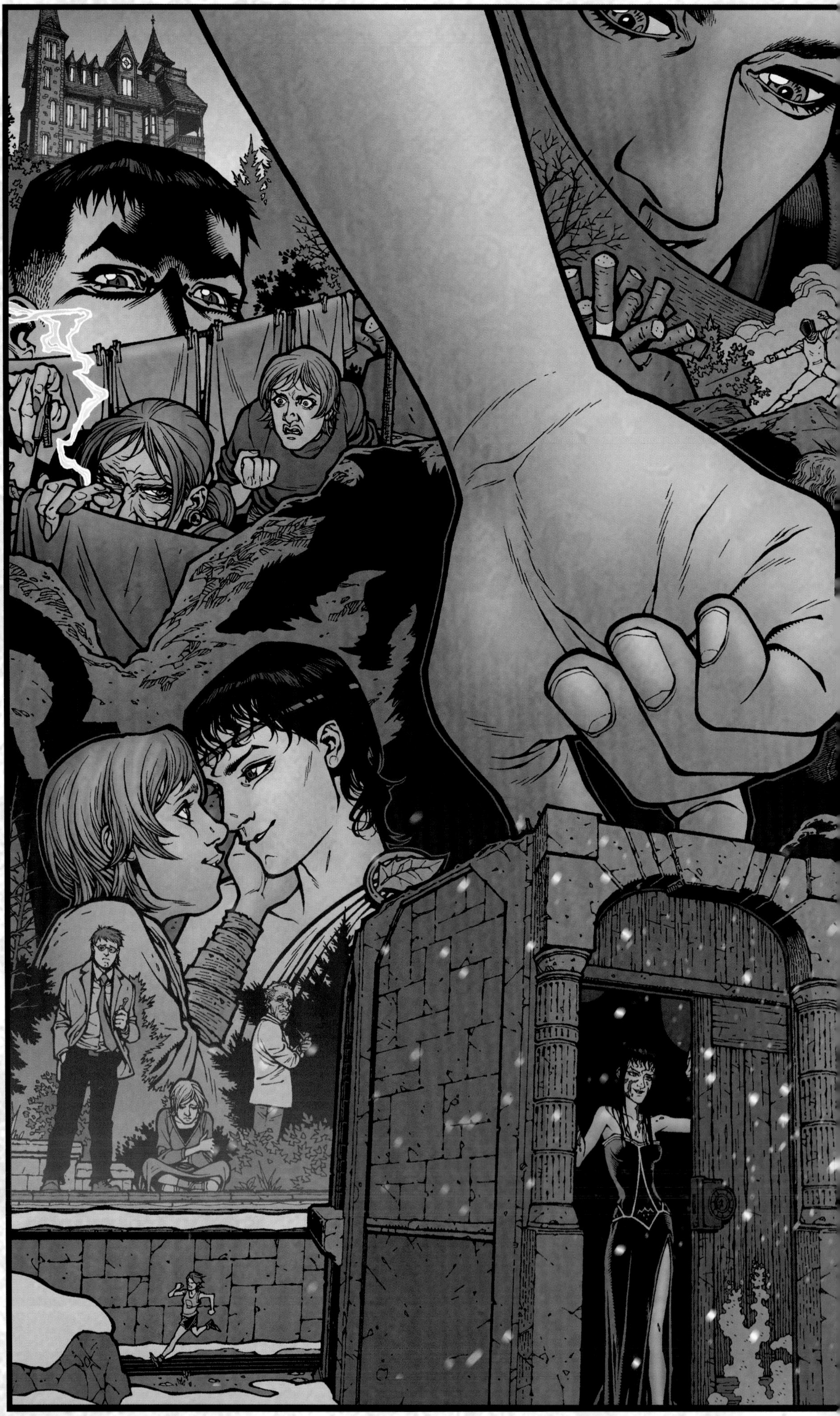

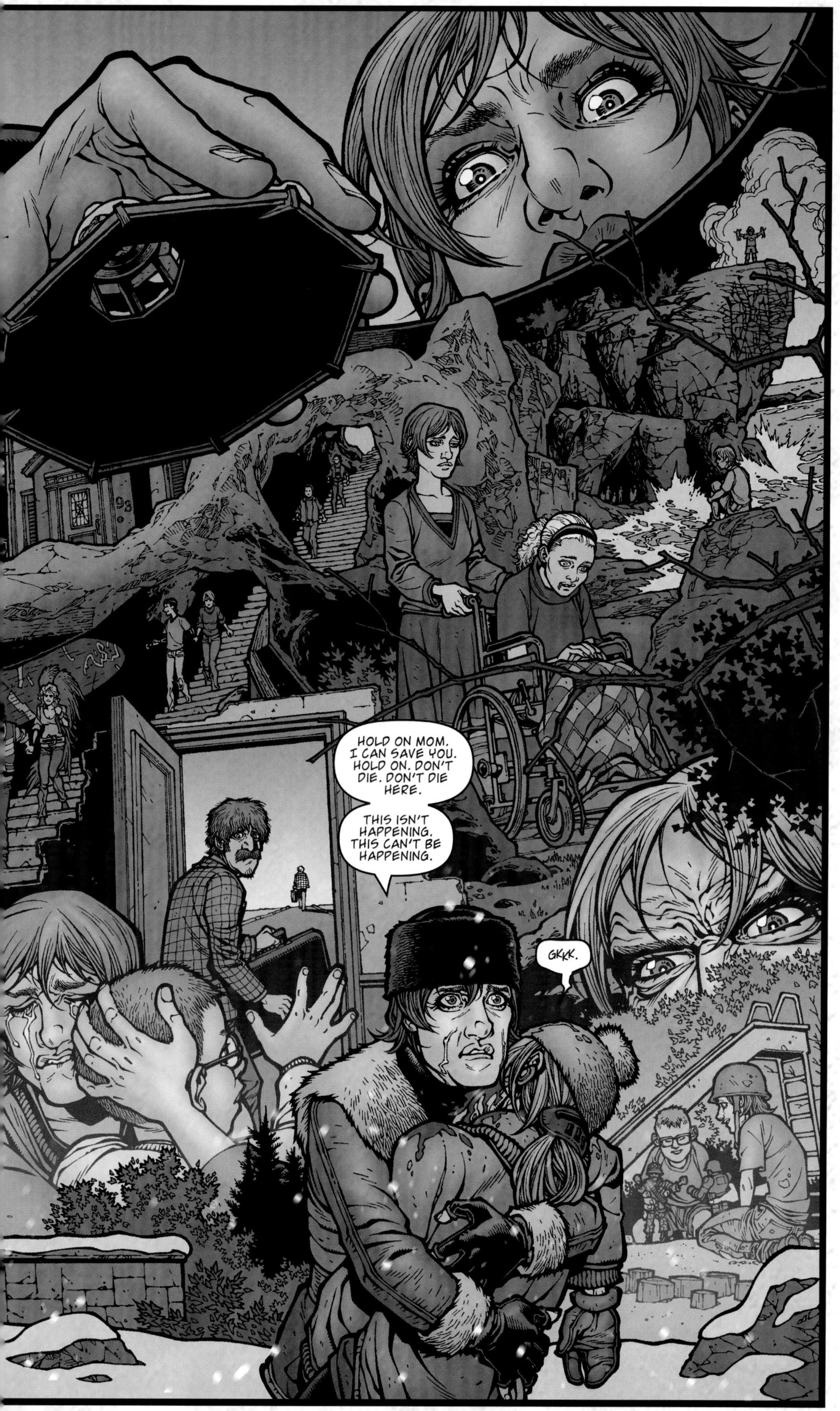
HOLD ON MOM. I CAN SAVE YOU. HOLD ON. DON'T DIE. DON'T DIE HERE.
THIS ISN'T HAPPENING. THIS CAN'T BE HAPPENING.
GKKK.

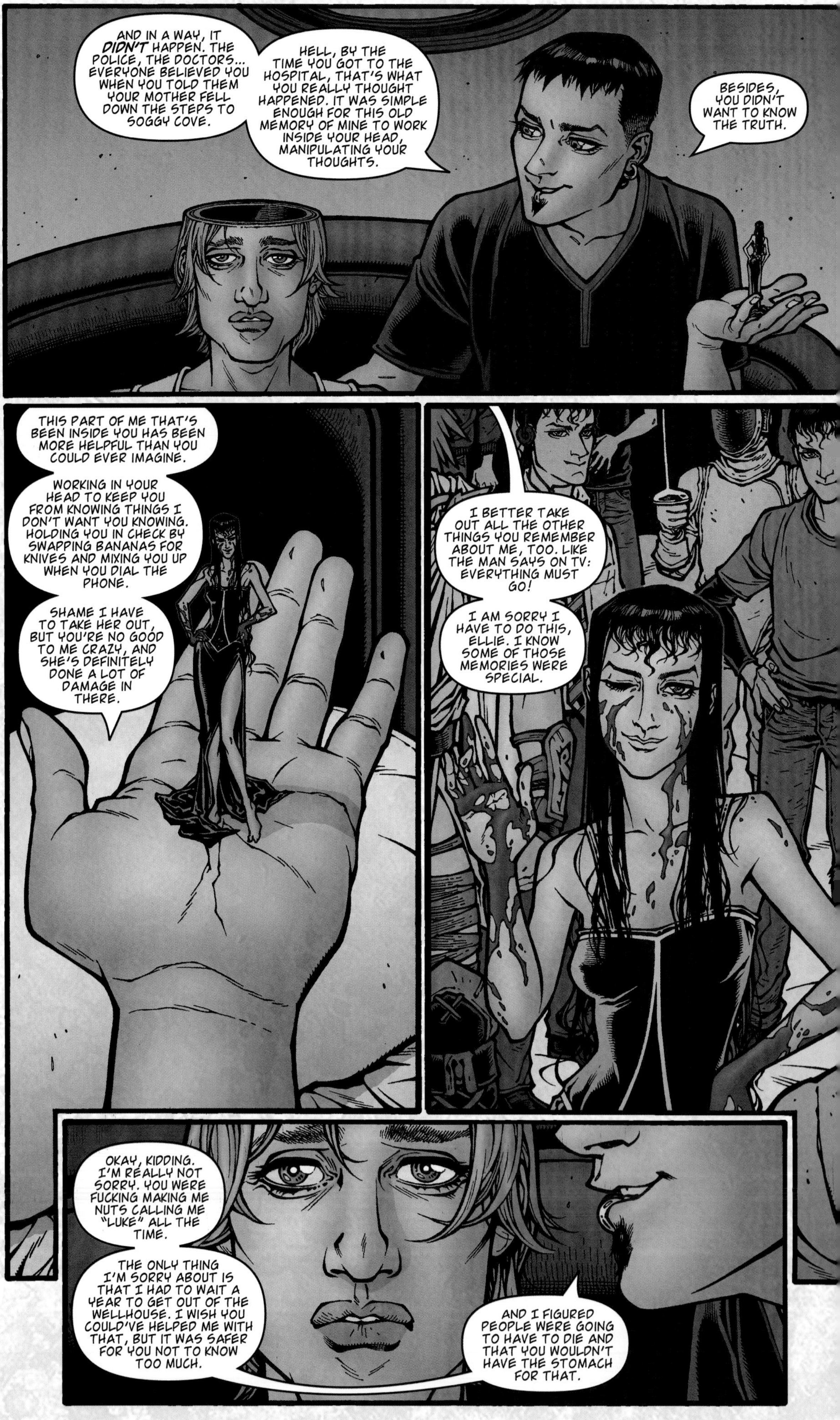
AND IN A WAY, IT DIDN'T HAPPEN. THE POLICE, THE DOCTORS... EVERYONE BELIEVED YOU WHEN YOU TOLD THEM YOUR MOTHER FELL DOWN THE STEPS TO SOGGY COVE.
HELL, BY THE TIME YOU GOT TO THE HOSPITAL, THAT'S WHAT YOU REALLY THOUGHT HAPPENED. IT WAS SIMPLE ENOUGH FOR THIS OLD MEMORY OF MINE TO WORK INSIDE YOUR HEAD, MANIPULATING YOUR THOUGHTS.
BESIDES, YOU DIDN'T WANT TO KNOW THE TRUTH.
THIS PART OF ME THAT'S BEEN INSIDE YOU HAS BEEN MORE HELPFUL THAN YOU COULD EVER IMAGINE.
WORKING IN YOUR HEAD TO KEEP YOU FROM KNOWING THINGS I DON'T WANT YOU KNOWING. HOLDING YOU IN CHECK BY SWAPPING BANANAS FOR KNIVES AND MIXING YOU UP WHEN YOU DIAL THE PHONE.
SHAME I HAVE TO TAKE HER OUT, BUT YOU'RE NO GOOD TO ME CRAZY, AND SHE'S DEFINITELY DONE A LOT OF DAMAGE IN THERE.
I BETTER TAKE OUT ALL THE OTHER THINGS YOU REMEMBER ABOUT ME, TOO. LIKE THE MAN SAYS ON TV: EVERYTHING MUST GO!
I AM SORRY I HAVE TO DO THIS, ELLIE. I KNOW SOME OF THOSE MEMORIES WERE SPECIAL.
OKAY, KIDDING. I'M REALLY NOT SORRY. YOU WERE FUCKING MAKING ME NUTS CALLING ME "LUKE" ALL THE TIME.
THE ONLY THING I'M SORRY ABOUT IS THAT I HAD TO WAIT A YEAR TO GET OUT OF THE WELLHOUSE. I WISH YOU COULD'VE HELPED ME WITH THAT, BUT IT WAS SAFER FOR YOU NOT TO KNOW TOO MUCH.
AND I FIGURED PEOPLE WERE GOING TO HAVE TO DIE AND THAT YOU WOULDN'T HAVE THE STOMACH FOR THAT.

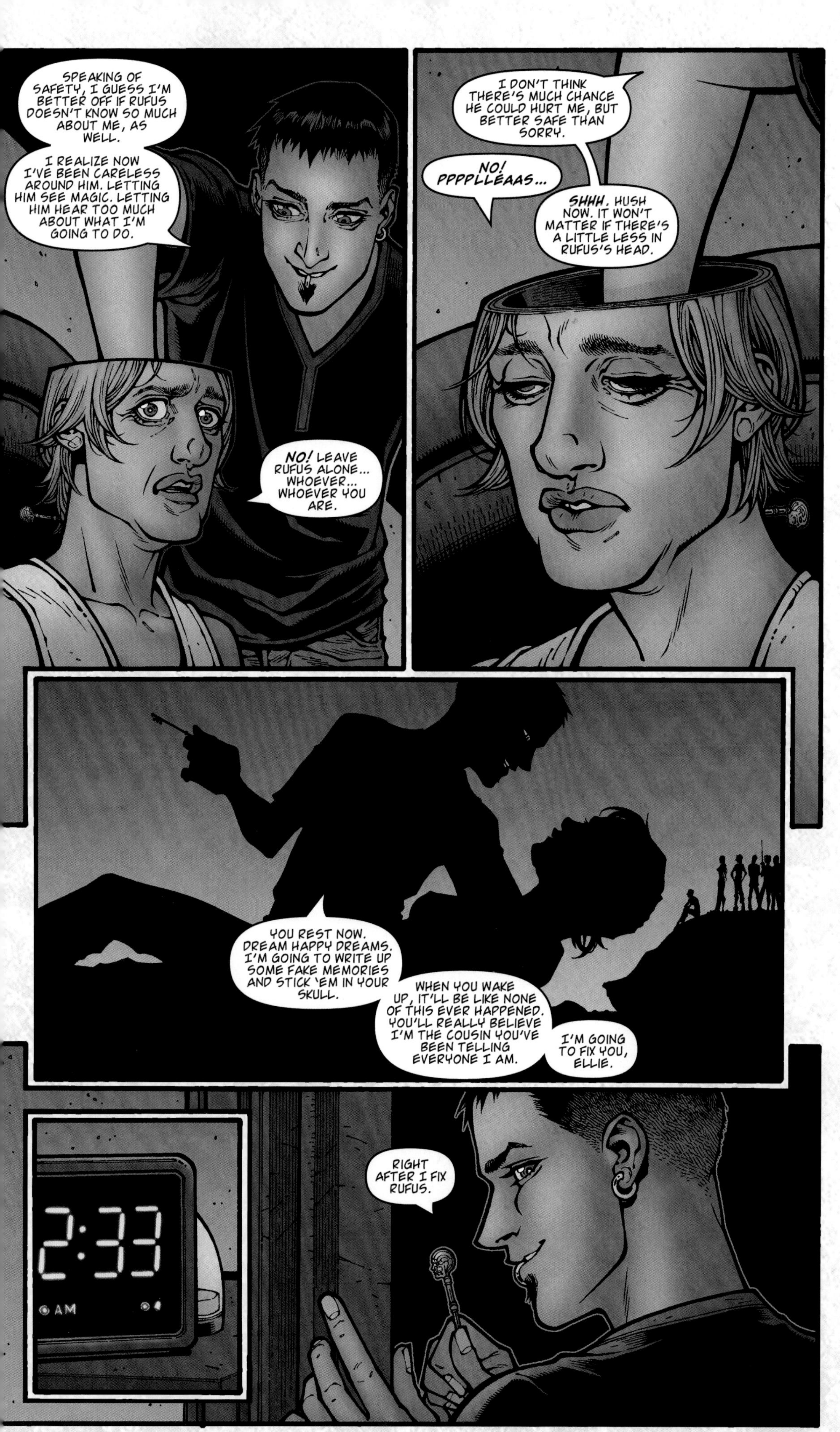
SPEAKING OF SAFETY, I GUESS I'M BETTER OFF IF RUFUS DOESN'T KNOW SO MUCH ABOUT ME, AS WELL.
I REALIZE NOW I'VE BEEN CARELESS AROUND HIM. LETTING HIM SEE MAGIC. LETTING HIM HEAR TOO MUCH ABOUT WHAT I'M GOING TO DO.
NO! LEAVE RUFUS ALONE... WHOEVER... WHOEVER YOU ARE.
I DON'T THINK THERE'S MUCH CHANCE HE COULD HURT ME, BUT BETTER SAFE THAN SORRY.
NO! PPPPLLEAAS...
SHHH. HUSH NOW. IT WON'T MATTER IF THERE'S A LITTLE LESS IN RUFUS'S HEAD.
YOU REST NOW. DREAM HAPPY DREAMS. I'M GOING TO WRITE UP SOME FAKE MEMORIES AND STICK 'EM IN YOUR SKULL.
WHEN YOU WAKE UP, IT'LL BE LIKE NONE OF THIS EVER HAPPENED. YOU'LL REALLY BELIEVE I'M THE COUSIN YOU'VE BEEN TELLING EVERYONE I AM.
I'M GOING TO FIX YOU, ELLIE.
2:33
AM
RIGHT AFTER I FIX RUFUS.

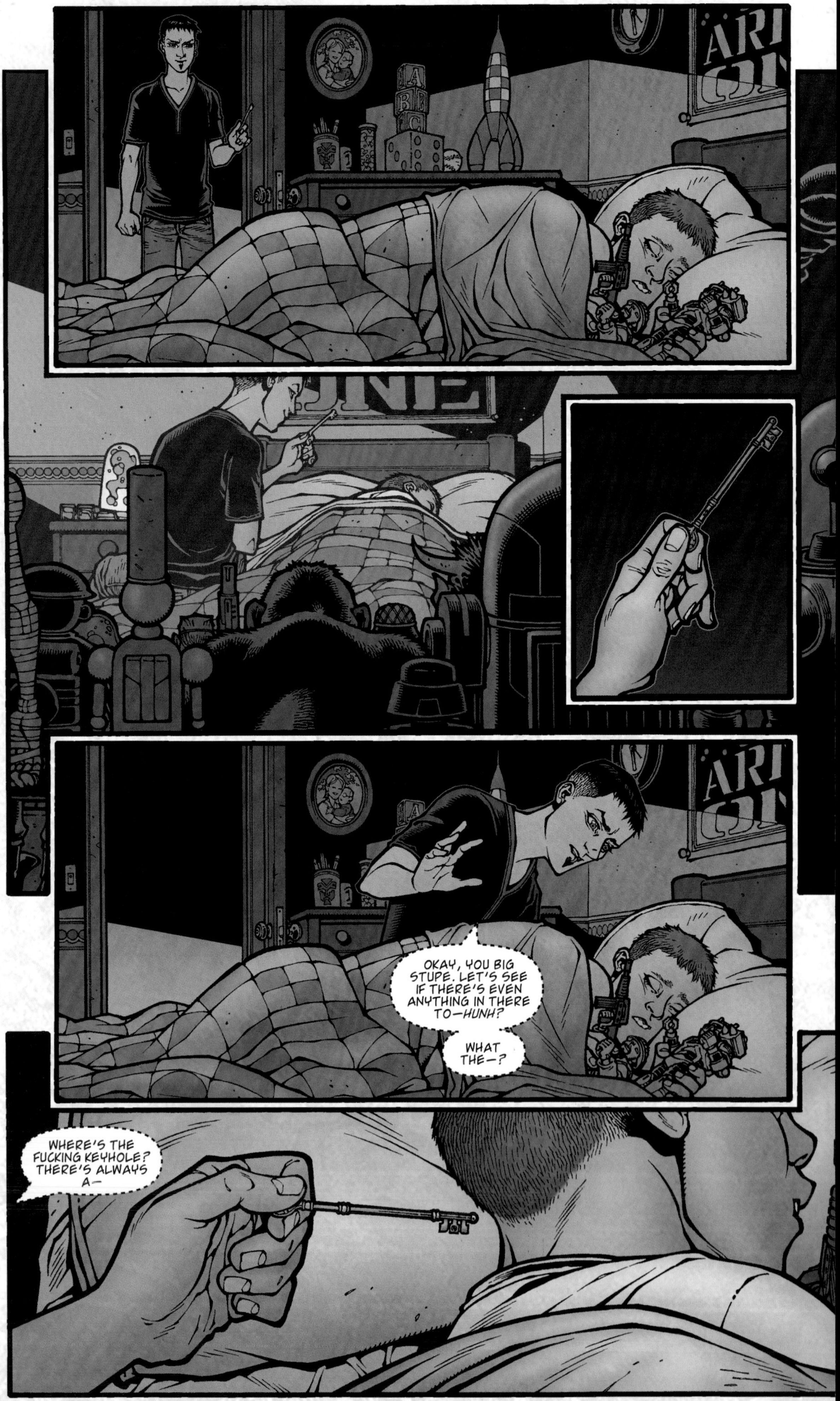

OKAY, YOU BIG STUPE. LET'S SEE IF THERE'S EVEN ANYTHING IN THERE TO—*HUNH?*
WHAT THE—?
WHERE'S THE FUCKING KEYHOLE? THERE'S ALWAYS A—

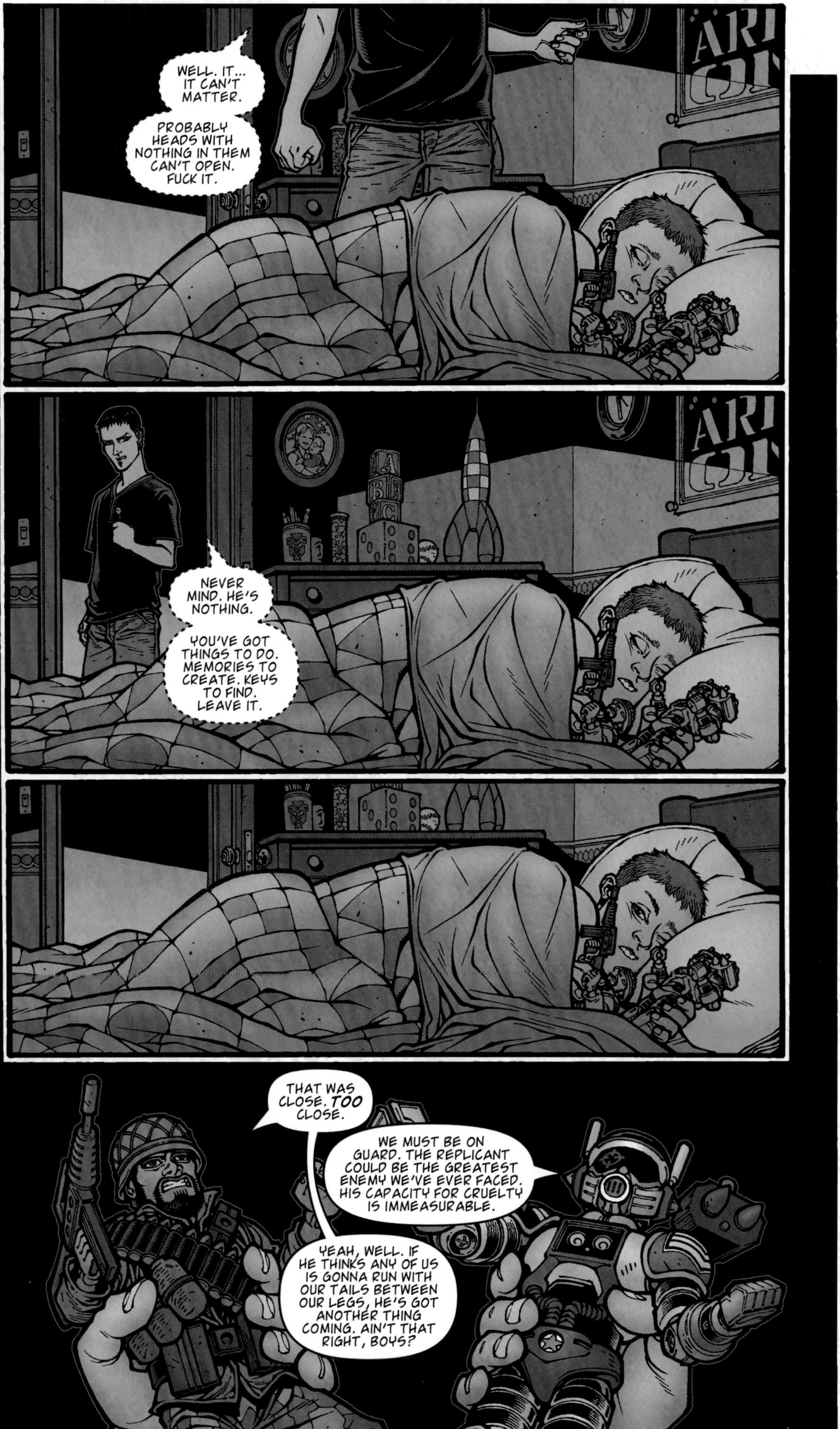
WELL. IT... IT CAN'T MATTER.
PROBABLY HEADS WITH NOTHING IN THEM CAN'T OPEN. FUCK IT.
NEVER MIND. HE'S NOTHING.
YOU'VE GOT THINGS TO DO. MEMORIES TO CREATE. KEYS TO FIND. LEAVE IT.
THAT WAS CLOSE. *TOO* CLOSE.
WE MUST BE ON GUARD. THE REPLICANT COULD BE THE GREATEST ENEMY WE'VE EVER FACED. HIS CAPACITY FOR CRUELTY IS IMMEASURABLE.
YEAH, WELL. IF HE THINKS ANY OF US IS GONNA RUN WITH OUR TAILS BETWEEN OUR LEGS, HE'S GOT ANOTHER THING COMING. AIN'T THAT RIGHT, BOYS?

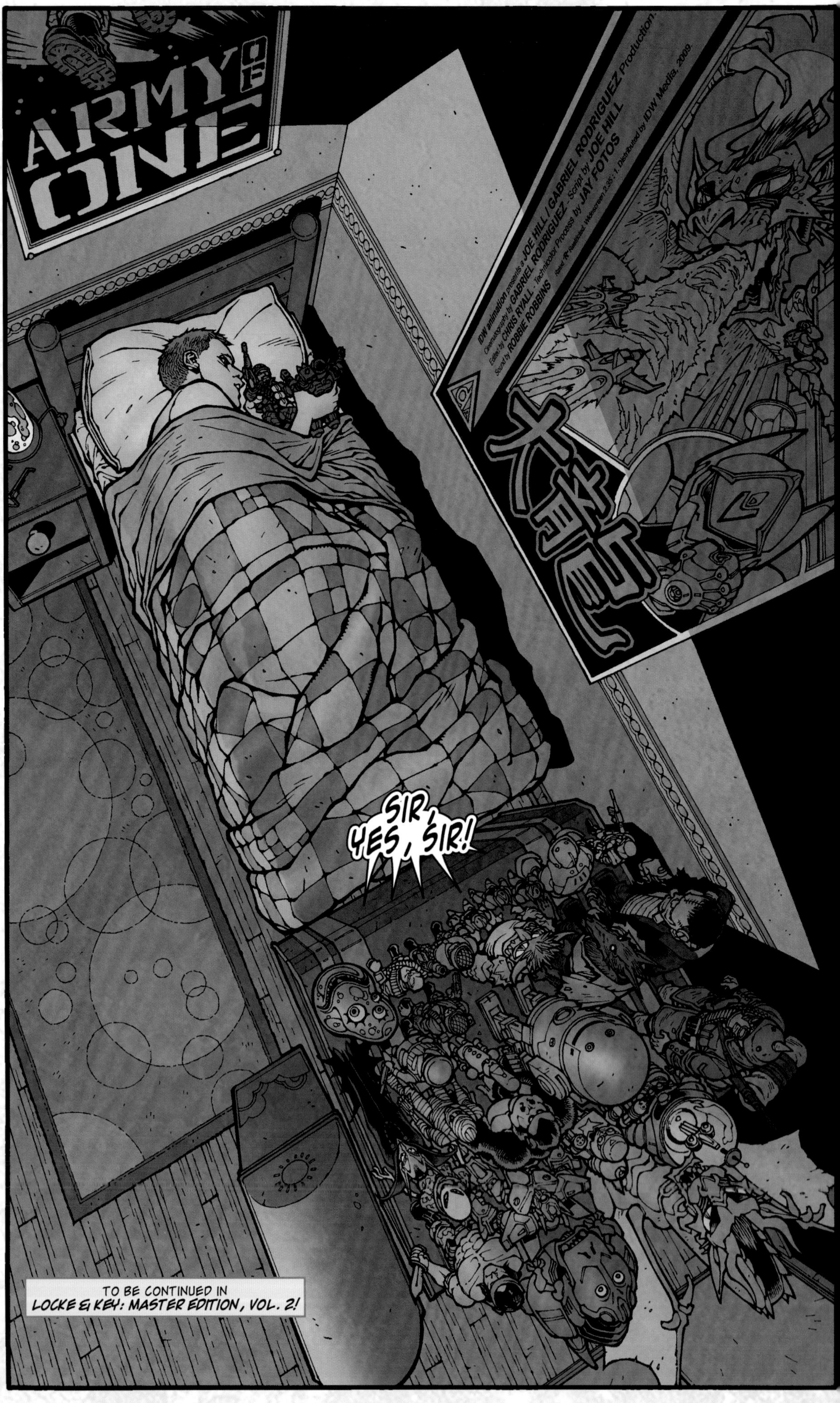
ARMY OF ONE
IDW animation presents a JOE HILL / GABRIEL RODRIGUEZ Production.
Cinematography by GABRIEL RODRIGUEZ · Script by JOE HILL
Edited by CHRIS RYALL · Technicolor Process by JAY FOTOS
Sound by ROBBIE ROBBINS
Rated "R" Restricted. Widescreen 2.35 : 1. Distributed by IDW Media, 2009.
SIR, YES, SIR!
TO BE CONTINUED IN
LOCKE & KEY: MASTER EDITION, VOL. 2!

LOCKE & KEY
- VOLUME ONE -

Editor - **Chris RYALL**
Master Edition Editor - **Justin EISINGER**
Letterer - **Robbie ROBBINS**
Colors - **Jay FOTOS**
Storytellers - **Joe HILL** & **Gabriel RODRÍGUEZ**

Locke & Key created by
JOE HILL & GABRIEL RODRÍGUEZ

aNYWHeRe KeY

us'd the key to anyplaice againe, to return to Boston, & gaither intelaigents for Crais. Tis an act of terryble wychcraift, but better I do it, than my sister, who is obssaissed with REVENGING herself upon the RED-COATS, for thair violence agin our faither & brother & belov'd maither. Aye, my dredd of beeing called to acconnt someday by SATAN HIMSELF is a trifling concern when maiched with my desyre to rid the worlde of the devylls who taik the King's Coyne to do raip & murdur...

GHoST KeY

onlee in occaisonull daith do I find peece now, for with the bode caste aisyde, it is possibull for one to know his own ETERNAIL SOULE. My spairt cannot leeve the grounds of Keyhowse, but heyre I walke laik an aingel! I aim everywhare and nowhare at once, from the tall's towair, to the deepst caves. It is hard to dreem thair could be any dore more terryble or wondairfulle than that wych dyvydes deth from lyfe, yet my expairances at the thraishold of the black dore have teach'd me thair are worse things than to dyye...

GeNDeR KeY

my sister - or should I now say my brother! - fights the shadow war with Crais in the streets of Boston whilst I wait at home, like a helpless maiden, praying to the ALLMAIGHTY! for her safe return. When first I fashin'd the key, I imagained she maight trainsform to a boy to protect her, if necessaire, from the unsavorie lusts of ENGLISHMEN should the King's foot-soldiers return to Lovecraft to abuse God fairing womain. Never did I think she wouldst WILLENGLY caist off the wardrobe of her femininitie for this ruggaid liberation among men...

HeaD KeY

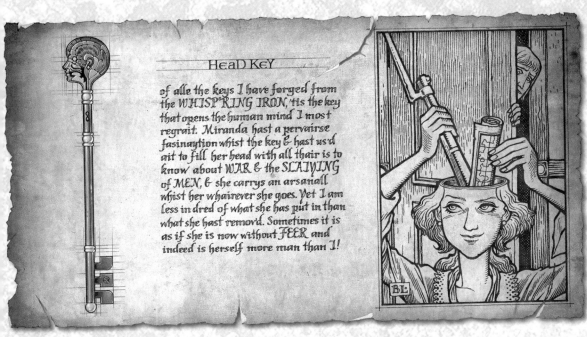

of alle the keys I have forged from the WHISP'RING IRON, 'tis the key that opens the human mind I most regrait. Miranda hast a pervairse fasinaytion whist the key & hast us'd ait to fill her head with all thair is to know about WAR & the SLAIYING of MEN, & she carrys an arsanall whist her whairever she goes. Yet I am less in dred of what she has put in than what she hast remov'd. Sometimes it is as if she is now without FEER and indeed is herself more man than I!

eCHo KeY

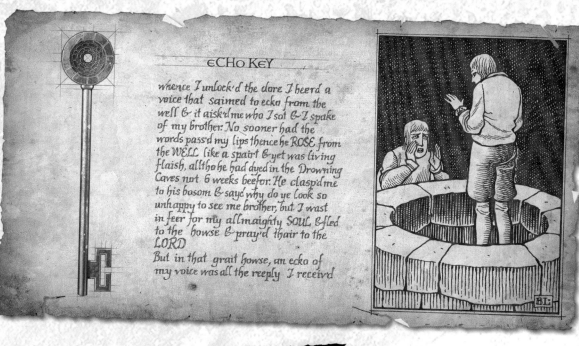

whence I unlock'd the dore I heerd a voice that saimed to ecko from the well & it aisk'd me who I sot & I spake of my brother. No sooner had the words pass'd my lips thence he ROSE from the WELL like a spairt & yet was living flaish, alltho he had dyed in the Drowning Caves not 6 weeks beefor. He clasp'd me to his bosom & sayd why do ye look so unhappy to see me brother, but I wast in feer for my allmaighty SOUL & fled to the howse & pray'd thair to the LORD

But in that grait howse, an ecko of my voice was all the reeply I receiv'd

ΩMeGa KeY

[text obscured by burn damage]

... er dead & ...
... ore open agains ...
... the tim ... sur'd ...
in our ... ...
& I resolved to ... them to ...
hazzarded such a lock wood ...
song I work'd in a fever ...
till finallie t'was cast & ...
oh how I feer'd! My he ...
in the gathr'd dai ...
straiked ou ...
held the dor ...
beig'd G ...
Gena ...
hol ...

THE KNOWN KEYS

Excerpts from the diary of Benjamin Pierce Locke (1757-1799)

LOCKE & KEY

- KEYHOUSE GALLERY -

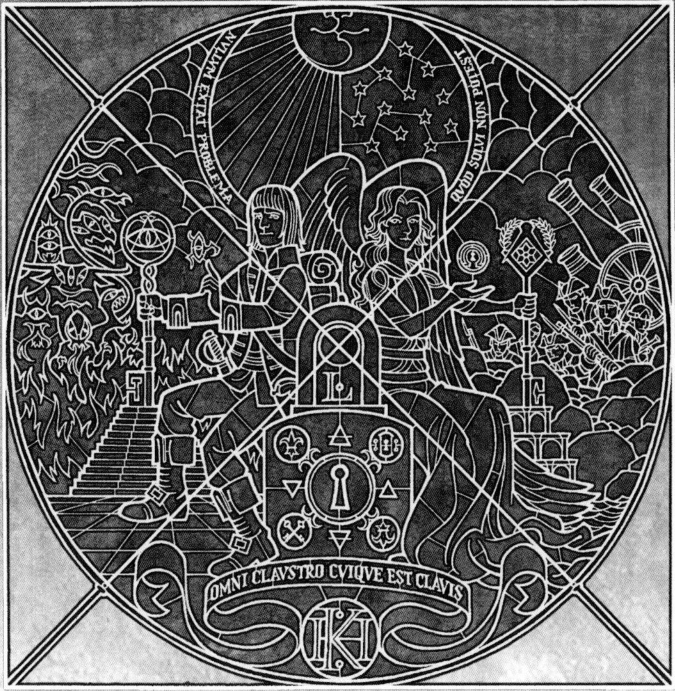
NVLLVM EXTAT PROBLEMA
QVOD SOLVI NON POTEST
OMNI CLAVSTRO CVIQVE EST CLAVIS

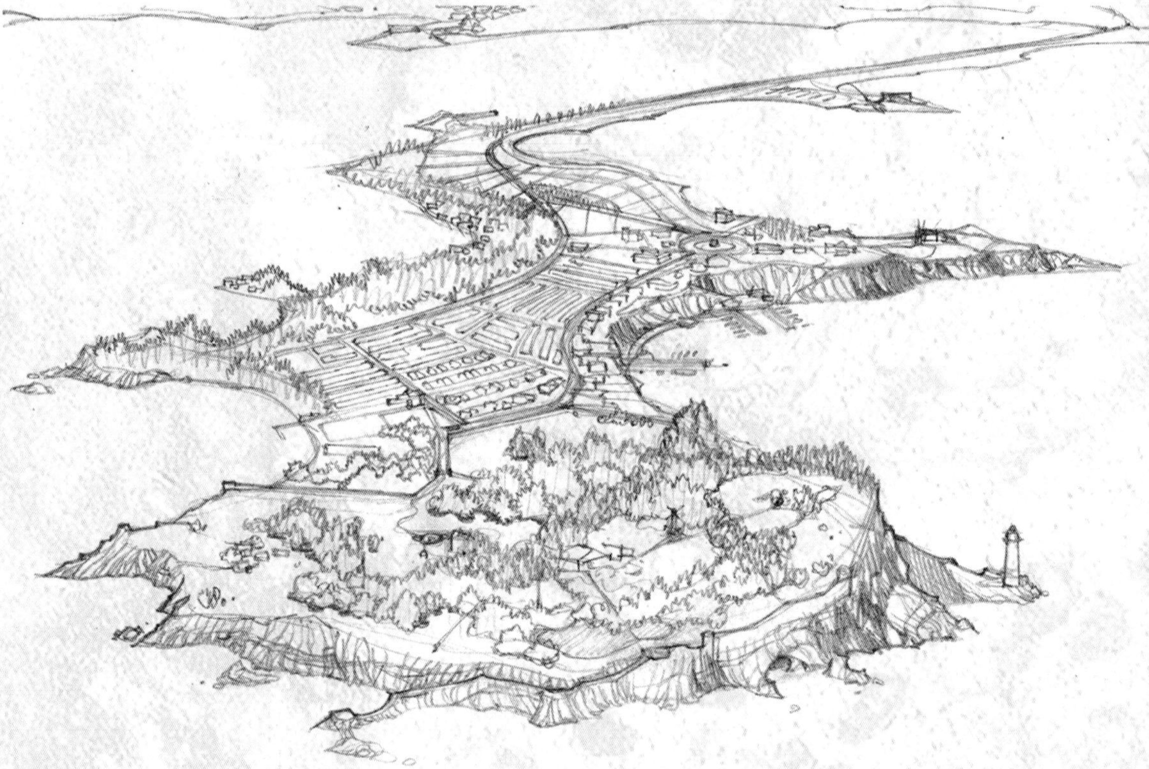

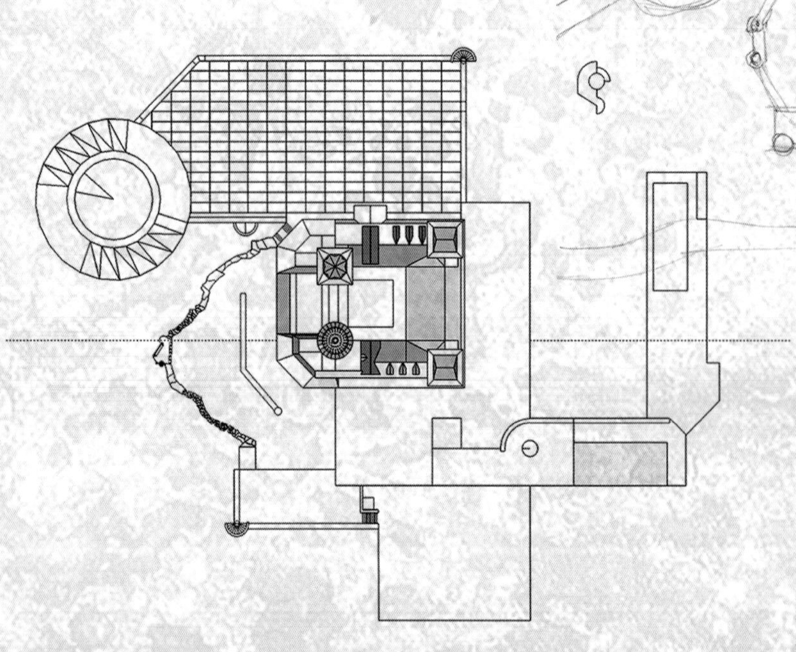

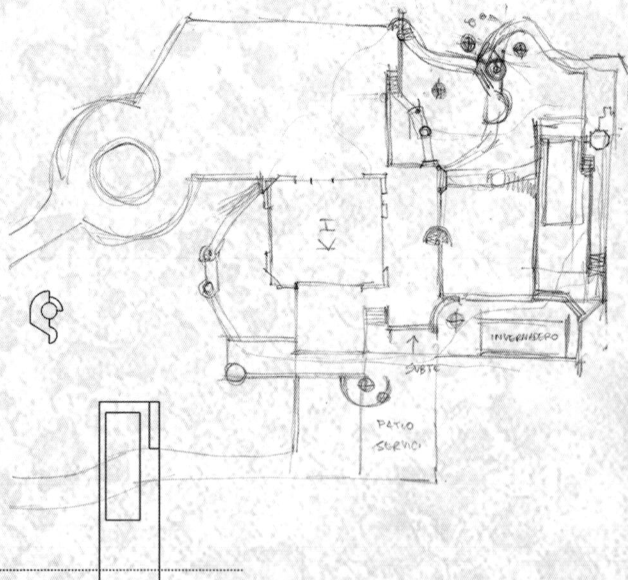
INVERNADERO
SUBTE
PATIO
SERVICI

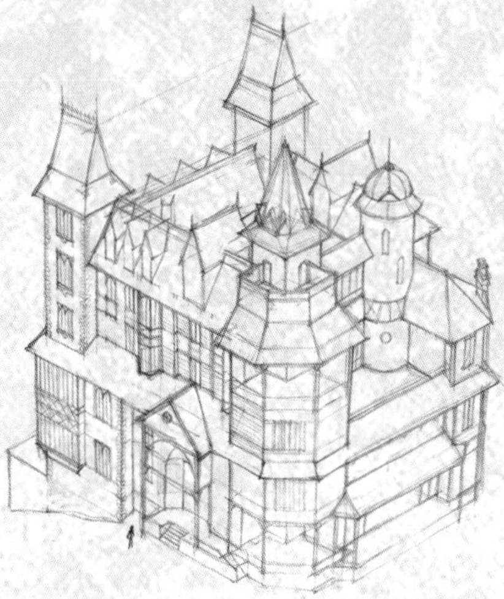

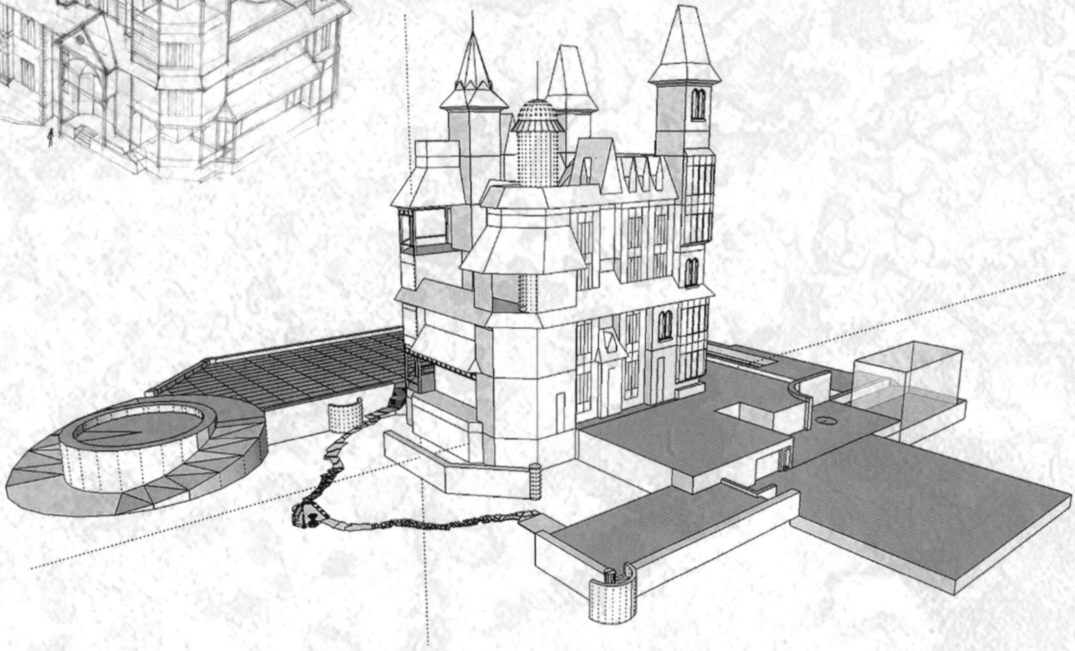

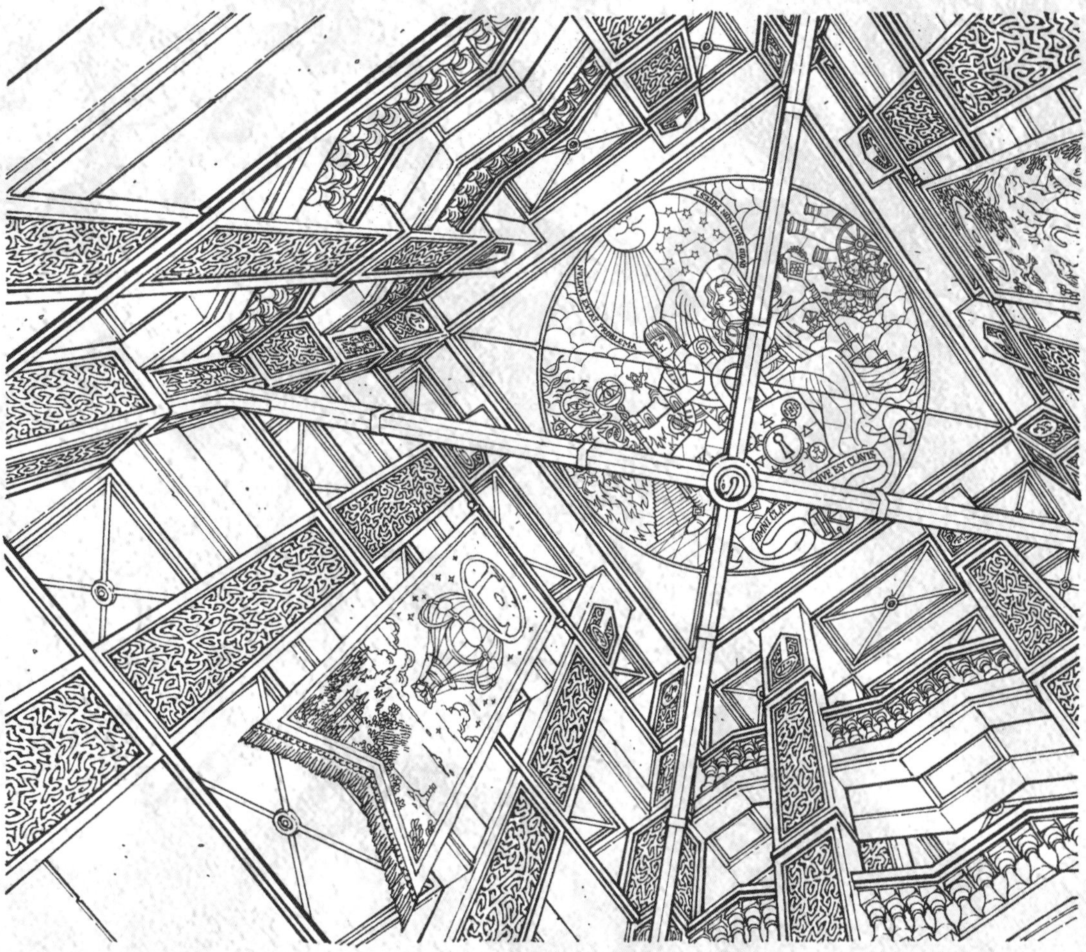

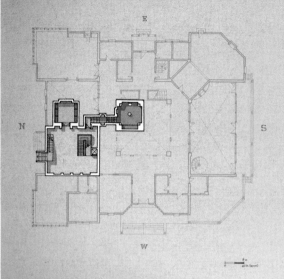

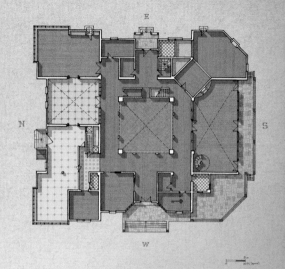

KEYHOUSE BASEMENT

KEYHOUSE GROUND FLOOR

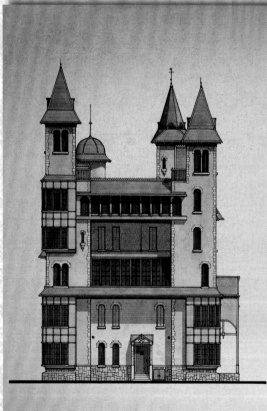

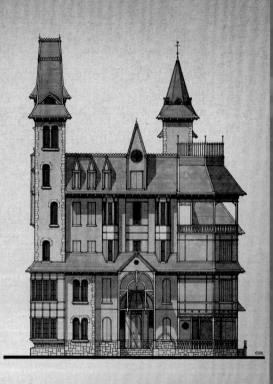

KEYHOUSE NORTH ELEVATION

KEYHOUSE WEST ELEVATION

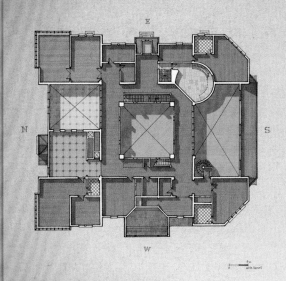

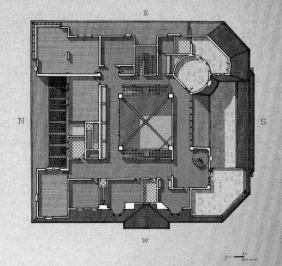

KEYHOUSE SECOND LEVEL

KEYHOUSE FOURTH LEVEL

KEYHOUSE SOUTH ELEVATION

KEYHOUSE EAST ELEVATION

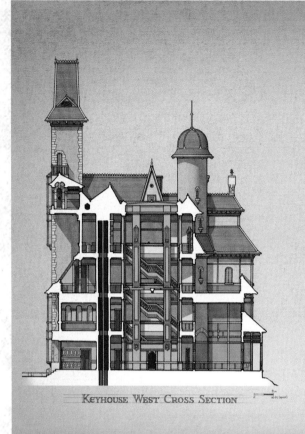

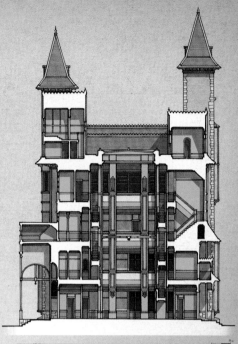

KEYHOUSE WEST CROSS SECTION

KEYHOUSE SOUTH CROSS SECTION

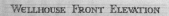

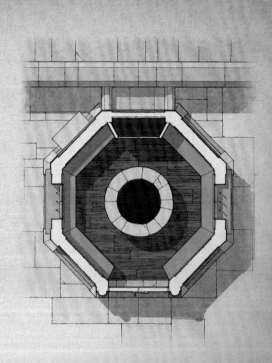

WELLHOUSE FRONT ELEVATION

WELLHOUSE PLAN VIEW

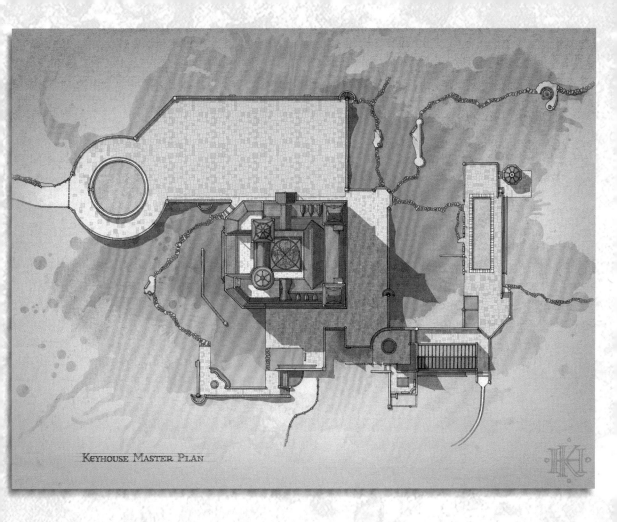

KEYHOUSE MASTER PLAN

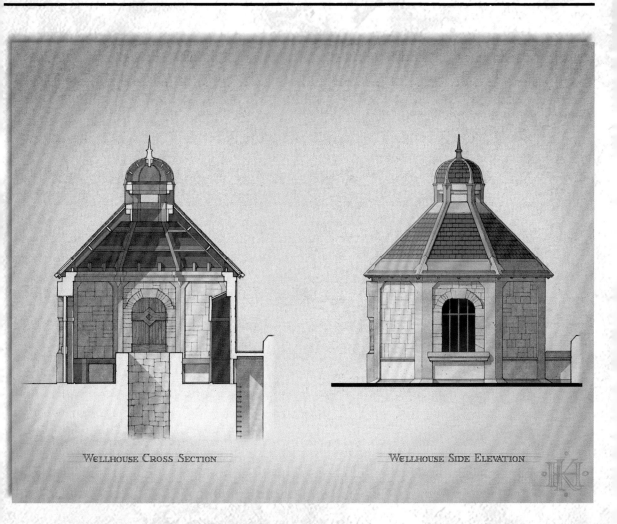

WELLHOUSE CROSS SECTION

WELLHOUSE SIDE ELEVATION

- END OF VOLUME ONE -

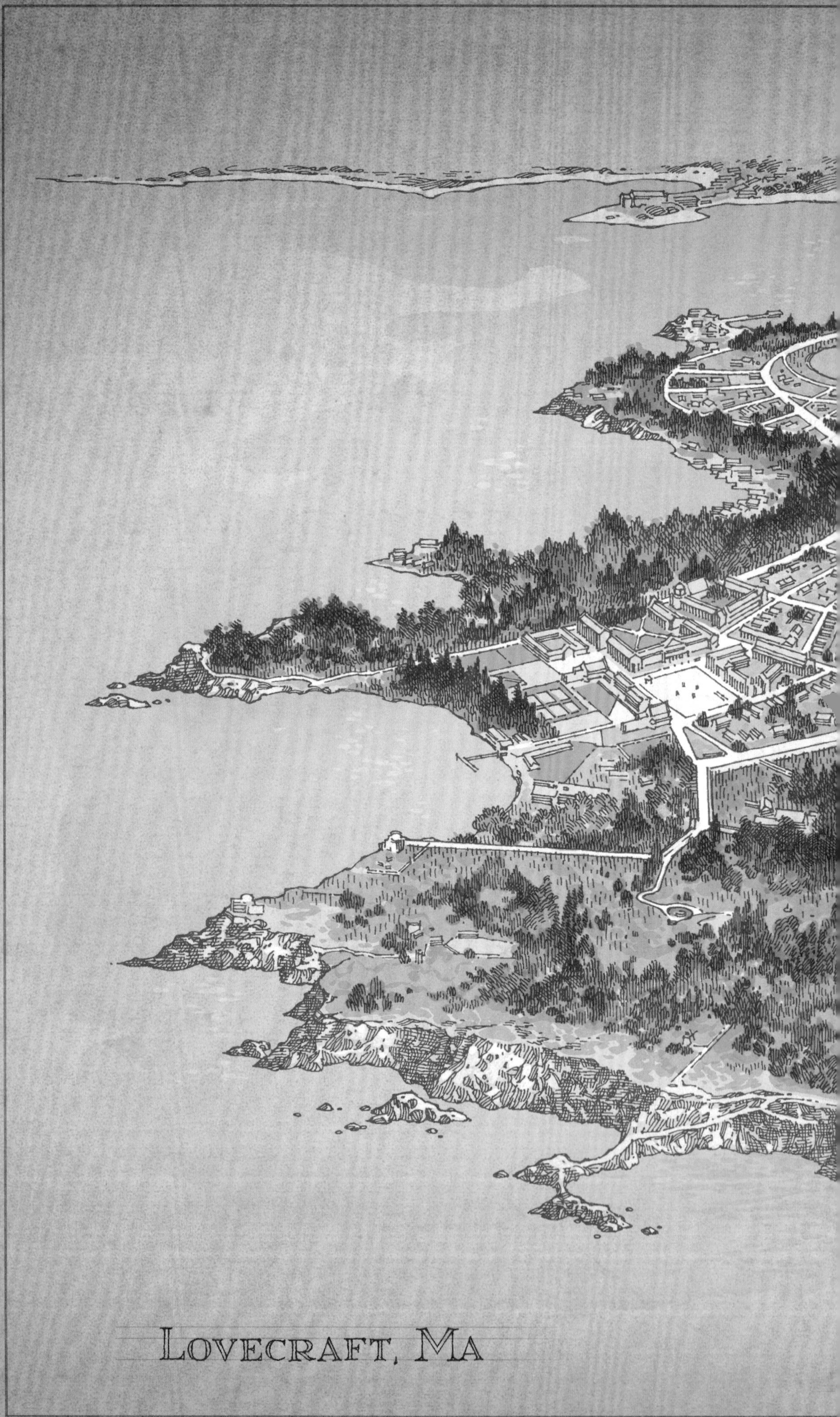
Lovecraft, Ma